The Law
Relating to
Activities
of Man in Space

The University of Chicago Press
Chicago and London

S. Houston Lay
and
Howard J. Taubenfeld

The Law
Relating to
Activities
of Man in Space

An American Bar Foundation Study

Standard Book Number: 226–46964–6
Library of Congress Catalog Card Number: 77–102747
The University of Chicago Press, Chicago 60637
The University of Chicago Press, Ltd., London
© 1970 by the American Bar Foundation
Published 1970
Printed in the United States of America

Contents

List of Members

Foreword

The general principles of international law apply to man and his activities in space to the same extent that they apply to man on earth, in air space, and on and under the seas. There remains a need for more detailed rules designed specifically for the circumstances of space, and we have here endeavored to set forth in a manner useful to scholars and students the general structure and content of the law relating specifically to space. We have analyzed the existing law and suggested to the extent possible the direction in which the law is developing. It must be recognized that dynamic space technology engenders a restlessness and uncertainty in the law, that since this volume went to the publisher humans have not only been in orbit around the moon but also have landed there.

Treaties already negotiated and in force set forth many guidelines for the behavior of man in space. Where there is no specific treaty on a specific subject, it is probable that the Treaty on Principles of 1967 covers the subject generally as for national sovereignty in space and on celestial bodies, accessibility of space to all nations on equal terms, treatment of space personnel, peaceful uses of space, and liability of nations for injuries resulting from activities in space.

The existence of the several treaties, United Nations resolutions, and some developed customary law does not signify that the detailed law has stabilized and will not undergo substantial changes. Much work remains to be done to prepare adequate and workable definitions of "peaceful uses," "fractional orbiting" weapons, military and economic surveillance, exploration and exploitation of resources of space and celestial bodies, and the use of space in the observation and control of weather and earth resources. Negotiations have already commenced, for example, for the purpose of revising the Intelsat Agreements of 1964, but the final outcome was not available at this writing. The major differences among the members of Intelsat will continue to be over the amount of control to be exercised by the United States and the amount of control to be divided among the other nations. The Soviet Union has proposed a competing satellite communications system based on a one-nation, one-vote control structure, a concept quite attractive to the underdeveloped nations but perhaps unlikely of final adoption in a communications system which is in fact oriented to the Soviet Union.

We owe special thanks to the National Aeronautics and Space Administration which, through John Johnson, former General Counsel, Walter D. Sohier, former General Counsel, and Paul Dembling, now General Counsel, all of whom were members of the project's Advisory Committee, made this study possible by providing generous assistance to the American Bar Foundation. E. Blythe Stason, former Administrator of the Foundation, gave great encouragement and assistance to us in commencing the lengthy research and writing required for this study, a policy continued by Geoffrey C. Hazard,

Jr., his successor as Executive Director of the Foundation.

Rita F. Taubenfeld worked constantly with Professor Taubenfeld in researching, drafting, and editing and was for him almost an alter ego. After Professor Lay's departure from the Foundation to join the faculty at California Western University Law School, Philip Hablutzel took over the indispensable task of coordinating activities at the Foundation related to this study. Prior to that he had worked on the project as a research assistant, drafting, checking authorities, checking drafts, and doing all the other tasks a member of a research and drafting team does. Richard Poole served as research assistant and prepared preliminary drafts of much of the material making up the chapter on liability. G. Perrine Walker worked on the communications materials and abstracted a great amount of material in the French language. George Yurchyshyn abstracted much material in the Russian language. Kurt Schaffrath, of Munich, Germany, abstracted materials in the German language, a task later taken over by Mr. Hablutzel. Prakash Sinha, who now teaches at the University of South Dakota Law School, researched various Oriental sources for space law materials. Frank Hill, now with the Department of Justice, helped with the research in the general law area. Several other students assisted in various aspects of the work both in Chicago and in Dallas. To all we express our deep appreciation and thanks. Mrs. Blossom Abrams of the Foundation secretarial staff is entitled to special recognition for her care and devotion to duty in repeatedly typing the manuscript. The similar work of Mrs. Margaret Seifert of Southern Methodist University was of the same high caliber.

Professor Mortimer Schwartz, now at the University of California at Davis, kindly made available an extensive bibliography which he had developed at the University of Oklahoma.

Kenneth Finch, of the Federal Communications Commission, and Peter Kehrberger, of Hamburg, Germany, both of whom have previously prepared and had published extensive space law bibliographies, spent many uncompensated hours preparing the bibliography included in this book, and we express full appreciation for their valuable contribution. Mr. Finch's appreciation and thanks go also to Miss Elizabeth Agnes Rademaker, formerly of the RAND Corporation and the United States Foreign Service, for her labor of love in typing and editing the drafts of the bibliography. Mr. Finch has also been very helpful in furnishing much unclassified information and commenting on the materials relating to communications. We also owe a special debt of appreciation to the members of our Advisory Committee, chaired by Mr. Arthur Dean, the names of whom are noted elsewhere, who gave generously of their time and great skills in reading and criticizing drafts of the manuscript. However, the authors of this book are solely responsible for its contents. The Advisory Committee, the National Aeronautics and Space Administration, and the American Bar Foundation, its officers and directors, have no responsibility for any statement of fact or opinion contained in the book.

S. Houston Lay
Howard J. Taubenfeld

Preface

In 1961 the American Bar Foundation published a small volume entitled *Report to the National Aeronautics and Space Administration on the Law of Outer Space,* by Professors Leon Lipson and Nicholas deB. Katzenbach. During the years since, the burgeoning space activities of the United States and other governments have revealed a need for an expanded and comprehensive treatment of the law of outer space.

This work represents research begun under the Foundation's auspices in 1964 and made possible by a research contract to the Foundation from the National Aeronautics and Space Administration. The Project Co-directors were Professor S. Houston Lay, then of the Foundation staff and now of California Western University School of Law, and Professor Howard J. Taubenfeld, of Southern Methodist University School of Law. Throughout the research project, they received invaluable advice and criticisms from an Advisory Committee under the chairmanship of Arthur H. Dean.

A draft form of the manuscript has been submitted to the National Aeronautics and Space Administration in compliance with contract NSR-041-001. The published work reflects editorial revisions and a last effort, inevitably imperfect, to bring text and references down to date. Change in the law of outer space continues to be as complex, if not as spectacular, as the rate of change in space technology. Yet the prospect of settled legal relationships concerning man's activity in space remains unfulfilled. The fault, of course, lies not in our stars but in ourselves.

Geoffrey C. Hazard, Jr.
Executive Director
American Bar Foundation

Introduction

The Lord God, who implanted in man's heart an insatiable desire for knowledge, did not place any limit on his efforts at conquest when He said: "Subdue the earth" (Gen. 1:28). It was rather the whole of creation which He offered for the human spirit to penetrate and thus understand more and more profoundly the infinite greatness of the Creator.

Pope Pius XII, Address at Castel Gandolfo to the Seventh International Astronautical Congress, Rome, 1956.

Writing in the late 1960s about the legal problems associated with man's activities in outer space has an air of solid reality about it which was almost totally lacking a single decade earlier. In ten years, what seemed at best a scientific and technological probability has become an everyday reality. With this in mind, it would indeed be rash to believe that all man's activities in outer space can now be identified for the decades to come. But the principal present and prospective space capabilities can be charted and analyzed, and in several areas at least, identifiable law already exists. It is the purpose of this study to analyze the law controlling or pertinent to man's activities in outer space and on the celestial bodies, whether derived from treaty, custom, statute, or related sources.

We here seek to study the law concerning outer space activities as it exists now and as it may develop. It is in no sense intended as a draft code of law governing these activities. Many writers have urged that a comprehensive code be drafted now.[1] Others—and most government representatives—have argued that codification would be premature.[2] What is clear is that nations have already indicated that a number of rules and principles are accepted as applicable to outer space activities, that rule-

---

[1] See Lipson & Katzenbach, *The Law of Outer Space* (study prepared for the American Bar Foundation), Abstracts 129–52, 179, 187, and sources cited; and see *infra* chaps. 3, 4.

[2] See Lipson & Katzenbach, Abstracts 180–82, 184, 186, 189–95, and sources cited; Report of the U.N. Ad Hoc Committee, 1959; and see *infra* chaps. 3, 4.

making by treaty in this field has begun, and that national legislatures in many countries have already considered one or more space-oriented problems. Although it is perhaps unwise to think in terms of comprehensive codification while we still know so little about the actual and potential uses of space and their significance to and impact on earth activities, it is certainly not too early to consider the alternative—overall legal regimes governing activities in space—since national and international choice here may well determine whether man's ability to penetrate outer space turns into a blessing or simply becomes a new way to extend and to escalate formerly earthbound conflicts.[3]

In the twelve post-Sputnik I years hundreds of satellites have been placed in orbit.[4] Men and a woman have made extended orbital flights. Satellite systems for scientific pursuits, for communications, and for meteorological, navigational, and military observation are in orbit. Probes have returned vast amounts of information about space; they have crashed into, landed on, and orbited the moon to photograph it, have photographed Mars, and impacted and returned information about Venus. Men have spent almost two weeks continuously in space.[5] Two manned lunar landings have occurred.

In this same decade, a vast amount of writing by legal and political scholars and an increasing amount of government attention have also been focused on this newest frontier. Nicholas deB. Katzenbach commented years ago on the number of lawyers already "in orbit" and,

while the pace of writing has slowed somewhat, the figures are still impressive. In August 1958 the *Index to Legal Periodicals* first added a "Space Law" heading to its survey of scholarly writing. By the end of 1967, there were over two hundred entries for this ten-year period,[6] and this represents only a part of the published materials.

Since it appears, as we shall see, that man's efforts to use his outer space capabilities will remain highly limited for decades, if not forever,[7] is this vast outpouring warranted? Are the basic problems, which are obviously political in the broadest sense rather than narrowly legal, new, or are they basically the same ones, set in a new milieu, with which men and nations have grappled through the centuries? Does the new milieu imply a difference in kind and in political tractability of problems? Is there now "law" governing human activities in outer space or making use of this outer space capability? What "law" exists; what is needed? This study, building on national and international "lawmaking" especially in the last decade, on the prior report of the American Bar Foundation to the National Aeronautics and Space Administration on the Law of Outer Space, and on the many distinguished scholarly works concerning legal problems associated with space activities, seeks to discover both the relevant rules which now appear to exist and the areas in which consensus and rule-making are now or soon will be essential, although presently lacking. We begin, however, not with "the law" but with a brief account of the new milieu, the space environment.

---

[3] Senator Gore at the United Nations in Dec. 1962 noted that "outer space is not a new subject, it is just a new place in which all the old subjects come up." As cited by Haughley, "Criminal Responsibility in Outer Space," *Proceedings of the Conference on Space Science and Space Law, June 18–20, 1963* at 146, 150 (Schwartz ed. 1964).

[4] By October 1967 some 3,000 objects had been placed in space; almost 1,300 of these are still in orbit. There had been 803 payloads. Of the launchings, 529 were by the U.S., 269 by the USSR, 4 by France, 1 by Italy. Payloads had been designed by Canada, the U.K., Australia, ESRO, and others as well. By the end of 1967, Australia had also launched a satellite. For the figures at the end of 1967, see *New York Times*, Jan. 31, 1968, at 12.

[5] The first manned orbital flight, by Gagarin of the USSR, took place on Apr. 12, 1961, and lasted 1 hour and 48 minutes. Glenn of the U.S. orbited on Feb. 20, 1962. In Dec. 1965 American astronauts Borman and Lovell made a flight of 210 orbits, lasting almost 14 days, the seventeenth human orbital flight. In the first 10 years, the U.S. made 14 manned orbital flights with 677 orbits and 1,933.4 man-hours; the USSR made 9 flights with 310 orbits and 532.5 man-hours.

[6] There were 77 items for 1958–61; 70 for 1961–64; 47 for 1964–67; and 22 more through May 1968. In addition, the *Index to Periodical Articles Related to Law* showed 29 entries from its inception in 1958 through Oct. 1966. There are now a number of bibliographies as well. See, e.g., Kehrberger, *Legal and Political Implications of Space Research* (1965), who lists 5,359 entries from all countries, although many are duplicates.

[7] For example, Hugh L. Dryden, then NASA Deputy Administrator, delivering the annual Robert Thurston Lecture of the American Society of Mechanical Engineers in Chicago, said that man would probably never explore the stars since a round trip to the nearest star would take 16,000 years. *Chicago Tribune*, Nov. 11, 1965, reported in *Astronautics and Aeronautics, 1965* (NASA), at 512.

1

The Physical Setting

Introduction

It is by now almost a custom of the trade to begin any serious treatment of the legal implications of man's newfound ability to begin the penetration of outer space with at least a brief review of the physical structure of space. The custom has its utility; it sets the nature of our legal problems in an appropriately limited context and, we hope, serves to make us less haughty over what are, while magnificent human efforts, only the puniest of assaults on the cosmos. It is well to keep in mind at all times that, as lawyers, we speak here not of "space law" but of national and international law concerning activities in outer space. The problems of human and international relationships are essentially the old and persistent ones; it is the milieu which is new. The interactions of the old problems in the constraints of the new setting are what challenge us.

The Space Environment

To understand at all the "dimensions" of the space environment is to wonder at the presumption of man in his talk of the "conquest" of space. The earth is the fifth largest of the nine planets known to be orbiting about the sun, a relatively minor star in the galaxy known as the Milky Way.[1] The earth's motion itself is impressive; it

---

[1] The authors claim no expertise as astronomers. For recent works in this field and for surveys of astronomical knowledge, see among others, RAND Corp., *Space Handbook* (rev. ed. 1963);

moves around the sun at some 66,000 miles an hour in its 580-million-mile orbit. The sun is itself in motion, orbiting, with some 100 or 200 billion other stars, about a central point in the galaxy. The sun's orbit takes about 200 million years to complete. The central point of the orbit is some 25,000 to 30,000 light-years[2] or about 150,000 to 180,000 trillion miles from the sun. Our solar system moves through space at 720,000 miles an hour or 17 million miles a day in its galactic orbit. Our galaxy is 10,000 to 20,000 light-years thick at the edge and some 80,000 light-years across. Our present largest optical telescope "sees" some 4 to 5 billion light-years away and shows more than 200 million, perhaps a billion—some say 10 billion—other galaxies across this expanse.[3] The total actual number of galaxies, each probably containing billions of stars, is of course unknown and is, in current theory, forever hidden from us. Moreover, the galaxies are all receding from us at stupendous rates, the farther from us, the faster. The most distant, at more than 4 billion light-years, is moving away at over 300 million miles

an hour, nearly half the speed of light. And to make "space" even less comprehensible to the lay mind, there is an estimated average distance of 4 million light-years between each of the visible hundreds of million galaxies.

To use another awe-inspiring set of figures, on a clear, dark night a human can see, with the unaided eye, the galaxy of Andromeda, some 9 billion billion miles away. Because of the geometry of space, its "curvature" and the related "expansion" of the universe, we can never see it all, even with the most powerful telescopes (yet this "limit" imposed by physical laws is 10,000 times further away than Andromeda).[4] This is the closest giant galaxy, but the light we see today when we look at Andromeda left there some 1.5 million years ago, long before man on earth learned to make tools, when mammoths roamed the earth. A change in Andromeda today will not be visible here until another 1.5 million years have passed.[5]

Travel times within the solar system are vast but feasible in most cases with present or foreseeable propulsion systems. A voyage to the moon at present speeds takes from 1.5 to 5 days. It is roughly 140 days to Venus, 210 days to Mercury, 260 days to Mars, 2.7 years to Jupiter, 6 years to Saturn, 16 years to Uranus, 31 years to Neptune, and 46 years to Pluto.[6]

Travel times to points outside the solar system have already been alluded to. The nearest star system to us is over 4 light-years away. At a constant speed of 25 miles per second (90,000 mph), far faster than present speeds, it would take a space vehicle 16 days to reach Mars at its nearest approach to earth (in contrast to Mariner IV's 7 months in 1964–65), but it would nevertheless take 30,000 years to reach our nearest star neighbor. A voyage to the center of our galaxy would take 560 million years and one to the nearest spiral galaxy, the Andromeda Nebula, would last 15 billion years.[7] These figures in a real sense make deep space travel appear to be impossible by presently attainable means of propulsion, and even vastly better techniques would seem to require a vehicle in which generations of explorers will live and die before a destination is reached.[8] As has been said,

---

NASA, *The Challenge of Space Exploration* (1959) [hereinafter cited as NASA, *Challenge*]; NASA, *Space: The New Frontier* (1962) [hereinafter cited as NASA, *Space*]; DuBridge, *Introduction to Space* (1960) [hereinafter cited as DuBridge, *Introduction*]; Lapp, *Man and Space* (1961); *Science in Space* (Berkner & Odishaw eds. 1961); Clarke, *The Exploration of Space* (rev. ed. 1959) [hereinafter cited as Clarke, *Exploration*]; Del Rey, *Rockets through Space* (rev. ed. 1960) [hereinafter cited as Del Rey, *Rockets*]; Weiser, *The Space Guidebook* (rev. ed. 1953); Ley, *Rockets, Missiles and Space Travel* (rev. ed. 1958); Gatland & Dempster, *The Inhabited Universe* (1959); Shapley, *Of Stars and Men* (1958); Baker, *When Stars Come Out* (rev. ed. 1960); Motz, *This Is Outer Space* (1960); Hoyle, *Frontiers of Astronomy* (1955); Hynek & Anderson, *Challenges of the Universe* (1962); Wilks, *The New Wilderness* (1963); Del Rey, *The Mysterious Sky* (1964) [hereinafter cited as Del Rey, *Mysterious*]. Some of these are "popular" rather than "authoritative" sources.

[2] The light-year is a measure of distance; it is the distance light will travel at its usually accepted speed of 186,300 miles per second in one calendar year. Thus "1 light-year" is a shorthand expression equal to just under 6 trillion miles.

[3] Radio telescopes appear to "see" 6 billion light-years' distance. In recent years, scientists have discovered sources of tremendously strong radio waves at distances which appear to be even greater. Too small to be galaxies and too large to be stars, these objects are called "quasars" (for quasi-stellar objects). For discussion, see Walter Sullivan, *New York Times*, March 30, 1964 p. 30, col. 1, and April 29, 1964 p. 15, col. 3 (report of discussion at the American Physical Society); Nicholson, "Galaxies, Quasars, and the Expanding Universe," 56 *Natural History*, No. 1, Jan. 1967, pp. 36–39, and *id.*, Feb. 1967, pp. 34–36.

[4] See Hynek & Anderson, *supra* note 1, at 708.

[5] *Id.* at 11.

[6] RAND, *supra* note 1, at 23.

[7] See DuBridge, "Space Exploitation: How and Why," *Science and Resources* 199, 203 (Jarret ed. 1959).

[8] Leonard, *Flight into Space* 273–74 (1953); Shepherd, "Interstellar Flight," *Realities of Space Travel* 395, 396 (Carter ed. 1957). Compare and see his discussion of the estimated effects predicted by the general theory of relativity. See also

distances in space are "utterly beyond our powers of comprehension, beside which our own solar system shrinks to the scale of an atom, the sun its nucleus and the planets circling electrons."[9]

The Solar System

Whatever the chances of acquiring much direct knowledge about the cosmos in its entirety in the next few decades, the chances now seem very good that man will at least be considerably more knowledgeable about his own solar system within the foreseeable future. All life in this system depends in the first instance on the star we call the sun. Although, as noted earlier, the sun is ranked by astronomers as only a minor star and is considered medium to small as stars go, its diameter is 108 times that of the earth; it is 330,000 times as massive as the earth; its surface temperatures at perhaps 50 million° F., effectively limiting the possibilities of a useful close approach.[10] It contains 99.9 percent of the material in the solar system.

Outward from the sun, the first planet in our system is Mercury, which is at a mean distance of 36 million miles from the sun. It is believed to be a small rocky sphere, about 3,100 miles in diameter or 1.5 times as large in diameter as earth's moon. There does not appear to be an atmosphere. Until recently it was believed that Mercury did not rotate on its axis but always kept the same face to the sun. There is now strong evidence, however, that Mercury rotates about every 58 days.[11]

Venus, the next planet, orbits at a mean distance of 67 million miles from the sun and comes at times to within 26 million miles of earth. It is surrounded by a dense, opaque cloud, apparently composed largely of carbon dioxide. It is somewhat smaller than earth with a diameter

of about 7,610 miles and a mass equal to about 82 percent of the earth's. It is now believed to rotate but in a retrograde manner, the only planet observed to do so. Its "day" is equal to about 118 earth days. Radar contacts, flybys by the American Mariner II space vehicle in December 1962 and Mariner V in mid-1967, a Russian flyby and impact by their Venus II and Venus III spacecraft in March 1966, and an apparent Soviet soft landing by their Venus IV in October 1967 have begun to produce information about Venus which has been denied to visual observers by the cloud cover; but our knowledge is still minimal.[12] Venus and Mars are nevertheless "first objectives because they are the first planets that technology makes available to our space probes; because they are the most 'earthlike,' and, most important, because of the possibility of adding information on the existence of life on these bodies."[13]

Mars is fourth from the sun, at a mean distance of 142

Saenger, *Space Flight,* chaps. 1, 2, 3, 7 (1965). Nobel Prize winning physicist Edward Purcell has stated flatly that this type of travel is in fact impossible. See Editors of *Fortune, The Space Industry* 166–68 (1962). See also *New York Times,* Oct. 26, 1966, p. 37, col. 6 (re comments by Dr. J. L. Greenstein that space travel is pure fantasy).

[9] Gatland & Dempster, *supra* note 1, at 19–20.

[10] NASA, *Space, supra* note 1, at 12. For a popular account of the sun and the solar system, see Del Rey, *Mysterious, supra* note 1, chaps. 5, 6.

[11] See McGovern, Gross, & Rasool, "Rotation Period of the Planet Mercury," 208 *Nature* 375 (Oct. 23, 1965) and *New York Times,* Nov. 20, 1965, p. 3. See also, e.g., 3 *Astronautics & Aeronautics* 108 (June 1965) [hereinafter cited as *Astro. & Aero.*]. Mercury's "year" is about 88 earth days.

[12] See the following in note 1, *supra:* DuBridge, *Introduction* 60, 62; RAND 12–13; NASA, *Space* 13. The Soviet Union launched an instrumented probe toward Venus in Feb. 1961, but the communications system failed. The first of several United States probes was launched in Aug. 1962. Mariner II passed within about 21,000 miles of Venus and its readings appeared to leave little hope for life as we know it, indicating a surface pressure perhaps 50 times that of earth at sea level, a lack of a detectable magnetic field, and surface temperatures of 700° F. to 900° F. These findings have been questioned as possibly incorrect. On Mariner V, which passed within 2,600 miles of Venus, see NASA Release 67–209, Aug. 1, 1967; *New York Times,* Aug. 30, 1967, p. 15; Oct. 20, 1967, p. 1; Oct. 22, 1967, p. 17. Some radio astronomers have tended to confirm the more pessimistic reports, showing a surface temperature of perhaps 675° F., too hot for life as we know it. See *New York Times,* Aug. 6, 1965, p. 7, col. 1. On the other hand, Plummer and Strong have argued that there are in fact large areas "where man would find the temperature comfortable." See *New York Times,* Apr. 18, 1966, p. 4, and *Washington Post,* Apr. 18, 1966, p. A7. For other reports on Venus's motion, seasons, etc., see 2 *Astro. & Aero.* 93 (Oct. 1964). On the Venus II and Venus III probes, launched in 1965, see *New York Times,* Mar. 2, 1966, p. 1; Mar. 6, 1966, pp. 66, 78; Mar. 14, 1966, p. 7. Neither operated or transmitted fully as planned. On Venus IV, see *New York Times,* Oct. 19, 1967, p. 1. On the continuing argument as to whether or not Venus is a "dead" planet, see *New York Times,* May 28, 1967, p. 20, col. 3. On U.S. radar mapping of Venus, see *New York Times,* Feb. 13, 1968, p. 30. In general, see also Bradforth Smith, "Rotation of Venus: Continuing Contradictions," 158 *Science* 114–16 (Oct. 6, 1967).

[13] NASA Authorization for Fiscal Year 1963, *Hearings on H.R. 11737 before the Sen. Comm. on Aeronautical and Space Sciences,* 87th Cong., 2d Sess., at 260 (1962); Wilks, *supra* note 1, chap. 10. See also Mayer, "Radioastronomy Studies of Venus and Mars," 4 *Astro. & Aero.* 13–25 (Apr. 1966).

million miles; at its closest approach, Mars is but 34.5 million miles from earth. It is about half the size of earth in diameter but only a tenth in mass. It has no oceans, so its land mass is about that of the earth. At least until recently, there has been a widely held belief that life, at least in some primitive forms, exists there, and it has been said that "although human life could not survive without extensive local environmental modifications, the possibility of a self-sustaining colony is not ruled out."[14] Temperatures ranging from +100° F. to −100° F. at different locations are not excessive by exploration standards. In July 1965 an American spacecraft approached to approximately 6,000 miles of Mars and sent back a series of photographs providing fascinating information on the structure and "surroundings" of Mars. Mars appears, for example, to have no radiation belts, making future exploration easier, and to lack a central molten core like that of earth, leading to conclusions that its surface structure is also much different from that of earth.[15] The possibility of life also received a setback when the moonlike appearance of Mars was revealed in the photographs, but some scientists still hold out substantial hope.[16] A more recent American flyby involving two spacecraft sent back equally fascinating and very similar pictures, showing a "moonlike" surface, though with features differing in part from the moon.

Since it is still the common belief that, if life will be found anywhere in our solar system it will be on Mars,[17] special care has been suggested to avoid contamination by objects from earth. Thus, even before the eventual questions of the establishment of bases on Mars for any purpose and of the conceivable use of Mars as a self-sustaining population center and source of locally used or exportable resources, the problem of proper control over preliminary probes and expeditions arises in a particularly acute form.[18]

Jupiter, Saturn, Uranus, and Neptune are giant planets with low densities, orbiting at mean distances ranging from 484 million to 2,800 million miles from the sun. They rotate rapidly and are believed to have small, dense cores surrounded by shells of ice and covered by thousands of miles of compressed hydrogen, helium, and other light gases. Temperatures range from −250° F. to −300° F.; thus, while their satellites may prove a bit more hospitable, these planets are not of any short-run interest as sites for human habitation. Pluto, the farthest from the sun and almost unknown, is at a mean distance of 3.5 billion miles and some 4.6 billion miles at its most distant point. It was discovered only in 1930. It is patently very cold and appears to have a small radius and a mass about 80 percent of that of the earth.

---

[14] RAND, *supra* note 1, at 13. See also *New York Times,* June 19, 1958, p. 20, and Nov. 13, 1958, p. 11, on the pros and cons of "life" on Mars. De Vaucouleurs asserted at the meeting of the American Physical Society in Apr. 1959 that the existence of life on Mars has already been established almost beyond question. See Sullivan's report, *New York Times,* May 1, 1959, p. 9. The issue is far from settled. See Sullivan, "Tantalizing Question Mark in the Sky," *New York Times Magazine,* p. 12 ff. (July 11, 1965) and *New York Times,* July 13, 1965, p. 12, col. 1. See also DuBridge, *Introduction, supra* note 1, at 62; Gatland & Dempster, *supra note 1,* esp. 73–74.

[15] See *New York Times,* July 15, 16, 17, 1965 (for the photographs). For background on the flight of Mariner IV, see 3 *Astro. & Aero.* 13–53 *passim* (Aug. 1965).

[16] See remarks of Nobel Prize winner Dr. Joshua Lederberg, supported by Dr. Carl Sagan of Harvard, *New York Times,* Aug. 8, 1965, p. 52, col. 4. See also 3 *Astro. & Aero.* 108 (June 1965) and Sagan, "Mars Opportunity Holds Up," 3 *Astro. & Aero.* 12 (Nov. 1965). Also on the Mariner flight, the ensuing controversy over life on Mars, and the problem of obtaining continuing support for exploration programs, see 3 *Astro. & Aero.* 20–44, 111 (Oct. 1965); 106 (Nov. 1965); 77–82 (Oct. 1965) for "Summary and Conclusions" of a study by NASA Space Science Board; 4 *Astro. & Aero.* 14 (June 1966) (review of the meeting of the American Institute of Astronautics and Aeronautics in Mar. 1966 on the subject: Stepping Stones to Mars). On Mars's surface, see *New York Times,* Aug. 30, 1967, p. 15. See also *New York Times,* Oct. 18, 1966, p. 17. On a Mars Symposium held Feb. 3–4, 1967, by the NASA Institute for Space Studies see *New York Times,* Feb. 12, 1967, p. 12E

(report by Sullivan). On life in the solar system, see also Pittendrigh, "The Path to Voyager," 4 *Astro. & Aero.* 76–89 (Nov. 1966).

[17] See the following in note 1, *supra:* DuBridge, *Introduction* 64–66; Shapley 55; NASA, *Space* 13; Clarke, *Exploration* 126, 140–42, 148–49; see also Vassilev, *Sputnik into Space* 154–58 (1958); Goodwin, *The Exploration of the Solar System* 97, 98, 99, 129–46, 152 (1960). Compare comments on Venus in note 12 *supra,* however.

[18] The subject of contamination is dealt with in chap. 7. After the Soviet announcement of an impact on Venus in 1966, Sir Bernard Lovell, the director of Jodrell Bank Experimental Station, called the landing "a vivid technical feat," but regretted that "the Russians should have endangered the future biological assessment of Venus by contaminating the planet." See *New York Times,* Mar. 2, 1966, p. 1; *Washington Evening Star,* Mar. 1, 1966, p. A1; *Washington Post,* Mar. 2, 1966, p. A1. Similarly, the smuggling by a Hughes Aircraft engineer of a small U. S. flag on NASA's Surveyor I spacecraft, which made a soft landing on the moon on June 2, 1966, was called both a breach of discipline and a violation of international space policy. See Dr. Joshua Lederberg in *Washington Post,* Aug. 7, 1966, as cited in *Astronautics and Aeronautics, 1966* (NASA) at 260–61 [hereinafter cited as *1966 A & A.* (NASA)].

The Moon

Earth's original and largest satellite, the moon, is a mere average 237,000 miles away. Its diameter is about 2,160 miles and it is, overall, about $\frac{1}{4}$ earth's size, although its mass is only about $\frac{1}{81}$ that of earth. Its surface gravity is only $\frac{1}{6}$ that of earth. Its surface is marked by craters and large mountains, and a shallow layer of dust appears to cover the entire surface. Temperatures range from $+272°$F. to $-250°$ F. There is no appreciable atmosphere: no water, no free oxygen, no vegetation. Space vehicles have impacted the moon, photographed its dark side, and landed on and sent detailed pictures of its surface since 1965.[19] In July 1969 American astronauts landed on the surface of the moon with a worldwide television audience, culminating this first major phase of space exploration, a major step for mankind.[20] The results of long-distance observation and deduction were confronted by on-the-spot observation of the moon's surface composition, and on-the-surface analysis of its whole physical makeup. This new confrontation of the empirical estimation procedures of modern astronomy itself is of great scientific interest.

The moon's interest and value to man must be noted here, although only in a preliminary way. To scientists, the moon offers the possibilities of study of the origin and evolution of the solar system—there is no erosion by wind or water, no decomposition or decay.[21] From the vast stable platform of the moon, telescopes will be able to peer into the cosmos unhampered by an atmosphere.[22] The moon may well serve as a base for further interplanetary travel. There may some day be modest self-sustaining lunar cities.[23] One potentially critical question, the utility of military bases of any sort on the moon, remains the subject of disagreement,[24] and the question is not made entirely moot by the self-denying statements of the space powers, by United Nations resolutions to date, and even by the treaty promulgated by the United Nations in December 1966 and signed by some sixty nations, including the space powers, on January 27, 1967 (discussed below in chapters 3 and 4).

In addition to the earth, astronomers have discovered that at least five other planets have their own moons. Jupiter has twelve; Saturn, nine; Uranus, five; and Neptune and Mars, two each. Some of these natural satellites are larger than our moon and may perhaps prove to be useful as bases for the exploration of these planets. Some are mysteries in themselves as well.

Four of Jupiter's twelve known moons, for example,

---

[19] On photographs taken in 1965 of the dark side by a Soviet space vehicle, see *New York Times,* Aug. 17, 1965, p. E9. An American Orbiter vehicle achieved a lunar orbit in 1966. On U.S. Lunar Orbiter I, see *New York Times,* Aug. 15–24, 1966, passim. For its pictures of the "back" side of the moon, see *New York Times,* Aug. 22, 1966, p. 8. See also 4 *Astro. & Aero.* 83 (Dec. 1966) and *id.* at 110 (Oct. 1966). On a map of the dark side made up from pictures from Lunar Orbiters I–IV and the Soviet Zone III, see NASA Release 67–220, Aug. 20, 1967. On Lunar Orbiter II, see, e.g., *New York Times,* Nov. 27, 1966, sec. IV, p. 7, and Dec. 1, 1966, p. 1, col. 3 (Sullivan). On the earlier detailed photographs taken by the U.S. Ranger VII, see *New York Times,* Aug. 29, 1964, p. 46, col. 3. On the Luna IX pictures, see Schoemaker, Batson, & Larson, "An Appreciation of the Luna IX Pictures," 4 *Astro. & Aero.* 40–50 (May 1966); Kuiper, Strom, LePoole, & Whitaker, "Russian Luna IX Pictures: Provisional Analysis," 151 *Science* 1561–63 (Mar. 25, 1966); *New York Times,* Feb. 4, 1966, p. 1, and Feb. 5, 1966, p. 1. On the later Ranger results see Smith, Vrelalovich, & Willingham, "Eyes on the Moon," 4 *Astro. & Aero.* 74–82 and sources cited (Mar. 1966). On Surveyor I, which "soft-landed" on June 2, 1966, see, e.g., 4 *Astro. & Aero.* 94 (July 1966). On Surveyor III, see, *New York Times,* Apr. 23, 1967 (editorial). On Surveyor VII, the last of the series, see *New York Times,* Jan. 8, 1968, p. 14, Jan. 12, 1968, p. 4, and Jan. 22, 1968, p. 17. On Lunar Orbiter V, see *New York Times,* Aug. 15, 1967, p. 1, and Aug. 13, 1967, p. 10E.

[20] On a manned lunar landing by 1970 as a national goal of the U.S. (at an estimated cost of over $20 billion), see e. g., *America's Race for the Moon* (Sullivan ed. 1962) [hereinafter cited as Sullivan, *Race*]; Holmes, *America on the Moon* (1962). For adverse comments, see, e. g., Etzioni, *The Moon Doggle* (1964). On the needs of a "moon colony," see remarks of Seaborg, AEC Press Release S–6–66 (Feb. 17, 1966).

[21] See DuBridge, *supra* note 1, at 56. Some Soviet authorities, following studies of the moon's surface achieved by Luna XIII, asserted that the moon "is not a dead body, but a living, breathing organism." See *New York Times,* Dec. 15, 1966, p. 34; *Tech. Wk.,* Dec. 9, 1966, p. 19. On Luna XIII, see *New York Times,* Dec. 25, 26, 31, 1966. On an AAS symposium on the moon in December 1966, see *New York Times,* Dec. 30, 1966, p. 7.

[22] Tifft, "Astronomy, Space and the Moon," 4 *Astro. & Aero.* 40–50 (Dec. 1966); Leonard, *supra* note 1, at 189.

[23] See Clark, "Down-to-Earth Survey of Space," *New York Times Magazine* 5 (Nov. 5, 1961); Del Rey, *Rockets, supra* note 1, at 142–49; Richardson & Bonestell, *Man and the Moon* 154–59 (1961); Holmes *supra* note 1, sec. VI; Sullivan, *Race, supra* note 20, at 87–96.

[24] For indications that the moon has little short-run military significance, see *Hearings on H.R. 11881,* 85 Cong., 2d Sess., 109, 781 (1958) (testimony of Dryden and DuBridge), and statement of Gen. Groves, *New York Times,* Dec. 7, 1963, p. 11. Compare also Von Braun, "Space Travel," 35 *For. Serv. J.* 20–21 (Apr. 1958); E. Teller, cited in Editors of *Fortune, supra* note 8, at 26.

are quite respectable in size. Io, with a diameter of about 2,300 miles, is slightly larger than our moon and is surprisingly dense, about four times as dense as water. Europa has a diameter of 2,000 miles and an ability to reflect light (albedo) that makes it sparkle like a jewel. No one is sure why it is able to reflect about 75 percent of the light which strikes it. Ganymede, with a 3,330-mile diameter, is larger than Mercury. Callisto is 3,200 miles in diameter, but, unlike Io, has an extraordinarily low density—no one yet has been able to explain the structure of so small a body with so low a density. As an added surprise, the four outermost moons of Jupiter, all small, have a clockwise or retrograde motion. The outermost of Saturn's nine known moons also behaves this way.

Other Areas of Interest

Three other areas warrant some special words: the atmosphere of earth itself, the stars and other bodies beyond the solar system, and "space" in general.

The Atmosphere

Earth moves through space wrapped in its own life-sustaining atmosphere. The atmosphere is generally described by scientists and writers in terms of four or five layers, each of which has its own characteristics.[25] Each blends into the next and statements about the "thickness" of a layer in fact vary depending on the characteristic being described. To limit or bound the atmosphere itself scientifically is totally arbitrary[26]—the atmosphere thins imperceptibly until the trace of "air" disappears.

In fact, half the entire mass of the atmosphere is found at a distance of not over 3.6 miles "above" or "out from" the earth and 97 percent of its mass is less than 18 miles above the earth's surface.[27] The layer of atmosphere closest to the earth is usually called the troposphere. It varies in thickness from about 10 miles at the equator to 3 to 5 miles at the poles. Most human activities are and will be confined to this area, which contains three-fourths of the air mass surrounding the earth. This blanket of air both distributes the sun's heat and serves to conserve it.

The next layer, the stratosphere, contains most of the remaining air in the atmosphere. It rises to a height of 20 to 70 miles above the earth depending on the classification used. Above the 50–70-mile height, there is insufficient aerodynamic lift to sustain any currently conceived heavier-than-air winged craft. This has led several writers to suggest that it is here that "outer space" begins.[28] The ozone of the stratosphere also serves as an essential shield, filtering out ultraviolet light.

Above the stratosphere is the ionosphere, which is sometimes subdivided into the mesosphere and the thermosphere.[29] It extends for several hundred miles, perhaps 400 to 500, depending on the quality used as a measure.[30] Higher-frequency radio and related waves, which travel in straight lines, are reflected back by the electrified layers of the ionosphere, thus making possible long-distance higher-frequency radio communications on earth.

Next comes the exosphere which gradually merges into interplanetary space.[31] Traces of atmospheric components have been located as far out as 60,000 miles. To the extent that the exosphere forms a true part of the atmosphere and rotates with the earth, national claims may well have to be treated differently from claims to outer space proper.[32]

The Stars

Regions beyond earth's atmosphere have been named by astronomers as well. Solar space refers to the area of the cosmos occupied by the solar system; galactic space includes solar space and the total area occupied by our galaxy; extragalactic space refers to all space beyond the Milky Way.[33]

---

[25] See Hogan, "Legal Terminology for the Upper Regions of the Atmosphere and for Space beyond the Atmosphere," 51 *Am. J. Int'l L.* 362 (1957); *Hearings on S. 1582,* 86th Cong., 1st Sess., pt. 1, pp. 127–53 (Apr. 7–10, 1959); Del Rey, *Mysterious, supra* note 1, 17 ff.

[26] *Hearings on H.R. 11881* at 109 (testimony of Hugh Dryden).

[27] Hogan, *supra* note 25, at 371.

[28] See *infra* chap. 3.

[29] Hogan, *supra* note 25, at 371. See Kallmann, *A Study of the Ionosphere* 368 (RAND).

[30] *Hearings on H.R. 11881* at 777 (testimony of DuBridge).

[31] Kaplan, "The Earth's Atmosphere," 41 *Am. Sci.* 49–65, esp. chart facing p. 49 (1953).

[32] Somewhat different "dimensions" for the layers are used in McDougal, Lasswell, & Vlasic, *Law and Public Order in Space* 33 (1963). For further technical information, see Strughold, "Definitions and Subdivisions of Space Dioastronautical Aspect," *First Space Law Colloquium* 110 (1958). See also Clarke, *The Making of a Moon* 51 (rev. ed. 1958); Zadorozhonyi, "The Basic Problems of the Science of Cosmic Law," *Cosmos and International Law* 23, 41, note 37 (1962).

[33] Hogan, *supra* note 25, at 374–75.

Beyond our solar system, the closest object is the star system Alpha Centauri, about 4 light-years or 25 trillion miles away. By contrast, Pluto, the farthest planet, is but 5+light-hours from us and earth's moon is but 2 light-seconds from earth. Alpha Centauri is a multiple star system and the stable formation of planets in any such system is not anticipated. Next are three red dwarf stars, followed by Sirius about 8.5 light-years away. Many astronomers consider Sirius too young and too hot to offer the chance of planets and life. Next are three more red dwarfs. Then comes a little star, Epsilon Eridani, at 11 light-years, the closest to our sun to have the features scientists consider necessary for the existence of planets. Planets appropriately placed within a system are needed for life as we know it. In all, within 15 light-years, there are only thirty stars and of these only two appear to have the conditions which indicate a chance for life.

Stars vary tremendously in size (Antares spreads out through hundreds of millions of miles of space; some "white dwarf" stars appear to be smaller than earth), and they vary in brightness (S Doradus is 500,000 times as bright as our sun). Yet all have about the same total mass.[34]

Observations of other stars have led to the widespread belief that many have planetary systems and thus offer the possibility of life, and therefore of intelligent life. Minimum estimates indicate perhaps one to ten billion stars with such systems in our galaxy alone and, as we have noted, man can already perceive hundreds of millions of galaxies. Thus life elsewhere is said to be "statistically" certain.[35]

While it is possible to discuss propulsion systems which, in theory, would at some distant time permit man to consider interstellar travel, it is clear that for decades and perhaps generations man will limit his practical planning to the solar system.[36] That is why this study deals only in passing with the question of eventual legal relations between humans from this system and "aliens," if any exist or are discoverable,[37] from other planetary systems.[38]

The Contents of "Empty" Space

In addition to the celestial bodies, space is in no scientific sense "empty." There are comets: "loose collections of orbital material" consisting of "rarefied gases and dust."[39] There are asteroids: a group of these planetoid bodies ranging in diameter from a few miles to almost 500 miles is found in our system largely in the region between the orbits of Mars and Jupiter. There are dust particles (micrometeorites); there are meteoric particles; there are such electromagnetic radiations as light, heat,

---

[34] On the stars, see, e.g., Del Rey, *Mysterious, supra* note 1, chaps. 10–15.

[35] In 1963, Peter Van de Kamp, director of Sproul Observatory at Swarthmore, announced the first clear-cut "sighting" of a companion to Bernard's Star which had the appropriate mass, etc., to have it reported as a planet. See Ley, *Missiles, Moonprobes, and Megaparsecs* 175 (1964).

In general, see Shapley, *supra* note 1, at 53–75; Posin, *Life beyond Our Planet: A Scientific Look at Other Worlds in Space* (1962); Oparin & Fesenko, *Life in the Universe* (2d ed. 1961); Jeans, "Life on Other Worlds," *A Treasury of Science* (Shapley ed. 1954); Haldane, "Genesis of Life," *The Earth and Its Atmosphere* at 287 (Bates ed. 1957). For an optimistic estimate, see 4 *Astro. & Aero.* 314 (Sept. 11, 1964). On "intelligent life," see also the comments of George Wald, *New York Times,* Mar. 8, 1966, p. 19, and Ponnamperuma, "Life in the Universe—Intimations, and Implications for Space Science," 3 *Astro. & Aero.* 66–69 and sources cited (Oct. 1965).

[36] See *Hearings on H.R. 11881* at 44 (testimony of Von Braun). See also *New York Times,* Mar. 29, 1958, p. 8. In NASA, *Challenge (supra* note 1, at 3) the investigation of the solar system alone is notes as "itself an assignment of awesome dimensions."

[37] There are several scientific studies aimed at eliciting direct knowledge of the existence of sentient beings in other planetary systems. Project Ozma, for example, focuses large-scale antennae elsewhere in the universe on the chance that radio transmissions in some recognizable form may be received. The time delays noted earlier with respect to the receipt of light from distant stars would also be significant if such a finding were made. See, generally, Sagan & Shklovski, *Intelligent Life in the Universe* (1966); "Report of the Search for Extra-terrestrial Life Symposium," noted in 4 *Astro. & Aero.* 40–44 (Aug. 1966). See also, e.g., Editors of *Fortune, supra* note 8, 174–78; Berrill, "The Search for Life," 212 *Atlantic Monthly* 35–40 (Aug. 1963). For a suggestion similar to Ozma by a Russian scientist, see *Washington Post,* Sept. 18, 1964, cited in *1964 A. & A.* (NASA) at 321. For more recent Russian proposals for massive searches for life elsewhere, see *New York Times,* Feb. 3, 1966, p. 2, and May 10, 1966, p. 19 (report by Sullivan).

[38] There is a treatment of this problem in McDougal *et al., supra* note 32, chap. 9, and in Haley, *Space Law and Government* (1963). Substantial space is devoted to the development of appropriate "metalaw" concepts, largely on natural law lines. See esp. chap. 12. See also the report of Lasswell's paper presented to the American Astronautical Society in May 1966, *Baltimore Sun,* May 26, 1966, cited in *1966 A. & A.* (NASA) at 190.

[39] RAND, *supra* note 1, at 14–15. In general see Wilks, *supra* note 1, chap. 1, and *Satellite Enviroment Handbook* (2d ed. Johnson ed. 1965).

radio and radar waves and X-rays and gamma rays; there are particle radiations such as the cosmic rays and the alpha and beta rays. We might also include what man puts into space—not only our probes and debris but also our signals, earthbound and space directed. This explains why some include "the spectrum of radio frequencies as well as a resource now common to the whole earth-space community."[40]

The atmosphere of the earth protects us from most of these outer-space "projectives," and the earth's magnetic field deflects the high-energy particles as well. These two shields make life possible on earth. Yet despite the shields the earth appears to gain several million tons of ash and particles a year.[41]

The radiations in space which today are a major concern of scientific investigation may someday be useful to man as sources of energy. At present, however, cosmic rays and such areas of charged particles as the Van Allen Radiation Belts (discovered during IGY space experiments) present a hazard to space travel rather than a resource to be tapped. The sun alone "radiates" 4 million tons of matter and energy into space each second. Indeed, space has been described as "a veritable sea of radiations."[42] Among these are cosmic rays and electromagnetic rays, including X-rays and gamma rays. The study of the sun's radiations is also of great scientific interest and may be of eventual help for the fields of communications and weather prediction. McDougal and his associates have catalogued the eventual possible direct uses of radiations, including those from the sun, and suggest that man may eventually tap them for the production of electricity for spacecraft and space platforms, for energy on other celestial bodies (for light, heat, processing of local raw materials, growth of plants) and for powering spacecraft in time.[43]

Of other "things" in space, molecules of matter, gases, dust, micrometeorites, meteors, and comets present subjects for scientific analysis but, in all likelihood, not for currently foreseeable use (or conflict over) by man. Such forces as magnetism and gravity are omnipresent in space but are, again, not foreseeably subject to ap-

propriation or legal concern.[44] Conceivably, sources of power might be found, it has been suggested, in two other phenomena closer to earth: the layer of monatomic oxygen above the 100-kilometer altitude and the electric currents of the upper atmosphere.[45] Of course, the important political and legal questions that seem likely to require resolution in the near future remain: (1) those of the permissible uses of outer space capabilities for more directly earth-oriented and traditional activities (communications, science, meteorology, intelligence gathering, war) rather than activities oriented toward harvesting space resources; and (2) those of the regime for space "within" our solar system and for its celestial bodies, which are of pressing concern.

It is this environment, dangerously hostile but infinitely rich, which man has at last penetrated. Since he is a social animal and since space penetration is a highly complex group activity requiring national support on a scale which, indeed, few nations can presently summon, human social organization and its law inevitably must go with the astronaut as well as his flag. Political and legal understandings on the regulation of space activities between the nations supporting space ventures are as essential to continued, peaceful progress as is their economic support.

---

[44] See Clarke, *Exploration, supra* note 1, at 116–17, 184–85; Motz, *supra* note 1, at 38–46; Wilson, *supra* note 42, at 187–98; Hanrahan & Bushnell, *Space Biology* 95–110 (1960).

[45] See Goodwin, *supra* note 17, at 168–69; Clarke, *Exploration, supra* note 1, at 117.

---

[40] McDougal *et al., supra* note 32, 751.

[41] Wilks, *supra* note 1, 33. See also Sullivan, *Race, supra* note 20, at 67–68.

[42] DuBridge, *Introduction, supra* note 1, 46–47. See also Wilson, *I.G.Y., The Years of the New Moons* 103–16 (1961); Burgess, *Frontier to Space* 103–36 (1956).

[43] See McDougal *et al., supra* note 32, 751–54 and sources cited.

2

Outer Space Activities: The Political-Legal Setting

Introduction

Man's ability to penetrate outer space and to conduct activities there has given rise to expectations of important benefits to man, but it has raised some doubts as well. Will space be, in President Kennedy's words, "a sea of peace or a new terrifying theatre of war"?[1] While the rate of development is clearly subject to fluctuation based on national estimates of short-run needs and long-range goals,[2] the great powers are com-

---

[1] Cited by Diamond, "That Moon Trip: Debate Sharpens," *New York Times Magazine,* July 28, 1963, at 10 ff.

[2] The United States has spent close to $10 billion overall annually on space or space-related activities, military and civil. The 1968 fiscal year direct budget was $7,242 billion. The 1969 budget has been cut except for the share of the Defense Dept. See *New York Times,* Dec. 28, 1967 at 6, and Normyle, "Space Budget Faces Hurdles in Congress," 88 *Av. Wk.* 123–25, 127, 129–30 (Mar. 18, 1968); "Apollo Applications Cut," *id.* at 21. On the magnitude, the challenges, the values, the hopes, the pioneering urge, see, among many: Statement of Pres. Johnson, *New York Times,* Mar. 2, 1968 at 21; DuBridge, "A Scientist Calls for Common Sense," 25 *Reporter* 22–23 (Apr. 27, 1961); Holmes, *America on the Moon,* esp. 20–21 (1962); Saenger, *Space Flight,* chap. 14 (1965); Webb, "Perspectives and Objectives of Our National Space Program," Conference on Space, Science and Urban Life, Oakland, Calif., Mar. 28–30, 1963 (NASA) 93–97 (1963); Joseph E. Johnson, "Introduction," *Space and Society* (1964); Welsh, *Astronautics and Aeronautics, 1964* (NASA), at 6–7 (1965) [hereinafter cited as *1964 A. & A.* (NASA)], and his remarks of Aug. 8, 1964, *id.* at 279–80; Berkner, "The Compelling Horizon," 19 *Bull. Atom. Sci.* 8–10 (May 1963); Jastrow & Newell, "Why Land on the Moon?" 212

mitted to a major development of outer space capabilities. It is the rapidity of change, pushed by national

desire to keep ahead or at least abreast of other nations,[3] to reap the military prestige and scientific and economic rewards of space, and to stay at the forefront of rapidly changing technology[4] which makes an approach to

---

Atlantic Monthly 41–43 (Aug. 1963); "The National Space Program—Its Values and Benefits," *House Comm. on Science and Astronautics,* 90th Cong., 1st Sess., Serial D (1967); "Summary Report: Future Programs Task Force of NASA," *House Comm. on Science and Astronautics,* 89th Cong., 1st Sess., Serial F (1965); "The Worth of the Space Program," Forum Issue, 6 *Astronautics and Aeronautics* 26 ff. (No. 2, Feb. 1968) [hereinafter cited as *Astro. & Aero.*].

On the costs and on the doubts of scientists and others, see 145 *Science* 368 (July 24, 1964); Saenger, *supra* note 2, chap. 13 (the "price" calculated in hours of work); Etzioni, *The Moon-Doggle* (1964); *America's Race for the Moon* 146 ff. (Sullivan ed. 1962) [hereinafter cited as Sullivan] (among those listed who questioned at least the rate of expenditure were former Pres. Eisenhower, Sen. Proxmire, Warren Weaver); Sen. Dirksen, comments of Oct. 2, 1964, *1964, A. & A.* (NASA) 337; *Cong. Rec.* 23061–23068 (Oct. 2, 1964); Pres. Eisenhower, Oct. 2, 1964, *Saturday Evening Post,* Apr. 11, 1964, at 17–19; Hutchins, cited in 2 *Astro. & Aero.* 120 (1964). See also *Reflections on Space* 117–20 (Rechtschoffen ed. 1964) [hereinafter cited as Rechtschoffen]; Diamond, *supra* note 1, at 10; Warren Weaver, "Dreams and Realities," 19 *Bull. Atom. Sci.* 11 (May 1963) (on alternatives); Smith, "Now It's an Agonizing Reappraisal of the Moon Race," *Fortune,* Nov. 1963, at 124 ff. On the alleged clash between NASA spending and the improvement of American cities, see *New York Times,* Dec. 5, 1966, at 1, and Dec. 6, 1966, at C34. See also *New York Times,* Oct. 2, 1967, at 47, and Oct. 14, 1967, at 26 (letter).

Deploring this use of great sums were also C. V. Raman, Indian Nobel Prize winner, and Pres. Senghor of Senegal. See *New York Times,* Aug. 1, 1966, at 42 and *Chicago Tribune,* Apr. 7, 1966, cited in *1966 A. & A.* (NASA) at 131 (1967).

Opposing a large space budget and arguing that funds should go to the cities or at least on getting vehicles to the planets rather than to the moon, see *Washington News,* July 28, 1967, at 16, *New York Times,* July 3, 1967, at 10, and Dec. 19, 1967, at 46. Some polls indicated that, while a slight majority of Americans favored a large space budget in 1966, by 1967 a majority opposed it. See *Washington Post,* July 31, 1967, at A2 (Harris poll), and *New York Times,* Dec. 3, 1967, at 28.

On American programs up to a moon landing and beyond, see 2 *Astro. & Aero.* 73 (Dec. 1964) (views of Newell, Dryden); *Washington Evening Star,* July 3, 1964, cited in *1964 A. & A.* (NASA) 238 (predicting at least a $7 billion annual cost to 1990). See also "Summary Report: Future Programs Task Force of NASA," *supra.* Report of the President's Science Advisory Comm. (PSAC), prepared by the Joint Space Panels, *The Space Program in the Post-Apollo Period* (Feb. 1967); Abraham Hyatt, "Beyond Apollo," *Int'l Sci. and Tech.* 30–39 (Mar. 1967); Karth, "Prospects for Progress: Space in the 1970's," 5 *Astro. & Aero.* 86 (No. 10, Oct. 1967); Luther J. Carter, "Post-Apollo: NASA's Plans Get Boost from LBJ and PSAC," 155 *Science* 1084–87 (Mar. 3, 1967); Dandridge M. Cole, *Beyond Tomorrow: The Next 50 Years in Space* (Amherst Press, 1965); Lewis, "Goal and No Goal: A New Policy in Space," 23 *Bull. Atom. Sci.* 17–20 (May 1967);

Brown, "The Post-Apollo Era—Decisions Facing NASA," 23 *Bull. Atom. Sci.* 11–16 (Apr. 1967). For criticism of the PSAC Report, see Abelson, "The Future Space Program," 155 *Science* 1367 (Mar. 17, 1967).

For other related problems, see, e.g. MacDonald, "Science and Space Policy: How Does It Get Planned?" 23 *Bull. Atom. Sci.* 2–9 (May 1967); Daddario, "Congress Faces Space Policies," 23 *Bull. Atom. Sci.* 11–16 (May 1967). On the implications of space policy, see *Technology and Social Change* (Mesthene ed. 1967) and E. Skolnikoff, *Science, Technology, and American Foreign Policy* (M.I.T. Press, 1967).

For a review of NASA's history, see Swenson, Grimwood, & Alexander, *The New Ocean* (NASA SP–4201; 1966). For a review of decision-making, see also Golovin, "U.S. Space Flight Affairs and Decisions: 1957–1967," 5 *Astro. & Aero.* 51 (No. 10, Oct. 1967).

On space goals (and their lack) see also *New York Times,* Aug. 11, 1966, at 13 (debate in the Senate over priorities and the NASA budget); remarks of Sen. Clark, *id.* at 22 (May 25, 1966) (space effort should not be on a "competitive basis"; priorities are "way out of order"); remarks of Rep. Teague urging "positive, bold decisions on future national goals in space," *id.* at 1 (Aug. 10, 1966); remarks of Webb, *id.* at 22 (May 30, 1966); *id.* at 18 (Jan. 25, 1967); Kerr, "Congress and Space: Overview or Oversight?" 25 *Pub. Admin. Rev.* 185–92 (1965); Ramo, "Space and National Priorities," 50 *Air Force & Space Dig.* 78 (Dec. 1967).

On the future generally, see Von Braun, "The Next 20 Years of Interplanetary Exploration," 3 *Astro. & Aero.* 24–34 (Nov. 1965); Friedman, "The Next 20 Years of Space Science," *id.* at 40–47; Ramo, "Space and the Automated Society," *id.* at 54–59; Hyatt, "A Future for Space Exploration," *id.* at 68–76.

[3] President Kennedy said: "We cannot possibly permit any country whose intentions toward us may be hostile to dominate space." Holmes *supra* note 2, at 20. President Johnson similarly stated: "We cannot be second in space and first in the world," *New York Times,* Sept. 16, 1964, at 11; and "We must be first in space and in aeronautics to maintain first place on earth," Letter of Oct. 1, 1964, *1964 A. & A.* (NASA) 335 (1965). With respect to the moon race, President Johnson said: "Our plan to place a man on the moon in this decade remains unchanged. It is an ambitious and important goal. In addition to providing great scientific benefits, it will demonstrate that our capability in space is second to no other nation's." *New York Times,* Jan. 22, 1964, 19–21.

[4] As James E. Webb has said: "You cannot afford to fall backward from what you are capable of doing in science and technology without finding that you have realized less than your potential, and frequently that someone has passed you by." Holmes, *supra* note 2, at 20. Of the need of all states for this technology, see, e.g., the Report of the British Interplanetary Society's Council to the Prime Minister, Apr. 1965, reprinted

agreed solutions for space-oriented problems of concern to us now.[5]

There is thus a national goal in space use which is vital, although it is not one with which legal rules can be directly concerned. Warranted or not, space achievement has become an index of technological and scientific prowess and, by implication, of national power.[6] What nations seek avidly through space technology is national prestige.[7] In this sense, prestige is a dummy variable representing not only national power but also all the other valuable resources, techniques, and uses not now foreseen or even foreseeable, but almost certain to come from a space capability. To avoid unforeseen, destabilizing, technical, political, or economic breakthroughs by their rivals, major powers believe, no doubt correctly, that they must stay at the forefront of human

---

in 3 *Astro. & Aero.* 70–73 (Sept. 1965); Saenger, *supra* note 2, at 4; Price, *What Space Means to Europe, passim* (mimeo., prepared for the European-American Assembly, Brighton, May 13–16, 1962).

[5] On Soviet accomplishments, see Heymann, *The USSR in the Technological Race* 1–14 (RAND P–1754; July 20, 1959); "Review of the Soviet Space Program," House Comm. on Science and Astronautics, 90th Cong., 1st Sess. (1967); "Soviet Space Programs, 1962–65: Goals and Purposes, Achievements, Plans and International Implications," *Senate Comm. on Aeronautical and Space Sciences,* Staff Report, 89th Cong., 2d Sess., *passim* (Dec. 30, 1966); and "Soviet Space Programs: Organization, Plans, Goals and International Implications," *Senate Comm. on Aeronautical and Space Sciences,* Staff Reports, 87th Cong., 2d Sess., *passim* (May 31, 1962); *New York Times,* Feb. 18, 1968, at 18. On the Soviet view of space programs, see 2 *Astro. & Aero.* 1 (1964); *Tech. Wk.,* Jan. 2, 1967, at 18 (on Soviet lunar colonies); Simmons, "The Russian Space Race," 4 *Astro. & Aero.* 4 ff. (June 1966).

For a proposal for shared U.S.–Soviet programs, see Sen. Young, 112 *Cong. Rec.,* pt. 8, on S. 6903 (May 16, 1967). On Russian coolness to cooperation, see speech of Meeker, "Organizing for the Exploration of Space," Aug. 17, 1967, at 12 ff. (typescript). See also Kash, "The Tyranny of Realism," 23 *Bull. Atom. Sci.* 16–20 (Feb. 1967).

For some indications of interest on the part of other countries, see also, on France and French satellites, *New York Times,* Nov. 27, 1969, at 1, 4; *Space Bus. Daily,* Dec. 11, 1965, at 172; *Washington Post,* July 6, 1966, cited in *1964 A. & A.* (NASA) 233; on a test German satellite, see *Washington Post,* May 13, 1966, at A23. On the U.K., see "A Space Policy for Britain," 10 *Spaceflight* 56–57 (Feb. 1968); on Soviet Proposals for a Soviet bloc program, *New York Times,* Dec. 14, 1967, at 26C. For negative comments, see, e.g., the statement of a member of the West German Bundestag, H-J. von Merkaty, that the U.S. was trying to "break up" western Europe's space program with "tantalizing" offers for joint U.S.–European planetary exploration: "In other words, the exploration of Jupiter could divert us from the essential economic benefits to be derived from space through the exploration of communications satellites. The American approach to date has definitely been aimed at insuring United States monopoly and leadership in this field as in the nuclear field." See *New York Times,* June 9, 1966, at 3.

On the rather apprehensive views of the new states, see Strickland, "Some Responses of New States to the Space Age," *Internal Working Paper No. 2* (Space Sci. Lab., Social Studies Project, U. of Calif., Berkeley; Oct. 1963).

[6] On the outcome of the "space race" as a test of the "free enterprise" system, see remarks of Webb, 2 *Astro. & Aero.* 391–92 (Nov. 17, 1964). On the Soviet use of outer space achievements for prestige purposes, see Senate Rpts., *supra* note 5.

Sen. Clinton P. Anderson has said: "Russian domination of the moon would equate in world opinion with the dominance of all space. We can't afford that false impression. The nation that retains space superiority holds an immeasurable psychological advantage. Space feats are an index of a country's strength." *Pageant,* July 1964, cited in *1964 A. & A.* (NASA) 268–69.

[7] On the prestige implications, see also Berkner, "Science, the Scientist, and Space," *Proceedings of the Conference on Space Science and Space Law,* at 5–6 (Schwartz ed. 1964) [hereinafter cited as Schwartz]. DuBridge, *supra* note 2, 22–23 (Apr. 27, 1961). On the "moon race," see also Library of Cong., Legislative Ref. Serv., *Soviet Space Programs, 1962–65: Goals and Purposes, Achievements, Plans and International Implications* (1967); *Tech. Wk.,* Jan. 2, 1967, at 18; Sen. Dirksen, in *Washington Evening Star,* Jan. 16, 1967, at A5 (critical); statement by Premier Kosygin, *New York Times,* Dec. 8, 1965, at C20.

On the dangers to human life of the "willingness to gamble for the sake of winning the race to the moon" see *New York Times,* Feb. 28, 1967, at 34; *id.* Mar. 27, 1967 (editorial). For other criticisms and comments on the "space race," see also Sen. Dirksen, *Washington Evening Star,* Jan. 16, 1967; at *New York Times,* Feb. 8, 1967, at 8 and Feb. 28, 1967, at 36 (editorial on the implications of the Apollo tragedy).

One possible example is in the area of space vehicle sterilization, discussed also *infra* in chap. 7. On the problems of sterilization and the need to avoid contamination of the celestial bodies and the earth, see, e.g., Magistrale, "Engineering Problems in Capsule Sterilization," 4 *Astro. & Aero.* 80–84, and sources cited (Feb. 1966). For criticism of U.S. insistence on severe sterilization procedures in that they may be slowing up the U.S. approach to space, see Horowitz, Sharp, & Davies, "Planetary Contamination I: Soviet and U.S. Practices," 155 *Science* 1501 (Mar. 24, 1967). See also Murray, Davies, & Eckman, "Planetary Contamination II: Soviet and U.S. Practices," *id.* at 1505.

On the possibility that U.S.–USSR competition is healthy in developing research, see remarks of Soviet Scientist Peter Kapitsa, *Washington Post,* May 5, 1966, at A20. On Soviet and U.S. competition and achievements, see also the remarks of Prof. G. Petrovich in *Trud,* reported in *Baltimore Sun,* Feb. 9, 1968, at A3.

knowledge, technology, and exploration, and today space is one of the great frontiers.[8] President Johnson has written,

> The orbiting of [Sputnik] was a feat of science. But the world-wide impact and importance was essentially political. Sputnik I was proclaimed by the Soviets as validation of Communist preachments and prophecies about the superiority of their political system. . . .
>
> The price of underestimating space explorations has been much more tangible than a "loss of status" in world opinion. . . . Fiscally, we paid an enormous price—of which the Berlin buildup, for example, was only a small part—to compensate for the political misjudgments of the early 1950's.[9]

Whatever benefits mankind derives from space activities, the initial thrust and much of the sustaining impulse has come from felt military needs, and this includes more than the ICBM and direct military systems in space. Superior knowledge and techniques reflect a genuine capacity to advance and to defend oneself under all circumstances and to get whatever turns out to be worth getting. Demonstrated space capabilities are taken as a measure of this ability. This is real power and it, in turn, yields prestige.

The present and prospective benefits of outer space capabilities, scientific, economic, and social,[10] are thus in part the fascinating by-products of capabilities which relied initially on military rocketry.[11] It is the continuing

dual nature of space competence, peaceful-hostile, which colors many important issues.

The Types of Space Vehicles

This study is concerned with the law applicable to man's activities in outer space. As a consequence, no special effort is made here to provide technical details on subjects, except to the extent that they possess or may lead to legal consequences.

Ballistic Missiles

Any analysis of the law applicable to space activities begins with a special problem. As we have noted, man's

---

[8] Secretary of Defense McNamara said in 1964: "[I]f a psychological victory that might result from the Soviets arriving at the moon first leads to a shift in attitudes in the world, tending to reduce the belief in the strength of the West, and in increasing the Soviet's view of the weakness of the West, this is bound to have a military effect. This is exactly what occurred in connection with our space programs, and it led to a very costly response by this country." *Av. Wk.*, July 20, 1964, cited in *1964 A. & A.* (NASA) 257.

[9] "The Politics of the Space Age," *Space: Its Impact on Man and Society* 4 (Levy ed. 1965) [hereinafter cited as Levy].

[10] On the social, theological, and other implications of space programs, see Barre, "The Human Implications of Space Activities," 30 *J. Air L. & Commerce* 355–68 (1964). See also Goldsen, *Research on Social Consequences of Space Activities* (RAND P-3220; Aug. 1965).

[11] On the military interest in space activities, see, e.g., Gen. Schriever, *Aero. Tech.*, Mar. 11, 1968, at 16; Adm. Raborn, Apr. 2, 1964, cited in *1964 A. & A.* (NASA) 126, and see the section on military activities *infra*. The U.S. Dept. of Defense now spends $1.5 billion annually on space research and development. See 2 *Astro. & Aero.* 116 (Nov. 1964). On early U.S. studies concerning rockets and satellites, see Hall, "Early U.S. Satellite Proposals," 4 *Technology and Culture* 410–34 (Fall 1963).

Some areas of anticipated benefit, not covered in this study of legal problems, but of interest as motivations for the space programs, include:

On medical advances, see, e.g., Strughold, "From Outer Space—Advances for Medicine on Earth," in Levy, *supra* note 9, 117–32; remarks of Pres. Kennedy, Nov. 21, 1963, in Rechtschoften, *supra* note 2, 173–75; *1964 A. & A.* (NASA) 178–79 (1965) (NASA program in space medicine and the biosciences).

On "spin-off" (advances to other industries, e.g., in the fields of miniaturized parts, production techniques, fuel cells, materials, design and development of computers, the general advance of science technology, reliability, bonding techniques, packing and packaged power, etc.), see, e.g., Sumner Goland, "The Aerospace Industry," in Levy, *supra* note 9, 38–49; Editors of *Fortune*, "Hitching the Economy to the Infinite," *The Space Industry*, chap. 6, at 94 ff. (1962); Silk, "The Impact on the American Economy," *Outer Space*, chap. 3 (Bloomfield ed. 1962); Silk, "Values and Goals of Space Exploration," *Space and Society*, chap. 3 (1964); Sumner Goland, "The Space Program: A Model for Technological Innovation," 14 *Looking Ahead* (Mar. 1966); George J. Howick, "Down-to-Earth Bonus of Space," 7 *Engineer* 6 (Winter 1966–67). See also Doctors, "Transfer of Space Technology to the American Consumer: The Effect of NASA's Patent Policy," 52 *Minn. L. Rev.* 789–818 (1968).

On economic effects generally, see also Downs, "The Economic Effects of the Space Program," Conference on Space-Age Planning 153–58 (NASA; Chicago, Ill., May 6–9, 1963); *Space Applications Summer Study*, 1967 Interim Report, Vol. 1 (1967); *New York Times*, Feb. 9, 1968 at 6.

On space impact, see also *The Railroad and the Space Program* (Maylish ed. 1966).

For views that there is little spillover, see Etzioni, *supra* note 2, chaps. 4, 5; Smith, *supra* note 2, at 124 ff.; for an argument that space research is a costly and inefficient way to advance civilian technology, see report of the Organization of Economic Cooperation and Development (OECD), *New York Times*, Dec. 19, 1965, at 20, and *Washington Post*, Dec. 2, 1965, at A24.

venture into space was initially borne on the wings of a military capacity and, despite other vital factors, it is the military-prestige potential which is vital in keeping the major powers around the globe interested and committed to the tune of many billion dollars annually.

It is the rocket vehicle, combined with a nuclear warhead, which is now the basis for the major powers' key offensive and retaliatory strength. Booster rockets for military missiles launched man's efforts into space. Our first problem in considering "space" vehicles then is whether or not to include the intercontinental ballistic missile in this analysis at all. Our decision is that it does not, in general, belong here. It is true that, during the launching phase, the vehicle follows the initial pattern of other launchings (a problem, in fact, for defense detection systems in other countries). It is also true that intercontinental missiles, at least, may spend some few moments at altitudes of 400 or 600 miles above the earth, an area which would be considered by almost all today as "outer space."

The problems of the control, inspection, and use of these vehicles is not, however, a problem for the "space" lawyer at this point. They are inextricably bound up in the broad problem of arms control and disarmament. Such problems will be touched on herein where relevant, of course, as in the cases of a United Nations resolution of 1963 and of the Outer Space Treaty of 1967, which deal with the orbiting of weapons of mass destruction, and of the Nuclear Test Ban Treaty of 1963, which prohibits testing of nuclear devices in the atmosphere and outer space. Common problems involved in launching and orbiting space vehicles and in testing long-range missiles, such as injuries caused by the vehicles and the like, will also be dealt with later under such broader categories as liability. Military missiles as such will therefore not be separately discussed; it is not their space-going capacity but rather their role in the complex world arms situation which is most important, and that is another study.

The vehicles we will be concerned with here can be conveniently placed in categories for analysis in terms of their means of propulsion and their "end location." Let us first consider the methods of propulsion available for penetrating outer space.

Propulsion Systems

While at the present time, with one exception, there appears to be little of legal significance to be derived from an analysis of propulsion systems, it seems useful as background to identify the existing and prospective techniques.[12] At present, rockets designed to boost intercontinental missiles and rockets for space launches are powered by chemical fuels, either solid or liquid. The fuels vary in capabilities, storability, and danger but essentially are similar in operation. They are all bulky; 90 percent of a typical present rocket's weight is fuel.

The distinguishing feature of the rocket, in contrast to the more familiar vehicles that depend on principles of aerodynamic lift, is that it does not depend on the atmosphere. In a real sense, it works best in a vacuum and is hence ideally suited for outer space activities. As Newton pointed out in formulating his laws of motion, action and reaction are of necessity equal—the force that a rocket exerts on its exhaust gases must be equaled by the force that they exert on the rocket. As the exhaust gases move backward, the rocket moves forward.[13]

Chemical liquid propellant rockets, which date from the end of the nineteenth century, dominate the field of space flight today.[14] Still awaiting perfection are rocket systems which will permit genuine maneuverable flight in space. Perhaps the first which will be available will employ nuclear energy in a convective fission system.[15]

---

[12] In general, see Johnson, "Launch Vehicle and Propulsion Program (NASA)," *A Review of Space Research* (S91-S103, NASA 1963); Wilks, *The New Wilderness,* chap. 4 (1963); Holmes *supra* note 2, chap. 3; Saenger, *supra* note 2, chaps. 11, 12; on solid fuel rockets, see, e.g., Thackwell, "Solid Rockets—a Maturing Technology," 3 *Astro. & Aero.* 74–77 (Sept. 1965).

[13] For a simplified account, see Ovenden, *Artificial Satellites,* esp. 41–53 (1960).

[14] On the historical background, see Saenger, *supra* note 2 at 68 ff.; Holmes, *supra* note 2, chap. 3.

[15] See, e.g., "Space Nuclear Power Generators," *Hearings before the Joint Committee on Atomic Energy,* 89th Cong., 1st Sess. (Aug. 6, 1965); Los Alamos Sci. Lab., *Nuclear Propulsion for Rockets* (Mar. 1965) (re Project Rover); Grey, "Where the Carrot Does Not Improve Vision—Nuclear Energy for Space," 4 *Astro. & Aero.* 68–72 (Mar. 1966); Saenger, *supra* note 2, at 88–91; Seaborg, "Atomic Power: The Key to Supremacy in Space," in Levy, *supra* note 9, 82–91; Johnson, "Beyond Apollo with Nuclear Propulsion," 2 *Astro. & Aero.* 22–28 (Dec. 1964); "Symposium," 3 *Astro. & Aero.* 34–52 (June 1965); Statement of F. E. Rom, NASA Lewis Research Center Release 64–88, summarized in *1964 A. & A.* (NASA) 337.

On U.S. progress with nuclear engines, see, e.g., the statement by H. B. Finger, Director of NASA-AEC Space Nuclear Propulsion Office, *Missiles & Rockets* 17 (Oct. 12, 1964).

On Soviet nuclear programs, see, e.g., *Missiles & Rockets* 21 (Dec. 14, 1964); *1964 A. & A.* (1964), 305.

On the legal and political problems involved, in view of the

With this, a one-step rocket flight and an aeronautical spacecraft may become possible with increasingly high proportions of payload to total weight at launch available for man's purposes.[16] In construction and performance, convective fission rockets will be very much like those using chemical liquid propellants but with the added risk of use of nuclear elements. Thus the problems of radioactive contamination of the atmosphere, enhancement of the radiation belt, and consequent need of protection of the crew will arise.[17] There is already some evidence of the problem, and this would become even more pressing with the possible advent of a proposed explosive nuclear-propulsion system (ORION).

In April 1964, for example, an orbiting reactor plunged into the atmosphere, dumping plutonium 238 into the air as it burned up. It was expected to take about two years for the stratospheric remains of that material to become uniformly distributed around the earth.[18] Of course, mixed stages in a rocket are possible—a chemical first stage might be mated to a nuclear second stage. Seaborg has in fact suggested that nuclear rockets should perhaps be launched only from outer space for safety's sake.[19]

Future systems involve the potentially economical nuclear hypersonic ramjet engine and, eventually, low thrust propulsion. Among the engines under study are those involving the use of ions or charged atoms as propellants; plasma-jet[20] techniques involving the sending of an electric arc through a propellant such as hydrogen; the use of photons, or particles of light; and the use of solar propulsion. All seem to be long-range possibilities at best.[21]

Earth Satellites

Since the Russians orbited Sputnik I in 1957, several hundred satellites have been placed in orbit about the earth (and a smaller number about other celestial bodies).[22] The vehicles can be classified in several different ways—by orbit, by purpose, by size, by weight[23]

1963 Test Ban Treaty, if the use of nuclear "explosives" rather than an atomic reactor is contemplated, see *Hearings on the Test Ban Treaty before the Senate For. Rel. Comm.,* 87th Cong., 1st Sess., at 26, on project "Orion" and Possony; "The Test Ban," *Cong. Rec.* 4365, 4367, 4368 (Mar. 21, 1967); *Missiles and Rockets* 34 (Nov. 4, 1965).

On the use of nuclear power in eventual colonies on celestial bodies, see the statement of AEC chairman Glenn T. Seaborg, AEC Release S-6-66 (Feb. 17, 1966).

[16] In a somewhat similar situation, the introduction of a nuclear power plant in the Antarctic has cut drastically into the need to devote shipping space to fuel oil which formerly occupied up to 85 percent of all supplies by weight delivered to the Antarctic for U.S. expeditions.

In mid-1964 the United States discontinued work on a low-flying, atomic powered missile, Pluto, which was reportedly near flight stage and might have been the forerunner of a nuclear powered aerospace vehicle. See *New York Times,* June 12, 1964, at 1, 23; July 13, 1964, at 11; Sept. 15, 1964, at 10.

[17] Von Braun said on Oct. 10, 1964: "The problems of man-made radiation connected with these [nuclear-propelled] space ships will prove far more challenging in the long run than those of the natural radiation in space." *New York Times,* Oct. 13, 1964, at 18.

[18] *New York Times,* Aug. 7, 1965, at 22. On reactors in development stages, see 3 *Astro. & Aero.* 85 (Aug. 1965).

[19] See Seaborg, in Levy, *supra* note 9, at 90–91. The U.S. Atomic Energy Commission has done work toward a reactor "designed to break apart and disintegrate" when it reentered the

earth's atmosphere. AEC Release G-1 (1964). On tests to determine the effect of an atomic engine falling into the ocean, see *1964 A. & A.* (NASA) 125.

[20] On experiments with electric-rocket engines, see NASA Press Releases 64–167, 64–264 (1964) (on the successful test on July 30, 1964, of the SER T I engine). See also *1964 A. & A.* (NASA) 359 (on Soviet use of an ion propulsion engine in the Voskhod I space vehicle). On ion engines, see also: NASA Press Release 66–662 (Oct. 4, 1966); *New York Times,* Nov. 5, 1966 at 12. On electric propulsion generally, see articles in 4 *Astro. & Aero.* 69–78 (Feb. 1966).

[21] See Saenger, *supra* note 2, 91–95 and chaps. 2–6.

[22] By mid-1965 successful launches were the rule, failures the exception. Both the United States and the Soviet Union had established rates of successful launch in excess of 80 percent (statement of Welsh, Mar. 20, 1964). See *1964 A. & A.* (NASA) 111–12. In 1967, NASA's rate of success was 20 of 22 attempts. Three objects were successfully placed in space by the U.S. in 1958; in 1967 the U.S. orbited 87 spacecraft while Russia orbited 67, France 4, Italy 1, and Australia 1. By the end of 1967, there were well over 1,000 objects in orbit—satellites, probes and "junk" (booster stages, etc.). Innumerable small rockets for various purposes were launched by countries around the globe as well. In the first 10 years of space activities, over 800 payloads were placed in orbit by the nations involved. For the U.S. and, reportedly, for the USSR as well, military vehicles in space outnumbered others widely. In 1967, for example, of the 87 U.S. spacecraft orbited, 66 were launched by the Department of Defense. See, e.g., NASA Release 67–301, Space Flight Record 1958–1967 (Dec. 1967).

On the continuing American effort, see esp. annual reports of Pres. Johnson, e.g., Report to the Congress, "United States Aeronautics and Space Activities 1967," Jan. 30, 1968.

[23] As another index of change, Explorer I, launched by the U.S. in 1958, weighed 31 pounds. By mid-1965, the Soviet Union was able to lift 26,840 pounds into orbit (the Proton space station) while the U.S. Titan 3C had lifted 21,000 pounds

and shape, and so on. Of these, the first two are perhaps the most important.

Orbits

The orbits of artificial satellites about the earth are limited in one sense by the earth's atmosphere. Objects from space encounter increasing friction as they move closer to the earth and tend to be destroyed or damaged by heat-caused friction. For practical purposes, artificial satellites are not by intent placed in orbits bringing them much closer than 100 miles to the earth at their perigee, or lowest point. For legal purposes, the concept of a "space vehicle" as one placed "in orbit" or beyond has been common as in U.N. Resolution 1721 B(XVI) and in the ELDO Convention (Art. 19).

For observing earth phenomena, for example, for scientific earth studies, for meteorology, for military observation (and for present human flight), satellites with low perigees and apogees are most useful. For observation of the whole earth, north-south orbits over the poles give assurance of complete coverage—the satellite will pass over all parts of the earth in time (or, as it can be put, the earth will turn under the satellite).[24] For some communications purposes, and perhaps others, satellites placed at about 22,300 miles on equatorial orbits will turn with the speed of the earth and thus appear to be stationary over one spot on the earth. Satellites have been placed in all these orbits.[25]

Missions

Classification of earth satellites by mission helps reveal the widespread nature of the problems we will be dealing with hereafter. A few types of United States vehicles are: satellites for geodesy (Anna, GEOS); for geophysics (Arents, Pogo, OGO, the Orbiting Geophysical Observatory); for communications, both passive (to have signals bounced off such as Echo and Rebound) and active (such as Telstar, Early Bird, Syncom I and II, HACS and MACS); for meterology (Tiros, Aeros, Nimbus); for astronomy (OAO, the Orbiting Astronomical Observatory, and OSO, the Orbiting Solar Observatory); for navigation (Transit), for technological studies (ATS, the Applications Technological Satellite);[26] for biological (BIOS) and technical studies, including manned flights (Mercury, Gemini, and Apollo) and landings on other celestial bodies; for military purposes (Midas); an infra-red early warning experiment (Samos); for photo reconnaisance (Saint); for detecting satellites (Vela);[27] for detecting atomic explosions (Bambi); a proposed missile-intercept satellite, EROS (Earth Resource Observation Satellite).[28] The list could go on and on.

For the foreseeable future, until inspection on earth or inspection in flight become politically and technically possible, we cannot identify with certainty the actual mission of any satellite. All we have is the unverified and unverifiable statement of the launching state. Although United States policy is to report all its vehicles to the United Nations, the classification by mission is in terms of four broad categories:[29]

a) development of spaceflight techniques and technology;

b) space research and exploration;

c) practical application of space based technology;

d) nonfunctional objects.

Far more information is normally available for nonmilitary vehicles through other reports and statements as, for example, in the annual publication of NASA, *Astronautics and Aeronautics,* which contains a long and detailed list of scientific and similar vehicles placed in space during the year.[30] Certain launchings, such as the manned

---

successfully. See, e.g., *New York Times,* July 17, 1965, at 6; 3 *Astro. & Aero.* 84 (Aug. 1965). Total weight placed in orbit by the Titan was 32,427 pounds, including the spent booster.

[24] A Soviet scholar has written: "The soviet artificial earth satellite does not violate the air sovereignty of any state, if only because it does not fly into space over other states. Instead, the territories of these states, by dint of the earth's rotation, pass so to speak under the satellite's orbit, which is fixed in relation to the earth and the stars." Zadorozhny, "The Artificial Satellite and International Law," *Soviet Russia* 3 (Oct. 17, 1957) reprinted in *Space Law: A Symposium,* 504 ff. (1961). See also the Int'l Radio Regulations, cited in Jenks, *Space Law* 189 (1965); Larsen, "A Sample of Space Law Opinion," 27 *Ohio St. L.J.* 462, 464 (1966).

[25] In mid-1965 a telephone call was made from Fort Monmouth, N.J., to Ethiopia via Saigon through the use of two synchronous satellites, Syncoms I and II. See 3 *Astro. & Aero.* 124 (July 1965).

[26] On the first ATS Satellite, launched into synchronous orbit on Dec. 6–7, 1966, see *New York Times,* Dec. 9, 1966, at 57 and Dec. 14, 1966, at 38.

[27] On Vela, see AFSC Release 205.66 (Oct. 16, 1966).

[28] On EROS and observation generally, see Clark, "High Ground View of Peaceful Space Activities," 4 *Astro. & Aero.* 8, 141–42 (Nov. 1966).

[29] See, e.g., Letter of May 6, 1965, U.N. Doc. A/AC.105/INF.95 at 2.

[30] See, e.g., *1964 A. & A.* (NASA) 445–68.

orbital flights, have also been carried out in full view of the world.

One type of classification by mission is already the subject of international controversy and, while discussed at various points hereafter, needs an early introduction. Both the Soviet Union and the United States are in agreement that outer space should be used exclusively for peaceful purposes. Both have thus far classified all of their own missions as "peaceful." Here, a divergence in language occurs if, perhaps, not in practice.

The Soviet Union, for its definition of a peaceful mission, rules out all "military" activities. It has thus charged that United States high-altitude nuclear tests, observation satellites, and the like, are military, aggressive, and contrary to the principal of peaceful use, although the Soviet Union has itself done all these things as well. The United States, on the other hand, argues that "peaceful" means only nonaggressive and not necessarily nonmilitary. Hence, military activities which are, on one basis or another, not hostile or aggressive, are permissible.

Space Probes and Interplanetary Vehicles

Both the United States and the Soviet Union have already launched a substantial number of vehicles designed to move into outer space without becoming near-in satellites of the earth. Space probes, as we have seen, have been designed to fly by Mars and Venus, to impact Venus, to orbit and to impact the moon, and to provide information on deep space, the solar environment, and the like.[31] The names of various probes and series have become familiar: Ranger, Mariner, Surveyor, Voyager, Lunar Orbiter, Lunik Mechta, Zond.[32] While failures have been frequent,[33] successes have been fascinating,

culminating in the moon landings achieved by the United States in 1969.[34]

Hybrid Vehicles

One of the difficulties, as we shall see, in defining outer space is that, as the former Chief of Staff of the U.S. Air Force, General White, has said: "In discussing air and space, it should be recognized that there is no division, per se, between the two. For all practical purposes air and space merge, forming a continuous and indivisible field of operations."[35] All space flight to date has originated on the earth, with the vehicles passing through airspace by intent or by being placed in too low an orbit for permanent space flight. To date, our vehicles are designed to operate either in familiar airspace or in increasingly familiar outer space.

In time, it seems clear that vehicles will be developed which can operate for sustained periods in either area at the choice of the pilot or controller. Both the United States and the Soviet Union[36] have shown an interest in vehicles capable of maneuver in the air-space continuum. Thus, the flight of the American X-15 was intended to mark the penetration of a "rocket-aircraft" to a height somewhere between 100 and 200 miles.[37] By the end of 1967, the X-15, in its first seven years of powered flight, had achieved a top speed of 4,537 mph (Mach 6.72) and an altitude of 354,200 feet, or about 67 miles.[38] By November 1967, four pilots had flown the X-15 higher than 264,000 feet (50 miles), the altitude administratively determined by the U.S. government to qualify one for astronauts' wings. These abilities have a significance in any consideration of a legal division between airspace and outer space.

Other hybrid vehicles planned or proposed for movement in and out of outer space have included the Saenger

---

[31] On Lunar Orbiter, see also *New York Times,* Jan. 14, 1967, at 12.

[32] The American manned lunar-flight program is designated Apollo; the Soviet parallel project is apparently named Voskhod (Sunrise). See, among many, Hyatt, "Will the USSR Reach the Moon First?" 3 *Astro. & Aero.* 114–16 (July 1965). On missions beyond the moon, see Bisplinghoff, "Advanced Research and Technology in the Space Program," 3 *Astro. & Aero.* 102 ff. (July 1965). For a report on the Lunar Orbiter program, see Helberg, "Lunar Orbiter" paper presented to the Stanford Conf., Aug. 16–18, 1967 (mimeo.).

[33] American observers estimated, e.g., that to mid-1965 the Soviet Union had suffered 14 deep space failures and 10 lunar failures, only a few of which were officially reported. See 3 *Astro. & Aero.* 124 (July 1965). Known casualties in space-connected operations have reportedly been limited to the three

Americans killed in a test on the ground and one Soviet cosmonaut killed on reentry.

[34] See *supra,* text and notes on the "moon race."

[35] White, "Air and Space Are Indivisible," *Air Force Mag.* 40, 41 (Mar. 1958).

[36] Chief Air Marshal Vershinin announced on Aug. 17, 1964, that the USSR was developing an "aerospace craft" and that "our generation will definitely witness the flight of such an aerial-spacecraft." *New York Times,* Aug. 18, 1964, at 17.

[37] See Hill, "Explorer of the X of Space," *New York Times Magazine,* Apr. 26, 1959, at 52; *Hearings on S. 1582* at 581–98.

[38] See NASA Press Release 64–265 (1964), summarized in *1964 A. & A.* (NASA) 320; and NASA Press Release 66–317 (Dec. 12, 1966).

bomber, the X-20-Dyna-Soar, the American "lift body,"[39] the Douglas Astro, the U.S. "Aerospace-Plane," the Russian T4A, the British Bristol-Siddley-Booster and Orbital Fighter,[40] the German Space Transporter, and the French Euro-space Glider.[41] Most of these, like the American Dyna-Soar, will probably never reach the flight stage, but interest, particularly in military circles, appears to remain high.

Activities in Outer Space: Form, Prospects, Issues

Scientific Activities

Among the studies which the tools of rocketry help make possible are those concerning the earth as a planet (its shape, gravitational and magnetic fields, its atmosphere and the meteorology of that atmosphere, its coupling into the interplanetary medium), the study of earth-sun relationships, the solar system (the planets, the moon, the planet-sun relationships, the interplanetary medium, etc.), the universe (e.g., celestial mechanics, particles, and fields, the extension of astronomy to wavelengths which cannot be observed from the earth's surface), the collection of data for cosmological studies, cosmic scale experiments (e.g., gravity-type experiments), life in space (both the search for life elsewhere and the study of terrestrial life carried out into space), meteorology, and others as well.[42] Thus satellites and sounding rockets have already helped to identify more accurately the size and shape of the earth as oblate, pear

shaped, out of round at the equator and with four "corners" and five troughs or depressions.[43] They have helped in mapping and calculating distances on earth more accurately.[44] They have investigated the upper atmosphere—its density, temperatures, pressures, chemical composition, the nature and strength of electrical charges there, the nature of the ionosphere. They have measured charged particles beyond the atmosphere. One of their most striking feats was the discovery of the Van Allen Belt, predicted decades ago.[45]

Satellites have studied primary cosmic rays, a task made very difficult on the ground by earth's atmosphere. Satellites and observatories on other celestial bodies will in time also permit observation of the universe undistorted by the atmosphere which both distorts and absorbs electromagnetic radiations from other bodies.[46] Counts can also be made of meteoric particles in space which normally disintegrate in the atmosphere.

Soviet space vehicles in 1959 and 1965 and American vehicles in 1966 and 1967 photographed the dark side of the moon.[47] In July 1965 an American vehicle photographed Mars from a distance of about 6,000 miles. In 1967 a Soviet vehicle impacted Venus. American and Soviet vehicles have orbited the moon at low altitudes, have "soft landed," and have returned close-up views of the moon's surface. These forerunners of automated reconnaissance vehicles to other celestial bodies make one impatient for an even closer look at our space companions.

---

[39] See, e.g., on lifting bodies, Love, "Manned Lifting Entry," 4 *Astro. & Aero.* 54 ff. (May 1966).

[40] On the U.K. aerospace plane, see 2 *Astro. & Aero.* 18–26 (July 1964).

[41] See Saenger, *supra* note 2, at 102–28.

[42] For a general survey, see NASA, *A Review of Space Research, passim* (1963), esp. Newell, "Program of the Office of Space Science," S–3 ff.; and see Jastrow & Cameron, "Highlights of Recent Space Research," 145 *Science* 1129 (Sept. 11, 1964). On science, the scientist, and space, see also Berkner, "Science, the Scientist and Space," in Schwartz, *supra* note 7, 1 ff.; Ovendon, *supra* note 13, chap. 6; RAND, *Space Handbook* 209–16 (rev. ed. 1963); Jastrow & Rossi, "Results of Experiments in Space," *Science and Space* 49 (Berkner & Odishaw eds. 1961) [hereinafter cited as Berkner]. Berkner, *passim;* Wilks, *supra* note 12, chap. 8; *A Review of Space Research* S114–S132 (1963); Jastrow, "Science, the Scientist and Space Developments," *Space and Society*, chap. 2 (1964).

On astronomy, see e.g., Nicholson, "Astronomy from Space," in Schwartz, *supra* note 7, 102 ff.; Briefing of Sept. 24, 1964 by N. Roman, NASA astronomy program chief, abstracted in *1946 A. & A.* (NASA) 327.

[43] See, e.g., 3 *Astro. & Aero.* 87 (Aug. 1965).

[44] On the use of satellites in geography see Risley, "Development in the Application of Earth Observation Satellites to Geographic Problems," 19 *Professional Geographer* 130–32 (May 1967). On oceanography see *U.S. Activities in Spacecraft Oceanography,* Report of the National Council on Marine Resources and Engineering Development (Oct. 1, 1967).

[45] The Van Allen Belt is a zone of high-energy radiation extending upward from a height of several hundred miles and substantially disappearing beyond 17,000 miles from earth. It ranges from at least 65°S., with highest intensities at the equator and gaps at the geomagnetic poles. There is some question of whether or not there is one belt with two radiation peaks at about 2,000 and 10,000 miles or two belts. The existence of the belt was predicted in 1931 by Chapman and Ferraro. See RAND, *supra* note 42, 16; *IGY and Space Reseach* 29–30; Del Rey, *The Mysterious Sky*, chap. 2 (1964).

[46] See RAND, *supra* note 42, 211, 215–16.

[47] Ovendon, *supra* note 13, 114–16. *New York Times*, Aug. 16 ,1965, at E9 and Aug. 17, 1965, at 30. It should be noted that the Russians claimed the right to name the features appearing in the photographs. *Ibid.*

In time, satellite stations may also be used as laboratories. Near perfect vacuums on a large scale could be obtained for experimental purposes, for example. The conditions for low-temperature and weightless experiments would also be at hand.

Clearly, the scientific interest is an important one, and scientists have vigorously asserted the benefits to human understanding to be derived from space activities. In general, scientists have for this reason demanded an undiminished, undistorted, freely observable outer space. These claims have been made both generally and with respect to specific national operations in space. Project West Ford, for example, the effort to place a band of copper needles in an orbit about the earth for communications purposes, was attacked by scientists in several countries and by government spokesmen in a few as a potential interference with radio astronomy and with other observation techniques as well. It was denounced as a "dangerous," unilateral interference with the cosmos and, when it was pointed out that such allegations were excessive, it was opposed as at least the forerunner of a scientifically undesirable "cluttering up" of space.[48] The Space Science Board of the National Academy of Sciences has concluded that the West Ford dipoles had not in fact interfered with radio or visual astronomy, but it was stated in the report that this "should not be taken either as an endorsement of the experiment or as tacit agreement to the launching of another similar belt without further discussion."[49]

In like manner, high-altitude nuclear explosions have been opposed by some scientists as creating distortions in the Van Allen Belt, for making the study of the earth's natural environment more difficult, for causing inter-ference with scientific and other satellites in orbit, and as a menace, present and future, to man in space.[50] Yet the high-altitude tests were themselves, in part, designed as an interesting scientific experiment.[51] There was a similar if milder controversy in 1966–67 over plans to orbit a reflecting satellite.[52]

---

[50] On the high-altitude tests, see. e.g., J. E. Johnson, *supra* note 2. For a Russian attack, see e.g., Pokrovsky, "Crime in Space," *New York Times* 9–11 (June 20, 1962) (on their illegality as interference with science, radio, health, cosmic flights, and as a projection of the arms race into space).

[51] On interference generally, see David Davies Memorial Institute of International Studies, *Draft Rules Concerning Changes in the Environment of the Earth, passim,* and sources cited (undated).

For other attacks on high-altitude needles and other experiments, see Stagg, "Possible Effects on Climate of Contamination of the Upper Atmosphere," *Report of Conference on Law and Science* 12–16 (Niblett Hall, U.K., July 1964) and Ryle, "The Effects on Astronomy of Tests in Earth's Environment," *id.* at 17–23.

For other comments of Sir Bernard Lovell on alleged interference with radio astronomy by U.S. military radar, see 2 *Astro. & Aero.* 340 (Oct. 4, 1964). For his views on the potential dangers of contamination of the earth's zone layer (through use of fluorine, carbon monoxide, etc.), see *Saturday Evening Post,* Feb. 22, 1964, at 10, 14.

[52] In 1966 there were at least proposals in the United States to orbit a reflecting satellite, a "space mirror" to illuminate the dark areas of the world at night. The Department of Defense was reportedly also "curious"; astronomers objected. See, e.g., Nelson, "Reflecting Satellite: NASA Study Causes Concern among Astronomers," 155 *Science* 304, 306 (Jan. 20, 1967). In May 1967 a report by the NRC Space Board on the concept of orbiting large reflecting mirrors concluded that there was no overwhelming evidence that scientific damage would result from the deployment of a single reflector system. It recommended, however, that such a satellite not be considered in the future unless the ability to destroy it by ground signals were an inherent part of the design and unless detailed studies of its effects on ecology, biology, and astronomy were previously conducted and made public. It said it could see no scientific merit for such a satellite system commensurate with its cost to the public and its nuisance to science. The report was prepared by the Board's Committee on Potential Contamination and Interference from Satellites as a result of NASA's 1966 announcement that it had asked five aerospace companies to study feasibility of orbiting large reflecting mirrors that could illuminate land masses at night. Donald F. Hornig, Special Assistant to the President for Science and Technology, confirmed in a letter to NASA President Frederick Seitz that the government no longer had plans for such a project. See NAS-NRC-NAE News Report (May 25, 1967). See also *New York Times,* May 26, 1967, at 4.

On proposals to do cloud experiments using colored vapors, see *Washington Star,* Mar. 31, 1967.

---

[48] On Project West Ford, see, e.g., Johnson, "Pollution and Contamination in Space," in *Law and Politics in Space* 37 ff. (Cohen ed. 1964) [hereinafter cited as Cohen]. The first attempt to discharge the needles failed. For an attack on West Ford, see Zhukov, "Problems of Space Law at the Present Stage," Proceedings, *Fifth Colloquium IISL* (Varna, 1962; mimeo); see also Lovell & Ryle, "Interference to Radio Astronomy from Belts of Orbiting Dipoles (Needles)" 3 *J. Royal Astro. Soc.* 100–108 (1962); and Blackwell & Wilson, "Interference to Optical Astronomy from Belts of Orbiting Dipoles (Needles)," *id.* at 109–14.

[49] See *NAC-NRC Press Release* (Mar. 26, 1964). To the same effect, see Shapiro, "Last of the West Ford Dipoles," 140 *Science* 1445 (Dec. 16, 1966). To avoid conflict in a later case, NASA launched its ATS–1 Satellite on Dec. 6, 1966, with one experiment turned off to avoid interference with radio telescopes. See Swenson & Bracewell, "Radio Astronomy: Conflict of Frequencies," 155 *Science* 518–21 (Feb. 3, 1967).

Other scientists have advanced special claims based on the "right" of scientists and indeed of mankind to learn.[53] Biologists and other specialists have demanded that vehicles used to impact and to explore the celestial bodies be sterilized to avoid contaminating them with earth forms of life and thus interfering with studies of life in other environments.[54] Radio astronomers claim a right to have left free for their use a substantial number of the highly valuable, limited radio frequencies.[55]

We do not here or hereafter seek to select among these claims. They are noted solely to illustrate that even here there are conflicts which may need settlement through "law" or other machinery of conflict resolution.

Claims of one group of scientists may conflict with claims of another group.[56] Scientific claims may compete for resources with claims of other groups having other socially useful ends, as is already apparent in disputes over radio frequency allocation. And the claims of scientists and other space users may conflict with various asserted national requirements, especially those involving military security in and from space.[57] It must be acknowledged that this last noted element is ubiquitous.

In our uncertain world the claims that states choose to put forth based on their felt need for security and prestige through space activities are apt to override all others, and the legal scholar as well as those who are charged with developing the law of space activities must proceed with this in mind. The potential interference with scientific activities is not likely to deter a state from any act in space considered vital to this central reason for being there. Yet claims stressed by others will, it is hoped, affect the military's choices both by compressing their area of decision as to what is truly essential and by narrowing the ways in which they pursue their irreducible needs in space. Of course other factors as well may produce end results considered desirable by other claimants. Thus, the Nuclear Test Ban Treaty of 1963 bars all nuclear tests above the earth's surface by parties obviously not merely to please those scientists who dislike interference with the earth's environment, but as a political policy decision dealing with the potential spread of a nuclear weapons capacity and as a measure in preventing dangerous contamination of the enveloping atmosphere as well.

Applied Activities

Communications

The use of satellite systems for communications purposes is with us already; it is also the subject of a vast literature concerning its scientific, technological, legal, commercial, social, and other significance. Chapter 5 of this study subjects the international legal aspects of these developments to extended scrutiny. Consequently, only the briefest introduction is offered here.

Satellite communications systems, in whatever form, vastly extend man's ability to transmit quantities of in-

---

[53] Compare, however, the views on the role and duty of scientists stated by Stone, "When Politics Is Harder than Physics," 32 *Am. Scholar* 431–44 (Summer 1963).

[54] On the problems of contamination of celestial bodies by vehicles from earth, on back-contamination of earth from returning space vehicles, and on sterilization techniques and problems, see Sullivan, *supra* note 2, 117–20; Berrill, "The Search for Life," 212 *Atlantic Monthly* 35–40 (Aug. 1963); Nicks, "Sterilization of Mars Spacecraft," 2 *Astro. & Aero.* 21 (Oct. 1964); COSPAR resolution of May 20, 1964, in *1964 A. & A.* (NASA) 185.

[55] See *infra* chap. 5.

[56] See, e.g., the demands for more life studies made by the American Institute for Biological Sciences, *New York Times,* June 11, 1964, at 2.

On disputes and dissent within U.S. science on the choice of programs and for the argument that the social and political pressures of the space race pose the threat of a "serious erosion in the integrity of science," see the Report of the Committee on Science in the Promotion of Human Welfare of the American Association for the Advancement of Science, reported in *Av. Wk.,* Jan. 4, 1965, at 18. For disputes over priorities in Soviet science, see *New York Times,* June 1, 1964, at 2.

On the problem of deciding between scientific experiments, see comments of AEC Commissioner Ramey, *Av. Wk.,* Jan 11, 1965, at 11; NASA Press Release 64–78 (April 15, 1964) (choice for the Gemini project); and remarks of R. L. Bisplinghoff, NASA Associate Administrator for Advanced Research and Technology, on Apr. 15, 1964, who noted that the choice was based on "an assessment of the scientific, social, economical, and political implications of these options." See *1964 A. & A.* (NASA) 139. On "excessive" demands for funds by space scientists, see remarks of Ralph Lapp, *Baltimore Sun,* Feb. 25, 1967. For an argument that $100 million from the Gemini program would solve the question of the orgin of the universe if spent on telescopes instead, see the statement of M.I.T. Professor P. Morrison, *New York Times,* Feb. 5, 1966.

[57] Even without the military claim, other interests may take preference. Thus it has been reported that sterilization requirements for the Ranger program were relaxed when it was suspected that the techniques used might be a cause of malfunctions which were causing delays and embarrassment in the program. See NASA Press Release 64–16 (Jan. 30, 1964), and *New York Times,* Jan. 31, 1964, at 1.

formation over great distances.[58] This includes television, telephone, data transmission, and cheaper long-range communications in general. For the first time, once the system is established, cost is independent of distance.[59]

A large number of uses, both civil and military, have already been successfully demonstrated and a commercial system, through the American Communications Satellite Corporation (ComSat) is already in operation in its early stages.

The total band width of land lines, cables, and low-frequency radio now in use is limited and short-wave radio bands tend to be crowded and unreliable due to atmospheric interference and ionospheric irregularity. Ultra-short-wave and microwave radio are usually limited to line-of-sight range. Satellites make possible round-the-world communications because the line-of-sight range at satellite altitudes is very great. The synchronous satellite, at an altitude of about 22,300 miles, is a particular example of this.[60] It is predicted that satellite systems, together with advances in other areas such as radio and cable technology, will go far toward solving foreseeable international communications needs.[61] For the United States this means primarily international communications needs; for the Soviet Union it is, at present, primarily a domestic need over the immense

---

[58] On satellite communications systems, see, e.g., NASA, *Review of Space Research* S32-S38 (1963); Forum Issue: "Communications Satellites—A New World Now," 6 *Astro. & Aero., passim* (No. 4, April 1968); Mitchell, "International Satellite Communications," in Levy 146–58; Clarke, "International Satellite Communications," 2 *Astro. & Aero.* 45–48 (Feb. 1964); Holmes, *supra* note 2 chap. 12. On the Early Bird satellite see Bentley, "Early Bird," 3 *Astro. & Aero.* 26–29 (Mar. 1965); Haley, "Communications in Space Existing Structures and Foreseeable Problems," *Eighth Colloquium, IISL* 33–99 (1966); Ivanyi, "The Topical Legal Problems of Space Communications," *id.,* 298–319 (1966); A. A. Cocca, "Legal Problems of Telecommunications by Satellites," *Report to the Ninth Colloquium, IISL* (mimeo., 1966). See also generally, Doyle, "Communications Satellites: International Organization for Development and Control," 55 *Cal. L. Rev.* 431 (1967); Note, "Future of Domestic Satellite Communications," 19 *Stan. L. Rev.* 1058 (1967); Throop, "Some Legal Facets of Satellite Communications," 17 *Am. U. L. Rev.* 12 (1967); Dirlam & Kahn, "Merits of Reserving the Cost-Savings from Domestic Communications Satellites for Support of Educational Television," 77 *Yale L.J.* 494 (1968); Paull, "Satellite Communications," *1967 Proceedings Am. Soc'y Int'l L.* 24 ff.; Johnson, "Satellite Communications: The Challenge and the Opportunity for International Cooperation," 19 *Fed. Com. B. J.* 88–96 (1964–65); Haley, "Space Age Radio Frequency Allocations," 4 *Astro. & Aero.* 66 ff. (May 1966); Leavitt, "Comsats: Galloping Technology and Lagging Policy," 49 *Air Force/Space Dig.* 61 ff. (July 1966); Schroeder, "The Communications Satellite Corporation: A New Experience in Government and Business," 53 *Ky. L.J.* 732–42 (1965); Hayes, "International Satellite Communications: Questions for 1969," and FCC Commissioner N. Johnson, "No Task More Challenging: Issues in Domestic Satellite Policy," speech at Stanford (mimeo., Aug. 16, 1967). For praise of the ComSat programs, see statement of Pres. Johnson, *Pres. Docs.,* Aug. 21, 1967, at 1146–54. For comment, see *New York Times,* Aug. 23, 1967, at 40M.

[59] On the potentially lower costs, see statements of Lloyd Berkner, *New York Times,* May 7, 1959, at 18. As the other side of the coin, there have been suggestions that a commercial space communications net could in time *earn* $100 billion a year. See *The Space Industry* 92 (1962). The officers and directors of the U.S. Communications Satellite Corporation have refrained from any precise predictions of either sort. See, e.g., ComSat, *Report, 1965 Annual Meeting of Shareholders* 10, 26. Initial receipts in 1965 were reportedly lower than was hoped for. See 3 *Astro. & Aero.* 102 (1965). On ComSat's progress, see also ComSat, *Annual Reports, 1966, 1967,* etc.

In general, see J. Johnson, "Satellite Communications: The Challenge and the Opportunity for International Cooperation," Work Paper, Washington World Conference on World Peace through Law (mimeo., Sept. 14, 1965).

[60] See RAND, *supra* note 42, 202 ff.; *Hearings on S.1582,* 251–65; on the functioning of American synchronous satellites, see, e.g., *New York Times,* Aug. 20, 1964 at 51 (Syncom III, in orbit Aug. 19, 1964) and ComSat, *Report, 1965 Annual Meeting of Shareholders* 14–20 (on Early Bird and Syncoms II and III). In space activities, nautical miles is the usual measure.

Even here, there are some "places" that are more useful than others and, if rival systems develop, there may well be contests for the choicest locations. Some Canadians have already suggested "staking out" outer space areas which may be especially significant for Canadian communications. In 1967, e.g., a committee established to report to the Canadian Prime Minister on the utility of a domestic satellite system delivered a report, the "Chapman Report," which, *inter alia,* recommended that Canada take immediate steps to stake out a claim to an 18,000-mile-long band between 75° and 115°W. longitude at 22,300 miles altitude lest the U.S. or some other country station a synchronous orbit satellite there causing that "territory" to be "lost forever." It went on to say: "This territory should be treated as prudently as Canada's water resources. It should be shared, rented or sold only on terms that are good for Canada." See K. Johnson, "Canadian Report Urges Domestic ComSat," 86 *Av. Wk. & Space Tech.* 69–71 (Mar. 27, 1967). See also *New York Times,* March 8, 1967, p. 21.

[61] See also, generally, Jessup & Taubenfeld, *Controls for Outer Space* 236–41 (1959); Michael, "Peaceful Uses," *Outer Space: Prospects for Man and Society* 33–42 (Bloomfield ed. 1962) [hereinafter cited as Bloomfield]. On the legal problems, see also Haley, *Space Law and Government,* chap. 7 (1963), and see *New York Times,* Mar. 8, 1967, at 21.

land mass,[62] and Russia has shown little interest thus far in participating in an American-sponsored international system.[63] For other, less developed countries, this offers a whole new approach to communications links for developmental, teaching, and other purposes, but little has thus far been done toward meeting this challenge.[64]

There are innumerable legal problems: assignment and preemption of the scarce, limited, valuable radio channels, potential direct broadcast into national territory,[65] interference, the advent of "private enterprise" into outer space, and so on. Economic and ideological conflicts of interest, both internationally and within the United States, are already apparent.[66] Communist writers

and government spokesmen denounce ComSat as an imperialist tool of the American government, of AT&T, or both, and they threaten to place their own international system in orbit, which they clearly have the right to do.[67] In time, other nations or the United Nations, perhaps as a social service to the developing nations, may place systems in orbit.[68] Certainly multiple world-

---

[62] In 1965, the Soviet Union established a communications satellite, Molniya I (lightning), in an orbit giving 10 hours a day visibility for a Moscow-Vladivostok link. See 3 *Astro. & Aero.* 109 (June 1965) and 3 *Astro. & Aero.* 85 (Aug. 1965).

[63] On U.S.-Soviet talks of June 15–16, 1964, which did not persuade the Russians to join the ComSat network, see, e.g., *New York Times,* June 16, 1964, at 3; June 17, 1964, at 3; and June 21, 1964, at 36; and *Missiles and Rockets* (June 22, 1964). On joint USSR-French experiments using the Molniya satellite, see e.g., 4 *Astro. & Aero.* 91 (Jan. 1966) and see also *Av. Wk.,* Oct. 30, 1967, at 13, *New York Times,* Oct. 4, 1967, at 3, and Jan. 18, 1968 at 52.

[64] For a very critical view, see Smythe, "On Thinking About the Effects of Communications Satellites," paper presented at the First Annual Meeting of the AIAA 1964 (mimeo.). UNESCO has proposed an international meeting on the use of satellites for mass communications use. See *New York Times,* Nov. 14, 1964, at 29.

[65] On direct broadcasts, see *infra* chapter 5 and see, e.g., Gen. Elec. Co., *Direct TV Broadcast from Space* (undated).

[66] Within the United States, various candidates for the privilege of exploiting a space communications network battled in the Congress. The conflict between proponents of a governmentally owned system and advocates of a communications-companies owned or dominated system was resolved eventually in the creation of the Communications Satellite Corporation, a hybrid private corporation with government overtones in a regulated industry which is already well on its way to establishing a world-wide communications chain, linked by satellites. See, among many, Taubenfeld, "The Status of Competing Claims to Use of Outer Space: An American Point of View," 1963 Proceedings, *Am. Soc. Int'l L.* 173, 176–77; Goldsen, *Research on Social Consequences of Space Activities* 5–7 (RAND No. 3220, Aug. 1965). On ComSat and its background generally, see Moulton, "Commercial Space, Communications," *Space and Society,* chap. 4 (1964); "Launching a Communications System in Space," *The Space Industry,* chap. 9 (1962); Feldman, "International Arrangements for Satellite Communications," in Cohen, *supra* note 48, at 23–26; ComSat, *Report, 1965 Annual Meeting of Shareholders* and *Annual Reports.* On ComSat and the FCC, see, e.g., *New York Times,* Jan. 8, 1967, at 12E.

For continuing critical comments, see, e.g., Sen. Long, *1964 A. & A.* (NASA) 79; Sens. Gore and Yarborough, *Washington Post,* Mar. 26, 1964, cited in *id.* at 116. On other continuing controversies, see, among many, Kirkpatrick, "Antitrust in Orbit," 33 *Geo. Wash. L. Rev.* 89–120 (1964).

On ComSat's disputes with communications companies over ownership of ground stations, see 2 *Astro. & Aero.* 74 (Dec. 1964) and ComSat, *Report, 1965 Annual Meeting of Shareholders* 29–31. On controversies with foreign partners, see 3 *Astro. & Aero.* 108–9 (June 1965). On other domestic disputes, see ComSat Corp. Release 67–38 (July 28, 1967) and *New York Times,* Dec. 29, 1967, at 43.

American military agencies, as we have noted, have also insisted on their own space communications net. On ComSat's unsuccessful efforts to sell its services directly to the armed forces which, despite predicted economies, were unwilling to risk a lack of protection "the technical and security requirements of the national communications system" due to foreign participation, and on the ensuing controversy, and other factors in this situation, see *New York Times,* July 14, 1964, at 15, July 16, 1964, at 3, Aug. 12, 1964, at 18 and Aug. 13, 1964, at 17 (Defense Dept. rebuttal); 3 *Astro. & Aero.* 95 (Mar. 1965) and *id.* at 98 (Apr. 1965). On later protests by U.S. communications companies of the Defense Department's use of Comsat, see *Wall Street Journal,* July 8, 1966, at 1.

On the problems of a single communications system for civilian and military uses, see Pritchard and MacGregor, "Military vs. Commercial ComSat Design," 2 *Astro. & Aero.* 72–77 (Oct. 1964). On the requirements of a military system, see also *Av. Wk.,* Aug. 17, 1964, at 19. On a military communications satellite system generally, see, e.g., Beecher, "Military Communications Satellites," 4 *Astro. & Aero.* 10–13 (May 1966). On the establishment of a functioning U.S. system, see *New York Times,* June 17, 1966, at 14 (launching of the first 8 of 23 planned satellites).

[67] The Soviet Union has already used satellites for domestic communications purposes.

For attacks on Comsat as a monopoly, see Stashevsky, "Communications Satellites and International Law," 34 *Sovet'skoe Gosudarstvo i Pravo* 57–66 (1964), and Ivan Cheprov, speaking at the 1964 Symposium of the International Institute of Space Law at Warsaw, reported in the *Washington Post,* Sept. 11, 1964, cited in *1964 A. & A.* (NASA) 313. Cheprov also said that the U.N. and the ITU could organize an international communications system "on the basis of equality." *Ibid.* No Soviet initiatives along this line appear to have been forthcoming. See also U.N. Doc. A/AC.105/PV.37 at 24 (Oct. 5, 1965).

[68] On early proposals for Canadian and European Comsat

wide systems, without centralized coordination, would lead to conflicts of interest between proponents of the different commercial systems and between them and military or U.N. systems over the allocation of the physically scarce resource in question, radio frequencies, on a global basis. Similarly, there is the potential conflict between space-satellite communications systems and such other claimants as radio astronomers and ground communications users. In addition, there is the potentially explosive version of a fundamental conceptual conflict which space communications activities have already brought to the fore. The Soviet Union once argued that only states (and possibly international organizations) should be permitted to use space capabilities; Telstar and ComSat mark the debut of private enterprise, of a sort, in space. The failure of the Soviet Union thus far to elicit much international support for its restrictive view has not stilled its attacks on "monopolies" in outer space, as we have seen.

Actually the role of private enterprise in outer space may prove minor for many years because of the huge capital inputs required and the lack of profit-making opportunities, but the formal limitation to states alone has been rejected by most of the world. Certainly this limitation has no precedent in the field of communications where private, regulated, and nationally owned systems have normally existed side by side and cooperated well.

National security interests are also involved in space communications activities as in almost every use of space. Conflicting claims are bound to arise if states assert a right to to use space systems, or simply use such systems without any special claim of right, to engage in activities considered by some or by many states as illicit in international law. This might in time include jamming another state's ground transmissions, or direct broadcasting

into home receivers when this becomes feasible, perhaps in the early 1970's or even earlier.[69] The Soviet Union has already proposed a rule barring the propagation of "national or racial hatred or enmity between nations," and the U.N. is on record as opposing hostile propaganda in all contexts.

Meteorology

Although meteorology is discussed here rather than under scientific activities in outer space, it is clear that this space capability offers us hope of an immense increase in man's understanding of the forces of nature and of how weather is made, as well as a better chance of predicting it and perhaps one day, at least on a small scale, of modifying it. The field of meteorology is one in which space activities are already playing an important role. It is also one in which the utility of international cooperation is readily apparent.

"All nations have an interest in accurate weather forecasting."[70] Weather phenomena have no knowledge of national boundaries. Until now, however, with only minuscule amounts of information available about conditions over the seas, about the mountains and deserts and the less developed countries which lack proper facilities and trained personnel, in fact about weather over 90 to 95 percent of the globe, we have lacked "one quality of observation most necessary to synoptic meteorology, that of complete continuity in time and space."[71] With satellite systems in operation, weather conditions over the entire world can be observed, reported on, worked into local forecasts, and studied for more basic scientific purposes.[72] Although estimates that this kind of coverage

---

systems, see, e.g., *Av. Wk.,* Nov. 21, 1960, at 35; *New York Times,* Nov. 25, 1966, at 4.

For more recent proposals of a Canadian system, see *New York Times,* June 1, 1967, at 71. For suggestions of a France-Quebec French language system, see *id.,* May 23, 1967. In early 1966, the Inter-American Development Bank made a $250,000 contract to find the most suitable ground stations in South America for connection through a satellite system.

On a Franco-German link, see *Av. Wk.,* July 24, 1967, at 27. On a European system, see *id.* at 29 (Aug. 28, 1967).

On Intelsat, see, e.g., R. R. Colino, "Intelsat: Doing Business in Outer Space," 6 *Colum. J. Transnat'l L.* 17 (1967). Intelsat had 61 members in January 1968, of which 40 were considered "developing nations." On Yugoslavia's interest, see *New York Times,* July 7, 1967, at 3.

69 See, e.g., statement of Charyk that it is likely by 1972. *Washington Post,* Apr. 18, 1967. See also 4 *Astro. & Aero.* 91 (Jan. 1966); Haley, "On the Track of Worldwide Satellite Communications," 4 *Astro. & Aero.* 56–89 (Feb. 1966). For a related but different problem, see W. G. Stolusky, "Unauthorized Interception of Space-Oriented Telecommunications," 25 *Fed. Bar J.* 412–21 (Fall 1965).

70 Lipson & Katzenbach, *The Law of Outer Space,* 30 (1961). On cooperation, see "Report of the Secretary-General of the United Nations," noted in U.N. Doc. A/AC.98/4 at 35–40 and Report of H. Wexler to WMO, reprinted as Annex I thereto; *Hearings on S. 1582* at 228–51; RAND, *supra* note 42, 192–98; Holmes, *supra* note 2, chap. 13. On the World Weather Watch, see, e.g., U.N. Ass'n, *Vista,* 30–34 (Sept.–Oct. 1965).

71 RAND, *supra* note 42, 192.

72 See Eidger & Tonart, "Utilization of Satellite Observations in Weather Analysis," 38 *Bull. Am. Meteor. Soc.* 531–33 (1957); Wexler, "Observing the Weather from a Satellite

could save the world billions of dollars in direct cost of damage to crops, in water resource conservation, in prevention of loss of life and property, and in shipping and aviation[73] have been subjected to some critical comment as overstatements,[74] there is no doubt of the general gain to knowledge as well as of specific utility.

A substantial number of weather satellites have been orbited by the United States and apparently by the Soviet Union as well.[75] American satellites have reported on cloud cover on a "real-time" basis, available for daily forecasts. They have taken remarkably clear pictures and have, in general, exceeded expectations.[76] They have

given warning of hurricanes and typhoons, shown capability for ice study, and provided basic scientific information on solar radiation of the earth's atmosphere.[77]

Most of the world's civilized nations are already members of the World Meteorological Organization (WMO) through which weather information is interchanged. The United States has made its satellite-derived weather information available to all requesting nations, and the processes of obtaining data and putting it in usable form have become increasingly rapid.[78] A modest cooperative program in meteorology already exists between the United States and the USSR as well.[79]

Three potentially important problem areas exist with respect to meteorological satellites. First, weather information is essential to military as well as civil operations. It was the weather which gave the Allied Command

---

Vehicle," 13 *Brit. Inter-Planetary Soc'y J.* 269–76 (1954); *Hearings on H.R. 11881*, at 910–11 (Reichelderfer); Wexler, "Meteorology," in Berkner, *supra* note 42, 139–155; Neiburger, "Utilization of Space Vehicles for Weather Prediction and Control," *Peacetime Uses of Outer Space* 153–73 (Ramo ed. 1961) [hereinafter cited as Ramo]; Library of Congress, *Meteorological Satellites* (Staff Report Prepared for the Use of the Senate Comm. on Aeronautical and Space Sciences), 87th Cong., 2d Sess. (Comm. Print 1962); *Review of Space Research* S26–S32 (1963); Saucier, "The Revolution in Meteorology," in Schwartz, *supra* note 7, 133–45. See also the report on a global weather system prepared at Stanford University, outlined in *Missiles and Rockets* 25 (June 22, 1964).

[73] For a Congressional estimate of a savings of $4 billion annually, see *New York Times*, Jan. 11, 1959, at 1, 50. It has also been stated that an "improvement of only 10% in accuracy [of prediction] could result in savings totaling hundreds of millions of dollars annually to farmers, builders, airlines, shipping, the tourist trade, and many other enterprises." *The Practical Values of Space Exploration* 51. In *The Space Industry* 93 (1962), figures of $3 billion per annum for water resources and $2.5 billion for farm products are noted, but so is a statement by Reichelderfer that the potentials cannot really be measured. The Russians are also engaged in this speculation. For an estimate of a saving of 500 million rubles through preventing crop failures on the basis of satellite observations, see Holmes, *supra* note 2, at 164.

[74] See Michael, *supra* note 61, at 42–48.

[75] American launchings include experiments in the Vanguard series, and the Tiros series (first launching Apr. 1, 1960). The Nimbus, first launched on Aug. 28, 1964, is a polar orbiting vehicle and Aeros involves a proposed "stationary" orbit. On the excellence of the Nimbus pictures, including those taken at night in infrared, see NASA Press Releases 64–195 (Aug. 28, 1964) and 64–243 (Sept. 23, 1964).

[76] They are expected, in the words of S. F. Singer, Director of the U.S. Weather Bureau's National Weather Satellite Center, to: "provide daily global coverage of weather; use vertical cameras for more complete pictures; aid in prediction of time and location of thunder-showers; determine if clouds are storm cover; aid in studying hydrology and geology, mapping earth's surface; aid airlines in tracking jet streams,

especially on transatlantic flights." See *Space Bus. Daily*, Feb. 13, 1964, at 239.

An extensive treatment of the Tiros series and the first Nimbus satellite, with pictures, and with a description of future systems is found in Tepper & Johnson, "Toward Operational Weather Satellite Systems," 3 *Astro. & Aero.* 16–26 (June 1965). On Nimbus see also 2 *Astro. & Aero.* 90 (Oct. 1964). See also Oliver, Anderson, & Ferguson, "Some Examples of the Detection of Jet Streams from Tiros Photographs," 92 *Monthly Weather Rev.* 441 (1964).

Tiros-derived weather maps were already in use regularly by international air carriers in 1964. See *Astro. & Aero. 1964*, 240 (1965).

[77] The Tiros and Nimbus satellites have observed and reported on a substantial number of hurricanes and typhoons. Tiros IV noted the severe hurricane Carla in 1961. Tiros VII reported on 16 hurricanes and typhoons in its first year. In a month of operation, Nimbus I observed and photographed three hurricanes and two typhoons. See, e.g., NASA Press Releases 64–243 (Sept. 23, 1964). On the help of satellites in locating ice formations, locusts, forest fires, etc., see Singer, "A Look at the Weather from Outer Space," in Levy, *supra* note 15, 141.

[78] On the ESSA 2 "Weather Eye" which is read out by 80 stations in 23 countries, see *Washington Post*, Mar. 1, 1966 at A4, and *New York Times*, Mar. 1, 1966 at 15. A receiving station can be built for $30,000. On the relaying of pictures from ATS 1 to the WMO conference in Apr. 1967, see NASA Release 67–77 (1967). On Nimbus, see H. Press and W. B. Huston, "Nimbus: A Progress Report," 6 *Astro. & Aero.* 56, No. 3 (Mar. 1968).

[79] On the beginning of the exchange of information in Oct. 1964, see *New York Times*, Oct. 29, 1964 at 58. See also *id.*, Mar. 4, 1967, at 7. The Soviets initially reported their data too late for maximum use. On recent progress and the exchange of Soviet weather pictures, see *Space Bus. Daily*, Mar. 20, 1968, at 109.

pause before D-Day in 1944, and weather information continues to be essential for normal operations although presumably not for the use of ICBMs.[80]

Second, weather satellites inevitably "see" or at least sense the areas beneath them. While cloud-cover cameras and other sensors are not designed to reveal human activities on the earth's surface and presumably normally do not, there have been reports of the "embarrassingly" clear pictures some of the satellites have obtained showing "unexpected detail,"[81] and the use of meteorological vehicles as "spies in the sky," whether intentional or not, has been attacked.[82]

Third, there is the fear, reportedly remote at this time, that outer space capabilities may lead to national attempts to modify the weather with conceivably adverse effects in other states.[83] Domestically, even minor attempts to influence rainfall have led to gunfire, and almost half the states of the United States now have legislated with respect to modification activities.[84] Internationally, attempts to modify control of a water resource, one of the chief goals of weather modification, have led to the brink of armed conflict; both Israel and Jordan, for example, have stated that the other's attempt to interfere with the waters of the river Jordan would constitute aggression.[85] Attempts to interfere drastically with the weather, which if successful would adversely affect another nation's way of life, even if inadvertently, might equally well serve as a *casus belli*.

Navigation

Satellite systems for navigation purposes are also a present fact. It was hoped that satellites could "provide the basis for all-weather, long-term navigation systems to determine with accuracy geodetic position, speed, and direction of a surface vehicle or aircraft, north reference and vertical reference."[86] The American Navy's Transit satellite has apparently lived up to these expectations.

Many older, alternative systems for fixing locations exist, of course, and, as has been noted, even without a satellite system ocean liners rarely get lost.[87] Nevertheless, high-speed aircraft will presumably be aided by more exact locations and, obviously, the military significance of highly accurate fixes, perhaps especially for missile-firing submarines, cannot be ignored. Here is another example of a brilliant new technology which is in itself neutral but which can be used to augment the world's system of international navigation aids[88] and to increase the efficacy of military operations.[89] Perhaps for these reasons, the U.N. Committee on the Peaceful Uses of Outer Space asked its Technical Subcommittee to make a study of the possibility of establishing a civil, world-wide, navigation satellite system on a nondiscriminatory basis.[90]

In peacetime at least, meteorological and navigation satellite systems present relatively few domestic or international areas of conflicting claims. They are services normally provided by governments and, with obvious minor exceptions, are not generally profit-yielding activities. There is thus little if any demand that they be allocated to private enterprise. Although both systems have important military significance, nations have not rejected the claim of other nations of a right to create such systems. Again, there are those who suggest that

---

[80] For criticism by Sen. Gruening of the alleged use of satellite-derived weather information to guide bombers in Viet Nam, see *New York Times,* April 15, 1967, at 1.

[81] See, e.g., Singer, *supra* n. 77.

[82] On U.S. meteorological satellites as "spy satellites," see, e.g., Petrov, "Spy Satellites and International Law," *Cosmos and International Law* (in Russian) 171, 176–77 (Korovin ed. 1962).

[83] See RAND, *supra* note 42, 198; Hearings on H.R. 11881 at 915 (Reichelderfer); Ball, "Shaping the Law of Weather Control," 58 *Yale L. J.* 213–44 (1949); Loebsack, *Our Atmosphere* (1959).

[84] See Taubenfeld, *Weather Modification Law, Controls, Operations* (Survey prepared for the Special Commission on Weather Modification of the National Science Foundation, 1966); Oppenheimer, "Legal Aspects of Weather Modification," paper presented at the Western Snow Conference, April 21, 1965 (mimeo.).

[85] See Doherty, "Jordan Waters Conflict," *Int'l Concil.* 35 (May 1965). In general, see Taubenfeld & Taubenfeld, *International Implications of Weather Modification Activities,* study prepared for the U.S. Dept. of State (Office of External Research, 1968).

[86] See RAND, *supra* note 42, 199. For a recent appraisal, see *Time,* Aug. 11, 1967, at 56–57.

[87] See, e.g., Michael, *supra* note 61, 48–49. On the expected benefits, see *New York Times,* Dec. 31, 1958.

[88] See Jessup & Taubenfeld, *supra* note 61, at 236.

[89] It should also be noted that geodetic satellites have made the problem of accuracy in locating places and distances on earth much easier. See RAND, *supra* note 42, 182–83. On NASA programs in geodesy, see NASA Press Release 64–236 (Sept. 22, 1964).

[90] *New York Times,* Nov. 8, 1964, at 12. On the use of navigation satellites by merchant ships, see *New York Times,* July 30, 1967, at 1, 28. On Japanese plans to create a navigation system, see *New York Times,* Apr. 1, 1966, at 59M. On the use of navigation satellites by commercial aircraft, see *New York Times,* Mar. 30, 1967, at 52.

such systems should be created by international organizations in another sphere; for example, ICAO already has authority to establish aids to navigation. Proponents of national systems have won the day but, in fact, there is substantial international cooperation in these fields and there is, as noted above, a limited U.S.-USSR cooperative agreement in the field of meteorology.[91]

Military Activities

The military uses of outer space have, on the whole, been relatively ignored by the public, if not by Congress in the United States except perhaps for observation satellites.[92] Even apart from the ICBMs, there are a substantial number of military uses of outer space, some of which are identical with or similar to scientific or commercial uses while some are distinctly military in nature. Among the former are geodetic surveys and meteorological, navigational, and communications systems, all of which have magnificent peaceful potentials and yet furnish information or services essential to military operations.[93]

In the field of space activities, even within the nation, it is extremely difficult to make and maintain a rigid distinction between civilian and military programs. The United States made a policy decision after Sputnik to place prime emphasis in its space program on a civilian agency, NASA;[94] yet what is developed for NASA programs is normally also of direct or applied use in military programs. NASA's astronauts, like the Soviet Union's cosmonauts, in general have been military officers. Several hundred Air Force officers serve with NASA.[95] There are joint NASA–Defense Department programs.[96] Boosters serve both programs.[97] This overlap and interchange is not unique. The Navy supplies the logistic support, and the majority of personnel engaged in Antarctic activities and such operations are exempted from the military ban of the Antarctic Treaty of 1959.[98] The problem nevertheless remains a prominent one with respect to outer space activities. In a real sense, as former Secretary of the Air Force Zucker has said, "There is no such thing as peaceful space or military space. There is just space. . . . This nation is holding to

---

[91] On U.S.-USSR programs in weather, communications, and magnetic field experiments, and the slow pace of reaching agreement, see *New York Herald Tribune*, Jan. 3, 1964 cited in *Astro. & Aero. 1964*, 2 (1965) (Dryden); *New York Times*, Jan. 19, 1964, at 33, and Jan. 27, 1964, at 12; NASA Release 64–21 (Jan. 27, 1964) with U.K.; *Washington Evening Star*, Feb. 22, 1964, cited in *1964 A. & A.* (NASA) 75; *id.* at 97 (Dryden); *New York Times*, June 6, 1964, at 1 (joint weather). On later difficulties with the June 1964 agreement on space medicine, see *Washington Post*, Oct. 6, 1964, cited in *1964 A. & A.* (NASA) 342. The meteorological link was ready for operation in 1965. See also note 79, *supra*.

[92] See, e.g., the somewhat acid comments in 3 *Astro. & Aero.* 101 (Sept. 1965) on the difficulties the Air Force has found in justfying the Manned Orbital Laboratory as designed for "peaceful" experiments rather than for its more obvious role as a vehicle for reconnaissance. On the military potentials of space, see J. S. Foster, "Space and Military Realities," 6 *Astro. & Aero.*, No. 2, 82–85 (Feb. 1968); W. C. Clemens, "Outer Space and Arms Control," MIT Center for Space Research, Doc. CSR TR–66–14 (Oct. 1966); Kantrowitz, "Some Military Potentials in Space," 3 *Astro. & Aero.* 36–38 (Nov. 1965); Singer, "The Case for Man in Space," 32 *Reporter* 25–28 (June 17, 1965). See also Baker, "The Military Implications of Space," *Current Problems in Space Law* 73–78 (Brit. Inst. of Int'l & Comp. Law 1966) [hereinafter cited as *Current Problems*]; Tager, "Legal Controls of the Military Uses of Spacecraft," *Current Problems* 79–82; and Comments by Bin Cheng & L. Bond, *Current Problems* 83–86.

[93] See generally, Jessup and Taubenfeld, *supra* note 61, at 222–25 (1959). Tiros VII pictures have been used to make

calculations in advance of missile launches. *Missiles & Rockets*, Jan. 6, 1964, at 16.

See also *supra* note 80 on the use of satellite-derived weather information in Viet Nam. For a survey of all uses, see S. Serebreny, *The Contribution of Satellite Viewed Cloud Cover to the Peaceful Uses of Outer Space*, Stanford Conf. (mimeo., Aug. 1967). The Syncom satellites have been used for military communications experiments. See *Bus. Wk.*, Sept. 12, 1964; *New York Times*, Sept. 29, 1964. On the Army's lunar mapping program, see *Washington Post*, June 24, 1964, cited in *1964 A. & A.* (NASA) 221.

[94] On the American decision to create a civilian space agency, see Griffith, *The National Aeronautics and Space Act* (1962) and, on the program generally see Van Dyke, *Pride and Power* (1964), esp. chap. 12 on NASA-DOD relations. See also, on NASA, its programs, and the NASA-DOD relationship, Rosholt, *An Administrative History of NASA, 1958–1963* (NASA 1966).

[95] See *Missiles & Rockets*, May 18, 1964, at 46; NASA Press Release 64–234 (1964); MSFC Release 67–107, July 1, 1967.

[96] See e.g., NASA Press Release 64–34 (Feb. 14, 1964) (concerning joint instrumentation ships); *Av. Wk.* (Mar. 13, 1967) at 18. NASA scientists are reportedly aiding in work for the war in Viet Nam. See *Washington Post*, Dec. 4, 1967 at A1.

[97] On the Titan as an ICBM and as a civilian launch vehicle, see *Missiles & Rockets*, Jan. 20, 1964, at 11.

[98] Discussed *infra* in chap. 3. Note also that, e.g., when the U.S. Navy's icebreaker Northwind engaged in peaceful exploration of the "Soviet" Arctic sea in 1965, "canvas covers were placed over the ship's twin five-inch guns," upon entering the eastern Barents Sea "to emphasize the scientific aspects of the voyage." *New York Times*, Aug. 2, 1965, at 29.

peaceful objectives in space, but we also know that the military services will have to do the same thing in space that they have always done in the media of the land, sea, and air."[99]

This difficulty of keeping military and civilian missions separate was again demonstrated by the Gemini V flight of eight days in 1965. As the Russians noted and as the *New York Times* observed:

> To a limited extent, some . . . military experimentation is being carried out in the Gemini program.
> In the Gemini flight, for example, the two astronauts have made visual, photographic and infra-red observations of a Minuteman ballistic missile being launched. They have also conducted relatively crude photographic reconnaissance of the earth and experimented with rendezvous radar.[100]

In fact, some of the photographs at least were astoundingly beautiful and quite clear.[101] Moreover, as Lipson has pithily put it with respect to an earlier Soviet manned flight: "We do not know whether Gagarin's camera looked up, astronomically, or straight out, navigationally, or inward, clinically, or downward, curiously."[102]

Operations that are clearly military include observation for early warning, military and civilian defense, and target spotting, the placement of weapons in orbit (bombardment systems), the detection of nuclear explosions in space and elsewhere,[103] and the development of rocket bombers, military space stations in satellites and on celestial bodies,[104] of anti-missile missiles and satellites,[105] of anti-satellite satellites, of antispace station satellites, and so on. The list is limited only by one's imagination.[106] This does not mean that many of these

---

[99] Cited by Rechtschoffen, *supra* note 2, 213 (1964). See also remarks of Meeker, Apr. 13, 1963, 48 *Dept. State Bull.* 746, 749–50 (May 13, 1963). In 1968, the U.S. Air Force Air Defense Command was renamed the Aerospace Defense Command. See *Space Bus. Daily*, Jan. 3, 1968, at 1.

[100] Aug. 26, 1965. For at least sporadic Soviet attacks on earlier manned flights as "military" and "aggressive," see *1964 A. & A.* (NASA) 118 (comments of Col. G. Terent'yev, Mar. 26, 1964). On the ability of the astronauts to observe rocket launchings and reentry of a missile, see 3 *Astro. & Aero.* (Oct. 1965), and *New York Times*, Aug. 25, 1965 at 24. For a recent Soviet attack on the whole U.S. space program ("346 of 455" payloads to mid-1967 were for espionage), see *Philadelphia Inq.*, Oct. 8, 1967, at 13C. See also note 137 *infra*.

[101] On Soviet statements that the Gemini V flight of Aug. 1965 was a "spy" flight, see *New York Times*, Aug. 26, 1965, at 15. See also *Washington Post*, Aug. 31, 1965 at A3 (Cuban reaction). The astronauts on the flight did take pictures of Cuba which were described as "just scenic shots." See *New York Times*, Aug. 26, 1965, at 1. On the "embarrassment" of NASA and the Pentagon over pictures taken by Gemini Astronauts, using a long focal length Questar camera, see 4 *Astro. & Aero.* 90 (Jan. 1966). See also the pictures taken of Dallas, Texas, from an orbiting satellite in which streets, railroad tracks, and runways, etc. at Dallas' airport, Love Field, are quite clear. *Dallas Morning News*, Oct. 8, 1965, at 9A. On "170 usable terrain photographs" from Gemini V, see also text of Jan. 6, 1966, "Report at NASA," *1966 A. & A.* (NASA) 7. On the clarity of pictures taken from a Gemini spacecraft, see *Earth Photographs from Gemini III, IV, and V*, June 18, 1967. Note the pictures of the streets of El Paso, Texas, taken from 115 miles up.

[102] *1963 Proceedings, Am. Soc. Int'l L.* 175 (1963).

[103] On the success of U.S. detection satellite under Project VELA, see DOD Press Release 30–64 (1964); *New York Times*, July 20, 1964, at 27; *Missiles & Rockets*, Apr. 27, 1964, at 11; 3 *Astro. & Aero.* 102 (Sept. 1965) (on the launching of a third pair). On a project to intercept messages from Soviet reconnaissance satellites (U.S.-Australia), see e.g., *New York Times*, Aug. 29, 1967, at 24.

[104] On the moon as a military base, see *supra* p. 5. On the controversy as to its utility, see also Saenger, *supra* note 2, 136; Levy, *supra* note 9, 202–5.

[105] On Sept. 17, 1964, Pres. Johnson asserted that the United States had achieved an operational system to intercept and destroy satellites. This was explained and expanded by Sec. McNamara. See, e.g., *1964 A. & A.* (NASA) 320; and DOD Press Release 673–64 (Sept. 18, 1964).

[106] In Oct. 1965 in discussing "The Military Implications of Space," Gen. Bernard A. Schriever, AFSC commander, said: "Our military efforts in space can be placed into three broad categories; first, the development of space systems to support military missions on earth; second, the development of defense measures against possible enemy actions in space; and third, the conduct of experimentation and of programs aimed at pushing technology forward. . . ." He noted two examples of unmanned satellite systems: (1) the Nuclear Detection Program consisting of six Vela satellites gathering information on radiation backgrounds in far space and defining an operational nuclear detection system; and (2) communications satellites. Speech to the Governor's Conference, Oct. 1–2, 1965, reprinted in *1965 A. & A.* (NASA) 459.

On military possibilities generally, see, e.g., Saenger, *supra* note 2, chap. 8; Sullivan, *supra* note 2, at 149–51; *The Space Industry*, chap. 2 (Military Challenge) (1962); Gen. Schriever, "Does the Military Have a Role in Space?" in Levy, *supra* note 9, at 59–68; Berg, "Weapons and Space," in Schwartz, *supra* note 42, at 54; Schultz, "Weapons in Space," *id.* 60; and Forman, "Why a Military Space Program?" *id.* 68; Wilks, *supra* note 12, chap. 9; Van Dyke, *supra* note 94, chaps. 3, 4. See also Foster, "Space and Disarmament," in Levy, *supra* note 9, at 50–58. Gen. Schriever stated that the military then had no programs beyond 22,300 miles (*id.* 61). For a partial list of U.S. military space projects, see Appendix A. In Nov. 1965 Col. Gen. Tolubko, First Deputy Commander of the Soviet Strategic Rocket Forces told Tass that Russia was developing maneuverable long-range ICBMs. See *New York Times*, Nov. 14, 1965, at 74.

more exotic suggestions are imminently practicable.[107] On the other hand, military space systems for observation, communications, navigation, and meteorology are in existence.[108]

Moreover, space is also being used for other, near-in, directly military purposes. Nations with ICBM capabilities have tested and presumably will continue to test these systems.[109] As already suggested, under most present definitions this involves at least a brief passage through outer space. There do not appear to have been protests about or conflict over the space traverse of these weapons undergoing testing. It would be difficult now to keep others from testing similar products. The testing of "conventional" weapons must therefore at present be considered an acceptable or at least accepted use.

One military system, the placing of weapons of mass destruction in orbit, was the subject of a condemnatory U.N. resolution in 1963 and was barred by the 1967 Space Treaty. Both the United States and the Soviet Union had persistently suggested such a ban on this activity.[110] Yet, why should this particular weapon be less controversial than the existence of national fleets on the seas, submarines under the high seas, or missile sites on one's own or on friendly territory? Russia and the United States, apparently not needing these perhaps unstable systems now, agreed to the ban, but what of other smaller potential space powers for whom they might be far more valuable, and what of other emerging major powers, wishing to catch up fast? The claim of a right to orbit weapons of mass destruction as "equalizers" cannot be said to have been finally eliminated for all nations.[111]

Indeed, a potential related threat on the part of the space powers themselves was identified in 1967 when a series of Soviet satellite test flights were indicated by Secretary of Defense McNamara to be at least the possible forerunners of a Fractional Orbital Bombardment System (FOBS). While an ICBM follows a ballistic trajectory from launch to impact with an apogee of perhaps 800 miles, the FOBS would be fired into a very low orbit, and, before the first orbit was completed, a rocket engine would slow down the payload causing it to drop out of orbit and into an ICBM-like reentry path. Flight time to target could be much less than for an ICBM and might yield as little as three minutes' warning time. The Secretary stated that this system would not violate the outer space treaty since *testing* a system was not barred by the treaty, assuming that no nuclear weapon was carried, and indeed that, even with a weapon of mass destruction on board, there might technically be no violation since not even one orbit was completed.[112] Whatever the present state of the law on this particular point, issues of this sort seem destined to recur.

Another set of issues involves the right to test nuclear devices at high altitudes and in deep space. Both space powers have conducted such tests. They do interfere with scientific observation, ground communications, and natural phenomena, thus competing with other claims to a free use of space. Although the facts are unclear, they may also have some effects on health through fallout, leading to a claim on behalf of all men to an undistorted survival. This last, the right of man to survive, even

---

[107] For suggestions on the possibility of war in space, see Golovine, *Conflict in Space* (1962); Siekman, "A Running Start Toward Cosmic War," *Life,* Sept. 10, 1962. For a suggestion that the space race may in time *replace* war, see the statement by Webb, *New York Times,* June 8, 1964, at 22.

[108] The Navy's Transit navigation system was declared operational in Dec. 1964. See 3 *Astro. & Aero.* 95 (Mar. 1965).

On the military ComSat program, see *supra* note 66; *New York Times,* Oct. 10, 1964, at 1, 14. *Missiles & Rockets,* Oct. 12, 1964, at 10; *New York Times,* July 2, 1967, at 20.

On the success of the military geodetic surveys by satellite (SECOR) in pinpointing exact locations on earth, see DOD Press Release 776–64 (Oct. 27, 1964). On its secret launching in Jan. 1964, see *Space Bus. Daily,* Feb. 19, 1964, at 274 and DOD Press Release 156–64 (Feb. 21, 1964).

On the general problems of observation satellites, see also Morenoff, *World Peace through Space Law* (1967); Soragham, "Reconnaissance Satellites: Legal Characterization and Possible Utilization for Peacekeeping," 13 *McGill L. J.* 458 (1967).

[109] There are some special problems connected with testing and the closing off of target areas. These are discussed *infra* chap. 3. On the extensive Soviet tests from Aug. 1964 to the end of the year near Christmas and Howland Islands, see *1964 A. & A.* (NASA) 268, 333. On tests in 1967, see *Washington Evening Star,* Nov. 27, 1967, at A5.

[110] See the comments in Nov. 1965, when the Soviet Union displayed "orbital missiles" at a military parade. *New York Times,* Nov. 8, 1965, at 36; *Washington Evening Star,* Nov.10, 1965, at H2. *Washington Post,* Nov. 19, 1965, at A10.

On the technical and other problems of such a system, see, e.g., "Summary Report: Future Programs Task Force of NASA," *supra* note 1.

[111] Indeed, in Aug. 1967, the Soviet Union was reported to be testing, or planning to test, reentry systems for such vehicles. Orbiting is barred by the treaty; testing is not.

[112] On the FOBS, see DOD Release 1060–67, Nov. 3, 1967 (Sec'y McNamara); *New York Times,* Oct. 17, 1967, at 1; *Av. Wk.,* Nov. 13, 1967, at 31; "Review of the Space Program," *House Comm. on Science and Astronautics,* 90th Cong., 1st Sess., Serial J, 138 (1967).

against the claimed right of the nations to defend themselves, is in our world the hardest of all to specify operationally and to promote.[113]

The 1963 Nuclear Test Ban Treaty prohibits atmospheric and outer space tests for participants. Without this agreed ban, it does not seem that the charter or the U.N. resolutions make testing illegal in any accepted sense.[114] Communist China and France have refused to agree to the treaty's terms. Eventually there may be claims by other states as well to try this facet of military experimentation and preparedness in outer space when they acquire the capability. Perhaps we may someday welcome unavoidable tests in deep space as an alternative to tests in the atmosphere.

In addition, the military of both space powers continue to have a strong interest in all outer space activities and potentials.[115] In the somewhat dramatic words of leading Air Force officers, military control of outer space may mean, in time, control of earth as well.[116] Whether or not this is so, the military cannot ignore the possibility.[117] As one Defense Department speaker has said: "We in the Department of Defense have always looked upon space less as a matter of adventure and more as a matter of necessity; we explore its potential not because it is 'there' but because we have needs that are 'here.' "[118]

Soviet leaders have taken similar positions. A high percentage of Soviet space launchings are estimated to be military in nature.[119] In 1961, Premier Khrushchev told the world: "You do not have 50 and 100 megaton bombs. We have bombs stronger than 100 megatons. We placed Gagarin and Titov in space, and we can replace them with other loads that can be directed to any place on earth."[120] Marshal Sokolovsky, writing in 1962, stated: "Soviet military strategy takes into account . . . the use of outer space and aerospace vehicles."[121] And American interest is certainly great.[122] Both countries have shielded their military programs in secrecy. An indication of the scope of these programs is impressive, however. For this reason, a partial listing by agency of the military space programs of the United States is included in Appendix A. Despite its length, this listing is indicative rather than complete. Moreover, on August 25, 1965, President Johnson formally announced approval of the Air Force Manned Orbiting Laboratory (MOL) program designed to test the usefulness of space stations for military purposes. As explained in a Department of Defense statement, the project was designed to "learn more

---

[113] The attacks on the high-altitude tests are noted *supra*.

[114] See, e.g., Taubenfeld, "Nuclear Testing and International Law," 16 *Sw. L. J.* 365 (1962).

[115] On the interplay of military and political factors, see also Frey, "The Military Danger," 212 *Atlantic Monthly* 46–50 (Aug. 1963); Leavitt, "Mixed Hopes for the Military Space Mission," 46 *Air Force/Space Dig.* 71 ff. (Sept. 1963); Puckett, *The Military Role in Space—a Summary of Officials, Public Justifications* 1–29 (RAND P–2681; Aug. 1962); Knorr, "On the International Implications of Outer Space Activities," in Goldsen, *International Political Implications of Activities in Outer Space* 133 (RAND, 1960); Rechtschaffen, *supra* note 99, 213–16 and sources cited. See Siekman, "The Fantastic Weaponry," *Fortune*, June 1962, at 56 ff. On Soviet views, see "Soviet Views on the Military Implications of Space," in "Soviet Space Programs," *supra* note 5.

[116] Gen. Gerhart, noting that manned Soviet satellites have repeatedly passed over the United States, has said that "strong modern aerospace defenses are indispensable; they are a vital part of deterrence—they are essential to survival and they are our insurance to victory." *J. Armed Forces* 6 (Oct. 24, 1964).

Gen. Power, former Commander of SAC, declared: "There can be no doubt that the possibilities of military space operations are indeed staggering. It would, therefore, be folly to assume that the Soviets would fail to recognize these possibilities and would hesitate to exploit them for both their political and military ends." Former Air Force Chief-of-Staff General LeMay said: "A nation that has maneuverable space vehicles and revolutionary armaments can indeed control the world. For peace or for aggression." See Rechtschaffen, *supra* note 99, 213.

[117] As the Air Force Chief of Staff, Gen. McConnell, said

---

on Jan. 13, 1966: "[H]istory shows that military weapons and strategy tend to exploit every possible medium for offensive action, and we must assume that this might also be true for space. Our only alternative, therefore, is to learn as much as we can about the space medium so that, if and when a threat should begin to materialize, we have the knowledge and 'building blocks' to develop a proper defense against it." Cited by Menter, "Government Regulations of Space Activities," 7 *JAG L. Rev.* (Air Force) 5, at 22.

On the lack of knowledge of the present military importance of space, see *Christian Sci. Mon.* Oct. 13, 1965, at 14.

[118] DDR&E Deputy Director (Strategic and Space Systems) D. J. Fink, address to the National Space Club, Wash. D.C., Apr. 1966, DOD Release 341–66 (April 26, 1966).

[119] On aid afforded to the Venus IV probe by Soviet military rocket experts, for example, see *Baltimore Sun,* Nov. 17, 1967, at A11.

[120] Cited in Rechtschaffen, *supra* note 99, 213–14.

[121] Cited in Levy, *supra* note 9, 59.

[122] See also Gen. Schriever, *supra* note 106. In 1963, e.g., 70 percent of U.S. orbital shots were made by the U.S. armed forces. *Space Bus. Daily* 18–19 (Jan. 6, 1964) (Welsh). In 1967 the U.S. orbited 87 spacecraft of which 66 were launched by the Defense Department.

about what man is able to do in space and how that ability can be used for military purposes."[123]

Thus, the experimental program was designed to seek to determine the feasibility of using manned satellites as command posts for military operations on earth, to inspect and destroy hostile satellites, to conduct photographic studies of the earth, and to monitor enemy radio and radar transmissions. It was also meant to furnish further information on how well man can function over prolonged periods in space. It was reported as probable that the MOL would at least on occasion pass over the Soviet Union, in the same way that Soviet manned vehicles have passed over the United States.[124] For stated reasons of economy, the Air Force MOL program was cancelled in 1969, though NASA's similar program was expected to continue.

While it may be attractive to imagine a world without military space systems, it is as well perhaps to sum up the words of President Johnson:

Our knowledge of outer space, and of activities in space, allows us to say with sad conviction that space systems can be of direct defense importance. Indeed, some defense functions can be conducted with unique advantage in space. . . . Space programs have benefits which can apply to both civilian and military efforts. It is not useful to pretend that arbitrary distinctions can or should be made between the two. . . . If I could get but one message to you it would be this: the future of this country and the welfare of the free world depend upon our success in space.

He nevertheless went on:

[O]ur American dream for outer space is a dream of peace and a dream of friendly cooperation among all the nations of the earth.

We believe the heavens belong to the people of every country. We are working and we will continue to work through the United Nations . . . to extend the rule of law into outer space.

We intend to live up to our agreement not to orbit weapons of mass destruction and we will continue to hold out to all nations, including the Soviet Union, the hand of cooperation in the exciting years of space exploration which lie ahead for all of us.[125]

Of the space military systems just noted, it is the satellites which "see" or sense the earth's surface that have caused the greatest international stir, no doubt because they are already in orbit.[126] Many nonmilitary sensor systems are also in orbit. Scientists "observe" the earth to gain more basic knowledge of its size, shape, and physical characteristics and for meteorological and other purposes as well. Some of these observations, however innocent, give information, even if inadvertently, on states and cannot avoid violating the sanctity, in this sense, of their national territory. Most, as we have seen, have some inherent military significance. None thus far has raised violent opposition, although the Soviet Union has condemned "spying" by meteorological satellites.[127]

On the other hand, systems employed on national peacekeeping missions, such as the American early warning system against surprise attack, have led to conflicts of definition and interpretation of their true purposes. The United States insists that to know of warlike preparations within a closed society like the Soviet Union is essential to the security and even the survival of the free world and is therefore a legal right.[128] Such systems are, in the

---

[123] *New York Times,* Aug. 26, 1965, at 30M. On the MOL as a $2 billion project, see *Tech. Wk.,* May 8, 1967 at 14 (DOD satellites); see also *Av. Wk.,* Mar. 13, 1967, at 12.

[124] For objections to and explanations of the use of and need for a manned military orbital vehicle, see among many: Air Force Chief-of-Staff LeMay, Feb. 3, 1964, Air Force Info. Pol. Letter, Feb. 1964; See also *Army-Navy-Air Force J. and R.,* Jan. 25, 1964, at 21, 30; *New York Times,* Aug. 26, 1965, at 30M; Rechtschaffen, *supra* note 99, 215. On the disutility of secrecy, see Editorials, *Missiles & Rockets,* Nov. 22, 1965 at 46; and *Washington Post,* Oct. 22, 1965, at 24. On the slowdown in MOL development, with a tentative 1969 date set for the first, see 4 *Astro. & Aero.* 96 (Apr. 1966). On legal issues, see Cooper, "The Manned Orbiting Laboratory: A Major Legal and Political Decision," 51 *A.B.A.J.* 1137–1140 (Dec. 1965). Many of the canceled Dyna-Soar experiments were apparently planned for the MOL.

[125] Cited in Rechtschaffen, *supra* note 99, 216.

[126] See Cooper, "Some Crucial Questions Concerning the Space Treaty: A Commentary," 48 *Air Force/Space Dig.* (Mar. 1967).

[127] There are many reports as to the excellent quality of present pictures taken from outer space. There may in fact be more of a problem with the clarity of pictures taken by meteorological satellites. The American government has stated, e.g., that Tiros pictures have been found clear enough to show life on earth in only 2 of 350,000 cases. See 2 *Astro. & Aero.* 179 (May 17, 1964). At the same time, there have been reports of the "remarkable" infrared images of the ground taken by a Nimbus satellite which, while not having a high ground resolution, showed, even at night, a river in Russia, mountains in Italy, etc. See 2 *Astro. & Aero.* 90 (Oct. 1964).

On observation from space, see also RAND, *supra* note 42, 174–176. On the developing field of the use of aerial photography in law, see Wolf, "Aerial Photography as a Legal Tool," 52 *A.B.A.J.* 543 ff. (1966).

[128] On the "right to know" with respect to Cuba, see remarks of President Johnson, *New York Times,* June 3, 1964, at 25. See generally Meeker, "Observation in Space," in Cohen, *supra* note 48, and 75; and in 48 *Dept. State Bull.* 746, 749–50 (May 13, 1963).

American view, defensive only and are hence permissible under the U.N. Charter, wherever placed.[129] To this, Russia objects on the ground that in her view it is the United States who is the potential aggressor, and such a system must in reality be designed for attack purposes and is itself aggressive.[130] In any event, Russia has more or less consistently rejected the "use of artificial satellites for the collection of intelligence information in the territory" of a state as, under all circumstances, espionage, and illegal wherever conducted.

Indeed, the Soviet government attempted in 1963 to have the idea that "the use of artificial satellites for the collection of intelligence information in the territory of a foreign state is incompatible with the objectives of mankind in its conquest of outer space" included in a General Assembly declaration.[131] They also initially opposed an unconditional obligation to assist spaceships and their crews to return home safely since this meant that "states must undertake to return spy satellites, safe and intact, to their legal owners with intelligence data which affect national security interests."[132]

Without an international treaty to this effect, it is far from clear that collecting information in peacetime is an international crime,[133] and the term may well not be at all applicable to many types of national information gathering for peacekeeping through warning systems, for example. The collection of data on incoming missiles from outside the potential aggressor's territory, however defined, would more clearly seem in the nature of self-defense than of espionage activities. Like so many lines, of course, the conceptual division may by nature be arbitrary. Questions remain in any event as to which elements of information gathering can be included as peacekeeping, which are "essential" in different likely circumstances, and who should perform them in each case.

At one extreme, a universal arms control and inspection system, using satellites, would be legal and its information-gathering activities could not constitute espionage. Indeed, one of the most productive peaceful uses of space may well be information gathering for

---

On observation generally, see also Quigg, "Open Skies and Open Space," 37 *For. Aff.* 95–106 (1958); Young, "The Aerial Inspection Plan and Air Space Sovereignty," 23 *Geo. Wash. L. Rev.* 565–89 (Apr. 1956); Beresford, "Surveillance Aircraft and Satellites, a Problem of International Law," 27 *J. of Air L. and Commerce* 107 ff. (1960).

On some of the political implications, see Knorr, "On the International Implications of Outer Space," *RAND Report R–362–RC,* 133, 145 (1960).

The David Davies Institute has similarly stated that, while space vehicles designed as weapons of conventional, nuclear, chemical, or bacteriological warfare should be banned in outer space, this prohibition "does not extend to surveillance or reconnaissance satellites, which may primarily serve military purposes, yet have the advantage that they contribute to an open world and so increase rather than diminish security." Comment xviii, Draft Convention I.

[129] This is, of course, not exclusively an "American" view. Professor Meyer has stated: "Neither can the ordinary use of reconnaissance satellites launched in peace-time be regarded as non-peaceful. They have a military connotation, but are not launched for aggressive purposes in peacetime." Int'l L. Ass'n, *Report of the 50th Conference* 42 (Brussels, 1962).

[130] See Crane, "Soviet Attitude towards International Space Law," 56 *Am. J. Int'l L.* 685, 704 ff. (1962). Crane points out: "Soviet condemnation of specific types of US satellites as aggressive began shortly after the May 1960 U–2 case . . . but the Soviets did not label any specific satellite as aggressive until the July 23, 1961, issue of *Krasnaya Zvesda* specifically included Midas III and Tiros III in the same legal category as the U–2 planes and designated them as 'acts of aggression.' " See Colonel B. Aleksandrov, "Spies in Space," *Krasnaya Zvesda,* July 23, 1961, at 3.

For consideration of the Samos and other systems as potentially destabilizing influences, whether legal or not, see Falk, "Toward a Responsible Procedure for the National Assertion of Protested Claims to Use Space," *Space and Society,* chap. 5 (1964).

[131] See the Soviet draft, U.N. Doc. A/AC.105/C2/L.6, at para. 9 (Apr. 16, 1963). See also Zhukov, "Practical Problems of Space Law," 9 *Int'l Aff.* 27, 29 (Moscow, May 1963). Soviet spokesmen have generally condemned "espionage" (with which observation is equated) as illegal in international law; see, e.g., Korovin "International Status of Cosmic Space," 5 *Int'l Aff.* 53 (Moscow, 1959); Zhukov "Space Espionage Plans and International Law," 6 *Int'l Aff.* 53 (Moscow,1960), comments by Goedhuis, 1962 *ILA Report* 79. They have occasionally treated it differently as in Tunkin's comments with respect to the Soviet spies tried in Canada in 1956; *id.* at 80–81. "The Proposals on the Assistance to and Return of Astronauts and Spacecraft," submitted by the USSR in 1964, did not expressly except observation vehicles as such. See U.N. Doc. A/AC.105/C.2/L.2/Rev. 2 (1964).

[132] Zhukov, "Practical Problems of Space Law," 9 *Int'l Aff.* 27 (Moscow, May 1963).

[133] See Note, "Legal Aspects of Reconnaissance in Airspace and Outer Space," 61 *Colum. L. Rev.* 1074, esp. note 1 (1961); 2 Oppenheim, *International Law* 408 (Lauterpacht ed., 7th ed.); Beresford, *supra* note 128, 107, 114 (1960). See also on gathering information from the seas the views of the Canadian and British delegates, U.N. Doc. A/AC.105/C.2/ SR.21 at 7 and SR.24 at 12 (1963). Contra: Mr. Federenko (USSR), U.N. Doc. A/AC.105/C.2/SR.22 at 5 (1963).

peace preservation, whether the systems are nationally or internationally directed.[134]

For observation systems then, there is a possible, admittedly arbitrary, distinction that can be made. Space activities which are very productive in peacetime—scientific, meteorological, or other systems, for example—can be usefully considered basically peaceful space activities even if there is also a military or observation potential. This category would also include information gathering of the stabilizing, peacekeeping type.

Another category of observation systems, those used specifically for targeting and other military fact-finding missions, has also been defended as legal by the United States. To the inherent need for and right of self-defense, there is added the additional claim that the systems' locations in outer space, outside the territorial sovereignty of any state, permit the characterization as legal. This may, of course, represent an implied support for the view that such surveillance is illegal when conducted elsewhere, notably in national airspace. Such surveillance activities in space are characterized by the United States as military, but defensive and nonaggressive, and do not, in the American view, in any sense run afoul of the principles of the U.N. Charter. They are equated with observations from the "free" high seas, or from "free" airspace, or from friendly countries which the United States considers permissible in law.[135] Since surveillance from

outer space is apparently effective,[136] predictably, Soviet spokesmen have tended to label all observation (at least of the Soviet Union) as illegal and aggressive wherever conducted.[137]

Observation for any nonaggressive purpose from outer space is then permissible in the American view and, indeed, at least at one time Secretary Quarles asserted that the United States would not object to Soviet surveillance satellites.[138] In practice, both the United States and the

---

[134] On satellites for inspection for disarmament purposes, see, e.g., Foster, "Space and Disarmament," in Levy, *supra* note 9, 50–58, esp. 55 ff. For doubts of their value, see *Av. Wk.,* Dec. 17, 1962, at 33 and *The Space Industry* 26. See also McNaughten, "Space Technology and Arms Control," in Cohen, *supra* note 48, 63.

Others who have commented on this potential role include: Brennan, "Arms and Arms Control in Outer Space," in Bloomfield, *supra* note 74, 123, 127; Bloomfield & Henkin, "Inspection and the Problem of Access," *Security in Disarmament* 107, 110 (Barnet & Falk ed. 1965) [hereinafter cited as Barnet & Falk]; Bloomfield, "Politics of Administering Disarmament," in *id.,* 123, 128; Berkner, "Space Research—a Permanent Peacetime Activity," in Ramo, *supra* note 72, 1, 4; Doolittle, "Impact of the Present World Situation on the Development of Peaceful Uses of Outer Space," in *id.,* at 17, 24–25.

[135] See Meeker, *supra* 128, sources cited; Sen. Gore, U.N. 1st Comm., 17th Sess., Dec. 3, 1962; Goedhuis, *supra* note 131, 78; and Cheng, 1962 *ILA Report,* at 52.

On June 13, 1962, the U.K. Representative (Miss Gutteridge) said, at the first session of the Legal Subcommittee of the United Nations Committee on the Peaceful Uses of Outer Space, U.N. Doc. A/AC.105/C.2/SR.10 (Aug. 21, 1962): "Principle 8 [of a Soviet proposal] constituted, in substance, a ban on the

use of space vehicles for observation purposes and was, again, so closely connected with controversial political questions as to be quite unsuited to a declaration of basic legal principles. Moreover, in contradiction to the assertion by the representative of the Soviet Union, the United Kingdom held that observation from points outside the territory of any State was not contrary to international law; nor did such observation offend against Art. 2(4) of the United Nations Charter, since it involved neither the use nor the threat of force." To the same effect, see the comments of the Canadian Representative, U.N. Doc. A/AC.105/C.2/SR.21/7 (1963).

On Soviet complaints about radio and radar monitoring along its borders from countries friendly to the United States as "espionage," see *New York Times,* June 11, 1964, at 10. On the U.S. Ferret system, designed to "listen in" on communications within a country from overhead, and to intercept radar, radio, and microwave transmissions, see Van Dyke, *supra* n. 94, at 36. On the prospective use of the Manned Orbiting Laboratory "to monitor radio and radar transmissions," see *New York Times,* Aug. 29, 1965, at 1E.

[136] In Mar. 1967, Pres. Johnson, while asking not to be quoted, stated flatly that he knew "how many missiles the enemy has." See *New York Times,* Mar. 17, 1967, at 13.

[137] See Zhukov, "Practical Problems of Space Law," 9 *Int'l Aff.* 27, 28, 29 (Moscow, May 1963); Korovin, "Peaceful Cooperation in Space," 9 *Int'l Aff.* 61 (Moscow, 1963); Zhukov, "Problem of Outer Space Qualifications," 1963 *Proceedings, Am. Soc'y Int'l L.* 193, 195; Korovin, "Aerial Espionage and International Law," 6 *Int'l Aff.* 49 (Moscow, June 1960); Korovin, "Outer Space Must Become a Zone of Real Peace," 9 *Int'l Aff.* 92 (Moscow, Sept. 1963); Gabrovski, "Some Legal Aspects of Space Exploration" 9 *Int'l Aff.* 92 (Moscow, Feb. 1963); Timerbaly, USSR representative at the Legal Subcommittee of the U.N. Space Committee, said: "All attempts to reconcile the collection of intelligence information by artificial satellites with the principles of international law were completely unfounded. Espionage in any environment was inadmissible and it was prohibited by every system of national law." Summary Record of the Twentieth Meeting, May 3, 1963, U.N. Doc. A/AC.105/C.2/SR.28/13 (1963). See also note 100 *supra.*

[138] See *Hearings on H.R. 11881,* at 1107 (1958). At least at one time in 1960, Khrushchev is reported to have been agreeable to some photography of the USSR. See Eisenhower, *Waging Peace* 556 (1965). Thus far, neither nation has interfered with the satellites of the other though both probably

Soviet Union now reportedly maintain surveillance space craft on a regular basis.[139] The American Samos series has reportedly been "remarkably successful."[140] The Samos system has been credited with giving information on the progress of the Chinese nuclear weapons program. It has been said that, based on Samos pictures, the United States was able to give advance warning of the test in the fall of 1964.[141] By that time, the Air Force budget no longer identified the costs of the reconnaissance satellite program, but observers estimated the outlay at $400 million annually.[142]

The Russian Cosmos series has also apparently had camera-equipped satellites in it, and Premier Khrushchev said in 1964: "If you wish, I can show you photos of military bases taken from outer space. I will show them to President Johnson if he wishes."[143] This fact is

probably responsible for the recent, relatively low-key Soviet complaints about observation satellites. It may, in time, require a change in the Soviet view that observation *is* espionage and that espionage (though universally practiced) is an international wrong constituting interference in a state's internal affairs and hence is illegal both under general and charter law. There is thus at present a major, if perhaps diminishing, political conflict over claimed legal rights to utilize some of the most important potentials of space, a question we return to in the following chapters.

Other Uses

Other uses of satellites include the search for earth resources, including mineral deposits, soil with high growth potential, and fish at sea; the monitoring of such diverse phenomena as ice movements on the oceans, forest fires, mass insect movements (e.g., locusts) on land, river and flood prediction, and similar worldwide collection of warning data, collision avoidance, and distress relay and rescue.[144] The delivery of mail by rocket has been attempted experimentally.[145] Cargo rockets

---

have some capacity to do so even now. This is true despite such earlier Soviet statements as that by Korovin, who wrote: "It is scarcely to be expected for Governments to be indifferent to acts of foreign intelligence directed against them, solely because they are conducted not in the air but in outer space." "International Status of Cosmic Space," 5 *Int'l Aff.* 53 (Moscow, 1959). Similarly, he wrote in 1960 that penetration by illegal satellite could be "paralyzed and rebuffed" and that "such action will be fully justified under the existing rules of international law and the United Nations Charter." "Space Espionage and International Law," 6 *Int'l Aff.* 53 (Moscow, Oct. 1960). In 1962 Zadorozhnyi stated that "the right of a state to destroy a satellite-spy and in general every spacecraft whatsoever interfering with the security of this state is indisputable." Quoted by Woetzel in *Space and Society* 130.

Note that it has also been said, with respect to the legal effects of an interference, that whatever the USSR should do to an American reconnaissance satellite "it is sufficient to observe that . . . this . . . will not appear to be violative of international law." Note, "National Sovereignty of Outer Space," 74 *Harv. L. Rev.* 1154, 1174 (1961). Nevertheless, by 1964, the Soviet writer Vereschetin, in an article not specifically mentioning reconnaissance satellites, denounced the theory that article 51 of the U.N. Charter allowed preventive attack upon a spacecraft, noting that Article 51 only applies in the case of an armed attack. "Outer Space—a Realm of Peace," 10 *Int'l Aff.* 98 (Moscow, June 1964).

An attack would certainly appear to be an "unfriendly" act if an unmanned vehicle were involved and, in view of practice to date, perhaps more than that if the vehicles were manned. On the earlier Soviet view of antisatellite warfare, see Crane, *supra* note 130, at 704 ff.

[139] See, e.g., 2 *Astro. & Aero.* 281 (Aug. 10, 1964).

[140] See, e.g., *New York Times,* Aug. 26, 1965 at 1 (on the "remarkable" pictures).

[141] See 2 *Astro. & Aero.* 74 (Dec. 1964).

[142] *Ibid.*

[143] See *New York Times,* May 30, 1964, at 1 (interview with

Sen. Benton). On Soviet reconnaissance satellites, see also *ibid.* and 2 *Astro. & Aero.* 90 (Oct. 1964) (which talks in terms of "routine Soviet reconnaissance missions"). On the Soviet statements, see also 5 *Astro. & Aero.* (1967), at 139–40.

[144] On the possible uses of earth-orbital satellites for prospecting for earth resources, minerals, fish, etc., see Stanford Research Inst., 1, 2 *Priority Analysis of Manned Orbital Research Applications* (prepared for Douglas Aircraft Co., Inc., 1965), and *Proceedings of the American Astronautical Society, Feb. 1966, passim.* For speculation on the potential legal problems involved in such observation, see Taubenfeld, "Legal Aspects of the Use of Satellites in the Exploitation of Earth Resources," *id.* See also Manned Space Flight Center Release 66–167 (July 26, 1966); *New York Times,* Jan. 25, 1967, at 18 (DOD Budget); *Av. Wk.,* Jan. 30, 1967, at 23–38; *New York Times,* Feb. 16, 1968, at 1; *Space Bus. Daily,* Dec. 20, 1967, at 257.

On the analogous discovery of the "Carlin Mine," the second largest present gold mine in the United States, through use of radar and infrared sensors in an airplane, which mapped the unusual rock formation, see *Washington Post,* Dec. 3, 1966, at A3.

On all these issues, see *Reports of the AAS Meeting* (Dallas, Tex., May 1967). See also "U.S. Activities in Spacecraft Oceanography," *Report of the National Council on Marine Resources and Engineering Development,* Oct. 1, 1967.

[145] *New York Times,* June 9, 1959, and see *id.,* Mar. 5, 1967 at 30.

have been predicted for the near future.[146] Commercial transport of humans between points on earth to the celestial bodies seems to lie much further off, but proposals for the movement of military personnel by rocket are already in hand. It has been suggested, for example, that a system for the transportation by rocket vehicle of 1,200 troops or of cargoes of over 100 tons between earth points could be operational by 1975[147] if funding were made available. This use of satellites to discover *earth* resources and to aid in operations *on earth* has been a major source of interest in the mid-1960s.[148]

As noted earlier, we will not devote attention here to the specific use of the more distant resources of outer space or, in general, to the resources of the celestial bodies.[149] Some years ago, DuBridge summed up the value of some suggestions for the short-run use of an outer space capability in these terms:

As to the valuable materials to be mined on the moon or other planets, I have been unable to think of a single conceivable substance of sufficient intrinsic value to warrant hauling it in, even from the moon, to say nothing of more distant sources. It is hard to imagine that in the foreseeable future we could get to the moon and ship materials back to the earth at a cost less than hundreds of thousands or millions of dollars per pound.

We can dismiss with equal ease the idea of using space as a repository for the earth's excess population. I am sure that over coming years we can find a few hundred, or possibly a few thousand, astronauts who would be glad to make exploratory journeys to the moon, to Venus, and to Mars and even to establish small colonies, if possible. But to plan on shipping off twenty or thirty million people each year does not sound like a very promising enterprise. When thriving cities exist at the South Pole and on top of Mount Everest, then one might begin asking whether the even more inhospitable surroundings of the moon, Mars, or Venus

might be made fit for human habitation. Since the moon has no atmosphere at all and the atmospheres of Venus and Mars appear to contain no oxygen, the problems, even of survival, on such bases clearly present horrifying difficulties. To think of millions of people living under such circumstances clearly is getting close to the borders of insanity.[150]

While the long-run possibilities are not so clearly negative, we will hereafter deal with them only in passing.

Summary

We have looked at the range of possible space activities, the nature of some of the claims which have arisen and are likely to arise from space capabilities, and the groups and entities which are involved in present or potential conflicts of interest. We will soon explore which rules now exist to regulate and to adjust these conflicts and which institutions and techniques of conflict resolution already exist or can be envisaged.

Clearly, in looking at the range of conflict over claims to use outer space, it appears that the potentially most deadly are the claims of nation against nation. These may be for free access, or fair access to space itself on the part of smaller nations, cramped for launching room, and to space resources as against claims to exclusive use. They may be for self-defense, including warning against surprise attack and a "right to know" of a potential enemy's activities, as against a claim to national secrecy, which is itself a part of self-defense. They may be for the use of resources for development of the poor nations on earth as contrasted with hurling resources into space.

Another group of claims is that of economic and professional interest groups within and across nations. Which projects will receive preference? What decision-making institutions exist to choose between alternative space projects which for financial or scientific reasons may be mutually exclusive? Which groups will operate the space facilities decided on? For whose gain? On whose performance standards? With what systems of control or regulation?

Broadly speaking, both categories also may involve the claims of man as against self-seeking national states —the right to survival, to avoid genetic distortion, to freedom from starvation. Human goals conflict and hence imply the necessity for compromise and for institutions to effect and make effective the agreed divisions. There is thus the problem of identifying and of furthering man's

[146] *Hearings on H.R. 11881* (1958) in Ramo, *supra* note 72, at 496. Cf. the more pessimistic comments of Gen. Boushey, at 585. See generally Johnson, "Cargo by Rocket—How Soon?" *Air Transportation* 14–24 (Nov. 1965).

[147] See *J. Armed Forces* 2 (July 11, 1964). On transport potentials, see also comment of E. C. Welsh on Jan. 11, 1965, cited by Menter, *supra* note 117, at 14.

[148] In addition to the materials cited above see, among many, sensing soil conditions and moisture crop yield and incidence of disease, drought, and insects: see *Baltimore Sun,* May 29, 1967 (speech of G. W. Irving, Jr.); *New York Times,* March 21, 1967 (speech of Sec. of Agriculture Freeman); Sen. Magnuson, "Earth Laboratory in Space," 1 *Airworld* 16–17 (Oct. 1966). On sensing ice movements on lakes, rivers, and oceans, see *New York Times,* Nov. 13, 1966, at 46.

[149] On possibilities of manufacturing in space, see *New York Times,* Feb. 27, 1966, at E7.

[150] DuBridge, *supra* note 2, at 22–23. See also Michael, *supra* note 6, at 49.

goals in a world divided by power and conflicting concepts and emotions.

The law developed to cover any aspect of human or international relations is inevitably responsive not only to the physical facts but to the interaction of these pressures brought by interested claimants to rights, privileges, and protection in the developing area. With respect to space activities, McDougal and his associates and other writers and government spokesmen as well have already developed at length some of these patterns of interaction.[151] They will be noted in later chapters.

The Resolution of Conflicts

Within any nation the framework of organized government offers the possibility for resolution of most major controversies through the use of power but without a resort to violence. In the United States, for example, the Executive and the Congress, responding to the private and public pressures most forcefully presented, and basing their judgment on what seems the best possible compromise within, in Theordore Sorenson's words, "the limits of available resources . . . available time . . . previous commitment . . . available information . . . and the laws of the land" decide on allocations between military and civilian space goals, on the forms of satellite communications nets, on the allocation of resources among scientific programs.[152] Administrative agencies, such as the Federal Communications Commission, make legally binding allocations among scientific, commercial, and other claims for radio frequencies and other valuable resources. The government thus provides the legal-political frame-

work within which even difficult conflicts over the use of non-shareable resources can be adjusted and the resolution carried out. This may also be done by courts if no one group can marshal enough power in Congress or the Executive or if some person or segment of the public is denied a claim fairly made under the law. Even the waters of the Colorado, if not of the Jordan, can be divided peacefully. In a sense, the existence of a solution-giving and enforcing mechanism is more important than its abstract equity or conformity with some abstract notions of individual preference or justice. As Lord Mansfield said of the commercial law two centuries ago, it is often most important to have a stable, understood legal situation. Behavior can then be adapted to it to make the best of it. Arizona may use the Colorado's waters less fruitfully than California, but they will be fruitfully used. By analogy, the same appears to be true of space communications system, for example. American decision-making could be improved but the vital thing is that it exists and functions without general warfare, if also without achieving perfect equity.

Internationally, decision making is decentralized. Institutions for reaching solutions, enforcing them, and forcefully channeling conflicting pressures and claims into nonviolent patterns of accommodations are not of comparable status. As the legal framework for resolving conflicting claims respecting outer space activities, we have in formulation general international law, the United Nations Charter, a few directly relevant U.N. resolutions, the Nuclear Test Ban Treaty of 1963, the 1967 Outer Space Treaty, the 1968 Treaty on Rescue and Return, a large number of bilateral and several unilateral agreements dealing with space and communications, and other draft treaties. There are also statements by many national leaders approving a concept of free, peaceful use of outer space (if also reserving essential national positions) and dealing with other space matters. There is a limited amount of unprotested practice. There are innumerable writings by scholars dealing with developing rules of customary international law for space activities.

There are also some international institutions already in existence which will help to resolve some of the important but not militarily crucial competing claims. Claims between groups of scientists for priorities can in part be evaluated through COSPAR (the Committee on Space Research), the international scientific unions, and through informal consultations between scientists of different nations. Provision for sterilization of spacecraft has been discussed, for example, in CETEX during the IGY and now in COSPAR. The United States has used

---

[151] See McDougal *et al., Law and Public Order in Space, passim* (1963); Van Dyke, *supra* note 94, *passim;* Taubenfeld, "The Status of Competing Claims to Use Outer Space: An American Point of View," 1963 *Proceedings, Am. Soc. Int'l L.* 173–86.

Briefer overviews of the patterns have been presented by Professor McDougal, "The Emerging Customary Law of Space," 58 *Nw. U. L. Rev.* 618 (1963), and Schwartz, *supra* note 7, 151–76. See also Levy, "Conflict in the Race for Space," in Levy, *supra* note 11, 188–211; Holmes, *supra* note 2, chaps. 5, 8 (for U.S. intragovernmental rivalries); Meeker, "Avoiding Conflict in and over Space," in Schwartz, *supra* note 7, 78–81; Taubenfeld & Taubenfeld, *Man and Space: Politics, Law, Organization* (Arnold Foundation Monograph, 1964).

[152] See, on various domestic space conflicts and on U.S. decision-making, Van Dyke, *supra* note 94, *passim,* esp. chaps. 6, 10, 12, and 16. See also Killian, "Shaping a Public Policy for the Space Age," *Outer Space,* chap. 8 (1962).

these techniques in connection with Project West Ford and with some of the high-altitude tests and has suggested a more extensive use of COSPAR's apparatus. The United States nevertheless rejects as a "veto" device Soviet proposals for prior discussion of and agreement upon *any* measures undertaken in space which might in an undefined way hinder the use of space for peaceful purposes.

The International Telecommunications Union (ITU), similarly, deals with the claims of scientists, with communications systems, and with all others needing radio frequencies and is charged with making allocations of these scarce, valuable rights.[153] Other agencies may have roles to play as well. The U.N.'s General Assembly and its Outer Space Committee may be able to suggest useful principles, or begin the process of treaty formulation, in questions of nationality of space vehicles, of liability, and of return-to-earth covenants.

Fortunately, many of the current and foreseeable uses of outer space are not only shareable by nature; in some cases they require the participation of many nations to make the operations feasible at all or at least to make them most productive. Science as a field has a notable record of endeavor shared by people from many nations. To at least a considerable extent, the information obtained through outer space capabilities has already been broadly shared.[154] Nations and scientists from many countries have shared in part, at least, in the meteorological progress to date. Communications users in several score countries are linked through a satellite system. These cooperative and shareable operations are considered further under various headings in the chapters which follow.

The gap in the decentralized international community is found, of course, in those remaining areas which are security suffused. Is there, for example, a "legal" basis for a peaceful decision between the American claim of a right to know in a nuclear-missile age and the Soviet claim of a right to inviolable secrecy? The record of resolution of this type of security-suffused conflict is extremely poor to date. At least at some time, every state

seems to believe that, as Dean Acheson said on April 27, 1963, "the survival of states is above the law—it must be."[155]

Nationally, many basic conflicts of interest are settled by executive or legislative decision, by a form of imposed, negotiated compromise between competing power groups. Sometimes the courts are also involved. While each group aims for a social decision by the organ— executive, legislative, or judicial—where, considering its power base, it is most favored, the decision is made within an agreed, orderly framework by the maximum use of power, perhaps, but not of force. We will investigate in the pages that follow the role of law, present and prospective, in structuring, resolving, and preventing conflicts within the nation and internationally with respect to outer space activities.

---

[155] Press Report. In 1963 *Proceedings, Am. Soc'y Int'l L.* 14, the statement reads: "The survival of states is not a matter of law."

---

[153] See *infra* chap. 5 and, e.g., on the role of the ITU see Estep, "International Law-making in a Technological World," 33 *Geo. Wash. L. Rev.* 162, 164–75 (1964) (esp. on the ITU's 1963 meeting).

[154] Jessup & Taubenfeld, *supra* note 61, 225–32; Peavy, "International Cooperation in Space Science," in Schwartz, *supra* note 7, 89–101; Odishaw, "International Cooperation in Space Science," *Outer Space*, 105 ff. On the IGY, COSPAR, etc., see *infra* chaps. 3, 4 and sources cited.

3

The General Legal Regime,
Background,
and Analogies

One of the most frequently discussed issues in the literature of the law concerning human activities in space is the delimitation of outer space for legal purposes. While the position of the national states continues to be reasonably uniform in agreeing to defer any generalized legal characterization of where outer space begins in favor of an approach based on the nature of the activity in question, the utility of a definition for some purposes at least seems clear.

Sovereignty Based on an Extension of Territory Outward

Airspace: The Air Law Background

The conception of a relation between a subjacent state and outer space based on some projection of altitude "above" or out from the earth's surface is a natural outgrowth of existing law concerning sovereignty in airspace.[1] At least from Roman days, the right of private landowners to an uninterrupted use of their property both up and down from the ground level was formally recognized by the law.[2] Nevertheless, before the twentieth century, in the days before controlled movements above

---

[1] See, e.g., Lipson & Katzenbach, *The Law of Outer Space* 8 and Abstracts 540–643 (1961).

[2] On the Roman law maxim *cuius est solum eius est usque ad coelum* and its "place in the modern world," see e.g., Jessup & Taubenfeld, *Controls for Outer Space* 205 and sources cited (1959) and United States v. Causby, 328 U.S. 256, esp. at 260–61, 66 S. Ct. 1062 (1946).

the surface of the earth became a real possibility, those few discussing the problem appear to have agreed that airspace, at least that area above what was needed for ordinary activities on the ground, was free for the peaceful use of all. Grotius, for example, maintained this position.[3]

This view continued to be held by some scholars, including Fauchille, into the twentieth century[4] despite the fact that others had already envisioned the airplane's military capabilities.[5] Although the Englishman Westlake and his supporters urged a recognition of national sovereignty in airspace, subject at most to a right of "innocent passage," the International Conference of 1910 on Air Navigation was still able to "agree" on a right of an airplane of one nation freely to overfly the territory of another, provided there was no threat to national security.[6]

The proof of the military utility of aircraft in the First World War, combined with the demands of economic nationalism, led to universal agreement that each state had absolute sovereignty in the airspace above its territory.[7] Signed in Paris in 1919, the Convention for the Regulation of Aerial Navigation, and its amending Protocols,[8] expressly recognized this "complete and exclusive sovereignty over the airspace above" national territory and the right of the subjacent state to exclude foreign aircraft from this area and to impose its jurisdiction over persons, things, and acts in "national" airspace. Limited rights of innocent passage for planes of contracting states were granted by the convention but, in practice, many states insisted on prior consent to entry.[9] The United States and the Soviet Union were not parties to this convention, but some thirty states had ratified it by 1939. In addition, the Ibero-American Convention of 1926 and the Pan American Convention of 1928, to which the United States was a party, recognized an exclusive national sovereignty in airspace. National legislation in every country which has considered the problem reflects the same claim.[10] State practice was and remains uniformly in conformity with the principle of national sovereignty.[11]

---

[3] *De Jure Belli ac Pacis* (trans.) II, ii, sec 3, p. 190 (Carnegie Endowment for International Peace, *The Classics of International Law,* Series No. 3, 1925).

[4] See, e.g., Fauchille, "Le Domaine aérien et le régime juridique des aerostats," 8 *Revue Générale de Droit International Publique* 414 (1901). Fauchille recognized state sovereignty for security purposes up to 330 meters, however. See also Shawcross & Beaumont, *Air Law* 3–9 (2d ed. 1951); Kislov & Krylov, "State Sovereignty in Airspace," 2 *Int'l Aff.* 35–44 (reprinted in *Legal Problems of Space Exploration: A Symposium* 1037–1046 (1961) [hereinafter cited as *1961 Symposium*]. For an interesting early comment on Fauchille's work, see Korovin, "La conquête de la stratosphère et le droit international public," 41 *Revue Générale de Droit International Public* 682 (1934).

[5] At the First Hague Conference in 1899, a measure was adopted prohibiting the discharge of projectiles from balloons "or other new methods of a similar nature." U.S. Department of State: "Freedom of the Air," 1 *Docs. and State Papers* 303 (Aug. 1948). See also *Survey of Space Law* 16–18 (1959).

[6] See Goedhuis, "Civil Aviation after the War," 36 *Am. J. Int'l L.* 596, 598–99 (1942). See also the 1906 resolution of the Institute of International Law, 21 *Annuaire de l'Institut de Droit International* 293 (1906). See generally Young, "The Aerial Inspection Plan and Air Space Sovereignty," 24 *Geo. Wash. L. Rev.* 565–89 (1956).

[7] Even during World War I neutral states insisted on the right to use such force as was necessary to keep foreign aircraft out of their airspace. See, e.g., Swiss Declaration of Neutrality, Aug. 4, 1914, sec. 17(b). This was also true in World War II. In 1940, Germany advanced the claim that its aircraft could overfly neutral territory if flown above a three-mile limit. This was rejected by the Netherlands and Belgium. See Kuhn, Note, 34 *Am. J. Int'l L.* 104 (1940) and, in general, see Spaight, *Aircraft in Peace and the Law* 203–15 (1919). For a more recent survey of the unanimity on these issues, see Lipson & Katzenbach, *supra* note 1, 8, Abstracts 270–312, and sources cited.

[8] 11 *L.N.T.S.* 173 (1922). For British proposals, see Cooper, "Some Historic Phases of British International Civil Aviation Policy," 23 *Int'l Aff.* 189, 191 ff. (1947). See also Lissitzyn, *International Air Transport and National Policy* (1942) and Goedhuis, "Sovereignty and Freedom in the Air Space," 41 *Trans. Grot. Soc'y* 137–52 (1956).

[9] "Art. II. Each contracting State undertakes in time of peace to accord freedom of innocent passage above its territory to the aircraft of the other contracting States, provided that the conditions laid down in the present Convention are observed."

[10] See, *e.g.,* U.S. Air Commerce Act of 1926 (44 *Statutes at Large* 568; 49 *U.S.C.,* secs. 171, 174–177, 179–184) and Civil Aeronautics Act of 1938 (52 *Statutes at Large* 973, 980); 49 *U.S.C.,* sec 401 (33); Air Code of the USSR, Art. 1, 1932 and 1935 in *Collection of Laws,* U.S.S.R., 1935, No. 43, at 359b ("To the Union of Soviet Socialist Republics belongs complete and exclusive sovereignty in the airspace above the Union . . ."). See Kislov and Krylov, *supra* note 4, at 35–44; British Air Navigation Act and Orders in Council of 1920 ("full and absolute sovereignty and rightful jurisdiction . . . over the air superincumbent on its territory") and Aerial Navigation Acts of 1911 and 1913.

[11] For example, see Van Zandt, *Civil Aviation and Peace,* esp. 57–59 (Brookings Inst., 1944). On the treatment by neutrals of belligerent aircraft in World War II, see Spaight, *Air Power and War Rights* 424 ff. (3d ed. 1947).

The conference on civil aviation held in Chicago in 1944 produced the basic current international arrangements which fully confirmed national control in national airspace. While President Roosevelt expressed the hope "that you will not dally with the thought of creating great blocks of closed air, thereby tracing in the sky the conditions of future wars and that you will see to it that the air which God gave to everyone shall not become the means of domination over anyone,"[12] the 1944 Convention on Civil Aviation, as adopted, set forth, in Article 1, that "the Contracting States recognize that every State has complete and exclusive sovereignty over the airspace above its territory."[13] A right of innocent passage remains, in Article 5, limited to nonscheduled civil aircraft, which can fly over a nation and make nontraffic stops without prior permission.

As has also been typically the case in national legislation, the Chicago Convention does not, either in its body or in the Annexes, define "airspace" or "air," nor does the convention regulate any vehicles other than civil aircraft.[14] Annexes to the convention have defined "aircraft," for purposes of the Annexes only, in language derived from the Paris Convention of 1919, as "any machine which can derive support in the atmosphere from the reactions of the air" (Annexes 6, 7, 8). This definition does not appear literally to be applicable to satellites or to most other space craft. National legislation is in general also devoid of useful definitions of these terms although the U.S. Federal Aviation Act of 1958[15] defines "aircraft" as "any contrivance now known or hereafter invented, used, or designed for navigation of or flight in the air."

For future reference in considering space activities, it should be stressed again that national concern over superjacent airspace is based both on security and on economic grounds. States create and then protect their own commercial airlines; the demand for a *quid pro quo* for entry into the national airspace has been unremitting; broad, general rights of economic access by one state into another have consistently been denied.[16] In the case of aircraft with military capabilities, the dominant factor has been security; the matter is so clear that it has been little discussed since World War I.

The right to self-defense has been used to extend claims to rights of observation and control in airspace beyond areas that are under national sovereignty. The airspace over the high seas is, by all, considered free for the flight of aircraft of all nations. Indeed, "that the airspace over the open sea and over unoccupied territory is

---

[12] U.S. Department of State, *International Civil Aviation Conference: Final Act and Related Documents* 4–5 (Conf. Series No. 64, Pub. 2282; 1945).

[13] 61 *Statutes at Large* 1180 (1944); *T.I.A.S.* No. 1591; 15 *U.N.T.S.* 295. For parties, this convention replaces the Paris and Havana conventions. The Soviet Union is not a party but 109 nations were, as of Jan. 1, 1966. "China" is a party but is represented, at present, by the Nationalist government.

Article I of the Paris Convention was quite similar: "The High Contracting Parties recognize that every Power has complete and exclusive sovereignty over the air space [*espace atmosphérique, spazio atmosferico*] above its territory. For the purpose of the present Convention, the territory of a State shall be understood as including the national territory, both that of the mother country and of the colonies, and of the territorial waters adjacent thereto."

As a matter of fact, states claim the right to prohibit all entries into their territory—aircraft, tourists, even radio waves—although, in the case of Herzian waves, enforcement has always been a problem. The principle of complete national sovereignty is nevertheless clear. See, e.g., General Communications Regulations attached to the International Telecommunications Convention, Madrid, Dec. 9, 1932, and the Revisions of Feb. 1 and Apr. 9, 1938; European Broadcasting Conventions, June 19, 1933, and Sept. 15, 1948, Cmd. No. 7946 (T.S. No. 30 of 1950); Aaronson, "Space Law," 1 *Int'l Rel.* 416–27, esp. 423 (1958) (reprinted in *1961 Symposium, supra* note 4, at 221–31).

[14] E.g., Art. 3(a): "This Convention shall be applicable only to civil aircraft, and shall not be applicable to State aircraft."

[15] 49 *U.S.C.* 1301(5). As we will see, this has been taken as broad enough to cover *all* flights, at least in airspace, and the act's legislative history so indicates.

[16] In 1944, two additional conventions were prepared, the International Air Services Transit Agreement ("Two Freedoms") (84 *U.N.T.S.* 389) and the International Air Transport Agreement ("Five Freedoms"). The former gives scheduled services only the right to fly over without landing and to land for nontraffic reasons. It is in force, as of Jan. 1, 1967, for 73 states. The broader Air Transport Agreement gives more commercially valuable rights for mail, cargo, and passenger aid.

In general, see Colclaser, "The New International Civil Aviation Organization of Air Transport," 8 *Free World* 503 (1944); Beresford, "The Legal Control of Outer Space," *ABA, Sect. of Int'l Law* (Aug. 1958), reprinted in *Space Law, a Symposium,* 410 ff. (1958); Feldman, "An American View of Jurisdiction in Outer Space," paper delivered at the Int'l Astronautical Fed. meeting, the Hague, August 1958, reprinted in *id.,* at 428 ff.; Goedhuis, *supra* notes 6 and 8; Lissitzyn, *supra* note 8.

On the air regime, see also Hayton, "Jurisdiction of the Littoral State in the 'Air Frontier,' " 3 *Philippine Int'l L.J.* 369 ff. (July-Dec. 1964); Cooper, "The Chicago Convention—after Twenty Years," 19 *U. Miami L. Rev.* 333–44 (1965); 2 Whiteman, *Digest of International Law* 270–80 (1963).

free and in the former case incapable of appropriation may be taken as almost universally accepted,"[17] as Lauterpacht has asserted. Nevertheless, even in this area, the United States and Canada have established air defense identification zones (ADIZ) off their coasts in which aircraft are required to identify themselves when not less than one hour's cruising distance from the coasts.[18] Penalties for failure to comply include interception. With Mach I jets, this could mean a "duty" to identify when 600 or more miles away from the nations involved, and Mach II and Mach III aircraft extend the distance by hundreds and, eventually, by more than a thousand miles. Legally, this is not a claim to sovereignty or even to jurisdiction, but only the claimed right to impose a presumably minor inconvenience in a "free" area to protect the national welfare.[19] And the fate meted out to "strays" and other casual intruders in airspace proper, particularly by the Communist states, needs little documentation.[20]

The Upward Extent of Sovereignty

Since it is by now clear that every national state claims and, to the extent it can do so, exercises complete sovereignty in superjacent airspace, and since airspace remains legally undefined for most purposes with no generally accepted limit to its extent, we come directly to a multifaceted dilemma. Of course, the term "airspace" or "atmospheric space" is found in most treaties, but it is only in the last decade that man has been able to send objects and humans beyond what all could readily agree is "airspace." We should also note here, although we will consider it in detail later, that there is now a broadly accepted principle that no nation shall lay claim to outer space (or to the celestial bodies) as such. Where then does "airspace" end? And is this a critical question for pursuit at this time?

There have been in recent years, as noted earlier, a number of attempts to define airspace so as to determine more precisely the applicability of existing treaties and legislation, to limit formally the outward extent of general national sovereignty, and to begin to lay the basis for a regime for those activities which are primarily or wholly "outer space" activities.

Arguments advanced in favor of a formally declared low ceiling to national sovereignty include:[21]

1. The increased difficulty for states in exercising effective control over a huge area.

2. The penalties of high ceiling to small states whose geographical position would make it impossible to launch or retrieve a space vehicle from the national homeland without violating the "territory" of an adjacent state, thus placing them in an unequal position with respect to individual national access to the resources of outer space. It has been suggested that a "way of necessity" or a "right of transit" might be created,[22] but experience with the position of landlocked countries on earth is not encouraging on this score,[23] although the possibility of effectively blocking (intercepting) the use of space and upper airspace, as compared to overland routes, near-in airspace, and waterways, suggests that such a right of transit might well be easier to assert effectively, at least given the short-run foreseeable technology.

3. The freeing of near-in space for useful scientific and peaceful national pursuits regardless of whether they are purely "outer space" ventures or employ hybrid vehicles.

The efforts to place a ceiling on national sovereignty

---

[17] Oppenheim, *International Law* 517 (Lauterpacht ed., 8th ed. 1955).

[18] See, e.g., Civil Aeronautics Act of 1938, sec. 1201, as amended Sept. 9, 1950, 64 *Statutes at Large* 825, 49 *U.S.C.*, secs. 701, 703; 15 *F.R.* 9180, 20 *F.R.* 8184, 14 *C.F.R.* 620, 621–23. For the U.S. Regulations of 1955 and those of Canada, see Murchison, *The Contiguous Air Space Zone in International Law* 79–94, Appendixes I and II (Canadian Dept. of Nat'l Defense, 1956); U.S. Naval War College, *International Law Situation and Documents 1956*, 577 ff. (1957); Cooper, "Space above the Seas," *JAG J.* (Navy) 8 ff., esp. 31 (Feb. 1959); Reiff, *The United States and the Treaty Law of the Sea* 365–68 (1959); Note, "Legal Aspects of Reconnaissance in Airspace and Outer Space," 61 *Colum. L. R.* 1070, 1087–95 (1961). See also Federal Aviation Agency, *Regulation of the Administration, Security Control of Air Traffic*, P. 620 (Nov. 16, 1961); "ADIZ, International Law, and Contiguous Air Space," 2 *Harv. Int'l L. Club* 1 (1960).

[19] On rights of self-defense, even without claims to sovereignty, see e.g., Craig, "National Sovereignty at High Altitudes," 24 *J. Air L. and Commerce* 384, 388 (1957).

[20] See, e.g., Lissitzyn, "Treatment of Aerial Intruders in Recent Practice and International Law," 47 *Am. J. Int'l L.* 559–89 (1953); Lissitzyn, "Some Legal Implications of the U-2 and RB-47 Incidents," 56 *Am. J. Int'l L.* 135 (1962).

[21] See, e.g., McMahon, "Legal Aspects of Outer Space," 1962 *Brit. Yrbk. Int'l L.* 339, 355–57 and sources cited.

[22] See Goedhuis, in International Law Ass'n, *Report of the 52d Conference*, Annex A, p. 10 (Brussels, 1962).

[23] See, e.g., the records of the United Nations Conference on the Law of the Sea, 1958, Vol. 7, Fifth Comm., "Question of Free Access to the Sea of Landlocked Countries" and of the U.N. Conference on Transit Trade of Land-locked Countries, 1965.

have nevertheless been almost exclusively the work of scholars,[24] and, although we will soon examine their various suggested approaches at some length, it is the views of the states to which, in any study of existing law, we must first turn. In one sense, the division between "states" and "writers" is rather artificial, and this effects both this section and those which follow. Clearly the Soviet Union is far less prone than the United States to speak officially, and there is no equivalent to the wealth of *official* material and statements found in testimony before and reports of Congressional committees and the like. On the other hand, Soviet writers are presumptively less free than those in democratic communities and would tend not to be published if their positions were clearly inconsistent with the policy or at least the apparent best interests of the Soviet Union. They may, therefore, suggest the current stage and status of official thinking. For this reason, we have made use of the works of various Communist writers here; we simply accept as a working limitation the comparative lack of more formally official Communist statements of position.

Government Views: The United States

It is clear from the outset that, despite the suggestions of many commentators, the states, at least the major powers, have been quite unready to set specific limits by altitude to their claims to sovereign rights. Unlike the case of lower reaches of airspace, it appears to be the security problem almost exclusively, rather than a mixture of economic and security issues, which has led to this result.

But in the early post-Sputnik period, at least a few states took the position that an airspace boundary should be set and set soon. Sweden, for example, urged a decision as to "the altitude where this [outer] space . . . begins."[25] At different times, representatives of Spain, Canada, France, Chile, and Italy have all suggested a formal limitation by altitude on the extent of national sovereignty in space.[26]

Formal statements of the United States' position on the outward extent of its sovereignty in space indicate a notable shift in the course of the first space decade. In the earlier years, official policy called for a slow, step-by-step approach to space problems with the "utmost flexibility and freedom of action with regard to future events" retained for the United States.[27] It was acknowledged that the Chicago Convention left it unclear where "airspace" and national sovereignty ended and that, since traces of the atmosphere might be found up to 10,000 miles, "it follows that it would be perfectly rational for us to maintain that under the Chicago Convention the sovereignty of the United States extends 10,000 miles from the surface of the earth."[28] The analogy to Antarctica was also noted. Thus, while the United States had rejected or would reject claims made by others and had made none of its own, Loftus Becker said, with respect to outer space:

The United States has already engaged in activities which, it could be asserted, have given to it certain rights, as distinguished from those states which have not engaged in such activities. Up to this time, the United States has made no claims based upon such activities. Nor does it seem expedient or necessary at this time for the United States to either assert or expressly or impliedly waive any such claims which it might have.[29]

Even at this time, it was argued that the celestial bodies and outer space, wherever it began, were free for the peaceful use of all. At the United Nations, in 1958 Lyndon Johnson stated: "Today outer space was free; no nation held a concession there; and it must remain that way."[30] Similar views have been expressed in the

---

Doc. A/C.1/PV. 982 at 56 (Nov. 12, 1958) (Italy); *id.* at 41 (Chile). See also John Johnson, "Freedom and Control in Outer Space," address to the American Rocket Society's Space Law Conference, New York City, Apr. 24, 1962, p. 11 (mimeo.), concerning the views of France.

[27] Loftus Becker, "United States Foreign Policy and the Development of Law for Outer Space," *JAG J.* (Navy) 4 (Feb. 1959). For other statements of Becker, then legal adviser to the Department of State, see also: *Hearings on H. R. 11881,* 85th Cong., 2d Sess., at 1269–1303 (1958); "Major Aspects of the Problem of Outer Space," in *1961 Symposium, supra* note 4, 396–403. See generally Lissitzyn, "The American Position on Outer Space and Antarctica," 53 *Am. J. Int'l L.* 126–31 (1959).

[28] Becker, in *1961 Symposium, supra* note 4, at 401.

[29] Becker, "United States Foreign Policy . . . ," *supra* note 27, at 4, 29.

[30] U.N. Doc. A/C.1/SR. 986 at 208 GAOR, 1st Comm., 13th Sess., 986th meeting (Nov. 17, 1958).

---

[24] Compare, however, the comments of John Johnson, former General Counsel of NASA, "Freedom and Control in Outer Space," in *Proceedings, Conference on Space Science and Space Law* 141–42 (Schwartz ed. 1964) [hereinafter cited as Schwartz].

[25] See U.N. Doc. A/C.1/PV.984 at 7–10 (Nov. 13, 1958). See also U.N. Doc. A/C.1/SR.1079 at 7 (Dec. 16, 1959).

[26] See, e.g., U.N. Doc. A/C.1/PV.992 at 17 (Nov. 20, 1958) (Spain); address by Howard Green, Canadian Minister of External Affairs, 11 *External Affairs* 302 (Ottawa, 1959); U.N.

U.N.'s various organs and elsewhere on many occasions.[31] These, as we shall see further, have been persistently accompanied by calls for regulation by type of activity rather than by location.[32]

In more recent years, although the United States has continued to note its right to defend itself wherever an apprehended source of danger might be located, there has been a shift away from the notion that this might call for an extension of "sovereignty" outward. The boundary line between airspace and outer space is still undetermined, but it is taken as a fact that all satellites orbited to date operate in "outer space" and that, hence, "airspace" must be at least limited below the orbital height of satellites.[33] As we shall see, the United States now persistently relies in many contexts on this concept that orbiting satellites are now in "free" outer space and are not within any state's "territory" nor subject to any state's "territorial" jurisdiction.[34] Thus, while the United States has given little support to the notion of drawing any single "line" and certainly to a very close-in line, there is evidence of tacit support for the principle that outer space begins (and "sovereign" airspace at a maximum must consequently end) at some point equal to or more probably somewhere below that at which an unpowered satellite can be maintained in orbit.[35] We will return to this theme briefly hereafter.

Government Views: The Soviet View

Soviet writers have suggested a wide variety of approaches to the question of the upward extent of sovereignty.[36] The Soviet claim to complete sovereignty in airspace is the basis for all discussions and received thorough airings both in connection with the alleged appearance of United States weather balloons in Soviet airspace in the mid-1950's and with the U-2 incident.[37] Throughout the mid-1950's a commonly expressed view was that there was no limit to the upward extent of national sovereignty.[38]

If all nations made unlimited claims upward, the flight of Sputniks would of course have violated the sovereign rights of every subjacent state and Soviet writers were quick to shift their approach. In 1958 and thereafter, there were suggestions of a limit based on aerodynamic lift,[39] on "effective control,"[40] and on "national security."[41] Although this last is hardly a limiting definition, it does avoid the dangers to national security found by Soviet writers in the other two.[42]

In their quest for security, Soviet authors have rejected a search for traces of the atmosphere or the "density of the gas cloud at one or another distance from the earth" and all other alleged physical criteria. Soviet writers in general, however, have not made claims to the infinite; they seem to agree that at some point in space, out "far enough" from earth, a nation would be sufficiently secure to permit the "free" use of these reaches by all for activities beyond that point.[43] For most activities, the "peaceful" ones, this might be the area where satellite orbits

[31] E.g. First (Political) Committee: U.N. Doc. A/C. 1/SR. 1210 at 245, 246 (1961); the U.N. Committee on the Peaceful Uses of Outer Space: U.N. Doc. A/AC.105/PV.2 (May 1962); the Legal Subcommittee of that Committee: U.N. Doc. A/AC.105/C.2/SR.1 (Aug. 21, 1962).

[32] Becker, "United States Foreign Policy . . . ," *supra* note 27, at 7.

[33] See, e.g., Gardner, "Extending Law into Outer Space," address to the Twelfth Annual Conference of National Organizations, Mar. 12, 1962, in 56 *Am. J. Int'l L.* 797–99 (1962).

[34] For the use of these arguments with respect to observation satellites, see *supra*, p. 29 and *infra*, pp. 87 ff.

[35] See, e.g., speech by Leonard Meeker, Dept. of State legal adviser, Aug. 17, 1967 at Stanford Symposium, p. 11 (typescript).

[36] For a survey, see Crane, "Soviet Attitude toward International Space Law," 56 *Am. J. Int'l L.* 687–723 (1962).

[37] See Kislov & Krylov, *supra* note 4; Lissitzyn, *supra* note 20, both articles.

[38] Kislov & Krylov, *supra* note 4, at 1045, citing British and French authors: Korovin, *International Law* 190 (undated): "an unrestricted height."

[39] Zadarozhnyi, "The Artificial Satellite and International Law," *Sovetskaia Rosiia* 3 (Moscow, Oct. 17, 1957) (reprinted in *1961 Symposium, supra* note 4, at 1047); Kovlev & Cheprov, "Artificial Satellites and International Law," 1 *Soviet Yrbk. Int'l L.* 128–45 (Moscow, 1959).

[40] *Ibid.*

[41] *Ibid;* Galina, "On the Question of Interplanetary Law," 7 *Sovet'skoe Gosudarstvo i Pravo* [hereinafter cited as SGP] 52–58 (Moscow, July 1958) (reprinted in *1961 Symposium, supra* note 4, at 1050); Golnia, "For Equal Collaboration in the Peaceful Use of Cosmic Space," *Izvestia* 5 (Sept. 17, 1958); Osnitskaya, "International Law Problems of the Conquest of Space," 2 *Soviet Yrbk. Int'l L.* 65–71 (1959).

[42] *Ibid.;* Kovalev & Cheprov, *supra* note 39.

[43] See, e.g., remarks of Zhukov in "Conquest of Outer Space and Some Problems of International Relations," *Int'l Aff.* 88–96 (Moscow, Nov. 1959) (reprinted in *1961 Symposium, supra* note 4, 1082). For a criticism of the Soviet "security" theory, see Markov, "On the Question of the Boundaries of Air Space in International Law," 32 *SGP* 95 (1962).

begin,[44] thus again protecting the Sputnik flights as "legal" and according with more recent United States views.

Recently, the emphasis has been, as in the United States, on the nature of the activity, not on the altitude at which it takes place.[45] Thus, to Soviet spokesmen, "espionage," as they define it, whether by land, by sea, by U-2, or by reconnaissance satellite, is "illegal" in international law.[46] In their words, high-altitude nuclear tests by the United States, even before the Test Ban Treaty of 1963, are "illegal" as is the scattering of copper needles by the United States (Project West Ford);[47] private "monopoly" enterprise in outer space is "piratical" and incompatible with the concept of "free" space.[48]

Certainly, however, the Communist writers have been as consistent as those in the West in urging that, at least at some point, outer space and the celestial bodies are free for the peaceful activities of all men.[49] As the Polish scholar Machowski put it: "The . . . question, whether state sovereignty extends into outer space, has already been tacitly answered negatively by practice and lack of protests on the part of any states in connection with the orbiting of space objects over their respective territories."[50] Thus, the official view of the United States and that of the Soviet Union, as far as it can be determined, are similar on most points. Both agree that national sovereignty ends at some point "out," but each retains its right to counter deleterious acts, wherever they occur. Neither encourages the formal drawing of a line delimiting sovereign claims based on a territorial concept, but both agree that satellites fly in nonsovereign outer space, although there is no overall agreement on all issues concerning legally permissible activities. The views of other powers conform, in general, to the position of the major space powers.

The Writers

The literature concerning the desirability of establishing a precise overall boundary to the outward extent of national sovereignty is vast and its beginnings predate the flight of Sputnik I. While it seems clear that the nations are not likely to adopt any single line or division for all purposes, a brief review of the suggestions proposed on various bases by writers around the world is still useful since the argument is a continuing one.[51] The

---

[44] Remarks of Zhukov, *supra* note 43, at 1083.

[45] Zhukov, "Problems of Space Law at the Present Stage," *Proceedings, Fifth Colloquium on the Law of Outer Space* 12–13 (Haley ed., Varna, 1962).

[46] For a discussion and the authorities, see *supra,* 29–32. Compare the statement reportedly made by Khrushchev to President Eisenhower that he would show pictures of U.S. military bases taken from satellites. On the need for "security," see also Gabrovski, "Some Legal Aspects of Space Exploration," 9 *Int'l. Aff.* 92 (Moscow, 1963).

[47] Note that the Soviet Union reportedly conducted similar nuclear tests. See, e.g., Frutkin, *International Cooperation in Space* 148 (1965); Davies, *Environment* 8 (undated). On the effects of nuclear tests in the atmosphere, see Report of U.N. Scientific Committee on the Effect of Atomic Radiation (1962), U.N. O. R., 17th Sess., A/5216, para 48.

For Soviet comments, see, e.g., Note, "American Diversion in Space," 7 *Int'l Aff.* 117 (Moscow, Dec. 1961); Korovin, "Outer Space Must Become a Zone of Peace" (letter), 9 *Int'l Aff.* 92 (Moscow, Sept. 1963).

The "needles" experiment reportedly did not in fact cause any interference as was indicated in a statement by COSPAR's Consultative Group on Potentially Harmful Effects of Space Experiments on May 16, 1964. See Liller, "Optical Effects of the 1963 Project West Ford Experiment," 143 *Science* 437 (Jan. 31, 1964). The COSPAR statement is reprinted in "International Cooperation and Organization for Outer Space," *Staff Report Prepared for the Senate Committee on Aeronautical and Space Sciences,* 89 Cong., 1st Sess., Doc. No. 56 (Galloway, ed.) 396–97 (Aug. 12, 1965). For earlier British criticism, see Lovell and Ryle, "Interference to Radio Astronomy from Belts of Orbiting Dipoles (Needles)," 33 *J. Royal Astro. Soc'y* 100–108 (1962); Blackwell and Wilson, "Interference to Optical Astronomy from Belts of Orbiting Dipoles (Needles)," 33 *J. Royal Astro. Soc'y* 109–44 (1962).

[48] See e.g., Cheprov, "Monopolies Reach Out for Outer Space," *Int'l Aff.* 35 (Moscow, Dec. 1963); Korovin, *supra* note 39; Wasilebskaya, "Questions of Space Law in Recent American Literature," *The Cosmos and International Law* 109 (Zhukov ed. 1960); Cheprov, "Some Legal Problems of

International Space Communications," *Proceedings, Seventh Colloquium on the Law of Outer Space* 10 ff. (Haley & Schwartz eds. 1965).

[49] See, e.g., Korovin, "International Status of Cosmic Space," 5 *Int'l Aff.* 53, 59 (Moscow, Jan. 1959); Kovalev & Cheprov, *supra* note 40.

[50] 1961 *Proceedings, Am. Soc'y Int'l L.* 164, 169.

[51] For other general analyses of the varying views, see Lipson & Katzenbach, *supra* note 1, 11–18 and notes; McDougal, Lasswell, & Vlasic, *Law and Public Order in Space,* chap. 3, esp. pp. 323–59 (1963); Jenks, *Space Law* 107–11, 175–76, 189–91 (1965); McMahon, *supra* note 21, at 340–57; Note, "National Sovereignty of Outer Space," 74 *Harv. L. Rev.* 1154 ff. (1961); Jessup & Taubenfeld *supra* note 2, 204–21; Haley, *Space Law and Government,* chap. 4 (1963); Sand, Pratt, & Lyon, *An Historical Survey of the Law of Flight* (Institute of Air and Space Law, McGill University, Montreal, Pub. No. 7, 1961). Kovalev & Cheprov, *Toward Cosmic Law* (Na Puti k Kosmiches Komu Pravu), chap. 1 (1962).

reasons for this strongly held view that a formal line is at present essential for continued progress were summed up in *The Law of Outer Space* in these terms:

(1) That formal agreement would help to preclude states from making unjustified claims in the future to sovereignty in large regions of space "above" their territory on the contention that it is "air space. . . ." (2) That given certain possible interpretations of existing conventions, there is always the possibility that some states will protest space activities as violative of their sovereignty. Acceptance of such contentions would greatly hamper space activities favored by scientists and military specialists alike, and would permit relatively small states to exercise what could amount to an arbitrary veto over particular activities. (3) That disputes as to the extent of air space could lead to international tensions and serious controversy. (4) That the United States, supporting as it does the Rule of Law internationally as in domestic matters, should avoid being put in the position of making unilateral decisions on the interpre-

---

In Lipson & Katzenbach, *supra* note 1, major proposals through 1958 were tabulated as follows (in each case, the author has been supplied; see that report for full citation):

Height	Author and Source (No. in study)	Remarks or Reasons Given
30 miles	Murphy (185)	400 miles for neutrals in wartime
275,000 feet	"Legal Aspects" (154)	Objects traveling at 35,000/sec
52 miles	Helfer (109)	Limit of atmospheric lift
53 miles	Wuigg (204)	Von Karman line
60 miles	Bohme (28)	Loss of earth's gravitational pull; air travel becomes impossible
100 miles	Herzfeld (111)	
200–300 km	Azrges (272)	Limit of air-filled space
150–225 m	Meyer (178)	
300 km	Von Hanover	Limit of area filled with air layers
250 miles	Neumann (note 68)	Too little air
200–300 miles	Martial (173)	Analogy to 3-mile limit at sea
300 miles	*The Times* (211); Cooper (52)	Limit of "contiguous space"
300–500 m	Cheng (35)	Assumptions as to atmosphere
310–620 m	Cheng (34)	Limit of atmosphere
500 miles	Horsford (123)	
650 miles	Danier (62)	Limit of atmosphere
7,000 miles	Galina	Citing Western meteorologists
Infinity	Meyer (176); Hingorani (115)	

tation of existing conventions and should urge resolution through international agreement and other cooperative means. (5) That the resolution of this fundamental legal question would help to induce cooperative attitudes toward building law in regard to space and that these attitudes could help to shape desirable technological trends.

Granting that nations are sovereign in superjacent airspace, a vast number of scholars have for these and other reasons proposed limiting the extent of this iron control by limiting the definition of airspace itself. Of course the definition varies depending on the criteria used for calculation. Scientists themselves agree generally that "atmosphere" itself has no single scientific meaning, and indeed the various sciences disagree since they look to different characteristics.[52] Recall, too, that the Chicago Convention of 1944 itself nowhere defines airspace.

To proceed logically (if naively from the political point of view), it is possible to suggest a "scientific" limitation in airspace as the height at which a human can live without artificial breathing apparatus, conceivably as high as ten miles.[53] With perhaps more *operational* meaning, the maximum height to which aircraft can ascend has been offered as a definition, at least within the outlook of the civil aviation conventions, for airspace or "atmospheric" space. This would place it, given present technology, at about twelve miles for conventional aircraft or perhaps twenty to twenty-five for the ram jet.[54] Several years ago, for example, Cooper wrote: "After many years of careful research, I am convinced that the term airspace, as used in the Paris Convention in 1919, was there meant to include only those parts of the atmosphere above the surface of the earth where gaseous air is sufficiently dense to support balloons and airplanes, the only types of aircraft then in existence."[55]

Focusing more directly upon the somewhat elliptical terminology of the conventions has not in itself led to

---

[52] Ley, *Rockets, Missiles and Space Travel* 362 (rev. ed. 1958). See also, e.g., Blessel, "Données scientifiques techniques des problèmes qui pose la réglementation de l'utilisation de l'espace," 25 *Politique Etrangère* 300 (Nov. 4, 1961).

[53] See Haley, "The Law of Space . . . ," *N.Y.L. Forum* 262, 264–65 (1958) and Danier, "Les Voyages Interplanetaires et le Droit," 15 *Revue Générale de l'Air* 422 (1952).

[54] See David Davies Memorial Institute, *Draft Code of Rules on the Exploration and Uses of Outer Space* 6 (1962).

[55] "Flight-space and the Satellites," 7 *Int'l & Comp. L.Q.* 82, 84–85 (1958). See also Lipson & Katzenbach, *supra* note 1, 18; Schachter, 1956 *Proceedings, Am. Soc'y Int'l L.* 105. Cooper earlier stated these views in "High Altitude Flight and National Sovereignty," 4 *Int'l L.Q.* 411–18 (1951) (reprinted in *1961 Symposium, supra* note 4, at 1, 3).

uniformity. Thus airspace or atmospheric space might be limited, for purposes of sovereignty and jurisdiction, to what scientists tell us is the "geophysical limit of the atmosphere";[56] or it is "infinite, at least in theory"[57] or "without limit of height";[58] or it is all regions "accessible to man";[59] or it is the outside limit of the earth's atmosphere, perhaps 60,000 miles,[60] etc.

Actually, it is reasonably clear that those who drafted the Chicago Convention, and certainly those who created the Paris Convention, simply never considered the problem of vehicles moving above what would be considered by all to be airspace.[61] As noted above, the vast majority of writers and most official pronouncements also reject the infinite extension of national sovereignty outward, whether based on the air conventions or not, and also reject the direct applicability of these conventions to space flight as such, at least while the space-going vehicles are in outer space.[62]

One special problem of the use of the concept of aerodynamic lift and "aircraft," whether considered under the terms of the civil air-law conventions or not, is that, due to technological change, it no longer has an operationally clear justification. Thus, "hybrid" craft, the American X-15, and others noted earlier in chapter 2, possess the characteristics of both aircraft and spacecraft; the X-15 has already flown at heights over 65 miles above the earth. Its performance does not fit neatly within the proposed definitions and limitations,[63] and several of its pilots have won American astronaut wings by piloting it at or above an altitude of 50 miles,[64] the altitude administratively established by military regulation as the basis for qualifying a pilot for such award.

Other "scientific" definitions of "airspace," not necessarily tied to the conventions, have also been offered to support altitudes greater than those at which conventional aircraft can fly. Ambrosini has suggested a height of about 100 kilometers as supported by "physical" considerations.[65] Reintanz, of East Germany, has also supported this height of about 62 miles as "the upper limit of national airspace."[66] Professor Cheng at one time found the limit of airspace at the base of the exosphere, perhaps "300–500 miles above the surface of the earth," and offered this as "the upper limit of national airspace."[67] Others, thinking in terms of "air" or "atmosphere" also reach distances of 10,000 miles or more, since at least oxygen particles can be found a great distance from the earth.[68] At such distances, the "line" then becomes func-

---

[56] Goedhuis, "Air Sovereignty and the Legal Status of Outer Space," Int'l Law Ass'n, New York Conference 7 (1958).

[57] Pinochet (Chile), U.N. Doc. No. A/C. 1/PV.982 at 41 (Nov. 12, 1958). See also Lapradelle, "Les Frontiers de l'Air," *Recueil des Cours,* [II] 121, 126–27 (1954).

[58] Shawcross & Beaumont, *supra* note 4, at 175.

[59] Lemoine, *Traité de Droit Aérien* 83 (1947); Peng, "Le vol à haute altitude et l'article de la Convention de Chicago, 1944," 12 *Revue du Barreau de la Province de Quebec* 277, 292 (1952); Saint-Alary, *Le Droit Aérien* 66 (1955). See also Hingorani, "An Attempt to Determine Sovereignty in Upper Space," 26 *U. Kan. L. Rev.* 5, 11–12 (1957).

[60] Aaronson, "Space Law," in 1961 *Symposium, supra* note 4, at 221, 225. Earlier, Oscar Schachter had suggested that a reasonable interpretation of the conventions might put this limit at about 42 miles. See Special Senate Comm. on Space and Astronautics, 85th Cong., 2d Sess., *Space Law* 8, 15–16 (Comm. Print, 1958).

[61] See Latchford, "The Bearing of International Air Navigation Conventions on the Use of Outer Space," *1961 Symposium, supra* note 4, at 493, 495–96; McDougal *et al., supra* note 51, at 328–30, esp. 329, and sources cited; Lipson & Katzenbach, *supra* note 1, at 15–16; *Hearings on H.R. 11881* at 1266 (1958).

[62] Many writers who advocate the drawing of an altitudinal limit on airspace also reject the conventions as a legal basis for drawing the line. See, e.g., Haley, "Survey of Legal Opinion on Extraterrestrial Jurisdiction," reprinted in *1961 Symposium, supra* note 4, at 719, 722–23; Goedhuis, *supra* note 56, at 3–4; Cooper, "Flight-Space Law," 1 *Handbuch der Astronautik* 55 (1960).

[63] On some of the legal issues, see David Davies Memorial Institute, *supra* note 54, at 8; Haley, *supra* note 62. For an argument that the issue of "hybrid" craft is a false one, see Haley at 102 ff.

[64] See e.g., FRC Release 2–66 (Feb. 7, 1966).

[65] A/C.1/PV.982, at 56 (Nov. 12, 1958).

[66] Reintanz, "Air Space and Outer Space," *1961 Symposium, supra* note 4, 1134, 1138, 1139.

[67] Cheng, "From Air Law to Space Law," 13 *Current Legal Problems* 228, 229 (1960).

[68] In general on this approach, see Goedhuis, "Some Trends in the Political and Legal Thinking on the Conquest of Space," 9 *Nederlands Tijdschrift voor Internationaal Recht* 113 at 121, n. 9 (Apr. 1962). Writers who share Goedhuis's opinion that airspace, in the meaning of international conventions and national laws, is synonymous with atmospheric space, include Meyer, Address to the Third International Astronautical Congress (Sept. 1952); Welf Heinrich, Prince of Hanover, "Luftrecht und Weltraum" [Air Law and Space] (dissertation, Goettingen U., 1953); Aaronson, *supra* note 13, at 420; Roy, 1958 *Proceedings, Am. Soc. Int'l L.* 97; Pepin, "Space Penetration," *id.;* Milde, "Considerations on Legal Problems of Space above National Territory," 5 *Rev. Contemp. L.* 5 ff. (June 1958); Korovin, *supra* note 49, at 53; Sztucki, *Security of Nations and Outer Space* (Warsaw, 1959); Cheng, *supra* note 67, at 229; Becker, in *1961 Symposium, supra* note 27, at 401.·

tionally meaningless; most important, close-in space activities will take place within the area bounded by such a line and such regions will be difficult to police, or at least it would be too expensive, given the foreseeable risks.[69]

Other suggestions for fixing a "natural" or "scientific" or "logical" boundary have called for combinations of physical factors including velocity, gravitation,[70] centrifugal force, and the like. One of the more vigorously asserted proposals is that espoused by Haley[71] and others[72] and called generally the Von Karman line. As noted in *The Law of Outer Space*:

[I]t accepts the basic concept of aerodynamic lift but argues that such lift need not be the only "support" and that present law could be interpreted as extending sovereignty up to the point where any aerodynamic lift is available. For an object traveling at 25,000 feet per second, that line is said to be about 275,000 feet from the earth's surface. While this line is thought to have more stability than the proposal first put forward, it would also vary with atmospheric conditions and with design changes and other factors affecting the flight of objects.[73]

Others have suggested about the same height for similar or related reasons.[74] Moreover, the International Astronautical Federation now classifies all flight above 62 miles (100 km) as "space flight."[75] It should also be noted that the David Davies Memorial Institute in both its Draft Code of Rules on the Exploration and Uses of Outer Space and in its Draft Rules Concerning Changes in the Environment of the Earth defines airspace as "the volume of space between the surface of the earth at sea level and an altitude of 80,000 meters above it." This

would place the upper line at about the distance of the Von Karman line.[76]

One other suggestion deserves special mention. It was perhaps first advanced in recent times by Kelsen in commenting, in 1944, on the Paris Convention and suggests that claims to sovereignty reach as far out as a state can exercise effective control.[77] There would thus be several boundaries, since some states are more technologically advanced than others. The diversity question could be eliminated by placing the line at maximum height which *any* state could exercise control.[78] This same problem was extensively debated at the time of the U-2 incident.[79] The instability of any such boundary or set of boundaries has been often remarked and the proposal is infrequently heard today.

Limits based on technology, whether it is the technology of flight characteristics or of the ability of a ground state to interdict the flight, have the great defects of instability and uncertainty. New materials, new techniques, new military developments might alter the line significantly, eliminating the alleged certainty which proponents offer as the basic utility of having a known, "scientifically" sound line.[80] In general, the critics appear to have become convinced, as a note in the *Harvard Law Review* put it:

[T]he imposition of a ceiling . . . keyed to control capacity would, in attempting to prohibit a nation from retaliating against air flight directly above its territory, be unresponsive to national security needs . . . [It] would exacerbate international tensions, since effective control could only be convincingly manifested by the destruction of an intruder.[81]

A few writers have also suggested the use of more than

---

[69] Of current and currently foreseeable activities, only the "stationary orbit" satellites (at about 22,300) miles would normally be "above" a line at 10,000 miles.

[70] This approach, while involving what most believe is unscientific speculation, considering the immense distances at which the earth's gravitational pull is felt, is nevertheless revived from time to time. See, e.g., Rine "Recht im Weltraum" (lecture); Verplaetse, *International Law in Vertical Space: Air–Outer Space–Ether* 143 (1960). For comment (scathing) see McDougal *et al.*, *supra* note 51, at 346–47.

[71] See Haley, *supra* note 51, 75 ff., 96–107.

[72] See, e.g., Dr. Belaunde, U.N. Doc. No. A/C.1/PV.1211 at 42 (Dec. 5, 1961).

[73] Lipson & Katzenbach, *supra* note 1, 12–13.

[74] See, e.g., Roberts, "Outer Space and National Sovereignty," 12 *Air U.Q.Rev.* 53, 59 (1960); Schofield, "Control of Outer Space," 10 *Air U.Q.Rev.* 93 (1958). See also Wright, "Legal Aspects of the U-2 Incident," 54 *Am. J. Int'l L.* 836, 847 (1960).

[75] Haley, *supra* note 62, at 719, 724.

[76] C. L. Sulzberger of the *New York Times* has also suggested a height of 50 miles, but his reasons remain unclear. See, e.g., *New York Times*, Nov. 19, 1960, at 20; June 1, 1960, at 36; Feb. 24, 1958, at 18.

[77] Kelsen, *General Theory of Law and State* 216–17 (1949). On this approach generally see McDougal *et al.*, *supra* note 51, at 338–46. McDougal and his associates are especially critical of Kelsen. Compare Giannini, "Diritto Spaziale o Astronautico," 34 *Rivista Aeronautica* 1993 (1958), who argues that sovereignty is vertical and goes as high as a state can exercise it. See also his "Juridical Problem of Space Navigation," 35 *Rivista Aeronautica* 879 (1959).

[78] See, e.g., Cooper, *supra* note 55.

[79] See McDougal *et al.*, *supra* note 51, at 430 ff., and sources cited.

[80] Thus see Haley, "The Law of Space and Outer Space," 33 *S. Cal. L. Rev.* 370, 373–74 (1960).

[81] "National Sovereignty of Outer Space," 74 *Harv. L. Rev.* 1154, 1165 (1961).

one line, a division into zones. There might be, for example, a fairly low area of complete national control, an intermediate zone free for nonmilitary transit or other internationally agreed uses, and "outer space," free for the peaceful use of all.[82] Haley, for example, also, suggested at one time that states should continue supreme in airspace (up to about 37.3 miles), that in the area of the "astronautic regime," starting about 3,728 miles (except for earth satellites which are in it at any altitude), states should have a limited competence, and that the "escape corridor" between the two altitudes needs further study and consideration.[83] Despite the possible lure of these proposals as analogous to known patterns on the seas, they have thus far attracted little national support.

Airspace and Outer Space: Division by Line or Function

Most of the earlier comprehensive studies in this field have advanced reasons pro and con for accepting or rejecting each or all of the types of proposals suggested by various groups of writers.[84] Since it now seems clear that no single line will prove acceptable to the nations in the foreseeable future and that, if one should ever be accepted by international consensus, it will be based on mutual political accommodation rather than on the "scientific" merits of the proposal,[85] we here conclude this discussion by noting briefly the disclosed views on why drawing any line is unpalatable to the nations of the world.[86]

(1) That the absence of explicit agreement has not yet led to international tensions and does not appear likely to do so. (2) That an attempt to reach explicit agreement on establishment of an altitude boundary would invite many states to make claims to sovereignty which, in analogous cases such as the high seas, have led to immoderate demands. Pandora's box might be harder to close than to open. (3) That any boundary set might have to be set too high. An altitude beyond that which seems to be the maximum being established by custom (the roughly one hundred mile figure . . .) would seriously hamper some space activity. A figure of a hundred miles, while less serious in effect, might also hamper at least some future activities. The possibility of getting anything less through agreement would seem to be negligible, primarily because fear of the unknown would lead states to claim as much as they could. On the other hand, future activities at lower altitudes may be acceptable if there is no explicit agreement on the extent of airspace. (4) That an agreed altitude once achieved will be next to impossible to reduce. States will not gladly give up sovereignty over territory. (5) That an agreement reached later is likely to fix on a lower altitude than an agreement reached sooner, and that the lower figure would be in the general interest. (6) That an arbitrary line, even if low enough to permit more space activity, might encourage rather than avert disputes because it might provoke technical complaints about violations which at high altitudes would be difficult to verify.[87]

The arguments against drawing (or accepting) a line or lines as the boundary for airspace (or outer space) have also been summed up more concisely in the terms "arbitrary, artificial, vulnerable to fluctuation with new scientific data, difficult to formulate in practice, difficult to enforce and . . . not even [able to] serve as an effective guarantee of a State's security."[88] It is also, after a decade

---

[82] See, e.g., Cooper, "Contiguous Zones in Aerospace—Preventive and Protective Jurisdiction," 7 *JAG J.* 15 ff. (Sept.–Oct. 1965); Cooper, "International Control of Outer Space (Additional Remarks)," 10 *Zeitschrift fuer Luftrecht und Weltraumrechtsfragen* [hereinafter cited as *ZLW*] 102 (1961); "Legal Problems of Upper Space," 1956 *Proceedings, Am. Soc. Int'l L.* 85, 91 ff.; Kopal, "Sovereignty of States and the Legal Status of Outer Space," reprinted in *1961 Symposium, supra* note 4, at 1122; Seara Vasques, "The Functional Regulation of the Extra-atmospheric Space," *Proceedings of the Second Colloquium on the Law of Outer Space* 139 (Haley & Welf Heinrich eds., London, 1959); Hyman, "Sovereignty over Space," *Proceedings, 3d Colloquium on the Law of Outer Space* 33 (Stockholm, 1960); Schofield, *supra* note 74, at 93, 104; Knauth, "1959 Proceedings," *ABA Sec. Int'l & Comp. L.* 232–33 (1960).

[83] See Haley, *supra* note 80, at 370, 375–77.

[84] As is no doubt to be expected, a proponent of a particular line has not only pointed out its virtues but has indicated why it alone is the most legally useful and why its competitors should be rejected. At least a few of the leading authors have found it necessary and have been willing in public to advance modifications of their initial proposals involving somewhat different theories as time and technology have advanced. See, e.g., the works of John Cobb Cooper, cited, *passim,* in this section. This itself suggests one reason why the contentions must be expected to continue.

[85] See e.g., the remarks of Meyer, Int'l Law Ass'n, *Report of the 50th Conference* 41–42 (Brussels, 1962).

[86] The situation is certainly not unique to outer space developments. As Justice Frankfurter stated in a totally different context: "In law, as in life, lines have to be drawn. But the fact that a line has to be drawn somewhere does not justify its being drawn anywhere. The line must follow some direction of policy, whether rooted in logic or experience. Lines should not be drawn simply for the sake of drawing lines." Frankfurter, J., dissenting in Pearce v. Commissioner of Internal Revenue, 315 U.S. 543, 86 L. Ed. 1016, 62 S. Ct. 754 (1941).

[87] Lipson & Katzenbach, *supra* note 1, at 17.

[88] McMahon, *supra* note 21, at 356, note 1. To the same effect see Meyer, "The Present Situation of Space Law,"

of practice, still referred to almost invariably by state officials as premature. The Report of the Legal Committee of the U.N.'s Ad Hoc Committee on the Peaceful Uses of Outer Space in 1959 termed this a matter of low priority,[89] and the Ad Hoc Committee itself noted:

It was generally believed that the determination of precise limits for airspace and outerspace did not present a legal problem calling for priority consideration at this moment. The Committee noted that the solution of the problems which it had identified as susceptible of priority treatment was not dependent upon the establishment of such limits.[90]

In 1961, in introducing a draft resolution[91] entitled "International Cooperation in the Peaceful Uses of Outer Space," cosponsored by Australia, Canada, Italy, and the United States, Ambassador Stevenson observed:

The members of the [First] Committee [of the General Assembly] will note that we have not attempted to define where outer space begins. In our judgment it is premature to do this now. The attempt to draw a boundary between airspace and outer space must await further experience and a consensus among the nations.

Fortunately the value of the principles of freedom of space and celestial bodies does not depend on the drawing of a boundary line. If I may cite the analogy of the high seas, we have been able to confirm the principle of freedom of the seas even in the absence of complete agreement as to where the seas begin.[92]

There is no evidence of any important change in outlook since then.

Similarly, in the British Parliament it has been stated:

It cannot, however, be said that the international law has yet determined the exact limit to be placed on the extension of sovereignty upwards. In her Majesty's Government's view, it would be premature to attempt such a definition at present.[93]

An Australian representative has said:

It would be wiser, in view of the illustration from air law, to postpone any attempt to formulate a criterion of demarcation, which might even in the end turn out to be functional and not spatial at all.[94]

The United States has also acted on the belief, noted in chapter 2, that:

In discussing air and space, it should be recognized that there is no division, *per se,* between the two. For all practical purposes air and space merge, forming a continuous and indivisible field of operation.[95]

It has been suggested that it is unnecessary and may even be dangerous to rush into a premature boundary or set of rules; that we lack the requisite scientific knowledge; that it is not possible to foresee all the effects of any overall division; and that premature action might prove dangerous for national security and for future international accommodation and cooperation as well.[96]

For Soviet spokesmen, arguments for avoiding a fixed boundary and favoring flexibility in limiting sovereignty by altitude and in establishing rules by function rather than by location are primarily based on the physical problems of devising any useful single fixed standard and on national security interests. Various authors and spokesmen have put the matter in similar ways. Zhukov, for example, has stated: "from the standpoint of the security of states the height to which sovereignty extends above land is not of decisive importance. A state will not feel itself more secure because military preparations are being conducted against it at a greater altitude."[97] He also said that "space craft, operating at immense altitudes which dwarf terrestrial distances, are not less dangerous

---

16 *Neue Juristisch Wochenschrift* 193 (1963) [hereinafter cited as *NJW*]; Economides, "Quelques réflexions sur le régime juridique de l'espace extra-atmosphérique," 13 *Revue Hellenique de Droit International* 246 (1960).

[89] See U.N. Doc. A/AC.98/2, *passim.*

[90] Report of the Ad Hoc Committee on the Peaceful Uses of Outer Space, A/4141, July 14, 1959; U.N. Gen. Ass. Off. Rec. 14th Sess., Annexes, Agenda Item 25, pp. 1, 25.

[91] A/C.1/1.301, Dec. 2, 1961.

[92] Statement of Dec. 4, 1961, before the First Committee of the General Assembly. The text of Ambassador Stevenson's remarks is reproduced in 46 *Dept. State Bulletin,* No. 1179, 180, 181 (Jan. 29, 1962) and in U.N. Doc. A/C.1/PV. 1210 at 2, 7 (Dec. 4, 1961).

[93] See Hansard, 653 *House of Commons Debates,* cols. 192–93 (Feb. 16, 1962).

[94] U.N. Doc. A/AC.105/C.2/SR.4 at 4, Legal Subcommittee on Outer Space (Aug. 21, 1962). See also Zhukov, "Problems of Space Law at the Present Stage," presented to the 5th Colloquium, IISL (Varna, 1962), mimeo, p. 11.

[95] Then Chief of Staff, U.S. Air Force, White, "Air and Space Are Indivisible," 41 *Air Force Mag.* 40, 41 (Mar. 1958).

[96] See, e.g., testimony of Becker, *Hearings on H.R. 11881* at 1273 (1958(; Becker, "United States Foreign Policy . . . ," *supra* note 27; Ward, "Projecting the Law of the Sea into the Law of Space," *JAG J.* (Navy) 3–8 (Mar. 1957), and "Space Law as a Way to World Peace," *id.* at 10 ff. (Feb. 1959); Keating, "Reaching for the Stars," 45 *A.B.A. J.* 54 ff. (1959). See generally McDougal & Lipson, "Perspectives for a Law of Outer Space," 52 *Am. J. Int'l L.* 407 ff. and sources cited (1958).

[97] Korovin, Pobedonostsev, Zadorozhniy, Zhukov, and Osnitskaya, "Conquest of Outer Space and Some Problems of International Relations," *1961 Symposium, supra* note 4, at 1072, 1082.

merely because they are not precisely perpendicular to target areas."[98]

An unlimited extension of sovereignty would not in itself guarantee security, and this has been generally recognized by Soviet writers and spokesmen. Even without sovereignty in or over an area, states may, as history shows, resist attack on the ground of the inherent right of self-defense, limited only in part by Article 51 of the U.N. Charter, which speaks in terms of defense against an "armed" attack.[99]

Such state practice as exists, including the banning of nuclear tests in the atmosphere and in outer space by the 1963 Nuclear Test Ban Treaty, the limitation on placing weapons of mass destruction in orbit (found in a UN resolution of 1963; in the Space Treaty of 1967 described below; and in the form of Soviet protests concerning U.S. "espionage" from outer space), all point to the control, if any, of activities in outer space on functional rather than on "territorial" or "boundary" bases.[100] There seems little point therefore, at this stage in the development of legal principles concerning outer space activities, to devoting further attention to the boundary issue as such. A stable, workable legal definition of outer space is not yet politically acceptable, partly because not enough is known definitely about potential strategic uses and controls over space technology to offer promise of making a legal definition both "safe" for all nations and operationally reliable. Even so, three issues should be noted briefly before moving on to the problem of the regime in outer space as such—an outer limit to airspace, the possible "inner limit" of outer space, and the status of space vehicles while in airspace.

An Outer Limit to Airspace

For the reasons just reviewed it appears unlikely that the nations will formally define and delimit outer space in the near future. These arguments nevertheless do not fully meet the continuing pressure by John Cobb Cooper (now deceased) and others who urge that, in any event, *airspace,* at least for purposes of existing air law treaties, arrangements, and regulations, should be formally defined.[101] A definition for limited and stated purposes would leave outer space as free of regulation as the nations seem at present to desire and at the same time clarify certain present problems of jurisdiction, the limits of the authority of the International Civil Aviation Organization, etc. While proponents of drawing a line for all purposes have clearly failed to convince the states of the wisdom of their contentions, the issue of defining airspace alone for specific purposes warrants special attention. It can in fact be separated from the question of a general boundary, although perhaps at present even this discussion would inevitably raise questions of the creation of a safe, dependable, enforcible, and enforced regime of fair behavior beyond the line, which the major powers are apparently not interested in considering at this time.

An "Inner" Limit to Outer Space

Again in noting the rejection by the nations and many writers of the utility of drawing a boundary or boundaries between airspace and outer space, we have nevertheless observed a present general acknowledgment that satellites now in orbit have not violated the sovereign territorial rights of any state. Such substantially unpowered flights are then, by common consent, in outer space.

Robert Jastrow early suggested a lower limit of about 100 miles (162 km.), where "the density of the atmosphere is sufficiently low to permit the completion of one circuit by an orbiting vehicle, without destruction by

---

[98] Zhukov, "National Sovereignty of Outer Space." See also Lipson & Katzenbach, *supra* note 1, at 13. Also on the problem of security as a consideration in extending or limiting sovereignty, see Gabrovski, "The Cosmos, Peace, and Sovereignty," 32 *SGP* 84 (1962); Galina, *supra* note 41 (reprinted in translation in RAND Corp. Translation T–98, Sept. 25, 1958); Kovalev & Cheprov, *supra* note 39, at 145, and "On the Working-Out of the Legal Problems of Cosmic Space," 30 *SGP* 130 (1960); Osnitskaya, *The Conquest of Space and International Law* (State Publishing House of Legal Literature, Moscow, 1962), and *supra* note 41, at 65. See also Reintanz, "The Legal Status of Air Space and Cosmic Space," 11 *Neue Justiz* 507 (1957).

[99] See, e.g., Katzenbach, "The Law in Outer Space," in *Space: Its Impact on Man and Society* 69, 75 (Levy ed. 1965) [hereinafter cited as Levy].

[100] Note again that this discussion does not include activities on the celestial bodies. On the "functional" approach in general, see again Report of the Ad Hoc Committee, A/4141 at 68 (July 14, 1959); McDougal & Lipson, *supra* note 96, at 164; Gal, "Space Law Science in Hungary," 7 *Varia* 177, 178 (1965); Verplaetse, "Methodological Considerations on the Law of Space," 26 *Revue Générale de L'air* 243 (26th year, N. S., 1963).

[101] See e.g., Cooper's comments in "The Boundary between Territorial Airspace and International Outer Space," *Int'l Symposium on Space Law* (Fed. Bar Ass'n, Sept. 11, 1964), and in "Contiguous Zones . . . ," *supra* note 82, *passim.* See also, for "pro-boundary" statements, Int'l Law Ass'n, *Report of the 51st Meeting* 639–42 (Cheng) and 679–82 (Cooper, 1964). Contra, see *id.* at 63 (McDougal) and 700 (Zhukov).

atmospheric friction."[102] Satellites have now in fact orbited successfully with apogees somewhat lower in the 70- to 80-mile altitude range. Cooper also, at one time, suggested as an inner boundary for outer space the "lowest altitude above the earth's surface at which an artificial satellite may be put in orbit around the earth" and this he estimated then at "80 to 100 miles,"[103] and later at perhaps 70 miles. Thus, the lowest limit at which an unpowered artificial satellite's flight can be sustained—something between 70 and 100 miles above the earth—might be taken as the lower limit to whatever regime is accepted by states for outer space.[104]

This idea has drawn some of the same criticism as other suggestions based on technological factors; it may be subject to change as space vehicle design changes and as space functions, capacities, and potential defense activities change, but it is an interesting basis for speculation because it is already a part of state practice, however informal and temporal. Even so, this can be suggested only for the activities already undertaken. If a functional approach is applied, as is the case to date and as seems inevitable, other problems arise. This line would clearly not set a boundary to the concept of airspace in any event; the limit to the airspace regime of state sovereignty would remain undetermined, although it would, if this view prevailed, end somewhere lower than the then-current orbital altitude.

Space Vehicles in Airspace

Whatever the significance of the fact that there is no agreed upper limit to airspace and that present orbital flight now appears to be accepted as taking place in outer space, no *state* has asserted that even a customary or treaty rule freeing outer space for use by all extends the right to innocent passage through the lower limits of still-sovereign airspace. States can at present generally be expected to reject such a notion. While in sovereign airspace, however defined, space vehicles will presumably be held fully subject to the airspace regime.[105] This may, of course, include special treatment of space vehicles, especially manned vehicles, which are patently on peaceful missions and which are clearly in distress.

Since there do not appear to be any states whose spokesmen have commented favorably on a right of free transit for space vehicles through national airspace, it is interesting to note that several authors now argue that there exists "at the present time . . . a customary rule of international space law permitting the innocent passage of space vehicles through national airspace."[106] It may be that some have taken the U.N. resolutions of 1961 and 1963 as inferring a general international acceptance of a concept of innocent passage for flight of nonhostile spacecraft through a subjacent state's air space incident to its takeoff or landing.

The argument that transit through another state's airspace cannot be illegal is largely based on the allegation that no protests have thus far been made.[107] Yet it is not at all clear that practice to date is in fact relevant, since the lack of protest has been keyed to flights at orbital heights. It is also clear that no such right of "innocent passage" exists today for aircraft and other airborne devices; such freedom was urged in the early days of aerial flight, as we have noted, but was rejected by all states, particularly with the lesson of the First World War's use of aircraft in all minds.[108]

---

[102] Jastrow, "Definition of Air Space," *Proceedings, 1st Colloquium on the Law of Outer Space* 82 (The Hague, 1958). Ley, another distinguished scientist, has suggested 50 kilometers (31 miles) as reasonable and 250 kilometers (155 miles) as possible. Ley, *supra* note 52, at 360.

[103] Cooper, "International Control of Outer Space," 9 *ZLW* 288, 290 (1960). Before Sputnik, it was commonly believed that 300 miles was the inner limit for a successful satellite.

[104] For this concept in the literature, see Katzenbach, in Levy, *supra* note 99, at 69, 74; Cooper, "Fundamental Questions of Outer Space Law" 3 (Lecture given at Leiden University, Oct. 1960); Leopold & Scafuri, "Orbital Space Flight under International Law," 19 *Fed. Bar J.* 227–41 (July 1959); Jastrow, *supra* note 102, at 82; Cooper, *supra* note 103, at 340; David Davies Memorial Institute, *supra* note 54, at 7.

[105] Note that in the present regime, airspace over the high seas is free for the peaceful use of all. No discussion of the complexities of the airspace regime, other than that of the sovereignty of the subjacent state, is included in this study. For the United States, Loftus Becker suggested simply that any infringement of airspace by a satellite or missile would be covered by existing law as equivalent to infringement by an airplane. See *Hearings on H.R. 11881* at 1297–1303. Special rights or privileges may of course be granted under treaty or by compliance with the principles suggested in United Nations resolutions. See *infra* chap. 4, at 73 ff.

[106] See, e.g., Christol, "Innocent Passage" in the "International Law of Outer Space" 7 *JAG L. Rev.* (Air Force) 22, 29 (Sept.–Oct. 1965). See also Int'l Law Ass'n, *Report of the 51st Conference* 624 (1964) and see generally Rehm, "The Legal Character of the Flight of Rockets and Satellites," 14 *Weltraumfahrt* (Zeitschrift fuer Astronautik und Raketentechnik) 76–77 (1963).

[107] Da Costa, "Air Domination of the Nation and of Space," 83 *Revista de Servico Publico* No. 2, Year 22 (May 1959); Ikeda, *Space Law* (1961); Meyer, *supra* note 88.

[108] The Paris Convention of 1919 purported to grant a right

Other writers have simply asserted that air law must apply to space vehicles while in the atmosphere.[109] They have pointed out "that under existing international law there is no such thing as a general freedom of transit through the territories of other States."[110]

To date American and Soviet launches and descents (and those of other nations as well) have been designed to avoid low-altitude passage over other nations. This factor presents a problem for smaller nations with neighbors on their borders who want or will want to conduct launch or recovery operations from within national boundaries. Presumably, cooperative programs such as those in Europe will, through agreements, permit the brief transit on ascent and descent of outer space vehicles through the airspace of states other than the launching state.

Absent such international arrangements, from the point of view of domestic law and the regulation and control of airspace, it seems clear that national states will seek to exercise control over low-flying "spacecraft," and the 1967 Space Treaty offers no exemptions. Thus, the congress of the United States, in August 1958, in enacting the Federal Aviation Act, concerned itself with the question of missiles and launch vehicles transiting airspace as well as other rocketry and balloons. In the Senate Report on the then-proposed Federal Aviation Agency, the Committee on Interstate and Foreign Commerce declared:

> It was the view of the committee that in order for the Administrator of the new Agency to properly discharge his responsibilities under the new act, particularly those in connection with the allocation of airspace, that his jurisdiction should extend not only to vehicles commonly considered as

aircraft, but also *during their flight through airspace,* to other vehicles such as rockets, missiles and other airborne objects. [Italics added.]

It will be recalled that an aircraft was defined as "any contrivance now known or hereafter invented, used or designed for navigation of or flight in the air." The committee also considered whether the then-existing statutory definition of aircraft was adequate:

> After due deliberation, the committee concluded that no change in the definition of the term "aircraft" was necessary in order to achieve this objective, since all vehicles, rockets and missiles, as well as aircraft, are in fact used at least in part for navigation of the airspace.[111]

Pursuant to its statutory responsibility, the FAA has undertaken a series of agreements with NASA and the Department of Defense to assure airspace protection from and for missiles and launch vehicles. The relevant documents indicate that the temporary "restricted airspace," necessary for the safe launching of space vehicles in the United States, is obtained by rule making, NOT-AMS, and other advisements, and by visual and radar observation.

Although the airspace jurisdiction of the FAA is generally limited to areas of United States sovereignty, "it may be assumed that the Agency would nevertheless exercise control over vehicles in outer space that are approaching the United States with intent to enter United States' airspace."[112] This control could be a condition imposed for permitting ingress into United States airspace, similar to that currently exercised over aircraft above the high seas flying an airway into the United States. United States jurisdiction over spacecraft on an "aerospaceway" into the United States, however, would not extend to a spacecraft in outer space which does not intend entering United States airspace unless the problem of self-defense exists.

---

of innocent passage through airspace, but its effect was vitiated by extensive qualifications. See 1 Oppenheim, sec. 197. The Chicago Convention of 1944 recognizes no such right.

[109] Hartwig, "The Present Situation in Space Law," 15 *NJW* 15 (1962); Homburg, "Droit astronautique et droit aérien," *Revue Générale de l'Air* 11 (21st year, No. 1, 1958).

[110] Cheng, in Int'l Law Ass'n, *Report of the 50th Conference* (Brussels, 1962). See his analysis of these points at that page. See also Goedhuis, "Report on General Questions on the Legal Regime of Space," *Report of the 50th Conference,* Annex A, at 77, 84 (1962).

For expressions of the view that there is no right of transit at present and that it may be premature to attempt to create one, see Int'l Law Ass'n, *Report of the 51st Conference* (1964); 631 (McDougal); 700–701 (Zhukov); 693 (Meyer); 768 (Cooper). See also 624, 658–62.

On "transit" in general, see E. Lauterpacht, "Freedom of Transit in International Law," 44 *Trans. Grot. Soc'y* 313 ff. (1958/59).

[111] See *Senate Report 1811,* 85th Cong., 2d Sess., 20 (1958). On these points, see ABA Committee on the Law of Outer Space—1965, Final Committee Report, "Registration and Traffic Control of Space Vehicles" 3–7 (3d draft, mimeo., June 25, 1965) [hereinafter cited as *ABA Report*]. See also Menter, "Government Regulations of Space Activities," 7 *JAG L. Rev.* (Air Force) 5, 12 (Sept.–Oct. 1965).

[112] See *ABA Report* 5. In Aug. 1966, for example, the FAA warned amateur rocket launchers that firings were subject to FAA aviation regulations; that firings were prohibited into airspace where aircraft were controlled by the FAA, or within 5 miles of airport boundaries, or within 1,500 feet of persons or property not involved in the launching, or into clouds, or at night. See FAA Release 66–83 (Aug. 23, 1966).

While an agreement providing for passage rights might help the progress of the development of space capabilities for some nations, the problem of identifying the vehicle, assuring that its passage is in fact "innocent" and/or that its entry and descent are due to accident or distress, will prove difficult both in legal definition and in practice.[113] The proposals of the David Davies Memorial Institute to deal with this problem thus seem to reflect current realities and likely state responses:

4.1 No spacecraft launched from the territory of any State may at any stage of its flight enter the airspace of another State without the consent of that State: provided that
  a. such consent shall not be withheld if prior notice has been shown to its satisfaction that the flight is solely for scientific and peaceful purposes and shall be so controlled as to obviate danger to aircraft;
  b. any craft capable of operating both as a spacecraft and as an aircraft shall for the purposes of its use of the airspace be deemed to be an aircraft;
  c. a manned spacecraft may enter the airspace without prior consent for the purpose of making an emergency landing, but shall be subject to the provisions of Section b. . . .
4.2 Save in the case provided for in Section 4.1c, any State may divert or destroy any spacecraft which enters its airspace without the consent prescribed in Section 4.1.

As long as the security issue remains paramount, in view of the short reaction time available, states are simply apt to feel obliged to treat all low-flying space vehicles, at least those on incoming trajectories, as potential threats, without some form of satisfactory advance assurances.

Without further consideration here of the problems of defining a boundary between airspace and outer space, we can proceed on the assumption that at some point there is a limit or limits to the extension of terrestrial sovereignty and that in time practical international necessities will lead to a relinquishment of at least extreme claims.[114] Whether it will turn out to be one line or several lines, or several zones, etc., will depend on the future of space technology and the fruits of space activities and exploration and on the nature of the space regime which evolves. We turn therefore to a consideration of the law applicable at present to the status of outer space, however that concept is defined.

The Regime in Outer Space: Background

In examining activities in outer space from the legal point of view, it is interesting to note that a legal regime which governs man's operations there, at least to a limited extent, already exists in recognizable form, although in certain important particulars it is essentially negative. It is a regime of self-denying, self-policed rules accepted today by most if not all of the states of the world.

For analytical purposes, we will continue to deal separately throughout this and the following chapters with national claims to sovereignty or control on or over the celestial bodies. Clearly the questions of sovereignty in "space" and over the celestial bodies in space have elements of similarity: statesmen speak of the two in one breath; United Nations resolutions and the 1967 Space Treaty deal with both. Yet the distinctive features of two permit separate consideration.[115]

Claims to Sovereignty or Control in or over Outer Space

To note the most extreme case first, it is still conceivable that a state might, at some time, lay claim to all "space" measured by projecting its national borders outward into the cosmos.[116] Such a claim would not only be presumptuous by all known standards of creating valid claims in international law; it would be physically absurd as well. In the words of the late Soviet airspace legal expert, Korovin, it would be "unscientific geocentrism, a return from Copernicus to Ptolemy."[117] In addition to

---

[113] For early discussion of reentry and landing in distress, see Report of the Ad Hoc Committee, A/4141 at 67 (July 14, 1949).

[114] See, e.g., Jessup & Taubenfeld, *supra* note 2, 209.

[115] While the positions taken by nations with respect to sovereign claims to outer space and to claims to the celestial bodies are more similar than not, certain differences do exist. No state thus far appears to have done any act predicated on a claim to or forming the possible basis for a claim to sovereignty over some portion of outer space, although the rights to defend oneself at any distance and perhaps to extend "airspace" for vast distances outward for this purpose have on occasion been asserted, as we noted above. The record with respect to the celestial bodies is slightly, but only slightly, less clear although the potentials are different. There has been, for example, some special concern with the moon, particularly because of its conceivable military value. The problem is discussed *infra* in chap. 4.

[116] On techniques for projecting the boundaries, see, e.g., Jessup & Taubenfeld, *supra* note 2, 206–7.

[117] "International Status of Cosmic Space," 5 *Int'l Aff.* 53–59 (Moscow, Jan. 1959), reprinted in *1961 Symposium, supra* note 4, at 1062–71. As Meyer noted in 1962: "[T]here seems to exist no longer any controversy of importance concerning the question of the legal status of outer space . . . the question is nearly unanimously answered in the sense that outer

the difficulties we even now face in determining where a nation's borders are located when projected upward in airspace from the earth's surface, a basic physical difficulty in projecting claims to sovereignty outward indefinitely is that "objects" in space do not rotate with the earth and maintain no constant relationship with any nation.[118] In a very real sense this same observation could be made about *space,* within which the atmosphere turns, though not about the earth's *air* envelope itself, but it serves to point out the inherent difficulty, not to say absurdity, of any such limitless claims.[119]

This is not to say that such claims may not even be put forth by states or by writers on their behalf.[120] But it is only fair to observe that the official position of all major states, including the two major present space powers, and the overwhelming majority of writers flatly reject such claims to unlimited sovereignty. The practice of states to date and the expressions of consensus embodied in United Nations resolutions and the 1967 Space Treaty are all in accord.[121] The only prospective exception, if indeed it can be called that, is the normal one in international relations; that is, it seems clear that if any space power *does* resort to making claims, others would feel free to protect their own interests.[122] In summary

then, while states express sovereign claims in airspace and will assert and exercise sovereign rights with respect to their vehicles, personnel and, no doubt, in time, to their bases while in outer space, for physical as well as legal-political reasons, they do not now assert claims to areas of outer space as such.

Space as Res Communis

If we lay aside national claims to outer space as physically absurd and, in any event, barred legally by tacit and/or treaty agreement among the states, the choice of an overall descriptive term for the status of outer space becomes simpler. If outer space is not "owned" by a state or states and is not, for reasons more fully developed elsewhere herein, *res nullius*[123] and hence subject to national claims, our choice is narrowed. There remain basically the statuses of *res omnium communis* and *res extra commercium*. In time, an internationalized regime might be developed which would offer another alternative. This possibility, and its various possible forms, has received much attention from commentators.[124] However desirable such an approach might be even now, current political realities, including the precedent involved in the form of regime developed for the apparently far less strategically important Antarctic continent and for the form of the 1967 Space Treaty, indicate that little time should be devoted to this possibility in any study which, like this one, is devoted to present law and foreseeable trends.[125] The major nations are opposed

---

space is to be considered a free area like the high seas." *Int'l Law Ass'n, supra* note 85, at 40.

[118] See Jenks, "International Law and Activities in Space," 5 *Int'l & Comp. L.Q.* 99, 103–4 (1956).

[119] See also Jessup & Taubenfeld, *supra* note 2, 205–7; Welf Heinrich, *supra* note 68, at 64–66.

[120] See, e.g., Mateesco, "A qui appartient le milieu aérien?" 12 *Revue du Barreau de la Province de Quebec* 227–42 (Apr. 1952).

[121] These matters are all discussed individually hereafter. For the writers, see, e.g., Lipson & Katzenbach, *supra* note 1, at 11, 15–16 and sources cited, esp. Abstracts 663–86; McDougal *et al. supra* note 51, esp. 328–30; Jessup & Taubenfeld, *supra* note 2, at 205–7; McDougal & Lipson, *supra* note 96, at 407, 422; Jenks, *supra* note 51, *passim;* Christol, *The International Law of Outer Space, passim* (1965); Goedhuis, "Reflections on the Evolution of Space Law," 13 *Nederlans Tijdschrift voor International Recht* 109–49 (1966); "Keeping Law and Order in Space," *Time,* Sept. 30, 1966, at 26–27; Mankiewicz, "The Regulation of Activities in Extra-Aeronautical Space, and Some Related Problems," 8 *McGill L.J.* 193–95 (1961–62); Quadri, "Droit International Cosmique," *Recueil des Cours* [III] 509, 539–49 (1959); Johnson, "Remarks," *1961 Am. Soc'y Int'l L.* 165, 166–67; Hildred Tymms, "The Case against National Sovereignty in Space," *1961 Symposium, supra* note 4, at 264, 266–67, 270; Korovin, "International Sovereignty in Space," *id.* at 1062, 1064.

[122] See e.g., Korovin, *supra* note 97; Romashkin, "Technical

Progress and Soviet Law," 30 *Soviet State and Law* 14–24 (1960).

[123] *Res nullius* is normally used to denote an area in which there is no national sovereignty, although unfettered freedom is not necessarily the alternative principle. See 1 Hackworth *Digest of International Law* 396 (1940); 1 Hyde *International Law Chiefly as Interpreted and Applied by the United States* 392 (2d ed., 1945). For a formal definition, see Black, *Law Dictionary* 1470 (4th ed., 1951).

[124] See, e.g., Jessup & Taubenfeld, *supra* note 2, chap. 9; Clark & Sohn, *World Peace through World Law,* chap. 6 at 296–305 (2d. 1961); Black, "Outer Space—The Prospects of International Regimes," AIAA Summer Meeting, June 17–20, 1963, No. 63–244 (mimeo.).

[125] For the view of one of the authors, see Jessup & Taubenfeld, *supra* note 2, *passim,* chap. 9; Taubenfeld, "A Regime for Outer Space," 56 *Nw. U. L. Rev.* 129 ff. (1961); Taubenfeld, 1961 *Proceedings, Am. Soc'y Int'l L.* 176. Especially for criticism of a self-policed, self-denying, self-inspected status quo approach, see also Taubenfeld & Taubenfeld, *Man and Space: Politics, Law, Organization* (Arnold Found. Monograph, 1965).

and, at least for the foreseeable future, the matter ends there.[126]

As some writers have noted, the concept of *res omnium communis* has usually been interpreted as involving a sort of community "ownership" rather than simply a general right to use, but the term is not defined in existing international law.[127] Many of the early statements by national spokesmen used language which seemed to imply a *res omnium communis*. It was said that outer space and the celestial bodies were "owned" by or belonged to or were the common property or the common domain of all people of the world.[128] From the early days of consideration of outer space at the U.N. "the idea of the international character of outer space as a *res communis omnium* seemed to have been generally accepted."[129] Yet this rather romantic notion has not been followed by any attempt to create international institutions to reflect any genuine concept of international ownership or control of space, of the celestial bodies, or of their resources.

The concept of *res extra commercium* as applied typically to the peacetime use of the high seas has indicated a common freedom to use an area without claims of ownership, special exclusive interests, or unilateral control. National spokesmen speaking of outer space and the celestial bodies have frequently used such terms as the rights of equal access, equal enjoyment of benefits, and total permissibility of peaceful use by all, which have been applied to the seas under this broad concept.[130] The real meaning of this regime is discussed below on pages 57 and 74–77.

In point of fact, most national spokesmen and most writers as well have in practice made no distinction in their use of terms. They have described the new milieu as *res omnium communis* or *res extra commercium* or

[126] For a statement of the U.S. position, see letter dated Oct. 5, 1959, written by Assistant Secretary of State Macomber, to Representative Overton Brooks, chairman of the House Committee on Science and Astronautics, 86th Congress.

"On July 30, 1959, the House of Representatives Committee on Science and Astronautics referred House Concurrent Resolution 297 to the Department of State for its views and recommendations. Under this resolution, the Congress would express 'its willingness to internationalize the control, ownership, and exploration of all the Universe from fifty-three miles above the surface of the earth under the direction of the United Nations' and 'its willingness to place all points of interplanetary law under the control of the United Nations.'

"The Department of State does not favor passage of this resolution.

"The Department does not believe that sufficient information is presently available to make possible a determination that all space beyond a given distance from earth constitutes, for all purposes, outer space rather than air space. More knowledge is required before any such boundary can be rationally delimited. Moreover, it may ultimately be concluded that regulation of space activities could better be based on the types of activities involved than on jurisdiction according to fixed spatial limits.

"The United Nations has not been endowed with legislative power with respect to such matters as 'the control, ownership and exploration of all the Universe' or 'all points of interplanetary law.' The Department of State does not consider that it would be sound policy to seek to proceed in that way. The Department believes that a far sounder approach is represented in the Report of the United Nations *Ad Hoc* Committee on the Peaceful Uses of Outer Space. . . .

"The Department would also point out that questions of control in the area of outer space inevitably form part of the problems of disarmament, which can only be dealt with through enforceable internation agreements concluded among the countries necessary to make them effective." Ms. Department of State, file 701.022/7–3059; 2 Whiteman, *supra* note 16, at 1295.

[127] See the comment of the Austrian delegate, U.N. Doc. A/AC.105/SR.5 at 6 (June 5, 1962). In general, see Cheng, "The Extra-terrestrial Application of International Law," *Current Legal Problems* 123, 143 ff. (1965).

[128] See, e.g., remarks of the representations of Venezuela, Iran, Italy, Greece and El Salvador, U.N. Docs. A/C.1/SR.982 at 10 ff.; 988 at 7; 990 at 2; 991 at 4; 992 at 3. The term *res communis* was also used by Communist spokesmen as a basis for attacking U.S. high altitude nuclear tests. See, e.g., U.N. Doc. A/AC.105/PV.16 at 12 (Sept. 14, 1962) (Czechoslovakia).

[129] Mr. Matsch (Austria), rapporteur of the First Committee, U.N. Doc. A/PV.792 at 615, GAOR, Plenary Meeting, 13th Sess., 792 meeting (Dec. 13, 1958).

The David Davies Memorial Institute's Draft Code, *supra* note 54, along this line, provides:

2.1 Outer Space, and the celestial bodies therein, are recognized as being *res communis omnium,* free for exploration and use by all States in conformity with the provisions of this Draft Code, and neither outer space nor the celestial bodies in it are capable of appropriation or exclusive use by any State.
COMMENTS

vii. This Section attempts the outline of a regime for outer space. It makes no distinction between peaceful and military purposes, beyond what is implied in the applicability of U.N. Charter provisions. It has been brought into line with General Assembly Resolutions on the uses of outer space.

viii. The principle that outer space is *res communis* seems now to be generally accepted. . . .

[130] See, e.g., statements of the Argentine and Italian representatives, A/AC.98/SR.4 at 5, 34, July 17, 1959; Report of the Ad Hoc Committee . . . , A/4141 at 64.

have used the terms interchangeably.[131] Despite objections by purists, it seems likely that the practice will continue. In any event, the distinction between the two is neither clear nor immutable; the already developing pattern for outer space activities has some elements of both. Clearly the nations are not prevented from proceeding with space activities on a consensual basis, without any great regard for the formal nomenclature applied by scholars to the overall regime.

Allocation of Authority in an "Area" Lacking a Territorial Sovereign

Bases for Jurisdiction

We turn now to a consideration of the question of allocating authority between states for acts occurring outside the territory of any state.[132] We do not deal here with the question of what portions of the law of any particular nation are applicable to the activities of its citizens or nationals in outer space or on the celestial bodies. For United States personnel, for example, if the question of the commission of a "crime" should arise, it seems clear that "criminal" conduct by military personnel is subject to the provisions of the Uniform Code of Military Justice[133] which is, by its terms, applicable to all "members of a regular component of the armed forces"[134] and "applies in all places."[135] There is no similar general federal criminal code to apply to the activities of U.S. government nonmilitary personnel or to U.S. private citizens in outer space although, presumably, certain statutes (e.g., the Internal Revenue Code) do so apply.[136] The same problem exists with respect to

U.S. activities in Antarctica and existed until recently for acts committed in registered U.S. aircraft while flying over the high seas,[137] etc. For informational purposes, a brief analysis of some of these matters is included in Appendix B and a general discussion of "analogous" areas follows this section.

The question of defining the permissible limits of state power to prescribe or enforce rules governing individual conduct is a recurrent, difficult, and partially unresolved problem for international law.[138] What are the limiting factors? Must there be some rational relation between a state seeking to control particular conduct and either the conduct itself or the persons engaging in or affected by it? What sort of relation will suffice, and how strong and direct must it be? Are any categories of relationship per se sufficient to justify such exercises of jurisdiction? Are such categories exclusive, or does international law permit the exercise of jurisdiction in other situations? Can more than one state with equal propriety under international law regulate the same conduct? What priorities should be accorded to the claims of states to enforce where the claims overlap?

The eventual problems in human relations in outer space are not resolved by the current approach to a regime. Claims to national territorial sovereignty are apparently now ruled out for outer space as such and probably, although less certainly, for the celestial bodies, as we will see. Yet much of national law as we know it is

---

[131] See, e.g., Taubenfeld, "Consideration at the United Nations of the Status of Outer Space," 53 *Am. J. Int'l L.* 400–405 (1959).

[132] The problem of jurisdiction over acts committed on spacecraft, on artificial satellites, and on the celestial bodies has already been noted by commentators. See, for instance, the comprehensive and stimulating discussion in McDougal *et al.*, *supra* note 51, chap. 6, esp. 695–705 (1963). The moot court case argued before the Apr. 1965 annual meeting of the American Society of International Law had as its topic the murder of an English astronaut-scientist by an American astronaut-scientist on the moon.

[133] 10 U.S.C., chap. 46, secs. 801–940, 70A. Stat. 37 *et seq.*

[134] Art. 2, 10 U.S.C. sec. 802.

[135] Art. 5, 10 U.S.C. sec. 805 and see Thompson v. Willingham, 217 F. Supp. 901 (D.C., Penn., 1962).

[136] For a suggestion that this is the case, see Katzenbach, in Levy, *supra* note 99, at 70.

[137] See 18 U.S.C. sec 7, para. 5 (added by 66 Stat. 589 on July 12, 1952).

[138] Action by a state in prescribing or enforcing rules that it has no jurisdiction to prescribe or enforce may constitute a violation of international law. *Restatement*, sec. 8. For a definition of jurisdiction, see *id.* at 25.

On the general problem of jurisdiction, especially with respect to crime, see Bishop, *Cases and Materials on International Law,* chap. 6 (2d ed. 1962); Becket, "Criminal Jurisdiction Over Foreigners," 1927 *Brit. Yrbk. Int'l L.* 108; Harvard Research in International Law, "Draft Convention on Jurisdiction with Respect to Crimes," 29 *Am. J. Int'l L.,* pt. 2, at 439 (Supp. 1935); Berge, "Criminal Jurisdiction and the Territorial Principle," 30 *Mich. L. Rev.* 238 (1931); Levitt, "Jurisdiction over Crimes," 16 *Am. Inst. of Crim. L. & Criminology* 316, 495 (1925–26); Sorkar, "The Proper Law of Crime in International Law," 11 *Int'l & Comp. L. Q.* 444 (Apr. 1962); Baxter, "Extraterritorial Application of Domestic Law," 1960 *U. Brit. Col. L. Rev.* 333; Katzenbach, "Conflicts on an Unruly Horse: Reciprocal Claims and Tolerances in Interstate and International Law," 65 *Yale L. J.* 1087 (1955/56); *Restatement*, pt. 1 (Jurisdiction); McDougal *et al., supra* note 51, esp. Chap. 6; Brown, "Jurisdiction of U.S. Courts over Crimes in Aircraft," 15 *Stan. L. Rev.* 45 (1962/63).

based on the concept that the law governing an act or event is that of the territory in which the act takes place. Under what law would an agreement between two persons on the moon or an act of violence there by one or the other be judged?

There are already well established, if not always agreed upon, patterns for allocating responsibility on other than territorial principles. Without attempting to analyze all potential situations and all prospective claims to authority, it is still necessary to indicate the types of approach that states will take under traditional international law, while outer space and the celestial bodies still lack an agreed regime which includes a rule-making, decision-making authority to allocate these responsibilities.

States have traditionally sought to assert jurisdiction on certain bases or principles. As usually identified,[139] these include:

1. *The Territorial Principle*—A state may exercise jurisdiction with respect to an act occurring in whole or in part in its territory.

2. *The Nationality Principle*—A state may exercise jurisdiction with respect to its own national, wherever he may be.

3. *The Protective Principle*—A state may exercise jurisdiction with respect to certain types of acts wherever, and by whomever, committed where the conduct substantially affects certain vital state interests, such as its security, its property, or the integrity of its governmental processes.

4. *The Universality Principle*—A state may exercise jurisdiction with respect to certain specific universally condemned crimes, principally piracy, wherever and by whomever committed, without regard to the connection of the conduct with that state.

5. *The Passive Personality Principle*—A state may exercise jurisdiction with respect to any act committed outside its territory by a foreigner which substantially affects the person or property of a citizen.

These are generally regarded as concurrent rather than as exclusive bases of jurisdiction; in any given situation more than one state may thus appropriately prescribe rules governing the same conduct.[140] In such case,

customary international law provides no firm rules for determining priorities with respect to trial and punishment of the offender, although there has in practice been a frequent recognition of the claim to such priority, first, of the territorial state, and, second, of the state of nationality.[141]

Generally speaking, the territorial[142] and nationality[143] principles are almost universally acknowledged by states as fundamental and legitimate bases for the exercise of legislative jurisdiction. International practice has also utilized these principles in seeking solutions for more or less analogous situations respecting jurisdiction over vessels or aircraft, which for some purposes at least are generally treated as either part of the "territory" or, in more recent jurisprudence, as possessing the "nationality" of the flag state.[144] There has also been wide acceptance of the legitimacy of the protective principle,[145] although its appropriate scope has been in dispute, and of the universality principle, with respect to the very few crimes, such as piracy and perhaps war crimes, to which it has been considered applicable.[146] On the other hand, there is much dispute over the passive personality prin-

---

[139] The leading such attempt is that of the Harvard Research in International Law, see, e.g., "Jurisdiction with Respect to Crime," Arts. 3–10, 29 *Am. J. Int'l L.* 435 ff. (Supp. 1935), and Dickinson's comment thereon as reporter. The same general framework is adopted by the *Restatement*.

[140] *Restatement,* sec. 105.

[141] In significant particular situations of concurrent jurisdiction, states may of course establish priorities by special agreement. See, for instance, the NATO Status of Forces Agreement, and similar Status of Forces Agreements, and the Tokyo Convention on the Legal Status of Aircraft.

[142] See *Restatement,* secs. 17, 18; Schooner Exchange v. McFadden, 11 U.S. (7 Cranch) 6, 136 (1812); American Banana Co. v. United Fruit Co., 213 U.S. 347, 356 (1909).

[143] See *Restatement,* sec. 30; Harvard Research, *supra* note 139, Art. 5; Blackmer v. U.S., 260 U.S. 94 (1922); Cook v. Tait, 265 U.S. 47 (1924); Skiriotis v. Florida, 373 U.S. 69 (1941); Kawakita v. U.S., 343 U.S. 717 (1952); *The Nottebohm Case* (1955) *I.C.J. Reports* 4.

[144] See *Restatement,* sec. 31 and, generally, Colombos, *International Law of the Sea* 261–64 (5th rev. ed. 1962). See also McDougal, Burke, & Vlasic, "The Maintenance of Public Order at Sea and the Nationality of Ships," 54 *Am. J. Int'l L.* 25 (1960).

[145] See *Restatement,* p. 94; Garcia-Mora, "Criminal Jurisdiction Over Foreigners for Treason and Offenses against The Safety of the State Committed Upon Foreign Territory," 19 *U. Pitt. L. Rev.* 567 (1957–58); U.S. v. Rodriguez, 182 F. Supp. 479 (1960) *aff'd sub nom* Rocha v. U.S., 288 F. 2d 545 (9th Cir. 1961); Skiriotis v. Florida, *supra* note 143 at 737. And see, for a foreign example, French Code of Criminal Procedure, Art 7.

[146] See *Restatement,* sec. 34. Piracy is the only crime uniformly recognized under this principle. See Arts. 15 ff. of the Convention on the High Seas. Some attempts have been made to broaden the principle to other crimes. See, e.g., the U.N. Convention on Genocide.

ciple.[147] Six of the judges (the technical minority) of the Permanent Court of International Justice in the "Lotus" case rejected it.[148] Many states, including the United States, expressly deny the existence of such a principle.[149]

In areas where no territorial sovereign exists, as on the high seas, states have tended to be liberal in recognizing the jurisdictional claims made by other states in which a reasonable connection could be demonstrated between the act or person and the claimant state. Moreover, the majority opinion in the "Lotus" case makes it clear that, where the jurisdictional claim is challenged, it is incumbent on the challenger to demonstrate that the claim violates an international standard—the claimant does not have to prove a rule of law in support of each claim. In the words of the court:

Far from laying down a general prohibition to the effect that states may not extend the application of their laws and the jurisdiction of their courts, to persons, property and acts outside their territory, it leaves them in this respect a wide measure of discretion which is only limited in certain cases by prohibitive rules; as regards other cases, every state remains free to adopt the principle which it regards as best and most suitable. . . .

In these circumstances, all that can be required of a state is that it should not overstep the limits which international law places upon its jurisdiction; within these limits, its title to exercise jurisdiction rests in its sovereignty.

It follows from the foregoing that the contention of the French Government to the effect that Turkey must in each case be able to cite a rule of international law authorizing her to exercise jurisdiction, is opposed to the generally accepted international law.[150]

Presumably, then, where a state could demonstrate that its claim to jurisdiction was convenient, practical, efficacious, and necessary to avoid a situation in which no law could apply, this totality of considerations would be convincing to an impartial tribunal.[151] Thus, for activities in outer space and on the celestial bodies, where the territorial basis for jurisdiction is absent,[152] even without specific international arrangements, it appears that the lawful application of some nation's law is possible in almost all likely cases, based on one or another of the traditional principles of international law.[153]

The Legal Regime: In "Analogous" Areas

In seeking rules to apply to activities in outer space, it is inevitable that states and lawyers will borrow directly and by way of analogy from developments in other areas which appear to the decision-maker to be relevant. The dangers of the improper use of reasoning from inappropriate analogy have frequently been noted and are as real here as elsewhere.[154] The temptation is nevertheless great and not entirely unwholesome.

As was stated in *The Law of Outer Space:*

The futility of mechanical adoption [of rules developed for other areas] does not mean that experience of decades or centuries in these other fields is irrelevant to the control of space. On the contrary, reflection on that experience *mutatis mutandis* will help to anticipate problems of space and suggest ways of dealing with them. Particular solutions or devices may commend themselves for adaptation; historic

---

[147] See, e.g., Art. 6 of the Turkish Penal Code involved in the *Case of the SS "Lotus", P.C.I.J.* Ser. A, No. 10 (1927).

[148] See *P.C.I.J.*, Series A, No. 10 (1927).

[149] The *Restatement* sec. 30 categorically rejects the passive personality principle. In the Cutting case, the U.S. strongly objected to an attempt by Mexico to assert jurisdiction over an American citizen for a libel published in the U.S. injuring a Mexican national in Mexico. See 2 Moore, *International Law* 231–40 (1906); Moore's "Report on Extraterritorial Crime and the Cutting Case," 1877 *U.S. For. Rel.* 761 and 1887 *U.S. For. Rel.* 757. See also Harvard Research in International Law, "Jurisdiction . . . ," *supra* note 139.

[150] The S. S. "Lotus" (France and Turkey), P.C.I.J., 1927. P.C.I.J., ser. A, no. 10, 2 *Hudson World Court Repts.* 20 (1935).

[151] For use of such considerations in cases involving jurisdictional questions, see, e.g., Lauritzen v. Larsen, 345 U.S. 571, 582 (1953); Romero v. Int. Terminal Operating Co., 358 U.S. 354 (1959); McCullock v. Sociedad Nacional, 372 U.S. 10 (1963). For the views of commentators, see, e.g., Falk, *The Role of Domestic Courts in the International Legal Order*, chaps. 3, 4 (Syracuse U., 1964); Jessup, *Transnational Law* 35–71 (1956); McDougal & Burke, "Crisis in the Law of the Sea; Community Perspectives versus National Egoism," 67 *Yale L. J.* 539, 570–73 (1958). See also, ALI *Restatement* (Second), *Conflict of Laws*, sec. 42 (1).

[152] Except for vehicles and bases which, for some purposes at least, can lawfully be assimilated to the home territory.

[153] Of course, some states are presumably barred from making claims based on some particular principle. Thus, the United States, having consistently rejected the "passive personality" principle, might now be loath to advance a claim based on that approach.

For a review of the jurisdictional problem, see Saint-Hilaire, "Reflections on the Penal Law of Air and Space," 28 *Revue Général l'Air et de l'Espace* 84–91 (1965).

[154] In Justice Frankfurter's words: "One of the most treacherous tendencies in legal reasoning is the transfer of generalizations developed for one set of situations to seemingly analogous yet essentially very different situations." Frankfurter, J., dissenting, in Braniff Airways v. Nebraska Board, 347 U.S. 590, 603, 74 S. Ct. 765 (1954).

failures may enable us to guard against repetition. The law of the sea may afford some hints for the accommodation of inclusive uses like navigation (space flight), fishing (exploration of mineral or energy resources), and cable-laying (communications) to defensive or exclusive uses like naval manoeuvres, protection of customs, and protection of neutrality, and vice versa. Rules of space navigation may draw upon the experience of the law of the sea and of the law of air space. Decisions on the registration of space vehicles, and on the consequences of registration, may be facilitated by a look at the successes and failures of similar efforts in air law and maritime law. Recent experiences in Antarctica may tend to show that in certain circumstances international cooperation and national enterprise are furthered by the conscious and agreed abstention from pressing claims to sovereignty.[155]

In general, then, the analytical rather than a direct "legal precedent" use of historical analogies is called for. It can well contribute to a predictive theory (or analysis) of what will be. It will also indicate what could be; that is, it can instruct rational choice by displaying the likely significant relationships which, insofar as the situations are in fact analogous and the relationships can be viewed as systemic, will tend to be repeated and can and should be analyzed for the implications for the future before irreversible commitments are made.

It is interesting therefore to consider briefly the law as it has developed for certain areas—the high seas, airspace, and Antarctica—which are frequently cited as appropriately analogous to outer space.[156] Others which might be mentioned, the Mandates and the Trust Territories, for example, are noted at most in passing.[157]

The Legal Regime: The High Seas

To say that outer space is to be considered as *res communis* or *res extra commercium*, "like the high seas," is to echo the words of many statesmen and commentators.[158] It is to be hoped that this amounts to an affirmation of a policy of encouraging all nonexclusive or shareable uses of space on a basis of equality of access for all nations. Even landlocked nations by now appear to have won universal recognition of their right to use the seas, to have ships under their flag, and to have access across neighbors to the seas, although naturally there is still a dispute about the relative merits of the right of access and transit contrasted with the rights of the neighboring states to be crossed.[159]

It is also true that present uses of the high seas and of outer space are substantially different. Both are of great military importance, but in ordinary times the commercial uses of the seas far outweigh their military significance, although missile-firing submarines on station perhaps make this balance less one-sided than it formerly was. Indeed, objection to the use of the seas as an analogy has centered on the nature of the military risks from outer space.[160] Both areas are of great scientific interest, but space is receiving the overwhelming bulk of national scientific investment, a point linked, it would appear, to the military prestige factor just noted. The oceans are a great medium for transportation and communication; space is just beginning to serve as a communications medium. Only a few states are presently

---

155 Lipson & Katzenbach, *supra* note 1, at 23.

156 Naturally, there are few suggestions that "the law" applicable to one or another of these areas be *directly* applied to outer space. On the areas generally, see Lipson & Katzenbach, *supra* note 1, Abstracts 313–64, and sources cited.

157 See, generally, on "areas" under joint, multiple, or international control, and on the analogies, Jessup & Taubenfeld, *supra* note 2, chaps. 1, 2, 4 and, on the "Antarctic Analogy," chaps. 5, 6.

158 On this analogy, see, in particular, McDougal *et al.,* *supra* note 51, *passim,* esp. 294–306; Jessup & Taubenfeld, *supra* note 2, 210 ff.; Lipson & Katzenbach, *supra* note 1, at 22 and Abstracts 339–44, 360.

In the words of Zadorozhnyi *supra* note 39, at 1049: "By analogy to the principle of freedom of the open seas, which beyond the limits of territorial waters and special maritime zones do not belong to anyone and are in general use by all nations, the upper atmosphere . . . can likewise be considered a zone of open air, in general use by all nations."

The analogy of the high seas was particularly emphasized in many of the earlier articles on the legal status of outer space. See also on the utility of the sea law analogy: Cooper, "Letter to the Editor," 3 *Spaceflight,* 99 (1961) and "The MOL: A Major Legal and Political Decision," 51 *A.B.A. J.* 1137–40 (Dec. 1965); Ikeda, *supra* note 107; Poulantzas, "Imperium or Dominium within the Framework of Space Law," 15 *Revue Hellenique de Droit International* 95 (1962); Hartwig, *supra* note 109, at 1593; Markov, "Liberté de l'Espace et Stations Interplanétaires," 24 *Revue Générale de l'Air* 327 (1961).

On the seas, see also Marsh, *Developments in the Law of the Sea, 1958–64* (Brit. Inst. of Int'l and Comp. Law, Int'l Law Series No. 3, 1965).

159 See, e.g., U.N. Conf. on the Law of the Sea, 1958, Fifth Committee, "Questions of Free Access to the Sea of Landlocked Countries," 3 *Off. Rec., passim.*

160 Arguing that the sea law analogy is a poor one since the risks and dangers differ are: Bueckling, "The Legal Status of Artificial Satellites," 15 *Oesterreichische Juristenzeitung* 533 (1960); Homburg, *supra* note 109; Korovin, *Osnovnye Problemy Sovermennykh Mezdunarodnykh Otnosheniy* 219 (Publishing House of Social-Economic Literature, Moscow, 1959); Osnitskaya, *supra* note 41, at 65; Verplaetse, *supra* note 100.

directly concerned with the use of space; the great majority of nations express a national concern but are not as yet participants in space, as almost all are on the seas. Whether many others ever will be enticed into major space activities is at present unclear. It depends on the potential economic and political yields, and the regime that is established to partition these fruits.

It must also be remembered that the high seas have only in comparatively recent times been acknowledged as "free." Until the seventeenth century at least, national claims to sovereignty over vast areas of ocean were common. Even today, a few states assert claims to sovereignty over offshore seas almost as great as those controverted by Grotius.[161] Moreover, in a real sense there is no single "law" of the sea; it is, rather, a "checkerboard of variegated regions and legal rules."[162]

Thus, there is still no agreement on the width of the belt of the territorial sea. There is controversy over the legal right to make extensive, preemptive, even if temporary, use of the seas for missile ranges and nuclear tests. All major powers continue to close off large areas of the seas (as they did and do for fleet maneuvers) for missile tests.[163] There is little left of the concept of "freedom of the seas" for neutrals in time of war. And the history of warfare on the seas and for possession of islands is not at all reassuring. In short "the principle of the freedom of seas permits sovereignty over portions of adjacent waters and a variety of national uses of the still vast stretches which are truly *res communis.*"[164]

There are nevertheless broad areas of consensus which might serve usefully as background analogies, as they did for the use of airspace. The 1958 Geneva Conference on the Law of the Sea did achieve agreement on four freedoms—navigation, fishing, laying cables and pipelines, and overflight—and noted that there might be others recognized in international law.

> [Important areas of] international cooperation can be found in establishing rules of the road, rescue arrangements, provisions against piracy and slaving, navigational and meteorological aids, cable laying and maintenance, responsibility for collisions and other injuries, ownership of craft through registration, recognition of authority in each state to exercise jurisdiction in the high seas over its own nationals and vessels, and many other arrangements or agreed procedures indicative of a balancing of the concepts of *res communis* with the claims of states to protect their police, security, and other arrangements through reasonable exercises of authority in but not over the high seas.[165]

Again, as McDougal has put it:

> The principles of jurisdiction developed for the relatively unorganized arena of the oceans would appear, again, to afford an excellent model for a regime of unorganized, exclusive competence in space. One set of these provides . . . protection of freedom of access, that every state may decide for itself whether to send ships out upon the oceans and that no state may arbitrarily preclude access to another state. A second set of principles—designed to establish with certainty what ships belong to what states, and, hence, to identify both who is responsible for the activities of a ship and who may protect it against unauthorized assertions by others—provides that no state may unilaterally question the competence of another state to confer its nationality upon a ship and that, in cases of conflicting claim, simple priority in time in conferment of nationality is to prevail.[166]

Thus, while a mechanical extension of the law of the sea to outer space, even if "the law of the sea" were itself

---

[161] See, e.g., U.N. Conference on the Law of the Sea, *Off. Rec.* Doc. No. A/Conf.13/37–43. Some years ago, at least, a Soviet lawyer, N. Vishnepolski, apparently stated (41 *Trans. Grot. Soc'y* 149 [1955]): "Historical, political, and legal facts give us a claim to full sovereignty over the Arctic seas. The international rules governing the open seas cannot be applied to the Arctic. The Arctic seas are our national waters whose legal status must rest on unconditional recognition of the USSR's sovereignty."

[162] *Survey of Space Law* 15. See also Ward, *supra* note 96.

On the law of the seas, generally, see Reiff, *supra* note 18; McDougal & Burke, *The Public Order of the Oceans* (1962).

[163] The areas have been quite large, hundreds of thousands of square miles for nuclear tests. Tests by parties to the 1963 Nuclear Test Ban Treaty are barred, but France conducted nuclear tests in the Tahiti area in 1966. On French plans and on protests by other nations, see, e.g., *New York Times,* May 23, 1966, at 32. On the use of the seas in general, see McDougal *et al., supra* note 51, at 297–99. On Soviet rocket tests in the Pacific from Aug. through Dec. 1964 and Soviet warnings to ships and aircraft to stay clear, see *Astronautics and Aeronautics,* 1964, at 268 (NASA, 1965). On Soviet Pacific firings from Apr. to July 1966 see *Tass,* Apr. 25, 1966; from April-July 1966, see *New York Times,* July 5, 1966 at 28.

On the legal controversy over earlier nuclear testing see Taubenfeld, "Nuclear Testing in International Law," 16 *Sw.L. J.* 365 (1962); McDougal & Schlei, "The Hydrogen Bomb Tests in Perspective," 64 *Yale L. Rev.* 648 (1955); McDougal, "The Hydrogen Bomb Tests and the International Law of the Sea," 49 *Am. J. Int'l L.* 356 (1955); Reiff, *supra* note 18, at 363 ff.

[164] Jessup & Taubenfeld, *supra* note 2, at 212.

[165] *Ibid.* See generally Schachter, "Who Owns the Universe," *Across the Space Frontier* (Ryan ed. 1952), reprinted in *Space Law: A Symposium* 8 ff. (1958) and "Decatur's Doctrine—A Code for Outer Space," *U.S. Naval Inst. Proc.* 931–37 (Sept. 1957).

[166] Schwartz, *supra* note 24, 160.

a tidier package, would appear to be undesirable, these rules are an interesting example of patterns of national control and protection in areas outside national boundaries without the complications inherent in "sovereignty."[167] Many of the sea law concepts (freedom of use, access, registration, etc.) have already found their way into the emerging law of outer space activities.

The Legal Regime: Airspace

Another area often referred to as analogous to outer space is airspace. The general regime for airspace is, as we have noted, tied to the sovereignty of subjacent states.[168] Between airspace and outer space, the distance, speeds, times, methods of launching, methods of landing, effects of gravity and radiation, the nature of the military threat, and the commercial and economic possibilities for transportation are all greatly different.[169]

To a certain extent, the regime for airspace over the high seas is a closer analogy to outer space.[170] There, too, no states claim to regulate activities on the basis of territorial sovereignty. The status of acts on board aircraft, the creation of rules of the road, the provision of navigation and rescue facilities—these and other similar problems are detached, in airspace over the high seas and in outer space, from solution on the basis of territorial location alone.

As with the high seas, the current practice of states with respect to airspace reveals many areas of close cooperation in apolitical, functional activities which might be adapted to a regime in outer space. These have been described as including

. . . airworthiness, registration and identification, competence of personnel, proficiency of operations, rules of the air, navigational aids, safety of life and property, rescue at sea, access to airports, routes, transit over national territory, customs, spread of disease, civil liability for damage, competition, discrimination, communications and meteorological information.[171]

One special point can be noted. With respect to airspace over the seas as with the seas themselves, the nations assert the right of protection and self-defense at whatever distance or height technology seems to make essential in their view. We have noted the air defense zones (ADIZ and CADIZ) off American coasts. No formal protests concerning this assertion of right appear to be of record.[172] In the course of the French-Algerian conflict of the early 1960s, France also established a "zone of special responsibility" extending some 80 miles seaward from the Algerian coast, although, perhaps because of the French technique of operation, several states protested this alleged harassment.[173] Whatever the merits of the rather special Algerian case, the claimed right of states to protection at even great distances from their shores appears to be generally accepted, especially as no claims to "sovereignty" are involved. We have already noted the existence of similar claims with respect to outer space activities.

The Legal Regime: Antarctica

A third area often treated by nations and writers as an interesting analogy for the development of legal patterns for outer space activities is Antarctica.[174] Indeed, this point was given special emphasis in 1965–66 as United States spokesmen, in calling for a treaty regime to govern the exploration of the celestial bodies, pointed with

---

[167] For suggestions that the seas be made a "U.N. area" (as has also been suggested for outer space), see, e.g., Eichelberger, "The Promise of the Seas' Bounty," *Saturday Review,* June 18, 1966, at 21–23. Comm. to Study the Organization of Peace, "New Dimensions for the United Nations," *Seventeenth Report* 41–46 (May 1966).

[168] On the general regime for airspace, see Billyou, *Air Law, passim* (1965).

[169] See Lipson & Katzenbach, *supra* note 1, at 23, Abstracts 313–30 and sources cited; see also McDougal *et al., supra* note 51, *passim,* esp. 306–11, 583–87, 725–27; Cheng, *supra* note 67, 228–54; Smiroff, "The Analogy of Space Law with Air Law: A Latent Danger," *Proceedings, 5th Colloquium on the Law of Outer Space* 348 (Varna, 1962).

[170] On the regime of the airspace above the seas, see report by G. Pepin, U.N. Conf. on the Law of the Seas, "The Law of the Air and the Draft Articles Concerning the Law of the Sea Adopted by the International Law Commission at its Eighth Session," Doc. A/Conf.13/4 (original text, Oct. 4, 1957).

[171] See Reiff, *supra* note 18, at 34–35. On sea law analogies in air law, see McNair, *The Law of the Air* 233–62 (Kerr & MacCrindle eds., 2d ed., 1953).

[172] See McDougal *et al., supra* note 51, 306–11, esp. note 356 at 310.
This is not meant to imply that nations do not have the right to protect themselves from incipient attack across land frontiers as well.

[173] See McDougal *et al., supra* note 51, at 311. Protesting states included the USSR, Yugoslavia, Bulgaria, and West Germany.

[174] See, e.g., Jessup & Taubenfeld, *supra* note 2, chaps. 5, 6 (on Antarctica); Lissitzyn, *supra* note 27; Jenks, "The International Control of Outer Space," reprinted in *1961 Symposium, supra* note 4, at 734, 745–48; McDougal *et al., supra* note 51, *passim,* esp. 798–803.

pride to the 1959 treaty for Antarctica as a possible model.[175]

Outer space and Antarctica are alike in that both are, for man, desolate, difficult to reach, difficult to survive in, free of permanent population, at least thus far, and only recently accessible in any significant way.[176] The differences are in practice of potentially far greater importance than any apparent similarities, however. Almost every activity in outer space has potentially a military prestige importance; the Antarctic is considered today militarily unimportant.[177] Space is vast, and its potentials for human activity may be great and may some day tempt extensive development programs; the Antarctic, when examined carefully, at best offers little present temptation for costly inputs for the purpose of development.[178] Given foreseeable techniques, the *limits* of Antarctica's potentials and resources are better known. It has been widely examined and explored, and there is therefore less need for international competition to be there first, or soon thereafter, in case something important strategically, politically, or economically turns up. Antarctica is already a more delimited, finite, international issue and is obviously, to the major powers, not very important.

In another way, the Antarctic also differs in that seven nations are now on record as having formal claims to territory in the Antarctic, although the Soviet Union and the United States characterize these claims as inadequate in law. Both Russia and the United States have reserved the right to make claims of their own, based on prior activities, but neither has thus far made any.[179] No claims have as yet been made in outer space by any nation. In this sense, Antarctica is also a worthy case study since, as the Australian representative said in the United Nations First Committee in November 1958: "Experience in Antarctica may suggest how difficult it may become to consider the problems of outer space impartially and on a universal plane if decision is left until states have established themselves permanently in the field."

In 1959, following a very successful period of cooperation by twelve countries, including the United States and the USSR in the IGY-coordinated program for Antarctica, a treaty was entered into to assure the pro-

---

[175] For the initial U.S. draft treaty of June 16, 1966, see A/C.105/32 (June 17, 1966).

[176] Compare McDougal, Lasswell, Vlasic, & Smith, "The Enjoyment and Acquisition of Resources in Outer Space," 111 *U. Pa. L.Rev.* 521, 589 (1963), who note:

"There would appear, on the other hand, striking similarities in relevant features with Antarctica. Neither Antarctica, nor the more immediately accessible celestial bodies have, as far as we know, a permanent population. Both areas are unsuitable for the type of habitation established in the temperate regions of the Earth. From neither area is man likely for some time to be able to extract the basic necessities of life in sufficient quantities; such necessities must be transported great distances at extremely high costs. In both areas, it is probably necessary for man to live within special shelters. . . . Research stations and settlements both in Antarctica and on the celestial bodies will therefore likely be few and dispersed through vast expanses for many years to come. In both areas the extraction of minerals and other riches will probably continue to be technologically difficult."

[177] See Jessup & Taubenfeld, *supra* note 2, 162–63; McMahon, *supra* note 21, at 396, esp. note 2.

[178] See e.g., Taubenfeld & Taubenfeld, "Independent Revenue for the United Nations," 18 *Int'l Org.* 241, 242–46 (1964); Taubenfeld, "A Treaty for Antarctica," *Int'l Council* 262–65 (Jan. 1961).

[179] States making claims include France, the U.K., Australia, New Zealand, Argentina, Chile, and Norway. In addition to the U.S. and the Soviet Union, Belgium, Japan, Sweden, Germany, Czechoslovakia, and Poland are interested in Antarctica or in arctic research but have made no territorial claims or given up any potential claims.

For the Soviet position, see the Soviet delegate's opening statement at the Antarctic Conference, and Toma, "Soviet Attitude toward the Acquisition of Territorial Sovereignty in the Antarctic," 50 *Am. J. Int'l L.* 611 (July 1956). For the evolution of the U.S. position, see 1 Hackworth, *supra* note 123, 449–76 (1940); 2 Whiteman, *supra* note 16, at 1232–70 (1963); Becker, "Major Aspects . . . ," *supra* note 27.

The traditional U.S. position has been that claims could not be validly asserted in polar areas where settlement is impossible. A recent U.S. position was set forth in the "U.S. Invitation to the Twelve-Nation Antarctic Conference," May 2, 1958, which, after citing the record of U.S. activities in Antarctica, stated: "In view of the activities of the United States and its nationals referred to above, my Government reserves all of the rights of the United States with respect to the Antarctic region, including the right to assert a territorial claim or claims." See *President's Special Report,* Annex III, Doc. 1, p. 23. However, the U.S. has never made a formal territorial claim or recognized such a claim by any other country in Antarctica.

For background on the claims problems in the Antarctic, see, e.g., Christie, *The Antarctic Problem* (London, 1951); Jessup & Taubenfeld, *supra* note 2, chaps. 5, 6; Daniel, "Conflict of Sovereignties in the Antarctic," *Yearbook of World Affairs* 241–72 (London, 1949); Carl, "Claims to Sovereignty in Antarctica," 28 *So. Cal. L. Rev.* 386 (1955); Hannesian, "Antarctica: Anent National Interests and Legal Realities," 1958 *Proceedings, Am. Soc'y Int'l L.* 145; Waldock, "Disputed Sovereignty in the Falkland Islands Dependencies," 25 *Brit. Yrbk. Int'l L.* 311 (1948); Hayton, "The American Antarctic," 50 *Am. J. Int'l L.* 583 (July 1956).

gress of peaceful scientific exploration in the Antarctic. The United States was the moving power behind the treaty, which is now in force for all of the IGY participants in Antarctica and a few other states as well.[180]

Although the analogy is inexact, or even largely inappropriate, until the nations come to believe that space and the celestial bodies are as strategically unimportant as the Antarctic continent,[181] the treaty regime needs some mention, in part because of the frequent use of its terms as a model for outer space.[182] The treaty was important because of its position as a first agreement, including an arms control arrangement, involving both the Soviet Union and the United States. It remains of "local" importance in that it helps to assure the highest possible present use of Antarctica—i.e., scientific exploration—by states which can afford to use it best, the two great powers.

In brief, then, the treaty provides for demilitarization of the Antarctic (Article 1) with full unilateral rights of inspection (Article 7),[183] the promotion of scientific investigation and cooperation (Article 3), a "freezing" of the status of territorial claims (Article 4), a ban on nuclear explosions and the dumping of radioactive wastes (Article 5), peaceful settlement of disputes concerning the treaty (Article 11), and the accession by other states (Article 13). To facilitate the accomplishment of these aims, it provides a conference mechanism for consultations between the parties (Article 9). It does not make any arrangements for joint operations in scientific, exploitative, and developmental ventures at all, nor does it provide any elements of "government" for the area, which remains substantially an international administrative vacuum.[184] As the treaty is written, scientists are left relatively unhindered; provisions to maintain the peace are included; the Southern Hemisphere nations are reassured on missile bases and nuclear testing; and it is intended that the status quo for territorial claims, although not eliminated, be maintained for at least three decades.[185]

The treaty thus provides for free, peaceful, unhindered scientific exploration in an unarmed, difficult environment. It has great appeal as a model of a limited, noncomprehensive, noninternationalized regime which might be applied at least to the celestial bodies. The Report of the National Citizens' Commission on Space, presented to the White House Conference on International Cooperation in November 1965, for example, suggested:

---

[180] There is already a substantial literature concerning the treaty, the treaty regime, and Antarctica. We do not here propose to repeat its contents. See, e.g., McDougal *et al., supra* note 51, *passim,* esp. 799–801 and sources cited therein; Taubenfeld, "A Treaty for Antarctica," *Int'l Concil.* No. 531 (Jan. 1961) and sources cited therein. In addition to the IGY participants, the treaty has been acceded to by Poland (June 1961) Czechoslovakia (June 1962) and Denmark (May 1965).

[181] Soviet authors have not in the past been especially happy with the Antarctic analogy. See, e.g., Korovin, *supra* note 160, esp. chap. 7. Compare, however, Zhukov, "The Moon, Politics and Law," 12 *Int'l Aff.* 32, esp. 36–39 (Moscow, Sept. 1966).

The Soviet writer Zadorozhnyi has stated in "Basic Questions of Space Law" (mimeo., Nov. 9, 1960), that "the neutralization of Antarctica can not serve as an exact analogy for outer space." Referring to this opinion, Crane comments in "Soviet Attitude toward International Space Law," 56 *Am. J. Int'l L.* 685, 697 (1962), that Zadorozhnyi adopts this point of view "probably because Article VII of the Antarctic Treaty provides that any state with participating rights in the Consultative Conference may nominate a representative who has full freedom to anywhere in Antarctica, and that all parts of the Antarctic and stations and equipment and all ships and planes at points of loading and unloading are subject to inspection. An analogy to outer space, of course, would give complete freedom to inspect all rocket launching facilities and equipment in the Soviet Union and possibly industrial points of loading as well."

[182] See, e.g., David Davies Memorial Institute, *supra* note 54, which specifically uses in whole or in part Arts. 1, 2, 3, and 5 of the Antarctic Treaty as models; McMahon, *supra* note 21, at 359, note 2, who suggests the applicability of Art. 4 (2) with respect to claims.

Schuster, "Can the Antarctic Treaty Point to a Treaty in Outer Space," paper prepared for the Summer Meeting, AIAA, 285 (June 17–20, 1963).

[183] See Simsarian, "Inspection Experience under the Antarctic Treaty and the International Atomic Energy Agency," 60 *Am.J. Int'l L.* 502–10 (1966).

[184] We do not imply here that more is necessarily presently essential. Most operations are conducted subject to the long arm of *national* control over citizens. Compare Bilder, "Control of Criminal Conduct in Antarctica," 52 *Va. L. Rev.* 231 (1966). Despite the problems, there may be as much administrative arrangement as can presently be utilized in an immense area where there are only a limited number of very widely separated and very small scientific stations, where the contacts are normally not between stations and their personnel but primarily between the stations and the home countries, and where the inspections of each other's stations have been conducted by personnel from the home countries rather than from the neighboring bases. There are of course occasional visits; a limited number of scientists have operated at stations of other countries; and a few stations have been manned by nationals of two countries.

[185] For problems with regulation of activities under the treaty in 1966, see articles reprinted in *Polar Times* 13 (June 1966).

With multiple manned landings on the moon in prospect within the next several years, the United Nations Committee on the Peaceful Uses of Outer Space could direct its Legal Subcommittee to draft a convention to serve as a guide for nationally sponsored exploratory expeditions there. The Antarctica Treaty stands as a model providing the essential elements of such a convention: suspension of sovereign claims, free access by all for scientific purposes, exclusion of military maneuvers and weaponry, and a verification procedure. Such a convention would give substance to the principle, already adopted by the UN General Assembly, that celestial bodies are not subject to national appropriation. It would become in effect, a code for human activity on the moon.[186]

And indeed it served·in part as a direct model for some of the provisions of the 1967 Space Treaty.[187]

The analogy holds up, as noted earlier, only if the major powers become convinced that the moon and the attainable celestial bodies are not of sufficiently great value for military-political prestige, or other factors, to warrant the forceful presentation of claims or the development of other exclusionary devices for national control. Ultimately, this probably requires that exclusive entry will not be worth the costs of maintaining it. Apparently this will be true even if space activities prove very valuable, if they also prove readily sharable or available for equally good parallel developments (i.e., if entry would not be a scarce right), or if successful development proves so difficult that it requires cooperation of all participants and the parties, at least, become convinced, as in Antarctica, that denying the military use of the area,

if any, to all is sufficient protection to each, because such denial can be policed effectively, preferably unilaterally, and breaches can be expected to involve little danger to major powers. Given the present and foreseeable disposition of all states to avoid a comprehensive internationalized regime and the memory of past scrambles for valuable new areas, perhaps we are "to be left to hope for great waste so that the gains from space will prove small and not destabilizing."[188]

---

[188] Taubenfeld & Taubenfeld, *supra* note 125.

---

[186] Report of the Commission, 31 (mimeo.). *New York Times,* (Nov. 30, 1964) at 4, commenting favorably, stated:

"An important precedent for a code of lunar law exists in the Antarctic Treaty of Dec. 1, 1959. That pact, to which both the United States and the Soviet Union adhere, provides that Antarctica shall be used only for peaceful purposes and shall contain no military bases. It suspends all territorial claims to the Antarctic and establishes the principle that all settlements and activities in the area are open to inspection by observers designated by the nations ratifying the treaty.

"The contracting nations agree to make available to each other all scientific information gathered there, and to exchange personnel among their expeditions and stations.

"Adoption of an analogous code for the moon would be a major triumph of international cooperation."

[187] See Meeker, *supra* note 35, at 5. For earlier suggestions of the Antarctic analogy by a former legal advisor, see Becker, "United States Foreign Policy . . . ," *supra* note 27, at 4, 7, 29, 30; and testimony on May 14, 1958, *Hearings on S. 3609 before the Senate Special Committee on Space and Astronautics,* 85th Cong., 2d Sess., at 315, 320–22 (1958), and on Mar. 6, 1959, *Hearings before the House Committee on Science and Astronautics,* 86th Cong., 1st Sess., at 73, 76–78, 92 (1959).

4

The Legal Regime, The Present Legal Order

The Content of the Present Legal Order

Two comments can be made at the outset about the existing legal order for activities in outer space. First, the nations have thus far been reluctant to attempt to develop any comprehensive, overall treaty regime that would include the allocation of authority and control for outer space activities to any entity other than the states themselves. The treaty proposed by the General Assembly in December 1966, after initiatives by the United States and the USSR, signed by over sixty nations in January 1967, and ratified by mid-1967 by the United States, the Soviet Union, and the United Kingdom, among others, is not, in our view, an exception to this statement, although, if widely adopted and accepted by states, it will clarify many of the issues now outstanding.[1] Second, even without the treaty,

---

[1] The Treaty on Principles Governing the Activities of States in the Exploration and Use of Outer Space Including the Moon and Other Celestial Bodies, signed Jan. 27, 1967, is included in Appendix E. The relevant portions are noted throughout these materials. The treaty, of course, forms an important part of the legal regime. On the background and drafting of the treaty, see Appendix D and "Space Treaty Proposals by the United States and USSR," *Staff Report Prepared for the Use of Senate Committee on Aeronautical and Space Sciences,* 89th Cong., 2d Sess (July 1966); R. G. Dembling & D. M. Arons, "The Evolution of the Outer Space Treaty," 33 *J. Air L. & Commerce* 419 (1967). For an interesting alternative suggestion, see David Davies Memorial Institute, *Draft Treaty on Outer Space, the Moon and Other Celestial Bodies* (Aug. 1966).

outer space activities are subject to a fairly broad legal regime in many respects. Although much of the law governing special problems arising from space activities remains to be made, there is certainly no "legal vacuum" in space despite the lack of a "sovereign" for the "area" of space and the celestial bodies.[2]

On the first point, representatives of the leading space powers and of most other nations, while rejecting national claims to outer space or the celestial bodies, have also rejected the present creation of an overall code of law governing space activities and have given little heed to calls for broadly based, internationalized operations or controls.[3] From the earliest days of international consideration of outer space activities, the United States has

[2] On the question of the "vacuum" and on existing rules governing outer space activities, see, e.g., Lipson & Katzenbach, *The Law of Outer Space* 21–27 and sources cited (1961); McDougal, Lasswell, & Vlasic, *Law and Public Order in Space, passim* (1963); McDougal, "Law and Public Order in Space," 1964 *Proceedings of the Conference on Space Sciences and Space Law* 151 ff. (Schwartz ed. 1964) [hereinafter cited as Schwartz]; McDougal, "The Emerging Customary Law of Space," 58 *Nw. U.L. Rev.* 618 ff. (Nov.–Dec. 1963).

On the general regime, see also, e.g., 2 Whiteman, *Digest of International Law* 1281–1321 (1963); Goldie, "Extraterrestrial Privileges, Immunities, and Exposures," 36 *So. Cal. L. Rev.* 396 (1963); Menter, "The Developing Aerospace Law," speech of Feb. 20, 1967 (mimeo.); Meeker, "Organizing for the Exploration of Space," speech of Aug. 17, 1967 (typescript); Fasan & Gross, "Sovereignty in Air Space and Outer Space," 17 *Oesterreichische Juristenzeitung* 1–7 (1962); Sorinj, "To Whom Belongs Outer Space?" *1962 Oesterreichische Zeitschrift fuer Aussenpolitik* (Austrian Journal for Foreign Policy) 131–41; Goedhuis, "Legal Regime of Space," Annex I to the *Report of the Space Law Committee of the International Law Ass'n* (Tokyo, 1964); Sontag, "Sovereignty in Outer Space," 12 *Jahrbuch fuer Interactionales Recht* 272–300 (1965); Menter, "The Developing Aerospace Law" (mimeo., Mar. 12, 1966).

For the older oft-repeated lay view that there is no law in space see, e.g., the editorial in the *New York Times,* July 12, 1962, at 28, which stated: "Yet the cosmos today is a lawless dimension and there is no universal agreement even on so elementary a question as where space begins—no boundary line between the region in which existing national and international law holds sway and the region in which it does not.

"But in the absence of space law, the cosmos bears some resemblance to a jungle. Each nation with space capabilities does as it pleases. Such license must surely become intolerable with the rapid expansion of man's capabilities in this new arena of human action and with the certain increase in the years ahead of the nations able to launch satellites, luniks, and the like."

See also Hyman, *The Magna Carta of Space* (1965), but cf. McDougal's view in Schwartz, *supra* note 2, at 151 ff., esp. text and notes 1 and 2.

For *earlier* views that space *was* a legal vacuum see, e.g., statements by the representatives of Austria, Chile, Italy, and Yugoslavia, U.N. Docs. A/C.1/SR.982 at 8–10, 10 ff., A/C.1/SR 990 at 5 (1958) and see Bueckling, "Space Law and International Jurisdiction," 18 *Juristenzeitung* 500 (1963). Contra, see Gal, "Space Law Science in Hungary," 7 *Acta Juristica* 177, 178 (1965). See also Simeone, "Space—a Legal Vacuum," 16 *Milw. L. Rev.* 43 (1962); Schrader, "National Sovereignty in Space," 17 *Milw. L. Rev.* 41 (1962).

[3] As we have noted, there are numerous bilateral arrangements and there are organs for European cooperative launchings and other ventures. What is meant here are operations or controls by or under the aegis of the U.N. or similar entity representing the world community. For proposals for a code of law or community operations, see sources cited in chap. 3, *supra,* and see Hyman, *supra* note 2, *passim* (1965).

For various suggestions about a space agency to control all or part of man's activities in outer space, under the U.N. or otherwise, or at least to resolve disputes between states over outer space activities, see also Clark & Sohn, *World Peace through World Law* (2d and 3d eds, 1960, 1966); Jessup & Taubenfeld, *Controls for Outer Space,* chap. 9 (1959); Shepherd, "Needed for the 1970s: International Space Control Agency," 4 *Astro. & Aero.* 56–59 (Nov. 1966); Bueckling, *supra* note 2, at 500; Ikeda, *Space Law* (1961); Madl, "The Conquest of Outer Space and Some Questions of Pecuniary Responsibility," 17 *Jogtudomaryi Kozlong* 200 (Apr. 1963); Pourcelet, "La Création de bases spatiales dans l'espace extra-atmosphérique," 12 *Themis* 33 (1962); Rivoire, "Ebauche d'un droit spatial," 14 *Revue Défense Nationale* 1559 (1958).

On record as opposing a supra-national organization are G. A. Osnitskaya, "International Law Problems of the Conquest of Space," 2 *Soviet Yrbk. Int'l L.* 65 (1959) (reprinted in *Legal Problems of Space Exploration: A Symposium* (1961) [hereinafter cited as *1961 Symposium*]); Zhukov, "The Moon, Politics and Law," 12 *Int'l Aff.* 32, 37 (Moscow, 1966).

Supporters, at least at an earlier time, of drafting a comprehensive code include: Ikeda, *supra;* Rivoire, *supra;* Reintanz, "The Legal Status of Air Space and Cosmic Space," 11 *Neue Justiz* 507 (1957); Smirnoff, "Astronautics," 22 *Revue Générale de l'Air* 31 (1960) (a report on the Second Colloquium on Astronautic Law held in London in September 1959 containing a draft for a convention on supra-atmospheric space law); Tempesta, "Juridical Problems of Navigation in Extra-atmospheric Space," *VII Congresso Internationale delle Communicazioni* (mimeo. Geneva, Oct. 1959).

Writers arguing against the drafting of a comprehensive code at an early date also include: Economides, "Quelques reflexions sur le régime juridique de l'espace extra-atmosphérique," 13 *Revue Hellenique de Droit International* 246 (1960); Korovin, "Outer Space Must Become a Zone of Real Peace" (Letter to the Editor) 9 *Int'l Aff.* 92 (Moscow, Sept. 1963); Kovalev & Cheprov, "On the Working-out of the Legal Problems of Cosmic Space," 30 *Soviet'skoe Gosudarstvo i Pravo* 130 (Nov. 7, 1960) [hereinafter cited as *SGP*]; Nikolayev, "International Cooperation for the Peaceful Uses of Outer Space," 6 *Int'l Aff.* 76 (Moscow, May 5, 1960).

rejected the need for a comprehensive code, calling it not only premature, but unwise.[4] It has also been pointed out repeatedly that "the rule of law is neither dependent upon, nor assured by, comprehensive codification."[5]

The American position was reflected in the Report of the U.N.'s Ad Hoc Committee of July 14, 1959.

The Committee considered that a comprehensive code was not practicable or desirable at the present stage of knowledge and development.

. . . It was pointed out that the rule of law is neither dependent upon, nor assured by, comprehensive codification and that premature codification might prejudice efforts to develop the law based on a more complete understanding of the practical problems involved . . . the Committee also recognized the need both to take timely, constructive action and to make the law of space responsive to the facts of space. . . .[6]

Similarly, the Soviet Union has rejected a broad code at present for the same reasons. In 1962, for example, it was said:

The Soviet delegation considered that the subcommittee should not draw up a comprehensive code of space law but should rather concentrate on stating general basic principles. Mankind's knowledge and experience of outer space were too limited for detailed regulation.[7]

Other nations have been equally opposed.[8]

The second set of problems, the existence of rules already applicable to space activities, has been subjected to substantial international analysis.[9] It seems obvious from the outset that, in searching for rules of international law applicable to human activities in outer space, existing international law, where appropriate, would be no less pertinent to outer space than to earth-bound activities of states, since it is essentially only the milieu which is novel.[10] As the Soviet expert, Korovin, wrote:

All universally accepted rules of international law (inadmissibility of the use of force in solving international disputes, non-injury of foreign citizens, and their property, governmental responsibility for the activities of their representatives, etc.) apply to the cosmos as well. The presence or absence of separate specialized legal systems corresponding, for example, to international maritime control, cannot abolish the generally recognized principles of law prevailing in our time wherever people are active on land, sea, air or space.[11]

Ambassador Stevenson put it in a similar if less formal

---

[4] In 1959, for example, the legal adviser told the U.N. Ad Hoc Committee: "We are not asked how to build substantive rules which, because of the limited content of our factual information about this widening world, might prove to be ill-adapted and unrealistic in its peaceful exploration. The Members of the United Nations well know what happens in a society in which the substantive content of the rule of law has no relationship to the facts of social life and to changing climates of social consciousness. . . .

"[T]he rule of law is neither dependent upon, nor assured by, comprehensive codification. At present we know very little about the actual and prospective uses of outer space in all their possible varieties of technical significance, political context, and economic utility. In this situation, an effort to agree upon any comprehensive code might either come to naught, or yield a small set of maxims of extreme generality, or produce an unworkable regime which would be dangerous in its giving a temporary illusion of certainty" (statement of May 7, 1959, before the Ad Hoc Committee, U.S.-UN Press Release No. 3179 at 2 (May 7, 1959). See also 40 *Dept. State Bull.* 885, 886 (No. 1042, June 15, 1959) and see Lipson & Katzenbach, *supra* note 2, at 28.

[5] Statement of Becker, May 7, 1959, *supra* note 4.

[6] A/4141.

[7] See A/AC.105/C. 2/SR. 7 at 4 (Aug. 21, 1962).

[8] See, e.g., Summary Records, Legal Subcommittee on Outer Space, Aug. 1962 (A/AC. 105/C. 2/SR's *passim*).

[9] In a sense, such massive works as that by McDougal *et al.*, *supra* note 2, are devoted to investigating what parts of existing rules and techniques of decision-making are now or are likely to be relevant to space activities.

[10] See Jenks, *Space Law,* chap. 25 (1965). Among other writers who have argued that the principles of international law apply to outer space activities are Katzenbach, "The Law in Outer Space," in *Space: Its Impact on Man and Society* 69 (Levy ed. 1965); Hartwig, "The Present Situation in Space Law," 15 *Neue Juristisch Wochenschrift* 1593 (1962) [hereinafter cited as *NJW*]; Karth, "Some Legal Problems Concerning Outer Space," 3 *Indian L.J. Int'l L.* (1963); Korovin, *Osnovnye Problemy Sovermennykh Mezdunarodnykh Otnospheniy* (Publishing House of Social-Economic Literature, Moscow, 1959); Korovin, "Aerial Espionage and International Law," 6 *Int'l Aff.* 49 (June, 1960); Kovalev & Cheprov, "Artificial Satellites and International Law." 1 *Soviet Yrbk. Int'l L.* 128–45 (1958); Lachs, "The Principles of Cosmic Law Are Studied," before the Legal Subcommittee of the United Nations, 9 *Monog. Dipl.* 13 (1962); Markov, "On the Question of the Limits of Air Space in International Law," 31 *SGP* 95 (1961); Poulantzas, "Imperium or Dominium Within the Framework of Space Law," 15 *Revue Hellenique de Droit International* 95 (1962); Rehm, "Acquisition of Territory in Outer Space," 9 *Zeitschrift fuer Luftrecht und Weltraumfragen* 1 (1960) [hereinafter cited as *ZLW*]; Smirnoff, "The Legal Status of Space (The Theories Compared)," 25 *Revue Générale de l'Air* 147 (1962); Suontausta, "Legal Problems of Rights to Outer Space" (reprint); Zhukov, "American Plans for the Use of Outer Space with Aggressive Purposes and the Security of States," *Soviet Yrbk. Int'l L.* 202 (1961).

[11] Korovin, "International Status of Cosmic Space," 5 *Int'l Aff.* 53 (Moscow, Jan. 1959) (reprinted in *1961 Symposium, supra* note 3, at 1070).

way when he said that we should "state explicitly that the rules of good international conduct" follow man "wherever he goes."[12] Of course, not all existing rules might be appropriate;[13] for example, appropriation by states of new territories will apparently be barred,[14] and some concepts of current legal practice might be too limited in scope.[15]

As indicated in the Statute of the International Court of Justice,[16] the core of rules would in any event be found in:

   a. international conventions, whether general or particular, establishing rules expressly recognized by the contesting states;
   b. international customs, as evidence of a general practice, accepted as law;
   c. the general principles of law recognized by civilized nations. . . .

For members at least, the United Nations Charter is perhaps the single most important overall treaty arrangement concerning their relations with other states, a point we return to shortly.

In general, it is argued that such admittedly vague concepts as equality of access, respect for the integrity of other sovereigns, and peaceful use free of restraint, except for the presumed obligation to avoid aggressive, harmful, and unnecessarily exclusive activities, which are generally accepted for non-national areas such as the seas, are appropriate for space uses.[17] This is also the approach accepted by the nations which approved the concept of an Outer Space Treaty at the United Nations in December 1966 and signed it in January 1967. That treaty provides, for example, in Article I, with respect to freedom of access and "equality":

> The exploration and use of outer space, including the moon and other celestial bodies, shall be carried out for the benefit and in the interest of all countries, irrespective of their degree of economic or scientific development, and shall be the province of all mankind.
>
> Outer space, including the moon and other celestial bodies, shall be free for exploration and use by all States without discrimination of any kind, on a basis of equality and in accordance with international law, and there shall be free access to all areas of celestial bodies.
>
> There shall be freedom of scientific investigation in outer space, including the moon and other celestial bodies, and States shall facilitate and encourage international cooperation in such investigation.

This implies an extension to space activities of the going international system on earth; the implications of such a "free competition" regime are discussed below.

---

[12] Address to the United Nations, Dec. 4, 1961, reprinted in 46 *Dept. State Bull.* 180–85 (1962).

[13] For a suggestion of the need to determine just which rules are applicable, see remarks of the U.A.R. delegate, A/AC.105/C.2/SR. 19, at 4 (Apr. 18, 1963), and of Brazil, A/C. 1/SR. 1346 at 101 (Dec. 5, 1963).

[14] This is true under the terms of the 1967 Outer Space Treaty. On Aug. 21, 1962, the French delegate at the Legal Subcommittee on the Peaceful Uses of Outer Space noted that "not all rules of international law could apply to outer space; for instance, its rules for the appropriation of unclaimed territories." A/AC.105/C.2/SR.3, at 5 (1962).

[15] Ambassador Jha of India stated, for example, before the UN General Assembly's First Committee, on Dec. 7, 1961 (A/AC.1/PV.1213, at 31, 38–40 [Dec. 7, 1961]): "But are we sure that extension of international law, as we know it on earth, to outer space has not a somewhat limitative connotation? International law is based on the concept of the sovereignty of States and concepts of nationality. . . . When the day comes that men of various nations, through international cooperative efforts, journey into outer space and to the planets, the concepts of nationality, territorial affiliations, etc., should perhaps be forgotten and will indeed be out of place in outer space. One might feel, therefore, that to transpose the whole of international law, as we know it here, and not merely certain principles, to celestial space might not be enough and not wholly suitable. International law may indeed need radical adaptation, conceptual or otherwise, for application to outer space."

[16] Statute, Art. 38. See generally Parry, *The Sources and Evidences of International Law* (1965).

[17] See, e.g., Richard Gardner, cited by Johnson, "Freedom and Control in Outer Space," in Schwartz, *supra* note 2, at 142–43.

Among other writers not elsewhere cited herein who have agreed over the years that space is free for the peaceful use of all nations are: Arpea, "Il Diritto Spaziale," 35 *Revista Aeronautica* 883 (1959); Bergern, "Some Legal Problems of Men and Vehicles in Space," *The Shingle* (Philadelphia Bar Ass'n, Mar. 1961); Bueckling, "The Legal Status of Artificial Satellites," 15 *Oesterreichische Juristenzeitung* 533 (1960); Castren, "The International Legal Status of Airspace and Outer Space," *Lakimies* 461 (1958); Hartwig, *supra* note 10, at 1593; Welf Heinrich, Prince of Hanover, "Souveraineté et espace," *Revue Internationale Française du Droit des Gens* (1960); Homburg, "Introduction to the Law of Space," *Revue Générale de l'Air* 187 (1960); Karth, *supra* note 10; Lachs, *supra* note 10; Markov, "Liberté de l'espace et stations interplanetaires," 24 *Revue Générale de l'Air* 327 (1961); Meyer, "La Réalité et la nécessité de la souveraineté aerienne et de la liberté de l'espace extra-atmospherique; Wirklichkeit und Notwendigkeit der Staatshoheit im Luftraum und Freikert des Weltraumgebietes," 12 *ZLW* 2 (1963); Poulantzes, *supra* note 10, at 95; Pourcelet, *supra* note 3, at 33; Rinc, "Recht im Weltraum" (lecture, 1960); Rivoire, *supra* note 3, at 1559; Smirnoff, *supra* note 10, at 147; Sountausta, "Legal Problems of Rights to Outer Space" (reprint); Vago, "On Behalf of a Space Law," 36 *Revista Aeronautica* 185 (1960).

Some similar general rules are already broadly accepted as "binding" on the basis of customary law. We know, for example, that an orbital space vehicle on a peaceful mission in outer space is free of the jurisdiction of the subjacent state and does not violate that state's sovereign territory while in outer space (although outer space remains undefined).[18] Thus, although the lack of national protest to the earliest flights of satellites was attributed by some scholars to a tacit or express consent to such flights under IGY arrangements,[19] it was argued almost from the outset that:

Up to the present, the community of states appears to have been following the principle that the transit over any state of orbiting space objects or vehicles of any nation, so long as they are not equipped to inflict injury or damages, does not infringe the rights of other states and is reasonable and in the common interest of mankind. It is perhaps not too bold to suggest that we are here viewing the initial stage of development of a principle of customary international law permitting the orbiting of satellites of this nature.[20]

Over the years, representatives of most of the world's nations have expressed similar sentiments. In addition, while only a few states have thus far placed satellites directly in orbit, a substantial number of other states have participated in the preparation of satellites and satellite experiments,[21] and there have been no prior requests for permission to overfly connected with any of the post-IGY satellites either. No protests about the "overflights" have been registered. Even the informal protests by the Soviet Union concerning U.S. observation satellites never questioned the general right of vehicles to orbit freely in outer space over the Soviet Union; the attacks were on the specific use, intelligence gathering, which was called illegal wherever it occurred.[22]

Soviet commentators have expressed agreement over the general approach described above with certain special additions. They have suggested these inclusions: recognized principles of peaceful coexistence, sovereignty, equality, and noninterference in domestic affairs.[23] The meaning of "peaceful coexistence" is uncertain to non-Soviet lawyers, at least, and of doubtful import as a "legal" concept.[24] It seems clearly to omit "wars of national liberation" from its ban.[25] Its particular purpose is perhaps obvious as used by Korovin:

It seems to me that the most valuable part of the resolution is the extension to outer space of the principles of peaceful co-existence between states. This means that no state should undertake such activities as the organization of temporary or permanent military bases (for example, American plans for developing bomber satellites, bomber orbital stations,

---

[18] It has, of course, been pointed out that "there may in some instances be a special and intimate relationship between a particular space activity and a particular subjacent state" which would require an exception to this rule. See Lipson & Katzenbach, *supra* note 2, at 21.

For other comprehensive overviews of the regime, see also Mankiewicz, "Some Thoughts on Law and Public Order in Space," 2 *Canadian Yrbk. Int'l L.* 259 ff. (1964); Babinski, "Quelques reflexions sur les rapports entre le droit des gens et le droit astronautique," 24 *Revue Générale de l'Air* 59 (1961).

[19] Thus, the Soviet writer Korovin stated: "Some experts . . . assume that since no country has protested, since the U.S.S.R., just as the U.S.A., launched its satellites this may be interpreted as 'freedom of outer space' established by universally recognized precedent. But this view may be contested, since the U.S.S.R., just as the U.S.A., launched its satellites under the previously agreed programme of the International Geophysical Year, or, in other words, with the preliminary consent of all the countries concerned." Korovin, "The International Status of Cosmic Space," 5 *Int'l Aff.* 53–55 (Moscow, Jan. 1959).

[20] Rear Admiral Clark, "Programming for Space Defense," *JAG J.* (Navy) 20, 20 (Feb. 1959). See also, testimony of Deputy Secretary of Defense Quarles, Apr. 30, 1958, before the House Select Committee on Astronautics and Space Exploration, *Hearings on H. R. 11881* at 1102, 1107. To similar effect, see Report of the Ad Hoc Committee, UN Doc. A/4141 at 63–64 (July 14, 1959).

[21] On joint and multilateral projects, see *infra* Appendix D.

[22] On surveillance and its problems, see chap. 2 and *infra* at 99 ff.

[23] See the statement by Morozov at the Committee on the Peaceful Uses of Outer Space, U.N. Doc. A/AC. 105/PV 3 (3d meeting, Mar. 20, 1962) at 23–25 (May 7, 1962). See also the citation by John Johnson, *supra* note 17.

[24] On "peaceful coexistence" in our context, see, among many, Lerner, "The Historical Origins of the Soviet Doctrine of Peaceful Coexistence," 29 *Law & Contemp. Probs.* 865 ff. (1964); "Juridical Aspects of Peaceful Coexistence," 1964 *Proceedings, Int'l L. Ass'n* 777–821; Crane, "Basic Principles in Soviet Space Law: Peaceful Coexistence, Peaceful Cooperation, and Disarmament," 29 *Law and Contemp. Probs.* 943 ff. (1964); C. Karpov, "The Soviet Concept of Peaceful Coexistence and Its Implications for International Law," *id.* at 858 ff. See also, e.g., McDougal *et al., supra* note 2, at 448–49; Crane, "Soviet Attitude toward International Space Law," 56 *Am. J. Int'l L.* 685, 710–23 (1962); Lachs, "Law Making for Outer Space and Its Peaceful Use," *Disarmament: An Information Bulletin* 1–4 (Paris, Dec. 1965).

[25] On the sanctity of "wars of liberation," see Khrushchev, "For New Victories of the World Communist Movement," *Kommunist*, Jan. 25, 1961, at 3–7, translated in 13 *The Current Digest of the Soviet Press* 8 (Feb. 22, 1961); and Ginsburgs, " 'Wars of National Liberation' and the Modern Law of Nations—the Soviet Thesis," 29 *Law and Contemp. Problems* 910 ff. (1964).

for setting up a military missile base on the moon, etc.), the launching into space of instruments designed to collect and transmit reconnaissance information about the territory of other states and the contamination of outer space with objects that might create impediments to scientific observations, free movement and radio communications. These and similar actions should be regarded as international delicts for which the respective states should bear responsibility in all the forms envisaged by contemporary international law.[26]

Thus, peaceful coexistence seems also to imply a type of regime to be adopted in space that would include free political, economic, and structural ideological competition between those·nations which have the power to compete. This is not necessarily desirable. Political competition between powerful sovereigns in the world community has not produced dependable peace in the past.[27]

At best, peaceful coexistence raises the hope of some mutual unilateral disarmament in the sense that direct aggression and direct military confrontation between the powers will be barred officially (and by the balance of terror) while the powers will remain free to pursue their goals by other means. These, unfortunately, may include subversion, indirect aggression, national civil wars of liberation, intervention, and the like, all for the same stakes but with "war" as such eliminated.

The problems of this "strategy" as a basis for a truly peaceful regime are evident once its potentials for conflict are subjected to analysis. Peaceful free competition, as applied to a political regime, can be a workable system of conflict resolution *within* a stable (static equilibrium) political structure and also when small, evolutionary changes in the power structure can and will be tolerated by all participants without international compensation for losses of power, without an armed fight in the form of direct confrontation, without indirect confrontation on the field chosen by the growing state or other aggressive "retaliation" (indirect or direct aggression), or without increasing pressure elsewhere to restore the intolerably threatened balance. This could be the case among friends, those states which do not fear each other because they are allied and in this sense share their power, particularly if the changes are small or otherwise nonthreatening.

---

[26] Korovin, "Peaceful Cooperation in Space," 8 *Int'l Aff.* 61, 63 (Moscow, 1962).

[27] On the possible value to both of scientific competition, however, see the statement of the Soviet physicist Peter Kapitsa, *Washington Post*, May 5, 1966, at 20.

In sum, such a regime probably cannot work on earth for any important *interbloc* competition because, assuming the West is willing, the Communists appear to be unready to accept stability and perhaps ideologically cannot even espouse stability or a stable division, or even an evolutionary process of growth of nationalist "socialism," unaided by them. At present, the Sino-Soviet struggle over leadership inhibits Soviet freedom to maintain an ideologically less aggressive pose, but even without China it seems likely that some other group of genuine "left deviationist" Marxist believers would be pushing Russia's hand, although perhaps less dramatically. This seems to be an endogenous phenomenon in the Marxist world. They have no strategy for dealing with their own success.

More relevant, in space the Soviet leaders can pursue stable free competition, as long as no potentially important stakes are involved. If any are discovered, the regime of free competition—meaning at present competitive, bilateral, monopoly exploration of a limitless resource—will end.

Self-policed demilitarization will be unilaterally honored, at best, only while some major convenience is found therein. The United States will respond both to direct threats *and* to legal subterfuges; for example, to forms of indirect aggression devised for space operations. It is therefore important that the rules of the game of peaceful cooperation in space be understood to be "guidelines" of *reciprocal* good conduct in normal times, as defined by the parties, and no more, and thus should not be viewed as inflexible legal rules. It should be made clear, by the United States in particular, that (1) it cannot tolerate binding obligations to disarm unilaterally in any milieu; (2) it is a peaceloving state in all arenas, but on a reciprocal basis only.

This regime may not be as good as a forceful, internationalized, multilaterally policed approach in a better world, but it avoids the risks of being duped, given the intentions of all the sovereigns not to create a more unified world at present. Reserving the unequivocal legal right to respond as the United States sees fit, at least against observed transgressions, is more sensible than having to denounce "unfair" legal encumbrances, which conflict with self-defense needs later. A self-defending, nonintegrated system cannot safely allow the development of more inflexible legal regulation than what we have described in potentially important conflict situations. In any event, the drive toward a formal "law of peaceful coexistence" appears to be receiving less attention now since more specific problems have occupied legal representatives.[28]

Returning to the more limited "special" law of outer space activities, we note that some, communications in particular, are already subject to legal regulation. There is, in addition, the Outer Space Treaty of 1967. It is worth noting here preliminarily the contents of that treaty.

The treaty, in seventeen articles, all of which are discussed hereafter where appropriate, lays down general principles covering much of present space activity.[29]

After Article I's declaration that space shall be free for exploration and use by all states and that states shall facilitate and encourage international cooperation in such investigations,[30] Article II expressly states that outer space, the moon, and other celestial bodies are "not subject to national appropriation by claim of sovereignty, by means of use or occupation, or by any other means." Article III provides that a nation's activities in exploration and use of outer space shall be in accordance with international law, in the interests of maintaining international peace and security and of promoting international cooperation and understanding. Article IV prohibits stationing in outer space any object carrying a nuclear weapon, or any other weapon of mass destruction and installing such weapons on celestial bodies, or in outer space in any other manner. It also prohibits establishing military bases and fortifications, testing weapons, or conducting military maneuvers on celestial bodies. Military personnel may be used for scientific research or for any other peaceful purposes. Article V expressly calls astronauts "envoys of mankind" and provides that

---

[28] On the application of the "law of peaceful co-existence" to outer space: see *Cosmos and International Law: Collection of Articles* (Korovin ed. 1962); Kovalev & Cheprov, *On the Road to Cosmic Legislation* (1962). "Peaceful co-existence," which was adopted as a policy by the 22d Party Congress in Oct. 1961, was interpreted by Inozemtev in "Peaceful Coexistence—the Most Important Present-day Problem," *Pravda,* Jan. 17, 1962, at 5, as "The most subtle and most effective expression of the party principle of proletarian internationalism. . . . Peaceful co-existence of states with different regimes is not the abandonment of the class struggle in the world arena, but the selection of such deployment areas for this struggle as are best suited for the interests of all mankind." With reference to the bipolar framework of "peaceful co-existence," Crane suggested, in "Law and Strategy in Space," 6 *Orbis* 281–300 (July 1962), that the free democratic countries pursue a policy of "peaceful cooperation under law."

[29] On the treaty, for an article-by-article analysis, see "Treaty on Outer Space," *Hearings before the Senate Committee on Foreign Relations,* 90th Cong., 1st Sess., on Exec. D (Mar. 7, 13, 1967, & Apr. 12, 1967). See also "Treaty on Principles . . . Analysis and Background Data," *Staff Report* prepared for the use of the Senate Committee on Aeronautical and Space Sciences, 90th Cong., 1st Sess. (Mar. 1967). For President Johnson's message urging prompt ratification to assure the peace essential for the longer journey to peace, see *Pres. Doc.* Feb. 13, 1967, No. 196–9. On the signing, see *New York Times,* Jan. 28, 1967, at 1. For the matter before the Senate, see *Hearings,* in this note. The Treaty was approved by the Senate on Apr. 25, 1967. See *T.I.A.S.* No. 6347 (1967).

For testimony by Gen. Wheeler, Chairman of the Joint Chiefs of Staff, that the treaty would enhance U.S. security and that the U.S. preferred to do its own observation and "inspection" of space vehicles and stations, see *Hearings,* in this note, *passim,* and *New York Times,* Apr. 13, 1967, at 52. On the treaty as an arms control measure, see also *New York Times,* May 10, 1966, at 18. See generally Eisendrath, "The Outer Space Treaty," 44 *For. Serv. J.* 27 (May 1967); Dembling & Arons, *supra* note 1, at 419; E. Galloway, "Interpreting the Treaty on Outer Space," paper prepared for the *10th Colloquium, IISL,* 1967 (mimeo); Wehringer, "The Treaty on Outer Space," 54 *A.B.A.J.* 586 (1968); Menter, "The Developing Law for Outer Space," 53 *A.B.A.J.* 703 (1967); Cooper, "Some Crucial

Questions About the Space Treaty," 48 *Air Force/Space Dig.* 104 (Mar. 1967); Finch, "Outer Space for 'Peaceful Purposes' ", 54 *A.B.A.J.* 365 (1968); Vlasic, "Space Treaty: A Preliminary Evaluation," 55 *Cal. L. Rev.* 507 (1967).

For a Soviet view, see A. Peradov & Y. Rybakov, "First Space Treaty," 13 *Int'l Aff.* 21–26 (Moscow, Mar. 1967), and remarks of the Soviet scientist G. Zhukov, *New York Times,* Mar. 2, 1967.

For a Chinese Communist assertion that, by signing the treaty with the U.S., the Soviet Union had betrayed the Vietnamese people, see *New York Times,* Jan. 29, 1967. On the Communist Chinese view of "space law" in general, see Chiu, "Communist China and the Law of Outer Space," 16 *Int'l Comp. L.Q.* (1967).

[30] At the insistence of Sen. Albert Gore (D-Tenn.), the Senate Foreign Relations Committee agreed to qualify in its report its interpretation of two clauses in the space law treaty. One clause questioned said benefits of space exploration "shall be the province of all mankind"; the other said that each nation would be liable for damages to another caused by its space vehicles. The Committee specified that (1) nothing would "diminish or alter the right of the United States to determine how it shares the benefits and results of its space activities"; and (2) damage "pertains only to physical, non-electronic damage." Gore suggested that if there were two competing U.S. and Soviet space communications networks, one nation might sue the other for damage from electronic interference of one system on the other. See *New York Times,* Mar. 14, 1967, at 20, and *Washington Post,* Mar. 14, 1967 at A7. The meaning of a senatorial "interpretation" has been unclear. It does not constitute a legal reservation in existing practice.

in event of accident, distress, or emergency landing on the territory of another state, or on the high seas, they shall be given all possible assistance, including safe return. On celestial bodies, astronauts of different states are to render all possible assistance to one another.

Article VI places international responsibility on a state for its activities in space, whether by governmental or nongovernmental entities. Nongovernmental entities must have authorization and "continuing supervision" by the state concerned.

Article VII provides that the launching state, and the state from whose territory or facility an object is launched, shall be internationally liable for any resulting damages to the persons of another state.

Article VIII provides that jurisdiction and control is retained by the state on whose registry an object launched is carried and over the personnel thereof in outer space or on a celestial body. Such objects or component parts are to be returned to the state of registry if found in another state.

Article IX also is concerned with the application of the principle of cooperation and mutual assistance among states in their exploration and use of outer space. States are to have due regard to the corresponding interests of other states parties to the treaty and are to avoid harmful contamination of celestial bodies and of the environment of the earth in the space activities. If potential harmful interference with activities of another treaty state is foreseen, appropriate international consultations are to be undertaken upon the request of any of the states concerned before proceeding with the activity planned.

Article X calls for opportunities for states to observe the flight activities of other states, as determined by agreements between them. Article XI provides for informing the Secretary General of the United Nations, as well as the public and the scientific community, to the greatest extent feasible and practicable, of the nature, conduct, locations, and results of a state's activities in outer space. Article XII advances this concept by providing that all space vehicles and installations on the moon or other celestial bodies will be open for inspection by other states parties to the treaty, who will be limited, however, by the need for advance consultation to assure that adequate safety precautions are taken and to avoid interference with normal operation of the space facility.

Article XIII deals with the role of international organizations. Articles XIV through XVII are concerned with ratification procedures, withdrawal, and the like.

Other treaties have already been under discussion for some time, and one on the rescue and return of space personnel and vehicles was signed in 1968 and is discussed as appropriate in this chapter and in Appendix D. Work is in progress also on a treaty concerning liability for outer space activities.

There is also a special treaty arrangement concerning a space use which requires note: In 1963, when most of the nations of the world agreed to end nuclear testing in the atmosphere, they concluded a Nuclear Test Ban Treaty which included a ban on tests "in the atmosphere; beyond its limits, including outer space. . . ." Since that treaty is biased in favor of those already possessing substantial nuclear capability, two of the major have-nots, France and the People's Republic of China, are not parties.[31] All other important states are parties, but several already seem anxious about being left out of nuclear weaponry. This list includes Germany, India, and even Japan. For parties to the treaty, the debate over the permissibility of high-altitude nuclear tests is now moot,[32] but the issue is not at all a dead one.[33] Neither the use of nuclear weapons in war anywhere, nor the use of atomic reactors which do not involve explosions for onboard power, for power for stations on the celestial bodies, or for propulsion systems, is affected by the treaty.[34]

In the area of "customary" law, there are the potential

---

[31] The Treaty is *T.I.A.S. 5433 (Treaty Banning Nuclear Weapon Tests in the Atmosphere in Outer Space and under Water)*. The literature concerning the treaty is voluminous but not especially in point for this study. On the treaty and outer space activities, see Taubenfeld & Taubenfeld, "Man and Space: Potentials, Politics, Legal Controls," *Space and Society* 1, 23 ff. (Taubenfeld ed. 1964).

[32] Barred also is the proposal to use outer space as a "safe" testing place for nuclear devices by the current nuclear "have-not" nations (and others), which has been proposed at times as being relatively safe by such eminent authorities as Edward Teller.

[33] *Aviation Week and Space Technology* reported, on Feb. 7, 1966 at 31, for example, that the AEC had developed standby capability to test nuclear-weapon research devices at high altitudes and in space if the 1963 International Test Ban Treaty were abrogated. The standby capability, based on large launch vehicles developed as nuclear device carriers and on small instrumentation rockets for diagnosis, would concentrate on the atmospheric testing of ICBM and anti-ICBM systems and on the effects of nuclear detonations on these systems. Testing experimental devices to explore new concepts of nuclear weapons could begin 3–9 months after the end of the U.S. commitments.

[34] All these uses are the subjects of present experimentation. Nuclear power is now in use in Antarctica, where a treaty also bars all nuclear testing.

legal effects of General Assembly resolutions dealing with broad principles of state conduct in outer space, which have been referred to in this section and which are analyzed further below.[35] In addition, Resolution 1884 (XVIII) of 1963 calls on all states:

    a) To refrain from placing in orbit around the Earth any objects carrying nuclear weapons or any other kinds of mass destruction, installing such weapons on celestial bodies, or stationing such weapons in outer space in any other manner;

    b) To refrain from causing, encouraging or in any way participating in the conduct of the foregoing activities.

The legal effect of this unanimously adopted resolution is also discussed below. On its face, it does not purport to state existing law or to create a new rule,[36] and it is also a self-policed, status-quo biased arrangement with all that that implies.[37] To the extent that it becomes accepted as placing on a noncomplying state "a responsibility equivalent to the violation of a legal obligation,"[38] it represents a departure for the nations of the world, a partial arms control arrangement limited, of course, to outer space.[39] Although the overall defects of this approach will remain, for parties at least the legal situation is largely clarified by the Outer Space Treaty of January 1967, which provides in Article IV:

States Parties to the Treaty undertake not to place in orbit around the earth any objects carrying nuclear weapons or any other kinds of weapons of mass destruction, install such weapons on celestial bodies, or station such weapons in outer space in any other manner.

The moon and other celestial bodies shall be used by all States Parties to the Treaty exclusively for peaceful purposes. The establishment of military bases, installations and fortifications, the testing of any type of weapons and the conduct of military maneuvers on celestial bodies shall be forbidden. The use of military personnel for scientific research or for any other peaceful purposes shall not be prohibited. The use of any equipment or facility necessary for peaceful exploration of the moon and other celestial bodies shall also not be prohibited.

The treaty is thus broader than the U.N. resolution and is more specific in its limitations and its exceptions. Like the resolution, it depends essentially on national good faith, plus unilateral inspection and detection, for compliance, but the legal obligations for parties are made clearer.[40] We have nevertheless already discussed, in chapter 2, an early question of interpretation caused by the apparent testing by the Soviet Union of vehicles designed to serve as a fractional orbital bombardment system.[41]

We need to say a few words about the applicability of the United Nations Charter as a whole to national acts in outer space. The applicability of the Charter was noted by the space powers from the beginning of public discussions of outer space activities. Legal Adviser Becker told the U.N.'s Ad Hoc Committee in 1959, for example, that:

[I]t is desirable to make explicit the essential understanding that the application of the Charter of the United Nations and the Statute of the International Court of Justice is not limited to the confines of the earth; these instruments are applicable to the relations of earthly states in outer space as well.

It is hardly necessary to remind oneself that Article I of the Charter succinctly sets forth the purposes of the United Nations. Yet it may be of value, in this context, to refer to paragraph 1 of that Article which reads as follows:

    1. To maintain international peace and security, and to that end: to take effective collective measures for the prevention and removal of threats to the peace, and for the suppression of aggression or other breaches of the peace, and to bring about by peaceful means, and in conformity with the principles of justice and international law, adjustments or settlement of international disputes or situations which might lead to a breach of the peace.

Can it be suggested that this complex goal has no relevance to an extraterrestrial situs?

That question is intentionally rhetorical. It seems undeniable that outer space questions do not affect only outer space, but are of primary interest to us, now and in the future, as they relate to Earth and to our universal interests

---

[35] See pp. 81–87.

[36] See generally, Jenks, *supra* note 10, chap. 60 (1965).

[37] See Taubenfeld & Taubenfeld, *supra* note 31, *passim,* for discussion of the likely effects of this form of arms ban.

[38] Jenks, *supra* note 10, at 303.

[39] The Antarctic Treaty of 1959 has for its parties "demilitarized" that continent. See *supra,* chap. 3. On weapons in outer space and on the effects of this resolution, see Gotlieb, "Nuclear Weapons in Outer Space," 3 *Canadian Yrbk. Int'l L.* 3–35 (1965). See also Zhukov, *Iadernaia Demilitarizarsiia Kosmosa* (Nuclear Disarmament of Outer Space), 34 *SGP* 79–89 (1964).

In November 1965 the Soviet Union displayed an "orbital missile" allegedly capable of delivering a surprise blow from space. In response to U.S. queries, the Soviet Union, through its ambassador, A. F. Dobrynin, gave assurances that it was abiding and would continue to abide by this 1963 U.N. resolution. See *New York Times,* Dec. 11, 1965, at 1.

[40] For earlier U.S. and Soviet draft treaty provisions, see A/AC. 105/32, June 17, 1966 (U.S. draft of June 16, 1966) and A/6352, June 16, 1966 (Soviet draft of June 16, 1966).

[41] See chap. 2 at 27.

upon Earth. The goals of developing friendly relations among nations and the achieving of international cooperation in solving international problems are of no less urgency and no less significance because the nations of this sphere have begun to develop interests in other spheres.

Similarly, Article 51 of the Charter which recognizes as a principle of international law the inherent right of individual or collective self-defense against armed attack is not restricted to the terrestrial arena.

These principles may seem obvious to us. Nevertheless, it is eminently desirable to make it plain to all that there exists no legal problem as to the universality of the spatial scope of the Charter. When the representatives of many of our countries met in San Francisco in 1945, and, since that time, when new nations entered this Organization, we were intending to lay down, and did lay down, the beginnings of an international order limited neither in time nor space.[42]

The Ad Hoc Committee in turn reported that, as a matter of principle, the Charter and the Statute of the Court "were not limited in their operation to the confines of the earth."[43] Other nations were in agreement.[44]

These views were given formal expression in General Assembly Resolution 1721 (XVI), which commended to states for their guidance the principle: "International law, including the United Nations Charter, applies to outer space and celestial bodies . . ."; and in the General Assembly's Declaration of Legal Principles of 1963 (Resolution 1962 [XVII]) which provides: "4. The activities of States in the exploration and use of outer space shall be carried on in accordance with international law, including the Charter of the United Nations. . . ." Once again, the 1967 Space Treaty follows this pattern. Article III provides:

States Parties to the Treaty shall carry on activities in the exploration and use of outer space, including the moon and other celestial bodies, in accordance with international law, including the Charter of the United Nations, in the interest of maintaining international peace and security and promoting international cooperation and understanding.

The issue can hardly be said to be in doubt. Thus, states today agree that general international law and the U.N. Charter are applicable to outer space activities. The con-

tent of the applicable rules remains subject to specification and refinement as space activities increase.

Although it is apparent that many articles of the Charter have no special relation to outer space activities, it has been suggested that Articles 1 and 2 concerning the general principles behind the U.N.'s existence are directly applicable to space activities and that nations are to "refrain from the threat or use of force" in their relations with other nations concerning space matters. Article 2 is also of interest, and chapters VI and VII of the Charter, concerning the peaceful settlement of disputes and the prevention of acts of aggression, breaches of and threats to the peace, and Articles 51 (self-defense), 55, 56, and 59 are of prime importance.[45] Chapters IX and X concerning the specialized agencies, and Articles 102–5 are also relevant. The Statute of the International Court of Justice should equally be applicable. The specific applicability of Articles 1 and 51 (self-defense) has repeatedly been noted by the major space powers.[46]

The right of self-defense is common to all systems of law: *vim vi repellere omnia permittunt.*[47] During the drafting of the Kellogg-Briand Pact, as an example, the United States stated:

There is nothing in the American draft of an anti-war treaty which restricts or impairs in any way the right of self-defense. That right is inherent in every sovereign state and is implicit in every treaty. Every nation is free at all times and regardless of treaty provisions to defend its territory from attack or invasion and it alone is competent to decide whether circumstances require recourse to war in self-defense. If it has a good case, the world would applaud and not condemn its action. Express recognition by treaty of this inalienable right, however, gives rise to the same difficulty encountered in any effort to define aggression. It is the identical question approached from the other side. Inasmuch as no treaty provision can add to the natural right of self-defense, it is not the interest of peace that a

---

[42] Statement of May 7, 1959, *supra* note 4, at 2–3.

[43] *Report*, A/4141, July 14, 1959, at 62.

[44] See, e.g., statement by the Indian representative, Dec. 7, 1961, A/C. 1/PV 1213 at 31, 38, 40 (Dec. 7, 1961): "We entirely agree that the principles of the United Nations Charter, which are the highest expression of moral principles and truths, are universal and should appropriately be applicable to outer space." Compare the statement of the Indian representative cited *supra* note 15.

[45] See, e.g., David Davies Memorial Institute, *Draft Code of Rules of the Exploration and Uses of Outer Space* 9–10 (1962); Jenks, *supra* note 10, chap. 26. Of course, the content of the rules and the charter terms is no clearer for space activities than for those on earth. What is a "peaceful" move to one nation may be "hostile" or "aggressive" to another. This problem is elaborated on hereafter. See generally Brownlie, "The Maintenance of International Peace and Security in Outer Space," 40 *Brit. Yrbk. Int'l L.* 1 (1964).

[46] See Becker's statement of May 7, 1959, *supra* note 4, and see generally De Saussure and Reed, "Self-Defense—a Right in Outer Space," 7 *JAG L. Rev. (Air Force)* 38 ff. (Sept.–Oct. 1965).

[47] *Decretals,* Book V, tit. XXXIX, chap. 3.

treaty should stipulate a juristic conception of self-defense since it is far too easy for the unscrupulous to mold events to accord with an agreed definition.[48]

As noted in the last chapter, the needs of self-defense have caused states to create air-defense identification zones in air space far out over the high seas, and national spokesmen have been uniformly clear that self-defense requirements will be pursued with respect to outer space activities, even if no claims to sovereignty are made.[49] Loftus Becker stated years ago: "The United States is prepared at all times to react to protect itself against an armed attack, whether that attack originates in outer space or passes through space in order to reach the United States."[50] The Soviet writer Osnitskaya stated early: "In the event of the improper use of cosmic space any state has the right to take the measures permitted by modern international law including, in the event of armed attack through space, measures of individual or collective self-defense as provided for in Article 51 of the U.N. Charter.[51] In October 1960 the Executive Secretary of the Space Law Commission of the USSR Academy of Science similarly declared: "In case of need the Soviet Union will be able to protect its security against any encroachments from outer space just as successfully as it is done with respect to air space. . . . Such action will be fully justified under the existing rules of international law and the United Nations Charter.[52]

It certainly is no surprise that nations feel obliged to look to their own defenses with respect to outer space activities by others. Since the ordinary concept of self-defense is broader than that of Article 51 of the Charter, which formally limits individual and collective self-defense activities to a response to an "armed attack,"[53] it

remains to be seen whether or not, once they have the technological capability to resist, states will continue to ignore what they consider "aggressive" acts directed against their own security interests, which are nevertheless not armed attacks. In the event of a major threat, whether or not an armed attack in the terms of the Charter's Article 51 is in progress, we may have to accept the idea we saw suggested earlier, that "law simply does not deal with such questions of ultimate power. . . . The survival of states is not a matter of law."[54]

In summary, subject to a tentative acceptance of certain assertions made in the following sections of this chapter, the status of rules concerning general national activities in outer space appears to be as follows:

1. Under customary international law, international conventions, and municipal legislation, acts within the airspace over a nation and its territorial waters are subject to the exclusive sovereignty of the subjacent state.

2. There is no agreed limit to the height to which such sovereignty extends.

3. There is no agreed point at which "outer space" begins but orbiting satellites, while in orbit, except presumably when in landing orbits, are "in" outer space.

4. Under present treaty rules and/or customary law, as demonstrated in practice, national statements, and United Nations resolutions:

   a) International law, including the United Nations Charter where appropriate, applies to acts in outer space. This expressly includes the right of self-defense against threats from outer space and threats to national interests (space vehicles, personnel, stations) in outer space and on the celestial bodies.

   b) Outer space is free for the peaceful use of all nations on the basis of initial equality of access to those with the capacity to gain access. Space as such is not subject to claims of national sovereignty.

   c) A state may place a satellite in orbit for peaceful and scientific purposes without obtaining the consent of any other state at least to its orbital flight.

   d) Objects and persons placed in space and on the celestial bodies remain subject to the jurisdiction, ownership, and control, as appropri-

---

[48] *U.S. Foreign Rel.* 36 (1928).

[49] See also remarks of McDougal, "50th Annual Meeting," 1956 *Proceedings, Am. Soc'y Int'l L.* (Apr. 25–28, 1956); U.S. Rear Admiral C. Ward, "Projecting the Law of the Sea into the Law of Space," *JAG J. (Navy)* 4 (Mar. 1957). On Soviet views on "sovereignty," see also Kucherov, "The USSR and Sovereignty in Outer Space," 12 *Inst. Study USSR Bull.* 25–33 (1965).

[50] Becker, "Major Aspects of the Problem of Outer Space," 38 *Dept. State Bull.* 962, 965 (June 9, 1958).

[51] In *1961 Symposium, supra* note 3, at 1088, 1092.

[52] Zhukov, "Space Espionage Plans and International Law," 6 *Int'l Aff.* 53, 57 (Moscow, Oct. 1960).

[53] The meaning of Article 51 is the subject of continuing debate among statesmen and scholars as well. See, e.g., Stone, *Aggression and World Order* (1958).

[54] Remarks of former Secretary of State Acheson, *1963 Proceedings, Amer. Soc. Int'l L.* 13, 14.

ate, of the launching (or otherwise appropriate) state.

5. The first stages in the creation of a rule barring nations from claiming sovereignty over celestial bodies have occurred. The 1967 Space Treaty removes all legal doubt for parties by providing in Article II that: "Outer space, including the moon and other celestial bodies, is not subject to national appropriation by claim of sovereignty, by means of use or occupation, or by any other means." *This does not necessarily prevent states from exercising control over areas without claims to sovereignty.*

6. The first stages in the creation of a self-policed rule barring nations from orbiting weapons of mass destruction have occurred. Again, the 1967 Space Treaty would make this a firm (if unpoliced) rule for parties.

7. By an international convention—the Nuclear Test Ban Treaty of 1963—most nations are now legally barred from conducting nuclear tests in outer space, but important nations remain outside the treaty and parties may denounce it for themselves if matters of national importance so require.

8. It also appears clear that, absent an overriding international rule, nations will apply their own rules to activities in outer space, to the extent they can do so, if such activities impinge on their territory (e.g., by radio transmission) or if their nationals are involved (e.g., if a national commits treason, fails to pay an income tax, etc.).[55]

9. States have accepted responsibility for their acts and the acts of their nationals in the outer space milieu.

A Note on the Regime of Free Competition

From the lawyer's point of view, space is not a vacuum, but to the political analyst's eye the regime of outer space can at present be called "empty." It has, nevertheless, a well-known history; it is the regime of international free competition. There is equality of initial rights of access but only for those having the capacity, including at present the ability and the willingness, to allocate major resources to the task. This is also the international legal-economic regime for certain non-national regions on earth, principally the seas but also, to a degree, Antarctica. We can now estimate reasonably

well what conditions are necessary for such a regime to work; where there are no scarce resources to appropriate, parallel activities of different sovereigns can take place side by side. The "area" remains non-national, although ships and land stations on earth and space vehicles, space stations, and stations on the celestial bodies remain national. *They* are not shared (as they could be, for example, in a U.N.-operated or U.N.-controlled regime).

The earth and space free-competition regimes may thus be thought of as providing a license to all, by all, to go anywhere. The license is not absolute; ports on earth and moon stations, ships and earth satellites remain national. Access to them can be restricted, and they cannot be freely invaded or displaced. Most important, the concept of sharing is not normally applicable to any valuable *yield* from activities at sea (primarily fish and minerals at present),[56] nor is it necessarily to be expected that a valuable yield from space will surely be shared.

If the resources are valuable but not removable, except piecemeal, or if they need to be hunted or fished out of the "shared" regions in a competitive extraction process, they need not be shared, "fairly" or otherwise; everyone is traditionally "free" (if able) to grab. The incentives, therefore, of those with capacity in this regime of equal access for competition is to take as much as possible which, it is true, may kill off the resource base if it is exhaustible.[57] Latecomers take nothing.

If the resources are stationary or fixed and support the other activities carried on in or via the medium (fueling stations, sea bases on your "lifeline" to your empire, moon stations for self-defense or aggression or for support of nationally important space activities), they have not normally been subjected to unregulated free access,

---

[55] See Katzenbach, *supra* note 10, at 69, 70.

[56] There is a notable minor example of sharing the fur seals of the North Pacific. On the history of the shared arrangements, involving a limit to catches, sanctions against violators, and enforcement by the naval vessels and customs inspectors of all participants, the United States, Russia, Canada, and Japan, see Jessup & Taubenfeld, *supra* note 3, at 93–94 and sources cited. For recent developments and texts of recent treaty arrangements, see "Fur Seals–Pribilof Islands," *Hearings on S. 2102 before the Senate Committee on Commerce,* 89th Cong., 1st and 2d Sess., ser. 89–57 (Sept. 6, 1965 and Feb. 18, 1966).

[57] The sad history of whaling in Antarctic waters is a current example of obvious greed destroying a resource despite the obvious facts and of ineffectual international attempts to alleviate the problem. See Jessup & Taubenfeld, *supra* note 3, at 92–93 and sources cited.

whatever the legal label given to the "sovereign's" right to exclude others. This seems likely to be a recurring phenomenon. *But* if they are shareable, at least in the sense that equally good sites are not scarce and there is no special strategic or other value to one such site, there may be no need to compete for any single location and, of great importance, latecomers may do as well as the original entrants. The usual political problems of late-arriving, powerful have-nots, sovereign competitors with a sense of their own "destiny" to join or dominate the haves, need not arise if this proves possible. Then the regime will not suffer from the dangers which have beset other inflexible status-quo oriented political, economic and legal regimes because it will not be status-quo biased. It will be flexible enough to accomodate all. Once a state can become a "member" of the club, it will have "free access" to equally desirable space locations and uses (which we have here assumed to be inexhaustible, within the needed range).

This is the regime thus far chosen for outer space exploration and activities. It is the type to be perpetuated under all American and Soviet proposals to date for further treaty arrangements and under the 1967 treaty. It is unhelpful to label it as "free" and "equal" without examining to whom it is free and in which ways and under what assumptions they can expect to be equal. It may well prove to be adequate for the needs of the nations in space, although that seems to depend on the variables already noted and, of course, there *are* alternatives, which will not be examined in detail here.[58]

It is perhaps enough to summarize the political reasons why no more ambitious regime has been possible. The nations do not fully know the various types of "value" they can expect to obtain from space. If these prove to be shareable, meaning nonunique, homogeneous, and inexhaustible, they do not need more. This is also true if they prove shareable by tolerance or by mutually convenient tacit or express agreement.[59]

In sum, if the fruits of space activities are nonshareable, unique, valuable (scarce), each nation apparently wants to be able to be free to utilize them for itself alone or in some way yielding maximum benefit to itself. There is no desire to make the approach multilateral and thus require a contest over the shares of the yield. Yet, if these values exist, other nations will join the competition. The later they start and the less well prepared they are, the less they will get of such exhaustible resources and of any resource base that could possibly be dominated. History indicates that other major powers will not be delayed very greatly after any such valuable discovery. They will "borrow" from the already existing research and development work of other nations and will catch up quickly if the rewards appear to be great enough.

In short, if appropriable, unique resources (i.e., resource bases) exist which can be dominated and controlled, an attempt can be expected by the great powers to appropriate them, although this need not necessarily involve a traditional claim to sovereignty as we know it. The outcome is potentially highly dangerous. It implies (1) an initial competitive struggle (which need not, of course, involve arms) by the current space powers; and (2) a later fight by the current appropriator or appropriators to keep other "aggressive" latecomers out.

Thus it might be rational from the world point of view to internationalize at least the resource bases of unique value, if any exist. In a world where major powers want to avoid confrontations, they may share the desire for peaceful development, even if this means some internationalization, but the question then becomes how to internationalize in one's own favor.

In one sense, the development of commercial space telecommunications (a "natural" monopoly) to date may provide a formula, although international communications by definition require at least two states to cooperate, whereas the exploitation of other resources may not. The first state to develop the system enjoys special privileges and presumably scores an economic coup while it has de facto monopoly control. Yet others can share in the system with a measure of control and little (comparative) risk of resources. And competing systems can be sustained and bargains made between the systems if the nations want it that way.[60] Thus, accommodation is

---

[58] For suggestions as to the range of alternatives, see, e.g. the sources cited in note 3, *supra*.

[59] This seems to be true even for such activities as gathering strategic information by earth satellites. Both major powers are flying such satellites and, even if they avoided overflying each other, they would presumably find it useful to keep track of activities in other countries, e.g., China. Moreover, *all* photographs of the earth have some strategic value, and this value cannot be divorced from materials gathered for other purposes. The alternatives, giving up all space activities or accepting some form of internationalized (U.N.?) information-

gathering monopoly, are not presently desired by any major power.

[60] Yet compare the criticism of the dominant role of ComSat in Intelsat, e.g., in the speech of H. G. Darwin of the U.K., "A British Perspective," Stanford Conference (mimeo.,

probably possible if desired, especially if not too fixed a division between the members exists so that fights over who loses from a necessary redistribution to accommodate latecomers can be avoided.

Near-space activities as we now see them and scientific exploration of the universe must be shared to be used most fruitfully. The only question is who pays the incremental costs. Essentially, the current highest uses—communications, scientific discovery, meteorology, navigation—are also shareable and are recognized as such. Military uses are, of course, the obvious exception to sharing as the world is now organized.

Thus far, then, nothing seems to require more internationalization than has been achieved to date or is likely under existing and proposed treaty arrangements. As soon as something does—a resource to be "harvested," the shares in the pie to be fixed, a space disarmament to be reliably enforced—more positive international arrangements will be necessary. They will nevertheless be achieved, if at all, on a piecemeal basis in accordance with the traditions of a functionalist approach to the development of the rules of international law, leaving each state great flexibility to bargain and maneuver.

Each space power's strategic overkill capacity on earth does not at present seem threatened by prospective space uses, even those of an information-gathering or military space-station type.[61] So long as exclusionary rights to major new power bases (strategic or resource) are not involved, so long as a centralized international coercive enforcement power is not necessary for adequate performance of the international functions involved (as in Antarctica today), the present non-national, noninternational regime will probably be adequate. In the short run at least, this seems the likely prospect for outer space and the attainable celestial bodies.

The Regime for the Celestial Bodies

While it is difficult, for physical reasons, to conceive of effective national claims over areas of outer space itself —except, perhaps as such areas could in time be policed

from natural or artificial satellites or maneuverable space vehicles—the same difficulties do not exist with respect to the celestial bodies. Here, the physical possibility of national claims to sovereignty at some time exists; occupation and control are possible, although admittedly vast technological progress remains necessary before man will be able to "occupy" a celestial body with any ease.

Historically, claims to new areas on earth have been based on discovery, contiguity, continuity, occupation, effective use, and annexation. It seems unnecessary here to review this experience in the light of recent surveys.[62] It is perhaps enough to say that, for the celestial bodies, "discovery" is neither factually nor legally sufficient to support claims to sovereignty, if it ever was on earth.[63] The same is true of acts of a type regularly performed on earth such as planting flags or markers, photographing areas, mapping, or exploring, or performing "administrative" acts at a distance—such as issuing regulations, printing postage stamps, or formally incorporating the areas claimed into the national homeland, as has occurred with Antarctica.[64] Doctrines of continuity or

---

[61] This is stated by American authorities to be so even if the Soviet Union in fact develops a "fractional orbital bombardment system." See statement of Sec'y McNamara, DOD Release 1060–67, Nov. 3, 1967 and *New York Times*, Oct. 17, 1967, at 1. For discussion, see *supra* chap. 2, at 27.

[62] See e.g., Lipson & Katzenbach, *supra* note 2, at 19–21 and sources cited; Jessup & Taubenfeld, *supra* note 3, chap. 5; McDougal, *supra* note 2, chap. 7.

[63] See, in general, Becker, "The Control of Space," 39 *Dept. State Bull.* 416–20 (1958); Keating, "The Law and the Conquest of Space," 104 *Cong. Record*, Appendix, pp. A1029–A1031 (1958); McDougal & Lipson, "Perspectives for a Law of Outer Space," 52 *Am. J. Int'l L.* 407–31 (1958); G. S. Rhyne, "The Legal Horizons of Space Use and Exploration," 104 *Cong. Rec.* 6152–55 (1958); Schacter, 1958 *Proceedings, Am. Soc'y Int'l L.* 245 (1958).

Discovery has always meant more than mere sighting. It has been described as a "purposeful act of exploration or navigation accompanied by a visual apprehension, a landing or some other act marking or recording such visit, but not acts expressive of possession." Aaronson, "Aspects of the Law of Space," 224 *Law Times* 219, 220 (1957). In the Island of Palmas Arbitration, discovery was said to give at most an "inchoate title." Island of Las Palmas Case (U.S. and the Netherlands), Perm. Ct. of Arb., Scott, *Hague Ct. Rpts.* 2d Ser. 83 (1932); 2 *U.N. Rpt. Arb. Awds.* 829. Compare, however, Helfer, "Who Owns Outer Space?" *Family Weekly Mag.*, Mar. 30, 1958, at 12; "Space Lawyers Ponder Ownership of Moon, Plot Spatial Borders," *Wall Street Journal*, Jan. 20, 1958, at 1.

[64] See Jessup & Taubenfeld, *supra* note 3, chaps. 5–6. See also Keller, Lissitzyn, & Mann, *Creation of Rights of Sovereignty through Symbolic Acts, 1400–1800* (1938). In general, on discovery, effective occupation, etc., from the U. S. point of view, see 2 Whiteman, *supra* note 2, at 1028–46; 1 Wharton, *Int'l L. Digest,* chap. 1, secs. 1–5 (2d ed. 1887); 1 Moore, *Int'l L. Digest,* chap. 4, at 255–611 (1906); I Hackworth, *Digest of International Law,* chap. 4, at 393–567 and chap. 13, at 357–59 (1940).

Aug. 1967). Note also a Canadian view on the need for a Canadian ComSat system and a "staking out of a part of outer space," *supra* Chap. 2, note 60.

contiguity, via sectors or otherwise, have little relevance in view of the physical facts of space noted earlier.[65] The United States, the Soviet Union, and other states as well have rejected claims based on such acts and doctrines in Antarctica and presumably would do so for claims made to celestial bodies as well.[66]

Perhaps the majority of writers and organizations studying the problem have simply argued that bodies in space must, like outer space, be treated legally as *res communis* or *res extra commercium* and are not subject to appropriation whatever the acts of particular states.[67] It has been urged that continuing freedom of access on a basis of equality is essential to avoid conflict initially and between initial occupants and latecomers. The celestial bodies, like space itself, should thus be considered a vast shareable resource.[68] This type of approach has led also to many suggestions that the United Nations or some new international organization be given special competence in outer space and on the celestial bodies including perhaps complete "ownership" of space resources in trust for all nations and men.[69] This question of a positive regime to prevent clashes between nations on and over the celestial bodies receives special treatment hereafter.

At the United Nations, the Ad Hoc Committee in 1959 took the position that present activities would not be a basis for claims to exclusive sovereignty and that problems based on such claims could not arise until it became possible to settle on the celestial bodies and to exploit their resources.[70] Resolution 1721 of 1961 thereafter bracketed outer space and celestial bodies as "free for exploration and use by all States . . . and . . . not subject to national appropriation." Resolution 1962 of 1963 went on even more firmly to urge:

2. Outer space and celestial bodies are free for exploration and use by all states on a basis of equality and in accordance with international law.
3. Outer space and celestial bodies are not subject to national appropriation *by claim of sovereignty, by means of use or occupation, or by any other means.* [italics added.]

If this states a rule of present international law, its scope is all inclusive as to claims to sovereignty. The 1967

---

[65] Compare, however, Knauth, "Letter," 45 *ABA J.* 14, 16 (Jan. 1959), who discusses the fact that the moon, for example, does not pass "over" certain countries (e.g., China) so that those over which it passes have a better basis for making a claim than these unfortunate few.

[66] On relevant aspects of the Antarctic analogy, see chap. 3. On the Antarctic Treaty of 1959 and its relevance, see sources there cited. In general, see Jessup & Taubenfeld, *supra* note 3, chap. 5–6. See also Korovin, *supra* note 19, at 53–59; Quigg, "Open Skies and Open Space," 37 *For. Aff.* 95–106 (1958). There have nevertheless been suggestions that very little in fact will be required in terms of effective occupation in uninhabited, inhospitable areas. See "The Clipperton Island Arbitration" 26 *Am. J. Int'l L.* 390 (1932) and the "Case Concerning the Legal Status of Eastern Greenland (Norway v. Denmark)," *Permanent Court of International Justice* [hereinafter cited as *P.C.I.J.*] *Reports*, Ser. A/B No. 53 (Apr. 5, 1933); see also note 81 *infra*.

[67] See Lipson & Katzenbach, *supra* note 2, at 19–20 and sources cited. The American Bar Association in 1959 resolved "That in the common interest of mankind . . . celestial bodies should not be subjected to exclusive appropriation."

[68] Lipson & Katzenbach, *supra* note 2, at 20 and sources cited. The David Davies Memorial Institute Draft Code (*supra* note 45) provides:

"2.1 Outer space, and the celestial bodies therein, are recognized as being *res communis omnium,* free for exploration and use by all States in conformity with the provisions of this Draft Code, and neither outer space nor the celestial bodies in it are capable of appropriation or exclusive use by any State.

"2.2 Subject to the provisions of this Draft Code, all States shall, for themselves and for their nationals, have equal rights in the exploration and use of outer space, including free navigation by means of spacecraft, the establishment of space stations and other like devices, astronomical and physical observations by optical radio and other methods, and the landing on and exploration and use of celestial bodies."

[69] See, e.g., Lipson & Katzenbach, *supra* note 2, 20 and sources cited. See also e.g., Horsford, "The Law of Space," 14 *J. Brit. Interplanetary Soc'y* 144, 147 (1955), who suggests an internationalized trusteeship for the celestial bodies. Compare the treatment of outer space in Clark & Sohn, *supra* note 3, *passim*, esp. 296–302 (2d ed.) (on a United Nations Outer Space Agency), and see "New Dimensions for the United Nations: The Problems of the Next Decade," *Seventeenth Report on the Commission to Study the Organization of Peace,* esp. 41–46 (1966). Jenks, in "The International Control of Outer Space," 1960 *Proceedings, Third Colloquium IISL* (Stockholm, 1960) stated: "We can perhaps envisage three successive phases, which for purposes of convenience I propose to describe as the Monroe Doctrine for the moon phase, the Antarctic Analogy phase, and the United Nations control phase." See also McDougal, Lasswell, Vlasic & Smith, "Enjoyment and Acquisition of Resources in Outer Space," 111 *U. Pa. L. Rev.* 521 (1963).

Soviet spokesmen have traditionally taken a dim view of transfers to the United Nations. See, e.g., Korovin, in 9 *Int'l Aff.* 100–102 (Moscow, July 1963), who refers to any transfer as "premature, to say the least."

[70] See *U.N. Report of the Ad Hoc Committee on the Peaceful Uses of Outer Space* (A/4141) (July 14, 1959).

Space Treaty is equally forthright in providing, as we have noted in Article II, that: "Outer space, including the moon and other celestial bodies, is not subject to national appropriation by claim of sovereignty, by means of use or occupation, or by any other means." The ability of states to use, occupy, and preempt an area without claims to sovereignty has nevertheless been repeatedly demonstrated in history.

For states which do not become parties to the treaty just referred to, a special problem exists in asserting that the principles of the United Nations resolutions of 1961 and 1963 concerning the celestial bodies bind them as rules of customary international law.[71] While national statements plus such practice as has already occurred seem to support a view that outer space as such is not subject to national claims, it can hardly be said that there is much practice, as distinct from national avowals, with respect to the status of the celestial bodies.

The states, in United Nations resolutions and elsewhere, have nevertheless called for the moon and the other celestial bodies to be free of national claims of sovereignty. Russian jurists have pursued this theme. They have said that: "As for appropriating celestial bodies, only American speculators trade in lots on the moon. . . ."[72]

Man has now landed on the moon and there have been limited impacts on Venus. Soviet impact vehicles have carried the Soviet coat of arms and Soviet pennants and, at one time, Chairman Khrushchev stated that a Soviet impact had demonstrated a Soviet "priority."[73] In other statements, he indicated that there would be no attempt to make property-type claims, indicating: "We regard the launching of a space rocket and the delivery of our pen-

nant to the moon, as our achievement. And when we say "our" we imply all the countries of the world, that is, we imply that it is also your achievement and the achievement of all living people on earth."[74] Moreover, in advance of the General Assembly's 1963 resolution, a Soviet Draft Declaration provided that: "Sovereignty over outer space or celestial bodies cannot be acquired by use or occupation or in any other way."[75] This language is similar to that employed in Resolution 1962 as unanimously adopted. The Soviet Union is also an original signatory of the 1967 Space Treaty.

American officials have reflected the same approach. At the United Nations, in 1962, it was stated expressly that "we have rejected the concept of national sovereignty in outer space. No moon, no planet, shall ever fly a single nation's flag."[76] Certainly the few impact missions to date do not qualify under any known and accepted theory as establishing the basis for claims to ownership, even without the U.N. resolutions. The scattering of plaques by an impact rocket meets none of the tests of "effective occupation,"[77] nor does the planting of a single American flag. Can we say then that public statements by government officials, plus the U.N. resolutions discussed herein—but without even the limited "practice" now cited to support the "rule" that space is free for all peaceful uses—are enough to make the "principle" that nations should not lay claim to the

---

71 See generally Cooper, "Who Will Own the Moon? The Need for an Answer," *Princeton Quart.* (Winter 1965–66), reprinted in 32 *J. Air L. & Commerce* 155 (1966).

72 Cited in McMahon, "Legal Aspects of Outer Space," 1962 *Brit. Yrbk. Int'l Law* 393. With regard to Soviet policy on this subject, Crane has stated in his *Soviet Attitude toward International Space Law* 29–29 (World Rule of Law Center, Duke U., Mar. 1, 1962) that "the Soviets oppose the establishment of territorial claims to celestial bodies for two reasons: 1) because of the difficulty of applying to these bodies the traditional international law on territorial acquisitions, and 2) because any territorial acquisition at all of celestial bodies would conflict with the new law of peaceful coexistence." See Osnitskaya, *supra* note 3, at 64.

73 It is not contended that this could ever be an "effective occupation." See McDougal, "Law and Public Order in Space," in Schwartz, *supra* note 2, at 151, 170, and Taubenfeld, "Comment," 1961 *Proceedings, Am. Soc'y Int'l L.* 177.

74 Khrushchev, *World Without Arms, World Without Wars,* Bk. 2, at 110 (Moscow, Aug.-Dec. 1959). See also Zhukov, "Problems of Space Law at the Present Stage," 1962 *Proceedings, Fifth Colloquium IISL* 23 (mimeo., Varna); Osnitskaya, *supra* note 3, at 1088, 1094; Korovin, "Conquest of Outer Space and Some Problems of International Relations," *1961 Symposium, supra* note 3, at 1072, 1074; Korovin, *supra* note 25, at 61, 63. To the same effect see Khrushchev's comments reported in *Washington Post,* Sept. 17, 1959, at A17. For views of the U.S. State Department, see 2 Whiteman, *supra* note 2, at 1312–13, and sources cited.

75 Cited in Schwartz, *supra* note 2, at 140.

76 See A/AC.105/PV.2 at 13–15 (May 3, 1962). See also the address by President Eisenhower to the General Assembly, Sept. 22, 1960, *1961 Symposium, supra* note 3, at 1009. Note that, despite the fact that the United States is clearly one of the first to "perform acts" on the moon, there does not appear to be the same sort of formal reservation of the right to make claims based on priorities as has been maintained with respect to Antarctica. See also Becker, "United States Foreign Policy and the Development of Law for Outer Space," *JAG J. (Navy)* 4, 29 (1959). To the same effect, see also *Report of the Ad Hoc Committee, supra* note 70, at 63–64, 68; Lipson & Katzenbach, *supra* note 2, at 20–21.

77 See Taubenfeld, *supra* note 73, at 177.

celestial bodies a legally binding rule in international law without a formal treaty to this effect? At the present time, practice, if it is necessary to the creation of rules of customary law in this new nuclear space age, is embryonic. Nevertheless, in view of the anticipated difficulties in any major use of the moon and planets by substantial populations in the near future, and of the likelihood that there will be no scarcity of equally good opportunities to develop parallel, if not shared, programs for the exploitation of any foreseeable uses, without strong incentives or the capacity to monopolize access, a customary rule keeping the celestial bodies free is likely to be established and useful especially with a confirming treaty to the same effect.[78] What happens to such a rule if circumstances change drastically (e.g., if the technology of exploitation and exploration becomes "cheap" and widespread) is of course another issue.[79] We have already discussed the regime of "free competition" as the world has known it in the last section.

Having said this, it is necessary to add comments on certain potential problem areas, although, since this study is concerned primarily with the legal situation as it is and not with the multiple possible permutations of future alternatives, only a brief introduction is warranted here. First, if the major powers should ever, for reasons not now apparent, overthrow the present treaty and customary law regime and insist that the celestial bodies are *res nullius* and subject to national appropriation, the principal difficulty in assessing national claims, after some form of occupation and effective use, would be to determine "the degree and kind of possession effective to create a title and to define the area of territory to which such a possession might be said to apply."[80]

The degree of effectiveness required depends on the circumstances of the case[81] and the time in history when the matter arises. With the major powers as legal contestants, presumably a high degree of effective use and actual occupation and control of areas claimed would doubtless be required, unless, of course, they simply divided space and the celestial bodies between themselves as treaty or *de facto* allies. Effective prior occupation and use gives a title valid against the world, but "on account of the expenditure required and the technological difficulties involved it may well be some time before any State exercises a sufficient measure of activity on the moon to satisfy the requirement of effective occupation."[82] It is hoped that these issues will never in fact arise.

Second, if nations do not advance formal claims to sovereignty over the celestial bodies, as now seems likely, history on earth indicates that there may nevertheless be effective preemptions of areas or resources, whether or not these can be fitted neatly into a "legal" category. We have already noted such common preemptive, but usually temporary, uses of non-national areas as are involved in fleet maneuvers and nuclear and missile testing. The establishment of bases in unclaimed areas, as in Antarctica, is often of even longer duration. Nations normally exclude or seek to exclude others while operations are in

---

[78] For a learned discussion of the creation of "instant" customary law, see Cheng, "United Nations Resolutions on Outer Space . . . ," 5 *Indian J. Int'l L.* 23, 35 ff. (1965). See also, e.g., Note, "National Sovereignty of Outer Space," 74 *Harv. L. Rev.* 1167–68 (1961); McMahon, *supra* note 72, 339, 354–55.

Cheng also points out that, even if there is no "rule" making claims improper, the major space powers and other states accepting the U.N. resolution may simply refuse recognition to such claims as are made. Since recognition is so important in the theory of title to territory this may serve the same purpose as a treaty rule. See generally Jennings, *The Acquisition of Territory in International Law* (1963); Schwartzenberger, "Title to Territory," 51 *Am. J. Int'l L.* 308, 316–18 (1957); Cheng, "The Extra-terrestrial Applications of International Law," 18 *Current Legal Problems* 132, 150–51 (1965).

[79] The question of apparent acquiescence in a developing rule by states which simply lack the capacity rather than the will to take a different stand has no clear answers. On this issue generally, see Lissitzyn's excellent study, *International Law Today and Tomorrow, passim* (1965).

[80] Jennings, *supra* note 77, at 20.

[81] Waldock, "Disputed Sovereignty in the Falkland Island Dependencies," 25 *Brit. Yrbk. Int'l L.* 336 (1948), states: "All are agreed in holding that the degree of state activity required to confer a valid title varies with the circumstances of each territory."

Waldock notes elsewhere (p. 317), that: "The cases make it plain that today the decisive test of the effectiveness of an occupation is whether the claimant has in fact displayed state functions in regard to the territory sufficiently to assure to other states 'the minimum of protection of which international law is the guardian.' Accordingly it is effective activity by the state either internally within the territory or externally in relations with other states which is the foundation of a title by occupation, not settlement and exploitation." See 1 Oppenheim, *International Law* 557 (8th ed. 1955), on "Possession and Administration as the Prerequisites for Occupation."

See also note 66, *supra,* and Island of Palmas case, *Annual Digest, 1927–28,* Case No. 72; Eastern Greenland case, *P.C.I.J. 1933,* Series A/B. No. 53; Minquiers and Ecrehos case, *I.C.J. Reports* 68–70 (1953).

[82] See McMahon, *supra* note 72, at 339, 395. See also Jennings, *supra* note 78, at 38–39; McDougal *et al., supra* note 69, at 635.

progress, often for the intruder's own safety. Occasionally, too, occupation of a particular piece of land has permitted *de facto* control or regulation over extensive areas of the high seas, as was the case with British licensing and taxation of the whaling industry in the early 1900's through control of South Georgia and the Falkland Islands.[83]

Of more importance potentially is the uninspiring record of the nations as mandatory powers, administrators of trust territories, "protectors" in protectorate arrangements, and the like in which no claims of sovereignty were made. Other states, however, rarely received rights of equal access, even when these were called for by international agreements.[84] Other limitations and obligations on the tutors in favor of their wards were unevenly or poorly respected. Even without claims to sovereignty, this history suggests that, if technological change and discovery make acquisition possible and attractive, it is likely that there will be grave difficulty in asserting an international interest or direct international control over major nations which establish preemptive positions, even after an Antarctic-type treaty.[85] As Leon Lipson put it in a discussion of probable future Soviet behavior:

It seems probable that Soviet diplomatic and legal policy will be governed by two characteristics: 1) they will refrain from claiming sovereignty or jurisdiction over the moon, 2) they will consistently claim the operating rights and benefits that would be expected to result from a successful claim to sovereignty or jurisdiction. Thus they could reap maximum political and practical benefits.[86]

It is also clear that, even without sovereign claims to territory, states have at times asserted exclusive rights to use the resources of an area. This has been true for fish on the high seas and may be for mineral and other resources in space and particularly, in time, on the celestial bodies.[87] To avoid conflict, it has also been suggested by many writers that title to space resources be placed in an international organization which could then issue licenses, etc.[88] These issues, while potentially of grave importance in some foreseeable circumstances, are not the subject of any present international arrangements or negotiations. The question of resource appropriation is open today, and, despite self-denying rules agreed to by states, when and if important resources become available a conflict over shares seems likely. The limited nature of the Antarctic Treaty of 1959, which does not deal with the issue of ownership or control of resources, is probably indicative of the difficulty of obtaining serious consideration by the nations of the relinquishment, in advance, of unknown (and perhaps nonexistent) resources.[89] The 1967 Space Treaty is equally barren of provisions dealing with this issue.

Even with the best of good will, the concept of sovereignty or at least of continuing national ownership will remain relevant to some aspects of outer space activities. It has been noted, for example, that:

The absence of the right to ownership of celestial bodies does not exclude the right of a state to own scientific instruments launched into space and research stations which might be set up on celestial bodies. We may give the analogy of the Antarctic, whose international status does not preclude the setting up by states of their own scientific stations whose personnel and property are subordinated to them.[90]

---

[83] Jessup & Taubenfeld, *supra* note 3, at 143–44.

[84] These arrangements are discussed in *id.,* chap. 1.

[85] See, *supra* chap. 3 on the Antarctic Treaty of 1959. For additional speculation on problems of control, exclusive operations, the applicability of an "Antarctic-type" treaty, and permissibility of various types of activities, see *Report of the Committee on the Law of Outer Space of the International and Comparative Law Section, American Bar Association* (July 20, 1966), esp. the remarks of Haley, Crane, Bishop, Davitt, Maggs, and McChesney; Markov, "Moon Landing and International Law," 3 *Diritto Aereo* 23–46 (Rome, 1964).

[86] Leon Lipson, "International Political Implications of Activities in Outer Space" (Report of a Conference, Joseph M. Goldsen, Chairman, Oct. 22–23, 1959), RAND Corp., *Report R 362-RC,* 79–89 (May 5, 1960). See also Goldie, "Special Regimes and Preemptive Activities in International Law," 11 *Int'l & Comp. L.Q.* 670–700 (July 1962).

[87] See, e.g., McDougal *et al., supra* note 2, chap. 7, *passim;* McDougal *et al., supra* note 69, at 521 ff. See also Gorove, "Prohibition of National Appropriation in the Outer Space Treaty," paper prepared for the 15th Conf., Interplanetary Space Law Comm., Inter-Amer. Bar Ass'n (mimeo., April 1967).
On oyster beds outside the territorial waters of Europe, see Fenwick, *International Law* 420 *et seq.* (1948).

[88] *Supra* note 3, and see, e.g., Jenks, *The Common Law of Mankind* 397–98 (1958); "New Dimensions for the United Nations: The Problems of the Next Decade," *Seventeenth Report of the Commission to Study the Organization of Peace* 41–46 (May 1966).

[89] See discussion of the Antarctic analogy in chap. 3. For a suggestion that the Antarctic settlement should have gone further, see Taubenfeld, "A Treaty for Antarctica," *Int'l Concil.,* No. 531 (1961).

[90] Korovin, "Peaceful Co-operation in Space," 8 *Int'l Aff.* 61, 63 (Moscow, Mar. 1962); see also David Davies Memorial Institute, *supra* note 45, which provides:
"3(5)(a) a State which establishes or permits its nationals to establish a manned station, may exercise jurisdiction over all persons in the station and in

The 1967 Space Treaty preserves these rights as well in providing, in Article VII, that:

A State Party to the Treaty on whose registry an object launched into outer space is carried shall retain jurisdiction and control over such object, and over any personnel thereof, while in outer space or on a celestial body. Ownership of objects launched into outer space, including objects landed or constructed on a celestial body, and of their component parts, is not affected by their presence in outer space or on a celestial body or by their return to the earth. Such objects or component parts found beyond the limits of the State Party to the Treaty on whose registry they are carried shall be returned to that State, which shall, upon request, furnish identifying data prior to their return.

An American draft of the treaty, dated June 16, 1966, provided that the bases on celestial bodies should, on the Antarctic pattern, be freely and fully "open" to all, and that all "findings" by those using these bodies should be promptly and fully reported to the U.N. and the world community,[91] but Soviet objections made a compromise necessary. As a result, the 1967 treaty, in a more limited way, makes the following provisions:

Article XI

In order to promote international co-operation in the peaceful exploration and use of outer space, States Parties to the Treaty conducting activities in outer space, including the moon and other celestial bodies, agree to inform the Secretary-General of the United Nations as well as the public and the international scientific community, *to the greatest extent feasible and practicable,* of the nature, conduct, locations and results of such activities. On receiving the said information, the Secretary-General of the United Nations should be prepared to disseminate it immediately and effectively. (Italics added.)

---

that area around it over which the movement is necessary for the maintenance and use of the station;

"3(5)(b) an international body which establishes such a station, may exercise a similar jurisdiction by international agreement."

[91] The U.S. draft provided that:

"Article 4

"A state conducting activities on a celestial body shall (a) promptly provide the Secretary-General of the United Nations with a descriptive report of the nature, conduct, and locations of such activities and (b) make the findings of such activities freely available to the public and the international scientific community.

"Article 6

"All areas of celestial bodies, including all stations, installations, equipment, and space vehicles, on celestial bodies, shall be open at all times to representatives of other States conducting activities on celestial bodies."

Article XII

All stations, installations, equipment and space vehicles on the moon and other celestial bodies shall be open to representatives of the other States Parties to the Treaty on a basis of reciprocity. *Such representatives shall give reasonable advance notice of a projected visit,* in order that appropriate consultations may be held and that maximum precautions may be taken to assure safety and to avoid interference with normal operations in the facility to be visited. (Italics added.)

Thus, the openness of the Antarctic Treaty regime has given way, perhaps inevitably in this potentially more strategically important area, to a milder set of obligations imposed on the parties. As one perceptive commentator, Nicholas Katzenbach, noted earlier, we may here be witnessing the development of a broad substitute for the old tradition of claims, a demand not for sovereignty but for recognition of the "primary rights of a nation in a localized facility created by its own efforts."[92]

If the concept of national bases is, as in the Antarctic, not overly extended, this approach seems both necessary and not harmful to the interests of other states. It is, nevertheless, a gap through which the content of the concept of exclusionary sovereignty might some day pour if useful to the great powers.

United Nations Resolutions concerning Outer Space Activities as Present Law

At various points throughout these chapters, we have referred to certain resolutions of the General Assembly as if at least some of the principles enunciated therein represent present rules of international law. These are, primarily, Resolutions 1721A (XVI) of December 20, 1961; 1962 (XVIII) of December 13, 1953; and 1884 (XVIII) of October 17, 1963 (weapons of mass destruction). Since it is clear from the charter and consistent United Nations practice that, with the exception of matters of internal U.N. administration specifically assigned to the General Assembly (e.g., the budget), resolutions of the General Assembly are recommendations only and are not formally binding on members,[93]

---

[92] Katzenbach, in Levy, *supra* note 10, at 69, 78.

[93] "[A] resolution or declaration by the General Assembly was certainly not law-making in the sense that a treaty, convention or declaration formally ratified by Governments was." Australian representative, U.N. Outer Space Comm. A/AC.105/ C. 2/SR. 23 (Apr. 25, 1963), p. 4.

On the effects of U.N. resolutions generally, see Lande, "The Changing Effectiveness of General Assembly Resolutions," 1964 *Proceedings, Am. Soc'y Int'l L.* 162 ff.; Higgins, *The*

a brief special analysis of the outer space resolutions is necessary, although for parties to the 1967 Space Treaty much contained in the resolution will now be "treaty law."

No one of these resolutions purports, by its own terms, to be legally binding on members. Thus, Resolution 1721A "commends" to states "for their guidance" certain "principles." Resolution 1962 is a "Declaration" in which the General Assembly *"solemnly declares* that . . . States should be guided by [certain] principles."[94] Resolution 1884 calls upon all states "to refrain" from placing weapons of mass destruction in outer space. No new legal obligation was created, a point noted and regretted at the time by some representatives at the United Nations.[95]

Nevertheless, at least the first two resolutions just noted have been called the "first chapter in the book of space law."[96] And Jenks, while noting that the declara-

tion (Resolution 1962) "is somewhat less than a treaty," goes on to call it "rather more than a statement of custom" and uses it in his noteworthy volume on *Space Law* as "the Twelve Tables of the Law of Space."[97]

The argument that the principles of these resolutions are *now* the law rests on a combination of factors. All agree that General Assembly resolutions are normally in themselves only recommendations, but the "space" resolutions were unanimously accepted and it is argued that they thus indicate the view of all these states with respect to appropriate state action. The United States Representative, Ambassador Plimpton, told the U.N.'s Committee on the Peaceful Uses of Outer Space that the principles in the resolution (1721) were "the basic foundation of a legal regime for outer space,"[98] and that "in the General Assembly's unanimous approval of the outer space resolution, all the Members of the United Nations have committed themselves to basic principles

Development of International Law Through the Political Organs of the United Nations (1963); Bindschedler, "La délimitation des compétences aux Nations Unis," 108 *Hague Recueil* 305 (1963); Vallat, "The Competence of the United Nations General Assembly," 97 *Hague Recueil* 203 (1959); Tammes, "Decisions of International Organs as a Source of International Law," 94 *Hague Recueil* 265 (1958); Gross, "The United Nations and the Role of Law," 19 *Int'l Org.* 537, 555 ff. (1965); Virally, "La valeur juridique des recommandations des organizations internationales," 2 *Annuaire Français de Droit International* 66 (1956); Johnson, "The Effect of Resolutions of the General Assembly of the United Nations," 32 *Brit. Yrbk. Int'l L.* 97–123 (1955–56); Schwartzenberger, 1 *Int'l L.* 539 ff. (2d. ed. 1949); Sloan, "The Binding Force of a Recommendation of the General Assembly of the United Nations," 25 *Brit. Yrbk. Int'l L.* 1–33 (1948); Falk, "On the Quasi-Legislative Competence of the General Assembly," 60 *Am. J. Int'l L.* 782 (1966). See also Tunkin, *Droit International Publique* 101–12 (1965).

[94] On the lack of special significance of the use of the term "declaration," see Cheng, "United Nations Resolutions on Outer Space . . . ," *supra* note 78, at 23, 31 ff.

[95] See, e.g., comments by the representatives of Austria and India, A/5549/Add. 1 at 21, 28 (Nov. 27, 1963).

[96] See the comment of the Canadian representative, A/C. 1/SR. 1346 at 189 (Dec. 5, 1963) (*in re* Res. 1962). To the same effect, see also, e.g., Gardner, "Outer Space: A Breakthrough for International Law," 50 *ABAJ* 30 (1964); speech of Quincy Wright, U. of Texas Law School, Mar. 12, 1966. Cf. *contra* F. B. Schick, "Problems of a Space Law in the United Nations," 13 *Int'l Comp. L.Q.* 969 (1964). See generally Lissitzyn, *supra* note 79. For extensive consideration of the effects of Resolution 1962, see also the report of Goedhuis, *supra* note 2, including his memorandum and the text of replies to his questionnaire received from various members of the committee, including Bodenschatz, Chauveau,

Cooper, Fasan, Guerreri, Huber, Lissitzyn, Meyer, Pepin, Zylics, and Zhukov. Opinions differed among members of the committee as to whether the resolution was binding. There was also a lively discussion at the ILA's 1964 meeting. Ghanem (U.A.R.), for one, argued that the declaration was not the equivalent of legal rules. Lissitzyn, Chauveau, and Zylics were more affirmative. See 1964 *Proceedings, Int'l L. Ass'n (Tokyo)* 638, 666–68. See also McMahon, *supra* note 72, at 352–536; Csabafi, "The U.N. General Assembly Resolution on Outer Space as Sources of Law," 1965 *Proceedings of the Eighth Colloquium on the Law of Outer Space* 357–61 (Haley & Schwartz eds., Sept. 1965) (strong evidence of interpretation of international law); Schachter, "The Relation of Law, Politics and Action in the United Nations," 109 *Hague Recueil*, Vol 2, 185, 187–88 (1963); Vallat, *supra* note 93, at 230; and Vlasic, "Law and Public Order in Space: A Balance Sheet," paper prepared for the Washington Conference on World Peace through Law, 1965, who states that the U.N. resolutions are "the appropriate channel for setting standards of conduct in this new medium."

As regards Resolution 1721 A, see, e.g., Schachter, in *Law and Politics in Space* 96 ff. (Cohen ed. 1964) [hereinafter cited as Cohen], and McDougal, in *id.*, at 115; Jenks, "Le droit international des espaces célestes—rapport preliminaire," 50 *Annuaire de l'Institut* 321 ff. (1963).

[97] *Space Law,* 186 (1965).

[98] A/AC. 105/PV. 2, at 33–35 (May 4, 1962). Commenting generally on unanimously adopted resolutions, the Office of Legal Affairs of the United Nations stated in a 1962 memorandum that while a resolution cannot be made binding upon member states in the sense that a treaty is binding upon them "in view of the greater solemnity and significance of a 'declaration,' it may be considered to impart, on the part of the organ adopting it, a strong expectation that members of the international community will abide by it. Consequently, in so far as the expectation is gradually justified by state practice, a

of the greatest significance." Moreover, as Oscar Schachter has written:[99]

I do not think that the only alternative to customary law is treaty law, even though in a formal sense these are the two sources of international law. It seems to me that the declarations adopted with general approval by the United Nations General Assembly which purport to set in terms of legal authority standards of conduct for States, can be regarded as an expression of "law" which is regarded as authoritative by governments and peoples throughout the world. The formalist may say these declarations are "only" evidence of international custom, but whether one characterizes the declarations in these terms or in terms of accepted law the effect is substantially the same. We have seen this manifested in regard to resolution 1721 dealing with outer space.

Even before the resolutions, Becker, commenting on the failure of states to protest the passage of satellites, stated that: "It is perhaps not too bold to suggest that we are here viewing the initial stages of development of a principle of customary international law permitting the orbiting of [peaceful] satellites."[100]

To this uniform concurrence in an expression of what the law is (or at least should be) is added the uniform practice of states before and after the resolutions. Several hundred satellites have been orbited without prior requests for permission and without formal objection by subjacent states during the IGY and thereafter, and scores are in orbit now. This admittedly limited but uniform practice, coupled with the intent made clear in the resolutions and public statements of government officials, have already given rise to rules not of principle but of law in the view of many governments, including that of the United States, as well as of the many commentators noted.

Arguments against this rapid development of customary law include the following:[101] (1) no state has thus far indicated at what exact heights its sovereignty ends;

(2) only two states have engaged in *major* outer space activities and what suits those who have not participated may not suit them when they begin to participate; (3) one major space power, the USSR, and one minor space power, France, are at least doubtful that "law" has been thus created; (4) the time is too short—there must not only be general practice, but an opportunity for states to convince themselves that the practice is reasonable and suitable to their probable needs; (5) the alleged rules are not clear enough to be workable rules leading to an inviolate custom—how we distinguish the permissible ("peaceful") uses of space, for example. These issues are not novel. On the question of numbers and time, Lauterpacht once wrote:

. . . the lengths of time within which the customary rule of international law comes to fruition is irrelevant. For customary international law is not yet another expression for prescription. . . .

. . . A consistent and uniform usage practiced by the states in question—to use the language of the International Court of Justice in the Asylum case—can be picked within a short space of years. . . .

. . . assuming that we are confronted here with the creation of new international law by custom, what matters is not so much the number of states participating in its creation and the length of the period within which that change takes place, as the relative importance, in any particular sphere, of states inaugurating the change.[102]

It is not just the United States and the Soviet Union which have participated. Many others are partners and participants in space activities: France, Italy, and Australia have launched satellites; all states have refrained from objecting or even reserving positions when satellites have passed overhead; almost all have participated in U.N. discussions and resolutions. Unless it can be shown that all this conduct was not accompanied by the intention that it have legal significance, "it would appear that the accurate principle . . . consists in regarding all uniform conduct of Governments (or, in appropriate cases, abstention therefrom) as evidencing the *opinio necessitatis juris.*"[103]

It is also true that, in history, states have on occasion

---

declaration may by custom become recognized as laying down rules binding upon states."

[99] Cohen, *supra* note 96, at 98.

[100] Becker, *supra* note 76, at 4, 29 (1959). To the same effect, see also *Report of the Ad Hoc Committee on the Peaceful Uses of Outer Space*, A/4141 at 63–64, 68 (1959); Lipson & Katzenbach, *supra* note 2, at 20–21.

[101] For a learned discussion of the creation of "instant" customary law, see Cheng, "United Nations Resolutions on Outer Space . . . ," *supra* note 78, at 23, 35 ff. See also, e.g., Note, "National Sovereignty of Outer Space," 74 *Harv. L. Rev.* 1167–68; McMahon, *supra* note 72, at 354–55.

---

[102] Lauterpacht, "Sovereignty Over Submarine Areas," 27 *Brit. Yrbk. Int'l L.* 393–95 (1957). See also Brierly, *The Law of Nations* (Waldock ed., 6th ed. 1962); "The Asylum Case," *I.C.J. Reports* 276–77 (1950).

[103] Lauterpacht, *The Development of International Law by the International Court* 380 (1958). See also *id.* at 379–81, 386–92; MacGibbon, "Customary International Law and Acquiescence," 33 *Brit. Yrbk. Int'l L.* 115, esp. 125–31 (1957).

been held to be bound even by unilateral declaration.[104] Thus, states voicing approval of these resolutions might be confronted by the argument that, binding or not in an original formal sense, they are "estopped" from deviating from the policies announced in the resolutions.[105] The Charter of course says nothing about such effects of Assembly resolutions.

The United States, at least since Resolution 1721 of 1961, has espoused the view that the principles of the freedom of outer space, the nonappropriability of celestial bodies, the applicability of international law to outer space activities, and other broad principles enunciated in the resolutions, are already rules of customary international law. On August 6, 1962, the Secretary of State told the Senate Foreign Relations Committee:

. . . although the resolution "commends" the principles to member states, the United States takes the position that these principles are presently the law; the unanimous action of the General Assembly in adopting the resolution, as action by the governments of the world assembled, confirmed this view.[106]

The next year, Leonard Meeker, the legal adviser of the Department of State, in representing the United States in the April 22, 1963, meeting of the Legal Subcommittee of the U.N. Committee on the Peaceful Uses of Outer Space, stated similarly:

When a General Assembly resolution proclaimed principles of international law—as Resolution No. 1721 (XVI) had done—and was adopted unanimously, it represented the law as generally accepted in the international community.[107]

In the General Assembly's First Committee, it was said:

[The United States Government] considered the legal principles contained in the operative part of the draft declaration reflected international law as accepted by Members of the United Nations. The United States intended to respect them and hoped the conduct they recommended in the exploration of outer space would become the practice of all nations.[108]

The key principles were thus again referred to as "international law."

Many other states seem more or less to accept the view that the resolutions by and large may by now be taken as evidencing what *is* the law,[109] whether they are "law creating" or "evidence" of customary law.[110] The principles of Resolution 1721 were "supported" by some countries including Poland,[111] and "subscribed to" by the United Kingdom.[112] The British representative noted at another time that "although . . . resolutions of the General Assembly were not . . . binding upon Member States—a resolution if adopted unanimously, would be most authoritative."[113] At one time at least, an Indian representative was more direct and argued that "a declaration had moral force and, when adopted unanimously, was generally accepted as part of international law."[114] And the Canadian representative said of the draft which became Resolution 1962: "The legal principles contained in it reflected international law as it was currently accepted by Member States."[115] A more traditional and careful view was expressed by the Australian representative: "It is our view that a declaration of legal principles by the General Assembly, especially if universally adopted and adhered to in practice, may be valuable evidence of international custom, which in turn is a most important source of law."[116]

It is also interesting that the Office of Legal Affairs of the United Nations, while noting that "there is probably no difference between a 'recommendation' or a 'declaration' in United Nations practice as far as strict legal principle is concerned," went on to say that there is a "greater solemnity and significance" to a declaration and that, consequently, "a declaration may by custom be-

---

[104] On the "Ihlen Declaration," see the Eastern Greenland Case, *supra* note 66.

[105] See, e.g., Cheng, *supra* at note 78, for arguments pro and con.

[106] Testimony of Secretary of State Rusk, *State Press Release, No. 490,* Aug. 6, 1962, at 8–10; *State Dept. Bull.* 315, 318 (No. 47, 1962), reprinted in 57 *Am. J. Int'l L.* 127–28 (Jan. 1963). See also U.N. Doc. A/AC. 105/PV 2 at 13–15 (Mar. 19, 1962).

[107] See A/AC. 105/PV. 2/ SR. 20 at 10–11 (Apr. 22, 1963).

[108] A/C. 1/SR. 1342 at 159 (Dec. 2, 1963). A somewhat stronger statement appears in the provisional records to the

effect that "[The United States Government] considered that the legal principles contained in the draft Declaration reflected international law as accepted by Members of the United Nations, and it was prepared to accept them." See A/C. 1/PV. 1342 at 3, 12 (Dec. 2, 1963).

[109] See generally Jenks, *supra* note 10, at 183–85.

[110] See statement of the Italian representative, A/AC. 105/PV. 38 at 49 (6 Oct. 1965).

[111] A/AC. 105/C. 2/SR. 6 at 7 (June 6, 1962).

[112] A/AC. 105/PV. 3 at 33–40 (Mar. 20, 1962) and A/AC. 105/C. 2/SR. at 3 (Mar. 30, 1962).

[113] A/C. 105/C. 2/SR. 17 at 9 (Apr. 17, 1963). See also A/C. 105/C. 2/SR. 24 at 13 (Apr. 29, 1963).

[114] A/AC. 105/C. 2/SR. 22 at 10 (June 24, 1963).

[115] A/AC. 1/SR. 1346 at 189 (Dec. 5, 1963).

[116] A/AC. 105/PV. 24 at 18 (Nov. 22, 1963). See also U.N. Doc. A/5549/Add. 1 at 15 (Nov. 27, 1963).

come recognized as laying down rules binding upon States."[117] This tends at least to be sympathetic to the rapid emergence of customary rules in this field.

A lesser number of states has more consistently urged that the resolutions are mere recommendations and do not necessarily reflect already accepted binding rules. Among these, the most noteworthy is France, with respect to Resolutions 1721[118] and 1962.[119] Romania also expressed this view.[120]

The French representative, for example, in contrasting the effects of a "recommendation" with those of a treaty, noted that the latter would have

. . . the advantages of conferring incontestably binding force on any regulations adopted. It was quite possible that with time the current enthusiasm about the achievements of astronauts might wane. When damage was caused by a space vehicle which made an emergency landing, the State in whose territory he landed might be tempted to treat the astronaut involved as a criminal, to arrest him and to impound the space vehicle. A General Assembly resolution might in such circumstances not be a legally operative instrument for ensuring different treatment.[121]

In 1963 the French representative also stated that, "while supporting the principles set forth in the draft declaration. . . , he wishes to stress that the latter could not be looked on as more than a statement of intention; legal obligations *stricto sensu* could only flow from international agreements, and an international law of outer space had yet to be created."[122] The U.A.R. and Czechoslovakian representatives also would have preferred a "more binding document" in 1963,[123] but no other representative agreed formally with the French position that the declaration was a mere "declaration of intent."

Russian writers and government spokesmen have not been entirely consistent about the development of customary rules of law for outer space. Initially, in general, they have been unsympathetic. Korovin, for example,

felt that there was little hope that customary international law would soon emerge.

First, one of the requisites for the formation of rules of customary law is the long duration and universality of their application, a requirement clearly inapplicable with regard to a new, just emerging field of law, actually practiced by only two states. Second, the approach to the exploration of space by these two states [USSR, U.S.] is far from identical.[124]

Similarly, Zhukov has written:

The opinion, expressed by a number of authors, that irrespective of the existence or absence of international agreements on concrete questions rules of customary international space law could be formed on the basis of activities of separate states in outer space, does not rest on sufficient grounds.[125]

And yet the same author has written that the combination of a declaration through the United Nations, coupled with supporting statements by the United States and the Soviet Union, meant that the states had imposed certain commitments on themselves and that the 1961 resolution represented "important principles of space law."[126] In 1962, after the adoption of Resolution 1721 (XVI), the Soviet representative came closer to granting the principles embodied in the resolution the force of present law. Thus, at one point, Tunkin stated:

Resolution 1721A (XVI) laid down certain principles which were binding upon all States with respect to activities in outer space. The States Members of the United Nations had clearly shown by their unanimous approval of the resolution that they recognized the need to lay down binding legal principles. But surely such general principles should not be confined to those laid down in the General Assembly resolution.[127]

At another time, it was said:

In its declaration the Soviet Union proposed as a tenet of international law that no state could claim sovereignty over outer space or celestial bodies, and reaffirmed that they

---

[117] Memorandum of the United Nations Office of Legal Affairs on the use of the terms "Declaration and Recommendation," U.N. Doc. E/CN. 4/L. 610 at 1–2 (Apr. 2, 1962).

[118] See A/AC. 105/PV. 3 at 48 (Mar. 3, 1962).

[119] See A/C. 1/SR. 1345 at 183 (Dec. 5, 1963). Alex Meyer apparently concurs in this view. See Meyer, "Comments on 'Space Law' by G. W. Jenks," 14 *ZLW* 347–50 (1965).

[120] A/AC. 105/PV.8 at 13–15 (Mar. 27, 1962).

[121] A/AC. 105/C.2SR. 9 at 2 (June 12, 1962).

[122] A/C.1/SR.1345 at 183 (Dec. 5, 1963).

[123] A/C. 1/SR.1345 at 182 (Dec. 5, 1963); A/C. 1/SR. 1342 at 163 (Dec. 2, 1963).

[124] Korovin, *supra* note 25, at 61.

[125] Zhukov, *supra* note 74, at 10–11.

[126] Zhukov, "Practical Problems of Space Law," 9 *Int'l Aff.* 27 (Moscow, May 1963).

[127] A/AC. 105/C. 2/SR. 14 at 2 (June 19, 1962). He has elsewhere stated that General Assembly resolutions adopted by unanimous vote or with the concurrence of the major world power groups can operate as stages in the development of rules of international law. Tunkin, *Voprosy Teorii Mezhdunarodnogo Prava* [Problems of the Theory of International Law] 134 (1962); *accord*, Kozhenikov in *Mezhdunarodnoe Pravo* [International Law] 43 (Kozhevnikov ed. 1964).

were free for exploration and use by all States. The Soviet Union regarded its success in outer space as an achievement not only of the Soviet people but of all mankind, and reaffirmed its support of the principle contained in Resolution 1721 (XVI), which should be given the force of an international treaty.[128]

Other statements concerning Resolution 1721 are perhaps more typical of the general Soviet view toward General Assembly resolutions. At various times, it has been said that Resolution 1721, in accordance with the provisions of the charter, is merely a "recommendation"[129] and that it "unfortunately is not yet a legal obligation on the part of States."[130]

Later in a somewhat ambiguous statement in the outer space committee which was discussing the draft of Resolution 1962, the Soviet representative also stated: I must remark with great satisfaction that the majority of the members of the Committee who took part in the debate did not challenge the propositions included in the draft declaration, and consequently it may be assumed that they are acceptable to all the members of the Committee. Therefore, giving all the remarks made here their due, I think we must assume—indeed, those who made the remarks proceeded on this assumption—that in the matter of international legal regulation it is impossible to compel any State to accept a particular proposition, if for any reason it is still not prepared to do so.[131]

Perhaps for the Soviet Union also, the unanimous approval of a resolution apparently gave it a special status. Thus, with respect to the draft which emerged as Resolution 1962, the Soviet representative stated:

The United States representative had said that in his Government's view the legal principles contained in the draft declaration reflected international law as accepted by the Members of the United Nations and that the United States for its part intended to respect them. The Soviet Union, in its turn, undertook also to respect the principles enunciated in the draft declaration if it were unanimously accepted.[132]

Discussions in the Legal Subcommittee in 1965 also found the Soviet representatives, as well as those from the United States and other countries, treating the declaration as if it embodied existing rules of international law.[133] One rather curious fact must also be noted with respect to Resolution 1884 (XVIII) concerning the placing in space of weapons of mass destruction. Here, the form was definitely an exhortation, which followed U.S.-USSR concurrence in this approach. "This resolution does not purport to state the existing law or to create any new obligation."[134] Yet Zhukov has written that this resolution, plus the oral declarations of the United States and the Soviet Union, have created a "peculiar form of international agreement, judicially binding for the sides party to it."[135] If this is current Soviet thinking, it gives substantial status to the General Assembly's action at this point in history.

These statements are not as clear as one might wish. Soviet practice has in fact been consistent with the principles of the resolutions. The Soviet Union has never sought permission beforehand from any state to orbit its satellites "over" that state; it has not formally protested the passage over it of satellites; it has not made claims to the celestial bodies.

Overall then, the major principles of the outer space resolutions to date are accepted as present customary law in the official statements of one of the major space powers and of many other nations, and it is not clear that this concept is rejected by the Soviet Union. Between "customary" law and estoppel, it would seem to be arguable that most nations are legally bound by at least the major, broad, general principles contained in the United Nations resolutions discussed above. The implications of this technique of the creation of what is almost "instant" customary law are not limited to rules concerning outer space activities and need far more detailed legal-political study than is appropriate here. The efficacy and danger of this technique must, of course, also be scrutinized more carefully since the events of the summer of 1965 when the United States dropped its fight to compel all U.N. members to pay peacekeeping costs and pointed out to the membership that, from then on, it reserved its right to refuse recognition even to assessments by the Assembly if it had strong and compelling

---

[128] A/AC. 105/C. 2/SR. 7 at 4 (Aug. 21, 1962).

[129] A/AC. 105/PV. 10 at 41 (Sept. 10, 1962), and see A/C. 1/SR. 1289 at 215 (Dec. 3, 1962).

[130] A/AC. 105/PV. 15 at 11 (Sept. 14, 1962).

[131] A/AC. 105/PV. 24 at 23 (Nov. 22, 1963).

[132] A/C. 1/SR. 1342 at 161 (Dec. 2, 1963). See also the Soviet comments on the need for and effect of unanimity in the Outer Space Committee, A/AC. 105/PV. 15 at 28 (Sept. 14, 1962).

[133] See, e.g., A/AC. 105/C. 2/SR. 46 (Sept. 23, 1965). USSR: A/AC. 105/C. 2/SR. 48 (Sept. 29, 1965). USSR: A/AC. 105/C. 2/SR. 52 (Sept. 1965). Czechoslovakia: A/AC. 105/C. 2/SR. 46 at 3 (Sept. 23, 1965). U.S.A.: 4/AC. 105/PV. 37 (Nov. 5, 1965).

[134] Jenks, *supra* note 10, at 303.

[135] Zhukov, "Atomic Demilitarization of the Cosmos," 34 *SGP* 79, 80 (1964). Generally on the weapons in space resolution see Gotlieb, *supra* note 39, *passim,* esp. 20–24, 28–34 (a "moral" obligation at least).

reasons for doing so. Although these comments were not addressed specifically to Assembly declarations of legal principles,[136] they inevitably cast a shadow over any assertion of even a quasi-rule-making power in the United Nations.

The Legal Status of Artificial Bodies in Space and of Space Stations and Equipment on the Celestial Bodies

The Status of Space Vehicles

In considering the legal status of artificial bodies in space, including orbiting satellites, space platforms, stations and, in time, powered spacecraft, there are again analogies, depending on the type of vehicle. For the orbiting vehicles, there are anchored lightships and Texas towers. For manned maneuverable vehicles, in particular, there are the ships on the high seas and aircraft over the high seas. For portions of launch assemblies, nonfunctioning vehicles, fragments, debris, and the like, there are the rules of salvage.[137]

The status of man-made bodies in space which are "national" in origin presents a different set of problems than does the status of celestial bodies since initial problems of control and exclusive possession will arise.[138]

The aim of writers addressing themselves to this issue has been essentially to create techniques that will avoid conflict and interference in what states now regard, or may come to regard, as their exclusive rights.[139]

The question of status is important for resolving such questions as jurisdiction over the spacecraft proper and over acts committed on board. Analogies from air law and the law of the sea, both of which place primary emphasis on the "nationality" of the craft, the country of its flag or registration, or perhaps today its actual ownership will prove helpful.[140] State aircraft, for example, have the nationality of the state, whereas civil aircraft have that of the state of "registration." At times it has also been suggested that jurisdiction over acts aboard a civil aircraft might be taken by the state over which the craft was flying when the act occurred, by that of the last takeoff, or by that of the first landing.[141] As we have seen, some states have been slow to apply their own laws on the basis of the nationality of an aircraft. Thus, the United States made its law applicable to American planes over the high seas only in 1952, establishing the jurisdiction of the United States courts over *some* crimes on board.[142]

---

[136] The actual terms used were addressed to the financial crisis at hand but were broad in scope: "[the United States] must make crystal clear that, if any member can insist on making an exception to the principle of collective financial responsibility with respect to certain activities of the organization, the United States reserves the same option to make exceptions if, in our view, strong and compelling reasons exist for doing so. There can be no double standard among the members of the organization." Statement by Ambassador Goldberg in the Special Committee on Peace-keeping Operations, Aug. 16, 1965. For text see *New York Times,* Aug. 17, 1965, at 6.

[137] On salvage and the legal implications of the removal of man-made objects from space, see Hall, "Comments on Salvage and Removal of Man-Made Objects from Outer Space," 33 *J. Air L. & Commerce* 288 (1967); Haley, "Space Salvage—Artifacts and Personnel in Space and on Terrestrial Jurisdictions," 1966 *Proceedings of the Eighth Colloquium on the Law of Outer Space* 119–30 (Haley & Schwartz eds. 1966). These issues are discussed only in passing herein.

[138] See Lipson & Katzenbach, *supra* note 2, at 20–21 and sources cited. McDougal *et al., supra* note 2, deal with these problems at length in their chap. 5 which should be consulted for all questions of the nationality of and control over space vehicles. See also Verplaetse, "Definition and Legal Status of Spacecraft," 29 *J. Air L. & Commerce* 131 (1963) and "Previews on the Legal Status of Spacecraft," 14 *Transporte*

Aerei 3–13 (1965); Jennings, "The Legal Status of Space Vehicles," *Report of the Space Law Committee to the International Law Association,* Annex III (1964). See *Report, id.,* at 710–15 and 715–25. See also, among papers (mimeo.) submitted to the Ninth Colloquium of the IISL (1966): Horsford, "The Need for a Moon Treaty and Clarification of the Legal Status of Space Vehicles" and "The Juridical Regime of Craft and Space Installations." See also Sztucki, "Legal Status of Space Objects," in *Proceedings of the Eighth Colloquium on the Law of Outer Space* 444–55 (Haley & Schwartz eds. 1966).

[139] Among writers on the issue of space vehicles not otherwise cited herein, see: Gabrovski, "The Cosmos, Peace and Sovereignty," *SGP* 84 (1962); Korovin, *supra* note 26, at 61; Hartwig, *supra* note 10, at 1593; Markov, *supra* note 17, at 327; Osnitskaya, "The Conquest of Space and International Law" (State Publishing House of Legal Literature, Moscow, 1962), and *supra* note 2, at 63; Vago, *supra* note 17, at 185. For an early discussion of the problems of a space station, see Romano, *Proceedings, Seventh International Astronautical Congress* 145–54 (Rome, 1956).

[140] See McDougal *et al., supra* note 2, chap. 5. On aircraft, see especially *Report on Nationality and Registration of Aircraft with Special Reference to Article 77 of the 1944 Chicago Convention. . . . ,* John Cobb Cooper, Rapporteur, with Preface by Bin Cheng, Int'l Law Ass'n, 1966 Conference.

[141] See generally Fenston & De Saussure, 1 *McGill L.J.* 66 (1952).

[142] See 66 Stat. 589, added July 12, 1952. For comment, see "Draft of a Convention on the Legal Status of Aircraft

Ships "have the nationality of the state whose flag they are entitled to fly," and on the high seas the exclusive jurisdiction of the flag state is normally recognized over the ship and acts occurring thereon.[143] One problem which is still largely unresolved today is the regime applicable to a vessel flying the flag of an international organization, since the organization lacks a "legal system" like that of a state.[144] This problem may in time arise for international spacecraft as well.[145]

In the General Assembly's major space resolution of 1963 (1962, XVIII), the problem of "ownership" was dealt with in these terms:

7. The State on whose registry an object launched into outer space is carried shall retain jurisdiction and control over such object, and any personnel thereon, while in outer space. Ownership of objects launched into outer space, and of their component parts, is not affected by their passage through outer space or by their return to earth. Such objects or component parts found beyond the limits of the State of registry shall be returned to that State, which shall furnish identifying data upon request prior to return.

Similarly, the 1967 Space Treaty in Article VIII provides:

A State Party to the Treaty on whose registry an object launched into outer space is carried shall retain jurisdiction and control over such object, and over any personnel there-of, while in outer space or on a celestial body. Ownership of objects launched into outer space, including objects landed or constructed on a celestial body, and of their component parts, is not affected by their presence in outer space or on a celestial body or by their return to the earth. Such objects or component parts found beyond the limits of the State Party to the Treaty on whose registry they are carried shall be returned to that State, which shall, upon request, furnish identifying data prior to their return.

In addition, the treaty on Rescue and Return of Astronautics and Space Objects,[146] signed on April 22, 1968, by forty-four nations, provides absolutely in its Article V that objects launched into outer space or their component parts, when found in another state or anywhere beyond the territorial jurisdiction of the "launching authority,"[147] "shall be returned to or held at the disposal of representatives of the launching authority." While certain provisos are included, e.g., that expenses incurred in recovering or returning a space object shall be borne by the launching authority, the treaty makes it clear that the object at all times remains the property of the launching authority. This treaty thus elaborates on the 1967 Outer Space Treaty.[148] Even without the more formal international conventions covering the matter, there appears to have been international agreement that a space vehicle belongs to the launching state or the state causing the launch,[149] although in formal terms it belongs to the

---

and of Crimes Committed on Board of Aircraft," 25 *J. Air L. & Commerce* 455 ff. (1968).

[143] Convention on the High Seas, Arts. 5, 6 (1958); Jacobini, 6 *West. P.Q.* 680 (1953); Jenks,. "International Law and Activities in Space," 5 *Int'l Comp. L.Q.* 99, 109 (1956); Reiff, *The United States and the Treaty Law of the Sea* 34–35, 76–80 (1959); 1 Oppenheim, *International Law* 541 (Lauterpacht ed., 8th ed. 1955). On piracy, see Convention on the High Seas, Arts. 14–22; "Piracy Laws of Various Countries," 26 *Am. J. Int'l L.* 893–902 (Supp. 1932); Reiff, *supra*, at 76. On other problems and analogies, see Convention on the High Seas, Arts. 14–22; Ward, *supra* note 49, at 3–8.

[144] Article 7 of the Convention on the High Seas of 1958 provides that: "The provisions of the preceding articles do not prejudice the question of ships employed on the official service of an inter-governmental organization flying the flag of the organization."

[145] See also report by François, Special Rapporteur for the Int'l Law Comm., "The Right of International Organizations to Sail Vessels under their Flags," A/CN. 4/104 (May 8, 1956). Some trawlers built with the aid of UNKRA flew the U.N. and Korean flags in 1955. I *UN Rev.* (1954). Note that the 1968 Treaty on Rescue and Return, discussed in the pages which follow, clearly expects international organizations to be around the "launching authorities." For an introduction to these problems in U.N. space discussions, see *infra* Appendix D.

[146] The Treaty is in General Assembly Resolution 2345 (XXII), Dec. 19, 1967, printed in 58 *Dept. State Bull.* 85 (1968). For a full analysis, see Dembling and Arons, "The Treaty on Rescue and Return of Astronauts and Space Objects," 9 *Wm. & Mary L.R.* 630 (1968). On the treaty see also Report of the Legal Sub-committee of the U.N. Space Committee, U.N. Doc. A/AC. 105/43 (15 Dec. 1967), *New York Times*, Dec. 17, 1967, at 1, Dec. 18, 1967 (editorial) and Dec. 21, 1967, at 29. The text is included in Appendix E.

[147] Note that this treaty defines "launching authority" in Article 6 so as to include international organizations. For discussion, see Appendix D and Dembling and Arons, *supra* note 146, at 658–59.

[148] For comment, see *id.,* at 653–57.

[149] See Haley, "Basic Concepts of Space Law: The Unmanned Earth Satellite," presented at the 25th Meeting of the American Rocket Society, Chicago, Illinois, in Nov. 1955; and the following in *1961 Symposium, supra* note 3: Galina, "On the Question of Interplanetary Law," at 1057; Osnitskaya, "International Law Problems of the Conquest of Space," at 1094; Korovin, "Conquest of Outer Space and Some Problems of International Relations," at 1074.

Some earlier suggestions were to the effect that satellites at least be considered as *res derelicta,* or as a shipwreck or a bottle in the sea (Danier & Saporta, "Un nouveau problème de droit aérien, les satellites artificiels," 18 *Revue Générale*

state of "registry"; presumably the terms normally apply to the same state for the foreseeable future. Representatives of the United States and the Soviet Union have been in general accord on this point, at least since the Geneva meetings on outer space in 1962.[150]

Return of Spacecraft

A concomitance of national ownership would appear to be the right to demand the return of a space vehicle or its remains which had been forced to land or had crashed on another state's territory. As noted just above, this is dealt with in the Treaty on Rescue and Return of 1968. The launching authority would also have a duty to pay necessary costs of the recovery and would have some duty to make recompense for damages caused by a space vehicle. The latter point is covered in Article VIII of Resolution 1962 and in Article XI of the 1967 Space Treaty, and it is dealt with extensively in chapter 6 of this study. The problem of the return of space vehicles and personnel is also dealt with in part in Appendix D.

In considering the problems inherent in the return of downed spacecraft, the Soviet Union at one time insisted that an exception should be made for "space vehicles aboard which devices have been discovered for the collection of intelligence information of another state" and insisted that such vehicles need not be returned.[151] The United States was unwilling to accept this exception,[152]

and Resolution 1962, the 1967 Outer Space Treaty, and the 1968 Treaty on Rescue and Return have no such limitations in their texts.

In practice, off-course or damaged civil aircraft and ships are usually returned by friendly nations but this is often said to be a matter for specific agreement or of comity.[153] The United States has urged, with respect to craft downed by Communist bloc countries, that there is a *duty* to return aircraft forced off their path in distress. There is also a general policy of return for craft stolen in another nation or seized by pirates or mutineers.[154]

Such "space" practice as exists includes at least one return of a portion of an orbital vehicle. The part of Sputnik IV which was found in Manitowoc, Wisconsin, in September 1962, was returned to Russia through the Soviet Embassy in Washington in January 1963.[155] As noted earlier in this study, the Soviet Union's treatment of aerial "intruders"—aircraft and balloons—has not been encouraging from the point of view of early return, but an occasional space intruder may be placed in a different category.[156]

---

de l'Air 297, 301 [1955]) or that they should be analogized to balloons, meteorites (Levitt, "Space Age Questions: Who Owns a Fallen Satellite?" *U.S. Military Rev.*, pt. 1 [July 19, 1958] and *U.S. Military Rev.*, pt. 3 [July 26, 1959] or even to a bullet or a buoy on the sea (Machowski, "The Legal Status of Unmanned Space Vehicles," *1959 Proceedings, 2d Colloquium IISL* [London, 1959]). For post-treaty comment, see Dembling and Arons, *supra* note 146, at 655, note 77.

[150] See, e.g., USSR Draft International Agreement on the Rescue of Astronauts and Spaceships Making Emergency Landings, Art. 7, A/AC. 105/L.3 (Sept. 10, 1962) [hereinafter cited as USSR Draft Agr't]; U.S.A. Draft Proposal on Assistance and Return of Space Vehicles and Personnel, Art. 2, A/AC. 105/L.4 (Sept. 11, 1962). See also U.A.R. Code for International Co-operation in the Peaceful Uses of Outer Space, Art. 5, A/AC. 105/L.6, (Sept. 14, 1962).

[151] See USSR Draft Agr't, Art. 7 (2), A/AC. 105/L. 3 (Sept. 10, 1962).

[152] See, however, the earlier statement made by Becker in 1958 that the return of such vehicle would require a "policy" decision.

Fragments of American rockets have apparently fallen on Cuba (1960), South Africa (1962), and Venezuela (1967). No damage has been reported (except for the claimed destruction of a Cuban cow) nor has the disposition of the remnants been

an issue. See McDougal *et al.*, *supra* note 2, at 519, note 6. On reports of Russian debris in Spain, see *Washington Evening Star*, Dec. 22, 1965. On American debris in Venezuela, see *New York Times*, Jan. 26, 1967 at 14.

On the status of a downed spacecraft, esp. under German law, see Rudolf, "Are Unmanned Spacecraft or Parts Thereof, Fallen on Foreign Territory, To Be Returned?" 9 *ZLW* 273–86 (1960).

[153] See Memorandum of the Secretariat: Conventions and International Agreements on Rescue of and Assistance to Aircraft and Vessels in Distress and Their Personnel, A/AC. 105/C. 2/2 (June 12, 1962). See also Goedhuis, "Assistance to, and Rescue of, Astronauts and Space Vehicles in Distress," Annex VI to *Report of the Space Law Comm. to the Int'l Law Ass'n* (Tokyo, 1964).

On personnel, the Report of the Ad Hoc Committee stated that: "It was also considered that certain substantive rules of international law already exist concerning rights and duties with respect to aircraft and airmen landing on foreign territory through accident, mistake, or distress. The opinion was expressed that such rules might be applied in the event of similar landings of space vehicles." A/4141 at 67 (July 14, 1959). See also statement of Legal Adviser Becker of May 7, 1959, at 7–8; *Dept. State Bull.* 885, 890 (No. 1042, June 15, 1959).

[154] Lissitzyn, "Treatment of Aerial Intruders in Recent Practice and International Law," 47 *Am. J. Int'l L.* 559 ff. (1953). With respect to ships in distress, see Jessup, *The Law of Territorial Waters and Maritime Jurisdiction*, 194–208, 220–21, 254–55, 258–63, 450, 466 (1927).

[155] On the Manitowoc fragment, see Frutkin, *International Cooperation in Space* 148–49 (1965).

[156] See Lissitzyn, *supra* note 154; Cheng, "International

Identification of Spacecraft

As with ships and aircraft, the mere statement that a spacecraft belongs to the launching state or launching authority, or to the state for which a vehicle is launched, or to the state of registry does not resolve all difficulties. How are vehicles to be identified, especially before the day when overhaul and inspection in space becomes possible? What of launches which states deny? What is the status of vehicles prepared by one country and launched by another? The United States, for example, has several times placed satellites in orbit for other countries and the Soviet Union has proposed doing the same. There will also, prospectively, be launches by multinational and perhaps by broad-based international organizations.

In the 1959 report of the U.N.'s Ad Hoc Committee, it was suggested that the identification of space vehicles was a current problem:

[I]dentification . . . could be obtained by agreement on an allocation of individual call signs to these vehicles . . . Another means of identification is by orbital or transit characteristics. . . .

18. As part of the problem of identification, there arises the problem of placing suitable markings on space vehicles so that . . . they may be readily identified.

19. Identification would be facilitated by a system of registration of the launching of space vehicles, their call signs, markings, and current orbital and transit characteristics.[157]

The United States thereafter supported the concept of a registry at the United Nations.[158]

In general international law it has long been argued that "a State is absolutely independent in framing the rules concerning the claim of vessels to its flag,"[159] and this important concept is at the base of the identification problem. At the present time the two major space powers apparently use markings of some sort on all the space vehicles they launch.[160] In 1962, the United States ob-

jected to the proposal that this type of identification be a condition precedent to the return of a downed spacecraft, however.[161] Note that the 1968 Treaty on Rescue and Return provides, in Article 5(3), that the launching authority which claims the return of a vehicle is obliged to furnish "identifying data" on request.

As noted, artificial satellites may also be identified through orbital characteristics which could be registered. It now seems more likely that spacecraft will be subjected to the practice of having nationality based on registration.[162] Thus, as we have seen, the 1963 U.N. resolution (1962) and the 1967 Space Treaty speak of a listing on a registry as the basis of control.

Aviation law offers well-known precedents. The 1944 Chicago Convention, for example, provides:

Article 17

Aircraft shall have the nationality of the State in which they are registered.

Article 19

The registration or transfer of registration of aircraft in any contracting State shall be made in accordance with its laws and regulations.

In sea law, registration is also the key to the benefits and privileges of nationality. In general, in the terms of the International Load Line Convention of 1930,[163] Article 3(a), "a ship is regarded as belonging to a country if it is registered by the Government of that country." Moreover, the 1961 U.N. resolution (1721), *inter alia*:

Calls upon states launching objects into orbit or beyond to furnish information promptly to the Committee on the Peaceful Uses of Outer Space, through the Secretary-General, for the registration of launchings;

Requests the Secretary-General to maintain a public registry of the information furnished in accordance with paragraph 1 above.

This resolution does not provide for the *effects* of regis-

Law and High Altitude Flights: Balloons, Rockets and Man-Made Satellites," 6 *Int'l & Comp. L.Q.* 487 (1957).

[157] A/4141 at 6. Reprinted in 2 Whiteman, *supra* note 2, at 1306.

[158] See, e.g., statement of Ambassador Stevenson of Dec. 4, 1961, *Dept. State Bull.* 180, 182 (No. 46, Jan. 29, 1962).

[159] Oppenheim, *supra* note 143, at 29. See Art. 5 of the Convention on the High Seas. For comment, see McDougal *et al., supra* note 2, at 550 ff.

[160] Zhukov, *supra* note 74, at 29. On identification through use of visual markings, call signs, orbits, or orbital characteristics and registration, see Report of the Legal Committee, at

6. See also McDougal, "Artificial Satellites: A Modest Proposal," 51 *Am. J. Int'l L.* 74 (1957). In general, see also ABA Comm. on the Law of Outer Space, "Registration and Traffic Control of Space Vehicles," *Final Committee Report* (mimeo., June 25, 1965) [hereinafter cited as ABA Comm. Report].

[161] A/AC. 105/C. 2/SR. 7 at 10 (Aug. 21, 1962).

[162] On registration of spacecraft, see ABA Comm. Report, *supra* note 160, in *1965 Proceedings of the Section of Int'l and Comp. Law* 248 ff.; and Cheng, "From Air Law to Space Law," 13 *Current Legal Problems* 228, 244 (London, 1960).

[163] Hudson, *International Legislation* 639 (1936). It is also apparently the case that an unregistered vessel may be arrested by the vessels of any nation.

tration, in which area there is the analogous, extensive experience of ships and aircraft;[164] and the 1963 resolution and the 1967 Space Treaty provide for control based on a *national* registry. In any event, compliance has not been perfect. Both the United States and the Soviet Union have accused the other of failure to provide full information and of failing to register all launches.[165] The existing registry, even if all states comply with the suggestion for registration, leaves questions open.[166] One issue, the meaning of "launching state" in the sense of the assignment of rights and obligations was, as we have seen, clarified in part by the language used in Resolution 1962, which seems to indicate that "ownership" is attached to the "State on whose registry an object launched into outer space is carried" (para. 6), whereas liability for damage can be assessed against "each State which launches or procures the launching of an object into outer space, and each state from whose territory or facility an object is launched" (para. 8). The 1967 Space Treaty uses the same language (Articles VII, VIII). Doubtless, "further clarification of the position in cases in which there may be doubt which State is responsible and entitled to jurisdiction and control will be necessary."[167]

---

[164] This experience in analogous fields is, by intent, not reviewed here. See, e.g., McDougal *et al., supra* note 2, at 549 ff.

[165] On the U.S. charge that the USSR had failed to register at least 6 space vehicles, see letter of June 6, 1963, A/Cc. 105/15 at 2, 3. See also Zhukov, *supra* note 74. The United States reports its military launchings but by code designation without particulars. On the types of information given by various countries and the like, see Jenks, *supra* note 10, 219 ff. and sources cited. The term "promptly" is taken to mean *after* the launch only. See, e.g., Korovin, *supra* note 26, at 61, 63. Note that France, Italy, and Australia have registered launches with the U.N.

[166] On the possible confusion between registration purely for "census" purposes and for attribution of nationality purposes see McDougal *et al., supra* note 2, at 564 ff.

[167] Jenks, *supra* note 10, at 236. See also pp. 236–39 for comments on the problems of an international registry. See also his criticisms of the resolution of the Institute of International Law on this point. Note too the language used in the 1968 Rescue and Return Treaty, discussed hereafter.
The David Davies Institute has proposed a comprehensive agreement on these points as follows:
5.1. Subject to the provisions of Section 5.2, every spacecraft shall be registered in a State, in accordance with its laws and regulations, and also with the United Nations Committee on the Peaceful Uses of Outer Space.
5.2. Every spacecraft to be launched by an international body shall be registered with the Committee on the

In one major situation, the 1968 Treaty on Rescue and Return provides a distinct clarification. Article 6 provides:

For the purposes of this Agreement, the term "launching authority" shall refer to the State responsible for launching, or, where an international inter-governmental organization is responsible for launching, that organization provided that that organization declares its acceptance of the rights and obligations provided for in this Agreement and a majority of the States members of that organization are Contracting Parties to this Agreement and to the Treaty on Principles Governing the Activities of States in the Exploration and Use of Outer Space, including the Moon and Other Celestial Bodies.

Thus, an international organization may receive the benefits and incur the obligations of the treaty. Note that this definition makes no mention of any "registry" of a space vehicle, so rights and duties do not depend on whether or not a vehicle is listed on a particular registry.

One special point which is also discussed in chapter 6 must be noted. Whatever the original markings, it is possible that space vehicles which remain in orbit for a long time may lose all possibility of identification from the orbit. Also, if the satellite or parts of it come back to earth, external identification is very likely to be burned off. There have been suggestions that the only method of making positive identification of the metal parts of spacecraft would be to use some trace element in a specified quantity as a specific signature.

Probably until such time as space technology has advanced far beyond what it is at present, the difficulties of identification will be with the spacecraft's return to earth, rather than while it is in orbit. As long as it is in orbit, the external markings will probably suffice, provided the spacecraft can be sighted and inspected while still in orbit, before it has suffered the erosion of a fiery entry. Nevertheless, it is also possible that registration

---

Peaceful Uses of Outer Space, which shall issue a registration mark.
5.3. For all purposes including that of any claim concerning the activities of a spacecraft:
a. every spacecraft to which Section 5.1 applies shall be deemed to have the nationality of the State in which it has been registered, and whose nationality and registration mark it bears, or in the absence of such registration, of the State responsible for its launching and
b. throughout its life shall, with its component parts, so long as they are identifiable, be deemed, in the absence of special agreement, to be the property of the State concerned under Section 5.3a or of the international body registering it, as the case may be.

will prove inadequate because of the danger that a nation not wanting to be identified with its particular spacecraft would fail to register it, and it might be extremely difficult to prove the origin of the craft. Even with the trace-element signatures in the metal, it would be extremely difficult because one nation might use the signature of another nation with the deliberate intent of avoiding identification. In the event of deliberate attempt at confusion, the molecular-structure identification of metal by the process of determining how the metal was worked would be unreliable.

There are no further provisions in United Nations resolutions or in the 1967 Space Treaty on the point of the form of markings, although a state claiming the return of a space object is to "furnish identifying data upon request" (para. 7, 1963 resolution, Article VIII of the 1967 Treaty, respectively; and see Article 5(3) of the 1968 Treaty). The Institute of International Law has proposed that "every space object shall bear marks of identification showing its origin and use call signals making it possible to identify the State under the authority of which the launching took place."[168] Ships, aircraft, motor vehicles are all now required by international practice and regulations to carry identifying marks and, where appropriate, to use identifying signals. There is no reason to doubt that, in time, space vehicles will be treated similarly.

Commercial Spacecraft

One division in attitudes between East and West over spacecraft became particularly acute following the American decision to permit the creation of a commercial satellite-communications corporation. This dispute was of wider scope than a simple communist-capitalist divergence. It also involved the right of international organizations to have space-going capabilities.

The 1962 draft declaration of principles proposed by the Soviet Union provided: "All activities of any kind pertaining to the exploration and use of outer space shall be carried out solely and exclusively by states."[169] The Soviet representative argued:

Another important need was to ensure that scientific and technological advances, such as communication satellites, were used exclusively for the betterment of mankind. His delegation therefore proposed that there should be an agree-

ment providing that outer space was not to be used for propagating war, national or racial hatred, or enmity between nations. If no such agreement were reached, the whole system of long-distance communication by means of artificial satellites would be jeopardized. In capitalist countries radio corporations intended to explore outer space on their own account. If they could do as they wished, private capitalistic competition would displace international co-operation. His delegation therefore considered that all exploration and use of outer space should be carried out solely and exclusively by States.[170]

Soviet writers and spokesmen have continued this approach with their sharpest barbs aimed at the Communications Satellite Corporation and the American Telephone and Telegraph Company.[171]

Not surprisingly, this effort to introduce socialist principles of exclusive state ownership into outer space activities was rejected by the Western states.[172] The attempt to exclude international organizations, the United Nations and regional groups such as ESRO and ELDO, was not acceptable either, and the 1963 U.N. resolution (1962, para. 5) mentions "non-governmental" entities and international organizations only to the effect that:

States bear international responsibility for national activities in outer space, whether carried on by governmental agencies *or by non-governmental entities,* and for assuring that national activities are carried on in conformity with the principles set forth in the present Declaration. *The activities of non-governmental entities in outer space shall require authorization and continuing supervision by the State concerned. When activities are carried on in outer space by an international organization, responsibility for compliance with the principles set forth in this Declaration shall be borne by the international organization and by the States participating in it.* [Italics added.]

Similarly, the 1967 Space Treaty, Article VI, provides:

States Parties to the Treaty shall bear international responsibility for national activities in outer space, including the moon and other celestial bodies, whether such activities are carried on by governmental agencies *or by non-governmental entities,* and for assuring that national activities are carried out in conformity with the provisions set forth in the present Treaty. *The activities of non-governmental entities in outer space, including the moon and other celestial bodies, shall require authorization and continuing supervision by the State concerned. When activities are carried*

---

[168] Resolution on the Legal Regime of Outer Space, para. 4, Sept. 11, 1963, reprinted in Jenks, *supra* note 10, at 416.

[169] A/AC. 195/L.2, para. 7 (Sept. 10, 1962).

[170] Tunkin, A/AC. 105/C. 2/SR. 7 at 5 (Aug. 21, 1962).

[171] See, e.g., Zhukov, *supra* note 74, at 25.

[172] See, e.g., A/AC. 105/C. 2/SR. 10 at 3 (Aug. 21, 1962) (U.K.); A/AC. 105/C. 2/SR. 9 at 3 (France); A/AC. 105/C. 2/SR. 9 at 6 (Canada); A/AC. 105/C. 2/SR. at 9 (U.S.A.).

on in outer space, including the moon and other celestial bodies, by an international organization, responsibility for compliance with this Treaty shall be borne both by the international organization and by the States Parties to the Treaty participating in such organization. [Italics added.]

These provisions for state responsibility would seem to meet the legitimate questions raised by the Soviet Union in connection with private space uses. Presumably, the nations will be able to comply with an international standard through internal controls and regulation of domestic corporations and individuals engaging in such activities.[173] Chapter 5 explores these matters further.

Application of Certain Laws Involving Other Definitions

Although not necessarily helping to resolve problems of definition respecting spacecraft, provisions of some other existing laws may have to be taken into account, a few of which are merely noted here. The relevance of the 1944 Chicago Convention on Civil Aviation, for example, has been discussed generally earlier. There is in Article 8, however, a provision that "no aircraft capable of being flown without a pilot shall be flown without a pilot over the territory of a contracting state without special authorization by that state." Does this encompass spacecraft, at least while at low altitudes?[174] As noted earlier, the problem of spacecraft while in airspace has already brought forth a substantial literature.

The definition of aircraft in American law also tends to be broader than in the law of many countries. At one time, Loftus Becker stated, with respect to the meaning of aircraft in U.S. domestic law: "Aircraft means any contrivance now known, or hereafter invented designed

for navigation . . . in the air. . . . I would take the position that that provision, regardless of any provision of the Chicago Convention, would cover a missile or any object regardless of the method of propulsion."[175]

Doubtless as spacecraft and airspace hybrid vehicles become more common, more questions of definition will be found. Some are noted throughout this study. There is no "space" practice to date to point the way to specific solutions, however.

Stations and Instruments on the Celestial Bodies

Although the major powers have, as we have seen, apparently been prepared to date to create a non-national regime for the celestial bodies, their view has always been that objects they placed on those bodies and stations there would be owned and/or controlled by them and would be "national" in that sense. This position has been uniformly taken and held, and there is no reason at present to doubt that it is the operating concept for space operations today.

Article VIII of the 1967 Space Treaty, for example, provides that, *inter alia,* jurisdiction and control over space objects remain in the state of registry while the objects or their parts are on celestial bodies, including objects constructed there. The control is modified somewhat by Article XII:

> All stations, installations, equipment and space vehicles on the moon and other celestial bodies shall be open to representatives of other States Parties to the Treaty on a basis of reciprocity. Such representatives shall give reasonable advance notice of a projected visit, in order that appropriate consultations may be held and that maximum precautions may be taken to assure safety and to avoid interference with normal operations in the facility to be visited.

There is thus no absolute right to unlimited free inspection, a question discussed above.

The acceptance of national character eliminates many of the possible questions of ownership, liability, and responsibility (e.g., for avoiding contamination, for removing debris, for jurisdiction for many purposes) which would, in time, be sure to arise. If national character is subordinated in fact to a duty to share internationally the fruits of national operations, it is a reasonable way to proceed, although it partakes of the potential difficulties inherent in a self-policed, self-denying regime discussed earlier.[176]

---

[173] On the controls over the operations of the ComSat Corporation, see chap. 5 *infra.* The David Davies Draft Code on exploration suggests that "no spacecraft shall be operated by private persons or corporations save by license granted by the State of which they are nationals."

As noted in the text, it should be recalled that the 1968 Treaty on Rescue and Return expressly provides that international inter-governmental organizations can be included as "launching authorities" for purposes of the Treaty.

[174] See, e.g., Verplaetse, "The Relation of Air Law to Space Law," paper presented to the Seventh Colloquium IISL 12–13 (mimeo. Warsaw, 1964), who rejects Article 8 as controlling on the basis that spacecraft simply are *not* aircraft or state vehicles in any event. On the applicability of the Chicago Convention to missiles and satellites, see also Machowski, *supra* note 149, in *1961 Symposium, supra* note 3, at 1204–12; Cheng, *supra* note 162, at 228–54; and the International Law Association, *Report on the 50th Conference,* Annex II, p. 288 (Hamburg, 1960).

[175] *Hearings on H.R. 11881* at 1275.

[176] As is discussed more fully in Appendix D, the 1967

The Astronaut

In the present, difficult stage of space exploration, the astronaut has been, and for some time no doubt will continue to be, an international hero and the subject of wide international goodwill. Problems of jurisdiction over and control of the astronaut's actions are not especially difficult with only a few states conducting space operations, and would not be much more complex if small, multinational expeditions should succeed the present national efforts. This area of jurisdiction over personnel and acts on board a space vehicle or at a space station is closely related to the well-known problems of control over nationals outside the national territory and of jurisdiction over ships, aircraft, and bases in remote, "non-national" areas such as Antarctica.[177] These points have all been discussed earlier in chapter 3.

The issue which is currently of most international concern with respect to astronauts is that of ensuring their safe return in the event of an error or mishap in landing, either in a country other than their own or in a remote area. The U.N.'s 1963 resolution (1962, para. 9) indicated the existing high regard for astronauts and the concern over their recovery by providing:

> States shall regard astronauts as envoys of mankind in outer space, and shall render to them all possible assistance in the event of accident, distress, or emergency landing on the territory of a foreign State or on the high seas. Astronauts who make such a landing shall be safely and promptly returned to the State of registry of their space vehicle.

At present, the state of registry, as used here, coincides in all cases with the state of the astronaut's nationality. This may change in time with multinational crews, but by then more formal treaty arrangements are likely to be in effect which can easily avoid any problems of this type.

There has been remarkably little discord over the general principles of assistance and safe conduct.[178] This approach was suggested in the literature[179] and in earlier suggestions by states. A Soviet Union draft, International

---

Space Treaty, for example, does *not* require parties to share *all* information. Article XI thus provides: "In order to promote international co-operation in the peaceful exploration and use of outer space, States Parties to the Treaty conducting activities in outer space, including the moon and other celestial bodies, agree to inform the Secretary-General of the United Nations as well as the public and the international scientific community, *to the greatest extent feasible and practicable,* of the nature, conduct, locations, and results of such activities. On receiving the said information, the Secretary-General of the United Nations should be prepared to disseminate it immediately and effectively." [Italics added.]

There is no specific provision for the sharing of *other* gains from space operations.

[177] It should be recalled that Resolution 1962 (XVIII) of 1963 provided, inter alia, in para. 7 that: "The State on whose registry an object launched into outer space is carried shall retain jurisdiction and control over such object, *and any personnel thereon,* while in outer space. [Italics added].
Article VIII of the 1967 Space Treaty uses the same language emphasized above.

In these early days, the launching State in all manned flights and the state of nationality have been one and the same. In time, this may well change. Other bases for asserting jurisdiction over the astronaut could include: nationality, launching state, state procuring the launch, state of landing, state affected by the astronaut's acts, any state, if the acts are equivalent to piracy or the like. See discussion on bases of jurisdiction in chap. 3.

By way of comparison, the Antarctic Treaty of 1959 provides in Art. 8 that:

"1. In order to facilitate the exercise of their functions under the present treaty, and without prejudice to the respective positions of the contracting parties relating to jurisdiction over all other persons in Antarctica, observers designated under Paragraph 1 of Article 7 and scientific personnel exchanged under Subparagraph 1(b) of Article 3 of the treaty, and member of the staffs accompanying any such persons, *shall*

be subject only to the jurisdiction of the contracting parties of which they are nationals in respect to all acts or omissions occurring while they are in Antarctica for the purpose of exercising their functions. [Italics added.]

"2. Without prejudice to the provisions of Paragraph 1 of this . . . the contracting parties concerned in any case of dispute with regard to the exercise of jurisdiction in Antarctica shall immediately consult together with a view to reaching a mutually acceptable solution."

On the subject of criminal jurisdiction in Antarctica, see the comprehensive article by Bilder, "Control of Criminal Conduct in Antarctica," 52 *Va. L. Rev.* 231 (1966).

[178] There may, however, be some confusion over the use of the term "envoys" in the 1963 resolution and the 1967 Space Treaty since the term has a normal usage in international dealings. It presumably was not meant to confer a diplomatic status on astronauts for any real purpose. For discussion, see Jenks, *supra* note 10, at 246–47.

[179] The Institute of International Law, for example, suggested in its 1963 resolution that states take appropriate measures for mutual assistance among astronauts, for mutual cooperation among states on behalf of astronauts, and for prompt repatriation (Para. 8). On the 1963 resolution of the Institute of International Law, see Chaumont, "The Brussels Resolution on Space Law . . . ," 15 *ZLW* 20–35 (1965) and Briggs, 58 *Am. J. Int'l L.* 114–22 (1964). See also McDougal *et al., supra* note 2, at 580 ff.; Jenks, *supra* note 10, at 246–50; memoranda by Goedhuis, *supra* note 153; and Zhukov, Annex VI to *Proceedings of the 51st Annual Meeting,* Int'l L. Ass'n, and *id.,* at 771–76 (1964).

Agreement on the Rescue of Astronauts and Spaceships Making Emergency Landings, presented in 1962, provided (*inter alia*):

Art. 1. Each contracting state shall render assistance to the crews of spaceships which have met with an accident and shall take steps to rescue astronauts making an emergency landing; to this end it shall employ every means at its disposal including electronic and optical facilities of different kind.

Art. 2. A contracting state which discovers that the crew of a spacecraft of another contracting state has met with an accident shall do its utmost to notify the launching state without delay.

Art. 3. In the event of astronauts of a contracting state making an emergency landing on the territory of another contracting state, the latter shall immediately inform the launching state of the occurrence and shall take all possible steps to rescue the astronauts making the emergency landing and to render them the necessary assistance.

Art. 4. If the astronauts are presumed to have made an emergency descent on high seas, a joint search for them shall be made, if necessary, by those contracting states to which the launching state may make application.

Art. 5. The assistance to be furnished when necessary by one contracting state to another contracting state shall in no way differ from the assistance which could be furnished to its own astronauts.

Art. 6. Such contracting state shall do its utmost to facilitate the early return to their own country of any astronauts of another contracting state who may make an emergency landing on its territory or who may be rescued on the high seas.

Art. 7. The expense incurred by a state in fulfilling the obligations provided for in article 6 . . . of the agreement shall be reimbursed by the launching state.[180]

At the same time, the United States proposed:

1. All possible assistance shall be rendered to the personnel of space vehicles, that land by reason of accident, distress or mistake or otherwise than as planned.

2. Space vehicles, and their personnel in the case of manned vehicles, that land by reason of accident, distress or mistake or otherwise than as planned shall be safely and promptly returned to the state or states or international organization responsible for launching.

3. Any expense incurred in providing assistance to or return of space vehicles and their personnel shall be borne by the state or states or international organization responsible for launching.[181]

In 1963, after adopting the broad resolution on space activities, the General Assembly asked its Committee on the Peaceful Uses of Outer Space to arrange, as a matter of priority, for the prompt preparation of a draft convention on international assistance.[182] In October 1964 that committee's legal subcommittee reached tentative agreement on the notification of accidents and assistance within the territory of a party. Included were specifications for notification to the launching state and to the UN Secretary-General by any state with knowledge of an accident or the like, for rescue and assistance on the basis of treatment it would accord its own nationals, and for cooperative efforts where needed. While no overall agreement could be reached for several years on certain more general obligations about the return of astronauts, the efforts to reach agreement were successful in 1967 with the results noted hereafter.[183]

This subject is also included in a broad statement in the 1967 Space Treaty. Article V thus provides:

States Parties to the Treaty shall regard astronauts as envoys of mankind in outer space and shall render to them all possible assistance in the event of accident, distress, or emergency landing on the territory of another State Party or on the high seas. When astronauts make such a landing, they shall be safely and promptly returned to the State of registry of their space vehicle.

In carrying on activities in outer space and on celestial bodies, the astronauts of one State Party shall render all possible assistance to the astronauts of other States Parties.

States Parties to the Treaty shall immediately inform the other States Parties to the Treaty or the Secretary-General of the United Nations of any phenomena they discover in outer space, including the moon and other celestial bodies, which could constitute a danger to the life or health of astronauts.

The 1968 Treaty on Rescue and Return deals specifically with this subject as a prime concern.[184] Its first four articles provide:

Article 1

Each Contracting Party which receives information or discovers that the personnel of a spacecraft have suffered accident or are experiencing conditions of distress or have made an emergency or unintended landing in territory under its jurisdiction or on the high seas or in any other place not under the jurisdiction of any State shall immediately:

(a) notify the launching authority or, if it cannot identify

---

[180] A/5181, Annex III at 2 (Sept. 27, 1962).

[181] A/5181, Annex III at 4 (Sept. 27, 1962). A draft code submitted by the United Arab Republic at the same time was similar. *Id.* at 6. See also note 150 *supra.*

[182] Resolution 1963 (XVIII) of Dec. 13, 1963.

[183] See Appendix D for a full discussion. A convenient summary of various early proposals and tentative agreements is in Jenks, *supra* note 10, Appendix XII, 446 ff.

[184] For background and comment, see Appendix D and Dembling & Arons, *supra* note 146, at 630–63.

and immediately communicate with the launching authority, immediately make a public announcement by all appropriate means of communication at its disposal; and

(b) notify the Secretary-General of the United Nations who should disseminate the information without delay by all appropriate means of communication at his disposal.

Article 2

If, owing to accident, distress, emergency or unintended landing, the personnel of a spacecraft land in territory under the jurisdiction of a Contracting Party, it shall immediately take all possible steps to rescue them and render them all necessary assistance. It shall inform the launching authority and also the Secretary-General of the United Nations of the steps it is taking and their progress. If assistance by the launching authority would help to effect a prompt rescue or would contribute substantially to the effectiveness of search and rescue operations, the launching authority shall co-operate with the Contracting Party with a view to the effective conduct of search and rescue operations. Such operations shall be subject to the direction and control of the Contracting Party, which shall act in close and continuing consultation with the launching authority.

Article 3

If information is received or it is discovered that the personnel of a spacecraft have alighted on the high seas or in any other place not under the jurisdiction of any State, those Contracting Parties which are in a position to do so shall, if necessary, extend assistance in search and rescue operations for such personnel to assure their speedy rescue. They shall inform the launching authority and the Secretary-General of the United Nations of the steps they are taking and of their progress.

Article 4

If, owing to accident, distress, emergency or unintended landing, the personnel of a spacecraft land in territory under the jurisdiction of a Contracting Party or have been found on the high seas or in any other place not under the jurisdiction of any State, they shall be safely and promptly returned to representatives of the launching authority.

The emphasis on humanitarian concern is clear; unlike the provisions respecting the return of space vehicles, the issue of reimbursement for rescue operations is not even raised. The duty of notification is made clear and express; *all* personnel aboard space vehicles are covered; the need for speed is asserted; states are to take "all possible steps" to effect a rescue; [185] "unintended" as well as land-

ings due to accident are included; the resources of the launching authority will be available as needed;[186] and rescue operations on the high seas and "any other place not under the jurisdiction of any State," which would seem to include Antarctica and the celestial bodies, are included.[187] Moreover, the duty to return is unqualified, though cynics may note that no specific definition of a "prompt" return is included.[188] The intent seems clear, nevertheless. The return need not be to another country; the astronaut may be turned over to representatives of the launching authority.

Overall, the intents and purposes of the 1968 Treaty are in most cases readily determinable. For the foreseeable future, the major potential problem areas are likely to be those caused by landing on the territory of a non-party to the Treaty (e.g., Communist China) and by the test of good faith which will be occasioned by an accident to an astronaut on a demonstrably "military" mission.

It is important that the Soviet Union has not to date raised the same issue about astronauts that it argued about space vehicles; that is, it has not tried to categorize astronauts by the nature of their mission or by the type of spacecraft used. Yet there is no evidence that this more generous attitude would extend to astronauts engaged in a specifically hostile mission, as defined by the Soviet Union.[189] Considering the consensus to date and the past history of cooperation in search and rescue work on earth, it appears likely that the 1968 Treaty on Rescue and Return will give astronauts the same broad assistance as has been the case in similar humanitarian pursuits in other fields.[190]

---

[185] For aircraft, analogous provisions of treaties (e.g., Article 25 of the 1944 Chicago Convention, 61 Stat. 1180, *T.I.A.S.* No. 1591 [1947] generally provide only for such assistance as states "may find practicable." In practice, there will probably be little difference.

[186] The territorial sovereignty of the state of landing is nevertheless not subject to uninvited infringement. See statement of Ambassador Goldberg, U.S./U.N. Press Release 246, Dec. 16, 1967.

[187] On rescues on the seas in general, see Dembling & Arons, *supra* note 146, at 649–651. On all these points, see *id.* at 641–653.

[188] See *New York Times,* Dec. 18, 1967 (editorial).

[189] On precedents from aerial approaches over or near the Soviet Union, see Lissitzyn, "Some Legal Implications of the U-2 and RB-47 Incidents," 56 *Am. J. Int'l L.* 135 ff. (1962); Cheng, "The United Nations and Outer Space," 14 *Current Legal Problems* 268–72 (1961).

[190] Compare the Safety of Life at Sea Convention, 164 *U.N.T.S.* 332 (1953) and the Search and Rescue Annexes (12 and 13) to the International Civil Aviation Convention. For comment on these precedents, see Jenks, *supra* note 10, at 249–50.

For the need of a space rescue service, see, e.g., *New York Times,* Mar. 21, 1966, at 30M. On the problems of locating and rescuing the astronauts of Voskhod II

A Special Problem in Definition:
Space Uses as "Peaceful," "Military," "Aggressive"

In chapter 2 we noted that the principal "actual and potential" military uses of a space-going capacity included the testing of ballistic missiles, which pass through "outer space" at least briefly; observation for military purposes; the placing of military stations or weapons in space; the establishment of military space communications, navigational and meteorological satellite systems; and the like. While it is obvious that national military-prestige interests engineered the initial thrust into space, most writers and government spokesmen are in agreement that man's use of outer space should be confined to "peaceful" uses. Thus, the question of the definition of "peaceful" has frequently been raised by officials as well as by commentators. In this, the problem is identical with or similar to other political problems of definition: "peaceful coexistence," the "peaceful" uses of atomic energy,[191] the meaning of "aggression," and so on.

The problem is not eased by frequent use of the term "peaceful" in international conferences, presentations, and arrangements dealing with outer space uses. Specific reference to the banning of the use of outer space for military purposes was made, for example, both by the United States and the Soviet Union as early as 1957. In his State of the Union message on January 10, 1957, President Eisenhower said that the United States was willing to enter into an agreement to control outer space, missiles, and satellite development. Following this statement, U.S. representatives at the discussions on disarmament in the U.N. General Assembly's Political Committee proposed that the testing of outer space objects be subjected to international inspection and control.

This proposal was pursued during meetings of the U.N.'s Disarmament Commission in 1957. At the twelfth session of the General Assembly, a resolution was adopted calling for a "joint study of an inspection system designed to ensure that the sending of objects through outer space shall be exclusively for *peaceful* and scientific purposes."[192] Most states have continued to urge that the military use of outer space be treated as a part of the general problem of disarmament,[193] and both the American and Soviet draft treaties on general disarmament have dealt with arms in outer space.[194] Soviet writers have also carried the logic one step further and argued at times that general international cooperation in outer space cannot be divorced from the disarmament issue.[195]

The term "peaceful" was also used in the title and in the terms of reference of the U.N.'s Ad Hoc Committee on the Peaceful Uses of Outer Space and in those of its successor, the Committee on the Peaceful Uses of Outer Space, as well.[196] It appears in General Assembly Resolution 1721 (XVI) of 1961 on International Cooperation in the Peaceful Uses of Outer Space, in which the General Assembly recognizes "the common interest of mankind in furthering the peaceful uses of outer space." The 1963 Resolution on Legal Principles (1962, XVIII) does not use the term "peaceful" in its title or body but does in its preamble: "The General Assembly . . . [recognizes] the common interest of all mankind in the progress of the exploration and use of outer space for peaceful

---

Bulganin, Chairman of the Council of Ministers of the USSR, dated Jan. 12, 1958, 38 *Dept. State Bull.*, at 122, 126 (No. 970, Jan. 27, 1958); another letter from President Eisenhower to Chairman Bulganin, dated Feb. 15, 1958, 38 *Dept. State Bull.*, at 1035, 1037 (No. 991, June 23, 1958); statement of Ambassador Lodge in Committee I of the General Assembly of the U.N. on Nov. 12, 1958, 39 *Dept. State Bull.*, at 972, 974 (No. 1016, Dec. 15, 1958); "Five Power Working Paper on General Disarmament," dated Mar. 14, 1960, submitted to the Conference of the Ten-Nation Committee on Disarmament (Geneva, 1960), Dept. of State Press Release, No. 120, Mar. 14, 1960; address of President Eisenhower at the U.N., Sept. 22, 1960, 43 *Dept. State Bull.*, at 551, 554–55 (No. 1111, Oct. 10, 1960).

[193] See, e.g., A/AC. 105/C.2/SR. at 2 (Aug. 21, 1962).

[194] See, e.g., the 1962 draft treaties: Soviet draft, Art. 15; U.S. draft, Pt. D. On the U.S. draft, see A/C. 1/875 (Nov. 9, 1962).

[195] Korovin, *supra* note 26, at 61–62, quotes Premier Khrushchev as saying: "I can only conclude that the solution of any and every essential problem concerning the international regulation of space activity cannot be separated from general and complete disarmament which is the basic prerequisite of all-round international cooperation." See also, in general, Zhukov, "The United Nations and Peaceful Use of Outer Space," 3 *Soviet Yrbk. Int'l L.* 186 (1960).

[196] See also A/C. 1/L. 220, Nov. 13, 1958, at 2, and A/C. 1/L. 220/Rev. 1, 21 at 3 (Nov. 1958). Cf. statements by U.S. delegate H. C. Lodge and then-Senator Lyndon Johnson before the United Nations, in 39 *Dept. State Bull.*, at 972–81 (Dec. 15, 1958).

---

from a snowed-in area of the Urals, see *Washington Post*, Mar. 10, 1966, at A4.

[191] On the "space-atom" and the "space-seas" analogy, see Lipson & Katzenbach, *supra* note 2, at 24–27. It will be recalled that "peaceful coexistence" does not for the Communists rule out "wars of national liberation," that is, broadly speaking, anti-Western wars.

[192] Resolution 1148 (XII), Nov. 14, 1957 (italics added). See also, e.g., letter from President Eisenhower to Nikolai

purposes." There has not been any authoritative attempt to define "peaceful" in any of these proceedings.[197]

It may be argued that "peaceful" in the sense of the United Nations Charter and in normal use in international law means the opposite of "aggressive," no more.[198] It has been so used by the Congress of the United States in dealing with outer space activities.[199] The seas have always been considered available under international law for peaceful military uses including transportation, gunnery practice, and even the testing of missiles and naval maneuvers which close off whole areas of the seas, often for extended periods.[200] The Antarctic Treaty of 1959 which prohibits military activities in that continent nevertheless expressly exempts the use of military personnel and equipment "for scientific research or any other peaceful purpose."[201] In a similar way, United States military and naval forces aid NASA in its manned flight program. For the first Mercury flight, 24 ships, 126 aircraft, and 18,000 persons were involved; for Cooper's flight in May 1963, the figure rose to 29 ships, 171 aircraft, and over 18,000 persons.[202] Soviet complaints that the vast majority of U.S. space flights are in fact for "military" and "espionage" purposes have already been discussed in chapter 2.

For these and other reasons, the United States and many other nations have insisted that the term "peaceful" used in connection with outer space activities means nonaggressive, not nonmilitary.[203] It is also true, of course, that *all* United States missions are considered by the United States to be "peaceful." Thus, Edward G. Welsh, Executive Secretary of the National Space Council, stated: "All of our programs are peaceful. The Defense Department's activities are to maintain the peace; NASA's are to enable us to live better in peace."[204] To this, the Defense Department's Manned Orbiting Laboratory would not be an exception.[205]

---

[197] On the confusing use of the term "peaceful" in these and other resolutions and reports, see McDougal *et al.*, *supra* note 2, at 395–97.

[198] Lipson & Katzenbach, *supra* note 2, at 24–30; Katzenbach, in Levy, *supra* note 10, at 77; "By 'peaceful' we mean nonaggressive, not necessarily nonmilitary." McMahon, *supra* note 72, at 339, 360; Quadri, "Droit international cosmique," 89 *Recueil des Cours III*, 505 at 571 (1959); Feldman, "Report of the United Nations Legal Committee on the Peaceful Uses of Outer Space: A Provisional Appraisal," 1959 *Proceedings, Second Colloquium IISL* 19, 23 (1959); *Report of the Brighton Space Assembly* (May 1962); David Davies Memorial Institute, *supra* note 45, at 7; Goedhuis, Report, Int'l Law Ass'n, *Report of the 50th Conference*, at 78 and sources cited (Brussels, 1962); Meyer, *supra* note 119, at 347–50; Cooper, "The MOL: A Major Legal and Political Decision," 51 *A.B.A.J.* 1137–40 (Dec. 1965).

On "peaceful," see also McDougal & Lipson, "Perspectives for a Law of Outer Space," 52 *Am. J. Int'l L.* 430–31 (1958). Sir L. K. Munro, "The Control of Outer Space and the United Nations," *Space Law—a Symposium*, 380 (1958); Horsford, "Principles of International Law in Space Flight," 5 *St. Louis U. L. J.* 70–78 (1958); Rhyne, *supra* note 63, at 6152, 6154.

[199] E.g., sec. 102 (a) of the National Aeronautics and Space Act of 1958, provides: "The Congress hereby declares that it is the policy of the United States that activities in space should be devoted to peaceful purposes for the benefit of all mankind." 72 *Stat.* 426; 42 *U.S.C.*, sec. 2451.

[200] See Jessup & Taubenfeld, *supra* note 3, at 210–12; McMahon, *supra* note 72, at 361. On Soviet tests in 1967, see *Washington Evening Star*, Nov. 27, 1967, at A.5.

[201] Treaty, Art. I. On similar provisions in the 1967 Space Treaty, see *infra* at notes 215 and 219.

[202] See Levy, *supra* note 10, at 62–63. Of course, it is also true that NASA programs are of great help to the armed forces in developing boosters, techniques, instruments, materials, etc. *ibid.* On the utility of NASA's expertise in the Air Force MOL program, see speech of Oct. 28, 1964 by Welsh to the American Ordinance Association, Oct. 28, 1965, quoted in *Astronautics and Aeronautics, 1964*, at 494 (1965). See also *Tech. Wk.*, Nov. 14, 1966, at 54. In 1964, NASA and the DOD agreed to exchange experts for training in each other's programs. *Av. Wk. & Space Tech.* 25 (April 25, 1966) reported that by Apr. 1966, 184 USAF, 78 Army, 25 Navy, and 6 USMC officers had been assigned to NASA, while one NASA official was then technical director of the USAF's Manned Orbiting Laboratory (MOL) program. See also, *supra*, chap. 2.

[203] Katzenbach, in Levy, *supra*, note 10, at 77.

[204] Quoted in *Missiles & Rockets*, Jan. 8, 1962, at 12.

[205] With respect to the MOL, Welsh has also stated: "Since I have mentioned the Manned Orbiting Laboratory, it is worth pausing right now to challenge forthrightly those who have asserted or intimated that it has something to do with a weapons race. We expect misinterpretations of that sort to come from unfriendly countries and sometimes from ignorant domestic critics. However, I was disappointed to find that a few otherwise well informed publications and individuals have asserted that the MOL is a weapons carrier and a project contrary to our peaceful progress in space.

"I assert as positively as I can that the MOL is *not* a weapons system, is *not* a means by which aggressive actions can be perpetrated, and is in *no* way in conflict with the established peaceful policies, objectives, or methods of the United States. *Rather,* it is a program that will increase our knowledge of man's usefulness in space and will relate that ability to our national defense." Welsh, Speech of Oct. 28, 1964, *supra* note 202. On the MOL, see Cooper, *supra* note 198.

For other comments on the U.S. military programs, see "Air Force in Orbit," 216 *Economist* 873–74 (Sept. 4, 1965); Robison, "Self-Restrictions in the American Military Use

The Soviet Union makes claims that are precisely similar.[206]

As noted, the word *peaceful* has nevertheless also been used in other contexts. In the agreement establishing the International Atomic Energy Agency, for example, it was used to mean *nonmilitary*.[207] As we stated earlier, the Antarctic Treaty of 1959 also generally equates "peaceful" and nonmilitary.[208] Well into 1963, Soviet bloc spokesmen seemed to insist that "peaceful" meant "nonmilitary" for outer space activities as well; in May

1963 Zhukov stated that "the concept of the 'peaceful use' of outer space excludes any measures of a military nature,"[209] and in September 1963 Korovin remarked that the military use of space was illegal.[210] In this they received some support outside the Soviet bloc.[211]

Since 1963 (and in fact to some degree even in 1962), Soviet spokesmen have been more equivocal; there is less talk of "military uses" as such, and efforts to have such uses declared illegal in general have been abandoned. Their present view seems to be that the military use of space is without legal characterization, and will remain so until agreement is reached on general and complete disarmament, with which the issue is inseparably linked.[212] The reasons for the apparent shift can only be guessed at; it may be due to an effort to avoid the obvious potential criticism of the multiple Soviet military space efforts, or to clear the way for future Soviet military efforts. Yet without now declaring that military uses of space in general are illegal, Soviet spokesmen continue to attack most American space efforts, whatever their purpose, as "military," thus contrasting them with the solely "peaceful" activities of the Soviet Union.[213] Such "warlike" acts as observation from outer space, high-altitude nuclear explosions, the scattering of copper needles, and orbital weapon suggestions are, when done by the United States, all nonpeaceful and "illegal."[214] (It is

of Space," 9 *Orbis* 116–39 (1965). For other attacks on the U.S. space programs as "military" and hostile, see Larionov, "The Doctrine of Military Domination in Outer Space," 10 *Int'l Aff.* 25–30 (1964); "Outer Space," 17 *Current Dig. Sov. Press* 30–21 (Oct. 20, 1965); Mader, "U.S. Militarist Plans in Space," 11 *Int'l Aff.* 54–58 (Aug. 1965); Teplinsky, "Space Maniacs," *New Times* 7–8 (Moscow, Sept. 1, 1965).

[206] Crane, *supra* note 72, at 685, notes: "Accordingly, the Soviets make no distinction between military and non-military uses of space by Soviet Vehicles. It makes no difference that all Soviet space vehicles are sponsored by military organizations and are thus 'military,' nor that Soviet rockets have served as delivery vehicles for systems testing nuclear weapons in outer space, because the Soviets contend that all of their space vehicles are 'peaceful.' "

Clearly Soviet writers seem to assume that U.S. reconnaissance satellites are designed for aggressive purposes, while Soviet weapons serve peaceful objectives; see Zhukov, "Space Espionage Plans and International Law," 6 *Int'l Aff.* 53–57 (1960). Osnitskaya, "Legal Problems of Space Exploration," 7 *Revue du Droit Contemporain* 53, 56 (Dec. 1960). Crane indicates that "the lack of accepted objective standards has enabled the Communists to apply a subjective test, namely the test of peaceful purposes. This enables the U.S.S.R. to assert a priori that all actions by the U.S.S.R. are peaceful and that all actions by the United States contrary to Soviet interests are not peaceful. This approach is consistent with the whole concept of Communist criminal law, according to which intent is a very important element in the criminality of the act." Crane, *supra*, at 35–36.

[207] Statute of the I.A.E.A., Art. 2. See Cheng, "International Co-operation and Control: From Atoms to Space," 15 *Current Legal Problems* 266 ff. (1962).

[208] Art. 1 states that: "Antarctica shall be used for peaceful purposes only" and then prohibits *"any measures* of a military nature." [Italics added.]

On similarities to the Antarctic Treaty and the Charter of the International Atomic Energy Agency, see Zhukoy, *supra* note 135, at 79–89. Zhukov has also stated, *supra* note 74, at 17: "In conformity with this, the term 'peaceful uses' of outer space precludes any measures of a military nature and signifies the organization of exclusively scientific exploration in the upper layers of the atmosphere and outer space." See also Korovin, "Urgent Tasks of Space Law," *Fifth Colloquium on the Law of Outer Space* 1 (1962).

[209] Zhukov, *supra* note 126, at 27, 28.

[210] Korovin, *supra* note 3, at 92.

[211] For example, the text of a United Arab Republic proposal, entitled "Code for international co-operation in the uses of outer space," tabled on Sept. 14, 1962, in the Committee on the Peaceful Uses of Outer Space, provides in Para. 1: "the activities of Member States in outer space should be confined solely to the peaceful uses." A/AC. 105/L.6. (1962). For criticism of this language as perhaps excluding all activities of a military nature, see Johnson, in Schwartz, *supra* note 2, at 143.

Cheng has also argued that "peaceful" in many contexts means "nonmilitary" rather than nonaggressive, but he has agreed that, lacking a specific agreement to the contrary, military activities are permitted in outer space if allowable by the law of peace (i.e., nonaggressive). See Int'l L. Ass'n, *Report of the 50th Conf.* 50–51 (1962).

[212] See Crane, *supra* note 72 and Comment, "The Cosmos Must Be a Peace Zone," 9 *Int'l Aff.* 41 (Dec. 1963). For comments on arms control in general, see the interesting study by Abt, "The Problems and Possibilities of Space Arms Control," 1 *J. Arms Control* 18–43 (1963).

[213] E.g., Mader, *supra* note 205, at 55; Larionov, *supra* note 204, at 25.

[214] For Soviet charges that U.S. space activities are nonpeaceful, see, e.g., Mader and Larionov, *supra* note 205; Zhukov,

clear that for Soviet spokesmen, ICBMs are simply outside this range of discussion if their discussion is to be consistent.) It must also be noted that, while Soviet space flights have all been, in Soviet eyes, peaceful and non-military, there is no way to verify these claims; indeed Russian astronauts have, in general, been military officers. We have cited earlier Lipson's comment about Major Gagarin's flight in 1961.[215] Indeed, we know that the Soviet Union has also conducted high-altitude nuclear tests in the past and apparently now regularly orbits reconnaissance satellites.[216] The recent lessening of Soviet complaints in public about reconnaissance vehicles in outer space may be due to this fact of international life.[217] Of course, they have no obligation, as they view the world, to be consistent or candid in this manner and, indeed, as we noted earlier, they have not usually been so on this issue. From its inception, the Soviet program used military vehicles as launchers, used military personnel as

astronauts, and maintains military secrecy about most of its program. This seems not to have embarrassed Soviet spokesmen at all as they criticize the United States for pursuing identical patterns in part.

Even if propagandistic and purely self-serving definitions are left aside, grave problems remain if any action is to be based on the distinction between "peaceful," "military," and "aggressive" activities. The fact is that almost every use of outer space has a possible military connotation, and the military gain lessons from peaceful activities conducted by other agencies and even by other countries. Even when the mission would be uniformly considered peaceful, its launch vehicle may still be one designed for military purposes or be capable of such a use, and will, whether that is so or not, be at least briefly indistinguishable, during the launch and the powered stage, from a military vehicle and even an ICBM.[218]

For the parties, the 1967 Space Treaty bars certain specific types of military activity while leaving free, as did the Antarctic Treaty of 1959, the "peaceful" use of military personnel, equipment, and facilities. Article IV thus provides:[219]

---

supra note 52; Korovin, *supra* note 3, at 92; Zhukov, *supra* note 126, at 28; Gabrovski, "Some Legal Aspects of Space Exploration," 9 *Int'l Aff.* 92 (Feb. 1963); Glazov, "Cannibals in Space," *New Times,* June 19, 1963, at 11–12; Zolotov, "Space Rights and Obligations," 9 *Int'l Aff.* 92–93 (July 1963) (on espionage and space needles). See also Crane, "Soviet Attitude . . . ," *supra* note 24, at 685, 702–6. On the Soviet view of reconnaissance aircraft, see Lissitzyn, *supra* note 154, at 559; Wright, "Legal Aspects of the U-2 Incident," 54 *Am. J. Int'l L.* 836–54 (1960).

[215] "An Argument on the Legality of Reconnaissance Satellites," 1961 *Proceedings, Amer. Soc'y Int'l. L.* 174, 175.

As the French delegate once noted at the U.N. there are "dangers inherent in definitions," citing as an example the general consensus that military personnel employed as astronauts should not be denied the benefits of a convention on rescue and return simply because of their military status. See A/AC. 105/C.2/SR 47 at 9 (1965).

[216] See 4 *Astro. & Aero.* 920–21 (June 1966) and see chap. 2. On Soviet reconnaissance satellites, see also *New York Times,* Apr. 21, 1966, at 2, and *Time,* Dec. 30, 1966.

[217] On reconnaissance satellites see chap. 2 and McMahon, *supra* note 72, at 365–80 and sources cited; Jenks, *supra* note 10, at 305–6; McDougal *et al., supra* note 3, at 311–15; Beresford, "Surveillance Aircraft and Satellites: A Problem of International Law," 27 *J. Air L. Commerce* 107 (1960); Falk, "Toward a Responsible Procedure for the National Assertion of Protested Claims to Use Space," in Taubenfeld (ed.), *supra* note 31; Note, "Legal Aspects of Reconnaissance in Airspace and Outer Space," 61 *Colum. L. Rev.* 1074 ff. (1961).

On the lessening of statements about the illegality of reconnaissance satellites, see "Reconnaissance Satellites," *Interavia,* Jan. 1965 at 104–5. The 1964 Soviet draft on the return of spacecraft made no mention of vehicles carrying devices for the collection of intelligence data, unlike earlier proposals. See A/AC. 105/C. 2/L. 2/Rev. 2 (1964).

[218] For example, the U.S. Titan was both the backbone of the 1965 manned flights and a dependable ICBM. See *New York Times,* Aug. 10, 1965, at 1. On the interrelationships of "peaceful" and "military" activities, see also McMahon, *supra* note 78, at 361 ff.; McDougal & Lipson, *supra* note 198, at 409–10; Lipson & Katzenbach, *supra* note 2, at 24–27; "Survey of Space Law," *Staff Report of the Select Committee on Astronautics and Space Exploration* 26 (1959); Ward, "Space Law as a Way to World Peace," *JAG J.* (Navy) 10, 21 (Feb. 1959); Quigg, *supra* note 66, at 95; Becker, *supra* note 50, reprinted in *1961 Symposium,* at 396; Quadri, *supra* note 198, at 576–77; Jenks, "The International Control of Outer Space," *Proceedings, Third Colloquium IISL* 3–5, 16–20 (1960); Jessup & Taubenfeld, *supra* note 3, at 222–24; McDougal *et al., supra* note 3, 394–400; Taubenfeld & Taubenfeld, *Man and Space: Politics, Law, and Organization* (Arnold Found. Mono. 1964); Fiorio, "The Coexistence of Peaceful and Military Activities in Outer Space," paper presented to the summer meeting, June 17–20, 1963, of the AIAA, No. 63–245.

Korovin has written: "We cannot but agree with Professor Schick when he stresses the military significance of what are seemingly the most peaceful forms of space activity and points to the consequent difficulties of the international regulation of problems concerning space." "Peaceful Cooperation in Space," 8 *Int'l Aff.* 61 (Moscow, 1962).

On military uses, see also Woetzel, "Legal Aspects of Military Uses of Space in Soviet and American Eyes," in Taubenfeld (ed.), *supra* note 31, chap. 6.

[219] For earlier draft proposals, see A/6352, June 16, 1966 (Soviet draft, Art. IV) and A/AC. 105/32, June 17, 1966 (U.S. draft, Arts. 8, 9).

States Parties to the Treaty undertake not to place in orbit around the earth any objects carrying nuclear weapons or any other kinds of weapons of mass destruction, install such weapons on celestial bodies, or station such weapons in outer space in any other manner.

The moon and other celestial bodies shall be used by all States Parties to the Treaty exclusively for peaceful purposes. The establishment of military bases, installations and fortifications, the testing of any type of weapons and the conduct of military maneuvers on celestial bodies shall be forbidden. The use of military personnel for scientific research or for any other peaceful purposes shall not be prohibited. The use of any equipment or facility necessary for peaceful exploration of the moon and other celestial bodies shall also not be prohibited.

Although certain acts are plainly barred, the treaty does not help us with an overall working distinction, leaving many potential questions for future resolution as, and if, necessary.

The difficulty in separating peaceful from nonaggressive military pursuits in outer space has been recognized by spokesmen of the leading space powers. Premier Khrushchev stated, for example:

Prior to achievement of agreement on general and complete disarmament both our countries would still be limited in their possibilities to co-operate in the field of the peaceful use of outer space. It is no secret that military missiles and space ships, which are launched for peaceful purposes, are based on the same achievements of science and technology. True, there already exist some differences here as well; space rockets require more powerful engines as they have to lift bigger loads to greater heights, whereas military rockets do not, in general, require such powerful boosters. Engines already in existence are capable of lifting warheads of great destructive potential and delivering them to any part of the globe. But you, Mr. President, know as well as we do that the principles of designing and production are the same for both military and space rockets.[220]

Similarly, Senator Gore, representing the United States, commented: "It was impossible to draw a clear distinction between military and nonmilitary uses of space, for the same vehicles were involved."[221]

The United States asserts that the test is not and cannot be based on a definition of "peaceful" or "military." "The test of the legitimacy of a particular use of outer space is not whether it is military or nonmilitary but whether it is peaceful or aggressive,"[222] or whether it "is consistent with the United Nations Charter and other obligations of international law."[223] The charter, of course, bars acts of aggression and the threat or *use* of force but not "military" activities as a class and certainly not self-defensive military action.

Whatever the difficulties of the arbitrary partial charter system of peacekeeping with respect to earth activities, it seems unlikely that "military" space activities which do not involve an armed attack on another nation (and would, hence, give rise formally to the charter-approved right of self-defense [Art. 51]) would constitute an actual threat to the survival of another state and thus raise issues under the charter. Space probably raises few of the worst of the old problems, given the present technology. It does raise some new, serious problems of

---

The Soviet Union never accepted the U.S. view that "peaceful" means only "nonaggressive" and the 1967 treaty accommodates to the Soviet view in that the term "peaceful," to avoid controversy, appears only here in the treaty.

[220] A/AC. 105/PV. 4 at 12 (May 7, 1962). See also the remarks of Lt. Gen. Nikolai Kamanin, Commander of Soviet cosmonauts, who said, during a meeting with Moscow writers: "After the flight of GEMINI V, Johnson said officially that the United States was inviting representatives of the Soviet Union to the next flight so that they could see the U.S. rockets and rocket devices. We told him: Thank you, but we do not intend to visit your launching site. We do not intend to go because we know all too well that all space devices are as a rule launched into space with the aid of military rockets. You do it this way and we do it that way. While military rockets are used for these purposes we are unable to show you our Soviet rockets because we know all too well that our rockets

were, and we are convinced, will be the most powerful, with the greater distance and load capacity. This is of decisive importance for the defense of the country." Tass, Oct. 24, 1965, reported in *Astronautics and Aeronautics,* 1965, at 489 (NASA, 1966).

[221] A/AC. 1/SR. 1289 at 361 (Dec. 6, 1962). He also noted that: "The question of military activities on earth; to banish both, all efforts for general and complete disarmament must be continued. Until disarmament was achieved, the test of any space activity must not be whether it was military or non-military but whether it was consistent with the Charter and other obligations of international law. . . . The United States, like every other country, was determined to take every non-aggressive step it considered necessary to protect its national security and that of friendly countries until the day when such precautions were no longer needed." *Id.* at 3.

[222] Deputy Ass't Sec'y of State Gardner, "Cooperation in Outer Space," 41 *For. Aff.* 344, 359 (1963).

[223] Senator Gore, in Committee I, U.N. Gen'l Assembly, *Dept. State Bull.,* 21, 23 (No. 48, Jan. 7, 1963). To the same effect, see the statement of Ambassador Yost in the U.N. Outer Space Committee on Jan. 13, 1966: "It is clear that the question of military activities in space cannot be divorced from the question of military activities on earth. The test of any space activity must not be whether it is military or nonmilitary, but whether it is consistent with the United Nations Charter and other obligations of International law. Our space program entirely meets this criterion."

protection for the rights of mankind, of which we have already had intimations in the furor over nuclear fallout, interference with the earth's natural environment, and the like.

It is interesting to note that when dangers of this type have appeared to be clear-cut, that is, when scientific evidence already exists on the subject and has been given great publicity, as with the by-products of nuclear testing, it has been possible to achieve self-denying, self-policed promises on the subject, at least from the present major powers.[224] Although these promises are reversible if the need arises, they have had beneficial results to date.

On the other hand, when there has been no scientific agreement on the extent of potential damage from space activities (e.g., the copper needles: Project West Ford), or when the issue seems remote and is not clearly understood as dangerous to human survival (e.g., a sterile impact on a celestial body), the cost to the space program (in time or resources or loss of knowledge) has proved, on occasion, a more important consideration than the possible losses implied to man in general. If space problems are run as competitions between powerful states, by administrators who are strongly motivated to be first, the losses are apt to be risked, whatever the potential costs to humanity.

Some attempts have been made by scholars to achieve consensus on the concept of "peaceful," if not on "beneficial," uses. Among the writers, McMahon, for example, while "acknowledging the difficulties implicit in the attempt to disengage the military from the scientific and peaceful uses," suggests that despite their possible military implications:

[S]uch activities as meteorological satellites, communication satellites, satellites to study and collect information concerning the atmosphere, the intensity of cosmic radiation, the Van Allen belts, radio waves, biological data and similar subjects must, from any commonsense point of view, be essential peaceful and scientific activities.[225]

Others have written in similar manner. To date, however, the nations have preferred to avoid formal definitions and to move pragmatically in asserting the risks of other nations' space ventures, achieving consensus only on nuclear testing, on the orbiting of weapons of mass destruction, and on placing military installations as such on the celestial bodies. If no overall international regime, including inspection, matures in time, the nations will presumably continue to regard each others' acts in space, as they do those on earth, as inherently worthy of suspicion and potentially hostile, and acceptance of *comprehensive* definitions of permissible "peaceful" or impermissible "aggressive" activities are no more likely for space than for the earth milieu.

---

[224] For discussion of the Test Ban Treaty of 1963, see *supra* at 70. Benefits to mankind from the cessation of testing have been reported—fallout from strontium 90, which is suspected of being a possible causative agent of bone cancers or leukemia was decreasing by early 1966, while iodine 131, believed to be harmful to the thyroid gland, had virtually disappeared from the milk supply as early as 1963. See *Washington Post,* Mar. 20, 1966, at A6.

[225] 38 *Brit. Yrbk. Int'l L.* 339, 355 (1962). See also *id.* at 360 ff.

5

The Legal Regime of Satellite Communications

Introduction

The launching of the Early Bird satellite in 1965, officially renamed Intelsat I, heralded a major step toward achievement of an international communications satellite system and foretold the early commercial use of space facilities by man. Communications systems utilizing satellites have a tremendous growth potential[1]

---

[1] No effort will be made to include a complete citation of authorities in this field as the literature on the subject is very large, usually technical, and frequently repetitious. See, e.g., *Significant Achievements in Space Communications and Navigation 1958–64* (NASA SP–93; 1966); *Communications Satellite Systems Technology* (R. B. Marsten ed., 19 *Progress in Astronautics and Aeronautics,* AIAA Series [1966]). There is also much business and popular literature on the subject. See, e.g., John McDonald, "The ComSat Compromise Starts a Revolution," 72 *Fortune* 128 (Oct. 1965). Every book on uses of outer space has a chapter on communications. See *Peacetime Uses of Outer Space* 35 (Ramo ed. 1961). The semiannual reports of NASA and the reports of ComSat all cover activities and planning for satellite communications. The RAND Corp. has prepared a number of reports relating to space communications. The U.N. has taken a very active part in promoting development of a global communications satellite system available to all nations. See, for example, U.N. Docs. A/4141 (July 14, 1959); C. 1/L220/Rev. 1; U.N. Res. 1348 (XIII) Dec. 13, 1958; U.N. Res. 1472 (XIV), Dec. 12, 1959; UNA/RES/1721 (XVI), Dec. 20, 1961; A/AC.105/PV.3, May 7, 1962; U.N. Res. 1963 (XVIII), Dec. 13, 1963; A/5783, Nov. 13, 1964. Extensive congressional hearings and reports are cited in subsequent notes. There will be many more hearings and reports since many aspects of communications utilizing satellites are very controversial, domestically and internationally.

and will almost certainly result in substantially modifying the pattern of long-distance communications over land and water. The technological advances bring to the fore many old and new problems of law and legal relationships. The international Telecommunications Satellite Consortium,[2] the members of which are responsible for perhaps 90 percent of all present international telecommunications traffic,[3] and its manager, the Communications Satellite Corporation (ComSat),[4] are well known in the United States and throughout the world. In addition to Intelsat and the United States Military Communications System based on American technology,[5] there also exists the Soviet Union's Molniya satellite system, which in some form is a potential competitor for international telecommunications business.

Many other countries and private and public organizations are devoting much time and effort to the complex problems of communications satellites, although they have not matched the technological progress of the United States.[6] If communications satellites of the projected capacity are developed, there will probably be no *technical* need for more than one system.[7] But the technology of the industry gives no assurance that competing systems will not be established for nationalistic or other reasons, just as the United States Department of Defense system has been established. Also, if one system has a complete monopoly, it is certain that it will, as an alternative to competition, be subjected to very close regulation by individual nations as well as internationally. The Soviet Union, France, England, Germany, Japan, and other nations have the capacity, individually or collectively, to develop regional or global communications satellite systems if they have the desire and are willing to pay the cost in manpower and resources, which may prove difficult to justify on economic grounds alone.

Electromagnetic waves in the radio frequency range continue to receive primary attention, but the use of masers and of the much higher frequency laser[8] for com-

---

For a brief description of the subject see *A Survey of Space Applications,* chap. 2 (NASA SP–142; 1967).

2 Intelsat—International Telecommunications Satellite Consortium—established by "Agreement Establishing Interim Arrangements for A Global Commercial Communications Satellite System," Aug. 20, 1964, T.I.A.S. 5646 [hereinafter cited as Interim Agr't]; 15 *U.S.T.* 1705: Special Agreement, Aug. 20, 1964, *T.I.A.S.* 5646 [hereinafter cited as Special Agr't]; 15 *U.S.T.* 1745: and Supplementary Agreement on Arbitration, June 4, 1965, IV *International Legal Materials* 735 (July 1965) [hereinafter cited as Supplementary Agr't].

3 For list of members as of 1966, see note 101 *infra*.

4 Communications Satellite Corporation, a U.S. corporation established pursuant to Act of Congress, P.L. 87–624, 87th Cong., 2d Sess. (Aug. 31, 1962); 47 U.S.C. 701–44 (1962) and the Corporation Law of the District of Columbia.

5 Other agencies of the United States government also have one or more satellites for use in navigation, weather forecasting, crop study, geological studies, etc. These "systems" are so new that they should be considered experimental and are involved in communications to only a limited extent. NASA will use spacecraft to collect information and intelligence about the earth, plants, animals, resources, etc. See *Chicago Tribune,* June 26, 1967, at sec. 1A, at 12, quoting various NASA officials.

6 Among other countries or groups of countries which have considered the possibility of national or regional communications satellites are France and Canada. Among the organizations involved are the European Conference of Postal and Telecommunications Administration (CEPT) representing 23 European countries; Eurospace, a private association of about 150 industrial firms and professional bodies from 12 European countries; the Committee on Space Research of the International Council of Scientific Unions (COSPAR, ICSU); International Radio and Television Organization (OIRT); Organization for Cooperation in the Field of Communications of the Council for Mutual Economic Aid (COMECOM); European Space Reseach Organization (ESRO); Preparatory Commission to Study the Possibilities of European Collaboration in the Field of Space Research (COPERS); European Launcher Development Organization (ELDO); and other organizations encompassing membership from private and public sectors from both sides of the Iron Curtain and of the Atlantic. Some of the discussion has probably been generated by private companies hoping for business, and this seems to have been the case in Latin America where there has been considerable talk but little action. France is the only Western European country which appears to be seriously considering the expenditures to establish a separate system and there the nationalistic motivation is obvious. Germany and France have signed an agreement for joint efforts but whether only for experimental work or also for operations is not known.

7 See *infra* note 31 for statistics drawn from ComSat's 1966 annual report. In some instances there is little leeway for the placement of satellites for certain coverage, e.g., between Japan and England where there is only about a half degree, and the same is true for coverage of Mexico and Iran by the same satellite. Because of the distance between the earth and a synchronous satellite, the time lapse involved in two-way transmissions mitigates against transmitting messages successively via more than one satellite.

8 Laser, an acronym from "light amplification by stimulated emission of radiation," is a device for producing light by emission of energy stored in a molecular or atomic system stimulated by an input signal. Maser, an acronym deriving from an amplifier utilizing the principle of "microwave amplification by stimulated emission of radiation," emits energy stored in

munications are among the subjects of scientific research and development and may affect the course of communications satellite technology. A high level of technological and political activity will doubtless continue as capabilities are improved, and this will, if any major nation deems it advisable to develop the equipment and techniques, include satellite-to-home receiver transmissions. A brief description of radio communication is necessary to understand the nature and complexity of the legal-political and economic problems of communications utilizing satellites for relay.

Basics of Radio Communication

Radio waves, X-rays, gamma rays, and light waves are all electromagnetic waves controlled by the same natural laws relating to frequency, velocity, intensity, direction of travel, and polarization, but they vary enormously in penetrating power, carrying distance, reflectivity, freedom from interference, frequency or number of cycles per second, wave length, and the extent to which directionality may be controlled. The waves tend to go equally in all directions from the point of origin. Electromagnetic radiation is considered to travel at a uniform velocity of approximately 186,300 miles per second regardless of wave length or frequency,[9] and may be generated by nat-

ural phenomena or by man-made equipment. Reliable transmissions over interplanetary distances remain a serious technological problem and over interstellar distances an impossibility. There is presently no known method to reduce the time element.[10] A system for electromagnetic

Wave Length	Frequencies	Services
10 millimeters	300 gigacycles per second	Infrared spectrum
Band 11	Extremely high frequencies (EHF)	Experimental communications, telemetry
1 centimeter	30 gigacycles per second	Radio relay, radar, and radio
Band 10	Super high frequencies (SHF)	Navigational aides
10 centimeters	3 gigacycles per second	Meteorological telemetry aids
Band 9	Ultra high frequencies (UHF)	TV channels 14–83
1 meter	300 megacycles per second	TV channels 7–13
Band 8	Very high frequencies (VHF)	FM broadcasting TV channels 2–6
10 meters	39 megacycles per second	International short wave
Band 7	High frequencies (HF)	Communications and broadcasting
100 meters	3 megacycles per second	Radio navigational aids
Band 6	Medium frequencies (MF)	AM radio broadcasting
1 kilometer	300 kilocycles per second	LF radio navigational aids
Band 5	Low frequencies (LF)	LF radio communications
10 kilometers	30 kilocycles per second	Communications-frequencies audible by the human ear
Band 4	Very low frequencies (VLF)	
100 kilometers	3 kilocycles per second	

a molecular or atomic system by a microwave power supply stimulated by an input signal. Masers are normally within radio frequency range, whereas lasers, as indicated by the name, are or may be within the visible light range. National Aeronautics and Space Administration, *Dictionary of Technical Terms for Aerospace Uses* (1st ed. NASA SP–7; 1965).

[9] See Glasstone, *Sourcebook on the Space Sciences* 309–12 (NASA; 1965). When frequencies become high the units employed, all relating to cycles per second, are kilocycles (one thousand), megacycles (one million), and gigacycles (one billion), the last term probably first used at Geneva in 1959 insofar as the radio regulations were concerned. Wavelengths are normally stated in accordance with the metric system and, as indicated in the formula $W = V/f$, the higher the frequency, the shorter the wavelength. See Everett, *Fundamentals of Radio and Electronics,* chap. 19 (2d ed. 1958) for an extensive technical description of radio wave propagation. "Radio Frequency Controls in Space Telecommunications," *Report by Staff before the Senate Committee on Aeronautics and Space Sciences,* 86th Cong., 2d Sess. at 844 (1960). Also, see Seely, *Radio Electronics* (1956), for a detailed discussion of the technical aspects of telecommunications and equipment used. A general schedule of wavelengths and their uses follows as a matter of general information. Communications engineers do not agree on any one set of tables and this is no exception.

[10] "However, the heart of the difficulty of extending this [accurate high speed transmission of information] capability to deep space lies in the fact that the data rate capability for a given system varies inversely with the square of the distance between transmitter and antenna. For example, the capability of the Mariner system transmitting from Mars is only of the order of one bit each five seconds." This may be raised by the early 1970's to some 2,000 to 5,000 bits per second, but television requires 10 to 100 million bits of information per

communication between two stations at any distance apart consists of three primary elements: (1) a controlled source of electromagnetic wave emission or transmission, including an antenna for radiation; (2) a receiver to intercept and convert the signals to intelligible form; and (3) the transfer mechanism through which the energy is propagated from the transmitter to the receiver. A relay station such as a communications satellite may be required.

Although frequencies from a fraction of a cycle per second to billions of cycles per second can be produced, the usable spectrum is overcrowded and will probably continue to be for the foreseeable future. Frequencies from about 500 kilocycles to 1,600 kilocycles are adaptable for standard broadcasting because, with careful engineering, both local and rural service may be provided effectively without serious long-distance interference. The 5–25-megacycle range is most suitable for communications over distances of 1,000 to 12,000 miles via sky wave, but these frequencies must serve all nations of the world and must be restricted to services for which they are uniquely suitable. Frequencies from about 50 megacycles and upward to several hundred megacycles are best for television, as they are relatively free from long-distance interference, and the necessary wide channel of about 6 megacycles can be satisfactorily transmitted and received. For many applications of radar, frequencies of hundreds to thousands of megacycles are required so that highly directive antennas of moderate size can be used and satisfactory detail still be obtained. Use of frequencies in the gigacycle range is in the development stage.[11] Because of the extreme ranges at which interference may be caused for some frequencies, frequency sharing is limited for several of the frequencies. Frequencies above 30 megacycles are generally useful only for line-of-sight transmissions. There are some exceptions, however, in that microwaves will reflect if "aimed" at the appropriate layer of the troposphere or upper ionosphere at the proper angle.[12] Satellites are useful in relaying radio frequencies from 100 to 20,000 megacycles over extended distances, and 1965 U.S. Air Force tests showed that, given the proper aim and transmission power, some microwaves could be transmitted from a satellite around the world to another satellite between layers of the ionosphere.[13]

Activities in space, as might be anticipated, require a large number of frequencies for operational and experimental activities.[14] In transmitting intelligence by elec-

---

[13] *New York Times,* May 8, 1965.

[14] The Nov. 1963 Space Radio Communications Conference of the ITU, as reported in 50 *Telecommunications Journal* 367 (Dec. 1963) [hereinafter cited as *T.J.*], allocated for space use the following frequency bands:

FREQUENCY BANDS	SERVICE
15.762–15.768 kc/s	Space research (shared)
18.030–18.036 kc/s	Space research (shared)
30.005–30.010 Mc/s	Space research and space (satellite identification) (shared)
37.75–38.25 Mc/s	Radio astronomy (shared)
73–74.6 Mc/s	Radio astronomy (exclusive)
136–137 Mc/s	Space research (telemetering and tracking) (shared in regions 1 and 3, exclusive in region 2)
137–138 Mc/s	Meteorological-satellite, space research (telemetering and tracking), space (telemetering and tracking) (shared)
143.6–143.65 Mc/s	Space research (telemetering and tracking) (shared)
149.9–150.05 Mc/s	Radionavigation-satellites (exclusive)
267–273 Mc/s	Space (telemetering) (shared)
399.9–400.05 Mc/s	Radionavigation-satellites (exclusive)
400.05–401 Mc/s	Meteorological-satellites (maintenance telemetering), space research (telemetering and tracking) (shared)
401–402 Mc/s	Space (telemetering) (shared)
460–470 Mc/s	Meteorological-satellites (shared)
1400–1427 Mc/s	Radio astronomy (exclusive)
1427–1429 Mc/s	Space (telecommand) (shared)
1525–1535 Mc/s	Space (telemetering) (shared)
1535–1540 Mc/s	Space (telemetering) (exclusive)
1660–1670 Mc/s	Meteorological-satellites (shared)
1664.4–1668.4 Mc/s	Radio astronomy
1690–1700 Mc/s	Meteorological-satellites (shared)
1700–1710 Mc/s	Space research (telemetering and tracking) (shared)
1770–1790 Mc/s	Meteorological-satellites (shared)
2290–2300 Mc/s	Space research (telemetering and tracking in deep space) (shared)
2690–2700 Mc/s	Radio astronomy (exclusive)
3400–4200 Mc/s	Communication-satellites (satellite-to-earth) (shared)
4400–4700 Mc/s	Communication-satellites (satellite-to-earth) (shared)
4990–5000 Mc/s	Radio astronomy (shared in regions 1 and 3, exclusive in region 2)
5250–5255 Mc/s	Space research (shared)
5670–5725 Mc/s	Space research (deep space) (shared)

---

second. Bisplinghoff, "Today's Research Sets Tomorrow's Capabilities in Space," *Fifth National Conference on the Peaceful Uses of Space* 107 (NASA, 1966).

[11] See Everett, *supra* note 9, at 282–337.

[12] *Ibid.* High power is needed.

tromagnetic waves, amplitude, frequency, phase, and pulse modulations are used either individually or in combinations as the circumstances and use require, which means that a single communications channel utilizes a substantial frequency spread.[15]

FREQUENCY BANDS	SERVICE
5725–5850 Mc/s	Communication-satellites (earth-to-satellite) (only in region 1 and shared)
5850–5925 Mc/s	Communication-satellites (earth-to-satellite) (only in regions 1 and 3 and shared)
5925–6425 Mc/s	Communication-satellites (earth-to-satellite) (shared in all regions)
7250–7300 Mc/s	Communication-satellites (satellite-to-earth) (exclusive)
7300–7750 Mc/s	Communication-satellites (shared)
7900–7975 Mc/s	Communication-satellites (earth-to-satellite) (shared)
7975–8025 Mc/s	Communication-satellites (earth-to-satellite) (shared)
8025/8400 Mc/s	Communication-satellites (earth-to-satellite) (shared)
8400–8500 Mc/s	Space research (shared in regions 1 and 3, exclusive in region 2)
10.68–10.7 Gc/s	Radio astronomy (exclusive)
14.3–14.4 Gc/s	Radionavigation-satellites (exclusive)
15.25–15.35 Gc/s	Space research (exclusive)
15.35–15.4 Gc/s	Radio astronomy (exclusive)
19.3–19.4 Gc/s	Radio astronomy (exclusive)
31–31.3 Gc/s	Space research (shared)
31.3–31.5 Gc/s	Radio astronomy (exclusive)
31.5–31.8 Gc/s	Space research (shared in regions 1 and 3, exclusive in region 2)
31.8–32.3 Gc/s	Space research (shared)
33–33.4 Gc/s	Radio astronomy (only in region 1 and shared)
34.2–35.2 Gc/s	Space research (shared)

[15] See Everett, *supra* note 9, at 309–21, for an understandable discussion of the technical aspects of transmitting intelligence by electromagnetic waves. "When the carrier (electromagnetic frequency) is modulated for message transmission, frequencies higher and lower than the frequency of the carrier are produced. Since they are distributed over a finite portion of the spectrum on each side of the carrier frequency they are called side frequencies and are referred to collectively as sidebands. These sidebands contain all of the message information, and without them no message could be transmitted," although various devices permit the transmission and reception of only one sideband, thus substantially reducing the required transmission bandwidth and power. "It is apparent, then, that radio communications systems, to carry the message sideband frequencies as well as the carrier frequencies, require an irreducible amount of frequency spread which depends upon the highest modulating frequency to be transmitted." See also Seely, *supra* note 9, at 1–14 (1958).

The Radio Spectrum: A Limited Resource

The number of frequencies of electromagnetic waves that can be generated is virtually unlimited, but the number of radio channels of varying widths available for efficient communications is limited.[16] A message should be transmitted on a channel of frequencies which no other user within the geographical carrying range of that frequency will try to use at the same time,[17] but compromises have had to be made between optimum high fidelity transmission and reception and the number of channels available for use.[18] A shift from one frequency to another may require such expensive changes in equipment, including a new antenna system, that a considerable amount of interference and crowding would be accepted rather than a shift to a new, comparatively clear channel.[19] Thus, technological and other pressures must be

[16] The radio spectrum "must be regarded as finite and similar in all respects to other natural resources." "Policy Planning for Space Telecommunications," *Staff Report before the Committee on Aeronautical and Space Sciences,* 86th Cong., 2d Sess., at 33 (Comm. Print 1960) [hereinafter cited as *Staff Report*]. Television channel 4 extends from 66 to 72 megacycles. Channel 3 extends from 60 to 66 megacycles. A conventional double sideband and carrier system for speech utilizes a radio frequency bandwidth of about 6,000 cycles while a single-sideband suppressed-carrier system requires a bandwith of only 3,000 cycles, although in standard broadcasting a bandwidth of 15,000 cycles would be desirable in place of the 10 kc/s used to permit more stations. Thus, a voice channel requires about as much spectrum space as 22 telegraph channels, and a black and white television channel requires about as much spectrum space as 600 two way voice channels. A color TV channel requires almost 3 times as much spectrum space as black and white TV. See also note 31 for an optimistic view of probable scientific developments to increase the number of usable channels. See Everett, *supra* note 9, at 302–26.

[17] Many frequencies can be shared, that is, used in each of several geographical regions. Thus, in 1959 the band from 4 to 10 megacycles was used by 74,284 transmitters through the world. See *Staff Report, supra* note 16. See also Hughes Aircraft Company, Space System Division, *Study for a Video Data Distribution Satellite System for the ABC Network* 3–6 to 3–11 (July 1965; rev. Sept. 1965) suggesting that the nature of stationary communications satellites permits the same frequency band to be used simultaneously by a great many ground stations and satellites.

[18] Provision for the optimal bandwidths would sharply restrict the number of channels and, therefore, the number of radio stations. Thus, in the standard broadcast bands for AM radio there are no guard bands or unused frequencies between channels, and interference between stations may be observed.

[19] For a description of some of the problems of shifting

heavy to bring about any substantial shifting in uses of frequency ranges, and this has contributed to the problem of making frequencies available for communications utilizing space.

Technological advances have steadily increased the number of radio frequencies available for communications[20] and at the same time have continued to narrow the channels required for transmission of information. Nevertheless the rapidly growing demand for the use of radio frequencies continues to outpace technology and leaves only limited promise of eliminating the congestion of the radio waves and the competition for frequencies.[21]

Space research and development programs have brought their own new demands for radio frequencies: tracking, command of spacecraft, and communications with men in space require that channels be available on a worldwide basis. Navigation and weather satellites must have channels available for transmission of intelligence. Radio telescopes used in space exploration and astronomy require that the weak extraterrestrial signals be receivable without interference from man-made transmissions.

Lasers and Masers for Communications

Lasers utilize the infrared range of electromagnetic waves, and experimental work has been under way for some time.[22] Lasers, being highly directional, give promise for point-to-point transmissions rather than for general broadcast use. They are, as is true of visible light, interrupted or blocked by water vapor or any solid matter and thus require an unimpeded line of sight between transmitter and receiver. They apparently require less energy than radio transmissions except for reserve power for attenuated circumstances.[23] A laser beam is very narrow and if satisfactorily developed should provide a comparatively secure means of almost jam-proof communications.[24] Recent experiments give promise of being able to place 100 million bits of information per second on a visible laser beam,[25] and a recently patented device may ultimately make it possible to carry 50,000 telephone messages on a laser beam by using frequency modulation.[26]

The extent of and results of research work in the use of masers operating in the microwave range of frequencies have not been publicized sufficiently to judge

---

from one frequency range to another, see Coase, 13 *U. of Chi. L. School Record* 23 (No. 2) (1965). The first user rule for international allocation of frequencies has not contributed to a logical allocation of frequencies.

[20] International Telecommunications Regulations reflect this growth: Washington Regulations (1927), from 10 kilocycles to 25,000 kilocycles. Madrid Regulations (1932), from 10 kilocycles to 60,000 kilocycles. Cairo Regulations (1938), from 10 kilocycles to 200 megacycles. Geneva Regulations (1959) from 10 kilocycles to 40 gigacycles. Experimental work is being done in the 300 gigacycle or infrared range of frequencies. See chart, *supra* note 9. See also Glazer, "The Law Making Treaties of the I.T.U. through Time in Space," 60 *Mich. L. Rev.* 269, 316 (1962). Leonard Jaffe, Director of the Communications and Navigation Programs Division of NASA, indicated that the theoretical capacity of the radio frequencies allocated the space communications by the 1963 conference might be "over 500 television channels or 600 times that many telephone circuits but that the theoretical limits would have to be divided by 50 to give presently usable channels." Harris, "Report on Geneva Space Radio Communications Conference and Progress Made in Establishing Global Communications Satellite System," 110 *Cong. Rec.* 173, 178–9 (1964).

[21] The telephone with its broader band requirement tends to replace the telegraph. High-speed data transmissions utilize the equivalent of a voice channel. Government demands are steadily increasing. Facsimile transmission is a wide band requirement. See Slighton, *The Market for Overseas Telecommunications in 1970* (RAND Memo No. 3831-NASA; Sept. 1963). Overseas telephone calls rose from slightly over one million in 1950 to nearly four million in 1960. AT&T expects one hundred million overseas calls per year by 1980. *Hearings on S.2650 and S.2814 before the Senate Committee on Aeronautical and Space Sciences,* 87th Cong., 2d Sess., at 12–13 (1962).

[22] The *Washington Post,* Dec. 9, 1965, at A9, col. 1, contains a report of an unsuccessful attempt on Dec. 8, 1965, to communicate with a ground station via laser beams by the Gemini VII crew. On Dec. 11, 1965, a laser contact was established, although attempted voice communications were unsuccessful. *New York Times,* Dec. 12, 1965. For some general discussion of laser communication experiments see 32 *T.J.* 108, 270 (1965). 4 *Astro. & Aero.* 64 (Apr. 1967) contains a technical description of possible laser communications development by Reinbolt & Randall, who cite nine additional papers on the subject.

[23] See *New York Times,* Dec. 12, 1965.

[24] "Jamming" is accomplished by the transmission of a high volume signal on the same frequency as the signal being jammed. Estep & Kearse, "Space Communications and the Law: Adequate International Control After 1963?" 60 *Mich. L. Rev.* 873, 876–77 (1962) refer to jamming and shifting frequencies to avoid jamming as the "hide and seek" game well illustrated by Soviet jamming of Voice of America broadcasts.

[25] *Wall Street Journal,* May 19, 1966, at 30.

[26] *Washington Post,* Mar. 4, 1967, at A17.

whether or not they have a practical potential for communications.[27]

Communications Satellite Technology

A radio wave travels outward in all directions from a transmitting antenna, but varying amounts of directionality of transmissions on many frequencies can be accomplished by configuration of the antenna, reflectors, and shields. Depending on such factors as the electromagnetic frequency involved, the direction and power of antennas, transmitters, and receivers, the earth's configuration, the weather, the time of day or night, and the state of radiations from the sun or other sources, the transmission may arrive at its destination via one or more of several propagation paths.[28] The radio waves may go directly from transmitter to receiver; via reflection down from the troposphere or the ionosphere; via scattering from one of these layers; via reflection from the ground; or via ducts formed in part by the surface of the earth, low clouds, or other atmospheric layers. Frequencies higher than 30 megacycles may be aimed to penetrate the ionosphere, which is said to be transparent to waves at these frequencies. The higher the frequency, however, the greater the attenuation of the transmission from intervening moisture and other substances, with the consequence that frequencies above 20,000 megacycles per second have not previously been very satisfactory for space communications,[29] and it is not known how useful they can be in the future. The frequencies in the higher ranges have little surface "duct" propagation, and communication using such frequencies must ordinarily rely primarily on line-of-sight transmission using relay sta-

tions. In some circumstances, however, it is possible to use signals reflected from the ground or from layers of upper atmosphere.

For the frequencies between 100 and 20,000 megacycles per second, which can be made to penetrate the reflective layers surrounding the earth fairly easily, satellites provide very good relay stations, thereby extending line-of-sight transmission up to approximately halfway around the earth. Techniques for using much higher frequencies are being perfected. Other frequencies including the range from about 10 to 30 kilocycles per second can, at certain angles of incidence, also be used to penetrate the reflective layers.[30]

Satellites are in practical commercial use as a means of long-distance communications in addition to cables[31] and regular high frequency radio transmissions with ranges up to 12,000 miles. Present satellites, especially the American ones, utilize low power, transmitting com-

---

[27] For a discussion of the potentials of lasers and masers see "Lasers and Their Applications." Conference sponsored by I.E.E. Electronics and Science Division, The Institute of Electrical and Electronics Engineers (U.K. & Erie Section), The Institution of Electronic and Radio Engineers (Sept. 1964); A. E. Siegman, *Microwave Solid-State Masers* (1964). Hughes Aircraft Company has been working with lasers which it thinks hold promise for deep space communications. 32 *Telecommunications Reports* 29 (July 11, 1966) [hereinafter cited as *T.R.*].

[28] See Everett, *supra* note 9, at 615–39; and Buckheim, *New Space Handbook* 96–100 (rev. ed. 1963). As previously noted, lasers and masers are propagated in a very narrow, very highly directional beam suited for point-to-point transmission.

[29] Plans for the 1970's include use of frequencies in the gigacycle range. See ComSat Report to the President and Congress for the Calendar Year 1966, at 12, and *infra* note 31.

[30] See Dept. of Defense, *Annual Report for Fiscal Year 1961*, 21, 210, 263 (1962). Weppler, "Intercontinental Television Relaying by Satellite: Mondiovision," 29 *T.J.* 247, 249 (1962) contains a full discussion in nontechnical terms. Huszagh, "The International Law Making Process: A Case Study on the International Regulations of Space Telecommunications" 37–41 (J.S.D. dissertation, 1964, U. of Chicago Law Library.)

[31] The capacity of cables, even with modern transistors, appears to be limited in comparison to that of communications satellites. In May 1965, a vice-president of AT&T reported that the latest trans-Atlantic cable "has a capacity of 138 voice circuits, compared with 36 in the initial trans-Atlantic system." Hough, "Communications Progress and Problems," *Fifth Nat'l Conf. on the Peaceful Uses of Space* 145–46 (NASA, 1966). It is also reported that a modern cable with 720 two-way voice circuits could be built. Cf. Segal, "Communications Satellites—Progress and Road Ahead," 17 *Vand. L. Rev.* 677, 679 (1966). ComSat's 1966 annual report at 11 suggests four 1970 satellites with combined capacity of up to 84,000 voice grade channels, four 1973 satellites with combined capacity of twice the 1970 capacity, four 1978 satellites with five times the 1970 capacity. A ComSat press release of Dec. 16, 1966, projected the capacity of the four 1978 satellites together as providing simultaneously 96 full-time color TV channels and 360,000 voice grade channels. Since the same release refers to the use of frequencies in the gigacycle range, it would seem that the 1978 satellites would use highly directional transmissions with relatively little interference. If these ComSat estimates of technological advances are accurate, the overcrowding of the electromagnetic spectrum may become less acute. Although improvements in cable capacity are also anticipated, there is apparently a lower maximum capacity so far as present planning is concerned unless wave guides can be developed for practical and economic use.

paratively weak signals on wide frequency bands which give usable signals at powerful earth receiving and sending stations. Using low power lessens interference with reception by less sensitive receivers on the same frequencies.[32] The use of highly directional antennas and special amplifiers coupled with isolation of ground station transmitters contribute to minimizing interference with conventional radio operations.[33] Satellites offer alternative methods of communications not only for long distances over water, formerly limited to high-frequency and cable transmissions, but also for land relay networks.[34]

Proposals for overland communications, insofar as the United States is concerned, raise questions of domestic law and policy, but international questions are also involved. Does Intelsat, assuming it retains a monopoly of international communications via satellites, control all communications satellites, even if used for national domestic communications only? Overland satellite communications in Western Europe will obviously be international and if the United States elects to have a separate

domestic system spanning three thousand or more miles, the European countries can very well argue that they should have their own regional system. This problem is discussed in some detail later in this chapter and in Appendix C.

Passive and Active Relay Satellites

There are two basic types of satellites for communication purposes.[35] Echo II is an example of an experimental passive satellite which reflects signals transmitted toward it. Very high-powered transmitters and sensitive receivers are required on the ground to utilize the weak reflected signal. It is doubtful that any regular operational systems using passive satellites will be established since active satellites have proved to be much more satisfactory.

Active satellites, such as Intelsat I, differ from the passive in that they receive a signal, amplify it, and then transmit it on a different frequency to a receiver on the ground.[36] Such satellites must have a built-in power source, transmitters, and receivers. Transmitters and receivers on the ground do not require as much power to utilize the signals from active satellites as from passive ones. In addition to differences stemming from active versus passive satellites, there are also substantial operating differences depending on the altitude and orientation of orbit of the satellites.

Low- and Medium-Altitude Satellites

The plane of the ellipse of a satellite must pass through the center of the earth. Subject to this limitation the orbit of a satellite may have any orientation with reference to the earth and may be quite elliptical or almost a perfect circle. A medium- or low-altitude system, orbiting at 6,000 to 12,000 miles, requires the use of several satellites for global coverage, plus elaborate scanning, tracking, and high-powered receiving equipment. Each satellite is only within the line of sight or "view" of a particular pair of transmitting and receiving stations for a comparatively short time before it is hidden by the

---

[32] The Soviet Molniya satellites are reported to use 40-watt power, and the Intelsat II satellites 18-watt power (compared with 6-watt power for Intelsat I). *Chicago Tribune,* Mar. 19, 1967, sec. 1, p. 4, citing W. F. Hilton in the British publication "Spaceflight."

[33] See Weppler, *supra* note 30 and ComSat press release, "Earth Stations" of Oct. 19, 1966, for a description of ground station equipment for space communications. See also FCC, "Second Notice of Inquiry into the Allocation of Frequency Bands for Space Communications," Docket No. 13522, attachment pp. 6–7 (May 17, 1961). "Some Principles for Allocating the Radio Frequency Spectrum and Formulating Plans for Various Radio Services," 19 *Electrovyaz No. 3,* 1, 8–12 (from Russian) (NASA Accession No. N65–32276; 1965).

[34] Fiedler, "Television Service for Large Areas Using Satellites," 20 *Frequency* 222 (July 1966) (in German) suggests using a centralized antenna system similar to CATV in the U.S. In 1965, ABC requested FCC authorization to place a satellite in orbit to relay domestic TV programs to 200 affiliates from coast to coast. *New York Times,* May 14, 1965, at 1; *id.* at 23. ComSat considered placing satellites in orbit for the purpose of leasing channels to the TV companies. *Wall Street Journal,* Sept. 22, 1965, at 2. The Ford Foundation proposal for orbiting several satellites to be utilized for nonprofit educational TV has been extensively reported in the press. See, e.g., *Newsweek,* Aug. 15, 1966, at 76, 77; *New York Times,* Aug. 7, 1966, sec. 4, at 2, 7E; *Washington Post,* Aug. 7, at E4; see also Marsten, *supra* note 1. The cost of earth stations and the need for interference-free reception are obvious practical and technical limitations on the use of satellites for short-distance communications. However, once an earth station has been established for any reason, the distance involved in a transmission via satellite to another earth station has no bearing on the cost.

[35] See Hedreich, "Communications Satellite Technology," Fourth National Conference on Peaceful Uses of Space 155 (NASA SP–51; 1964). Marsten, *supra* note 1, at 681 describes systems concepts in several articles. Buckheim, *supra* note 28, at 259–64 discusses passive and active synchronous and nonsynchronous satellites. Glasstone, *supra* note 9, at 270–82.

[36] ITU regulations require a shift from an up to a down frequency.

curvature of the earth. To maintain continuous communication, a second satellite must be in "view" by the pair of stations before the first satellite passes from "view" below the horizon. Thus, a medium-altitude system may require a dozen or more satellites to insure "visibility" between pairs of stations most of the time. Launching costs may be reduced by launching several satellites from one booster, but this requires maneuvering the satellites apart in their orbits. Orbits for low- and medium-altitude satellites may be "phased" so that a satellite's position relative to that of other satellites in the system will remain constant; they may also be "random." Random orbits require sophisticated scanning equipment and entail some risk that there will be occasional periods when service to any given point on earth will fail temporarily because no satellite will be in view of the ground station.

Synchronous Satellites

An alternative to the low- and medium-altitude satellite system is the high-orbiting synchronous equatorial satellite. A synchronous satellite is placed approximately 22,300 miles above the equator and revolves around the earth at a speed synchronized with the rotation of the earth. Thus the satellite appears to be in a stationary position above a point on the earth, making it possible to utilize slightly less expensive but nonetheless complicated scanning and tracking equipment.[37] Since a perfect synchronous orbit can seldom be attained, however, some drift does occur and occasional "station-keeping" adjustments are required. In the synchronous system one satellite is able to cover 160° of the globe but cannot cover either of the polar caps, a limiting condition if complete communication coverage is required for any specific use. The system requires only three satellites to provide satisfactory world-wide commercial coverage, but each requires a precise separate launch by a more powerful booster than that required for the lower altitude satellites. ComSat, manager of Intelsat, has indicated a desire to place four or more synchronous satellites in orbit as part of a permanent operational global system;[38] more may

be required if traffic increases as expected. The extra satellites would be used for special communications requirements of the United States, and some would be held in reserve for quick launchings if one of the satellites in orbit ceased to function.[39]

Active satellites, presently relying on solar power and storage cells, are limited in power for onboard signal reception, amplification, and transmission.[40] The low-power levels aboard the satellites must be compensated for with high-powered, sophisticated, and consequently expensive ground equipment in order that signals of sufficient fidelity and magnitude for reliable communications may be obtained. Earth stations must also be isolated from areas of heavy electromagnetic traffic to transmit and receive signals without interference.[41]

The Outlook for Technological Development

The outlook for the 1970s and beyond is very impressive. Methods of increasing effective radiated power (ERP) from the satellites are under intense study, and developments include improvements in the power source, in increased antenna gain, and in spacecraft stabilization.[42] Color television[43] and facsimile and computer data[44] have been successfully transmitted. The feasibility of using satellites as navigational aids for ships and aircraft, for air traffic control, for air-sea rescue coordination, and for satellite tracking is being researched.[45] One

---

[37] Earth stations for synchronous satellites may cost approximately $5,000,000 while a comparable station for a nonsynchronous satellite may cost from $6,000,000 to $10,000,000. Operating costs of synchronous satellites also tend to be a little less. These figures do not include the cost of tying the earth station to the terrestrial communications system. McDonald, *supra* note 1.

[38] ComSat filed a petition with FCC for authorization to build six 1,200 voice-channel satellites, four of which would be orbited. *Wall Street Journal,* Mar. 1, 1966, at 4, col. 3. ComSat press release of Apr. 28, 1966, described a proposed contract with TRW, Inc. calling for delivery of six satellites between Feb. and May 1968.

[39] See ComSat press release of Oct. 19, 1966, Commercial Communication Satellite Service to Expand to Pac. & Atlantic.

[40] Intensive studies are under way to develop nuclear power and more efficient solar power for needed satellite power capacity. See *Significant Achievements in Space Communications and Navigation 1958–1964,* 55 (NASA, 1966).

[41] This may be an obstacle in heavily industrialized areas where radio wave emitting sources are numerous.

[42] *Supra* note 40, at 52. Technological progress in the satellite communications field is producing economic advantages over cable communications. See speech by Charyk, ComSat president, before Nat'l Ass'n of Broadcasters Annual Convention in Chicago in March-April 1966, reported in 32 *T.R.* 18 (Apr. 4, 1966).

[43] *Washington Post,* Dec. 14, 1966, at 48.

[44] *Wall Street Journal,* Jan. 16, 1967, at 1.

[45] Airlines insisted before Congress that satellite service is

of the far-reaching potentialities of space satellites is their use for direct broadcasting to home receivers.[46] FM broadcast is presently possible, and television and AM broadcasts will be feasible when satellites have engineered into them greatly increased power supplies, especially for television. Engineers are satisfied that facilities can be developed within a few years. The possibility of direct broadcast to home receivers raises important legal, political, and policy questions of ownership and control which will be discussed subsequently in this chapter. It is recognized that technological information is subject to early obsolescence as scientific advances are made, and thus decisions appropriate at the time made may be unrealistic soon thereafter.

Potential Conflicts and Cooperation

Development of telecommunication systems has required nations to elect between private and public or mixed ownership with the United States being one of the few to opt primarily for private ownership except for

some government requirements. It has also required extensive international arrangements. The first International Telegraph Convention was signed in Paris in 1865, and from the beginning the International Telecommunications Union (ITU) has developed with extensive responsibilities in the field of international telecommunications.

The development of communications satellites and the increasing demand for communications utilizing electromagnetic waves present steadily increasing problems of allocation and control of frequencies for the International Telecommunications Union.[47] The problems of frequency allocation are not peculiar to satellite communications although they are more acute. These problems are beyond the scope of this study, except for a brief summary to be found commencing at page 114. The problems are further complicated by the apparent and promised economics of communications by satellites which, if borne out, will transform the economic structure of communications systems, make obsolete costly equipment, and create a threat to many vested interests.[48]

Nations may, for security reasons or for nationalistic prestige or for political reasons, be concerned about a single world-wide communications system over which they would have little control and which might be under the control or domination of an unsympathetic power or

---

essential. *New York Times,* Oct. 2, 1966, at 88, col. 3. First communication between an aircraft and an earth station via satellite was in early 1965. Charyk, "The Coming Era of Satellite Communications," *Fifth National Conference on the Peaceful Uses of Space* 139 (NASA, 1966). See also: 32 *T.R.* 29 (Sept. 12, 1966) for reference to mobile radio service and satellites; 32 *T.R.* 31 (Oct. 3, 1966); 33 *T.R.* 51 (Dec. 19, 1966); 32 *T.R.* 25 (Nov. 28, 1966). ICAO members have been urged to participate in tests, 32 *T.R.* 38 (Nov. 14, 1966). FAA, in a status report to the House Government Operations Subcommittee for Military Operations, stated it saw a "positive need" for a satellite communications service to meet aviation requirements, 32 *T.R.* 20 (Sept. 6, 1966). ComSat requested bids for satellites for aeronautical service in Apr. 1966 but whether this was as manager of Intelsat is not entirely clear, 32 *T.R.* 10 (Apr. 4, 1966). Ford Motor Co. is studying the possibility of utilizing satellites in connection with automobile traffic control, 32 *T.R.* 27 (July 25, 1966). James W. Campbell of Technology Audit Corp. discusses the subject in "Possible Uses of Satellites for Navigation and Traffic Coordination," 31 *T.J.* 37–42 (Feb. 1964).

[46] "Broadcast satellites can further provide emergency and civil defense communications to an entire country. As an educational aid they can be used to bring the best of educational material to the remotest of communities. They can provide for global dissemination of information, and can ultimately serve to unite the people of large areas more rapidly than would conventional techniques," *supra* note 40, at 55. The subject has received considerable attention: *Washington Post,* Apr. 18, 1967, at 2; May 5, 1967, at 11, col. 7; *New York Times,* Nov. 30, 1965; *Chicago Daily News,* May 18, 1965; Haviland, "Space Telecasting for World Education," 16th IAF Congress (Athens, Sept. 1965).

[47] See Codding, *The International Telecommunication Union, passim* (1952) for a comprehensive account of the history, structure, and operations of the ITU. At the risk of substantially oversimplifying a very complex problem, the members of the ITU in periodic conferences allocate bands of frequencies to particular uses (*supra* note 9); within these uses the first nation to file a claim for and use a particular frequency has priority in the event of interference with another nation using the same frequency. There is no real enforcement authority, however, and ordinarily most complaints are resolved through negotiations within the ITU framework. In many instances neighboring countries enter into bilateral or multilateral agreements to provide additional controls over radio and television as between the contracting parties. See, e.g., Inter-American Arrangements Concerning Radio Communications, entered into force July 18, 1938, 54 Stat. 2514; E.A.S. 200; Inter-American Radio Agreement, entered into force April 13, 1952; 3 U.S.T. 3064. There are many similar agreements, all subject to frequent revisions as conditions change and as technology advances.

[48] 33 *T.R.* 29 (Apr. 30, 1967); 32 *T.R.* 18–21 (Oct. 10, 1966). These refer to the conflicts and arguments with communications carriers over costs, channels, etc., which reflect the possible impact on the existing structure. The press and periodicals contain innumerable references to various aspects of the problem.

an international organization not amenable to their direction, with the possibility that access to the system might be interrupted.[49] This factor is significant in the context of Intelsat, which is substantially influenced by the United States; the potential Soviet Molniya system; and the proposed French system. There has also been some discussion, perhaps primarily by would-be suppliers, of a possible Latin American system and of other regional systems. Although there may be no technological justification for more than one system, such suggestions have a strong nationalistic appeal. Presumably all systems will compete for the same frequencies, subject to such alleviation of the overcrowding as may be brought about by technical developments, including directionality and the use of gigacycle frequencies giving many more circuits.[50]

The organization and structure of Intelsat is scheduled to be renegotiated by 1970, and it is almost certain that some European countries will demand a greater voice in Intelsat matters.[51] France has announced her intention of launching a system, Saros, in 1970 which will be "open to European cooperation,"[52] but the problems of

NATO caused by French withdrawal has added to the attractiveness for its other members of the United States suggestion of a separate system for NATO.[53]

If all the systems which have been mentioned or suggested are established, the problems of competition, coordination, interchange, and frequency assignment will be aggravated, and the impact on cables is difficult to foresee.[54] Lack of adequate experience with and proof of reliability of satellite communications, as well as cost and problems of suitable locations for earth stations, has led some spokesmen for the communications industry to suggest that cables will still be essential in the satellite era.[55] For example, ComSat, on April 25, 1966, requested and received authority to construct an earth station on St. Croix, Virgin Islands, but this had to be changed to Puerto Rico on November 16, 1966, because of electronic interference.[56] During the same period a group of United States communications common carriers requested and received from the FCC authority to build

---

[49] Concern for security, absolute control, and possibly costs contributed strongly to the establishment of the Dept. of Defense Communication Satellite System. Political chauvinism plus distrust of the political potential of Intelsat doubtless were major factors in the decision of the Soviets not to join Intelsat, although it is questionable whether the Soviets will be able to establish a commercially viable system, either domestic or international. France has indicated an intent to establish its own system, presumably motivated by political rather than economic factors, but has nonetheless joined Intelsat. Canada's discussion of a separate system for domestic purposes is openly motivated by the political desire to avoid losing control of its domestic communications system to the United States or to Intelsat.

[50] Intelsat is utilizing frequencies at 3700–4200 and 5925–6125 Mc/s plus some frequencies just below 5925. The Soviets have used 3400–3700 and 4400 to 4700 Mc/s. In experimental work there are many exceptions, and as traffic increases the competition will increase.

[51] See editorial, "The ComSat Question," *Technology Week* (English) Oct. 24, 1966; see also E. W. Faller, "European Perspective on Satellite Communications" in Marsten, *supra* note 1. "It is pointed out that Europe's current demand for a role and voice in the development of a truly global satellite communication system should not be understood as a repetition of ancient patterns of wasteful competition, but as a plea for a joining of forces in the spirit of useful cooperation." The French views are well known.

[52] *Washington Post,* Feb. 23, 1967, at 43. It is possible that this announcement was made to strengthen France's hand in negotiating the new Intelsat agreement, but it seemed more

probable at this writing that France was determined to have a French system for prestige purposes.

[53] *New York Times,* July 31, 1966, at E8; 32 *T.R.* 31 (Oct. 3, 1966). The U.S. ambassador noted that the system would by-pass France, *Washington Post,* Sept. 29, 1966, at A22, col. 4.

[54] The most recently constructed trans-Atlantic cable has a capacity of 138 voice circuits. See Hough, *supra* note 31, at 145. At a cost of $11.9 million, IT&T is now laying a cable between England and Lisbon to be in operation by Spring 1969, with 480 channels. Existing satellites could presently supply this requirement or, for about the same cost, an additional satellite with about three times the capacity could be put in orbit with a life expectancy of several years. Technology and cost will doubtless restrain many countries from establishing separate satellite systems which, if used, would serve national pride but would not serve to expedite international communications.

[55] This was the tenor of testimony given by AT&T representatives to the House Government Operations Subcommittee in connection with anticipated circuit requirements for the next several years; see 32 *T.R.* 28 (Sept. 19, 1966). Lester, vice-president of Bell Tel. Co. of Canada, stated in a speech in Montreal Nov. 29, 1966: "But it is unquestionably by a combination [of satellite and microwave] that the general television public and broadcasting interests would be best served at the lowest cost," 32 *T.R.* 40 (Dec. 5, 1966). The same position has been adopted by the Telephone Association of Canada, 33 *T.R.* 37 (Feb. 8, 1967). It is hardly to be expected that a company such as AT&T would acknowledge that satellites could replace their long lines.

[56] See ComSat press releases of those days. Competition is very keen for interference-free sites for electronic installations of many types.

a 720-circuit cable from Florida to the Virgin Islands.[57] The FCC is obviously concerned with the problem, but there is insufficient experience to enable the FCC to define precisely what place satellite communications can fill satisfactorily. There are also heavy economic and political implications.

Satellites will have a heavy impact on the communication centers of Europe such as Paris and London since "virtually all international telephone calls from or to Asia, Africa, and the Middle East are routed through London or Paris, for which these cities collect substantial 'transit fees'—for example, a call from Abidjan, capital of Ivory Coast, to Lagos, Nigeria, five hundred miles or so down the coast, may be routed through both Paris and London."[58] A country with its own earth station could communicate directly by satellite with almost any other nation possessing an earth station. This fact may contribute to European reluctance to see rapid conversion to satellite communications.

Potential conflicts involving domestic law exist in many individual states, and probably more so in the United States than elsewhere because telecommunications is not a government monopoly there. These conflicts may have repercussions beyond national borders when more than one national communications entity wishes to participate directly in satellite communications operations or when a national agency attempts to control international activities through domestic regulation, such as establishing rates for using satellite channels. A somewhat analogous situation may develop in Europe, where the state communications monopolies have been troubled with private "pirate" broadcasts from the high seas. If and when direct satellite-to-home receiver transmission becomes a reality, any broadcaster with access to a satellite channel can reach almost any nation.

Allocation of Electromagnetic Wave Frequencies

The International Telecommunications Union, since 1947 a specialized agency of the United Nations, has played, and undoubtedly will continue to play, the lead-

ing role in the allocation of electromagnetic frequencies.[59] Basically, ITU allocates bands of frequencies for types of use rather than to specific users, and nations assign specific frequencies to their stations which are registered with the International Frequency Registration Board of the ITU on a "first come, first served" basis.[60] The ITU has not differentiated between military and nonmilitary uses, but in practice military users are likely to utilize, within the limits imposed by their equipment, the band which best meets their requirements at the moment, particularly if the band is not registered or not in use.[61]

The assignment and allocation of radio frequencies is at best an extremely complex technical problem made difficult by the overcrowding of a limited resource, and the advent of the space age has added many new demands for frequencies. Natural phenomena in air and space sometimes generate electromagnetic waves in a wide range of frequencies which interfere with man's efforts to transmit information, and man-made transmissions may interfere with efforts to receive information of natural origins coming in from space.[62]

Although most nations of the world are members of the ITU, violations of frequency assignments are frequent. Interference is usually inadvertently caused by crowded spectrum and changing atmospheric conditions or by inadequate equipment, but it is sometimes the result of disregard for rules or of deliberate jamming.[63] The

---

[57] *Wall Street Journal,* Dec. 8, 1966, at 3. It may be justified to query whether FCC approved a compromise solution because it did not think enough technological information was available to make a decision that might have extensive long term policy effects on the future structure of our communications system. Political pressures were obviously very heavy.

[58] Silberman, "The Little Bird That Casts a Big Shadow," 75 *Fortune* 109 (Feb. 1967).

[59] See generally for the structure and operations of ITU, "International Cooperation for Outer Space," Sen. Doc. No. 56, 89th Cong., 1st Sess., 263–84 (1965); Codding, *supra* note 47.

[60] Frequency uses are registered with the ITU's International Frequency Registration Board as they are received. Actual assignment of a frequency band to a user is made by the government of each member country in accordance with their domestic law. Detailed procedures are established in the ITU Radio Regulations.

[61] Art. 50 of the 1959 ITU Geneva Convention and Art. 51 of the 1965 Montreux Convention provide that "members and associate members retain their entire freedom with regard to military radio installations of their army, navy, and air forces."

[62] Since the natural transmissions from space are usually weak and frequency cannot be changed, the appropriate frequencies must be kept free from man-made interference if the natural signals are to be received for use in man's efforts to acquire knowledge from deep space.

[63] See *supra* note 42; *Significant Achievements in Space Communications and Navigation 1958–1964,* 55 (NASA, 1966); C. Christol, *The International Law of Outer Space* 398–99 (1966); Naval War College, *International Law Studies* (1962); Federal Communications Commission, *Annual Report*

need for the permanent allocation of bands for specific purposes was recognized by the ITU at its 1959 and 1963 meetings, and the table of frequency allocations now includes the entire spectrum between 3 kilocycles and 300 gigacycles.[64]

ITU has neither the police power nor the ability to apply effective sanctions against nations for frequency violations; but recognition that, if a substantial number of states disregard the rules, every state will suffer has prevented the situation from becoming chaotic. Although direct diplomatic representation and protests have been used, the most frequent recourse has been to the ITU and its consultative organs. In 1965 at Montreux an effort was made to strengthen the authoritative and legislative power of ITU and to provide more formal machinery for resolving disputes.[65]

Intelsat must obtain authority to use radio frequencies through governments and the ITU in basically the same manner as other communications carriers using radio frequencies. ComSat's use of frequencies is subject to Federal Communications Commission controls, and Intelsat's use of frequencies available to it is controlled by its representative ruling body, the Interim Committee.[66]

The Organizations for Utilizing Space Satellites for Communications

Satellite communications facilities may be organized and owned on a national or international basis, and ownership may be public, private, or mixed. Political factors and national policies will continue to exercise at least as much influence on the communications structure as the legal, economic, and technological factors. Even satellite communications systems intended to meet the domestic requirements of only one country have international aspects because the satellites are in non-national space; because it is necessary to coordinate the use of frequencies to avoid or minimize radio interference; and because any system can be given the technical capacity to reach across national boundaries wherever there are ground stations to receive. Limitations to national uses represent political as well as technological decisions.

Nations representing a very high percentage of all

---

161 (1965) for a discussion of handling of U.S.–Canadian interference problems; see also Korovin, "The Struggle for Space and International Law," *Kosmos i Meshdunarodnoye Pravo* 7 (Korovin ed. 1963) in which the author alleges that the U.S. used an "Echo" satellite for relaying Radio Free Europe programs. Sputniks I and II used frequencies assigned and registered for other purposes. Suggestions were made to give space communications priorities over all transmissions except distress calls. Svanyi, "Thoughts on Legal Provisions to Improve and Safeguard Space Communications," 30 *T.J.* 73–76 (1963).

[64] The chart from the 1959 ITU Radio Regs., Art. 2, para. 112, is reproduced *supra* note 9 and the 1963 chart taken from 30 *T.J.* 367 (Dec. 1963) is reproduced *supra* note 14; see also FCC *Annual Report* 47 (1964). Of the various cooperative agreements between the U.S. and other nations on experimental space communications work, tracking stations, etc., only one has been located which has a provision concerning frequencies available for use: Executive Agreement for Space Tracking and Communications Station at Antigua, between the U.S. and the U.K., signed Jan. 23, 1967, Art. 7. See also the Report of the Extraordinary Administrative Radio Conference of 1963.

[65] The 1959 ITU Convention with six annexes is in 12 *U.S.T.* 1761. Treaties in Force (1967 ed.) lists 118 signatories as of Jan. 1967. The 1965 Montreux Convention, which supercedes the Geneva Convention for those countries which adhere to it, including the U.S., added an Optional Additional Protocol on Compulsory Settlement of Disputes which was not signed by the U.S., USSR, France, or Great Britain (International Telecommunication Convention, Final Protocol to the Convention, Additional Protocol to the Convention, Resolutions, Recommendations and Opinions, Montreux, 1965). Gen. sec. ITU, Art. 28 of the ITU Convention provides for diplomatic negotiations or, in case of any existing agreements between the disputants or of failures to resolve the questions, for arbitration under Annex 3 which constitutes a brief conventional arbitration agreement couched in permissive terms. Underwood, "Problems of Participation in the Global Commercial Communications Satellite System," 18 *S.C.L.*

Rev. 796, 807–11 (1966) discusses the role of ITU and suggests at 808 that the situation "[M]ay be analogized to that of a policeman assigned to a street intersection under a set of instructions which state he may indicate to motorists the direction in which they must legally travel in order to avoid hitting one another, but that if they violate these legal requirements, then all he can do is stand on the street corner and cry 'foul'," *id.* at 808.

[66] Allocation of frequencies and enforcement of discipline are not peculiar to satellite communications and will not be treated in further detail in this study, although they will continue to be problems of major significance. For a record of some of ITU's activities relating at least in part to space communications see: the 8th, 9th, and 10th plenary assemblies of the CCIR (Warsaw, 1956; Los Angeles, 1959; Geneva, 1963); the ITU Plenipotentiary Conference (Geneva, Oct.-Dec. 1959); the ITU Administrative Radio Conference (Geneva, Aug.-Dec., 1959); and the ITU Extraordinary Administrative Radio Conference (Geneva, Autumn 1963). In 1959, CCIR established Study Group IV, "Space Systems." The ITU has made a number of reports to the U.N. in 1962, 1963, 1964, etc. and to the International Telecommunication Convention of Montreux in 1965, cited previously. Frequency allocation and control are very clearly of such significance that they warrant a separate, extensive study not possible in a single volume on the law of man's activities in space.

international telecommunications traffic have joined Intelsat in a cooperative effort to provide facilities for international commercial communications, but it is not yet known what other systems, domestic or international, may be established or what national services Intelsat or some other international organization may provide. There may be political pressures for bilateral communications satellite arrangements, but economic and technological factors will probably exert a controlling pressure for multilateral arrangements sanctioned by governments.[67] Earth stations will for the most part probably be subject to individual national ownership and control, although several small contiguous countries may jointly own, control, and use a single earth station. A nation with its own earth station will be freed from one form of dependency on other nations, which has been felt by those who did not have cable terminals on their own land or who found it necessary for their cables to cross the territory of another.[68] Conventional radio and cable transmitting and receiving facilities present many of the same problems presented by satellite communications and, in most instances, are or will be in direct competition. The space segment consisting of satellites and necessary tracking and control facilities has no real counterpart in conventional or cable communications, however. Even in a cable system requiring a multilaterally owned relay station the legal problems and technology are quite different because the space segment involves a large number of nations and the satellite is not on one nation's territory. Radio and cable communications require essentially bilateral arrangements with possibly intermediary third-party relay stations, whereas satellite communications facilities are, because of costs and technology, better suited to multilateral arrange-

ments even when the particular communication is only bilateral.

National, Regional, and International Systems

There are, in addition to Intelsat, at least three other satellite communications systems in operation. A United States military system is intended to serve national needs and to be available to allies under some circumstances.[69] The Department of Defense assumed responsibility in April 1965 for the operation of NASA's synchronous satellite repeaters, Syncom II and III, and for research and development of a military communications satellite system, which is now operational although still in the experimental stage.[70] This system is for command and operational purposes and will be of limited capacity, partly because it uses small portable-type earth stations.

The United States ambassador to NATO proposed, on June 29, 1966, to the NATO council that NATO develop its own satellite communications system.[71] The initial phase of the program was inaugurated in July 1967, and utilizes the U.S. military satellites already in orbit. The next phase requires a $45 million budget and, when approved, involves the launching of NATO's own satellites over the Atlantic. The need for reliable communications with the southern members of NATO is obvious, especially with the present uncertainties about whether or not France will permit the continued operation of communications across her territory since her withdrawal from NATO. France will probably not participate in the NATO satellite system.[72]

---

[67] For obvious reasons ComSat and Intelsat officials strongly oppose national or regional systems and argue that they are neither technologically nor economically feasible.

[68] This is a matter of cost and is of some practical importance, especially during periods of strained relations or of war with neighboring states. Use of Intelsat during war is not mentioned in either the Interim or Special agreements. In connection with Spain's plans for an earth station, a representative of the Spanish National Telephone System suggested that the new medium of satellite communications offers Spain, for the first time in history, the chance to have her own communications, without depending in any way on other countries. The Spanish comment may be overly optimistic since the space segment will not be under exclusive Spanish control. Canada is utilizing the U.S. Andover earth station. 33 *T.R.* 14 (Jan. 23, 1967).

[69] For general background, see "Government Use of Satellite Communications," *Hearings before the House of Representatives Subcommittee on Military Operations of the Committee on Government Operations,* 89th Cong., 2d Sess. 1–46 (1966); also 32 *T.R.* 9 (June 20, 1966).

[70] Seven communications satellites were placed in subsynchronous orbit on June 16, 1966 (*New York Times,* June 17, 1966, at A4, col. 1), but did not perform as well as hoped (*Wall Street Journal,* June 17, 1966). Additional launches have been made: see *Washington Post,* Aug. 27, 1966, at A3; *id.,* Jan. 19, 1967, at A7. The Dep't of Defense section of the U.S. Aeronautics and Space Activities 1966, Report to the Congress from the President of the United States, at 54–59 (Jan. 31, 1967) describes the Military Communication Systems: the Defense Communication Satellite Program Syncom (DCSP), the Initial Defense Communications Satellite Project (IDCSP), the Operational Defense Communication System (DSCS), the Tactical Satellite Communication Program (TacSatCom), and various other experimental programs.

[71] See references, *supra* note 53.

[72] *New York Times,* July 9, 1967, at 17, col. 1.

NASA operates communications systems of several different types for experimental purposes. As part of its own space activities, NASA provides support through the Space Tracking and Acquisition Network (STADAN) and the Smithsonian Astrophysical Observatory (SAO) optical tracking service. The NASA Communications Network (NASCOM) is the connecting link between the network stations and control centers.[73] The newer Applications Technology Satellite (ATS) Program includes experimental work in satellite communications technology, as well as in meteorology and geophysics.[74]

The Soviets have launched several Molniya communications satellites which are being used at least on an experimental basis for internal Soviet communications and for experimental work with other countries, especially France. The Soviets may also be using satellites for military communications, although their public statements place heavy emphasis on cultural exchanges.

A Molniya satellite was first launched on April 23, 1965, with other launches following: October 14, 1965, March 1966, October 1966, and May 25, 1967.[75] The 65° inclination orbits are elliptical with perigee of about 310 miles over the southern hemisphere and an apogee of about 24,500 miles over the northern hemisphere. The orbital periods are about 12 hours of which between 9 and 10 hours can be used for transmitting in the Soviet Union. Molniya satellites transmit with a power of 40 watts compared with 6 for Early Bird and 18 for Intelsat II series satellites. The limited information released by the Soviets and other available information indicates the Molniya satellites have been used for all types of communication, including an exchange of color television with France in November 1965 and telephone service between Moscow and Vladivostok since June 1965,[76] although it is not clear if service has been on a regular or experimental basis.

At the time Comsat was established as the United States entity to participate in international communications satellite development, it was uncertain to what extent other nations would participate. Intelsat was then quickly established and it took over much of what had been national United States satellite operations, although the United States has maintained a very strong cooperative program. Even before Intelsat the United States participated very actively in cooperative international

---

[73] See NASA section of U.S. Aeronautics and Space Activities, *supra* note 72 at 41–44.

[74] The first ATS satellite was launched Dec. 6, 1966, weighed about 1,550 pounds, and was placed in a near geostationary orbit (*id.* at 24). 33 *Telecommunications Report* 34 (Apr. 3, 1967) refers to the launching of a multipurpose experimental satellite for this program and notes that NASA hopes to have at least 4 satellites of this type in orbit by 1970.

[75] "Soviet Space Programs, 1962–65; Goals and Purposes, Achievements, Plans, and International Implications," *Staff Report for Senate Committee on Aeronautical and Space Sciences,* 225–26, 327–29 (Dec. 30, 1966); *New York Times,* Oct. 21, 1966, at 10, col. 1; *Chicago Tribune,* May 26, 1967, at 4. A conference was held in Moscow, Nov. 15–20, 1965, with Bulgaria, Rumania, Czechoslovakia, and the Soviet Union attending. They discussed, among other things, the possibility of establishing a Communist bloc communications satellite system based on Soviet technology. The reports emanating from the conference contained the usual criticisms of AT&T, ComSat, and Intelsat. A forthcoming book by Zhukov and Korovin (deceased) discusses the conference briefly. Tass reported that delegates from Russia, Bulgaria, Hungary, East Germany, Cuba, Mongolia, Poland, Rumania, and Czechoslovakia met in Moscow, Apr. 5–13, 1967, to discuss "cooperation in space research and peaceful uses of outer space." The delegates agreed to set up a satellite communications program "open to all countries willing to join" (*Chicago Tribune,* Apr. 17, 1967, at 7). It is probable that at some propitious moment the Soviets will announce the establishment of an operating system, although it seems doubtful that such

a system would attract enough traffic to be economically viable or to constitute any real competition to Intelsat. A brief description of the Molniya satellite taken from *Pravda* appears in 32 *T.J.* 192 (May 1965) and is also described by Fortushenko in 32 *T.J.* 422–24 (Oct. 1965). Lustiberg of the Soviet Press Agency, Apon, described the Molniya satellite in some detail in "Satellite Radio Communications in the U S S R" 33 *T.J.* 425–27 (Dec. 1966).

[76] *Soviet Space Programs, 1962–65 supra* note 75. See also *Chicago Tribune,* Mar. 19, 1967, at 4. The Soviet Union has not released much data about the capacity of the Molniya satellites. In the Soviet Space Program report it is stated at 226: "In spite of their possession of the capability, the concept, and the interest, the Russians have been content to let the transoceanic and intercontinental relay of teletype, facsimili, voice, data, and television, the erection of large structures in space and their use as passive reflectors of radio signals, and the active repeating of radio signals at various altitudes and orbits of interest to system designers become largely American achievements. The reason is very possibly a choice of priorities: the Russians could conduct an aggressive communications satellite program but have failed to do so, because they wished to do other things." It must be assumed that recently launched Soviet satellites reflect technological advances comparable to Intelsat developments, and ComSat acknowledges that the Soviets may have an operational system by 1969. See 33 *T.R.* 35 (May 8, 1967). But the Soviet Union has hardly enough commercial communication with the West to utilize a large capacity system if it provided only East-West service.

satellite experiments and development.[77] The Intelsat system is discussed in detail in subsequent sections of this chapter, but it should be noted that the other operating systems are in different stages of development, serve different purposes, and that only Intelsat is under international control. It may be argued that based on available evidence the Molniya satellites do not constitute an operational system. It is probable that additional "systems" will be established, although they may consist of only one or two satellites and may be of short duration. The factors which may lead to a multiplicity of systems are political rather than technical, economic, or geographic. In addition to the operational systems a number of other national and international systems have been under discussion or development, with three of them limited to the United States.[78]

There has been some discussion of the possibility of a Western European regional system and a British Commonwealth system, but whether these are intended seriously is difficult to assess.[79] France, Germany, Japan, and Canada have generated some publicity over the possibility of separate communications satellite systems.[80] Whether or not any of these systems materialize will depend on political rather than on technological and economic factors, since the nations concerned have or can develop the capacity if they are willing to meet the cost in priorities as well as money. Part of the publicity may be intended to improve prospects for obtaining contracts in connection with Intelsat and to improve bargaining positions in connection with the scheduled reconsideration of the Intelsat Interim Agreement by 1970. Suggestions for separate systems will doubtless recur from time to time partly because the prestige rewards are so dazzling, although very expensive, and partly because national leaders are convinced that the best interests of their nations will best be served by having a system exclusively under their own control or under the control of a small number of nations with an identity of interests. The establishment and structure of national communications satellite systems will be determined primarily on the basis of national law and policy, and, consequently, will not generally be discussed in detail in this chapter, although any such system does have distinct international implications.

There have been proposals for establishing an international communications satellite system under the aegis of the United Nations,[81] but thus far no substantial

---

[77] Frutkin, *International Cooperation in Space, passim,* especially 159–62 (1965). Other nations obviously desire to develop their own capabilities but are limited by financial and technological resources and many are pleased to work cooperatively with the U.S.

[78] See Appendix C for a brief description of the proposals by Carnegie, ABC, Ford Foundation, and ComSat. The Dept. of Defense system is also discussed. NASA also has experimental and operational communications satellites in orbit. NASA satellites are usually multipurpose. ComSat, as has been noted, would prefer to see no communications systems other than Intelsat but if regional or national systems are established they "should be carried out in proper relationship to and with the recognition of the international goal and the international plan" for a global system. Charyk, President of ComSat, quoted in 33 *T.R.* 21 (Mar. 6, 1967).

[79] See "The ComSat Question," editorial in *Technology Week,* Oct. 24, 1966 (a British publication).

[80] See, e.g., *New York Times,* Nov. 15, 1964, June 8, 1965, Nov. 21, 1965; *Washington Post,* Aug. 2, 1964, p. A19, July 29, 1965, Feb. 28, 1966, p. A2, March 4, 1966, p. A8, May 1, 1966, p. A13, Sept. 25, 1966; and *Wall Street Journal,* Oct. 27, 1966, p. 13. France is developing a major rocket-launching base in French Guiana, which has replaced its Algerian base. This new facility will be used by ELDO and ESRO in connection with their efforts to develop reliable launch capabilities for communications satellites. France has also announced plans to launch its own communications satellite in 1970 to handle traffic between France and the French-speaking nations of Africa (33 *T.R.* 10 [Feb. 27, 1967]). Whether France will find

this plan economically feasible is doubtful. It appears to be an effort on the part of France to retain its old position as an interchange point as it has been with cable communications, which the new technology makes quite unnecessary. France and Germany are planning a communications satellite by 1971 at an estimated cost of about $75,000,000 (33 *T.R.* 29 [May 8, 1967]). Canadian authorities have suggested they may wish to have their own satellites. The estimated cost for 2 satellites and 54 earth stations is about $80,000,000 (32 *T.R.* 38 [Nov. 14, 1966]; 33 *T.R.* 32 [March 13, 1967]; 33 *T.R.* 27 [June 5, 1967]).

[81] D. M. Smythe in "Freedom of Information: Some Analysis and a Proposal for Satellite Broadcasting," 6 *Q. Rev. Econ. & Bus.* 7 (Autumn 1966), sharply attacks the entire ComSat-Intelsat system because of U.S. domination and proposes a U.N.-owned system financed in the same manner as the U.N. and structured in a pattern similar to the BBC. See also Morenoff, *World Peace through Space Law* (1967), who strongly supports a communications satellite system under U.N. control. Zhukov, in a paper delivered at the 1966 Astronautical Federal, stated: "The organization of administration and operation of a worldwide system of telecommunications by satellites should incorporate a principle of equal cooperation of all States without any discrimination. Such cooperation might assume various forms: a special agency may be set up." He indicated Intelsat failed to meet these standards. *Ninth Colloquium on the Law of Outer Space* 91, 93 (1967). There has also been discussion of authorizing the U.N. or the ITU to license satellites for various purposes.

progress has been made and neither of the major space powers has given or appears likely to give the proposals official support.

The problem of receiving radio and television programs across international boundaries may be aggravated by direct satellite transmissions to home radio and television receivers which would greatly increase the potential for international broadcasts, using national and international systems.[82] The problem presently exists for standard and television broadcasts near international boundaries; these are frequently regulated to some extent by bilateral treaties relating primarily to interference. Short wave presents the problem on a worldwide basis, and if the countries concerned are not able to resolve differences by negotiations, the unwilling recipient jams the undesired transmission. This situation will probably continue, for the space powers do not appear to be ready for the alternative, which would be to place international telecommunications under the control of the United Nations, the International Telecommunications Union, or some other international organization. It is unlikely that any nation will voluntarily submit to censorship by another nation or by an international organization.

The implications of satellite-to-home transmission for domestic radio and television broadcasting are equally significant and will probably change the economic and operational structure of the industry. The subject requires a great amount of broad policy analysis to determine what structure will best serve the public interest.[83] The fundamental queston is whether a profit-oriented private business heavily regulated by the government is the most suitable entity to own and operate a communications system which can easily span the entire globe.

The Communications Satellite Legislation

Many nations have enacted legislation relating to communications satellites, but only the United States's domestic laws are examined here. It is apparent that ComSat's counterparts in other countries, for the most part government agencies, are subject to government controls and supervision comparable to or greater than those over ComSat.[84]

The ComSat Act providing for a privately owned corporation was passed by a large majority over the opposition of a few vocal members of Congress who

---

[82] There are indications that the development of direct broadcasting to home receivers is being played down for national and international political, as well as technological reasons. See *Hearings on S.2909 before the Senate Committee of Aeronautical and Space Sciences,* 89th Cong., 2d Sess., at 319 (1966), in which Associate Administrator Newell stated: "At this point it is emphasized that NASA does not have a program to develop a broadcast satellite system at this time, nor is there any intent to enter any phase of the broadcast business. We believe, however, that the application of space technology to the vast field of communications in all its forms is a very real technical possibility. NASA must be familiar with these applications of space and their technical requirements. It is with these applications in mind that NASA has undertaken a modest study program in the space broadcasting area." Charyk, ComSat president, stated that it is "more natural, logical, economical" and permits wiser use of broadcast frequencies to go from space to ground stations and then redistribute the broadcasts by existing television networks as they are now (*New York Times,* June 22, 1966, at 12). Why "more natural" is entirely unclear. Schramm, director of Stanford University's Institute of Communications Research, stated that "in 10 to 20 years it should be possible to broadcast television directly from satellites to home receivers. Just how soon this will occur depends more on economic and political considerations than on technology which is far outstripping the former" (*Chicago Tribune,* May 23, 1966, sec. 1A, at 11). John A. Johnson, Vice-president of ComSat, in a paper entitled "Satellite Communications: The Challenge & the Opportunity for International Cooperation," delivered Sept. 14, 1965, at the Washington World Conference on World Peace through Law, stated: "Perhaps the most revolutionary change promised by communications satellites will come about when direct broadcasting from satellites into the home receiver is realized . . . it is a possible development during the decade of the 1970's. . . . With the advent of direct broadcasting of television from satellites, a totally new situation will arise which will test the ingenuity and creativity of the architects of international order."

[83] Ownership and control of programs as well as of distribution systems are among the many problems U.S. policy-makers must decide. The press contains innumerable articles about Congressional and FCC hearings on the general subject. See, e.g., *Washington Post,* Oct. 25, 1965, at B13, in which Representative Cellar is quoted as saying: "I do not want CBS, nor NBC, or ABC to continue to be the pooh-bahs or panjandrums of what the public may see or hear, especially during the prize, prime hours." Views are strongly held, economic interests are very large, and the protagonists for different views will wage strenuous campaigns. See also Bishop's article in the *Wall Street Journal,* Sept. 26, 1966, at 1, col. 1, calling attention to the fact that direct broadcast could render obsolete most radio and TV broadcast equipment in the world while presenting the difficult problems of national sensitivity to foreign transmissions.

[84] The literature in the field is extensive. For some of the problems see Doyle, "Communication Satellites: International Organization for Development and Control," 55 *Cal. L. Rev.* 431, at 432–34 (May 1967); Schwartz, "ComSat, the Carriers, and the Earth Stations: Some Problems with Melding Variegated Interests," 76 *Yale L. J.* 441, 445–46 (Jan. 1967).

vigorously insisted that communications utilizing space should be a government operation. Arguments advanced were that the public, through a government operation, should receive the benefits of the enormous space research and development costs; that most other states treated communications as a government monopoly; that international negotiations might be expedited if a government agency handled the matter for the United States; and that private ownership might lead to monopoly and would give rise to antitrust and regulatory problems. The United States, however, has ordinarily followed the rule that private enterprise should be favored except where national security is involved or where it is evident that private enterprise is incapable or unwilling to act. In this case it was argued that, although much government financing had been used and would still be required, a private, profit-oriented, commercial system for United States participation in Intelsat offered substantial advantages, and that with increasing reliability of operations in space many of the necessary operating facilities could be put into the hands of private industry, resulting advantageously in greater efficiency and in greater private investment. Private industry insisted that the space program should not be a device for changing the American politico-economic structure by eliminating or substantially modifying the patent system, by establishing a major nationalized industry, or by increasing government and political control over the economic structure of the nation. The arguments covered the entire spectrum of private versus public ownership, sometimes heatedly and often repetitiously. The very extensive discussions also covered what private interest should be allowed to participate in the ownership of ComSat.[85] For those who wish to explore in detail the considerations leading to the decision for private ownership, the documentation is extensive.[86] At the time that

---

in the acquisition of equipment used in the system;

6. Structure of ownership or control which will assure maximum possible competition;

7. Full compliance with antitrust legislation and with the regulatory controls of the Government;

8. Development of an economical system the benefits of which will be reflected in overseas communication rates."

Levin in "Organization and Control of Communications Satellites," 113 *U. Pa. L. Rev.* 315, 335 (1965), suggested that the decision favoring private ownership was based in large part on the following assumptions:

"1. Private ownership of a global relay is legally possible and desirable notwithstanding the uncertain state of space law and the fact that orbital objects cannot be policed.

"2. Private ownership is crucial for speedy development and efficient operation even though the government also has the know-how and resources, and can alone provide necessary booster and tracking capability.

"3. Although satellites can accommodate far more varied services than cables, have unique foreign policy implications, and are far more expensive to install, they are essentially an adjunct of existing communications facilities and thus most suitably owned and operated by the international common carriers.

"4. The complex international negotiations needed for satellite communication are best handled by the common carriers—even though such negotiations, necessarily multi- rather than bilateral, involve the State Department and FCC in crucial ways.

"5. The great capital and operating costs of any system, added to the need to service uneconomic markets, virtually guarantee losses for a long time, and private common carriers rather than the government should bear these losses.

"6. The satellite and ground station components must be jointly owned, even though they are technologically distinct, and common ownership would open the door to government intrusion into both domestic and international communications."

[85] The President in a policy statement released July 24, 1961, declared: "Private ownership and operation of the U.S. portion of the system is favored, provided that such ownership and operation meet the following policy requirements:

"1. New and expanded international communications services be made available at the earliest practicable date;

2. Make the system global in coverage so as to provide efficient communication service throughout the whole world as soon as technically feasible, including service where individual portions of the coverage are not profitable;

3. Provide opportunities for foreign participation through ownership or otherwise in the communications satellite system;

4. Nondiscriminatory use of and equitable access to the system by present and future authorized communications carriers;

5. Effective competition, such as competitive bidding,

[86] These discussions relate primarily to domestic policy and law and will not be analyzed in detail here. R. J. Cordiner, "Competitive Private Enterprise in Space," *Peacetime Uses of Outer Space* 220 (Ramo ed. 1961) states: "If the space effort were only a minor activity, the dependence on government financing and control would have less economic impact. But the fact is that the military and peaceful needs of the space program are already employing a significant percentage of the industrial work force, and will make up an even larger proportion of the total production of the country as the years go by . . . we are not speaking of a minor element in the national economy but of its leading growth industries. These industries are subject to ever-increasing government influence by way of government contracts. And the Space Age is only beginning." Space activities could easily consume the entire productive capacity of the United States just as did temple building in some of the ancient civilizations. Levin, *supra* note 85, at 315. The RAND Corp. has prepared a number

it was decided ComSat should be privately owned, it was also decided that ownership should be broadly based and that ComSat would be subject to extensive government controls because of the many interrelations with existing communications systems and because of the far-reaching repercussions in foreign relations.

Several major areas of domestic law and policy have not yet been resolved. An extremely controversial area is whether ComSat may offer service only to common carriers.[87] An equally controversial question is whether

or not ComSat is to be the only entity in the United States which may have and operate a satellite communications system for domestic purposes.[88] The controversy over rates promises to be long continuing,[89] with ComSat seeking to have rates reduced for communications using satellites, and with the communications carriers generally endeavoring to spread the savings to all communications users and even resisting reductions to protect investments in conventional facilities. Foreign communications entities have shown the same reaction to the use of Intelsat facilities. Further legislative and judicial action may be required domestically and extensive international negotiations will doubtless take place before Intelsat is fully utilized. The decisions will inevitably be made on policy grounds rather than on technical, legal ones.

Policy of the ComSat Act

Only a general summary of the ComSat Act[90] and its relationship primarily to domestic law will be given. Several studies of the act already exist.[91]

---

of studies on various aspects of organization, ownership, and control. Among them are RAND Memo RM-2925-NASA (1963), "The Commercial Application of Communications Satellites: A Study of Major National Policy Considerations"; RAND Memo RM-3487-RC (Feb. 1963) by Reiger, Nichols, Early & Dews, "Communications Satellites: Technology, Economics and System Choices"; RAND Memo RM-3484-RC (Feb. 1963) by Schwartz & Goldsen, "Foreign Participation in Communications Satellite Systems, Implications of the Communications Satellite Act of 1962"; RAND Memo RM-3472-RC (Feb. 1963) by Nichols, "Submarine Telephone Cables and International Telecommunications"; RAND Memo RM-2925-NASA (Dec. 1961), by Goldsen, Lipson, Meckling, Moore & Reiger, "Communications Satellites & Public Policy."

Some of the major Congressional hearings were as follows: *Hearings on Space Communications and S. J. Res. 32 before Communications Sub-committee of the Senate Committee on Commerce*, 87th Cong. 1st Sess. (1961), which in sec. A, contains a statement of President Kennedy on Communications Satellite Policy indicating the administration's consistent position favoring private ownership; *Hearings on Space Satellite Communications before the Subcommittee on Monopoly of the Senate Select Committee on Small Business*, 87th Cong., 1st Sess. (1961); *Hearings on Antitrust Problems of the Space Satellite Communications System before the Subcommittee on Antitrust and Monopoly of the Senate Committee on the Judiciary*, 87th Cong., 2d Sess. (1962); *Hearings on S.2650 and S.2814 before Senate Committee on Aeronautics and Space Sciences*, 87th Cong., 2d Sess. (1962); *Hearings on S.2650 and S.2814 Amendment before the Senate Committee on Commerce*, 87th Cong., 2d Sess. (1962); *Hearings on H.R. 11040 before the Senate Committee on Foreign Relations*, 87th Cong., 2d Sess. (1962); *Hearings on S. Res. 258 before the Subcommittee on Antitrust and Monopoly of the Senate Committee on the Judiciary*, 87th Cong., 2d Sess. (1962); *Hearings on H. R. 10115 and H. R. 10138 before the House Committee on Interstate and Foreign Commerce*, 87th Cong., 2d Sess. (1962).

[87] FCC Doc. 66–563 (June 23, 1966) holds that, except in unique circumstances, ComSat may furnish satellite services and channels to none but other common carriers. This position was reiterated in FCC Doc. 66–677 (July 21, 1966) but a clear definition of "unique circumstances" has not been given. Para. 38 of the FCC ruling states:

"Our ultimate conclusions are:
(a) ComSat may as a matter of law be authorized to provide

services directly to non-carrier entities;
(b) ComSat is to be primarily a carrier's carrier and in ordinary circumstances users of satellite facilities should be served by the terrestrial carriers;
(c) In unique and exceptional circumstances ComSat may be authorized to provide services directly to non-carrier users; therefore, the authorization to ComSat to provide services is dependent upon the nature of the service, i.e., unique or exceptional, rather than the identity of the user. The United States Government has a special position because of its unique or national interest requirements; ComSat may be authorized to provide service directly to the Government, whenever such service is required to meet unique governmental needs or is otherwise required in the national interest, in circumstances where the Government's needs cannot be effectively met under the carrier's carrier approach."

See also FCC order of Feb. 2, 1966, Docket No. 16058. A great deal more is likely to be heard about this before it will be possible to judge in advance with reasonable certainty what the rule for a particular set of facts will be.

[88] See note 16, Appendix C. See also Mansbach, "Authorized Users," *20 Fed. Communication B. J.* 2 *passim* (1966).

[89] See, e.g., Smith's article in the *New York Times*, Sept. 18, 1966, sec. 3, at 1, col. 6. *Wall Street Journal*, Mar. 31, 1967, at 11, refers to one of a number of requests by ComSat to reduce rates to and from the satellite. The foreign partner controls the rates from the satellite to the foreign earth station. This subject is mentioned subsequently and in Appendix C.

[90] 47 USC 701–44 (1962).

[91] Levin, *supra* note 85 at 315; Rosenblum, "Regulations

Title I of the act expresses the broad "policy of the United States to establish in conjunction and in cooperation with other countries, as expeditiously as practicable, a commercial communications satellite system, as part of an improved global communications network, which will be responsive to public needs and national objectives, which will serve the communication needs of the United States and other countries, and which will contribute to world peace and understanding." Economically less developed countries are to receive the benefits of the new technology. "Authorized users" of ComSat facilities, an ambiguous term reflecting one of the unresolved problems previously noted, are to have nondiscriminatory access to the communications satellite system.[92] Competition is to be maintained in the provision of equipment and services for the system. The corporation created under this act is to be so organized and operated as to maintain and strengthen competition in the provision of communications services to the public;[93] United States antitrust laws are to be observed. The system may be utilized for domestic communications, and additional systems may be created if they are required to meet unique governmental needs or are otherwise in the national interest.

Federal Controls

Title II of the act provides for extensive supervision,

guidance, aid to, and control of ComSat by the President, Congress, NASA, the Attorney General, the Federal Communications Commission, and the Department of State. Other agencies such as the Department of Defense are greatly concerned with ComSat operations.

The impact of a satellite communications system on international affairs is recognized, and the President is directed to:

"(4) Exercise such supervision over relationships of the corporation with foreign governments or entities or with international bodies as may be appropriate to assure that such relationships shall be consistent with the national interest and foreign policy of the United States;

"(5) insure that timely arrangements are made under which there can be foreign participation in the establishment and use of a communications satellite system;

"(7) so exercise his authority as to help attain coordinated and efficient use of the electromagnetic spectrum and the technical compatibility of the system with existing communication facilities both in the United States and abroad.

"The FCC . . . shall . . . in any case where the Secretary of State, after obtaining the advice of the Administration (NASA) as to technical feasibility, has advised that commercial communication to a particular foreign point by means of the communications satellite and satellite terminal stations should be established in the national interest, institute forthwith appropriate proceedings under Section 214(d) of the Communications Act of 1934, as amended, to require the establishment of such communication by the corporation and the appropriate common carrier or carriers." This provision obviously infringes on the control of Intelsat by its Interim Committee, which is authorized to approve earth stations.[94]

in Orbit: Administrative Aspects of the Communications Satellite Act of 1962," 58 *Nw. U. L. Rev.* 216 (1963); Legislation Note, "The Communications Satellite Act of 1962," 76 *Harv. L. Rev.* 388 (1962); Schrader, "The Communications Satellite Corp.: A New Experiment in Government and Business," *Ky. L. J.* 733 (1965); Symposium on Satellite Act of 1962," 7 *Antitrust Bull.* 411 (1962); Schwartz, "Governmentally Appointed Directors in a Private Corporation —the Communication Satellite Act of 1962," 79 *Harv. L. Rev.* 350 (1965); Boskey, "Monopoly and Antitrust Aspects of Communications Satellite Operations," *Proceedings, Conference on the Law of Space and Satellite Communications,* NASA SP–44 at 80 (1963). See also the Congressional hearings cited *supra* note 86.

[92] The FCC has ruled on this question, but it seems probable that the matter will eventually be tested through the courts or that additional legislation may be sought. See FCC rulings July 21, 1966, 31 *Fed. Reg.* 10144, Docket 16058, FCC 66–677; and Feb. 8, 1967, 32 *Fed. Reg.* 2829, Docket 16058, FCC 67–164.

[93] ComSat efforts to prevent other entities in the United States from having separate communications satellites for domestic purposes indicates a strong opposition to competition in this particular area. Stated policies are not entirely compatible as far as competition is concerned.

[94] Special Agr't, Art. 7. The Dept. of State, the Dept. of Defense, and the FCC became involved in establishing circuits to S.E. Asia, and in testimony before the House Government Operations Committee, Military Operations Subcommittee, Ass't Sec'y of State Loy stated, "The timing of events and the way the FCC regulatory action appeared to our partners [consortium members] was that the U.S. was reviewing or second-guessing actions after they had been made with full U.S. participation. They objected to that at the meeting of the Interim Communications Satellite Committee." Loy went on to say that it was a question of principle and not of delay. Each country instructs its representative before action is taken, and then when a decision is made, "no country in essence should have a veto power." See 32 *T.R.* 22, 23 (Sept. 6, 1966). There are sharp differences of opinion between government

The role of NASA is defined primarily as that of technical advisor to the President, FCC, and the Department of State in addition to responsibilities to assist and advise ComSat.[95] The Federal Communications Commission is charged with extensive regulatory responsibilities over ComSat activities. ComSat must keep the Department of State advised of any business negotiations with any international or foreign entity, and the Department of State is to give ComSat foreign policy guidance and assistance in negotiations as appropriate.[96] It will take some years to establish a set of procedures which will operate smoothly and without friction, for the technology has presented many new questions and there are powerful contenders for communications traffic.

---

agencies over control and guidance of communications satellite operations.

[95] A contract between ComSat as manager of Intelsat and NASA dated Dec. 17, 1964, provides that NASA will furnish to ComSat on a reimbursable basis satellite launchings and related services as a contractor and not as an agent. ComSat is required to make appropriate payments. Although the contract as presently worded indicates that ComSat is the manager of Intelsat, there remain points of ambiguity about the obligations and relations between the members of the consortium. There are also ambiguities as to the relationship of members of the consortium to contractors and to third party strangers. Underwood, *supra* note 65, at 796–811 comments on the complicated international responsibilities of ComSat and states (p. 799): "At the present neither the United States itself nor foreign governments or communications entities can know entirely who is dealing with whom and with what authority."

[96] ComSat obtained FCC authorization to permit Canada to utilize "units of satellite utilization" via the Andover, Me., earth station, 33 *T.R.* 14 (Jan. 23, 1967). The Dept. of State conducted a survey of potential Intelsat earth station markets, 33 *T.R.* 22 (Feb. 20, 1967). FCC sharply criticized ComSat for obtaining Intelsat approval to construct Intelsat III satellites without having obtained prior FCC approval. Senator Pastore, chairman of the Commerce Subcommittee on Communications, suggested the need for hearings to find the cause and solution of the bickering between government agencies. FCC instructed, "ComSat shall not apply to [Intelsat] for any units of satellite authorization, nor use any units it may obtain, except in accordance with an instrument of authorization issued by the Commission upon consideration of an appropriate application duly filed by ComSat." 32 *T.R.* 3, 4 (June 27, 1966). See also 32 *T.R.* 28 (Mar. 28, 1966) referring to ComSat efforts to obtain modification of FCC rules which appeared to attempt to regulate foreign communication entities; 32 *T.R.* 18 (June 13, 1966) suggesting White House or Congressional action might be required; 32 *T.R.* 11 (July 11, 1966) referring to a ComSat letter to FCC pointing out the difficulty of its position as a domestic corporation and as manager of Intelsat. See also *supra* note 66.

Corporate Structure of ComSat

Congress extensively debated the structure of ComSat and the decisions made are fundamental in the context of the general economic structure of the United States. Consequently, a description of ComSat is pertinent, domestically and internationally. Title III of the ComSat Act authorizes the incorporation of ComSat in the District of Columbia, defines the corporate powers, and provides for its method of financing. Not over half the stock may be held by communications common carriers and the rest "shall be sold . . . in a manner to encourage the widest distribution to the American public."

ComSat, although subject to such extensive controls that it is a quasi-governmental or only a quasi-private operation,[97] has displayed a considerable degree of aggressive independent business judgment and initiative. It has not hesitated to press its claim to be the only United States entity authorized to have communications satellites. It has vigorously asserted its right to make circuits directly available to the government and to others rather than go through the intermediary of a communications common carrier. Its officials have been forthright in expressing disagreement with rules proposed by the FCC considered adverse to ComSat, but nonetheless, the future alone will indicate whether or not an entity so encompassed with governmental controls can function in the tradition of private American industry. The law, at present, places ownership in the private sector, but a determined administration could exercise very extensive influence over the business decisions of ComSat. A substantial part of the answer will depend on the restraint shown by the President and the FCC in the exercise of their statutory powers. In theory and, it is hoped, in substance there is reserved a role for private enterprise in an area where the scope of future development cannot easily be assessed.

International Communications Satellite Systems

The creation of ComSat and the negotiation of the Intelsat agreements are indicative of United States commitment to establishing under its leadership an international communications satellite organization. Efforts to develop an international system have been carried out with some urgency in the stated hope that a communications satellite system would contribute to world peace

---

[97] Underwood, *supra* note 65, at 796, 798 refers to ComSat as "a so-called mixed public-private corporation" and suggests the structure "in the potential for conflict."

and economic progress.[98] There is little doubt that a satellite system has many advantages[99] and that an international arrangement would facilitate its establishment.

Earth stations[100] owned and controlled by the countries where they are located will present comparatively few international problems. The United States is willing

to share internationally the benefits of technological advances with nations participating in the costs of developing the system as well as in its management. "Technically, a single worldwide system provides the most effective use and management of the limited frequency spectrum; avoids duplication of and interference between competing systems; improves operating efficiency; and reduces the technical and operating problems of compatibility between different space systems and other services."[101] There is, as we have seen, no assurance that only a single system will be established.[102] Intelsat, which presently includes no old traditional Communist countries, does include as members the nations responsible for a very high percentage, perhaps in excess of 90 per cent, of all telecommunications traffic.[103]

[98] See, e.g., the statement by Senator Long, "Public Policy Questions on the Ownership and Control of a Space Satellite Communications System," *Hearings before the Senate Subcommittee on Monopoly of the Select Committee on Small Business,* 86th Cong., 2d Sess., at 1 (Aug. 2, 3, 4, 10, 11, 1961): "Since this area of astronautical development is the first to assume commercial importance, decisions made yesterday, today, and tomorrow will have far-reaching political and economic implications because they will create a precedent for later solutions in other areas of human activity in space." U.N. Res. 1721 (XVI) calls for a communications satellite system as soon as possible and on a nondiscriminatory basis. The preamble to the Intelsat agreements referred to the desirability of "a single global commercial communications satellite system at the earliest practicable date." Prestige was also a consideration. See "Communications Satellites: Technical, Economic and International Developments," *Staff Report of the Senate Committee on Aeronautical and Space Sciences,* 87th Cong., 2d Sess., 25 (Comm. Print 1962). The first officially announced Soviet communications satellite, Molniya I, was launched Apr. 23, 1965, but there are suggestions Cosmos 41, launched Aug. 22, 1964, may have been an earlier attempt. See J. Morenoff, "Communications in Orbit: A Legal Analysis and Prognosis," in Marsten, *supra* note 1, at 1011, citing *New York Herald Tribune,* Apr. 24, 1965, at 11. Then-Deputy Attorney General Katzenbach speaking at the World Peace through Law Conference, held in Greece in 1963, said, "These interests especially included the Government's . . . responsibility to encourage satellite communications in order to improve communications among nations and assist in their economic development, which have long been major objectives of the United States foreign policy." Leonard Marks of the USIA at the same conference stated, "Communication is the lifeline of civilization. Without it, people live in small tribal societies, suspicious of strange and different customs. With improved communication comes better understanding and a removal of the barriers of suspicion and distrust. When we know our neighbors we are more likely to become friends philosophically and socially, and from this relationship may evolve a world dedicated to the preservation of law in an atmosphere of peace." Section 102(a) of the ComSat Act refers to "a commercial communications satellite system . . . which will contribute to world peace and understanding."

[99] See *Staff Report, supra* note 98, at 26–28 outlining some of the known and anticipated advantages.

[100] Defined as the ground equipment linking a satellite and terrestrial communications systems. It consists of an antenna to send and receive electromagnetic signals and facilities to track a satellite.

[101] Paper by Edwin J. Istvan, Director of International Development for ComSat, presented at the AIAA Communications Satellite Systems Conference, Washington, D.C., May 2–4, 1966, AIAA Paper No. 66–332.

[102] *Washington Post,* Oct. 29, 1965, at A6, reports that "The Soviet Union is cajoling France to become a partner in a French-Russian sponsored communications satellite system. One aim of such a partnership would be to compete against the American dominated system. . . ." French and Russian television is not compatible with U.S. television, and conversion equipment would be required for an interchange between the two systems. In answer to a question about a competing satellite system that might be launched by the Soviet Union, ComSat's chairman said he doubted two-way communications would be of much use to the Russians, but he added, "One way television would be very attractive to them and so we assume they will do it. We shouldn't kid ourselves that the U.S. will be the glorious leader in the only global communications satellite system over the next ten years." *Wall Street Journal,* Oct. 6, 1966, at 30, col. 2. France and Germany have announced the signing of an agreement to build a satellite for communications; whether for experimental purposes or for commercial use is unclear. A ComSat spokesman acknowledged that basic questions about the relationship of regional schemes such as the Franco-German proposal to Intelsat "are under serious consideration." AT&T indicated it thought the proposal perfectly legal. *Wall Street Journal,* June 7, 1967, at 14. This problem of multiple systems is referred to in several places in the text as it has an impact on many aspects of communications satellites.

[103] Names of the 48 countries in Intelsat as of May 1966 are given in Istvan, *supra* note 101. More countries have joined since that date. Istvan wrote: "These 48 countries account for at least 90 percent of the potential international world communications traffic which might be served by a global satellite system in the next few years." Istvan, *supra* note 101, at 3. It will be noted that neither the Soviet Union and Communist China nor any of their close allies are members of

Political and propaganda factors mitigate against Soviet or other Communist participation in a Western-controlled communications satellite system although the economics of the situation provide opposite inducements. The Communist nations cannot realistically hope to gain control of Intelsat, but the Soviets may hope to bargain for a disproportionate voice if they are able to establish an operational system capable of providing service on a worldwide basis. The orbit of the Molniya satellites is not so designed. Soviet failure to cooperate in Intelsat may prove to be solely a part of the cold war, and it can be anticipated that some of the "neutralist" members of Intelsat will wish to collaborate with the Soviets for political reasons.

The Soviet Union has been routinely very critical of United States activities in space communications.[104] Intelsat has shared in this criticism[105] in terms so inaccurate and so obviously politically motivated as to require little comment. It will be interesting to see what terms Russia offers for participation in a Molniya system

and to what extent it matches the internationalization of Intelsat. Soviet-Chinese relations may also influence the Soviet attitudes. The Soviet desire to maintain control of radio and television broadcasts into its own and satellite territories as evidenced from time to time by extensive jamming, doubtless plays a part in their attitude and undoubtedly is greatly strengthened by the potential capacity for direct home reception from communications satellites.

The Agreement Establishing Interim Arrangements for a Global Communications Satellite System speaks of a "single global commercial communications satellite system"[106] but, significantly, contains no express prohibition against a signatory participating in another communications satellite system. "Commercial" system is undefined and leaves the way entirely open for government purposes systems. The U.S. ComSat Act reserves the right to create additional systems "if required to meet unique governmental needs or if otherwise required in the national interest,"[107] which could be interpreted as encompassing all telecommunications traffic of Communist countries or other countries in which communications is a government monopoly.[108] There is no legally enforceable barrier to the establishment of any number of satellite communications systems, and withdrawal from Intelsat is technically simple, although it would cost the investment and possibly additional sums. Economics and politics rather than law will determine the extent to which Intelsat fulfills its goal of being a single, global, commercial communications satellite system. The problem will become increasingly difficult when additional powers or organizations possess the technological ability to put satellites in orbit. While recognizing that other systems may be established to serve international and various national requirements,[109] Intelsat

Intelsat, although most are members of the ITU. There have been discussions with Yugoslavia and other Communist countries concerning possible accession to Intelsat. *Washington Post*, May 3, 1966, at A4, col. 1.

[104] See for example, Kovalev & Cheprov, *The Way to Space Law* 70 (1962), suggesting that U.S. motivation is entirely military; Cheprov, *Some Legal Problems of International Space Communications;* 1964 *Proceedings, Seventh Colloquium on the Law of Outer Space* 10 (Haley ed. 1965), suggests a covert attempt by AT&T to rule earth and space. Zhukov's forthcoming book contains very sharp political criticism along the same line.

[105] "Behind the backs of these organizations [U.N. and ITU] they [U.S.] agreed with a narrow group of Western countries on the sharing of privileges from exploiting the system according to American conditions," Stashevsky *Soviet'skoye Gosudarstvo i Pravo* 57, 62 (Nov. 12, 1964) [hereinafter cited as *SGP*]. He continues: "countries which, due to their economic position are unable or do not wish to contribute capital to the creation of a system of communications on American conditions, who will only be users of that system and will build their own receiving stations, are completely excluded from deciding questions concerned with governing the system and also from defining general rules and principles of its activities.

"The organizational structure of the system creates almost limitless possibilities for discrimination in relation to those countries which shall be subscribers to the satellite communication system, although formally in the agreement there is a reference to the decision of the U.N. General Assembly that such discrimination must not be permitted." It is probable that a demand for one-nation one-vote will be heard although it is also probable that the Soviets would want veto power similar to that in the U.N.

[106] Interim Agr't, Preamble.

[107] *Id.* at sec. 102(d).

[108] If the U.S. permits the establishment of a national system for its own use, the U.S. will not be in a strong position to object if other nations or groups of nations wish to establish their own special purpose or regional systems. Even the establishment of a separate system for U.S. government purposes such as the military breaks the concept of a single global system.

[109] See FCC Docket No. 16495, Dec. 15, 1966, at 4 and 5 wherein AT&T states: "However, AT&T suggests that negotiations looking toward a definitive international agreement should proceed on the premise that domestic satellite systems or their regional equivalents are inevitable." This is a realistic view.

raises most of the anticipated legal, policy, and technical questions of space communications.

The Agreement for Interim Arrangements: The Special and Supplementary Agreements

An understanding of Intelsat requires a knowledge of the background of the basic documents which provide a structure of and methods for control and operation of an international space communications system. They are:

1. The Agreement Establishing Interim Arrangements for a Global Communications Satellite System. This is a permanent agreement contemplating revision— but also capable of being continued intact (hereinafter referred to as Interim Agreement);

2. Special Agreement;[110]

3. The Supplementary Agreement on Arbitration.[111] The documents are reproduced in Appendix E.

The Interim Agreement's objective of world-wide satellite communications coverage by 1967[112] has been achieved. European members have not used all available satellite circuits, however, at least partly because of investments in unused cable circuits and because of uncertainties about the reliability of satellite communications.

Signatories to the Interim Agreement are states, but signatories to the Special and Supplementary agreements are about equally divided among governments and governmental communications entities. The signatories for Canada, Japan, and the United States, and possibly others are corporations, but the Canadian signatory is a crown corporation, and the Japanese signatory is a private corporation, the Kokusai Denshin Denwa Co., Ltd., under the supervision of the Japanese Ministry of Post and Telecommunication. The government may own shares in the company.[113] Apparently, United States

ComSat is the only wholly privately owned entity involved in Intelsat.

The real distinctions between private and public entities are at least as much political as financial and legal, since ComSat's operations are almost as closely controlled by the United States as are most foreign governmental communications agencies. Private ownership of ComSat may have contributed to, but has probably not been a major factor in, the Soviet Union's decision not to participate in Intelsat. The Soviet Union has not yet been able to bring forth an alternate system capable of competing generally with Intelsat, and the first in the field has a distinct psychological and technical advantage. Indications are that Intelsat would welcome participation of the Soviet Union and other Communist countries on the same terms as for any other country; that is, voting power, etc., would correspond generally to the use made of the system and to the investment in the system.[114]

Amendment, Withdrawal, and Renegotiation of the Agreements

Amendments to the Special Agreement require approval of two-thirds of the signatories, not in committee votes or investment quota value, and no amendment may impose any additional financial obligation upon any signatory without its consent.[115]

The Interim Agreement contains no provision for amendment but includes provisions for negotiating a definitive agreement with a view to having it enter into force by January 1, 1970.[116] The Interim Agreement contains several instructions for negotiating the definitive agreement, but such mandates will at most have only persuasive weight as the negotiators are no more likely to consider themselves bound than would a future legislature consider itself bound by a prior legislature.

Any party may withdraw from the Interim Agreement on giving three months' notice,[117] which act also con-

---

[110] 15 *U.S.T.* 1705; *T.I.A.S.* 5646. Entered into force Aug. 20, 1964.

[111] 4 *International Legal Materials* 735 (June 4, 1965).

[112] Interim Agr't, Art. I(a) (2).

[113] The company monopolistically operates overseas telecommunications services in Japan under the supervision of the Ministry of Post and Telecommunication. Its activities were restricted by the Public Telecommunication Law and the Kokusai Denshin Denwa Co., Ltd., Law, besides the commercial code. The shares of the company may be possessed only by the government, local public entities, Japanese nationals or Japanese juridical persons. Letter to authors dated June 6, 1967, from K. Sase, 2d Secretary of Japanese Embassy, Washington, D.C.

[114] See, e.g., the article in *New York Times*, Aug. 30, 1965, noting President Johnson's comments calling for cooperation in space programs; an article in *Washington Post*, July 20, 1964, refers to an American invitation to the Soviets to join in forming the global system. To the same effect see Kohlmeier's article in *Wall Street Journal*, Feb. 23, 1965. A part of Soviet response is referred to *supra* notes 74, 75.

[115] Special Agr't, Art. 15.

[116] Interim Agr't, Art. IX(c).

[117] *Id.,* Art. XI(a). Failure to pay accounts may result in an automatic withdrawal as noted.

stitutes withdrawal from the Special Agreement. Accounts must be settled and the quota of the withdrawing member is distributed proportionately among the remaining signatories to the Special Agreement or as may otherwise be agreed; or, with the approval of the Interim Committee, the quota may be transferred to another party acceding to the Interim Agreement[118] and the Special Agreement.

Designated Communications Entities

Each party to the Interim Agreement is required to sign, or to designate a public or private communications entity to sign, the Special Agreement; this must be accomplished before the Interim Agreement is considered in force for that signatory, and no signatures may be affixed to the Special Agreement without a prior signing of the Interim Agreement.[119] Domestic law controls relations between a party to the Interim Agreement and its designee for the Special Agreement. The parties to the Special Agreement negotiate and enter directly into appropriate traffic agreements for use of communications channels.[120] Most of the signatories to the Special Agreement are subject to suit in the courts of the corresponding signatory to the Interim Agreement as they are either corporations, such as ComSat and a few others, or government agencies considered by their national authorities to be engaged in proprietary activities and thus subject to suit. Also, most modern nations permit some form of adjudication of claims against the government.[121]

Since ComSat, as manager of Intelsat, and other signatories to the Special Agreement may sign contracts in their own names[122] for the benefit of Intelsat, there would appear to be little doubt that they could sue in their own names for the same purposes in accordance with the law of the forum. The language apparently indicates that when a contract is to be let in the territory of a signatory to the Interim Agreement, the corresponding signatory to the Special Agreement will usually but not manda-

torily be the contracting party.[123] In practice, however, ComSat has signed all procurement contracts. Contracts are to be distributed in approximate proportion to the respective investment quotas of the signatories. Had the various signatories to Intelsat signed contracts in their own territories, most of the contract problems would have been kept within the jurisdiction of the courts of the individual members. As the practice has in fact developed, presumably for purposes of operational uniformity and good administrative practice, the general rules of international law will apply except as modified by the Intelsat agreements.[124]

Legal Status of Intelsat

Intelsat cannot easily be categorized because it is hardly possible to distinguish in all cases between the signatories to the Interim and Special agreements.[125] In several instances signatories are the same, and where they are not, the signatories to the Special Agreement are in all instances the designees or even the agents of the states signatory to the Interim Agreement.[126] Consequently, there is considerable justification to say that the activities of Intelsat are the activities of the states signatory to the Interim Agreement, although all states may have access to the system.[127]

The Interim and Special agreements may be compared with a corporation's articles and by-laws, respectively, and the Interim Committee[128] may be likened to a corporate board of directors,[129] although a juridical entity was not created. But subsequent actions by individual

---

[118] *Id.,* Art. XI(e).

[119] *Id.,* Art. XII(f). Any entity designated by a signatory to the Interim Agr't would doubtless be acceptable as a signatory to the Special Arg't although the agreement calls for a communications entity.

[120] *Id.,* Art. II(b).

[121] The United States Federal Tort Claims Act is a good example. 28 U.S.C. 1291–1346.

[122] Interim Agr't, Art. X; Special Agr't, Art. 10.

[123] *Id.,* Art. X.

[124] See *Washington Post,* at 71, for a brief comment on the question of liability of members of the consortium. Members of Intelsat are, of course, national entities.

[125] Both agreements must be signed before either is effective as to the signatory. Interim Agr't, Art. XII(f).

[126] *Id.,* Art. II.

[127] *Id.,* Preamble.

[128] Established by Interim Agr't, Art. IV.

[129] The Interim Committee is composed of representatives from each of the signatories to the Special Committee whose investment quota in Intelsat is not less than 1.5 percent. Signatories have the right to combine smaller quotas to gain representation. "Quota" means the percentage of financial contribution to the total cost of the system, as established in the Annex to the Special Agreement. Votes are proportioned to the size of the quota, but limitations are imposed to assure that the United States does not have unfettered control, because its quota is in excess of 50 percent of the total. Interim Agr't, Arts. V, VI and Annex to Special Agr't.

states have extended to Intelsat at least some of the attributes and benefits of a juridical entity.[130] Intelsat may be described as a consortium, a joint venture, or a partnership operation. By its own internal action it has adopted the name Intelsat.[131]

The reasons for not having established a juridical person have not been set forth but are probably related in part to the time which would have been required to negotiate the necessary provisions; and it was doubtless felt that Intelsat would receive more general acceptance and support if most of the nations expected to participate were allowed a voice in the formulation of definitive arrangements. There was also hesitancy on the part of some about creating a corporate structure subject to American domination. The way is left open to establish a formal juridical entity, if this is considered desirable, when definitive arrangements are negotiated.[132] But in the meantime states likely to participate in the negotiations have the opportunity to gain experience in Intelsat operations and to formulate policy.

In view of the ambiguity of Intelsat's status as a juridical entity it seems doubtful that it has the legal capacity to sue or be sued or to contract in its own name. Obviously, it has no standing in its own right before the International Court of Justice.[133] But the traditional concepts of international law are being modified, and natural and juridical persons have standing before some international tribunals.[134] Intelsat could easily be given unquestioned juridical personality in the territory of Intelsat members and, under some circumstances, the status would probably be recognized by other nations as well.[135] Existence or lack of existence of a juridical personality will have little to do with Intelsat's internal power structure and operations but will have a technical bearing on its external contracting and other business procedures and liability.

The Interim Committee has responsibility for the design, development, construction, establishment, maintenance, and operation of the space segment,[136] but ComSat is designated the manager of Intelsat "in the design, development, construction, establishment, operation, and maintenance of the space segment pursuant to general policies of the Interim Committee and in accordance with specific determinations which may be made by the Interim Committee."[137] The space segment consists of the communications satellites and the tracking, control, command, and related facilities and equipment required to support the operation of the communications satellite. It is owned in undivided shares by the signatories to the Special Agreement in proportion to their respective contributions to the costs of the design, development, construction, and establishment of the space segment.[138]

Although the Interim Agreement indicates that Intelsat is owned by the signatories to the Special Agreement rather than by those to the Interim Agreement, it is not clear what significance in international law this may have in view of the identity of or close relationship between the signatories to the Interim Agreement and those to the Special Agreement, the lack of a juridical entity in Intelsat, and the concept of state liability for all activities in space as reflected in U.N. resolutions and in the space

---

[130] The United States has, for various purposes, treated Intelsat as if it were a juridical entity. See E.O.11227, June 2, 1965, designating the Interim Committee as a Public International Organization Entitled to Enjoy Certain Privileges, Exemptions, and Immunities; and E.O. 11277, Apr. 30, 1966, designating the International Telecommunications Consortium as an International Organization Entitled to Enjoy Certain Privileges, Exemptions and Immunities. Other countries have taken somewhat similar actions.

[131] The caption used in the Interim Agreement initially was "Multilateral Communications Satellite System," subsequently modified to "International Telecommunications Satellite Consortium" (Intelsat).

[132] Interim Agr't, Art. IX, provides for the negotiation of definitive arrangements "with a view to their entry into force by 1st Jan. 1970," although the interim arrangements "remain in effect until the entry into force of the definitive arrangements." Interim Agr't, Art. XV. The agreements were negotiated and intially signed by only nineteen states. Members of the ITU in addition to the original signatories are eligible to participate in Intelsat subject to approval of quota and financial arrangements by the Interim Committee. *Id.*, Art. XII.

[133] Art. 34 of the Statute of the International Court of Justice requires all parties before it to be states.

[134] The Community Court of the European Communities is an example. Treaty Establishing the European Economic Community, arts. 4 and 188 and Statute of the Court, Art. 39; 5 *European Yrbk.* 438 (1959).

[135] See, e.g., Article 104 of the Charter of the U.N. which reads, "The organization shall enjoy in the territory of each of its members such legal capacity as may be necessary for the exercise of its functions and the fulfillment of its purposes." The statutes of suitable international courts would also require modification, a highly controversial political question so far as the International Court of Justice is concerned.

[136] Interim Agr't, Art. XII.

[137] *Id.*, Art. VIII.

[138] *Id.*, Arts. I (b), III.

treaty.[139] In the absence of an insulating corporate structure, and unless there is specific language in contracts which would be binding at least for the parties, it would appear that the parties to the Interim Agreement as well as to the Special Agreement are liable for the contracts, actions, and torts of Intelsat, whether or not the action complained of is specifically an activity in space or is only related to or preparatory for such activity.[140] Contracts entered into by ComSat as manager of Intelsat have specified that ComSat only is liable under the contract, but such a provision could hardly control if a satellite caused damage in the territory of a stranger to the contract.[141] Participants in Intelsat may divide responsibilities among themselves as they consider appropriate, but it is doubtful that injured third parties not bound by contract will consider themselves obligated under either the civil or common law to distinguish among or between signatories to the Interim and Special agreements.[142] Even in contract cases, if the party signing the contract defaults and other signatories to the special agreement are enjoying the benefits of the contract without paying their respective quota shares, a diplomatic claim would probably be made, and possibly an equity or third-party beneficiary-type action might be brought to force the defaulting party to exercise its rights under the Special Agreement for reimbursement from other members of the consortium for the benefit of the claimant.[143]

Financing, Ownership, and Costs

The estimated costs of establishing the international communications satellite system was set at $200 million,[144] although provision was made for a possible cost of $300 million without the necessity of a new agreement.[145] The funds are to be paid in dollars or dollar-convertible currencies by the signatories to the Special Agreement[146] in accordance with quotas of investment or ownership based on anticipated use of the system.[147] If these quotas reflect fairly accurately the usage of the system, there is no real basis for complaint, but if they prove to be erroneous, strong arguments for revising the quota pattern are sure to be heard when negotiations of the definitive agreement get under way. Further, it seems probable that the Soviets will not participate in Intelsat unless they are given a voice much stronger than their usage would justify if the current policy is followed. Some of the smaller nations may ask for a one-nation, one-vote rule as in the U.N. General Assembly.[148]

Payments into the fund administered by ComSat as manager are to be made at such times and in such amounts as may be established by the Interim Committee.[149] Failure to make timely payment results in suspension of the rights of the defaulting signatory and may result in its exclusion ("deemed to have withdrawn") from the Interim and Special agreements, subject to adjustment of accounts.[150] Costs cover the "design, development, construction and establishment of the space segment,"[151] including those costs incurred by ComSat

---

[139] See *infra* chap. 6 and Art. VII of the Treaty on Principles Governing the Activities of States in the Exploration and Use of Outer Space, Including the Moon and Other Celestial Bodies, signed Jan. 27, 1967.

[140] See generally *infra* chap. 6.

[141] Letter to the authors from John A. Johnson, vice-president, International ComSat, Aug. 25, 1965. "The form of all such contracts is such as to obligate only the Communications Satellite Corporation directly and not the other signatories to the Special Agreement. Under the terms of the Special Agreement, ComSat has the right to reimbursement by the other signatories in proportion to their respective capital commitments." The probability of damage across international borders from launch vehicles is not great. See *infra* chap. 6 for an extensive discussion of the subject.

[142] See Restatement of the Law, Agency 2d, secs. 20(e) and (f); also sec. 189, Ill. 2.

[143] The Special Agr't, Art. 3, requires each signatory "to

contribute a percentage of the costs of the design, development, construction and establishment of the space segment equal to its quota." Art. 4 requires each signatory to "make their respective proportionate payments in order to enable obligations to be met as they become due . . . Where a signatory other than the Corporation (ComSat) incurs obligations pursuant to authorization by the (Interim) Committee, the Committee shall cause payments to be made to that signatory."

[144] Interim Agr't, Art. VI. Indications are that the cost of establishing the system will be substantially less than the estimates.

[145] Special Agr't, Art. 4, (a).

[146] Interim Agr't, Art. VI(a).

[147] Special Agr't, Art. 1(e) and Annex. Initially eleven signatories held 97.5 percent of the quota of ownership or investment which gave them the same voting power. A reduction of these quotas by 17 percent would still leave eleven signatories with 80.3 percent of the quota and four members would control 67.7 percent of the quota.

[148] See *supra* note 105.

[149] Special Agr't, Art. 4(b) (c) and (d).

[150] Interim Agr't, Art. XI(b) and Special Agr't, Art. 4(d).

[151] Special Agr't, Art. 3. The space segment is defined as

prior to the opening of the Interim Agreement for signature, subject to agreement between ComSat and the Interim Committee.[152] The space segment is "owned in undivided shares by the signatories to the Special Agreement in proportion to their respective contributions,"[153] whereas the earth stations which receive and transmit the communications to and from the communications satellites are owned by individual members of the consortium.[154] Costs of earth stations, taxes, costs of design and development of launchers and launching facilities—except costs for the modification of launchers and launching facilities for the space segment—and expenses of representation for members of the consortium on the Interim Committee and its subcommittees cannot be included as charges to be shared by the signatories as consortium expenditures.[155]

Earth stations are essential parts of the total system, but their owners may not utilize the space segment without the approval of the Interim Committee.[156] Applications for earth stations will be made by the signatory to the Special Agreement "in whose area the station is or will be located or, with respect to other areas, by a duly authorized communications entity."[157] "Duly authorized communications entity" is inadequately identified. In context, it does not refer to the communications entity authorized by the concerned signatory to the Interim Agreement to sign the Special Agreement as its designee in accordance with Article II of the Interim Agreement. Neither does it refer to an "authorized carrier" defined in

the U.S. ComSat Act as a communications common carrier authorized by the FCC to provide services by means of communications satellites, since the ComSat Act is domestic legislation.[158] A number of nations interested in having satellite communications lack technical and financial resources with which to construct and operate earth stations. If they are to receive the benefits of modern technology, they must be assisted from external sources,[159] not only for earth stations but also for improving local communications which in some large areas are almost nonexistent.

"Duly authorized communications entity" relative to an area not in the consortium appears to mean a communications entity authorized by a nonmember to apply for authorization for an earth station. Under this interpretation a nonmember of the consortium might authorize ComSat, AT&T, or some other communications entity, public or private, domestic or foreign, to apply to the Interim Committee for an authorization for an earth station in an area not included in the consortium.

An application for an earth station in the territory of a member of the consortium is to be made by the signatory to the Special Agreement for the area in question even though the earth station is to be owned or operated by a different organization.[160] Thus if the United States wished to locate an earth station in Canada, a member of Intelsat, the Canadian signatory of the Special Agreement would submit the application to the Interim Committee.

It is doubtful that these provisions will cause any

"the communications satellite and the tracking, control, command and related facilities required to support the operation of the communications satellites," Interim Agr't, Art. I(b) (i).

[152] Special Agr't, Art. 5.

[153] Interim Agr't, Art. III. Also, Art. 10 of the Special Agreement provides that technical data and information arising directly from any work performed under contracts for design, development, and procurement of equipment for the space segment are to be available, insofar as possible to provide in the contract, for Intelsat use without payment of royalties. ComSat is obligated to use its best efforts to obtain the free use of technical information and data developed for the space segment under contracts signed prior to the effective date of the Special Agreement. Special Agr't, Art. 10 (f) (g) and (h).

[154] Special Agr't, Arts. 5, 6, 7, and 8 do not specifically mention that earth stations are to be owned by the individual members, but this is clearly the intent.

[155] Special Agr't, Art. 6.

[156] Special Agr't, Art. 7, and Interim Agr't, Art. VII.

[157] Special Agr't, Art. 7(b).

[158] There has been sharp debate in the U.S. over ownership of earth stations by communications entities other than ComSat; the controversy is still unresolved.

[159] Various international banks, U.S. AID, and some contractors have assisted undeveloped countries both financially and technically. 33 *T.R.* 28 (Feb. 22, 1967) notes an Export-Import Bank Loan to Thailand for an earth station.

[160] Special Agr't, Art. 7(c). Intelsat has approved more than 20 earth stations. 33 *T.R.* 2 (May 29, 1967). More than 40 may be approved by 1970. 33 *T.R.* 32 (Mar. 13, 1967) notes an AID loan to help finance a Malagasy communications improvement program not directly connected with communications satellites. NASA and AID have financed communications studies for Nigeria, Ivory Coast, Ghana, Togo, and Dahomey. The Peace Corps has financed a communications study in Botswana, 32 *T.R.* 12 (Dec. 5, 1966) and 33 *T.R.* 35 (Dec. 27, 1966). World Bank loans have gone to Kenya, Tanzania, and Uganda, 33 *T.R.* 28 (Feb. 22, 1967) and to Colombia, 33 *T.R.* 30 (June 12, 1967). For prestige, more earth stations than can be justified technically may be built with money that could better be spent on improving conventional communications.

difficulty, for the procedural interpretation placed on them by the Interim Committee will probably be accepted without argument since all earth stations must be approved by it. Considerations are technical rather than political. If more than one signatory to the Special Agreement and duly authorized communications entities are to use an earth station the application is to be submitted either individually or jointly on behalf of all. If an earth station within the territory of a state which has signed the Interim Agreement is to be operated by an organization other than the state's designated signatory of the Special Agreement, the application is nonetheless to be submitted by the signatory of the Special Agreement.[161]

Approval for earth stations to utilize the space segment will be based primarily on technical engineering, anticipated use, satellite capacity, geographical distribution, and use-efficiency factors. The recommended standards of the ITU's International Radio Consultative Committee and the International Telegraph and Telephone Consultative Committee are to be considered but are not controlling; the lack of established general standards does not preclude approval of an earth station.[162]

Earth stations are to be available for use on an equitable, nondiscriminatory basis to all signatories or duly authorized communications entities with due consideration to the quotas of the signatories to be served by each earth station.[163] Rates for the use of the space segment are controlled by the Interim Committee, and the income of Intelsat is, of course, from the use of the space segment. Individual members of Intelsat will receive on a pro rata basis any profits Intelsat may make and will also collect fees which they may establish for the use of their earth stations and local communications distribution systems.

Rates

The Interim Committee establishes rates for units of utilization of the space segment which are intended to cover amortization of the capital cost, compensation for the use of capital, and the estimated operating, maintenance, and administrative costs of the space segments.[164] Intelsat intends its rates to be competitive with existing communications systems, to the extent that vigorous and protracted opposition may be encountered from other communications companies such as American Telephone and Telegraph and foreign communications entities seeking to protect investments in cables and other facilities.[165] In informal private conversations with the authors, representatives of NASA and ComSat have suggested that an ultimate goal of 10 cents a call through synchronous satellites, plus the earth station and terminal charges, is not unreasonable. This figure does not include charges for research and development.[166] Rates for the use of earth stations and relays from earth stations to local communications users, although being of obvious and substantial economic interest to Intelsat and having a direct impact on the ability of Intelsat to compete and provide worldwide communications facilities, are under the control of the owner-operator of the station rather

---

[161] Special Agr't, Art. 7(c). Article 7 is not clearly drafted but is unlikely to cause difficulty as the interpretation given it by the Interim Committee will probably be accepted.

[162] Special Agr't, Art. 7(a).

[163] Special Agr't, Art. 8(b) and (c). States lacking finance may be able to obtain assistance from AID or one of the international banks. *Hearings on National Communications Programs Before the Senate Committee on Aeronautical and Space Sciences,* 89th Cong. 2d Sess., at 56 (Jan. 25, 26, 1966). See *supra* note 159.

[164] Special Agr't, Art. 9.

[165] *Newsweek,* Oct. 3, 1966, at 77, suggests Intelsat may propose rates which will be about half those charged for cable circuits, presently about $4,200 a month for an Atlantic circuit. Previously, ComSat had proposed a reduction of the Atlantic rate to about $3,800 per circuit. *Chicago Tribune,* July 8, 1966, sec. 3A, at 1. See ComSat press release of Oct. 3, 1966 for proposed Pacific rates. See *Staff Report, supra* note 98, at 34–35, 169–71 for early cost estimates for channels.

[166] European members of Intelsat have chosen to move slowly and circumspectly in utilizing space segments channels. Europeans have paid half the cost of an Atlantic cable opened in 1965 and want to see this investment protected before making heavy use of the satellite system. This Atlantic cable provides 400 circuits altogether, and with special equipment, 500. Also, Intelsat has not had adequate experience to be able to make guarantees of continuity of service equivalent to cable circuits. The competition will continue, and it has been argued that satellite communications should bear the burden of amortizing the cost of research and development which has been accomplished by the government. This is not likely to be done for past expenses nor is it possible to compute hidden subsidies, if any, received from government business. See 33 *T.R.* 46 (Apr. 10, 1967) for proposed rates for leased channels: $2,700 from Brewster Flat, Washington, to Paumalu, Hawaii; $3,800 from Paumalu to Japan, the Philippines, and Thailand; $4,900 from Brewster Flat to Japan; and $3,800 from Andover, Me., to Europe. The competition between cables and satellites shows clearly even in advertising; see advertisements of Submarine Cables, Ltd. in 31 *T.J.* 320 (Nov. 1964), which has a caption "Space for prestige—but cables for sure communications." The advertisements appeared repeatedly—even on the expensive back-page position.

than of Intelsat.[167] ComSat, as manager and part owner of earth stations, has considered it necessary to request the FCC's approval of rates for getting the message up to the satellite.[168]

The Interim Committee is given the authority to establish rates,[169] but the stakes are high. The economic viability of existing public and private communications entities with large investments in cables and other facilities may be at issue. Since many of the same entities are represented on the Interim Committee, it will not be surprising if they fight through political and economic channels. Any success at control of rates by individual members of the consortium would cause confusion and delay the full exploitation of communications satellite technology.[170]

Interim Committee Voting

Ratios of ownership, which represent investment in and anticipated utilization of the space segment and control voting power on the Interim Committee, are subject to adjustment to take into consideration the protection of the rights of new members of Intelsat.[171] But no member or group of members under the minimum 1.5 percent quota rule will be deprived of its voting rights on the Interim Committee because of a reduction of its quota to accommodate new participants.[172] Each

signatory or group of signatories with an investment quota of 1.5 percent or more has voting power on the Interim Committee equal to its quota,[173] with the United States' quota to remain in excess of 50 percent unless changed by the definitive agreement yet to be negotiated.[174] The voting procedure, however, is established in such a way as to require the affirmative vote of three or more signatories on matters of substantial significance.[175]

The Supplementary Agreement on Arbitration

A supplementary agreement on arbitration[176] for the settlement of legal disputes within Intelsat was opened for signature June 4, 1965, and entered into force on November 21, 1966. The arrangements are fairly typical of international arbitration agreements, providing a three-man arbitral tribunal, with one member appointed by each of the parties[177] and the third, to serve as president, selected by the first two from a seven-member panel of experts established by the Interim Committee, pursuant to the Supplemental Agreement.[178] The seven-

---

167 Special Agr't, Art. 8(a).

168 See, e.g., ComSat press release, Mar. 31, 1967, "ComSat Asks FCC for Permission to Reduce Satellite Phone and TV Rates for Atlantic Area."

169 Interim Agr't, Art. V(c) (v), relating to total vote required for approval provides "establishment of the rate of charge per unit of satellite utilization pursuant to article 9(a) of the Special Agreement." Special Agr't, Art. 9(a), provides, "The Committee shall specify the unit of satellite utilization and from time to time shall establish the rate of charge per unit at a level which, as a general rule, shall be sufficient, on the basis of the estimated total use of the space segment, to cover amortization of the capital cost of the space segment, an adequate compensation for use of capital, and the estimated operating, maintenance and administration costs of the space segments."

170 Arguments may be based at least in part on the concept that Intelsat should be charged for research and development work paid for by the U.S. Government—that otherwise space communications will receive the benefit of a huge hidden subsidy. See *supra* note 86. Such arguments may overlook the fact that many areas of private enterprise have received hidden and open subsidies from time to time. See also *infra* Appendix C, text and note 18.

171 Interim Agr't, Art. XII(c).

172 *Id.*, Art. IV(e).

173 *Id.*, Art. V(a).

174 *Id.*, Art. XII(c) provides that the quotas of all signatories to the Special Agreement other than the original 19 shall not exceed 17 percent. The original U.S. quota was 61 percent which, if reduced by 17 percent, would leave a U.S. quota of 50.63 percent.

175 *Id.*, Art. V. An Interim committee quorum consists of a number of votes exceeding the vote of the largest quota by not less than 8.5 percent of the votes. Thus, the votes of the United States plus an additional 8.5 percent of the total votes are required to make a quorum. The United Kingdom commenced with 8.4 percent of the votes; thus, the U.S. and U.K. are unable to make a quorum. The U.S. vote plus 12.5 percent of the total vote are required for major decisions relating to the type of space segment to be established, standards for earth stations, budget, adjustment of accounts for expenditures, charge per unit of satellite utilization, additional contribution, placing of contracts in excess of $500,000, the program for launching satellites, approval of quotas for new members, approval of financial conditions for accessions, withdrawals from Intelsat, recommendations for amendments to the Special Agreement, committee rules of procedure, and approval of compensation for ComSat's services as manager. In some cases the requirement drops to the U.S. vote plus 8.5 percent of the total vote after 60 days.

176 IV *International Legal Materials* 735 (July 1965). Reproduced in Appendix E.

177 Partisan-appointed members of arbitral tribunals seldom see their role as impartial jurists and are much more likely to conduct themselves as proponents of the position of the party appointing them.

178 The Communist countries normally favor a two-man

member panel designates its own chairman[179] whose most important functions are to appoint the presidents of the three-member tribunals and to appoint other members to the tribunals when the parties to a controversy or their members of an arbitral tribunal have failed to take action.[180]

The tribunals have competence to decide "whether an action or failure to act by the [Interim] Committee or by any signatory or signatories is authorized by or is in compliance with [Interim] Agreement and the Special Agreement,"[181] and to resolve "any legal dispute arising in connection with any other agreement relating to the arrangements established by the [Interim] Agreement and the Special Agreement where the signatories have agreed to confer such a competence."[182] Procurement, construction, and other contracts signed by ComSat as manager or by one of the other signatories to the Special Agreement will normally be subject to the domestic law of one of the signatories to the Interim Agreement, and thus are not likely to come within the purview of the Supplementary Agreement.

Procedures established by the Supplementary Agreement are simple and an arbitral tribunal may, consistent with the agreement, adopt additional rules of procedure as necessary.[183] Proceedings are private and are conducted in writing, but oral evidence may be heard. Only the Interim Committee and signatories to the Special Agreement may be parties before an arbitral tribunal established under the agreement.[184] When the Interim Committee is a party to the dispute, all parties to the Interim Agreement and all signatories to the Special Agreement may be present. When the Interim Committee is not a party to the dispute, only the parties to the dispute and their respective signatories to the Interim Agreement may be present and have access to the materials; but if any signatory to the Special Agreement or the Interim Committee believes it has a substantial

interest in the case it may petition the tribunal to become a party to the case.[185] Deliberations of the tribunal are secret and findings must be supported by not less than two members.[186]

The undesirability of having Intelsat controversies tried in the press and in national legislatures probably justifies secrecy. Also, business secrets and classified patents may be involved. There are, however, strong arguments in favor of furnishing signatories to the Special Agreement with copies of findings for use as guidelines for future tribunal actions.

It is contemplated that the parties to a controversy submitted to a tribunal will continue efforts to resolve their dispute by direct negotiation. Agreed settlements are to be incorporated in consent decrees.[187] To avoid multiplicity of actions, it would be appropriate to include a provision prohibiting institution of proceedings in more than one forum at the same time. Decisions are to be based on interpretation of the three agreements and on "generally accepted principles of law,"[188] but an arbitral tribunal has no enforcement authority. Sanctions such as are applicable under the Special Agreement for nonpayment of amounts owed might be appropriate.[189]

The Supplementary Agreement does not appear to give the arbitral tribunals competence over tort claims arising in the course of operations of Intelsat. Since Intelsat is not at present a juridical entity and also in view of the concepts expressed in U.N. resolutions and negotiations for a general convention on liability for injuries resulting from activities in space,[190] states are severally liable, in solidarity as expressed in civil law, for damages resulting from activities in space. The terms of the general treaty on liability for damages resulting from space activities, when finally completed and brought into force, will probably be controlling for damages founded in tort connected with these activities. Any existing arbitration arrangements between the parties or an international court can be utilized. If such facilities are not available and diplomatic channels have not provided a solution,

---

"arbitral tribunal" which requires unanimous approval for any finding. Such a "tribunal" is at best only a negotiating forum between representatives of the parties to the dispute. See discussion on this point in chap. 6.

179 Supplementary Agr't, Art. 3.

180 *Id.,* Art. 4(c) and (d).

181 *Id.,* Art. 2(a).

182 *Id.,* Art. 2(b).

183 *Id.,* Art. 5.

184 *Id.,* Art. 2(c). The right to appear before a tribunal, national or international, is an attribute of a juridical person, but possession of the right is not sufficient to make an entity a juridical person in the face of a contrary intent.

185 *Id.,* Art. 7. The closed nature of the hearings may make it very difficult to ascertain if there is a substantial interest.

186 *Id.,* Art. 5(g). Vacancies in the tribunal may be filled in accordance with procedures set forth in Art. 4(f) and (g) but in some circumstances the remaining two members may give a final decision, Art. 4(h).

187 *Id.,* Art. 11(b).

188 *Id.,* Art. 11.

189 *Id.,* Art. 4(d).

190 See *infra* chap. 6.

there would be no reason why parties to the Interim and Special agreements could not, on an ad hoc basis, utilize procedures similar to those provided by the Supplementary Agreement.[191] It would require a new protocol technically to utilize the Supplementary Agreement itself in such cases. Since parties to the Interim Agreement are all members of ITU, it would appear that they could utilize the Optional Additional Protocol Concerning Compulsory Settlement of Disputes of the 1965 Montreux ITU Conference.

Conclusions

Communications using satellites are providing peoples and nations with a new facility for national and international communications at greatly reduced costs in areas which have previously been largely isolated from conventional radio and surface communications. ComSat and Intelsat have been established; Intelsat is operating successfully in international communications, although many difficult problems lie ahead. Domestic utilization of communications satellites has not yet commenced.

Domestically, the unresolved legal, political, social, and economic problems are very difficult and have delayed development of a national satellite communications facility. In March 1967 the Ford Foundation requested the FCC to withhold for at least a year authorization for development of a domestic satellite communications system to give the President and Congress adequate time to consider the problems presented. At the same time, the President also gave Congress a proposal, or rather a series of questions, concerning educational television, a subject which cannot now be considered separate from communications satellites. The President asked for studies but offered no final solutions. The FCC has been unable to give definitive answers on questions of domestic ownership of earth stations, authorized users, rates, ownership of special domestic purpose satellites, and so on.

Other nations in which all communications are a government monopoly do not have the problems of deciding ownership of different segments of the system but have many of the same problems of the proper use and control of the new technology.

Intelsat represents a remarkable example of the development of international legal, economic, and administra-

tive arrangements and institutions by which the benefits of the new technology can be made available to any nation which wishes to participate, regardless of differences in politics or in the state of economic and social development. The many unresolved questions such as the determination of the relationships between Intelsat and national systems like the one the United States Department of Defense has established or the proposed French or the Soviet Molniya systems have not prevented Intelsat from becoming operational. There is no legal reason why competing or complementary international systems cannot be established, although present technological knowledge indicates that a single integrated system would probably be considerably more efficient and economical, even if some of its satellites were used for special purposes.

There is no assurance that Intelsat will continue to exist in its present structure, for the Interim Agreement is scheduled to be reviewed by 1970. Although it can be made permanent in its present form, it can also be revised very extensively. Probably several countries may be insistent on changing the power structure of the controlling committee, which may be converted into a board of directors or governors if a decision is made to give Intelsat a formal juridical personality. The Soviet Union and its allies have chosen for political reasons not to participate in Intelsat in its present form and are endeavoring to establish an international system based on the Molniya satellites, although they have only a limited amount of telecommunications traffic. France proposes to establish a separate system, and other nations have discussed the possibilities of national and regional systems. Justification for such systems would be basically political.

ITU has not been able fully to resolve questions of unintentional interference on either a scientific or a legal basis, although nations, recognizing the chaos which might develop, have generally resolved most serious questions of interference on a bilateral cooperative basis. Very little progress has been made toward resolving politically charged questions relating to broadcasts to which some nations object and to the extensive jamming to which they have resorted. This is not a problem new with satellites, but it will become increasingly acute as direct satellite-to-home-receiver broadcasting is perfected.

In the first few years of communications satellite operations we have seen capacity per satellite develop from just a few weak circuits to several thousand. By 1978 capacities are expected to approximate the equiva-

---

[191] It is recognized that parties in arbitration proceedings under the Supplementary Agreement are limited to signatories to the Special Agreement and the Interim Committee, Art. 3(c).

lent of 120,000 voice circuits. Equipment and techniques which will utilize frequencies into the billions of cycles per second (gigacycles) are now in the development stage and may provide many additional circuits with a very high degree of directionality. Other presently undeveloped techniques, such as the possibility of much greater use of cables for delivery of programs into homes, may bring about equally great changes. If this should come about, the pressure for circuits might become considerably less.

The usual rules relating to electromagnetic communications apply to the new technology, and the International Telecommunications Union has allocated frequencies for space communications in accordance with its customary procedures. These procedures will probably be inadequate within another few years and will require a substantial revision of the structure and authority of ITU just as the structure and authority of the FCC should be reviewed domestically. Both are in need of separate, extensive analysis.

The entire technical, economic, and political structure and law relating to communications is in the initial stage of enormous advances which give promise of great contributions to mankind. It is not presently possible to forecast the future with any degree of accuracy, but the changes will surely be as dramatic as those brought by the advent of radio itself. A single system under the auspices of the United Nations or some similar worldwide organization is unlikely in the foreseeable future and probably cannot be anticipated until some form of world government is acceptable to the great powers. But the area of communications has the potential to lead the way toward greater cooperation and understanding between nations. Technological progress should proceed as rapidly as possible and communications satellites should be used wherever technologically and economically feasible without artificial delays imposed for political reasons. "Permanent" decisions on matters of control, ownership, etc., may not come for many years, and it is quite probable that continuing technological changes will require frequent and sometimes major changes in the rules and regulations. Necessary interim dispositions can be made, subject to modification as experience and technology require, but efforts should be made to avoid changes unless there is justification other than the application of political pressures by first one interest and then another. On many points there is no assurance that agreement by a substantial consensus, let alone by unanimous consent, can be reached within the foreseeable future; there is neither justification nor need to delay the application of a beneficial new technology until all of the political, social, economic, moral, and legal implications are assessed and agreed upon to everyone's satisfaction.

6

Liability and Space Activities

Causes, Objectives, and Parties

Theories of liability and general questions of
international claims adjudication have been extensively
considered in numerous scholarly studies[1] and will be
discussed in relation to space activities only to the extent
necessary for analyzing specific problems. Questions
of liability under municipal law for damages incurred
by nationals of the state to which liability is assigned
internationally on any nexus are also generally outside
the scope of this chapter.[2] Even so, some proposals made

---

[1] In addition to the standard texts on claims, see Blum &
Kalven, "Public Law Perspectives on a Private Law Problem—
Auto Compensation Plans," 31 *U. Chi. L. Rev.* 641 (1964);
Calabresi, "The Decision for Accidents: An Approach to
Nonfault Allocation of Costs," 78 *Harv. L. Rev.* 713 (1965);
Keeton, "Conditional Fault in the Law of Torts," 72 *Harv. L.
Rev.* 401 (1959); Keeton & O'Connell, "Basic Protection—a
Proposal for Improving Automobile Claims Systems," 78
Harv. L. Rev. 329 (1964). For the general handling of
international claims, see, e.g.; L. B. Sohn & R. R. Baxter,
"Responsibility of States for Injuries to the Economic
Interests of Aliens," 55 *Am. J. Int'l L.* 545 (1961); 5
Hackworth, *Digest of International Law* 471–851 (1943);
Bishop, *International Law: Cases and Materials* 626–743 (2d
ed. 1962). Lipson & Katzenbach, *The Law of Outer Space* 31
and Abstracts 411–31 (1961); Goldie, "Liability for Damage
and Progressive Development of International Law," 14
Int'l & Comp. L.Q. 1189–1264 (1965), discusses theories of
liability with specific reference to claims arising from activities
in space.

[2] Several excellent studies of the domestic liability problems
arising out of United States government programs have been

in the course of United Nations negotiations would appear to cover all claims arising from activities in space, even by a national against his own state. Damage inflicted intentionally as an act of war or in violation of accepted rules of international law is better analyzed in a discussion of the maintenance of international order in space.[3]

Probable or desirable developments in international law concerning space activities are, of course, subject to modification in the light of scientific, political, social, and economic developments.[4] In particular, scientific developments may substantially change causative factors, and political developments may open the way to much greater international cooperation.

Occurrences Which May Give Rise to International Claims

A discussion of legal problems of international liability arising from activities in space[5] requires an

exploration of the occurrences which may result in international claims. Rapidly developing technology, much of which is classified, makes it imprudent to attempt to prepare an exhaustive list of the possible sources of liability, however.

Some acts, such as interference with communications and navigational aids, are so similar to nonspace occurrences that existing regimes of law covering such acts will probably be extended so that no separate set of rules need be devised to provide coverage for the space-oriented part of a general problem. Thus, the International Telecommunications Union (ITU) has already been utilized to allocate frequencies for use in space activities and to resolve some questions of communications interference.

The novel and experimental aspects of man's activities in space, the nationalistic competition for achievement of space goals, and the necessity of utilizing high-energy propellants, exotic atmospheres, and experimental techniques and materials make many types of accidents both conceivable and credible.[6] But a listing of possible types of accidental occurrences does not constitute an evaluation of the probabilities that damage will result. To date, no formal international claims based on damages and injuries resulting from activities in space[7] have been pre-

---

published, although many basic questions remain unanswered. See, e.g., Rosenthal, Korn, & Lubman, *Catastrophic Accidents in Government Programs* (National Security Industrial Association 1963); Haley, *Space Law and Government* 233–57 (1963); Stason, Estep, & Pierce, *Atoms and the Law* (1959); Berger, "Some Aspects of Civil Liability for Space Craft and Vehicle Accidents," 33 *Pa. Bar Ass'n Q.* 301 (1962); Parry, "Space Law: Surface Impact Liability of Space Vehicles," 14 *Okla. L. Rev.* 89 (1961); Schrader, "Space Activities and Resulting Tort Liability," 17 *Okla. L. Rev.* 139 (1964). Liability to the personnel of a space program is thus a question of municipal law. A member of the National Aeronautics and Space Council has called for a space rescue team, saying, "We intuitively know that we and/or the Soviets will suffer a manned space catastrophe." *Washington Post*, Dec. 2, 1966, sec. A, at 14.

[3] McDougal, Lasswell, & Vlasic, *Law and Public Order in Space* 387 ff. (1963); Jessup & Taubenfeld, *Controls for Outer Space* 222–30 (1959); Haley, *supra* note 2, at 136–58; Cohen, *Law and Politics in Space* 63–94 (1964).

[4] A developing sense of social responsibility by states to their residents is a significant factor in assessing what nations may be willing to do in the event of space accidents resulting in damages. Many nations have developed social welfare systems which are supposed to prevent acute suffering caused by lack of earning capacity; and no special rules are likely to be adopted or needed to extend the same protection to disabilities caused by activities in space.

[5] Unless indicated to the contrary, "space" is used to refer to outer space as distinguished from airspace. A precise line of demarcation between the two has not been established. A line of demarcation is not essential for a discussion of liability since, with the exception of possible damage to space vehicles in orbit, all the damages which will be the subjects

of discussion will probably occur on the surface of the earth or in airspace, although a result of activities in space. This includes efforts to put vehicles into space even if the vehicle does not leave airspace.

[6] Rosenthal *et al., supra* note 2, at 23–33; Arthur D. Little, Inc., *On Credible Catastrophic Eventualities in Selected Areas of Government Sponsored Activities* (1963); Hassialis, Bernstein, & O'Neill, *Some Major Hazards in Government Sponsored Activities* (1964). See *New York Times*, Jan. 28, 1967, at 3, for an account of the accident involving tests of a spacecraft at Cape Kennedy which resulted in the deaths of three astronauts in an oxygen fire on Jan. 27, 1967. The accident has been extensively investigated by Congress. See, for example, "Apollo Accident," *Hearings before Senate Committee on Aeronautical and Space Sciences,* 90th Cong., 1st Sess., parts 1–7 (Feb., Mar., Apr., May, June 1967).

[7] Fragments of an American navigation satellite fell in Oriente Province in Cuba, *New York Times*, Dec. 2, 1960, at 10, col. 1. A piece of the Soviet satellite, Sputnik IV, landed at Manitowoc, Wisconsin, in 1962 while at the same time a number of pieces of varying sizes fell into nearby Lake Michigan. Plimpton, representing the United States, placed the Manitowoc fragment weighing about 20 pounds before the Soviet Union representative at the United Nations but stated that no damage had been done; U.N. Doc. No. A/AC.105/PV. 15, at 33–34 (1962). The second and third stages of a

sented, but there is, of course, no way to eliminate the possibility of damage.[8]

Actions resulting in the spoliation of scientific endeavor, such as the introduction on a celestial body of terrestrial bacteria, viruses, or other living matter from a man-made spacecraft before it can be determined whether life exists there independently,[9] cluttering space with debris of dead spacecraft, boosters, copper needles, or other objects, and modification of radiation belts or other aspects of the space environment present special problems. Such actions are unlikely to give rise to specific claims for compensation on the part of individual states, although the nations of the world collectively have a substantial, if nonmonetary, interest in the conservation of the resources and scientific integrity of celestial bodies.

Falling Boosters, Spacecraft, and Debris

Contrary to the expectations of some scientists that fragments and parts from space vehicles and boosters placed in orbit or sent beyond the atmosphere will burn up in the atmosphere prior to reaching earth unless designed and fabricated for reentry, experience indicates that some fall back on earth as solid pieces of metal. As the number of objects put into outer space increases, the probability of damage from falling debris correspondingly increases, even though as previously noted, the incidence of damage is likely to continue to be low.[10] A more substantial risk is involved in the possible return to earth of a booster stage still containing unexpended fuel.[11]

Vanguard missile impacted 1,500 miles from its launch site Apr. 28, 1958; Senate Committee on Aeronautical and Space Sciences, *Legal Problems of Space Exploration; A Symposium,* Doc. No. 26, 87th Cong., 1st Sess., at 1307 (1961). The third stage of a Vanguard missile impacted near the east coast of the Union of South Africa on May 27, 1958; *id.* at 1308. The payload and third stage of a Vanguard missile fell into the Atlantic Ocean several hundred miles off Cape Kennedy, Apr. 13, 1959; *id.* at 1313. The third stage of a Vanguard missile fell into the Atlantic Ocean 300 miles northeast of the Atlantic Missile Range, June 22, 1959; *id.* at 1314. Pieces of the second stage of an Atlas-Able launch vehicle were found on a farm in Transvaal, South Africa, Sept. 25, 1960; *id.* at 1325. Fragments of the booster which propelled Col. Glenn into orbit impacted in South Africa in Mar. 1962; *New York Times,* Mar. 2, 1962, at 20, col. 3. The 4,000-pound first stage of the booster which propelled the Gemini V manned spacecraft into orbit was recovered from the Atlantic Ocean a few hundred miles from Cape Kennedy; *Washington Post,* Aug. 22, 1965, pt. 2, at 5, col. 2. An Agena-Atlas rocket, orbited Feb. 15, 1966, from the West Coast, returned at least 40 fragments to earth over a seven-day period; *Chicago Tribune,* Mar. 11, 1966, at 22, col. 5. Three heavy metal spheres, apparently pressure tanks from a Soviet spacecraft, were found near Seville, Spain; *Chicago Tribune,* Dec. 23, 1965, at 3, col. 8. An Agena-Atlas target for docking Gemini IX misfired into the sea several hundred miles southeast of Cape Kennedy; *Washington Post,* May 18, 1966, at 1, col. 4. It might be argued that the 1954 nuclear test explosions in the Pacific utilized space to some extent. One or two Japanese fishermen died and several were quite ill as the result of exposure to radioactive fallout from the Bikini hydrogen bomb tests, and Pacific Islanders are still showing the effects of exposure. Although disclaiming legal responsibility for the injuries resulting from the Bikini explosions, the United States, after negotiations with Japan, made *ex gratia* payments of two million dollars. Payments to the islanders were approved by Congress only in late 1965. In general, see McDougal & Schlei, "The Hydrogen Bomb Tests in Perspective: Lawful Measures for Security," 84 *Yale L.J.* 648 (1955).

[8] Unless the context indicates to the contrary, the term "damage" will be used to include property damage, death, and personal injury.

[9] Tass has given assurance that the Russian spacecraft which allegedly landed on Venus in early Mar. 1966, was properly sterilized. *Chicago Sun-Times,* Mar. 6, 1966, at 4, col. 1.

---

[10] An analogy to falling particles from man-made objects are natural meteorites. The Smithsonian Astrophysical Observatory indicates that approximately 5,600 meteorites of 2.2 pounds or more strike the earth every year. Murchie, *Music of the Spheres* 111 (1961) states: "There is no record of anyone's having been killed by a meteorite in all history." Murchie goes on to describe some instances of injuries and property damage and at 122 he refers to the huge meteorite which fell in Siberia in 1908. This meteorite, estimated to weigh 40,000 tons, completely devastated an area 50 miles in diameter. Scientists at Pa. State U. have located 42 "probable or proven" meteorite impact sites in the continental U.S. and southern Canada; see map, *Chicago Daily News,* Nov. 20, 1965, at 31. There is some popular support for the idea that Sodom and Gomorrah were destroyed by a similar meteorite; *True Magazine,* Dec. 1965, at 31. In contrast, the United States rocket S-11, expected to be used in the Apollo moon-landing program, weighs no more than 500 tons fully loaded. *Chicago Tribune,* May 11, 1965, at 3, col. 5.

[11] The fuel in the Aug. 1965 Gemini V booster which was recovered from the Atlantic Ocean had, of course, been consumed. *Washington Post,* Aug. 22, 1965, pt. 2, at 5, col. 2. In Hassialis *et al., supra* note 6, at 42 the opinion is expressed, without reference to classified data, that the upper stages of the Saturn V moon rocket and its Apollo spacecraft "is dynamically stable and therefore unlikely to destroy itself by violent maneuvers during descent. This opinion is strengthened by the fact that the structure is designed to survive substantial axial and transverse loads (the latter due to winds) during first stage burning." See also Arthur D. Little, Inc., *supra* note 6, at 67–83. It is unlikely, but not impossible, that United States boosters containing unexpended fuel will land on foreign territory. Some may very well land on the high seas. Smaller

The possible extent and probabilities of damage occurring depend on variables the most important of which are: the nature of the site of the accident, the kind of fuel used, and the amount of fuel remaining at the time of the accident. As distance from the launch site increases, the amount of unconsumed fuel will decrease with a corresponding reduction in the probable violence of an explosion on impact. Except in an erratic launch, the altitude of a spacecraft rapidly increases as its distance from the launch site increases, thus greatly augmenting the probabilities that the unexpended fuel can be exploded harmlessly by built-in safety devices. Also, as the altitude of the spacecraft increases, so do the probabilities that in the event of an unscheduled return of the vehicle and booster to the earth's surface, the remaining fuel will be ignited by the heat of friction and will be burned or exploded harmlessly as the spacecraft reenters the denser atmosphere, even if the safety destruct devices fail to function.[12] Consequently, questions of liability for large claims are likely to come under domestic law, unless a launching takes place near an international boundary close to sizeable cities. Areas in Canada, Mexico, and the Caribbean may be close enough to some United States launching sites to be susceptible to damage from errant missiles containing unexpended fuels. Similarly, Russian launch sites may create international risks for areas of eastern Europe and Asia.

Fuels and pure oxygen used in space may cause severe damage during almost every stage of activity, including periods prior to the actual flight of the vehicle. The risk commences with the manufacture and transportation of the highly inflammable propellants and liquid oxygen to storage sites and launching pads.[13] At the present time the risks of transporting and storing fuels are limited primarily to the territory of the launching state and are thus matters of domestic concern. International legal problems could arise when several countries participate in joint space activities, which are provided for in numerous agreements to which the United States is a party[14] and which are being undertaken by the European Space Research Organization (ESRO), the European Launcher Development Organization (ELDO), and other multinational groups.[15]

Liability questions involving launch-pad accidents are generally limited to the territory of one state,[16] although launches may be made from platforms at sea and new methods of placing vehicles in orbit may present substantially different factual situations.[17] Claims arising as a result of cooperative space endeavors, to the extent they cannot be disposed of by domestic law or by agreement among the participating states,[18] present the same types of legal problems as accidents caused by errant vehicles launched by a single country.[19]

If nuclear fuels are developed for spacecraft, as seems probable,[20] scientists and engineers foresee possibilities of

---

of the cooperative projects provide for joint launching responsibilities.

[15] See "International Cooperation and Organization for Outer Space," *Report of Staff of Senate Committee on Aeronautical and Space Sciences,* Senate Doc. No. 56, 89th Cong., 1st Sess., at 103–20 (1965). Also see Frutkin, *International Cooperation in Space* 132–41 (1965).

[16] The tragic death of three American astronauts at Cape Kennedy on Jan. 27, 1967, technically presents only domestic legal questions. See *Hearings, supra* note 6. The Apollo accident has been extensively reported in the press, as has been the death of the Russian astronaut on reentry. See *Wall Street Journal,* Apr. 25, 1967, at 5; *Washington Post,* Jan. 29, 1967, at 1; Apr. 25, 1967, at 1; Apr. 26, 1967, at A1; *New York Times,* Apr. 25, 1967, at 1.

[17] The use of very large bore guns as launchers is an example. See *New York Times,* Nov. 9, 1965, at 3, col. 1.

[18] Liability relationships between members of a cooperative space endeavor can be provided for in the agreement or understanding establishing the project. However, an examination of the hundred or so cooperative project agreements and arrangements to which the United States is a party indicates that none covers the question of liability specifically. On the other hand, NASA "operation support" agreements mention the question of liability in general terms. Cooperative projects anticipate direct foreign participation whereas operations support appear to contemplate only passive participation on the part of a foreign country. The line of demarcation is not clear.

[19] For a discussion of the risks of an occurrence such as the Texas City fire-initiated fertilizer ship explosion of 1947 which resulted in 600 deaths, 3,000 injuries, and $75,000,000 in property damage, see Hassialis *et al., supra* note 6, at 94–108.

[20] See Finger, "Space Nuclear Systems," NASA-Industry Conference, *passim* (1963); *New York Times,* Mar. 15, 1966, at 12, col. 2; *Chicago Tribune,* Apr. 14, 1966, sec. 1C, at 1, col. 1. The President has requested $91 million for use in developing a nuclear powered space engine with 200,000 to

---

countries are faced with the dangers of unexpended fuel falling across international borders.

[12] See discussion in Hassialis *et al., supra* note 6, esp. at 3, 4, 42, 43, 56, 66, 67, 70.

[13] For an extensive discussion of the risks involved in transporting highly volatile missile propellants, see Arthur D. Little, Inc., *supra* note 6, at 9–66.

[14] The United States is party to over 100 agreements providing for cooperation in space activities, but only a few

damages from radiation in the event of an accident and the return to earth of radioactive debris, even in the absence of a nuclear explosion.[21] Very little information about the use and hazards of nuclear power in space activities has been made public, but classified details of operations are not required to recognize the existence of a risk.[22] Radiation, with or without nuclear explosion, may constitute a hazard over an area many times larger than an impact area, and this hazard may continue to exist for a considerable time after the deposit of the material on the earth's surface.[23]

If explosive warheads, nuclear or other, are placed in space in spite of the U.N.-sponsored treaty to the contrary,[24] which appears possible,[25] their potential for causing damage to earthbound interests will be commensurate with the power of the particular warhead. Reentry heat shields and safeguards against accidental detonations reduce but do not eliminate the possibilities of unintended explosions that could effect widespread pollution as well as direct destruction.[26]

Collisions

The probabilities of collisions between spacecraft or between spacecraft and aircraft seem remote, given the vastness of airspace and outer space. At least one such collision has already occurred, however. To the apparent irritation of United States officials, an American scientist described a collision at the Seventeenth International Astronautical Congress in Madrid in October 1966. Eight satellites had been placed in orbit by a single rocket on March 9, 1965. More than a month later, two of them brushed together but with only slight damage.[27] The increasing number and greater maneuverability of satellites will progressively increase the probability of collisions. Collisions involving a spacecraft in early ascent stages and aircraft would most likely occur within the territorial jurisdiction of the nation initiating the launching; the claims arising therefrom would usually be cognizable under national rather than international law, but an abortive launch resulting in an undesired orbit or in the destruction of a space vehicle might drop fragments across airlanes anywhere around the world.[28]

250,000 pounds of thrust. See *Washington Post,* Mar. 1, 1967, at A3.

[21] Hassialis *et al., supra* note 6, at 91; Stoner, *The Next Ten Years in Space; 1959–1969,* H.R. Doc. No. 115, 86th Cong., 1st Sess., at 194 (1959). See also the statement of Harold B. Finger, Manager, AEC-NASA Space Nuclear Propulsion Office, in NASA Authorization for Fiscal Year 1966, *Hearings before the Senate Committee on Aeronautical and Space Sciences,* 89th Cong., 1st Sess., at 377 (1965); Glasstone, *Sourcebook on the Space Sciences* 135 (1965); O'Toole, "Radiation Causation, and Compensation," 54 *Geo. L. J.* 751, *passim* (1966).

[22] Knutson, *The Next Ten Years in Space: 1959–1969,* H.R. Doc. No. 115, 86th Cong., 1st Sess., at 102 (1959).

[23] Hassialis *et al., supra* note 6, at 89–93.

[24] Treaty on Principles Governing the Activities of States in the Exploration and Use of Space, Including the Moon and other Celestial Bodies, signed Jan. 27, 1967 (reproduced in Appendix E) [hereinafter cited as Treaty on Principles].

[25] The *New York Times,* Nov. 9, 1964, at 5, col. 1, refers to a military parade in Moscow on Nov. 7, 1965, in which was displayed a large three-stage rocket described by Tass as an orbital missile which can deliver a "surprise blow on the first or any other orbit around the earth." In response to a U.S. query, the USSR denied that there was any intent to engage in actions contrary to the terms of the U.N. resolution.

[26] There have been airplane accidents involving nuclear weapons, but no nuclear explosions have occurred. There is an unconfirmed report of a B-52 bomber jettisoning a 24-megaton weapon over North Carolina with five of the six safety devices failing; Hassialis *et al., supra* note 6, at 92. A bomber carrying nuclear weapons crashed over Spain in January 1966; one bomb was not recovered until late March 1966. Conventional

explosives in one of the warheads detonated and scattered some radioactive debris, but there was no nuclear explosion. *Washington Post,* Mar. 3, 1966, sec. 1, at 1, col. 6.

[27] *Washington Post,* Oct. 11, 1966, sec. A, at 1. See generally, Murchie, *supra* note 10, at 114–15: "Even when improved radio devices for 'homing in' and automatic speed-blenders designed to avoid . . . errors have become standard space equipment, the increase in speed differentials as astronautical evolution unfolds is bound to cause serious meeting mishaps, including collisions, and a space collision obviously will seldom be the gentle sideswipe of the earthly highway which you can 'see coming' but will more likely strike completely without warning producing a lightning-like disintegration from explosive friction and heat, with death mercifully instantaneous to all." An analysis of legal problems relating to the use of spacecraft for commercial passenger service would require assumptions of technological developments which cannot presently be anticipated with any degree of certainty, but a series of treaties similar to those applicable to commercial aircraft come to mind.

[28] See note 7 *supra* and Murchie, *supra* note 10, at 115: "Each succeeding crash (in space) must compound the over-all danger by adding new derelicts to the entropy of the universe." *Newsweek,* Oct. 17, 1966, at 73, reported: "Last Friday night at 2400 GMT, no fewer than 1,158 man made objects were orbiting around the earth, moon and sun. Among them were 274 intact satellites, including Vanguard I, the second U.S. satellite ever put in orbit (1958). The rest of the orbiting traffic—884 trackable pieces in all—can be classified as space junk: burned-out rocket bodies, a glove that floated out of Gemini IV, a Hasselblad camera lost by the Gemini X astronauts, and about 240 fragments of an Air Force Titan

Pollution

Pollution involves the introduction of substances capable of causing damage or undesired change by other than normal impact or fire.[29] Pollutants may include microorganisms, biological products, chemicals, radioactive debris, or other matter not found at the particular place except through the action of man. Claims, which may be in addition to or separate from those for impact damages, may arise for specific damages caused by pollution. Introducing microoganisms to earth or to a celestial body might upset the "balance of nature" in such a way as to have lasting and unpredictable consequences. Of the possible contaminants, those involving nuclear radiation have generally received the most attention from various disciplines.[30] Increasing ability to move about in space will carry the risks of damage from all types of pollution to celestial bodies and activities which may be centered there.

Interference with Communications

Communications utilizing electromagnetic transmissions may be disrupted or completely blocked for varying lengths of time by competing electromagnetic emissions from many types of man-made sources. The most frequent interference is from other communications signals on the same or on adjoining frequencies. Space activity is a potential major contributor to the problem of overcrowded radio channels, not only because of the increased need for communications channels but also because of the existence of nuclear- and sun-powered space vehicles which may continue transmitting indefinitely, even when their usefulness has long since ended.[31] Since spacecraft

are highly mobile, transmissions to and from them may result in interference anywhere in the world. Technological advances are being made with great rapidity, but the demand for communications facilities is increasing at such a rate that problems of interference will continue indefinitely into the future. In addition to competing communications signals, major interference may be caused by space activities which release electromagnetic emissions or otherwise disrupt the normal atmospheric and space electromagnetic patterns.[32]

Interference with communications is not a new phenomenon and claims and complaints will, in the absence of new or amended international agreements, probably continue to be made as they are at present.[33] Although international claims for interference with communications have not been successful as a device for collecting damages in the past,[34] it is possible that rules could be devised which would provide a basis for claims for compensation of actual damages resulting from interference. Proof of causation and of the extent of damage would be difficult, and the inflexibility of rules which would be required to control use of frequencies might interfere with advantageous use of available frequencies under naturally varying electromagnetic and climatic conditions. Damages could involve the loss of planes, ships, space-

---

III-C that blew up while carrying a brace of military communications satellites into orbit." See also 61 *Life* 23–32 (Aug. 5, 1966).

[29] Jenks, *The International Law of Outer Space* 167–74 (1962), contains an overview of types of pollution risks. See also Cohen, *supra* note 3, at 37–63 (1964). Chap. 7 contains a more detailed discussion of pollution.

[30] For a very good treatment of the origin and types of radiation injuries, see Stason *et al., supra* note 2, at chap. 1 (1959). A brief technical discussion appears in Hassialis *et al., supra* note 6, at 84–89.

[31] As early as 1959 the U.N. Legal Committee in its report of the Ad Hoc Committee on the Peaceful Uses of Outer Space, U.N. Doc. No. A/AC.98/2 (June 12, 1959) contained the following observation at p. 5: "Attention should . . . be given to the desirability of terminating transmissions from space vehicles once these transmissions have outlived their

usefulness. Such a measure would help conserve and make optimum use of the frequencies which are assigned for outer space communications."

[32] The United States and Russian high-altitude nuclear explosions are examples. The United States "Megaton-Plus hydrogen device exploded at more than a 200-mile altitude" caused "some communication disruption but less than predicted"; *House Comm. on Science and Astronautics,* 88th Cong., 1st Sess. (1965).

[33] The International Telecommunications Union (ITU) is basically a forum for the resolution of differences rather than a lawmaking institution. It has done excellent work in obtaining cooperation from nations and in obtaining observance of common-sense rules. See Huszagh, "The International Law Making Process: A Case Study on International Regulation of Space Telecommunication" 1–3 (unpublished doctoral dissertation, U. of Chicago Law School, 1964).

[34] See Huszagh, *The International Law Making Process* (1964): "The vast extent of damage possible and the likelihood of such interference due to the crowded radio spectrum necessitate a legal system of financial penalties to discourage unauthorized radio frequency use. Despite the thrust of these undesirable circumstances the 1959 Convention (ITU) did not establish provisions for payment of damages. Consequently, only the cumbersome mechanism of diplomatic negotiations is available to compensate injured parties and deter unauthorized frequency use."

craft, and attendant personnel or the loss of experimental data and commercial profits of a communications carrier.

Reporting and Modifying Weather

Space beyond the atmosphere is being utilized for observation of atmospheric phenomena, and future developments may make possible greatly increased use of air and space for weather observation and modification.[35] Activities relating to weather observation will involve both airspace and outer space; and it will probably not be possible to make any clear differentiation. Damages resulting from erroneous weather forecasts and from deliberately modified weather conditions may become serious problems. However, weather reporting and analysis is still such an imperfect science that it would hardly be possible to base an international claim for damages on inaccurate predictions. Weather prediction and modification have already been the subjects of some domestic litigation in the United States.[36] Although some of the crucial information and concepts may be by-products of space activities, modification at present is accomplished by activities in airspace and thus is not within the scope of a study of the law of activities in space.[37]

Earth Measurements and Navigation Aids

Spacecraft are being used extensively to make earth measurements and to provide additional information and fixes for navigational purposes.[38] Erroneous navigational information may result in damage to or loss of ships, aircraft, and spacecraft. Collection of damages resulting from acting on erroneous or inadequate information furnished as part of a government discretionary function has seldom been possible, and developments in space are unlikely to make a significant change in this situation. But the general trend of U.S. courts operating under the Federal Tort Claims Act is to place greater responsibility on the government when it is discharging an operational function.[39]

Other Claims, Nominal and Exemplary Damage

International claims are not necessarily limited to accidents involving death, personal injury, and property damage, and it is not possible to predict all the types of space activity which might give rise to claims. For example, the American Institute of Aeronautics and Astronautics commented: "We see orbital sightseeing tours within the reach of moderately affluent private citizens."[40] Claims may be made in an effort to establish that a particular space activity is wrong, or for exemplary damages to punish the perpetrator of wrongful behavior, or to compensate for mental anguish and degradation. United States courts recognize claims based on damages without contact such as sonic booms; non-physical damage such as mental anguish, pain and suffering; and claims without damages for technical violation of a pro-

---

[35] For a discussion of past accomplishments, present programs, and future possibilities, see Stroud, "Weather Satellites," *Fourth National Conference on the Peaceful Uses of Space* 113 (NASA, 1964); National Science Foundation, *Weather and Climate Modification* (1965); Taubenfeld, *Weather Modification: Law, Controls, Operations* (NSF, 1965).

[36] Oppenheimer, *Legal Aspects of Weather Modification* (Western Snow Conference, 1965); Taubenfeld, *supra* note 35, at 45.

[37] If technology develops to the point that weather modification as well as weather predicting is brought about by activities in space, the problem of damages will have to be considered. Proof of causation will remain difficult. See Hassialis *et al., supra* note 6, at 131–32 for a discussion of "Project Cirrus," the seeding of a tropical hurricane in 1947. Six hours after the seeding the direction of the storm changed so that a coastal area of Georgia was subjected to the storm. "It is by no means certain that the change in course of this storm was causally related to the seeding equipment. Such storms have been known to change their directions before. Contrariwise it cannot be said that the change in course was not due to the experimentation—the probability is that it was." See also Arthur D. Little, Inc., *supra* note 6, at 98–104; Taubenfeld, *supra* note 35, at 26–29.

[38] See Kershner, "Navigation Satellites," *Fourth National Conference on the Peaceful Uses of Space* 127–32 (NASA, 1964); *Significant Achievements in Satellite Geodesy, 1958–1964* (NASA SP-94; 1966); *Significant Achievements in Communications and Navigation, 1958–1964* (NASA SP-93; 1965).

[39] See Aero Enterprises, Inc., v. American Flyers, Inc., 167 F. Supp. 239 (N.D. Texas 1958) wherein the United States was held liable for the negligence of the CAA control tower operators which resulted in a midair collision of two airplanes causing four deaths. A 1960 United-TWA crash over Brooklyn resulted in an agreement for the U.S. to pay 24 percent of total damage; *New York Times,* Oct. 23, 1963, at 1, col. 2. The FAA denied that the decision implied admission of fault, however; *New York Times,* Oct. 26, 1963, at 14, col. 3. In U.S. v. Maryland, 257 F. Supp. 768 (DDC 1966), the court held the government liable for the actions of its employees at an air control center where their negligence contributed to a fatal accident; commented on in 33 *J. Air L. & Commerce* 364–65 (Spring 1967).

[40] *Washington Post,* Dec. 1, 1966, at 3.

tected right such as trespass. Although all these claims could be raised internationally, they would not be different in theory from similar claims based on nonspace causes. A space treaty on liability should specifically include or exclude these kinds of claims because there is no established rule of international law on them.[41]

The violation of national territorial sovereignty or privacy has received much attention since the development of aircraft, and questions concerning information-gathering activities from aircraft just outside the territorial limits of a country and from spacecraft far overhead continue to be subjects of discussion and some controversy, particularly among nongovernment, international law scholars. As ability to rendezvous in space is perfected, claims might be presented for simple trespass on a spacecraft, the same as for a ship on the high seas. Formal claims for damages alleged to arise from such space activities have not been made. It seems likely that, if objections are made, it will be through diplomatic channels or in military reaction rather than through legal forums, although the international law basis would be the same. If legal action is brought, it would seem that the basic purpose, particularly where military information is in question, would be to establish the wrongfulness of the action rather than to collect a specified amount in damages. A successful claimant could utilize a decision for propaganda purposes and justify forceful self-help in the event the other party did not discontinue the objectionable actions. However, since the United States and Russia both utilize satellites to collect military intelligence, it is rather unlikely that a case will be brought other than for propaganda purposes.[42]

If no international tribunal will find that the collection of military information by satellite provides a basis for collecting damages, it is no more probable that a tribunal will award damages for the collection of information of economic value. It is technically possible that a space power may be able to obtain better information about mineral deposits and other resources than the observed state lacking space capabilities has about itself. This would ordinarily be true only for comparatively undeveloped areas.[43]

Many legal systems utilize punitive damages as a deterrent to unlawful or undesirable conduct; this is clearly an objective of a Hungarian draft proposal concerning liability for damages caused by launching objects into space.[44] The processing of any such claims requires a prior political agreement as to which types of activities are undesirable. The nuclear test-ban treaty would serve as an example of such an agreement. However, the treaty does not provide for the assessment of damages.[45] In

[41] The Treaty on Principles, *supra* note 24, makes states liable for damages but does not specify the kinds of claims covered. It was ratified by the USSR, May 20, 1967; by the U.S., Apr. 26, 1967. Work on a treaty on liability continues and agreement may come at any time Soviet and American political considerations so permit.

[42] General Eisenhower quotes Soviet Premier Khrushchev at the 1960 Summit as saying that despite his violent objections to the U-2, any nation in the world that wanted to photograph the Soviet Union by satellite was completely free to do so. Eisenhower, *Waging Peace* 556 (1965). For a summary of the Soviet position, see "Soviet Space Programs: Organization, Plans, Goals, and International Implications," *Senate Committee on Aeronautical and Space Science,* 87th Cong., 2d Sess., 207–9 (Comm. Print 1962). For a discussion of the pros and cons of the use of satellites for intelligence purposes, see Falk, "Toward a Responsible Procedure for the National Assertion of Protested Claims to Use Space," *Space and Society* 91–120 (Taubenfeld ed. 1964); Lipson & Katzenbach,

supra note 1, at 31, 91. Innumerable papers have been prepared and given at various institutes and conferences on the information-gathering capabilities of satellites. For comprehensive lists, see the International Aerospace Abstracts published by the Technical Information Service of the American Institute of Aeronautics and Astronautics and also the Scientific and Technical Aerospace Reports published by NASA.

[43] See McDougal *et al., supra* note 3, at 54C. "It is conceivable that if a state acquires through unauthorized observation from space a more comprehensive or specific knowledge of the physical (including mineral) properties of state B than state B itself possesses, such knowledge on the part of state A may represent a deprivation for state B." Taubenfeld has stated that there is presently no rule requiring a state obtaining information through activities in space to pass such information on to any other state; "Legal Aspects of the Use of Satellites in the Exploitation of Natural Resources," paper delivered at American Astronautical Society Annual Meeting, Feb. 21, 1966, San Diego, Cal.

[44] U.N. Doc. A/AC.105/C.2/L.10 (1964) Art. 11, sec. 1 proposes a general rule that "Liability of the State shall not exceed [amount left blank in the draft]." Art. IV provides that "The State shall assume full liability for damages caused directly or indirectly on the ground, in the atmosphere or in outer space, if the State is exercising an unlawful activity in outer space." The draft does not define "unlawful" and is unlikely to be accepted because of the uncertain political implications.

[45] The Jan. 27, 1967, Treaty on Principles, *supra* note 24, provides for liability for damages without regard to whether or not the causative action was authorized or prohibited by any other treaty or rule of law. The questions of "legal" peaceful activities have provided the major political obstacles in the negotiation of a liability treaty.

case of violations leading to war, the only way to process claims for damages would be through provisions in a peace treaty when hostilities ceased. In the event damage claims arise as a result of violations not leading to hostilities, claims could be processed through such customary procedures as might be agreed. Presumably, proof of damage would have to be specific rather than general.

This discussion of occurrences out of which claims for damages may arise exemplifies the difficulties space activities contribute to the international rules of law relating to liability for deaths, personal injury, and property damages. The risk of damage is not limited to the nation carrying out the activity but may occur at any time anywhere on the surface of the earth, in airspace or in outer space. Consequently all nations, whether engaged in space activities or not, must participate in the establishment of legal rules or acquiesce in their promulgation if a uniform system of handling claims is to be developed. It is doubtful, to say the least, that this optimum goal will be achieved.

This discussion is not intended to indicate that the authors of this study are convinced that international claims arising from activities in space will constitute an intolerable burden on the economies of the space powers. Experience has thus far been very encouraging in that no significant damage across national borders has occurred and no international claims have been presented.

Objectives in Resolving Claims Arising from Activities in Space

Laws on liability for damages are part of the rules of conduct laid down by a society, either national or international, for the advancement of its social, political, and economic objectives. The less homogeneous the society, the more difficult it is to agree on a set of common objectives, but without such agreed objectives the task of drafting acceptable rules of conduct or laws is an especially difficult process of compromise which calls for mutual adjustment, i.e., good faith bargaining.[46] An

essential precondition to fruitful negotiation is that all necessary parties to an agreement have a sincere desire to make an agreement rather than a desire to prolong negotiations for political and propaganda purposes.[47] The existence of appropriate national policy guidelines and international political accommodations relative to activities in space are essential before an internationally acceptable draft on even a comparatively uncomplicated subject such as liability for damages can be prepared.[48]

Although the political and legal conceptual differences between Communist and Western countries produce the most difficult stumbling blocks, there are also some differences related to whether a nation has present or potential space capability. A nonspace power may tend to see the problems of liability for damages more from the point of view of a claimant than a defendant,[49] but this factor

---

[46] Several nongovernmental efforts have been made to draft codes of law for activities in space. See, e.g., William A. Hyman's "Magna Carta of Space," adopted by Resolution of the Inter-American Bar Association at its 12th Annual Conference, Feb. 2, 1961, 166–67 (1966). See also David Davies Memorial Institute of International Studies, *Draft Code of Rules on the Exploration and Uses of Outer Space* (1962). These drafts are general in nature but, even so, contain provisions not likely to be acceptable to nationalistic governments, including the U.S. See Lay & Poole, "Exclusive Government Liability for Space Accidents," 53 *A.B.A.J.*

(Sept. 1967) for discussion of objectives in determining liability questions involving activities in space.

[47] One American author suggests that "[T]he Soviets use international law not as a means to resolve and remove conflict but rather to manage and direct conflict in the interests of Communist global expansion." Crane, "Basic Principles in Soviet Space Law: Peaceful Coexistence, Peaceful Cooperation and Disarmament," 39 *Law & Contemporary Problems* 943, 955 (1964).

[48] An impasse based on political factors delayed U.N. negotiations relative to separate agreements on assistance to and return of astronauts and space vehicles, now approved, as well as on liability. Committee on the Peaceful Uses of Outer Space, U.N. General Assembly Doc. No. A/AC. 105/29 (1965). The Treaty on Principles, *supra* note 24, at Article V provides in broad terms that astronauts are envoys of mankind in outer space and are to receive "all possible assistance in the event of accident, distress, or emergency landing . . . they shall be safely and promptly returned to the State of registry of their space vehicle." Minor shifts in the political approach would allow approval of a liability treaty. The inability to devise a general agreement on disarmament is well known. Considerably better progress has been made in the negotiation of a treaty on liability for damages from space activities, but lack of agreement on objectives and policy in determining lawful and unlawful activities and several other points has prevented a final agreement. See, e.g., Hungarian draft proposal Art. V, Com. on the Peaceful Uses of Outer Space, Report, U.N. General Assembly Doc. No. A/AC.105/29, Annex II, p. 4 (1964).

[49] E.g., the Belgian draft proposal, U.N. Doc. No. A/AC.105/C.2/L.7/Rev. 2 (1964), provides for no limitation on liability. Orbiting spacecraft are peculiarly international and not susceptible to satisfactory bilateral arrangements. These factors furnish rather strong arguments in favor of establishing an international legal regime to cover the risks, even though as a practical matter the probability of numerous incidents is very slight.

has not appeared to play a part in the relationships between the United States and the Soviet government where the East-West political differences have been a dominant factor. The expressed willingness of present and aspiring space powers to make provisions for compensation for damages resulting from activities in space has reduced the differences which might exist between space and nonspace powers,[50] and some of the small nonspace powers have indicated an interest in limiting liability for damages so as not to be deterred from future participation in space activities.[51] It has also been argued that it may be desirable if the risk of liability for damages does serve as a deterrent to entry into space activities, because the less wealthy nations could concentrate on economic and social development rather than on prestige projects.[52] In fairness it should be said that few developing countries have shown any excessive interest in space projects. The promptness and fairness with which the first space damage claims are disposed of by the space powers will unquestionably have a sharp impact on opinion among the nonspace powers and may have a substantial impact on how soon an initial agreement requires revision. Contributing to the optimism that a detailed agreement on liability for damages can be achieved within the next year or two is the fact that space activities have thus far caused no deaths, injuries, or appreciable property damage cognizable under international law. Broad agreement on liability has already been reached in the Treaty on Principles.[53] It is possible that the general terms of this treaty may be considered sufficient and that details of application may be developed as cases arise. The Treaty on Principles makes states internationally responsible for all national activities, whether effected by a governmental or nongovernmental entity. An international organization may also be liable. The U.N. process of formulating rules for inclusions in a treaty has tended to place heavy emphasis on political factors, and as these are minimized the prospects for an acceptable treaty improve.[54]

In comparison, questions relating to liability of airlines to passengers still, after many years of commercial air operations, cause substantial disagreement between nations, but primarily economic rather than political.[55] Because of lack of agreement on the extent and terms of liability, the Rome Convention on Damages Caused by Foreign Aircraft to Third Parties on the Surface[56] is in

---

[50] See Rosenthal *et al., supra* note 2, at 147, who suggest that "While the harmful effects on this country's foreign relations [resulting from damages caused by space activities] could not be wholly undone, they might be significantly mitigated by arrangements that would speedily provide adequate financial compensation for the victims."

[51] See comment of the Mexican representative summarized in U.N. Doc. No. A/AC.105/C.2/SR.48, p. 13 (1965): "Since it was agreed that responsibility was absolute, then unlimited liability could spell financial disaster for a small country."

[52] See, e.g., the statement of George R. Woods, former president of the World Bank, to the annual meeting of the Bank's Board of Governors, Sept. 27, 1965: "It is useless to attempt to sugar-coat the fact that in many of the underdeveloped countries, economic performance can be greatly improved. It is essential that these countries take effective measures to increase the mobilization of capital through taxation and through incentive to investment, both domestic and international. It is urgent for many of them to cut down some of the biggest items of waste—excessive military expenditures, prestige projects, inefficient administration, overstaffing of railways and other public enterprises, and subsidies to public services that could and should be self-supporting."

[53] Treaty on Principles, *supra* note 24, at Arts. V and VII (reproduced in Appendix E).

[54] On Nov. 15, 1965, the United States renounced the Warsaw Convention of 1929, 49 Stat. 3000, *T.S.* No. 876, 3 *Air Laws and Treaties of the World* 3103 (1965) because the other nations party to it were unwilling to increase adequately the limits on liability (less than $10,000) for the death of passengers; 54 *Dept. of State Bull.* 580 (Apr. 1966). Pursuant to a subsequently reached agreement increasing to $75,000 the limit for death in flights involving the United States, the denunciation was withdrawn; 54 *Dept. of State Bull.* 956 (June 1966). Without such a treaty a plaintiff might find himself bound by foreign law even in a U.S. court. Recently, a widow suing for wrongful death of her husband in an airplane accident in Brazil was bound by the Brazilian maximum of $170. Tramontana v. S.A. Empresa de Viacao Aerea Rio Grandense, 350 F. 2d. 468 (1965) *cert. denied,* 383 U.S. 943 (1966). Negotiations on the new treaty provisions have not gone smoothly, and there is sharp disagreement between the U.S. government representatives and representatives of the various American airlines. See *Wall Street Journal,* July 10, 1967, at 1 for some speculation on the final outcome.

[55] Senate Committee on Commerce, 89th Cong., 1st Sess., 3 *Air Laws and Treaties of the World* 3147, 3221 (Comm. Print 1965).

[56] See Goldie, *supra* note 1, at 1191. "The great damage these [space] objects could cause to the victim State, and their close relation to the national defense and prestige of the launching State, may tend to predispose these incidents to becoming political questions—to be resolved in the atmosphere of heightened tensions which such questions tend to carry with them. Frequently these tensions may be intensified by the lack of objectively formulated definitions and rules to which both parties may make common reference. Reference to common standards and rules can, by contrast, reduce the tension of claims arising from disasters to 'objects of

force for only a few nations, not including the United States.

Each country's concept of its socioeconomic obligations to its own nationals will be reflected in its domestic laws of liability and in the efforts it makes to obtain compensation for its nationals for damages caused by foreign states or nationals. A sense of fairness and a recognition of requirements or reciprocity will result in comparable offers of compensation to aliens. The general objective of compensating victims of space accidents has been expressed repeatedly since activities in space commenced.[57] The statements of the negotiators at the United Nations indicate firm political commitments by all the nations, including Russia,[58] to this objective. Not everyone agrees that compensation to the damaged party is an absolute objective for systems of liability, and there may be advantages in keeping social welfare con-

cepts separate from concepts of liability for specific injuries.[59]

Deterrence of unsafe or improper conduct is also generally recognized as an appropriate objective, but if an attempt is made to base space liability on fault, the problems of defining conduct constituting fault are raised and the task of the claimant is made almost impossibly difficult. Too, the political issues posed by the Hungarian draft, which provides for unlimited liability when injury results from "unlawful" activity, are sharply accentuated.[60]

A major objective of any arrangement for handling claims must be the avoidance of unnecessary and emotionally charged conflicts and the provision of adequate compensation to injured parties in accordance with present social concepts, which seem to require compensation without regard to fault. As stated, this objective is compatible with encouraging activities in space, although it will increase the budget requirements.[61]

Parties and Sources of Compensation

Traditionally only states may be parties to actions before international tribunals,[62] but this concept is being modified and some treaties give nongovernmental entities and natural persons status before international tribu-

---

litigation,' and so help to avert the development of international tests of strength." Goldie has perhaps overemphasized the probabilities of major damage from activities in space cognizable under international law, but providing machinery to resolve only one serious incident would justify the efforts being made to draft a treaty.

[57] See, e.g., United States proposals for a convention concerning liability for damages caused by the launching of objects into outer space, U.N. Doc. No. A/AC.105/C.2/1.8 (1964): "The Contracting Parties . . . seeking to establish a simple and expeditious procedure to provide financial protection against damage . . . agree as follows . . ."; and U.N. Doc. No. A/AC.105/C.2/1.8/Revs. 1 and 2 (1964): "The Contracting Parties . . . seeking to establish a uniform rule of liability and a simple and expeditious procedure governing financial compensation for damage . . . . agree as follows . . ."; Belgium appears to have emphasized continuously the compensation objective. See Belgium's proposal in U.N. Doc. No. A/AC.105/C.2/L.7/Revs. 1 and 2 (1964): "The Contracting Parties . . . Recognizing that activities in the exploration and peaceful uses of outer space may from time to time result in damages, recognizing the need to establish rules governing liability with a view to ensuring that compensation is paid for damage thus caused, have agreed as follows . . . ." Some American writers have given strong support to the humanitarian concept of compensation as the basic objective. See, e.g., Estep, "Book Review," 17 *Yale L.J.* 343, 353 (1965): "The needs of business have to be taken into account, but surely the most important concern is how to provide the most compensation for the greatest number of people with the least amount of overhead expense."

[58] U.N. Doc. No. A/AC.105/C.21 S.R. 48, at 11 (1965). The Russian representative stated, "That provision [Items of General Assembly Resolution 1962 (XVIII) (1963)] was intended to safeguard the interest of those outside the launching State which might suffer injury as a result of the space activity."

[59] See Keeton & O'Connell, *supra* note 1 at 329, 331, where it is suggested that "an award is not to be made unless there exists some reason other than the mere need of the victim for compensation. Otherwise, the award will be an arbitrary shifting of loss from one person to another at a net loss to society due to the economic and sociological cost of adjudication." Blum & Kalven, *supra* note 1 at 641, 721 observe that "The welfare universe is not limited to victims of auto accidents but includes victims of all kinds of human misfortune. We can think of no ground for singling out the misfortune of auto accident victims for special welfare treatment." The same thought might be applied to space accident victims.

[60] U.N. Doc. No. A/AC.105/29 Annex IV, Hungarian draft, Art. V. See also Goldie, *supra* note 1, at 1189, for an analysis of strict and absolute liability applied to sovereign states.

[61] General Assembly Res. 1721 (XVI) (Dec. 20, 1961) begins by "Recognizing the common interests of mankind in furthering the peaceful uses of outer space."

[62] See art. 34, sec. 1, of the Statute of the International Court of Justice, *T.S.* 993 (1945): "Only states may be parties in cases before the Court." The Treaty on Principles *supra* note 24, supports this proposition in Art. VI: "States Parties to the Treaty shall bear international responsibility for national activities . . . whether such activities are carried on by governmental agencies or by non-governmental entities. . . ."

nals.[63] Some bilateral treaties, particularly those dealing with commercial relations, create arbitration procedures to which natural and legal persons other than states can be parties. No state has shown an inclination to depart very far from the traditional rules, however, and the traditional concept will probably continue to be the general rule applicable to space activities. United Nations resolutions relative to liability questions reflect this position,[64] as do the terms of the Treaty on Principles. They also represent a compromise between the United States position that private entities should be permitted to participate in some space activities and the Russian view that only states should be permitted to engage in space activities. Unfortunately these compromises do not resolve all the problems.

A related question is whether international organizations may be parties before international tribunals. The answer to this is usually found in international agreements establishing the organization and the tribunal in question.[65]

In the U.N. negotiations for a space liability treaty the United States initially proposed that only states could be signatories.[66] But it subsequently "clarified" its proposal to permit an international organization to present a claim for compensation and to be a respondent but not to become a signatory to the proposed treaty.[67]

A revised Belgian proposal[68] would allow international organizations to sign or accede to the proposed treaty on the invitation of the U.N. General Assembly, whereupon they would have the "same rights and obligations as states."[69] Other Western representatives proposed var-

---

[63] See Art. 175 of the treaty establishing the European Economic Community, 295 *U.N.T.S.* 2 (Mar. 25, 1957); "Any natural or legal person may submit to the Court of Justice . . . a complaint to the effect that one of the institutions of the Community has failed to address to him an act other than a recommendation or an opinion." Article 25 of the draft of the Convention for the Protection of Human Rights and Fundamental Freedoms, 231 *U.N.T.S.*, 221 (1950), provides that "(1) The Commission may receive petitions addressed to the Secretary-General of the Council of Europe from any person, non-governmental organization or group of individuals claiming to be the victim of a violation by one of the High Contracting Parties of the rights set forth in this Convention, provided that the High Contracting Party against which the complaint has been lodged has declared that it recognizes the competence of the Commission to receive such petitions." Art. 2(c) (i) of the Supplementary Agreement relating to Intelsat permits "any signatory" to be a party before the arbitral tribunal. Art. 1 (d) defines a "signatory" as "a government or communications entity which has signed the Special Agreement and in respect of which it is in force." See Article 28 and 36 of the Convention on Settlement of Investment Disputes between States and Nationals of Other States, signed Mar. 18, 1965, 4 *International Legal Materials* 532 (1965) which provide, "(1) Any Contracting State or any national of a Contracting State wishing to institute (conciliation/arbitration) proceedings shall. . . ."

[64] "States bear international responsibility for national activities in outer space whether carried on by governmental agencies or by nongovernmental entities, and for assuring that national activities are carried on in conformity with the principles set forth in the present Declaration. The activities of nongovernmental entities in outer space shall require authorization and continuing supervision by the state concerned. When activities are carried on in outer space by an international organization, responsibility for compliance with the principles set forth in this Declaration shall be borne by the international organization and by the states participating it." A/RES/1962 (XVIII) (1963), para. 5. Art. V of the Treaty on Principles, *supra* note 24, adopted this language with only minor changes. If and when a separate treaty on liability is adopted it is probable that this theory will be included. See discussion in Jenks, *Space Law* 210–11 (1965). For an excellent discussion of the U.N. negotiations on the subject of liability see Dembling & Arons, "Space Law and the United Nations: The Work of the Legal Subcommittee of the U.N. on the Peaceful Uses of Outer Space," 32 *J. Air L. & Commerce* 329, 349 (1966).

[65] See Bishop, *supra* note 1, at 257–58: "Theory and practice both suggest that any 'personality' which they [international organizations] may have in international law must be conferred upon them by states . . . either expressly or through customary development. . . . It . . . seems clear that an international organization may be given the capacity to sue or be sued before an international court." The Charter of the International Court of Justice would require amendment to permit other than a state to be a party before it.

[66] U.N. Doc. No. A/AC.105/C.2/C.2/L.8 (1964), Art. I(c) and Art. XIII reading in part, "This convention shall be open for signature by States. . . ."

[67] First revision to the United States draft, U.N. Doc. No. A/AC.105/C.2/L.8/Rev. 1. (1964), Art. I(d) defines a "Presenting State" as "a State which is a Contracting Party, or international organization which has transmitted a notification to the Secretary-General under Art. III, para. 1, of this Convention, which presents a claim for compensation to a Respondent State." Art. III, para. 1, provides that "If an international organization which conducts space activities transmits to the Secretary-General of the United Nations a declaration that it accepts and undertakes to comply with the provisions of the present Convention, all the provisions [subject to exceptions] shall apply to the organization as they apply to a state which is a Contracting Party." Art. XIII permits only states to accede to the proposed treaty. Subsequent revisions leave these provisions basically unchanged. U.N. Doc. No. A/AC.105/C.2/L.8/Rev. 3 (1965).

[68] U.N. Doc. No. A/AC.105/C.2/L.7/Rev. 2, Art. 5 (1964).

[69] Art. 6. The Belgian representative indicated "one of the main purposes of the Belgian provisions concerning international

ious modifications of the United States and Belgian suggestions[70] but generally accepted the position that international intergovernmental organizations should be permitted to receive the benefits and incur the obligations of the treaty without being treated in the same manner as states.

The Hungarian proposal,[71] apparently relying on the U.N. Declaration of Legal Principles Governing Activities of States in the Exploration and Use of Outer Space, imposed obligations on international organizations without regard to action by the organization. It stated: "Liability for damage shall rest with the state or international organization which has launched . . . the space vehicle."[72] The agreement was to be "open for signature to all states." The Western powers generally questioned the propriety of such an approach, while the Communist powers generally supported the Hungarian approach with some modification.[73] The space treaty signed January 27, 1967, is open to states for signature and appears to bind them for activities originating from their territory.

The procedural pattern established by the treaty could very well be followed on an ad hoc basis by nations or international organizations not parties to the treaty if they are faced with problems of the type covered by the treaty and if they rely on conventional international law and customary diplomatic negotiations for resolution of differences.

Liability of private or nongovernmental international organizations has received limited attention from government officials and legal scholars; they will probably be treated in the same manner as other nongovernmental entities such as natural persons.[74] The United States and Great Britain reserved their positions on this point, however, obviously concerned about entities such as the

United States Communications Satellite Corporation and Intelsat, whose members are governments, government entities, and private entities.[75]

Claimants: Relationships between Claimant States and Injured Parties

When states represent the injured parties, what relationships should exist between the state and the injured party? Traditionally, a state presenting a claim owns the award received and can do with it as it sees fit in the absence of an agreement or stipulation to the contrary,[76] although international tribunals obviously know that the real party in interest is ordinarily an individual.[77] All proposals suggested for outer space application provide that under some circumstances a state may espouse a claim for a noncitizen. If the claiming state refuses to pay the amount to the injured party, it is doubtful that any other state including the state of nationality of the injured party can, in the absence of treaty provision or other international commitment, demand that the compensation be handed over, either to be retained or to be paid over to the injured party. In international negotiations involving a number of claims, it is customary to agree on a lump-sum payment, with the receiving government giving the paying government an acquittance and accepting the task of distributing the money among the various individual claimants.[78] In the unlikely event of a space accident involving international claims by many individuals, there would be no reason why this procedure could not be used.

If the basic goal of a treaty on liability for damages arising out of activities in space is to compensate injured parties, then there is justification for including provisions

---

organizations was to enable and encourage States which were not parties to the Convention to participate in it by joining an organization which was a party." U.N. Doc. No. A/AC. 105/C.2/SR.52, at 7 (1965).

[70] U.N. Doc. No. A/AC.105/19, Annex II, at 14 (1964); U.N. Doc. No. WGII/6 (1964); No. A/AC.105/C.2/SR.52, at 3, 5, 9, 10–11 (1965).

[71] U.N. Doc. No. A/AC.105/C.2/L.10/Rev. 1 (1964).

[72] U.N. Resolution 1962 (XVIII) para. 5 (1963).

[73] U.N. Doc. No. A/AC.105/C.2/SR.52, at 4, 7, 10–11 (1965); U.N. Doc. No. A/AC.105/21, Annex I, para. 2 (1964); No. WGII/31 (1964); U.N. Doc. No. A/AC.105/C.2/SR.29–37, at 91 (1964).

[74] U.N. Doc. No. A/AC.105/C.2/SR.52, at 7, 10, 12 (1965); A/AC.105/21 Annex I, at 12, Doc. No. WG I/31 (1964).

[75] U.N. Doc. No. A/AC.105/C.2/SR.52, at 12 (1965) and see chap. 5.

[76] Bishop *supra* note 1, at 741: "The private claimant ordinarily has no *legal* right to any moneys recovered by his government as compensation or redress, but normally such sums will be paid to the claimant or to the persons properly entitled thereto." See also Borchard, *The Diplomatic Protection of Citizens Abroad* 383–98 (1927).

[77] O'Connell, *International Law* 121 (1965): "The pursuit of an international claim is an assertion of the primary right of the individual, so that the national State has the duty, albeit an unenforceable one, to hand over the proceeds of litigation to the claimants."

[78] Bishop, *supra* note 1, at 740–41: "Sometimes a lump sum settlement is made between the two states, and a domestic tribunal established to make the awards. This practice is not new, but seems to be growing in favor at present."

which will assure that the benefits of the payments are enjoyed by the injured parties. If the basic goal is to provide a means for the efficient settlement of international disputes, then the treaty can leave the question of compensation to the injured parties to the domestic laws and policies of the claimant state.

The discussion relative to the power of a claimant state to retain any sums recovered emphasizes the necessity for examining the circumstances under which a state may present a claim for damage suffered by a nongovernmental entity, natural or juridical. In some circumstances two or more states may have some basis for representing the same injured party.

Claimants: The Principle of Nationality

Traditionally, only the state of which the injured party is a national may advance a claim on his behalf.[79] In a claim involving three countries, A, B, and C, in which country A has engaged in space activities which caused an accident in country C, where nationals of A, B, and C were damaged, under the traditional rules C may espouse claims of nationals of C only. B may espouse the claims of nationals of B, even though the damage occurred in C, and the nationals of A would proceed directly against A in accordance with the domestic laws of A. In the U.N. negotiations the United States has proposed that the rule for A and A's nationals be continued.[80] Several other Western nations have supported similar positions,[81] and some representatives in the U.N. negotiations formulated proposals based on the idea that the provisions of the proposed convention should not apply to compensation for damages caused in the territory of the launching state or suffered by its nationals or permanent residents.[82] If this rule were accepted, the proposed treaty would not apply to damages caused by country A in the territory of A except possibly to transients. A revised Hungarian proposal[83] included the territory of the responsible state

in the coverage of the treaty. The Austrian[84] and French[85] representatives favored inclusion of the territory of the responsible state on the theory that a nation had a right to claim compensation for damages done to one of its nationals wherever they were, and both countries appeared to support the United States position that only nationals of the state causing the damage would not be covered by the treaty. The Hungarian[86] and Mexican[87] representatives stated the view that a state should be permitted to make a claim for damages occurring within its territory regardless of the nationality of the damaged party. Under the Hungarian proposal, C could espouse claims of nationals of A, B, and C, certainly an innovation in the law.

In all these proposals the state where the damage occurred would be permitted to make claims for nationals of a third state, which is a departure from the concept that nations may represent only their own nationals. In those instances where several states participate in a space activity resulting in damage in one of the participating states or in a nonparticipating state, the American proposal might result in a denial of the benefit of the treaty to nationals of all the participating states since they would all be respondents.[88] Parties to a joint launch could

---

[79] See 5 Hackworth, *supra* note 1, at 802: "It is well settled that the right to protect is confined to nationals of the protecting state."

[80] Art. V of the first U.S. draft, U.N. Doc. No. A/AC.105/C.2/L.8 (1964), states that: "A state shall not be liable under this convention for damages suffered by its own nationals." Subsequent revisions contain the same language. U.N. Doc. No. A/AC.105/C.2/L.8/Rev. 3 (1965).

[81] U.N. Doc. A/AC.105/C.2/L.7 (1964); U.N. Doc. No. A/AC.105/C.2/L.7/Revs. 1 and 2 (1964).

[82] U.N. Doc. No. WG. II/5 (1964); U.N. Doc. No. A/AC.105/C.2/SR.48, at 13 (1965).

[83] U.N. Doc. No. A/AC.105/C.2/L.10/Rev. 1 (1965).

[84] U.N. Doc. No. A/AC.105/C.2/SR.49, at 8–9 (1965).

[85] U.N. Doc. No. A/AC.105/C.2/SR.49, at 10 (1965): "It would be difficult . . . to abandon the existing principle of diplomatic protection with regard to aliens present in the territory of the launching state." It noted that the Belgian proposal would prevent a state from representing its nationals permanently residing abroad.

[86] U.N. Doc. No. A/AC.105/C.2/L.10/Rev. 1 (1965); U.N. Doc. No. A/AC.105/C.2/SR.49, at 809 (1965). The Hungarian representative, in commenting on his revised draft, noted that it did in fact cover the case of a national of the launching state resident in the applicant state.

[87] U.N. Doc. No. A/AC.105/C.2/SR.48, at 7 (1965). The Mexican representative suggested the convention should apply to damage caused in the territory of one contracting state by a space vehicle registered in another contracting state.

[88] It would hardly seem proper to permit the state where the damage occurred to seek recovery from all the states engaged in a cooperative endeavor except the national state of the injured party; this would result in an inequitable distribution of the burden. This problem would be overcome if the Hungarian proposal were accepted but the Austrian representative commented: "The Hungarian proposal went too far for it would enable the applicant state to claim compensation from the launching state for a national of the launching state permanently resident in the territory of the state which had suffered the damages." U.N. Doc. No. A/AC.105/C.2/SR.49, at 9 (1965). The Treaty on Principles, *supra* note 24, does not resolve this point. It is possible that a special treaty on

resolve by agreement between themselves the procedures for disposing of claims from their respective nationals, as well as from nationals of other states, but this could result in a different procedure for each launch, which would hardly seem as satisfactory as a recognized uniform procedure.

Neither the United States nor the Hungarian draft indicates if the espousal of a claim by a state of which the damaged party is not a national would prevent the state of which the damaged party is a national from presenting a claim. Permitting the state where the injuries occur to present claims regardless of the nationality of the injured party would tend to consolidate into one action all claims arising out of a single incident, although it would permit the imposition of a state between a national and his own state. Only one investigation and one basic presentation to the state liable would be required; this would be accomplished by the state having immediate and unfettered access to the site of the damages. Only the extent of damage would require individual determination. If state C where the injuries occur is permitted to espouse the claim of nationals of state B, there does not appear to be a theoretical legal justification to refuse state C to espouse the claims of nationals of the responsible state A. However, it may be argued that the relationship between a person and the state of his nationality is a domestic matter in which an intermediary is unnecessary and undesirable.

Unless the rule is adopted that state C may represent any injured party regardless of nationality and residence, it would be desirable, if not essential, that "residence" be given some definition within the meaning of the treaty.

The United States drafts provided that a nation might represent only its "permanent" residents, but not nationals of the state, liable. This position was adopted by Belgium in a revised draft,[89] with an added provision to allow a nation to make a claim for its permanent resident even if the resident was abroad at the time of the injury.[90]

Compensation paid to an intermediary government may never be received by the damaged party. This argument can obviously be applied to any payment made to a government rather than to the damaged party, but presumably paternalistic concern would be strongest where the damaged party is a national of the state making payment to an intermediary state. In some countries of the world where the social welfare function is highly developed in theory at least and the state is normally supposed to relieve the burdens of one who is injured or loses a spouse, there is a theoretical basis for payment to the state to recompense it for its expenses resulting from injuries to its nationals. At the present time this argument must be taken on faith since there is inadequate information from many countries about the functioning of their social welfare systems, even though the laws and national reports indicate an ideal situation. The state receiving payment of an award might be required to submit proof that payments were received by the injured party under conditions which afforded him the economic benefits of the payment within the framework of his country's laws.

Liability arising from activities in space is not of such a peculiar nature as to require a legal regime substantially different from that applicable to international claims in general, and if states are permitted to espouse claims of non-nationals in space activities, it might establish a precedent for general modification of international claims procedures. A provision authorizing a state in whose territory the damage occurred to present claims for residents, whether or not nationals, could result in presenting claims for nationals of states not parties to the convention. Such a result would doubtless be favored by some, but it might tend to reduce the incentive to become a party to the agreement under negotiation.

There remains the situation in which the damage occurs in the territory of the responsible state or states. In these cases states whose nationals suffer damage would presumably press the claims, since it would be illogical to have the state responsible for the damages press claims against itself. An alternative would allow resident nationals of other states to sue, which would presumably bring the claim into domestic law.

Allowing a state of residence as well as a state of nationality to represent an injured party in international claims raises a possibility of conflict over the right of representation which, under traditional rules, could arise only over dual nationals. This difficulty could be eliminated by assigning priorities to states that could be waived in favor of another state or by providing that only one state, presumably the one where the injury occurs, could represent all the injured parties, regardless of nationality or residence. The state where the injury occurs

---

liability can break new ground in international law and be a precedent for other situations.

[89] U.N. Doc. No. A/AC.105/C.2/L.7 and Rev. 1 (1964). The Belgian delegate justified the revision as "based on provisions which were not new and were to be found in the Rome Convention on Damage Caused by Third Parties on the Surface." U.N. Doc. No. A/AC.105/C.2/SR.49, at 9 (1965).

[90] The Hungarian delegate voiced disagreement. U.N. Doc. No. A/AC.105/C.2/SR.49, at 8 (1965).

will normally be in the best position to make investigations and will also be in a position to present the claims as a group, thus minimizing costs of investigation and adjudication.

It seems unlikely that the state where the damage occurred would refuse to represent a damaged alien,[91] although a provision might be included in the treaty which would authorize the state whose national is injured to make application to the state in whose territory the damage occurred to represent the injured national or, this failing, to demand that the state where the damage occurred compensate the injured national. Since legal systems, styles, and standards differ, it is unlikely that many countries will be willing immediately to give up the long-established right to represent their nationals in international claims.

There are strong arguments based on practical aspects of world politics and firmly established tradition against curtailing the right of a state to espouse the claims of its nationals, in spite of technical advantages which might be gained by a different rule. It is suggested that the state of nationality retain the primary right to present claims for its nationals. This right may be waived in favor of the state of residence or the state where the damage occurred.

Respondents: Individuals and Intra-national Organizations

In theory it is comparatively easy to ascertain what or who has suffered damages although, as has been shown above, it may be difficult in international law to determine which state will prosecute the claim if there is a departure from the traditional rule of nationality. It is equally difficult to determine who is to share the liability where more than one party or state has participated in the activity which caused the damage. Subject to identification of ownership or control of the causative activity, several basic questions must be resolved. Can states participating in multinational projects or international organizations, public or private, engaging in activities in space be held individually liable for injuries under inter-

national law? What should be the distribution of liability when more than one state participates in an activity causing damage? Can individuals or national nongovernmental entities be held liable under international law? Should sources other than the specific parties or states engaging in activities which cause damage be looked to for compensation?

The classic concept that only states may be parties to international litigation applies equally to respondents and claimants.[92] For the foreseeable future governments will sponsor or closely control significant space activities. Intelsat, a mixed private and government enterprise, is closely controlled by governments of the participating countries, including the United States, whereas organizations such as the European Launcher Development Organization (ELDO) are intergovernmental institutions. Organizations such as the Committee on Space Research (COSPAR) of the International Council of Scientific Unions (ICSU) may be considered private institutions engaged in space activities, but they are for the most part controlled, financed, and otherwise supported by governments to such an extent that it may be argued that they are quasi-governmental or only quasi-private entities. The present extensive involvement of governments in space activities provides substantial justification for accepting the concept of state liability for all injuries arising out of space activities.

Objectives of the payment of compensation for damages are the quick and peaceful resolution of international disputes and the humanitarian concept of reimbursing victims for injury they could not avoid by any amount of diligence and care. These aspects of the problem provide an additional justification for placing liability on states, which are more likely to be able to respond fully in damages than are nongovernmental entities.[93]

---

[91] See McDougal, "The Hydrogen Bomb Test and the International Law of the Sea," 49 *Am. J. Int'l L.* 355, 357–58 (1955): "The duality in function . . . or fact that the same nation-state officials are alternately in a process of reciprocal interaction, both claimants and external decision-makers passing upon the claims of others, need not, however, cause confusion: it merely reflects the present lack of specialization and centralization of police functions in international law generally."

[92] Bueckling, "State Liability for Damages in Outer Space," *Neue Juristisch Wochenschrift* 527, 530 (1964): "[O]n the basis of the principle of territorial integrity in international law the state, because of its duty to supervise and control, which has its counterpart in space-flight enterprises being dependent upon state concession, is liable for damages caused by private space-flight enterprises to subjects of other states." See also the comment of the Belgian representative in the U.N. discussion, U.N. Doc. No. A/AC.105/C.2/SR.25, at 7 (1964): "If private individuals or public entities were authorized by a State to launch space devices, the State authorizing such activities would be liable for any resulting damage to third persons."

[93] National law will ordinarily determine whether the state or states which are held liable or accept liability for international space claims have a right of reimbursement from a national

Distribution of Liability among Multiple
Respondent States

Many nations and various "private" and public entities are participating in space activities, usually with the United States or Russia providing the launch capability. Russian cooperative efforts have, of course, been limited to governments. In addition to ad hoc multilateral projects, international organizations have been established for the purpose of engaging in continuing space activities beyond the resources of individual members. Multilateral endeavors raise questions about the responsibility of participants, individually or collectively, or of the organization as an entity, whether or not it constitutes a formal international organization with a juridical existence of its own.

Respondents: Participation in Space Projects

In discussions of the amount of participation required to affix liability, vague phrases have been used, such as "a State undertaking activities in outer space"[94] or "States . . . responsible for the launching of space vehicles."[95] A United Nations resolution and the Treaty on Principles[96] were more specific, stating that "each state which launches or procures the launching of an object into outer space, and each state from whose territory or facility an object is launched, is internationally liable. . . ." Subsequent discussions reflect continuing efforts to clarify positions and also differences of opinion.

A revised Belgian draft defined launching state to include all participants in the activity and made launching states jointly liable.[97] Revised United States proposals

suggested that the launching state be liable and defined the term to include a state which "procures the launching" or "whose territory or facility is used in such launching,"[98] or which "exercises control over the orbit or trajectory of an object."[99] Where several states are liable, each state was to be liable to the claimant in the full amount.[100] A third United States revision included an attempt to spell out in precise terms what was intended by joint and several liability: "If under this convention more than one launching State would be liable the Presenting State may proceed against any or all such States individually or jointly for the total amount of damages, and once the amount of liability is agreed upon or otherwise established, each such State proceeded against shall be liable to pay that amount provided that, in no event shall the aggregate of the compensation paid exceed the amount which would be payable under this convention if only one Respondent State were liable."[101]

The Hungarian revised proposal[102] also proposed "joint and several liability" for "all the States participating in the undertaking or the State from whose territory or from whose facilities the launching was made, or the State which owns or possesses the space vehicles or object causing the damage." The Hungarian draft would

---

nongovernmental entity. Contracts between governments and nongovernmental entities should be precise in spelling out liability for damage.

[94] USSR Draft Declaration of the Basic Principles Governing the Activities of States in the Exploration and Use of Outer Space, Art. 11, U.N. Doc. No. A/AC.105/12, Annex I, at 2 (1963).

[95] U.S. Draft Proposal on Liability for Space Vehicle Accidents, Art. 3(a) & (c) U.N. Doc. No. A/AC.105/C.2/L.4 (1962).

[96] U.N. Doc. No. A/RES/1963 (XVIII) (1963). The Treaty on Principles, *supra* note 24, uses "Each State Party to the Treaty that launches or procures the launching . . . and each State Party from whose territory or facility an object is launched . . . " (Article VII). The treaty language is clearly copied from the resolution.

[97] U.N. Doc. No. A/AC.105/C.2/L.7/Rev. 2, Art. 2 (1964): "Launching State shall be understood to mean the State or

States which carry out the launching of a space device or whose territory is used for such launching." Proposals in U.N. Doc. No. W.K. II/27 (1964) suggested, "If several states participate in the launching of a space device, each of them shall be liable for the whole of the damage, and a claim for compensation may validly be addressed to any one of them."

[98] U.N Doc. No. A/AC.105/C.2/L.8/Rev. 1, Art. 1, 1.C (1964).

[99] U.N. Doc. No. A/AC.105/C.2/L.8/Rev. 2, Art. I(c) (1964) and U.N. Doc. No. A/AC.105/C.2/L.8/Rev. 3, Art. I(c) (1965).

[100] U.N. Doc. No. A/AC.105/C.2/L.8/Rev. 1, Art. II.3 (1964); U.N. Doc. No. A/AC.105/C.2/L.8/Rev. 2, Art. II.3 (1964); U.N. Doc. No. A/AC.105/C.2/L.8/Rev. 3, Art. II.3 (1965).

[101] In U.N. Doc. No. A/AC.105/C.2/SR.52, at 13 (1965), the U.S. representative stated: "That concept [joint and several liability] varied somewhat even in different jurisdictions within the United States itself and procedures varied widely in the different common-law countries. . . . The intention was to specify that the presenting State should proceed for the total amount at one time and not make a series of separate actions for various amounts of damages against different States; once the amount had been established, the Presenting State might seek payment of any amount from any of the liable states within any time period."

[102] U.N. Doc. No. A/AC.105/C.2/L.10, Art. VII (1964); U.N. Doc. No. A/AC.105/C.2/L.10/Rev. 1, Art. VI (1965).

also make international organizations liable, but one Hungarian writer disagreed with his government's official position and suggested using the single characteristic of territory to define the liable state.[103] The Rumanian representative questioned the territorial approach because of the problem raised by international organizations which have no territory and because of the possibility of launches from territory not a part of any state.[104]

Some progress in the negotiations was made by the end of 1965, and the Legal Subcommittee[105] reported that where only one state was involved in launching, that state should be liable, and that the term "launching" included attempted launching. With reference to joint launching involving two or more states, items discussed included territory and facilities for launching a space object; control, possession and procurement of launching; participating in the launching; and registration (international or national) of a space object. The Treaty of Principles, Article VI, makes states and the international organization responsible for activities of the international organization. Joint and several responsibility is apparently intended although not detailed.

In those situations where only states are involved in a space activity, there is no legal problem in having a single respondent to answer the claim or claims arising from a given incident. Unless the participants have registered the activity and designated a state to which all claims should be presented, a claimant state should be permitted to present its claim to any participant state. Even if the participating states have designated one state to handle claims, it would seem that a claimant state should not be bound and should be permitted at its discretion to present its claim to a different state. However, reasonable arguments based on uniformity of procedure and economy can be made in favor of requiring a claimant state to honor a designation made by a group of states participating jointly in a space activity.[106]

The Vienna Convention on Civil Liability for Nuclear Damage[107] provides that the operator of the nuclear plant is always liable.[108] The nearest equivalent position for claims arising from activities in space would presumably be to assign liability to the state controlling the activity. But practical and technical factors may make it difficult, if not impossible, to identify the controlling state in the absence of that state volunteering information; and it is questionable if a long-dead satellite or a fragment can be said to be under anyone's control.

An alternative might be to assign liability to the state from whose territory or facility the launch was made. This appears to be the theory followed in the Treaty on Principles in Article VII, although Article VIII refers to retention of jurisdiction and control by a state "on whose registry" an object is launched.

The claimant should not have the burden of identifying

---

[103] Ference Madl, 3 *Jogtudomanyi Kozlony* (1963), quoted in Szadeczky-Kardoss, "Activities of the Space-Law Committee of the Hungarian Lawyers' Association," *Seventh Colloquium on the Law of Outer Space* 259 (International Institute of Space Law of the International Astronautical Federation, Warsaw, 1964). "Liability must lie with the state the territory of which was used for launching the spacecraft. This is international liability, and the state will appear as the sole depositary of the faculties offered by sovereignty of the territories under its rule. It is the sovereign right of the state to decide whether, in addition to its own agencies, it will grant or deny the right to other states, to international organizations outside its sovereignty, or to private persons subjected to its sovereignty, to launch spacecraft from its territory. Inasmuch as the state grants such rights it is its own business under what conditions it will do so."

[104] U.N. Doc. No. A/AC.105/C.2/SR.51, at 3 (1965).

[105] *Report of the Legal Subcommittee on the Work of its Fourth Session (20 Sept.–1 Oct. 1965) to the Committee on the Peaceful Uses of Outer Space,* U.N. Doc. No. A/AC.105/29, at 4 (1964).

[106] It can be argued that permitting a binding designation of a state to receive claims would provide greater uniformity of procedures, simplify the allocation of costs between states jointly liable, and would probably result in less cost of administration in disposing of claims. Since there will doubtless be liability without fault, at least for some time, there will not be a moral issue of right and wrong. The respondent states would be in a better position to prepare replies to claimants, and it can probably be assumed that the state with the largest participation in the activity would usually be assigned the task of responding. It could also be assumed that the state registering the joint space activity usually would have the largest participation. Smaller states might feel more free to participate in space activities since they would be assured that they would not be saddled with the burden of defending against a substantial claim.

[107] 2 *International Legal Materials* 727 (1963).

[108] The official comment is as follows: "In order to facilitate, for the victims, the filing and litigation of claims, and for the persons liable the purchase of financial coverage for their liability, the Convention [Vienna Convention on Liability for Nuclear Damage] channels liability for nuclear damage to one person with respect to each incident. This person is the operator of the nuclear installation concerned, who shall always be liable for incidents occurring in his installations." The 1952 Convention on Damages Caused by Foreign Aircraft to Third Parties on the Surface (III Air Laws and Treaties of the World 3221 [1965], Art. 2) also places the liability on the operator.

relationships which may be known only to the participants. Consequently, the definitions of participants who may be respondents must be wide, and a claimant should be allowed to present a claim to any identifiable participant. A claimant should be required to make only one presentation.

If a claimant is allowed to present its claim to any state participating in a space activity resulting in injury, any participant which may be called upon to contribute to compensation awarded should be allowed to participate in the defense, although there should be only one action.

Whether a claimant is bound to present a claim to a designated respondent, or whether it may select one of several joint participants, does not control arrangements which the participants in the activity may make among themselves for sharing the cost of reimbursing claimants.[109]

Extensive discussions in the United Nations reflect a variety of ideas, but no final decision, about how best to resolve the complex questions related to responding to a claim for damages.[110]

Most academic commentators in Western countries seem to prefer that apportionment of liability among participants in an activity in space be left to individual agreements;[111] whereas at least some of the Communist countries suggest that the general agreement on liability should give a right to demand contribution among participants in an activity,[112] but allow the claimant to go

---

[109] Jenks, *supra* note 64, at 228, describes how such arrangements in fact have already been carried out. "[T]he Interim Agreement of May 6, 1964 between Australia, the United Kingdom and the European Organization for the Development and Construction of Space Vehicle Launches concerning ELDO firings provides that ELDO is to indemnify the Commonwealth of Australia and the United Kingdom against any loss or damage suffered by the Commonwealth or the United Kingdom and against any liability of any kind in respect of claims against the Commonwealth or the United Kingdom, their respective servants or agents for loss, damage or injury that occurs in any place, whether within or outside Australia arising howsoever out of any activity carried out on behalf of the Organization in Australia."

[110] The French representative emphasized, "one claimant to one respondent," U.N. Doc. No. A/AC.105/C.2/SR.53, at 8 (1965); and suggested, "(1) if 'launching State' meant the State to which the claim for compensation would be presented, his delegation was in favor of the largest possible number of liable states," U.N. Doc. No. A/AC.105/C.2/SR.51, at 9 (1965). The Austrian representative suggested (pp. 7, 9–10): "[T]he applicant State might be allowed to decide to which of the participating States—all such States being liable—it would make its claim, and the latter States would be responsible for apportioning the liability among themselves. . . . This solution would enable the injured State to choose from among the States that were liable the one which would be best able to bear the material burden of liability." The Austrian also mentioned the possibility of making the state whose territory was used for the launching liable for all claims, subject to reimbursement in accordance with agreement among the participants. The Belgian representative suggested (pp. 8–10): "[T]he Belgian draft was designed, for practical reasons and also to ensure the payment

of compensation for damage, to leave a broad range of alternatives open to the applicant State. Wealthiness should not be the determining factor, but the fact was that when two or more States took part in a launching in different capacities it was difficult to fix liability. . . . [I]f States agreed on a launching operation they should be allowed to make their own arrangements concerning liability. What was needed was a solution which would facilitate action by the applicant State." The Italian representative suggested the possibility of making the registering state liable. U.N. Doc. No. A/AC.105/C.2/SR.51, at 4 (1964) and A/AC.105/C.2/L.8/Rev. 1 (1964). The Rumanian representative stated: "The definition of 'launching State' must, in fact, be given the widest possible scope." U.N. Doc. No. A/AC.105/C.2/SR.51, at 4 (1965). In U.N. Doc. No. A/AC.105/C.2/SR.48 (1965) at 12–13 the Hungarian representative is reported saying: "[T]he motion of joint and several responsibility must be referred to . . . and . . . it [must be] equitable for respondent as well as for claimant States. It would in effect, induce member countries of organizations which were potential respondents to agree beforehand on the sharing of liability." The United States representative stated that it was necessary to define the degree of participation on the basis of which a State would be considered liable as a launching State. He wondered whether, for instance, a state which had sent a technical observer to cover a launching or which had taken advantage of a launching in order to carry out experiments on insects, would bear equal liability. Too broad a definition might affect international cooperation in the exploration of outer space. The meaning of substantial participation should be defined; the Italian–United States San Marco operation was a good example. On the other hand, if State A had built a space vehicle and State B had purchased it, paid for it and launched it, there could be no basis for saying that State A was liable. U.N. Doc. No. A/AC.105/C.2/SR.51, at 9 (1965).

[111] See the comment of the British representative in the U.N. discussions: "[T]he questions of the apportionment of liability between respondent states did not concern presenting states, which the convention was intended to protect." U.N. Doc. No. A/AC.105/C.2/SR.53, at 4 (1965). See Goldie, *supra* note 1 at 1189, 1254: "[A] general convention on space liability should not deal with the apportionment of liability. This is a matter which is better left to individual agreement. For in these the degree of liability should be proportioned to the degree of control, participation, and financial contribution. Hence, it may best be stipulated in terms of the mutual relations of the parties to the enterprise and to each other."

[112] U.N. Doc. No. A/AC.105/C.2/SR.53, at 3 (1965). The Rumanian representative stated: "[I]t would be useful to add a further sub-paragraph defining relations between co-debtor

against any participant.[113] Another variation suggested would permit the respondent making payment to demand contributions in the absence of an agreement on the point among the participants.[114]

International Organizations as a Source of Compensation

The status of international organizations as claimants or respondents in international litigation has been touched on previously and is, of course, the subject of considerable literature. Terms of agreements establishing international organizations are controlling for the parties to the agreements; and the questions considered here include whether agreements relating to activities in space should accord international organizations such juridical status as to permit them to be parties to international claims without at the same time making the member states parties.

Prior to the space treaty signed January 27, 1967, discussions in the United Nations had explored, but not resolved, the problem; the report of the Legal Subcommittee[115] indicated only the agreement that international

organizations should be liable. It is not clear how the responsibility will be enforced because no reference is made about parties to litigation. The Soviets would probably use diplomatic representation to member states. In the U.N. negotiations for a treaty on liability several countries appeared to favor immediate joint and several liability of the organization and its member states,[116] and a Belgian revision[117] provided that "the states members of . . . [an] international organization shall be held jointly liable for the obligation of the latter. . . ." A United States draft[118] provided a delay of one year before a claimant state could commence action against a contracting state, a member of a defaulting international organization. The year's waiting period is probably longer than necessary, and the Russian delegate suggested that the American draft did not provide for liability of a state which was a member of the international organization in question but not a party to the convention.[119] However, the British representative argued that this was in accord with the sovereign acceptance of individual treaties by states.[120]

It seems doubtful that it would be appropriate under international law to attempt, by a convention such as is contemplated for liability arising from space activities, to bind a nonsignatory state to its terms by such indirect means. If the state were not a signatory, it would be a valid assumption that it was not interested in the convention or objected to its terms, and the objections would not be lessened by such indirection. Few states would ordinarily consider themselves bound by a treaty to which they were not a party. The Austrian representative ques-

---

States where the presenting state claimed compensation from only one of the various jointly and severally liable States. That State would be obliged to pay, and if the agreements it had concluded with the other States liable did not entitle it to claim against them, the convention should give it the right to claim reimbursement of the amount it had paid in excess of its share of the total amount of compensation."

[113] U.N. Doc. No. A/AC.105/C.2/SR.53, at 4 (1965). The Soviet representative stated: "[T]he presenting State must be able to demand full or partial compensation for the damage either from all the respondent States or from any one of them. If it did not receive compensation for the total amount of the damages, it should be able to claim the balance of the compensation from the other respondent states. The latter would remain debtors until the total amount of compensation had been paid."

[114] U.N. Doc. No. A/AC.105/C.2/SR.53, at 5 (1965). The Australian representative suggested: "Nevertheless, the Convention might, without going into detail, say that if one of the launching states liable to pay compensation for damage had paid the full amount of such compensation, it would have the right of recovery against its co-respondents, it being understood of course that such a provision would be subject to and overridden by any agreement that might have been concluded between the participants which would have priority." This point is not mentioned in the Treaty on Principles, *supra* note 24, although the silence on the subject may be interpreted to mean joint and several liability with contribution required between the responsible States.

[115] The Report of the Legal Subcommittee, *supra* note 105, at 4: "There was general agreement that international

organizations engaged in space activities should be liable under the convention for damages caused by such activities. An exchange of views took place in respect of the relationship of the liability of an international organization to that of its constituent members."

[116] A Hungarian draft provided: "If liability for damage rests with an international organization the financial obligations toward States suffering damage shall be met by the International organization and by its member States jointly and severally." U.N. Doc. No. A/AC.105/C.2/L.10/Rev. 1, Art. VII (1965). The Czechoslovakian delegate expressed approval of the Hungarian draft while the Rumanian representative justified the position at length. The Russian representative strongly supported the Hungarian position. U.N. Doc. No. A/AC.105/C.2/SR.51, at 13 (1965). U.N. Doc. No. A/AC.105/C.2/L.7/Rev. 2, at 8–9 (1965).

[117] U.N. Doc. No. A/AC.105/C.2/L.7/Rev. 2, Art. 6 (1964).

[118] U.N. Doc. No. A/AC.105/C.2/L.8/Rev. 3, Art. III, para. 3 (1965).

[119] U.N. Doc. No. A/AC.105/C.2/SR.52, at 809 (1965).

[120] U.N. Doc. No. A/AC.105/C.2/SR.54, at 5 (1965).

tioned if even under the United States draft the *inter alios acta* defense could be utilized by a signatory state.[121] This argument hardly seems valid since parties to the convention would bind themselves to compensate injured parties if the international organization of which they were a member did not.[122] The Treaty on Principles makes international organizations *"and"* its member states responsible, however. The intent is probably to make the liability joint and several, and by its terms the treaty is probably not intended to apply to nonsignatories.

The better arguments and precedents tend to favor making members of international organizations liable only if the organization defaults, although the terms of the Treaty on Principles may be a controlling precedent to the contrary.[123] Other workable regimes can be devised, and ultimately decisions about the juridical status of international organizations in general will have a part in the final solution—which may be a number of years in the future. There should be substantial inducement for member states to agree in advance about the distribution of liability and to make provisions to enable an international organization to discharge its responsibilities promptly. A claimant should find the claims procedure simple,[124] and in the ordinary course of affairs the individual member states should not have the burden of negotiating a claim as respondents where the action had

been by an international organization.[125] To provide otherwise could set precedents for other organizations, including the United Nations, and this has doubtless contributed to some of the discussions in the United Nations.[126]

Despite the detailed discussion of these problems during the extensive United Nations negotiations on liability, the Treaty on Principles signed January 27, 1967, contains only one very general article, Article VII, providing that states "that launch or procure the launching . . . and each State—from whose territory of facility an object is launched, is internationally liable for damage," and another, Article VI, on the broad responsibilities of states for all national activities in outer space, whether conducted by states, nongovernmental entities, or international organizations. Article VI must be read in conjunction with all other operative provisions of the treaty, including Article VII, and thus the liability for

---

[121] U.N. Doc. No. A/AC.105/C.2/SR.54, at 5 (1965): "[I]f the international organization refused to pay, a member State liable under Art. III, para. 3, of the United States text could argue that it was a third party and that the provision had been raised *inter alios acta.*"

[122] The Swedish and Italian representatives endorsed the proposal for making the members of international organizations liable only if the organization defaulted. U.N. Doc. A/AC.105/C.2/SR.52, at 5, 10 (1965).

[123] The pertinent language from Art. VI reads: "[R]esponsibility for compliance with this Treaty shall be borne both by the international organization and by the States Parties to the Treaty participating in such organization." Use of the article "the" before "Treaty" is slightly ambiguous, particularly in view of the use of "this" in the preamble and in Arts. XIII, XIV, and XVII.

[124] "There would . . . be great procedural economy if the international organization itself was regarded as the launching State, since it would clearly be in the best position to deal with the claims. If the international organization did not give satisfaction as first debtor, there would of course be a residual right against individual states." Statement of the British representative, U.N. Doc. No. A/AC.105/C.2/SR.52, at 12 (1965).

[125] The Argentine representative commented, U.N. Doc. No. A/AC.105/C.2/SR.51, at 12 (1965): "When the United Nations, one of its specialized agencies or a similar organization generally recognized as having international status was involved, the liability of the organization took precedence over that of its members. In other words, the latter were required to answer for the activities of the organization only if it did not do so itself. If, on the other hand, a more limited organization which did not have the same international status was involved, the organization and its members were simultaneously liable. There were already a number of organizations of that type, which had been established for the specific purpose of promoting cooperation in space activities. Since they had no international legal status, they were bound only by their statutes and their declarations were authoritative only *inter partes* and not *ergo omnes;* some of them, such as COMSAT, had not yet set up any machinery to ensure compensation for those affected by any damage which they might cause on land." It might be noted that contracts let by ComSat on behalf of Intelsat are reported to contain since mid-1965 provisions specifying that as between the parties, only the maker of the contract (ComSat) is liable. It is doubtful that such a provision would be binding on a party not privy to the contract or agreement.

[126] U.N. Doc. No. A/AC.105/C.2/SR.48, at 19 (1965) and A/AC.105/C.2/SR.52, at 8 (1965). The Austrian representative suggested: "As the [Hungarian] text stood, it would seem to mean that a country claiming damages against the United Nations—say, Belgium in connection with the Congo operation—could present a claim against any individual member of the United Nations—say Hungary . . . Austria did not assume responsibility as an individual State for the activities of the International Atomic Energy Agency, of which it was a member and the host country; that was stated in the headquarters agreement. Similarly Switzerland had denied responsibility for the activities of the League of Nations during the Second World War."

damages, which are not defined, is quite broad. Neither Article VI nor Article VII establishes any machinery for the resolution of claims disputes; this would be left to customary claims procedures under international law, including the International Court of Justice, existing or ad hoc arbitration arrangements, and diplomatic negotiations.

Sources of Compensation Other than from a Party Engaged in Space Activities

Numerous suggestions have been made for providing compensation for damages from sources other than the identifiable participants in the space activity causing the damage. An international insurance or guarantee fund has been mentioned frequently.[127] Justification for establishing a fund is difficult in situations where there is an appropriate identifiable source from which to collect compensation. Questions of unwillingness, justified or not, to pay compensation will not be resolved by asking for payments before rather than after damage takes place,[128] although some authors have combined optimis-

tic idealism with realism in a somewhat illogical manner on this subject.[129] Moral and international legal justifications for creating such a fund are no more compelling here than in any other area of liability, and the expense and effort of maintaining such a fund should be taken into consideration.[130] Suggestions have also been made:

"[E]ach State should create a guaranty fund or otherwise obligate itself to compensate its nationals suffering damage from space vehicles up to a fixed minimum amount for each incident. Perhaps the Rome Convention limits should, for uniformity, be applied. In addition all States which are parties to the convention should agree to be subject to the compulsory jurisdiction of the International Court of Justice so that the State of the national suffering damage on the surface or in the airspace could proceed against the launching State or States, jointly or severally to recover: a) by recoupment the amount already paid by the complaining State to its nationals; b) such additional amount for the benefit of its nationals suffering damage as may be required for full compensation to cover the damage suffered; and c) such damage as the complaining State itself may have suffered. It is difficult now to fix any maximum amount to which the liability of the launching State or States ought to be limited. . . ."[131]

---

[127] See de Rode-Verschoor, "The Responsibility of the States for the Damage Caused by the Launched Space Bodies," *Legal Problems of Space Exploration: A Symposium,* Sen. Doc. No. 26, 87th Cong., 1st Sess., at 460 (1961): "One may consider the solution of an international guaranty fund for paying the damages caused by satellites. . . . Each state interested in astronautics will deposit a sum of money in this Fund. . . . Such a Fund could exist under control of the United Nations, a body that most experts have pointed out already as most competent to control the traffic in outer space." See also Valladoso, writing in the Brazilian periodical *Revista Forense* (Apr.–June 1961), who says that any damages caused by spacecraft should be borne ratably by all nations because space activity is for the good of all humanity. The Arab delegate to the Vienna Convention on Nuclear Damages advocated establishment of an international guarantee fund. The Soviet writer Osnitskaya, in *The Conquest of Space and International Law* 68 (1962), supports the idea of an international fund for accidents beyond the ability of an individual state to provide compensation. Hyman's resolution, "Magna Carta of Space," *supra* note 46, provides that "An international insurance fund shall be established through some appropriate international association such as the United Nations for the payment of compensation for . . . damage."

[128] In air law, payment of claims can be compelled by refusing permission to overfly territory until a bond is posted. See Art. 15, para. 1, of the Rome Convention on Damage Caused by Foreign Aircraft to Third Parties on the Surface, 1952, Senate Committee on Commerce, 89th Cong., 1st Sess., 3 *Air Laws and Treaties of the World* 3221 (1965). A similar method of enforcement for activities in space is not available.

[129] See Rauchhaupt, "The Damages in Space Law," *Fifth Colloquium on the Law of Outer Space* 5 (1962): "The usefulness of an international fund for the world space damages was also mentioned in discussions. But some states, as for instance Russia, are known for their neglect to pay their contributions to the United Nations: Therefore, it is to be feared that a new international fund might get into money difficulties soon and even get bankrupt, if the bad example should be copied by an increasing number of States. Nevertheless, it seems to be advisable that a special international authority should receive all necessary guarantees and money for the potential cases of world space damages and still better have them in their possession before the permission of the covered world space flight be granted."

[130] See Wimmer, "Suggestions for an International Convention on Damages Caused by Spacecraft," *Fifth Colloquium on the Law of Outer Space* 6 (1962). After reference to de Rode Verschoor's argument for an international fund Wimmer says, "An obligation to pay a contribution to the Guaranty Fund could be imposed on those States only which themselves operate or have licensed spacecraft. Simultaneously an obligation to pay additional contributions would have to be provided for in case the Guaranty Fund would be exhausted by payment of compensation. Those states, however, the spacecraft of which did not cause any damage will scarcely be prepared to pay any additional contribution to the Guaranty Fund."

[131] John Cobb Cooper, "Memorandum of Suggestions for an International Convention on Third Party Damage Caused by Space Vehicles," *Third Colloquium on the Law of Outer Space* 144 (Stockholm, 1961).

Where damage results from an unidentified activity in space, an international fund would be the only non-national source of compensation: Cooper observed that the plan he put forward at Stockholm in 1960 could easily be modified to provide for national compensation for damage from unidentified sources.[132]

If contingency funds are to be established, there is equal or greater justification for including damages from all unidentified sources and natural phenomena such as floods, earthquakes, etc. In the United States, at least, damage from any cause beyond the local capacity to handle is of immediate concern to state and national authorities and to voluntary organizatons such as the Red Cross. Establishment of special funds for damage from space activities away from the vicinity of the launching site might tend to exaggerate the risks involved and give rise to unwarranted fears. Although the possibility of a catastrophic accident across national boundaries cannot be arbitrarily dismissed, experience thus far—the Apollo accident and the Soviet loss to the contrary—indicates the probabilities of such an incident are very low.[133]

Consequently, it can be questioned whether the difficulty, cost, and complexity of establishing and administering such special insurance funds are justified at the present time. As it is, the Treaty on Principles has not adopted any fund as a source of payment but places the obligation directly on states, and through Article VI, on international organizations.

Some of the occurrences resulting from activities in space that may give rise to international claims have now been surveyed and related to the identification of claim-ants and respondents. Although the injured party may be a natural person and the party causing the injury may be only a quasi-governmental entity, states probably will ordinarily be the parties to litigation or negotiations. This traditional rule is implicit in the Treaty on Principles but could be modified by subsequent agreement. States will, for the time being, be the source of payment of compensation, although possibly the negotiators will devise a formula under which international organizations will be made initially responsible for payments for injuries which their activities have caused.

As has been shown, the probabilities are that there will be few international claims resulting from activities in space. Nevertheless, international accommodations in this area have a tendency to remove or at least to minimize a source of potential conflict.

Forum and Procedures for Presenting Claims

The dramatic nature of activities in space and the use of space activities for propaganda have led many to believe in the need for special procedures and tribunals to handle claims arising from activities in space, although there have been no claims to adjudicate thus far. Article III of the Treaty on Principles contains only the general mandate that space activities are to be carried on "in accordance with international law, including the Charter of the United Nations. . . ." Customary diplomatic negotiations between governments and arbitration pursuant to existing or ad hoc agreements are always available, and the International Court is open to those nations accepting its jurisdiction.[134]

The Forum

The selection of a forum, not referred to in the Treaty on Principles, for consideration of claims arising from activities in space presents no legal problems markedly different from general international claims law, and usually damage will have occurred in the territory of the state presenting the claim. Several writers have suggested

---

[132] Letter of Nov. 16, 1965, to the authors.

[133] Studies on the probabilities of major or catastrophic damage from space activities have not for the most part distinguished sharply between domestic and international liability, although they have noted the lessening danger as distance from the launching site increases. Thus, Rosenthal *et al., supra* note 2, at 119, say: "At the present time, the danger of exceedingly large accidents abroad is less than at home. The damage which could be done by the crash of an errant space vehicle might depend on the amount of chemical fuel still unconsumed at the time of the crash; the greater the distance from the launch site, the smaller would be the damage." See also Hassialis *et al., supra* note 6, at 19 ff. After discussing possible accidents, the authors note, at 33: "At this point, it is appropriate to emphasize once again that the events referred to [space accidents other than at the launching site] are possibilities, not likely events." Murchie, *supra* note 10, at chap. 5 (1961) minimizes the probability of injury from falling meteorites and artificial satellites.

[134] See Schrader, *supra* note 2, at 139, 153–54, for an analysis of some of the obstacles to the use of the International Court of Justice: limited jurisdiction, the Connelly Amendment, failure of the USSR and other Communist nations to accept the court, etc. As is true with agreements relating to liability for activities in the air, those relating to liability for claims resulting from activities in space will require periodic modifications to take into consideration changing political, economic, and technological conditions.

that nations should agree to submit all claims arising from space activities to an established tribunal, with the International Court of Justice being most frequently mentioned.[135] Justification for a single forum has been based on the supposed expertise which would develop and the uniformity of decisions which might be expected. But it is doubtful that nations, including the United States and the Soviet Union, which have steadfastly refused to accept mandatory jurisdiction of the World Court generally will make an exception for liability cases arising out of activities in space.[136] And as previously indicated, the number of cases to be adjudicated is likely to be so small that the cost of a permanent establishment specifically for space claims cannot be justified, nor can the development of great expertise be expected.[137]

Discussions in the United Nations indicated a willingness to allow the parties to a damage claim to adopt any peaceful procedure they find suitable for resolving the dispute, without recourse to formal international arbitration or litigation.[138] Since states will usually be the parties

in claims proceedings, it would be inconsistent with normal concepts of state sovereignty to give jurisdiction to national courts, which was done in the nuclear liability and third-party aircraft-liability conventions. There it was anticipated that respondents would be other than states or if states, they would be operating through a proprietary corporation or similar instrumentality.

The Communist nations and some others have not favored arrangements that would result in compulsory jurisdiction and conclusive judgment,[139] whereas most of the Western nations have proposed procedures which would.[140] In essence, the Communists favor continuation of argument with no possibility of a conclusive answer unless by unanimous consent even in an arbitral commission, their standard approach to all arbitration. An arbitral tribunal should be judicially independent, but unfortunately all too many arbitrators consider themselves partisans whose responsibility is to support a principal's position. The result frequently is that the only impartial member of a three-man tribunal will be the chairman appointed by an outside authority or selected by the two partisan members. It is doubtful that the Com-

---

[135] See Cooper, *supra* note 131, at 682: "[A]ll states which are parties to the convention should agree to be subject to the compulsory jurisdiction of the International Court of Justice so that the state of the national suffering damage on the surface or in the air space can proceed against the launching state or states, jointly or severally . . . ." See also Meyer, "Legal Problems of Outer Space," 28 *J. Air L. & Commerce* 339, 345 (1961): "[E]xclusively before the International Court of Justice." See Poulantzas, "The Chambers of the International Court of Justice and their Role in the Settlement of Disputes Arising Out of Space Activities," *Seventh Colloquium on the Law of Outer Space* 186 (1962); and "Legal Liability in Space," 104 *Solicitors Journal* 904 (1960).

[136] See Schrader, *supra* note 2, at 139, 153–54. "The first obstacle to the International Court of Justice's being the ideal forum for the injured plaintiff is the limited jurisdictional aspect of the court. In addition the Court may consider those cases in which jurisdiction is conferred on the Court by treaty outside the United Nations Charter . . . . [T]he United States has enacted the much discussed Connally Reservation, which, in effect, states that the *optional clause* [of the Statute of the International Court of Justice, Art. 36.2 (a), (c), (d)] does not apply to disputes with regard to matters which are essentially within the domestic jurisdiction of the United States of America as determined by the United States of America. [I]t is obvious that if neither the United States nor the Communist World accept compulsory jurisdiction, this eliminates the World Court as a present or future forum for the settling of international disputes arising from space exploration." Even without the Connally reservations, there are other methods of avoiding the jurisdiction of the court.

[137] See *supra* chap. 5 for a discussion of the arbitral arrangements established for the participants in Intelsat.

[138] Drafts of a proposed treaty submitted for U.N.

consideration assumed negotiations between the states concerned but provided for those situations where the parties are unable to resolve their differences. U.N. Doc. No. A/AC.105/C.2/L.7/Rev. 2 (1964); U. N. Doc. No. A/AC.105/C.2/L.8/Rev. 3 (1965); U.N. Doc. No. A/AC.105/C.2/SR.48, at 11 (1965) and U.N. Doc. No. A/AC.105/C.2/L.10/Rev. 1 (1964).
The Treaty on Principles, *supra* note 24, at Art. VII, appears to contemplate only states could be parties to claims proceedings arising from activities in space.

[139] U.N. Doc. No. A/AC.105/C.2/L.10/Rev. 1 (1964); U.N. Doc. No. A/AC.105/C.2/SR.13 (1962) at 5; U.N. Doc. No. A/AC.105/SR.29–37, at 88–89 (1965); U.N. Doc. No. A/AC.105/C.2/SR.48, at 11 (1965).

[140] U.N. Doc. No. A/AC.105/C.2/L.7/Rev.2, Art. 4 (1964). The Belgian draft reads: "[T]he State receiving the claim shall appoint one arbitrator, the applicant state shall appoint a second and the President of the International Court of Justice a third. If the State receiving the claim fails to appoint its arbitrator within a prescribed period, the person appointed by the President of the International Court of Justice shall be the sole arbitrator. The Arbitration Commission shall take its decisions according to law by majority vote . . . its decisions shall be binding." The United States drafts were similar in substance. U.N. Doc. No. A/AC.105/C.2/L.8/Rev. 3, Art. VII (1965); U.S. drafts in U.N. Doc. No. A/AC.105/C.2/L.4, Art. 3(e) (1964); U.N. Doc. No. A/AC.105/C.2/L.8/Rev. 3, Arts. IX and X (1965); Swedish position in U.N. Doc. No. A/AC.105/C.2/SR.11, at 2 (1962); Japanese position in U.N. Doc. No. A/AC.105/C.2/SR.13, at 9 (1962).

munist nations will abandon their historic opposition to international tribunals having mandatory jurisdiction to issue binding decisions. Also, even if most nations were willing to give the World Court or some other international tribunal compulsory jurisdiction to issue final judgments, the Connally reservation might present problems for the United States.[141] Procedural provisions, such as the right to refer a "dispute" to the Court of International Justice included in an early United States draft, in addition to raising jurisdictional questions, are subject to abuse as a delaying tactic.[142]

Situs of Proceedings

The geographic location of proceedings to resolve claims arising out of activities in space has received comparatively little attention, although it may have some political and economic as well as legal implications for claimant and respondent.[143] If provisions for ad hoc arbitral tribunals or panels drawn from membership of the World Court are established, there might be little justification for having all adjudications heard in one location. Selection of the location for the proceedings might be left to the parties to each controversy, which is the situation under the Treaty on Principles.

Injured parties, witnesses, and evidence will for the most part be located in the immediate vicinity of the incident causing the damages. Thus, there are practical advantages in holding the proceedings in the territory of the claimant state, but it can be argued that they should be held on neutral territory. If the theory of absolute liability is accepted, questions of negligence, for which the evidence would probably be in the territory of the respondent, will not require adjudication. Absolute liability has generally been favored by all nations, subject to some minor exceptions, and is the rule included in the Treaty on Principles.

If the proceedings are held in the territory of the claimant state, it would be comparatively simple under municipal law to provide a method for the compulsory attendance of most of the necessary witnesses. Compulsory attendance across international borders can be accom-

plished, but it is considerably more troublesome. Since the award of compensation will be based primarily on the presentation of the claimant state, it should not be necessary to require that state to make information available, as it must do if it wishes to recover. Having made a claim and presented some evidence, the claimant state should then be required to submit all pertinent evidence. There is little basis for requiring that claimants go to the territory of respondents who may not be fully identified except during the course of the adjudication.[144] The claimant, however, might be given the option of having the proceedings held in the territory of a known respondent, or at some other location agreed upon at the time, which is the procedure in the absence of a treaty.

The Proper Law

Vexing conflict of law problems will be presented unless there is an advance agreement identifying the law to be applied in resolving claims.[145] The Treaty on Princi-

---

[141] It is conceivable that treaties relating to space activities might be used as a vehicle for general review and modification of United States policy relative to the jurisdiction of international tribunals.

[142] See comment of U.S. representative, U.N. Doc. No. A/AC.105/C.2/SR.55, at 6–7 (1965).

[143] The subject is not mentioned in the Treaty on Principles, *supra* note 24.

[144] The Vienna Convention on Liability for Nuclear Damage (2 *International Legal Materials* 727 [1963]); International Atomic Energy Agency Document CN-12/46 (May 20, 1963) at Art. XI provides: "[J]urisdiction over actions for nuclear damage shall lie only with the courts of the Contracting Party within whose territory the nuclear incident occurred." The 1933 Convention for the Unification of Certain Rules Relating to Damages Caused by Aircraft to Third Parties on the Surface (Rome, Oct. 1952) (3 *Air Laws and Treaties of the World* 3147 [1965]) at Art. 16 gives jurisdiction to "the judicial authorities of the defendant's domicile and those of the place where the damage was caused, without prejudice to the injured third party's right of direct action against the insurer in a case in which it can be exercised." The Convention on Damage Caused by Foreign Aircraft to Third Parties on the Surface, signed at Rome on Oct. 7, 1952 (3 *Air Laws and Treaties of the World* 3221 [1965]) provides in Art. 20 that "Actions under the provisions of this Convention may be brought only before the courts of the Contracting State where the damage occurred. Nevertheless, by agreement between any one or more claimants and any one or more defendants, such claimants may take action before the courts of any other Contracting State, but no such proceedings shall have the effect to prejudicing in any way the rights of persons who bring actions in the State where the damage occurred. The parties may also agree to submit disputes to arbitration in any Contracting State." Identity of the respondents under these treaties will usually be known in advance, and the presence of the instrumentality causing the damage will usually be pursuant to specific agreement.

[145] See Cooper, *supra* note 131, at 680: "After thirty-five years of somewhat varied experience with flight law problems, I am convinced that practical uniformity in the field of liability can be accomplished in no other way than by

ples gives no guidance. Jurisdiction questions will probably be resolved on the basis of a general convention on space liability of the type under negotiation in the United Nations in 1965–69 or on the basis of some other agreement, general or ad hoc, entered into before a claim is submitted to a tribunal. Theories of liability without fault will, at least for the present, be applied, thus eliminating the extremely difficult, if not impossible, task of determining questions of negligence and due care. The question of causation will remain. When liability has been established, the amount of compensation to be paid will have to be determined. There is, however, a risk that any detailed rules presently formulated and based on existing technological information may become outmoded at any time or may encounter strong opposition by one or more countries.[146]

Consistent with the concept that law relating to activities in space is a part of international law and that codification should be approached slowly, the United States has supported the view that the measure of liability should be determined in accordance with applicable principles of international law, justice, and equity.[147] Use

of international law for general guidance was both supported[148] and objected to by other states.[149] Suggestions have been made that the law of the claimant state should be utilized,[150] but adoption of such a rule would not con-

---

international legislation. Waiting for eventual uniformity through the development of customary rules is impractical and much too slow in so dynamic a field of human action as flight."

[146] Schrader, *supra* note 2, at 139, 156: "[F]rom a practical aspect, the space age is not ready to accept international conventions as a solution to the problem of liability . . . . [A]ny international convention on the subject of liability would be enforceable only if the Soviet Union and the United States were in agreement and accepted the terms and responsibilities imposed thereby . . . . Both nations could promulgate domestic legislation without compromising their national sovereignty thereby allowing adequate recovery." McCollum, "Tort Aspects of Space Technology," 8 *Clev.-Mar. L. Rev.* 292, 304 (1959): "The exigencies of the matter make it necessary that agreement be reached *pro re nata*." Secretary of State Rusk in Hearings before the Senate Foreign Relations Committee on the Communications Satellite Act of 1962, at 177 (Aug. 6, 1962), stated: "I had always believed the genius of the common law was that it proceeded from case to case, refining its rules and norms out of the ore of experience and practice, solving problems pragmatically as they arise, rather than seeking to provide all the answers in advance through some sort of generalized code. We believe the law of space communications will grow in this organic way rather than by a process of abstract speculation. Where early international agreement— one might almost say 'legislation'—is needed to move ahead, as in the case of frequency allocation, we will be prepared to take our place at the conference table."

[147] U.N. Doc. No. A/AC.105/C.2/L.8/Rev. 3 (1965), U.S. draft, Art. II, para. 4. The American representative

indicated this "was designed to insure uniformity in the determination of damages by reference to international law" and where necessary to "equity and justice" (U.N. Doc. No. A/AC.105/C.2/SR.48, at 4–5 [1965]), and subsequently added that these were "the sort of claims which arbitral tribunals had been settling for years without any great difficulty on the basis of international law" (U.N. Doc. No. A/AC.105/C.2/SR.54, at 11 [1965]).

[148] "[T]he case for applying an international standard and avoiding the differences in particular national laws seemed very strong," U.K. representative, U.N. Doc. No. A/AC.105/C.2/SR.54, at 7, 14 (1965). ". . . seemed preferable," Canadian representative, U.N. Doc. No. A/AC.105/C.2/SR.54, at 8 (1965). "[O]nly the approach taken in the United States proposal was acceptable," Austrian representative, U.N. Doc. No. A/AC.105/C.2/SR.54, at 10 (1965). "The problems of collective responsibility seemed to point conclusively, as did many other arguments, to the use of international law as the law applicable under the Convention," Australian representative, U.N. Doc. A/AC.105/C.2/SR.54, at 10 (1965).

[149] "[N]ot satisfactory since international law did not give any precise rules for such calculation," Mexican representative, U.N. Doc. No. A/AC.105/C.2/SR.48, at 8 (1965). "[V]ague and possibly controversial notions of justice and equity . . . as was evidenced by the fact . . . that moral damage was provided for under some systems and not under others," Belgian representative, U.N. Doc. No. A/AC.105/C.2/SR.54, at 7–8 (1965). Even the Canadian representative questioned "whether the principles of international law on the subject were sufficiently developed for such a clause to require no further elaboration," and suggested the possible substitution of "ex aequo et bono" for "equity and justice," U.N. Doc. No. A/AC.105/C.2/SR.54, at 8 (1965). The Soviet, Rumanian, and Hungarian representatives considered that "equity and justice" and "principles of international law on such matters, if they existed, could hardly be considered precise enough to be made the point of reference . . . . To invoke international law was simply to defer the whole question." U.N. Doc. No. A/AC.105/C.2/SR.54, at 9, 11, 13 (1965).

[150] Belgian drafts, Arts. Ib, III, IV and Rev. 2, U.N. Doc. No. A/AC.105/C.2/L.7 (1964). The Rumanian, Swedish, Belgian, and French representatives variously supported applying the claimants law with the French representatives suggesting "[I]nterstate claims probably offered the best guide to the solution of the problem. When one State suffered damage as a result of the activities of another State, it submitted a claim in which the damage was assessed according to its own laws . . . [with] no fixed international compensation for particular damage or injury . . . . Only domestic law could settle such issues . . . . If a member of a Claims Commission was told not to apply the laws of the claimant state, he could only fall back on the laws of his own state . . . ." U.N. Doc. No. A/AC.105/C.2/SR.54, at 7, 9–12 (1965). Jenks, *supra* note

tribute to uniformity of results.[151] The possibility of utilizing the law of the respondent state has been mentioned,[152] but objections have been encountered.[153]

Comparatively little attention has been given to the possibility of setting forth in a convention the detailed rules of law. In few, if any, areas of the international law of claims has a detailed code been adopted, although the Conventions on Damage Caused by Foreign Aircraft to Third Parties on the Surface[154] gives jurisdiction to the courts of the country where the damage occurred,[155] limits the amount of liability,[156] establishes periods of limitation, and provides some additional guidelines.[157] The Vienna Convention on Civil Liability of Nuclear

Damage also limits liability and periods of limitation[158] while providing that, subject to the provisions of the convention, "the nature, form and extent of the compensation, as well as the equitable distribution thereof, shall be governed by the law of the competent court," which is generally "the courts of the Contracting Party within whose territory the nuclear incident occurred."[159] The Harvard Draft Convention on International Responsibility of States for Injuries to Aliens provides that "responsibility is to be determined according to this Convention; and international law," makes reference to the Statute of the International Court of Justice, and stipulates that "a State cannot avoid international responsibility by invoking its municipal law."[160] Treaties give the parties to a controversy an option of choosing the law to be applied, and it is not unusual to utilize both international and municipal law.[161] Most countries, including the United States,[162] recognize and accept international law as a part of the law to be enforced by their national courts, and so far as the international relations of the state are concerned, international law is superior.[163]

Analogies have been suggested for guidance, with air law most frequently mentioned,[164] but the laws of the

---

64, at 290: "[A]ny . . . tort committed in space but taking effect on Earth, on the surface or in territorial airspace, would appear to be governed, subject to the general rules of international law and of any applicable international agreements, by the law of the jurisdiction within which it takes effect."

[151] "Even though it might not be conducive to uniformity," Swedish representative, U.N. Doc. No. A/AC.105/C.2/SR.54, at 10 (1965). "It would be easier, furthermore, to obtain some uniformity among national provisions than to work out international rules," Romanian representative, U.N. Doc. No. A/AC.105/C.2/SR.54, at 11 (1965). "[T]he assessment of damages might then vary considerably according to the country where the damages occurred, and the possibility of special legislation being enacted by countries on the matter could not be discounted. The position would thus be uncertain, and States might be deterred from acceding to the Convention," Canadian representative, U.N. Doc. No. A/AC.105/C.2/SR.54, at 8 (1965). "[M]any practical and legal difficulties might arise if compensation was determined simply on the basis of the state whose nationals suffered the damage . . . practice varied from state to state," Soviet representative, U.N. Doc. No. A/AC.105/C.2/SR.54, at 9 (1965). "[T]he greatest diversity of solutions in the settlement of claims . . . ," Austrian representative, U.N. Doc. No. A/AC.105/C.2/SR.54, at 10 (1965). "[D]id not see how the collective liability of several States could be worked out on the basis of an amount arrived at in accordance with the municipal laws of any one of the States concerned," Australian representative, U.N. Doc. No. A/AC.105/C.2/SR.54, at 10 (1954).

[152] Hungarian draft U.N. Doc. No. A/AC.105/C.2/L.10, Art. 2 and Rev. 1, Art. 2 (1965) supported by Czechoslovakia and Russia, U.N. Doc. No. A/AC.105/C.2/SR.54, at 9 (1965).

[153] "[T]he anomalous situation of a State determining by its own national law the extent of its international obligations." U.K. and Austrian representatives, U.N. Doc. No. A/AC.105/C.2/SR.54, at 7, 9 (1965).

[154] 3 *Air Laws and Treaties of the World* 3147, 3221 (1965).

[155] Art. 20.

[156] Art. 11.

[157] Arts. 10–21.

[158] 2 *International Legal Materials* 727, Arts. IV, V, VI (1963).

[159] Arts. VIII, XI.

[160] Louis B. Sohn & R. R. Baxter, *The Harvard Draft Convention on International Responsibility of States for Injuries to Aliens,* Art. 78 (1961). See also Art. 2.

[161] The Convention on the Settlement of Investment Disputes between States and Nationals of other States, signed Mar. 18, 1965 (4 *International Legal Materials* 532, Art. 42 [1965]) provides: "(1) The Tribunal shall decide a dispute in accordance with such rules of law as may be agreed by the parties or in the absence of such agreement, the Tribunal shall apply the law of the Contracting State party to the dispute (including its rules on the conflict of laws) and such rules of international law as may be applicable. (2) The Tribunal may not bring in a finding of non liquet on the ground of silence or obscurity of the law. (3) The provisions of paragraphs (1) and (2) shall not prejudice the power of the Tribunal to decide a dispute ex aequo et bono if the parties so agree."

[162] The United States Constitution, Art. I, sec. 8, expressly recognizes the existence of international law: "The Congress shall have Power . . . To define and punish Piracies and Felonies committed on the high Seas, and offenses against the Law of Nations."

[163] 1 Hackworth, *Digest of International Law* 24 (1940).

[164] See, e.g., Berger, *supra* note 2, at 301, 303–4: "A Case involving damage caused by crashing aircraft seems to offer a situation similar to that of a wayward space vehicle and an analysis of the law applicable to this type of situation would be

sea, of nuclear damage[165] and of enterprise liability[166] have also been suggested.

To avoid disputes at the time of an actual incident, a treaty adopted should permit the parties to agree on the application of any regime of law they choose, whether it is the law of one of the parties or "international law" or a specially devised regime. The treaty, however, should identify the proper law to be applied if the parties do not agree on another within a limited time.

For those areas for which it is not feasible to provide rules in a treaty, it is suggested that the claimant state be allowed to utilize the claims laws of both the claimant and respondent states to supplement international law. Where there are conflicts in the laws of claimant and respondent, the claimant should be allowed to utilize the law most favorable to him. Interpretation of the law of

the respondent state should probably be by that state, and for the sake of uniformity where federal and local law exist, as in the United States, only the federal tort law should be considered.[167] A respondent can hardly complain if his own law is used, and he will be protected against any unjust law of a claimant by the requirement that only the general claims law and not special law be used and also by the limitations and rules set forth in a treaty to which both parties have agreed. Although some claims have been resolved by application of "general principles of international law," there does not exist, as previously noted, a body of international law with precise rules which give adequate guides by which to determine causation and measure of damages. National law is almost invariably relied upon heavily in the preparation of claims for international presentation.

If utilization of the laws of the claimant and respondent is politically unacceptable, international law should be utilized. This would provide flexibility for technological development and would contribute, to the extent that there are cases, to the development of international law adapted to the requirements of activities in space.[168] If Article III of the Treaty on Principles is interpreted as applying international law to damage claims, however, it should be recognized that arbiters will utilize their own national law to a considerable extent in determining what they think international law is or should be. It would have been helpful had the Treaty on Principles indicated whether or not there should be compensation for items such as interest from the time of the incident, consequen-

---

of some aid from the standpoint of possible precedent." See also Tager, "Liability for Space Activities" 25 (mimeo., McGill Univ., 1963): "[O]perationally and in consideration of the legal effects that flow from these operations, airspace and space are one, perhaps designable as 'aerospace,' and as one, are amenable to an existing regime of international law—air law." But see U.N. General Assembly Res. 1348 (XIII) 1958, para. 1(d): "[N]o international standard regarding safety and precautionary measures governing the launching and control of space vehicles has yet been formulated, and the fact could also be taken into account in studying analogies based on existing conventions." McCollum, *supra* note 146, at 292, 298: "If aviation is so different from land movement that a new body of law was deemed necessary, then certainly satellite movement is so different from that of aircraft that new law is necessary for this type of activity." Osnitskaya, *The Conquest of Space and International Law* 69 (State Publishing House of Legal Literature, Moscow, 1962): "While the principle of state responsibility for injury and damage can be applied, we cannot mechanically apply the concept of responsibility from air law. The cases in which responsibility will be recognized and what the scope of such responsibility will be, all need further study."

[165] See Jessup & Taubenfeld, *supra* note 3, at 242: "In the case of space vehicles used for peaceful purposes it is not to be anticipated that the damage from an accident would have the catastrophic proportions of one involving an atomic power plant, except perhaps when space vehicles are propelled by atomic power."

[166] See Goldie, "Some Problems of Liability Arising Out of Space Activities," *Sixth Colloquium on the Law of Outer Space* 17 (Paris, 1963): "The development of international law analogies to enterprise liability of operators of nuclear facilities, would assure to individuals due compensation for injuries and loss from falling 'space garbage' burnt up in the atmosphere thus creating a climate of confidence." The Treaty on Principles (*supra* note 24, at Art. III) states only that activities in space are to be carried on in accordance with international law, including the charter of the U.N.

[167] Erie R.R. v. Tompkins, 304 U.S. 64, 58 Sup. Ct. 817 (1938) would make it necessary to utilize the law of the District of Columbia to avoid variations in accordance with the laws of different states.

[168] See Goldie, *supra* note 1, at 1189: "Just as nuclear and space disasters provide examples of transnational laws. These transnational laws in their turn call for a greater degree of precision, a more rigorous standard of liability and a greater range of possible alternative rules than has been traditionally provided by public international law. . . . While the one [international law] is sufficiently wide in its geographical scope to cover the extent of such a disaster, it is too impoverished in concepts, power and reach against individuals, and the other [municipal law] is too parochial both in policy and jurisdiction." See 1 Lauterpacht, *Oppenheim's International Law* 533, note 1 (8th ed., 1955). "Measure of Damages and Interest. Great diversity of practice at present prevails amongst international tribunals upon these matters, and any general rules which might be laid down at present would need to be qualified by many exceptions." For a comprehensive discussion of all aspects of damages see Whiteman, *Damages in International Law*, 3 vols. (1937–43).

tial damages, costs of prosecuting the claim, pain and suffering, invasion of privacy, and simple trespass without injury. These problems can be treated in ad hoc arrangements if and when claims arise, but it would be well to have agreement in advance.

Methods of Presentment

Methods of presentment of claims need not and should not differ appreciably from methods used in other international claims. Significant questions involve (1) time limitations, (2) channels for presenting claims, (3) availability of remedies other than those provided by treaties, with requirements for efforts at settlement by negotiation prior to recourse to treaty machinery, and (4) necessity for joinder of actions.

Time of Presentment

The objective should be prompt resolution of disputes without imposing penalties for delays outside the ability of the parties to prevent. Reasonable time must be given in which to ascertain facts and prepare necessary documents. A year[169] or two years[170] has been suggested as the time within which to commence action after damage is or should be known,[171] but this has been criticized as being too short, particularly if it includes damage from nuclear radiation.[172] Difficulty in identifying the re-

sponsible party must also be taken into consideration.[173] It is apparent that time limitations should be fairly generous if concurrence of many nations to the treaty is to be obtained.

The possibility of nuclear radiation damage presents such long-term special problems that it has been suggested that a general convention on liability for space activities should exclude such damages,[174] and unless fairly extensive provisions for radiation damage are included, this seems to be a reasonable solution. Four major conventions on nuclear liability have been prepared,[175] and while none of them specifically purports to cover space activities, the Vienna Convention rules could be used, although it may be desired to give jurisdiction to a tribunal established in a space activities liability convention, rather than to the courts of the state in which the damage occurred, as in the Vienna Convention. Otherwise, two unrelated tribunals would be adjudicating different aspects of the same occurrence.

The comparatively short limits suitable for ordinary damage are unsuitable for radiation damage.[176] Damage

---

169 U.S. drafts submitted in connection with U.N. discussions for a treaty on liability suggested claims should be presented within a year (U.N. Doc. No. A/AC.105/C.2/L.4 [1962]; Doc. No. A/AC.105/C.2/L.8, Art. IV [1964]; Doc. No. A/AC.105/C.2/L.7, Art. V [1964]; Doc. No. A/AC.105/C.2/L.10, Art. X [1964], but doubts were expressed that this was a long enough period for "cases in which the damage caused or the nature of the damage could not be immediately apparent." U.N. Doc. No. A/AC.105/C.2/SR.29–37, at 54 (1964).

170 U.N. Doc. No. A/AC.105/C.2/L.8/Rev. 1, Art. IV (1964); U.N. Doc. No. A/AC.105/C.2/L.8/Rev. 2 (1964); U.N. Doc. No. WG II/29 (1964) in U.N. Doc. No. A/AC.105/21, Annex II, at 32 (1964); U.N. Doc. No. A/AC.105/C.2/L.8/Rev 3 (1965); U.N. Doc. No. A/AC.105/C.2/L.7/Rev. 2 (1964).

171 U.N. Doc. No. WG V/17 in U.N. Doc. No. A/AC.105/19, Annex II, at 27 (1964); U.N. Doc. No. A/AC.105/C.2/SR.29–37, at 64 (1964).

172 The Brussels Convention on Liability for Nuclear Ships 57 *Am. J. Int'l L.* 268 [1962]) and the Vienna Convention on Liability for Nuclear Damage (2 *International Legal Materials* 727 [1963]) provide ten-year periods. The Japanese suggested that the period commence when knowledge of the

damage is or should reasonably be known. U.N. Doc. No. WG II/17 at U.N. Doc. No. A/AC.105/19, Annex II, at 27 (1964).

173 U.N. Doc. No. WG II/28 in U.N. Doc. No. A/AC.105/21, Annex II, at 31 (1964).

174 Hungarian draft, U.N. Doc. No. A/AC.105/C.2/L.10/Rev. 1, Art. I, para. 1 (1964). The Treaty on Principles, *supra* note 24, does not mention the point. It "is internationally liable for damage—by such object or its component parts" which would almost certainly include nuclear radiation damage.

175 Convention on the Liability of Operators of Nuclear Ships (Brussels, 1962) (57 *Am. J. Int'l L.* 268 [1962]); OEEC Convention on Third Party Liability in the Field of Nuclear Energy (Paris, July 1960) (55 *Am. J. Int'l L.* 1082 [1960]; Convention of Jan. 1963, Supplementary to the Paris Convention of July 1960, on Third Party Liability in the Field of Nuclear Energy (2 *International Legal Materials* 685, 727 [1963]. See Goldie, *supra* note 1, at 1189, 1216, 1242 for brief discussion.

176 See Harvard Law School and Atomic Industrial Forum, Inc., *International Problems of Financial Protection against Nuclear Risk, 1959*, 10: "It is characteristic of many radiation injuries that they may delay for many years in manifesting themselves. Thus the traditional periods which obtain in the United States may deprive a substantial percentage of plaintiffs of the chance to secure compensation." Compare Stason *et al.*, *supra* note 2, at 512 where favorable reference is made to a "contingent injury fund" plan which enables a claimant to be compensated from a special fund even after a long period but without reopening litigation between the claimant and respondent. The Treaty on Principles, *supra* note 24, makes no reference to periods of limitation.

from unidentified man-made space objects is unlikely to be paid, unless an insurance-type arrangement can be established. This seems improbable on an international basis. A prolonged limitations period would substitute a long period of uncertainty for the probability of prompt settlement of disputes. Financially, this is not as significant to states as to private interests, but it might constitute a continuing source of political friction.

Identification of the proper respondent will become increasingly difficult, and sometimes impossible, as more nations engage in space activity and as increasing numbers of man-made objects orbit the earth. Consequently, assuming that radiation damage is separately provided for, it would seem that a two-year period of limitation from the time of occurrence or a year from the time of identification of the respondent, whichever is shorter, is a reasonable formula. A space power, by notifying a claimant of its responsibility, could limit to not much over one year the normal period during which the claimant would have to commence action. A respondent should be obliged to reply promptly; failure to reply should constitute an acknowledgement of participation in the activity in question. The problems of causation of and measure of damage remain to be resolved after the identity of the space activity is established.

The Channels for Presenting Claims

Since it is generally accepted that states are liable for damages resulting from activities in space, it follows that claims should initially be presented through diplomatic channels[177] by the claimant state or by a third state if there are no diplomatic relations between claimant and respondent. If the respondent state is willing, the actual party suffering the loss might be permitted to submit a claim directly to the respondent,[178] although some claimant states might object to such procedure since a recovery in foreign exchange might escape control. The Communist nations would probably object on principle. It could also be argued that a respondent state might take advantage of a private claimant. Barring an express agreement

to the contrary, diplomatic channels not only should but will be used to make the initial contact in all normal cases, and private parties will seldom be directly involved in the negotiations.

The Pursuit of Alternate Remedies

The basic concept of state-to-state claims renders recourse to national judicial systems inappropriate except by special agreement between the parties.[179] The customary rule of international law requiring exhaustion of local remedies[180] by injured parties before sponsorship by governments can give rise to delays and other abuses, although it eliminates most small claims. The cost of prosecuting an international claim will, in most instances, deter the presentation of inconsequential claims by states when local remedies are not first used. Activities in space present a different factual situation than in more familiar international claims, where most frequently the injury is to a foreigner or foreign interests within the geographic limits of the respondent state. In other instances, claims may arise out of contract or aerial or maritime collisions, which are for the most part covered by some form of treaty provision.

---

[177] All drafts submitted in the course of U.N. negotiations so provide: U.N. Doc. No. A/AC.105/C.2/L.8/Rev. 3, Art. IV, para. 3 (1965); U.N. Doc. No. A/AC.105/C.2/L.7/Rev. 2, Art. IV(a) 1964; U.N. Doc. No. A/AC.105/C.2/L.10, Art. X (1964). The Treaty on Principles, *supra* note 24, follows the state liability theory and, by implication from silence, the concept that diplomatic channels will be the initial channel of communication.

[178] See Sohn & Baxter, *supra* note 160, Art. 22, Draft 12.

[179] U.N. Doc. No. A/AC.105/C.2/L.4, Art. 3(c) (1964); but see Sohn & Baxter, *supra* note 160, Art. 1, para. 2(b), Draft 12, which requires exhaustion of local remedies as a method of limiting the number of situations in which a state becomes internationally responsible. The same problem is resolved in an opposite manner for space activities by making states primarily liable in all instances. Sohn & Baxter suggested: "If direct remedies should be made available to individuals, it may be expected that restrictions would be imposed upon the types of claims which might be submitted and that claims for insubstantial amounts might in particular be excluded." The Italian representative favored allowing the claimant access to municipal courts on the basis of simplicity of procedure and cost. U.N. Doc. No. A/AC.105/C.2/SR.29–37, at 68 (1965).

[180] 5 Hackworth, *supra* note 1, at 501–26. See Poulantzas, "The Rule of Exhaustion of Local Remedies and Liability for Space Vehicle Accidents," *Sixth Colloquium on the Law of Outer Space* 3–6 (International Institute of Space Law of the International Astronautical Federation, Paris, 1963). Latin American sensitivity to intervention by foreign governments in international claims has resulted in many of the constitutions containing provisions intended to prohibit or minimize assistance of foreign governments in such matters. Citations following are to OAS translations of constitutions available in 1965. Bolivia (1961) Art. 20; Columbia (1886), Art. 11; Costa Rica (1949), Art. 19; Ecuador (1946), Art. 177; El Salvador (1950), Arts. 19, 20, 21; Guatemala (1956), Art. 59; Honduras (1957), Art. 27; Mexico (1917), Art. 27 (1); and Venezuela (1961), Arts. 45 and 52.

The simplest possible procedure is obviously desirable. There is inadequate justification to require parties to a claims dispute either to follow a fixed procedure or to require them to exhaust other remedies before resorting to a tribunal constituted in accordance with treaty provisions. If the parties have agreed expressly or by clear implication and actions to be bound by an alternative method, they should obviously follow through. Use of procedures provided by treaty should be available on a compulsory basis if alternative methods, including direct negotiations between the parties, are unsuccessful or are making little or no progress.[181] Pursuit of a claim through two or more channels at one time should not be permitted. Initiation of alternative procedures should not be allowed to extend the time to institute action in accordance with the terms of the proposed space liability treaty. Neither should use of the treaty provisions be permitted to harass the respondent.

The Joinder of Actions

An objective of any procedure for the resolution of claims is to consolidate actions and parties so that there will be a single action for each incident resulting in damage. Ideally, all claims from a single incident should be handled in a single adjudication with all claimants represented by one state and all respondents represented by another.[182] The claimant state would distribute the award in accordance with the decision of the tribunal, and the respondent state would receive contributions in accordance with such arrangements as had been made by the participants in the space activity causing the damage.

What constitutes a single incident is open to argument. If a space vehicle breaks up and pieces fall in widely scattered areas, perhaps in several states and over a period of several days or even weeks, it seems doubtful that the resulting damages should be considered as having arisen from a single incident. If an adjudication utilized some parts of the domestic law of claimant states, the applicable law would be different; and even if the adjudication utilized international law, it must be recognized that in the area of claims different states have different views about what constitutes international law.

In those instances where several states have engaged in a joint venture or where two unrelated space activities have together caused damage in one place at one time, the claimant or claimants should be able to recover in a single action. If a rule of law permitting the claimants to take advantage of favorable provisions in the respondent's law is adopted, the claimants should be permitted to utilize the law of any of the respondent states.[183] Some may argue, however, that this gives the claimant undue advantage. A single regime of law, theoretically available if rules of international law only are applied, appeals strongly in its simplicity of joinder of actions and its encouragement in developing international law, but there will probably not be a sufficient number of cases to make this a significant advantage. Insistence on combining actions and parties where there is no common evidence and general mutuality of interests could result in confusion, extra expense, and delays—if not a denial of justice. Where the interests of the claimants and respondents do not coincide, the interests of the claimants should receive preference.[184] If procedures are adopted requiring joinder

---

[181] The U.S. position has been to bar other remedies as soon as adjudication under the terms of the proposed liability treaty were commenced. The Treaty on Principles, *supra* note 24, is silent on the subject. U.N. Doc. No. A/AC.105/ C.2/L.8, Art. VI (1964); but a 1965 draft, U.N. Doc. No. A/AC.105/C.2/L.8/Rev. 3 (1964) forecloses use of the proposed convention if alternate remedies are pursued. A Belgian draft did not permit simultaneous pursuit of alternate remedies. U.N. Doc. No. A/AC.105/C.2/L.7/Rev. 2 (1964) and the U.K. suggested an amendment to the U.S. draft similar in principle to the Belgian proposal. U.N. Doc. No. A/AC.105/19, Annex II, at 27 (1964).

[182] This will frequently not be possible for technical and political reasons. Thus, it seems unlikely that the United States and Communist China could be persuaded to join as claimants where both nations suffered damage as a result of a single incident. In situations where normal damage and also radiation damage occurred, the difference in the time in which damage became apparent would likely make it impossible to determine all claims in a single action. In some instances the same state may be at the same time both a claimant and a respondent.

[183] See *supra* at 163, and Horsford, "Liability for Damage Caused by Space Operations" in 2 *Int'l Rel.* 657, 667 (1964): "It is likely that many claims will be multinational in character, since an object struck in orbit does not immediately fall to Earth as in aircraft collisions, but will continue to circle the Earth until in the case of the larger fragments which are able to withstand reentry heat, these fall to Earth over a wide area involving many countries. International procedures could ensure the consolidation of actions in this event, except where they arise from different incidents or causation." The Treaty on Principles, *supra* note 24, being silent on the point, must be presumed to call for the application of general rules of international law in accordance with Art. III.

[184] Belgian proposals called for joinder. "There shall be joinder of claims where there is more than one applicant in respect of the damage due to the same event or where more than one state is liable and the damage was caused by more than one space device." U.N. Doc. No. A/AC.105/C.2/L.7/Rev.

of actions and of parties even to the "same event" narrowly construed, it will be essential that appropriate rules be established to protect the interests of each of the claimant and respondent states. Appointment of arbiters would require joint action, and any consent or compromise settlements would require the approval of each concerned party. Few states will be willing to commit themselves in advance to allow an unknown state to represent them as either claimant or respondent without being assured of a voice in the appointment of the arbiters and in the conduct of the litigation,[185] which would include presentation of evidence and arguments.

A "single incident" should include only the damage and injury resulting from a single piece of falling debris or a group of pieces falling within a comparatively short period in the same general locality and within the borders of one state. Actions for incidents involving the territory of more than one state could be joined by agreement of the claimants and respondents. This is considered necessary since, even under Article III of the Treaty on Principles, states will have substantially differing views over the content of the rules of international law under which states are to carry on activities in space.

Substantive Principles of Law for the Resolution of Claims

Substantive rules of law may be determined by selecting an already existing regime of law, international or national, by prescribing a fairly detailed code of law by treaty, or by leaving the determination to the tribunals hearing the claims. The Treaty on Principles applies international law to activities in space with almost no specific guidelines. Although it is desirable to provide as much guidance by treaty as can be agreed upon, there are substantive questions involving a mixture of law and fact—such as man-made causation, national identification,[186] and measure of damages—about which prior detailed agreements would be difficult to achieve. Some of the difficulties arise from political factors involving the world community, but a substantial problem arises from the necessity to keep rules flexible enough to allow for tech-

nological advances. It is desirable to establish simple and automatic procedures to accomplish periodic revisions of the substantive rules or to give the tribunal substantial authority to devise its own rules.

The Investigation of Claims

Parties to a claims case and the adjudicating authority must have access to the information necessary to make a determination and a basis on which to determine where the burden of proof lies.

Scope of Space Activity

It must be agreed what constitutes "space activity," from which claims for damages should be covered. The definition may be narrow, encompassing only damage done by the space vehicle,[187] or it may be expanded to include all related activities connected with launching,[188] orbiting, and landing or retrieval. It may be included in a treaty or be left to subsequent adjudication, as was done in the Treaty on Principles, although the terminology used seems to contemplate a fairly restrictive definition.[189]

---

[187] The Belgian and Hungarian drafts were rather narrow. U.N. Doc. No. A/AC.105/C.2/L.10/Rev. 1, Art. I (1965), the Hungarian draft, suggested "an object launched into outer space—caused in outer space, in the atmosphere or on the ground by any manned or unmanned space vehicle or any object after being launched, or conveyed into outer space . . . even if . . . the space vehicle or other object has not yet reached outer space." U.N. Doc. No. A/AC.105/C.2/L.7, Art. 1 (1964), the Belgian draft suggested "any device which is intended to move in space, remaining there by means other than the reaction of the air."

[188] A revised U.S. draft, U.N. Doc. No. A/AC.105/C.2/L.8/Revs. 2 and 3 (1964 and 1965, respectively). Article II, para. 1, provided "for damage on the earth, in air space, or in outer space, which is caused by the launching of an object into outer space, regardless whether such damage occurs during launching, after the object has gone into orbit, or during the process of re-entry, including damage caused by apparatus or equipment used in such launching." An Indian amendment endeavored to clarify the distinction between spacecraft and aircraft. U.N. Doc. No. W.G. II/20 (1964) at U.N. Doc. No. A/AC.105/21, Annex II, at 28. Earlier U.S. drafts were neither so broad nor so detailed: U.N. Doc. No. A/AC.105/C.2/L.8 (1964); U.N. Doc. No. W.G. II/1 (1964), Art. II, para. 1. A revised Belgian draft (U.N. Doc. No. A/AC.105/C.2/L.7/Revs. 1 and 2 [1964]) with Italian amendments (U.N. Doc. No. W.G. II/2 [1964] at A/AC.105/19, Annex II, at 13), while not as detailed, was about as broad as the later U.S. drafts.

[189] In the general articles of the treaty the phrase "the

2, Art. 4 (1964). Other proposals did not require joinder but some recognized the possibility. U.S. draft in U.N. Doc. No. A/AC.105/C.2/L.8/Rev. 3, Art. VII, para. 2 (1965).

[185] This problem was recognized in a U.S. draft providing for collective appointment of the arbiter. U.N. Doc. No.   . A/AC.105/C.2/L.8/Rev. 3, Art. VII, para. 1 (1965).

[186] Lipson & Katzenbach, *supra* note 1, at 87.

If a convention on liability is to accomplish the desired purposes of minimizing the risk of international friction from space-connected mishaps and of compensating injured parties, however, "space activity" should be defined and interpreted broadly to encompass all international claims arising from damages caused by a space vehicle or fragments and by other activities so closely related thereto as to be a part of the same activity. Fueling a booster would fall within this definition. Efforts to retrieve a space capsule which had just landed could be considered a part of the space activity. If the activity resulting in injury is closely related to the space activity proper, it should not matter whether the damages is caused by a space vehicle itself or whether outer space is reached. Unless covered by other arrangements, the mechanisms established by a convention should be available for handling international claims from mishaps involving surface or air transportation of space-vehicle components, including fuel. In most such instances, however, special arrangements on liability can and should be made in connection with obtaining permission of the host country for passage through its territory, unless the states concerned wish to include such matters under a multilateral space liability convention.

Causation

Even if a broad definition of space activities were adopted, the first task of a tribunal charged with responsibility for handling claims will be to ascertain whether the alleged damage has been caused by a "space activity." This primarily factual question will require access to the situs of the damage for investigation. The unsupported assertion of a claimant is unlikely to be accepted.[190] The situs of the damage should be blocked off to keep out souvenir hunters and other unauthorized persons. The claimant should be required to return to the respondent, as soon as they have served the needs of the tribunal, the space vehicle or fragments which caused damage. Unnecessary delay in accomplishing this might raise questions about the validity of the claim,[191] and timely access to the situs by the tribunal and respondent could appropriately be made a condition precedent to pursuit of the claim. Such a rule would raise the issue of inspection, which has been a continual stumbling block in negotiations involving Communist territory.[192] Possibly, however, the Communist nations will in most instances permit access to and inspection of the damage situs, since the situs would not per se be a sensitive security area. Inclusion of a provision requiring access should not prevent Communist nations from being parties to a convention since they could, by forfeiting their claim, forbid access.

Assuming that the claimant has control of the situs, the burden should be on the claimant to establish that a space activity caused the damage, although the respondent should cooperate in good faith by providing available information to assist in identifying the cause of the damage. Where fragments or residue of any kind are recovered, it may be comparatively easy to establish that the damage was caused by a space activity; but in the absence of tangible items, the proof may require lengthy and intricate computations of the trajectories and orbital paths of a number of space launchings and even then the results may be inconclusive. The technical problems are such that until additional experience has been acquired it would be unwise to formulate detailed rules of evidence in excess of placing a burden on the claimant to establish, with cooperation of the probable respondent or respondents, that a space activity of the respondent caused the damage.

Identification of Respondents

Evidence to establish the identity of the originator of

---

exploration and use of outer space" is used. Article 7 refers to "the launching of an object into outer space—by such object or its component parts on the earth, in air space or in outer space." The lack of clarity reflects the difficulty of obtaining agreement.

190 A meteorite or other natural phenomenon could be the cause. A nation might for propaganda or for obtaining foreign currency, present unsubstantiated claims. Too, less developed countries may not have the scientific and technical ability to make the necessary tests.

191 See Crane, "Soviet Attitude Toward International Space Law," 56 *Am. J. Int'l L.* 685, 708 (1962): "[I]t might [be] that the Soviets recognize liability for any damages their space ships might cause, *contingent,* however, upon the recognition by other states of a Soviet right to the return of any and all Soviet space equipment and crew which enter the territory of these states in connection with the incident causing the damage or at any other time."

192 Christol, *The International Law of Outer Space* 308 (1966): "The serious difficulties attendant upon the verification and inspection of nuclear tests conducted by one state are similar to the problems in the launching of space vehicles. Thus, for reasons of sovereignty, security and self-defense, seasoned by the Soviet's large passion for secrecy, it has not been possible to arrive at a process for prelaunch inspection and identification of artificial satellites."

the activity may be available only in the records of the originator. Such information consists of data relative to the metallic composition, structure, and orbit of space objects. Space powers could simplify the problem of identification of spacecraft and components by including a signature or identifying trace element in the metallic components of the spacecraft. A United Nations resolution[193] has called upon states "launching objects into orbit or beyond to furnish information promptly to the Committee on the Peaceful Uses of Outer Space, through the Secretary-General for the registration of launchings." Most nations have periodically registered their space activities, although no real enforcement machinery exists. Proposals for the space liability convention have included references to registration,[194] but the discussion[195] made it clear that failure to register could not be utilized as a device to avoid liability. Article XI of the Treaty on Principles requires reporting space activities to the greatest extent feasible and practical. Registration could be one helpful element in making identification of space activities, but it would obviously be unsatisfactory to place exclusive reliance on it since, even if mandatory, there would be no assurance that all states would observe a rule requiring registration any more than they would observe one requiring use of designated trace elements.

Shifting the burden to require the respondent to disprove that its space activity caused the claimant's loss has also been considered. But such a procedure is unrealistic and unworkable. A state desiring to conceal its own activities might use materials and designs pointing to another country that would have no way of disproving responsibility other than with self-serving denials.

Detection and identification methods may eventually be developed so that it will be technically impossible to conceal the identity of the state whose spacecraft causes damage, but at present it is probable that a state could deliberately render proof of identity impossible. Even with the fullest possible cooperation of all potential respondents, it may not be possible to establish the origin of a space-vehicle fragment which has been in orbit for a substantial period, or which cannot be identified as having come from the orbit of any particular space shot. In those instances where identification of the originator cannot be made, the claimant will be unable to recover unless some international fund or insurance is established or unless one of the space powers elects to make an *ex gratia* payment.

Extent of Damage and Measure of Compensation

A claimant must, in addition to establishing the identity of the state responsible for a space activity causing damage, prove the extent of damage and measure of compensation. The legal problems in this instance are similar to those involved in establishing the measure of compensation in any other international damage claim, subject to such provisions as may be specified in applicable treaties. The relevant information for property damage will almost invariably be at the situs of the accident. Information relative to personal injuries or to death claims will also ordinarily be located at or near the situs, and the claimant should be required to grant access to maintain the claim. The burden of proof, as is customary, should be on the claimant.

The Principle of Absolute Liability

The presentation of international claims arising out of activities in space will necessitate the selection and application of general theories of liability, subject to such modifications and exceptions as may be considered desirable.

Discussions held under the aegis of the United Nations indicated a general acceptance of the position that liability for damage should be absolute and without the requirement of showing fault on the part of the respondent state.[196] Thus the United Nations has by resolution rec-

---

[193] General Assembly Res. 1721 (XVI), U.N. Doc. No. A/5100 (1961).

[194] See U.N. Doc. No. W.B. II/19, at A/AC.105/21, Annex II, at 28 (1964); U.N. Doc. No. A/AC.105/C.2/L.8/Rev. 1 (1964) in which a launching state is identified as a "state which has notified the Secretary-General of the United Nations of the launching of a space device and given the data necessary for its identification." The draft suggests that a state failing to give notice of a launching "may not take advantage of the limitation of liability referred to in the following article."

[195] U.N. Doc. No. A/AC.105/C.2/SR.51, at 5, 6 (1965).

[196] Goldie, *supra* note 168, at 1189, 1216, 1229, 1240–41 suggests a general trend in all areas of international law toward the principle of absolute liability and notes "absolute liability has been imposed in four recent international agreements on liability to third parties in the field of nuclear energy. These agreements incorporate the concept of 'channelling,' which traces liability back to the nuclear operator, no matter how long the claim of causation, nor how novel the intervening factors [other than a limited number of exculpatory facts]." At p. 1231 he argues that the Trail Smelter and Corfu Channel cases represent a trend toward strict liability where one state creates unnecessary hazards for others and suggests that creation of risk may be

ommended absolute liability for space activities,[197] adopted in Article VII of the Treaty on Principles. In some recent instances international air law appears to have adopted a rule of absolute liability.[198] Most non-governmental authorities now support the absolute liability rule for space activities.[199]

The Reasons for Absolute Liability

Arguments justifying and explaining absolute liability and limitations thereon are varied and sometimes conflicting. It has been argued that automatic liability for space accident damage constitutes liability for intentionally caused damage,[200] but it would seem preferable to save "intent" liability for situations where there is a conscious plan or design to injure. It has also been argued that, by analogy to pilotless aircraft, launching any spacecraft is illegal—thus carrying with it penalties in the form of liability for any damage done.[201] Part of the

argument is based on the concept that the reentry of a spacecraft violates the sovereignty of the subjacent state.

Another justification for absolute liability is that injured parties do not assume the risk which is foreseeable and controllable solely by those in charge of the space activity.[202] This argument is almost equally applicable to any complex activity of the modern industrial society, and if the authority in charge of the activity could in fact completely control it, there would be no accidents and no damage. Another argument is that standards of care to assess fault in space activities have not been developed.[203]

It is also argued that the ultrahazardous nature of activities in space justifies and requires the application of absolute liability for any damages caused.[204] But even the

likened to expropriation. Sohn & Baxter, *supra* note 160, Draft 12, with Explanatory Notes, suggest that there are insufficient cases to justify an attempt to formulate any rigid principles purporting to govern cases which may arise in the future.

[197] U.N. Res. 1348 (XIII) (1958), para. 1(d); Convention on Damage, *supra* note 144; Meyer, *supra* note 135, at 339, 345 reports a German Legal Committee has recommended that: "Compensation should be paid upon proof only that the damage was caused by a spacecraft in flight or persons or things falling therefrom, or by collisions between aircraft and spacecraft."

[198] U.N. Res. 1962 (XVIII), para. 8 (1963) provides that "each. State which launches or procures the launching of an object into outer space, and each State from whose territory or facility an object is launched is internationally liable for damage to a foreign State or to its natural or juridical persons by such object or its component parts on the Earth in air space, or in outer space." See also draft proposals in U.N. Doc. No. A/AC.105/C.2/L.7/Rev. 2, Art. 1(b) (1964); U.N. Doc. No. A/AC.105/C.2/L.8/Rev. 3, Art. II, 1 (1965); U.N. Doc. No. A/AC.105/C.2/L.10/Rev. 1 (1965); and comments in U.N. Doc. No. A/AC.105/C.2/SR.50 (1965), all of which support the general concept of absolute liability.

[199] See, e.g., para. 13 of the Resolution on the Legal Regime of Outer Space, Institute of International Law, Brussels, (1963), reprinted in Jenks, *supra* note 64, at 416, App. 9: Hyman, *supra* note 46, at 304a, Art. 13 (1966); Csabafi, "The Questions of International Responsibility of States before the United Nations Committee on the Peaceful Uses of Outer Space and Some Suggestions," *Sixth Colloquium on the Law of Outer Space* 21 (1963); McMahon, "Legal Aspects of Outer Space," 38 *Brit. Yrbk. Int'l L.* 389 (1962).

[200] Parry, "Space Law: Surface Impact Liability of Space Vehicles," 14 *Okla. L. Rev.* 89, 93–94 (1961).

[201] Vasquez, *Cosmic International Law* 115 (Malley trans.

1965) citing the 1919 Paris and the 1944 Chicago conventions relative to aircraft liability.

[202] Rinck, "Damage Caused by Foreign Aircraft to Third Parties," 28 *J. Air L. & Commerce* 405, 407 (1961–62). Haley, "Space Vehicle Torts," 36 *U. Det. L. J.* 294, 298 (1959): "With the growth of the machine age which produced more numerous instances of serious property damage and personal injury it was felt necessary to extend the doctrine of absolute liability in order to place the loss on those who, though free from negligence or tortious intent, had control over the instrumentality causing the harm and who, in most cases, were better able to foresee the possibility of financial loss and protect against it." Harvard Law School Study, *supra* note 176, at 10: "[I]nsofar as any precautions and protective measures can be taken, those in charge of an atomic facility are in a position to take them whereas potential victims have relatively little ability to protect themselves."

[203] Schrader, *supra* note 2, at 139, 149; Haley, *supra* note 202, at 294, 298: "as technology advances and rockets become less of a novelty it is probable that the rule will be changed and that, as in the case of aircraft, liability will be based solely on fault"; Jessup & Taubenfeld, *supra* note 3, at 243–44; Goldie, *supra* note 1, at 1189, 1197.

[204] Haley, *supra* note 202, at 294, 298; de Rode Verschoor, *supra* note 127, at 460, and his "Recent Developments Regarding Liability for Damage Caused by Spacecraft," *Seventh Colloquium on the Law of Outer Space* 251 (1964); Harvard Law School Study, *supra* note 202, at 19; Schrader, *supra* note 2, at 139, 153; Csabafi, *supra* note 199, at 15; Vasquez, *supra* note 201, at 115, 123; Goldie, *supra* note 1, at 1189, 1212, 1214. "[T]heories of risk creation as expropriation. . . ." U.N. Doc. No. A/AC.105/C.2/SR.50, at 6 (1965): "[H]azardous activities were tolerated only on condition that the person engaging in such activities assumed responsibility for any damage resulting, whether attributable to fault on his part or to mere accident . . . ."; and at 9 and 10: the question of civil liability for handling a very dangerous or potentially dangerous object "anyone undertaking a dangerous activity had to accept absolute liability for the results."

best definition of an ultrahazardous activity is vague.[205] Aviation has apparently outgrown that appelation,[206] although many insurance policies continue to carry special exclusionary provisions for losses from certain types of activity in the air. Activities in space, whether or not ultrahazardous, have not yet resulted in international claims, although the theoretical potential for loss unquestionably exists. Justification for considering activities in space ultrahazardous comes from lack of knowledge of its dangers rather than from a record of damage-causing accidents.

It can hardly be argued that the very occurrence of an accident causing damage is unlawful and entails absolute liability or makes the activity ultrahazardous. "Unlawful," based on political concepts,[207] has also been applied to some space activities, but "unlawful" in this context is impossible to define[208] except on an arbitrary basis. Futhermore, the law of compensation for accidents should not be confused by the penal and political provisions, which have already given rise to considerable discussion and disagreement.[209] If a decision is made to include references to "unlawful" or "improper" activities in space in a convention on liability, it appears essential that great care be exercised in defining precisely what is meant, since the problems of conflicting interpretations between East and West are well known.

One of the stronger justifications for the principle of absolute liability, frequently argued in other areas of tort law, is that it places the burden on the party best able to absorb the loss.[210] Application of this argument for absolute liability assumes that the state responsible for the activity is in the best position to know the risks and, since as a general rule only the wealthier states will engage in extensive space activity, to absorb the loss. To the extent that a state is not in a position to accept the risk of absolute liability, it may be deterred from space activity, which is consistent with the idea that a state engaging in space activities should bear the full cost,[211] but it is not consistent with the concept that space activity is for the benefit of all mankind. In international law the loss is suffered by the claimant state rather than by the damaged individual, and even if the claimant state pays over to the individual promptly the sums received, traditional processes are almost invariably too slow to provide the injured individuals with emergency relief.[212] Thus, it is

---

[205] "An activity is ultrahazardous if it necessarily involves a risk of serious harm to the land, chattels or persons of others which cannot be eliminated by the exercise of the utmost care, and if it is not a matter of common usage." Restatement, Torts secs. 835 and 520.

[206] Berger, *supra* note 2, at 301, 304–5.

[207] A revised Hungarian draft, U.N. Doc. No. A/AC.105/ C.2/L.10/Rev. 1, Art. V (1965), read: "The State shall assume liability for damage . . . if the damage occurred while exercising an unlawful activity in outer space or the space vehicle or object was launched for unlawful purposes, or if the damage has otherwise resulted from an unlawful activity." See to the same effect U.N. Doc. No. A/AC.105/ C.2/SR.29–37, at 86 (1964) representing the Russian view. See comment by Crane, *supra* note 191, at 685, 709.

[208] McMahon, *supra* note 199, at 339, 387: "A third suggestion is that liability may well depend on the nature and character of the activity that is being pursued. If it is primarily of a military nature and for the benefit of one country, no doubt liability should be absolute. If it is of a commercial nature and such as to benefit a large number of States, liability may well be imposed only for negligent conduct . . . . However . . . the insoluble difficulty is to disengage a commercial from a military activity for this purpose."

[209] U.N. Doc. No. A/AC.105/C.2/SR.50, *passim* (1965).

[210] For discussions of the general principle see Keeton, *supra* note 1, at 401, 405: "[T]he gist of the argument is that in this way a loss will be spread more generally in the community among those who benefit from the activity out of which the loss arises." Stason *et al., supra* note 2, at 772: "In our society there is a definite trend toward the establishment of enterprise liability in conjunction with the sale of products in our economy . . . the supplier is more likely, than is the injured person, to be able to suffer the economic losses or to take steps to minimize them." Calabresi, *supra* note 1, at 713, 714. Keeton & O'Connell, *supra* note 1, at 329: "As the definition of negligence is broadened to include instances of conduct not morally blameworthy, the argument becomes stronger for treating such losses as costs of motoring to be distributed equitably among motorists through insurance, rather than to be borne by either of the parties to the particular accident." The analogy here is obviously not very strong as there is substantial difference between an individual driving a car and a state launching a space vehicle.

[211] Compare Goldie, *supra* note 1, at 1189, 1200: "As a general rule of policy for compensating harms caused by extrahazardous or security-cloaked activities, resort to making *ex gratia* payments on compassionate grounds constitutes a most unsatisfactory situation. At law fault liability would, in all probability remain the governing principle. But in practice this would mean little more than a legal fiction which closes the doors of the courts to injured parties and encourages them to seek redress from the legislature . . . . But if a standard akin to a principle of strict liability is developed *de facto* in administrative practice, why not accept the form of liability *de jure* to be applied by the courts as a rule of law."

[212] Compare Horsford, *supra* note 183, at 657, 659: "Where liability is readily attached legal procedures could ensure a swift settlement of claims, and in the present state of the art absolute liability would seem to be a reasonable proposition,

argued, the focal point is correctly on relations between states rather than on concern for individuals who must in any event look to their own states for emergency relief. Absolute liability will ensure that the claimant state is reimbursed for payments for damages caused by an identifiable space activity, and, as between states, it would seem more equitable to require the state initiating the activity to pay for the unanticipated consequences than to require a state with no connection with the activity to be burdened.

It is frequently argued that the imposition of absolute liability in international space law will reduce the number and severity of accidents.[213] However, the costs of space activities are so great that a very strong monetary inducement already exists to exercise the utmost care to avoid any accidents. National prestige for accomplishment and acceptance of space programs by nonspace powers are also deeply involved. From a realistic point of view it is doubtful that absolute liability rules will cause the space powers to exercise any greater care than they are now doing.[214] But acceptance of the principle of absolute liability will, primarily for psychological reasons, contribute to the acceptance of space activities by nonspace powers. This is true even though proponents of space activities argue that mankind generally is the beneficiary and that nonspace powers should be willing to contribute to the cost of these activities. Fault liability[215] for damages is al-most the equivalent of no liability because of the extreme difficulty of proof.[216]

Exceptions to the Principle of Absolute Liability

Sentiment favoring absolute liability for damages resulting from space activities is general and exceptions to the principle have been viewed with some skepticism.[217] No exceptions are expressed in the Treaty on Principles.

Contributory or Comparative Negligence

Drafts of conventions submitted for consideration in the United Nations negotiations have all suggested, in different language, some exception for damage which would not have occurred but for the negligence of the injured party.[218] Language used includes "a wilful act or from gross negligence," "wholly or partially from a wilful or reckless act or omission," and "wilful misconduct." India and the United Arab Republic have objected to any such exception.[219] Others have, as noted previously, questioned the language used but have indicated sympathy with the concept.

An apportionment of damages for contributory negligence is appropriate. In some instances involving property damage, such an exception may supply a major

---

especially if combined with a limitation on the amount of damages."

[213] See Calabresi, *supra* note 1, at 713, 715: "There are ways to reduce the primary cost of accidents—their number and severity—that can, indeed must, be an important aim of whatever system of law governs the field. One way is to discourage those activities that result in accidents and to substitute safer ones. Another is to encourage care in the course of an activity." Keeton, *supra* note 1, at 401, 439: "Responsibility for injuries caused to others serves as a selector of socially useful activities and methods . . . . Though economic incentive is only one factor among many in the complex motivation for accident prevention, it can be an important one. In the absence of responsibility for injuries caused, it tends to work against safety." De Rode-Verschoor, *supra* note 204, at 251, 252–53: "This effort [to avoid accidents] will also be furthered by the adoption of the principle of absolute liability." U.N. Doc. No. A/AC.105/C.2/SR.50, at 9 (1965). See generally Lipson & Katzenbach, *supra* note 1, Abstracts 411–18.

[214] See Blum & Kalven, *supra* note 1, at 701: "Whatever little we may know about deterrence, it seems plausible that liability rules will have a more marked impact on accidents due to fault than on those not caused by fault."

[215] See the early statement of McDougal, in "Legal Problems of Space Exploration," included in *1961 Proceedings of the American Society of International Law* at its Fiftieth Annual Meeting, 1956, Sen. Doc. 26, at 87 (1961): "If the purposes here are so advantageous that everybody wants to secure them, then Rylands v. Fletcher will not be the answer. There will not be absolute liability. Reasonableness will be the key to decision."

[216] Haley, *supra* note 202, at 294, 299; Berger, *supra* note 2, at 301, 303; Jessup & Taubenfeld, *supra* note 3, at 243; U.N. Doc. No. A/AC.105/C.2/SR.1 (1962); Schrader, *supra* note 2, at 139, 149; Crane, *supra* note 191, at 685, 709: "[O]ne might expect that the Soviets' opposition to inspection would influence them to accept absolute liability for any harm caused by their space vehicles, in order to avoid any investigations concerning the existence or absence of due care of negligence on their part." Many details of U.S. space activity are also highly classified.

[217] See, e.g., U.N. Doc. No. A/AC.105/C.2/SR.29–37, at 107 (1964). The Indian representative suggested: "It [absolute liability] was hedged by concepts of negligence, fault and vis major which virtually nullified the recognition of absolute liability." See Canada to the same effect in U.N. Doc. No. A/AC.105/19, Annex II, at 23 (1964).

[218] U.N. Doc. No. A/AC.105/C.2/L.7/Rev. 2 (1964); U.N. Doc. No. A/AC.105/C.2/L.8/Rev. 3 (1965); U.N. Doc. No. A.C. 105/C.2/L.10/Rev. 1 (1965).

[219] U.N. Doc. No. A/AC.105/19, Annex II, at 23 (1964).

motivation to the claimant state to avoid or minimize damage. Even for personal injuries and deaths, the contributory negligence exceptions may prove to be an inducement to some countries to take action to minimize the danger,[220] or at least to refrain from submitting claims for losses which would not have occurred, except for the claimant's lack of care.[221]

This exception, to be effective, obviously requires that the respondent state have access to pertinent information likely to be available only at the situs of the accident.

The degree of negligence required to make an exception to absolute liability would have to be spelled out, since no generally accepted guidelines exist in either national or international law. Ordinary or minor negligence is probably insufficient justification to invoke the exception, but reckless or willful disregard of safety will suffice.[222] It will be necessary to allow the tribunal considering the claim discretion since, at best, the most precise definition possible will be one of degree and the burden of establishing contributory negligence would probably have to be on the respondent. A contributory negligence exception should cover only the increase in the amount of damage resulting from the negligence of the claimant and should not defeat the entire claim, although there has been some sentiment in favor of complete exoneration.[223]

Force Majeure

There has been no uniform view as to whether or not *force majeure* should exonerate a respondent whose spacecraft causes damage;[224] the arguments are similar to those customarily raised in discussions of the subject in municipal law.[225] No separate justification such as encouraging care on the part of either respondent or claimant exists, as in the case of contributory negligence. There are no clear precedents of either municipal or international law to follow.

In any subsequent negotiations, the final decision will be one of practical policy rather than of legal theory. As the concept of absolute liability has been accepted, it would seem that the space powers would and should be willing to forego the defense of *force majeure*. The adjudication of claims would be greatly simplified, and the space programs would carry this part of their costs to society.

Other-Party Interference

This point has many similarities to *force majeure*. Presumably, the respondent as well as the claimant is unable to do anything to prevent the adverse consequence. And there has been no uniform view as to whether other-party interference should exonerate a respondent whose spacecraft causes damage.[226] Since the absolute liability theory

---

[220] The value of human life as such varies greatly in different cultures, and it is quite possible that in some areas authorities might be willing to trade lives for foreign exchange.

[221] See Prosser, *Law of Torts* 443–49 (1964) for a discussion of comparative and contributory negligence and of the lack of uniform usage of terms.

[222] Canada suggested: "[W]illfully and recklessly exposed himself to dangers of which he was warned and which he could have avoided." U.N. Doc. No. A/AC.105/19, Annex II, at 23 (1964). The U.S. stressed "'[W]illful or reckless act or omission' . . . did not mean mere negligence but was rather tantamount to 'gross negligence.'" U.N. Doc. No. A/AC.105/C.2/SR.50, at 6 (1965).

[223] Belgian comment to U.N. Doc. No. A/AC.105/C.2/SR.50, at 5 (1965) but see U.S.–U.K. comments to the contrary at 8.

[224] A Hungarian proposal specifically so provided, U.N. Doc. No. A/AC.105/C.2/L.10/Rev. 1, Art. III (1965); and the Hungarian representative suggested that the other proposed

drafts indirectly did the same, U.N. Doc. No. A/AC.105/C.2/SR.50, at 7 (1965). U.S. and Belgian representatives indicated their drafts were not intended to exonerate a respondent on the basis of *force majeure;* U.N. Doc. No. A/AC.105/C.2/SR.50, at 5–6 (1965). The U.K. representative indicated: "In his view the possibility of natural disaster was a risk which should be borne by the launching State." But for the launching would the damage have occurred? The Czechoslovak and Russian representatives favored at least partial exoneration in case of *force majeure*. U.N. Doc. No. A/AC.105/C.2/SR.25, at 9 (1964) and A/AC.105/C.2/SR.50, at 5 (1965). Onitskaya, *supra* note 164 at 5. *Id.* at 65 favors exoneration in cases involving *force majeure*. Vasquez, *supra* note 201, at 114 distinguishes between rockets intended to leave earth and those intended to return to earth and would apply a *force majeure* exception only as to the first category. The Treaty on Principles, *supra* note 24, does not mention an exception for *force majeure* or any other reason.

[225] In U.N. Doc. No. W.G.II/9 (1964) at U.N. Doc. No. A/AC.105/19, Annex II, at 14–15 (1964), Italy suggested no exception in the case of *force majeure* when the damage is on the surface of the earth because the victims have "no possibility of protecting themselves," but fault principles should apply when two space activities are involved. Canada agreed. U.N. Doc. No. A/AC.105/19, Annex II, at 23 (1964).

[226] A Hungarian proposal suggested that as between space activities there should be joint and several liability where a third state was a claimant for liability, U.N. Doc. No. A/AC.105/C.2/SR.50, at 7 (1965). But a Czechoslovakian statement suggested a respondent should be "relieved of liability if the

is to be followed with respect to damage caused to a third state as a result of the respondent's space activity which has been interfered with by a second state, a claimant should be allowed to proceed against either state. In the absence of a showing of negligence, the respondent against whom the claim is presented might be permitted to collect a proportionate share from the other state or states which were involved. Such other respondent state or states should be permitted to join the original respondent in the proceeding. If one of the respondents is able to establish negligence on the part of the other, then rules of contributory negligence should be applied to apportion the cost. This should not be a problem for the claimant, who should be able to recover from any of the respondents without waiting for them to determine their respective degrees of responsibility.

A problem remains as to liability for spacecraft collisions or other damage involving the space activities of two or more states. Application of absolute liability without an exception will require that each state pay for the damage of the other. Such a result has frequently been criticized,[227] but it has been included in a U.S. proposal,[228] with the suggestion that "it was better to formulate a clear and simple rule than to allow the unlikely possibility of a collision in space to affect the statement of the principle of absolute liability."[229] Although consistency

of policy may theoretically suffer, the simplest policy may be to let each party to a collision bear his own loss, except where negligence of the other party can be established.

We conclude, therefore, that provision should be made for absolute liability, subject only to the exception of contributory negligence of a willful variety on the part of a claimant and in the case of one space activity causing damage to another space activity.[230]

Types of Damage and Amount of Compensation

After it has been determined that the respondent's space activity has caused damage for which he is liable, the issues remaining are the elements of damage covered and the amount of compensation due. Although ideally a claimant should be restored to his condition prior to the injury or damage, for practical reasons monetary compensation is almost invariably used.[231] Among the adjectives used to describe proper compensation are "full," "fair," "adequate," "just," and "appropriate,"[232] all terms requiring subjective interpretations to some degree. The claimant state might also be allowed to recoup the amounts it had paid to its nationals,[233] plus such additional amounts as might be required for "full compensation" for the damages suffered by the nationals and damage suffered by the complaining state itself. This would give the claimant state substantial unilateral control over the amount of compensation. None of these problems were solved by Article VII of the Treaty on Principles.

---

damage was due to harmful acts of other states," U.N. Doc. No. A/AC.105/C.2/SR.25, at 9 (1964). The Soviets supported the Hungarian position, U.N. Doc. No. A/AC.105/C.2/SR.50, at 3–4 (1965). The U.S. proposals imposed absolute liability on the launching state for any accident whatever, U.N. Doc. No. A/AC.105/C.2/L.8/Rev. 3, Art. II (1965). See, for general discussion, McDougal *et al., supra* note 3, at 606–20.

[227] "In the case of collision of space vehicles in outer space, the idea of the absolute liability of the launching state made no sense at all." Mexican comment in U.N. Doc. No. A/AC.105/C.2/SR.50, at 3–4 (1965). For comments see McDougal *et al., supra* note 3, at 623–24: "[I]t would seem a sound policy to dispense in such situations [collisions] with the principle of absolute liability, recommended for surface impact damage." Csabafi, *supra* note 199, at 17: "In this case the application of the principle of absolute liability would result in the absurdity that the parties should be bound to refund mutually each other's damages."

[228] U.N. Doc. No. A/AC.105/C.2/L.8/Rev. 3, Art II (1965).

[229] U.S. comments in U.N. Doc. No. A/AC.105/C.2/SR.50, at 4–5 (1965), where it was also noted that: "If some willful or reckless act or omission was involved, the liability of one state would be wholly or partially extinguished under the United States proposal." The Austrians, supported by the British, pointed out the difficulty a claimant state would have in establishing negligence and questioned the advisability of

including a provision likely to be unworkable in practice. U.N. Doc. No. A/AC.105/C.2/SR.50, at 708 (1965). Under the Treaty on Principles *supra* note 24, it would seem that each state would have to pay the damage caused the other state in the event of a collision, etc.

[230] Liability arising from interference with communications is discussed in chap. 5. In general, no justification is seen for establishing a set of liability rules for space communications separate from rules for radio communications generally, as both airspace and outer space have been used for radio communications for some time.

[231] See Eagleton, "Measure of Damages in International Law," 39 *Yale L.J.* 53 (1929): "The ideal form of reparation, doubtless, is the restoration of the situation exactly as it was before the injury. . . . Such a solution, however, is rarely possible in international law. . . . The usual, and almost exclusive, method of reparation . . . is pecuniary payment." See also Csabafi, *supra* note 199, at 19.

[232] Fitzgibbons, "Compensation for Intangible Elements of Value of Expropriated Property under International Law," *Harv. Int'l L. Club J.* 177, 179, (1963).

[233] Cooper, *supra* note 131, at 680, 683.

It may be preferable to provide by subsequent treaty, to the extent possible, the types of damage for which compensation will be paid, the methods of evaluating the losses suffered, and the limitations, if any, on the amount of recovery.

Compensable Damages

Various definitions of "damage" have been proposed and discussed. Among them are that: damage means "loss of life, personal injury, or destruction or loss of, or damage to property";[234] "loss of life, personal injury or other impairment of health, and damage to property"; and "loss of profits and moral damage whenever compensation for such damage is provided for by the law of the State liable for damage in general," but excluding "nuclear damage resulting from the nuclear reactor of space objects";[235] and that the law of the situs of the loss be utilized to determine the compensable loss.[236] The diversity of views emphasizes the desirability of either specifying in a subsequent convention the types of damages for which compensation is to be made or specifying a regime or regimes of law to be applied. Silence in Article VII of the Treaty on Principles and Article III's prescription of general rules of international law merely postpone the decision until a claim arises. The decision will then of necessity be made by whatever tribunal is formed. This is not necessarily undesirable if the tribunal has sufficient authority to make binding decisions.

Article VII of the Treaty on Principles specifies that damages resulting from activities in space are to be compensable, although it was suggested that a convention on liability might cover only damage caused on the surface.[237] All the drafts of a liability treaty considered by the U.N. in 1965 included damage occurring on the surface, in the air and in outer space,[238] and this position[239] was accepted by the U.N. subcommittee considering the question and by the resulting Treaty on Principles.

Exclusion of nuclear damage from the types of losses to be covered has been extensively discussed.[240] There is no doubt that respondents should be liable for nuclear damage. The question is whether the subject should be covered in a separate agreement because of the difficulties and delays in determining the existence and extent of nuclear damage.[241] Also, a limit on liability for compensation could have been set more easily if liability for nuclear damage were handled separately from liability for damages from other causes. Maximum liability limits for nuclear damage would probably be higher, partly for psychological reasons, than for other kinds, and time limitations for presenting claims for radiation damage might be considerably longer than for readily identifiable damage.

Nuclear damage was not separately provided for in the general liability article of the Treaty on Principles. This provision would have avoided the inconvenience of separate conventions but would have made more difficult the task of obtaining agreement. As written, the Treaty on Principles doubtless encompasses liability for nuclear damage from space activities. Precedents for providing separate liability in the field of nuclear energy are found in the 1960 Paris Convention on Third Party Liability in the Field of Nuclear Energy, in the 1962 Brussels Convention on the Liability of Operators of Nuclear Ships, and in the 1963 Vienna Convention on Civil Liability for Nuclear Damage.[242]

Another possible area for exclusion from coverage in a convention are various categories of intangible and noneconomic losses.[243] Legal systems of the Western

---

[234] U.N. Doc. No. A/AC.105/C.2/L.8/Rev. 3, Art. I(a) (U.S.A.).

[235] U.N. Doc. No. A/AC.105/C.2/L.10/Rev. 1, Arts. I, II (1965) (Hungary).

[236] U.N. Doc. No. A/AC.105/C.2/L.7/Rev. 2, Art. 2 (1965) (Belgium).

[237] U.N. Doc. No. A/AC.105/C.2/SR.48, at 708 (1965). The Mexican representative suggested that inclusion of damage in air or outer space raised complicated issues of fault whereas liability for damage on the surface would be absolute. Demarcation of airspace and outer space was also raised.

[238] U.N. Doc. No. A/AC.105/C.2/L.8/Rev. 3, Art. II (1965). U.N. Doc. No. A/AC.105/C.2/L.8/Rev. 3, Art. 1 (1965). U.N. Doc. No. A/AC.105/C.2/L.7/Rev. 2 and Corr.

1, 2, and 3 and W.G. II/27, Art. II (1965). See comments in U.N. Doc. No. A/AC.105/C.2/SR.48, at 8, 9, 13 (1965).

[239] U.N. Doc. No. A/AC.105/C.2/SR.49, at 3, 4, 5 (1965).

[240] U.N. Doc. No. A/AC.105/C.2/SR.48, at 3–13 (1965).

[241] Stason *et al., supra* note 2, at 8–36; O'Toole, *supra* note 21, at 751–76; U.N. Doc. No. A/AC.105/C.2/SR.48, at 2–12 (1965).

[242] The decision as to how to cover liability for nuclear damage is primarily a policy rather that a legal question, but the Vienna Convention might well be used as a model.

[243] The Hungarian draft, by implication, would probably have excluded such damages unless they were covered by the law of the respondent. U.N. Doc. No. A/AC.105/C.2/L.10/Rev. 1, Art. II (1964). Emphasis has consistently been on physical damage caused by physical impact, although there are numerous situations under which damage other than that of physical impact might be suffered.

world often provide for such damages, whereas the legal systems of the Communist countries ordinarily do not.[244] Another problem is the inclusion of liability for consequential economic loss. The Treaty on Principles contains no guidelines for what should be included in "damage," and in view of the differences in national laws on the subject it is essential, if subsequent arguments are to be avoided, that the coverage intended be explicitly defined by agreement. There is little support for an argument that, because a state has more generous national laws, its obligation under international law should be greater than its neighbor's unless the parties agree on a reciprocal basis that the laws of both claimant and respondent may be utilized to give the claimant the benefit of whichever provision may be more liberal. Otherwise, if, for example, the Soviet Union and the United States were engaged in space activities that caused identical damage in each other's territory, there might be a substantial disparity in the awards, a result not likely to be considered appropriate.

An early Belgian draft[245] included as part of the damage "judicial and legal costs and interests." Assessments of costs and interest might encourage the respondent to expedite handling a claim. However, delays are also frequently the responsibility of the claimant, and if interest is to be included, provision should be made to avoid assessing it for periods for which the claimant is responsible. Inclusion of costs and interest as part of the damages is consistent with absolute and fault liability, although it may serve to encourage submission of minor claims where the cost of international adjudication is greater than any legitimate recovery. If costs are to be included, safeguards should be written in to prevent abuse.[246]

Valuation of the Losses

Negotiators of a separate detailed liability convention might consider establishing a set of values for each type of personal injury with fixed amounts for loss of life, loss of limbs, loss of work days, etc., as is generally the rule in workmen's compensation. Property damage could be fixed at original or replacement cost with straight-line depreciation for the age of the property. This would simplify the task of the tribunal, but the awards would not necessarily have a rational correlation with the loss suffered by the claimant state. Also, the task of obtaining agreements for specific amounts for each type of injury would be difficult and might take more time than is justified in view of the probability that there will be few claims. Even if agreement could be reached, amounts set would be quickly outmoded and the negotiations would have to be done over again,[247] unless provisions were included tying amounts to some international economic index or to a national economic index of the claimant and/or respondent.

The diversity of provisions for determining the amount of compensation to be paid for an injury or property loss, even within a single country, is so great that inclusion of a provision in a treaty to use national laws in determining the amount of compensation would require careful drafting to assure that only generally applicable laws would be utilized. Specific laws could hardly be cited because of excessively cumbersome numbers and because of the fact that such laws are subject to modification by national legislators.[248] Probably the most satisfactory method

244 See Gsovski & Rusis, "Liability under Soviet Law for Damages or Personal Injury Caused by Space Vehicles" 17 (Library of Congress mimeo., 1959). "The Soviet courts consistently followed the principle that compensation for non-property damage may not be adjudicated, and the same opinion prevails among Soviet writers. Compensation may not be granted for mental anguish, pain or other suffering not accompanied by material loss."

245 U.N. Doc. No. A/AC.105/C.2/L.7, Art. I(b) (1964).

246 Compare Sohn & Baxter, *supra* note 1, at 545, 583, where Arts. 36 and 38 of the proposed convention make provisions for interest and costs.

247 Amounts set by international agreement are frequently very difficult to revise. To obtain agreement to increase the liability for deaths resulting from aircraft accidents from less than $10,000 to $75,000, coupled with absolute liability, it was necessary for the United States to denounce the 1929 Warsaw Convention on the Unification of Certain Rules Relating to International Transportation by Air, 49 stat. 3000 (1934); *T.S.* 876, 53 *Dept. of State Bull.* 923 (Dec. 6, 1965); *Washington Post,* May 1, 1966, at A3. The negotiations are continuing and sharp disagreement between the U.S. government and U.S. airlines is quite apparent. The Treaty on Principles makes no reference to limitations on amounts which may be recovered.

248 The amount of compensation paid in the U.S. as a result of deaths from air accidents varies greatly. In a 1964 case, a New York court found Sabena guilty of "willful misconduct" on an international flight under the Warsaw Pact and awarded $202,705 to the estate of Leroy. *New York Times,* Mar. 19, 1964, at 66, col. 2. A 1960 case involving Kamlet's death called for a $600,000 settlement, with many other cases settled out of court. *New York Times,* Feb. 25, 1964, at 33, col. 7. Congress voted $25,000 to the estate of each member of a U.S.N. band killed Feb. 20, 1960, in a plane crash in Brazil. Brazilian law permitted a very small recovery of less than $200. *New York*

would be to provide the tribunal with standards as precise as possible, but allow it to make the final decision as to the amount of compensation to be paid for each injury or loss.[249]

Valuation of loss of life, if not to be done on the theory that all lives are worth the same amount, would logically require the ascertainment of the net loss in productive capacity resulting from the death of the individual. This involves a factor of net earning capacity and probable working-life expectancy discounted to present values. If this formula is adopted, compensation for lives of nonproductive persons would be nominal and theoretically a claimant state might be spared future expenses by the elimination of permanently nonproductive persons, requiring continuing institutional care. Theory and acceptability are obviously at variance. Maximums and also minimums could and probably

should be established by a subsequent agreement. Compensation for personal injuries could be computed on the basis of lost or lessened earning capacity and the cost of treatment and care.

Property losses can be computed on the basis of loss of net return, cost of replacement, or international market value. The question of compensation for consequential or indirect loss is the subject of much difference of opinion, nationally and internationally, and many subsequent arguments could be eliminated if rules could be agreed upon in advance.[250] If compensation for pain and suffering, sentimental value, trespass, etc., is to be included, a subsequent international agreement should so specify. It will be difficult, however, to show that the *state* has suffered a loss,[251] since compensation for such items is not required to give the claimant state the same resources as if the damage had never occurred.

It has been suggested that average recoveries for other international claims might serve as a starting point in the valuation process.[252] But it is also apparent that some items of compensation in international claims are in addition to what would be required if the only criteria were to restore the claimant state.[253]

Conduct of the respondent should not be a factor in determining the amount of compensation to be paid.[254]

Times, Aug. 3 1966, at 16, col. 8, and Oct. 6, 1966, at 14, col. 2. Other awards have exceeded $1,750,000. The three astronauts killed in the Cape Kennedy mishap Jan. 27, 1967, carried $100,000 private insurance in addition to regular military benefits.

However, compare this with 42 U.S.C. 2473 (13) (sec. 203[b] [13] of the U.S. NASA Act) which authorized NASA "to consider, ascertain, adjust, determine, settle, and pay, on behalf of the United States, in full satisfaction thereof, any claim for $5,000 or less against the United States for bodily injury, death, or damage to or loss of real or personal property resulting from the conduct of the Administration's function as specified." Claims for amounts in excess of $5,000 must be submitted to Congress for consideration. Congressional relief is very slow. See, e.g., *Public Law* 89–757 approved Nov. 5, 1966, authorizing the Secretary of the Army to settle claims for death or personal injury resulting from an ordnance plant explosion on July 8, 1963. Limit per claim was set at $25,000. An agreement dated Jan. 17, 1967, with the U.K. for a tracking station in Antigua refers to 42 U.S.C. 2473 as the basis on which claims arising from acts or omissions of U.S. personnel connected with NASA "will be considered and settled." Other claims arising from acts or omissions connected with the tracking station "may" be settled in accordance with applicable provisions of U.S. law.

[249] This conclusion is supported by many respected international law authorities. See, e.g., Borchard, *supra* note 76, at 423: "It is . . . difficult to bring within any established rule the measure of damage in tort cases, inasmuch as each case depends upon its own peculiar facts, and inasmuch as arbitrators exercise a wide discretion in determining the elements of loss which may enter into the allowance of compensation." Eagleton, *supra* note 231, at 75: "A large amount of freedom must be left to the judge." Fitzgibbons, *supra* note 232, at 211: "[T]he weighing of evidence of value must inevitably involve the use of discretion by the decision maker with principal reliance upon the particular circumstances of the controversy."

[250] See Prosser, *Selected Topics on the Law of Torts* 426 (1963).

[251] Compare Fitzgibbons, *supra* note 232, at 203–4: "Through a lump-sum payment, two States can do their compromising in one inclusive negotiation rather than in the course of a multitude of individual arbitrations. The claimant State is then able to distribute the amount received in settlement according to its own concepts of fairness and efficiency."

[252] See Eagleton, *supra* note 231, at 50, 52, 75: "Such precedents have fixed with fair accuracy the amount to be allowed for false imprisonment, or the measure of damages in death cases. The only principles which need be stated are that the judge is free to award indirect damages, but that he is limited in the award to damages proximately caused by the illegal act, and in the calculation of the damages to those reasonably capable of estimation."

[253] U.N. Doc. No. A/AC.105/C.2/SR.48, at 5 (1965), where the United States representative suggested, "[I]t was customary to take into account the nature and extent of the bodily injury, loss of earnings, and so on. In death, it was proper to take into account the amount which the deceased would probably have contributed to members of his family, the value of his personal services and the mental suffering sustained by the members of his family."

[254] Compare Fitzgibbons, *supra* note 232, at 211, on the practice in the area of expropriation: "The nature of the action of the expropriating State would also seem to have an effect on

The question of whether the respondent should be disciplined for its behavior should be determined outside the scope of any convention on liability.[255]

Limitations upon Recovery

It will probably be necessary, as a condition to obtaining general approval of a detailed agreement on liability, to establish a limit on recovery for a single accident and possibly also for recovery for a life.[256] Arguments favoring a limitation include analogies to other areas such as maritime and air law, which have limitations; and to international and domestic law relating to atomic energy.[257] Also advanced are the concepts that space activities are for the benefit of all mankind and an imposition of absolute unlimited liability could cripple or severely limit the activity, and that limitations are necessary to protect small countries from damaging liability and to encourage cooperative activities between states.

There is also support for unlimited liability, although most nations, as reflected in the discussion in the U.N., are uncertain about their final position.[258] The same objectives of compensating for losses of the claimant state which support absolute liability are cited also to support unlimited liability. It is argued that space powers do not need the extra encouragement of limitations on liability to engage in space activities which is required to encourage the use of nuclear energy for peaceful purposes by less developed countries. Probable costs of absolute unlimited liability are very small in comparison to amounts space powers spend on space activities. Nuclear energy technology has developed to the extent that some insurance can be purchased, but the same is true to only a limited extent for space activities, which lack any international standards of safety or precautionary measures. It has also been suggested that the deterring of small states from participating in space activities because of the possibility of liability is not necessarily undesirable, as they might better devote their resources to urgent social welfare problems.[259]

Establishing maximums by other than arbitrary means would be difficult, as it would be necessary to determine by international agreement if there should be a limitation for each accident, each launching, each claimant state, each individual victim, each year, each respondent, or some combination. It would also be necessary to determine if the limitations would be a percentage of loss or a flat ceiling. Since the Treaty on Principles appears to include liability for nuclear damage, it may be desirable to establish, in some manner, a special limitation for it. Before an agreement on limitation is reached, it would be desirable to know the possible extent and type of damage; this could best be supplied by space scientists, but even their information is inadequate for lack of technical experience. There are conventions such as those concerned with nuclear and aircraft liability which can be looked to for precedents. The extent of liability for collisions at sea is fixed according to the size of the respondent vessel, and conventions relating to liability for damage on the ground caused by aircraft contain limitations related to size of the aircraft.

Another approach to the question of limitation is to consider the need and status of the individual claimant.[260]

---

compensatory evaluation. Individual, and outwardly predatory takings receive less sympathetic treatment." See also Article V of the proposed Hungarian draft which imposes heavier liability for space accidents caused "while exercising an unlawful activity." U.N. Doc. A/AC.105/C.2/L.10/Rev. 1 (1965).

[255] Compare statement by Lowenfeld, chairman of the U.S. delegation to the Special International Civil Aviation Organization Meeting on Limits for Passengers under the Warsaw Convention and The Hague Protocol, Montreal, Canada, Feb. 1–15, 1966, 54 *Dept. of State Bull.* 580, 584 (1966): "The theory of Compensation is, after all, to restore the survivors, to the extent money can do so, to the position that they would have been in but for the accident. There is no attempt to punish the person responsible for the accident."

[256] The U.S. and Hungarian draft conventions considered by the U.N. in 1965 included provisions for overall limitations, although the amounts were left open. U.N. Doc. A/AC.105/ C.2/L.10/Rev. 1, Art. II (1965) and U.N. Doc. No. A/AC.105/ C.2/L.8/Rev. 3, Art. IX (1965). The Belgian representative indicated no objection to the principle, U.N. Doc. A/AC.105/ C.2/SR.55, at 3 (1965). Representatives of several other countries indicated interest and possible agreement although most were uncertain of their position. Czechoslovakia, U.N. Doc. No. A/AC.105/C.2/SR.29–37, at 80 (1964); Mexico, U.N. Doc. No. A/AC.105/C.2/SR.48, at 8, 13 (1965); Italy, U.N. Doc. No. A/AC.105/C.2/SR.29–37, at 69 (1964) and SR.50, at 3 (1965); Goldie, *supra* note 1, at 1189, 1218.

[257] The Price-Anderson Act of 1957, 42 U.S.C. 2210, included a $500 million ceiling.

[258] See discussions in U.N. Doc. No. A/AC.105/C.2/ SR.29–37, at 64, 107 (1964); U.N. Doc. No. A/AC.105/C.2/ SR.48, at 8, 9 (1965); U.N. Doc. No. A/AC.105/C.2/SR.49, at 3–8 (1965); U.N. Doc. No. A/AC.105/C.2/SR.55, at 3–6 (1965). See also Hinograni, "Damages by Satellite," 30 *U. Kan. City L. Rev.* 214, 217 (1962).

[259] Woods, *supra* note 52: "It is urgent for many of them [underdeveloped countries] to cut down some of the biggest items of waste . . . prestige projects."

[260] See Goldie, *supra* note 1, at 1189, 1218–1220: "It would

This ignores the concept that international space claims involve only states and adds complications of detailed agreement that probably makes the suggestion impractical. However, it would be possible to use current earnings and actuarial life expectancy, number of dependents, etc., as factors in computing compensation for a life; this is commonly done in the United States in cases not subject to statutory limitations.

An agreement for a ceiling on compensation for life should, if possible, include a provision for automatic adjustment upward or downward to avoid a hiatus, such as occurred under the Warsaw Convention on aircraft liability.[261] If a limitation is accepted, it should be clear that it is a ceiling which is not to be exceeded and is not an amount everyone will receive without proof of loss in that amount.[262]

---

seem consistent with the functional thesis of this article that the actual amounts of these maxima should be calculated upon the basis of types of social situations to which they are applicable. The suggestion is, furthermore, that different classifications of space activities, for example, should be agreed upon by treaty, and the maximum amounts which may be awarded should vary with these classifications. These classifications, and the relevant maximum amounts, should be seen as proportional to the degree of expropriation engendered, and in inverse ratio to the degree of sharability of the activity. . . . Variations in living standards and of the cost of living among nations, possible balance of payment and other currency problems, all provide political considerations which can best be solved by negotiations."

[261] 53 *Dept. of State Bull.* 924 (1965). McDougal *et al., supra* note 3, at 619 note that: "[T]he imposition of absolute liability for surface impact damage upon the operator, with limits as to the amount of liability, even though in many respects desirable, does, however, present certain problems. Maximums prescribed may be far from adequate to cover the actual loss suffered." Jessup & Taubenfeld, *supra* note 3, at 246, 348 refer to the Warsaw Convention: "In exchange for establishing a *prima facie* case on behalf of anyone showing a contract of carriage plus injuries sustained, and limiting the defenses available to an aircraft operator, the convention limited the maximum claim on behalf of a person injured or killed to . . . about $8,300. . . . The limitations . . . have been defended on the basis of a need to protect an infant industry against threat of catastrophic losses which would make it impossible to raise capital, uniformity of law, the availability of insurance to passengers—arguments that may be heard when commerical space vehicles for transport purposes become feasible."

[262] See Lowenfeld's statements, *supra* note 255, at 580 with reference to the Warsaw Convention: "[O]nly when the limit has been very low, as under Warsaw, has the limit tended to be the average—in fact generally the automatic sum at which claims are settled. . . . We propose that the limit of liability under Hague or under Warsaw be increased to $100,000 per

If a limit on liability is established, policy guidelines should be established for apportionment between injuries to persons and damage to property.[263] It should also be decided whether interest and costs are to be included in the maximum limits.[264]

Enforcement of Awards

Enforcement or collection of awards for damages presents the same problems as other international claims for which awards have been made. Problems of enforcement of decrees by international or foreign tribunals against natural or nongovernmental judicial persons are unlikely to arise for some time if, as appears probable, international claims continue to be handled on a state-to-state basis, either by diplomatic negotiation, adjudication under a general agreement, or by adjudication in accordance with the terms of an ad hoc agreement reached under the Treaty on Principles. It has been suggested that claims for compensation should not constitute grounds for sequestration of or the application of enforcement measures to such spaceships.[265]

The Treaty on Principles Governing the Activities of States in the Exploration and Use of Outer Space, including the Moon and Other Celestial Bodies, established a rule of absolute liability and made states liable for all activities in space, but normal rules of international law still control most aspects of liability for damages. No special procedures or forums have been established or identified, and questions relating to jurisdiction, limitations, types of injuries covered, and representation rights remain for resolution as cases arise or in a detailed treaty on liability. Although the probabilities of numerous claims are small, so that a low priority for negotiation of a liability treaty could probably be justified, the space powers and the other members of the United Nations

---

passenger. . . . We have no reason to believe that a limit set at $100,000 per passenger would tend to become the average recovery in the United States or anywhere else."

[263] U.N. Doc. No. A/AC.105/C.2/SR.55, at 3, 4 (1965). It may be argued that apportionment between personal injuries and property damage is a moral question, but decisions on such matters are ordinarily based on economic factors and public relations factors.

[264] Vienna Convention on Liability for Nuclear Damage, *supra* note 144, at 727. Article IV does not include interest or costs which may be added on.

[265] U.N. Doc. No. W.G.II/18 at U.N. Doc. No. A/AC.105/21, Annex II, at 28 (1964); and U.N. Doc. No. A/AC.105/C.2/L.10/Rev. 1, Art. XII (1965).

have indicated their intent to go forward with the negotiation of a treaty.[266] If, unexpectedly, a number of international claims for damages arise from activities in space, or if it becomes necessary to show accomplishment in international cooperation, it should be comparatively easy for the major space powers to complete the negotiation of a fairly comprehensive liability treaty within a short time, for precedents have been established in previous negotiations for several of the more difficult questions.

---

[266] U.N. Doc. No. A/Res/2222 (XXI) (Dec. 19, 1966) contains the following: "Requests the Committee on the Peaceful Uses of Outer Space

"(a) To continue its work on the elaboration of an agreement on liability for damages caused by the launching of objects into outer space and an agreement on assistance to and return of astronauts and space vehicles, which are on the agenda of the Committee."

This resolution was in the context of enumerating unfinished business following U.N. recommendations for ratification of the Treaty on Principles, *supra* note 24.

7

Natural Resources, Pollution, and the Law of Activities in Space

Resources in Space

The conservation, allocation, and utilization of earth resources affected by activities in space, which includes potentially the resources of airspace, of the earth's surface, of the oceans and as deep beneath the surface as man is able to penetrate, have an impact on many of the legal and political problems of space, but these resources must be considered separately from those in and from space, including celestial bodies.[1] Although all areas have much in common in that they involve relations between nations and problems of enforcing general international law and those special rules which may be agreed on for new situations, they have major, technological differences which have a substantial impact on the legal problem. An obvious difference is that land masses of the earth from which natural resources can be

---

[1] Chaps. 2 and 3 discuss the legal status of space, which includes the use of space for satellites of all varieties. The use of space to orbit satellites for communications is discussed in detail in chap. 5. See also *A Survey of Space Applications,* chap. 2 (NASA SP. 142; 1967), which gives a summary of communications utilizing satellites and includes a 23-item bibliography. The NASA report also has chapters covering earth resources, geodesy, meteorology, navigation, and future applications of space. Each unit has its own bibliography for a total of about 250 entries. The use of space vehicles for such purposes as weather reporting, navigational aids, military intelligence, science, etc., is discussed commencing on page 15. Chap. 6 analyzes the problems of liability and references to various uses of space are to be found throughout.

taken or observed are, for the most part, physically accessible and subject to the national sovereignty of a single nation. Even the high seas are readily accessible to mankind and have been since long before written history.[2]

Resources of space are not accessible in the same way, and are not yet subject to commercial exploitation or to national sovereignty. There are nevertheless important parallels. National sovereignty is not now, for example, generally considered applicable to the high seas although there is a lively controversy over the sea-bed below. The national ship, submarine, or space vehicle is, nonetheless, considered subject to national sovereignty and ownership, even if located physically outside the bounds of national sovereignty.[3] Strategic security interests, the rapidly developing capability to work at great depths beneath the surface of the sea, and the potential ability to exploit Antarctica present legal, policy, and economic problems similar in some respects to those which, if optimistic hopes are fulfilled, may be presented by activities in space. If so, this will almost certainly induce many changes in the applicable law,[4]

including the revision of existing treaties relating to space activities.

Ability to utilize the resources of space for purposes other than sending out spacecraft which can be used for communications, for observation of natural and man-made phenomena, and for impact of objects such as weapons on the earth's surface has not yet been achieved and may not be for a long time, if ever, but economic and strategic utilization of natural resources from space could become feasible as a result of some dramatic technological advance.[5] If this does happen and vital interests of

---

[2] See chap. 3 at 57.

[3] See Appendix E for text of: The Treaty on Principles Governing the Activities of States in the Exploration and Use of Outer Space, Including the Moon and Other Celestial Bodies (signed Jan. 27, 1967, and reproduced in Appendix E), which provides in Arts. VI and VII for national control of all activities in space; The Agreement on the Rescue of Astronauts, the Return of Astronauts, and the Return of Objects Launched into Outer Orbit reiterates throughout the concept of national authority and control over all space activities and vehicles; The draft treaty on Liability for Damage Caused by Objects Launched into Outer Space is based on the concept of national ownership and control over all activities in space. All United Nations resolutions including those reproduced in Appendix E (1721 [XVI] of Dec. 20, 1961; 1884 [XVIII] of Oct. 17, 1963; 1962 [XVIII] of Dec. 13, 1963; 1963 [XVIII] of Dec. 13, 1963) are based on the same concept. The location in space of the spacecraft or where the activity is taking place is not subject to national ownership or sovereignty, which is generally consistent with the law of the high seas.

[4] McDougal, Lasswell, & Vlasic, *Law and Public Order in Space* (1963). Chap. 7, at 749, deals with "Claims Relating to the Enjoyment and Acquisition of Resources" (also published in 111 *Pa. L. Rev.* 521 [1963]). Many other writers have devoted attention to the subject. See, e.g., Carl Q. Christol, *The International Law of Outer Space* 109 (1966); *Peacetime Uses of Outer Space* (Ramo ed. 1961), wherein Teller at 261 suggests the thing of value to be brought back from space is knowledge, not gold, uranium, or diamonds. If exploitation of resources does become feasible, there are analogies from which ideas may profitably be drawn. See chap. 3 *supra*. See also Jessup & Taubenfeld, *Controls for Outer Space*, chaps.

5, 6 (1959), which analyzes the Antarctic and space problems in comparative terms. National sovereignty claims have been made in Antarctica (and the Arctic), but they are not universally recognized; Antarctic claims are supposed to be more or less in abeyance for at least thirty years under the Antarctic Treaty of 1959 (12 *U.S.T.* 794). On conservation and control of the living resources of the high seas, the literature is voluminous and there have been a great number of international agreements negotiated. Problems relating to resources of the seabed are receiving ever-increasing attention from governments and scholars of all disciplines. Garcia Amador, *The Exploitation and Conservation of the Resources of the Sea* 86–167 (1963). Burke in his monograph, *Ocean Sciences, Technology, and the Future International Law of the Sea* (Ohio State U. Press 1966), poses many of the legal and policy problems likely to arise as ability to exploit resources of the sea and seabed are developed. See also McDougal & Burke, *The Public Order of the Oceans: A Contemporary International Law of the Sea*, chap. 7 (1962), which covers the problem of exploitation of resources in some detail. This interest is generated by the possibility that the seas may become an even more valuable source of foodstuffs for a continually increasing population. It presently seems unlikely, unless there is an unanticipated technological development, that space will provide any supplement to animal, vegetable, or mineral resources of the human race. If this supposition is correct, then, aside from space as a resource into which to send spacecraft for communications, for intelligence gathering, and for destruction, Teller is doubtless correct that the thing to be brought from space is knowledge.

[5] It would be injudicious to assert that man cannot develop the ability to exploit resources from celestial bodies, but it will require a scientific breakthrough in new means of propulsion to give any hope of commercial exploitation. Present estimates suggest costs of several hundred thousand dollars an ounce to bring materials from the moon to the earth with known methods of operation. Articles such as Cole's "Application of Planetary Resources" (AIAA International Aerospace Abstracts, Accession No. A66–13577; 1966) and articles on establishing colonies on celestial bodies are presently in the category of space science fiction rather than serious scientific literature. A display at the dedication of the Allied Chemical Tower in Times Square, New York, showed an animated model of a press agent's imaginary city called Copernicus on the moon as it

nations become involved, historical precedents indicate that previously asserted positions and views of the proper law for space will be sharply modified. Thus, the concept currently expressed by practically all states that national sovereignty does not and should not extend into space or to celestial bodies might be discarded in favor of concepts for celestial bodies similar to those applied to land masses of the earth.

Scientific information indicates that elements and compounds will be found on nearby celestial bodies generally in about the same proportions as on earth, but none of the celestial bodies of our solar system has an atmosphere comparable to earth's. Smaller celestial bodies also seem to have very little, if any, free water. Presently unknown elements may be found, although scientists do not anticipate finding any which do not fit within the periodic table of atomic weights nor do they anticipate any exceptional concentrations of elements rare on earth.

Resources have been divided into groups such as renewable or flow, nonrenewable or stock, and spatial extension,[6] but such differentiation is primarily a matter of degree. More importantly, where a particular resource is in abundant supply, regardless of category and value, there is less likely to be controversy between nations than when a valuable resource is in scarce supply. Utilization of electromagnetic radiation frequencies in space for communications is an example of a resource requiring extensive consideration and regulation because of overcrowding of the available wave lengths.[7] Solar energy in space is being utilized as a source of power for communications in connection with the investigation of space, but it is not presently of commercial value except for communications satellites using it as a source of energy for generating electricity. Solar radiations, including cosmic rays, while possessing enormous energy, are so diffuse that the size of the screen which would be required to collect usable amounts of energy for use on earth is not practical through present technology even if a way could be devised to place such a screen in space.[8] There is no

known method of collecting energy in space and transmitting it to earth for use. Gases in space are in the same category[9] as are the atmospheres of celestial bodies. However, for scientific reasons nations and writers have indicated a considerable interest in the application of rules which will prevent the contamination of space, celestial bodies, and earth, a subject discussed hereafter under pollution.[10] Resources such as water, nonpoisonous atmospheres containing oxygen (even if only 1 or 2 percent of earth's concentration), and other necessities for the support of earth-type life may have to be subjected to international regulation if they are not so diffused over and around celestial bodies as to render regulation of use impractical and unnecessary.[11]

If commercial exploitation of minerals, ores, or other substances from celestial bodies becomes feasible,[12] such striking technological advances will probably have occurred that it is also probable that radically new and presently unforeseeable economic, political, and legal factors will have developed just as in the development

---

might appear in the year 2000. *New York Times,* Dec. 3, 1965, at 3, Magazine Section.

[6] Ciriacy-Wantrup, *Resources, Conservation, Economics, and Policies* 25 (1963). McDougal *et al., supra* note 4, at 779.

[7] See chap. 5. While communications technology is making great advances, the demand for frequencies has been increasing even more rapidly. Satellites may make possible the utilization of an entirely new series of frequencies and thus alleviate an already existing shortage.

[8] The Mariner II Venus probe indicated a rather constant

radiation intensity of approximately 3.0 particles per square centimeter per second throughout the flight. Cosmic rays, x-rays, and other radiations in space are presently phenomena to be shielded from rather than phenomena to be utilized. They can be expected to raise no legal questions as long as this condition persists.

[9] See Dauvillier, *Cosmic Dust* 18 (1963).

[10] See p. 189. Article 9 of the Treaty on Principles, *supra* note 3 (reproduced in Appendix E), provides in part that the parties shall: "conduct exploration of them [celestial bodies] so as to avoid their harmful contamination and also adverse changes in the environment of the earth resulting from the introduction of extraterrestrial matter and, where necessary, shall adopt appropriate measures for this purpose."

[11] The capacity of celestial bodies other than earth in the solar system to support earth-type life is doubted, although still subject to interminable discussion. Scientists think it will be necessary to take along or manufacture an environment suitable for human life in areas likely to be visited from earth. The task is infinitely more difficult than supporting life in the Antarctic or far beneath the surface of the sea. In addition to the distances, the radiation hazards, and the lack of atmosphere, the temperature ranges are vastly greater than anywhere on earth. For discussion see Snider, "New Case for Life on Mars," *Chicago Daily News,* Oct. 13, 1965, p. 9; and "Scientist Says Life Could Not Exist on Mars," *Washington Post,* Oct. 13, 1965, p. 7; Glasstone, *Sourcebook on Space Sciences* 717 (1965).

[12] See *Handbook of Geophysics and Space Environments* (S. & H. Valley, eds. 1965), which indicates asteroidal meteorites are about 93 percent stone. The conclusions of Middlehurst & Kuiper eds. in *The Solar System: The Moon, Meteorites and Comets* at 41 (1963) are consistent.

of the resources of the seabed.[13] For reasons noted earlier in this volume, the legal analogy with the sea is neither precise nor broadly accepted. The probabilities of using space or celestial bodies for residence, even temporarily, are extremely small in the short run when the necessity of recreating earth's atmosphere and environment is considered.

Conflicts in connection with the utilization of resources of space and celestial bodies will be extensions of rivalries on earth. It may eventually be necessary to negotiate detailed agreements, but until the direction that developing technology will take is reasonably certain, general agreements on the conduct of the relations between nations are all that appear possible and may perhaps be all that is ever necessary. Where sufficient information is available, agreements can and are being negotiated.[14] The space treaties to date and U.N. Resolution 1962 (XVIII) are as specific as the Antarctic Treaty.[15] Some long-standing fisheries treaties provide for little more than that fishing boats shall not interfere in one another's operations on the high seas.[16] Numerous

writers and spokesmen of some governments have idealistically called for comprehensive international controls,[17] yet the concept that all nations should share equally in resources found or developed by any nation has never been applied to resources on earth, and none of the space powers has indicated any inclination to surrender control or benefits of expensive space projects.[18] While the United States, the Soviet Union, and other powers have thus far disclaimed any intent of making national claims to celestial bodies,[19] the bases for such claims may develop. Even without formal claims of sovereignty, history also confirms that extensive control of areas and resources has often been achieved by states unilaterally and in combination. Even though detailed rules of law relating to acquisition of resources from space and celestial bodies may not now be needed, we cannot ignore the fact that the generally expressed desires of some members of the community of nations have not to date

---

13 See John Cobb Cooper, "The Manned Orbiting Laboratory: A Major Legal and Political Decision," 51 *A.B.A.J.* 1137, 1139 (Dec. 1965): "Slowly and inexorably we are coming to accept the fact that the legal status of outer space and the high seas differs very little, if at all. Historically, it should be noted that air space above the high seas has long been accepted as having the same legal status as the seas themselves."

14 See, e.g., the Treaty Banning Nuclear Weapons Tests in the Atmosphere in Outer Space and under Water, Oct. 10, 1963, 14 *U.S.T.* 1313, although not all nations are parties. Also, it might be noted that this treaty may bar the use of nuclear explosions for peaceful purposes, such as digging a second canal between the Atlantic and the Pacific Oceans. See the series of agreements referred to in chap. 5 and the series of cooperative agreements between the U.S. and other powers, referred to in chap. 4. See also the comprehensive Outer Space Treaty discussed in detail in chap. 4, *passim,* described by Ambassador Goldberg as offering an opportunity to states "to lift themselves out and above current issues and interests and build a framework—if only skeletal in form—for the future pattern of mankind's activity." The relevant treaties are reproduced in Appendix E.

15 June 23, 1961; 12 *U.S.T.* 794.

16 See, e.g., the Convention (between Great Britain, Belgium, Denmark, France, Germany, and the Netherlands) for Regulating the Police of the North Sea Fisheries, signed at The Hague, May 6, 1882; Ratifications deposited at The Hague, Mar. 15, 1884; 73 *British and Foreign State Papers—1881–82,* 39, 43 (1889). Arts. XIV and XV in translation read: "(XIV) It is prohibited to any fishing boat to let down its nets, between sunset and sunrise, in the vicinity of other fishermen with nets already out.

"However, this ban does not apply to castings which may have happened due to accidents or to any other circumstances of *force majeure.*

"(XV) Boats arriving upon fishing spots are forbidden to place themselves or to cast their nets in such a manner as to interfere with each other or to disturb the fishermen who have already begun their operations."

Art. IX of the Space Treaty provides that States shall conduct their space activities "with due regard to the corresponding interests of other States." Lack of adequate controls has resulted in the practical elimination of whales and other denizens of the sea as resources.

17 See, e.g., Hyman, *The Magna Carta of Space* (1965). The David Davies Memorial Institute of International Studies, *The Draft Code of Rules on the Exploration and Uses of Outer Space* (1962); Smirnoff, MS., Report of Working Group III, *Proceedings, Fourth Colloquium on the Law of Outer Space* 361 (1963) proposing that all space activities be under the control of the U.N. and that any resources found in space be made available to all nations on an equal basis. These proposals encompass the whole of space activities, not just the problems relating to resources; Jessup & Taubenfeld, *supra* note 4, at chaps. 1–4.

18 International law and the U.N. Charter are based on concepts of sovereignty of states. A collection of excerpts from speeches of various U.N. delegates emphasizing this point is included in the paper given by Fasan, "Law and Peace for the Celestial Bodies," *Proceedings, Fifth Colloquium on the Law of Outer Space* 3–4 (1962) at the International Institute of Space Law of the International Astronautical Federation. The Jan. 27, 1967, Treaty on the Exploration of Space, Art. I, expresses the pious hope that the exploration and use of outer space "shall be carried out for the benefit and in the interest of all countries."

19 See p. 76 ff. and Article II of the Treaty on Principles, *supra* note 3, and reproduced in Appendix E.

normally overidden the desires of powerful states for exclusive control.

The general rules of international law, the United Nations resolution,[20] and the general agreements relating to the conduct of activities in space[21] furnish broad guidelines of conduct which should be adequate to avoid a dangerous confrontation over disputes arising from initial efforts to exploit spatial resources. It is essential, however, that the lawyers and statesmen of the world keep abreast of technological developments and press continually for negotiation of new agreements as scientific information indicating what problems are likely to arise becomes available.

The detailed rules, when drafted, must be acceptable to the great powers. They will probably provide that the first nation commencing to exploit a particular resource is not to be interfered with by other nations. This is already expressed in general terms in the various existing resolutions and treaties. What will constitute commencement of exploitation, the extent of the area protected, and how continuous the exploitation must be will depend on physical conditions and the terms of international agreements, which should be subject to frequent revisions or at least review.[22]

Space Activities and Natural Resources of the Earth

The less than promising prospects of immediate economic exploitation of natural resources from celestial bodies are far overbalanced by the potential and actual uses of space in connection with resources of the earth. Surveys, studies, and actual experience suggest a panorama of ways in which space vehicles carrying a variety of sensors aimed at the earth can and are helping us learn about conditions on and under the earth's surface. The legal implications of the development have received comparatively limited attention except as related to military intelligence.[23] Use of space in connection with navigational aids, cartography, geodesy, meteorology, oceanography, hydrography, physical geography, and geology is already clear.[24]

Where it can be established that spacecraft engaged in any of the activities just referred to cause damage to interests across international boundaries, it would seem that the nation from which the activity had originated would be absolutely liable in accordance with the provisions of Article VI of the Treaty on Principles Governing the Activities of States in the Exploration and Use of Outer Space, Including the Moon and Other Celestial Bodies.[25] However, the interpretation of the treaty language is open to substantial uncertainty and the records of debates in the United Nations committee cast no light on the subject. Must the injury be caused by a physical piece

---

[20] See U.N. Resolution of the General Assembly, para. 2: Declaration of Legal Principles Governing Activities of States in the Exploration and Use of Outer Space, A/Res/1962 (XVIII) (Dec. 13, 1963). "Outer space and celestial bodies are free for exploration and use by all states on a basis of equality and in accordance with international law. Outer Space and celestial bodies are not subject to national appropriation by claim of sovereignty, by means of use or occupation or by any other means." Text of the resolution is reproduced in Appendix E. See other related resolutions in that Appendix.

[21] See chap. 4 *supra* and the Treaty on Principles, *supra* note 2, reproduced in Appendix E.

[22] We have been using the resources of the sea for hundreds of years, but hardly a decade passes without at least one major new multilateral treaty on the subject. Within the decade just passed, four major multilateral conventions relating to the sea were negotiated, and there are still dangerous controversies over such a seemingly simple matter as the width of territorial waters.

[23] For a discussion of the nature of man's activities in space related to earth resources see p. 32 and note 144. See pp. 25–32 for a discussion of military use of space.

[24] The legal implications of these activities are as yet undefined, although there has been some speculation on the subject, primarily related to national law and surveys made by airplanes. See, e.g., Jack D. Oppenheimer, Exec. Sec'y Special Commission on Weather Modification, NSF, "Legal Aspects of Weather Modification" (Mimeo., Western Snow Conference, Apr. 21, 1965). The legal problems of depriving one party of precipitation and giving too much to another would appear to apply equally to weather modification achieved from outer space or from airspace. The damage resulting from the hurricane or typhoon storm systems can be enormous in both lives and property. What will be the liability if one nation diverts the storm from its territory to that of another nation? Glasstone, *supra* note 11, at 240, devotes about 20 pages to meteorology and 10 pages to navigational and geodetic satellites, but legal problems are not discussed. *Significant Achievements in Satellite Meteorology 1958–1964* (NASA SP. 96; 1966) reviews progress of those years and includes a 97-entry bibliography, primarily of government publications. See also Report of NSF Special Committee on Weather Modifications (1967); Taubenfeld, *Weather Modification: Law, Controls, Operations* (NSF, 1966).

[25] Art. VII provides for absolute liability of nations for "damage to another State Party to the Treaty or to its natural or juridical persons by such object or its component parts on the Earth, in air space or in outer space, including the moon and other celestial bodies." The proposed drafts of a treaty on liability (reproduced in Appendix E) also appear to refer to physical and related injury caused by a satellite or pieces thereof.

of the spacecraft or may the injury result from the use of information acquired by a satellite and used to the economic, political, or military injury of the subjacent country? With various kinds of space-borne sensors, it may be possible to obtain more detailed information about some of a nation's resources and economic and military activities than could be obtained by a slower and perhaps more expensive air or surface survey.[26] From a practical

point of view, it is impossible to draw a sharp line of distinction between information gathered for military purposes and information collected for commercial and economic reasons; consequently, the legal rules likely to be applied for both purposes will probably be similar, although possibly gathering military information will be more sensitive politically. Historically, even in time of war or serious international tension, it has generally been accepted that nations not at war legitimately obtain by radar, radio, photography, direct viewing, and other observational means any information possible about another country, as long as the curious nation did not trespass into the territory or defensive sea and air frontier of the observed state.[27] The Soviets have tended to es-

[26] The utility of satellites for such purposes has been demonstrated by photographs taken by Gemini IV and V astronauts, among others. See *New York Times,* Jan. 9, 1966; 218 *Scientific American* 54 (Jan. 1968). See also RAND publications: Buckheim, *New Space Handbook: Astronautics and its Applications,* chap. 21, at 217 ff. (1963); RAND Monographs, RM-2620-NASA, "Weather Information and Economic Decisions: A Preliminary Report"; RM-3412-NASA, "Automatic Pattern Recognition of Meteorological Satellite Cloud Photography"; RM-3536-NASA, "Some Satellite Orbits for the World Magnetic Survey"; RM-3986-NASA, "The Satellite Determination of High Altitude Prospects"; R-365, "Inquiry Into the Feasibility of Weather Reconnaissance from a Satellite Vehicle"; P-2193, "The Upper Atmosphere as Observed with Rockets and Satellites"; P-2580, "Report on a Symposium on Meteorological Rockets"; P-2623, "Aircraft Navigation by Satellite"; P-2635, "Review of Proceedings of the International Meteorological Satellites Workshop No. 13–12, 1961"; P-2762, "Selected Readings on Aerial Reconnaissance; a Reissue of a Collection of Papers from 1946 and 1948"; RM-3247-PR, "Some Implications of the Earth's Gravitational Field for the Internal Structure of the Earth"; Michael, *Proposed Studies on the Implications of Peaceful Space Activities for Human Affairs* 15, 79 (Brookings Institute, 1961), implications of a space-derived weather-predicting system. For some of the specific programs, see NASA Authorization for Fiscal Year 1967. *Hearings before the Senate Committee on Aeronautical and Space Sciences,* 89th Cong., 2d Sess., at 144–45 (1966). See also *A Survey of Space Applications* (NASA SP 142, Apr. 1967) "for the benefit of all mankind." Chap. 3 deals with earth resources and lists agricultural and forestry resources, geology and mineral resources, geography, cartography and cultural resources, hydrology and water resources, and oceanography as areas related to the earth's resources suitable for the application of space technology. Each of these subject headings has appended at the end of the discussion a bibliography of 15 or 20 articles and books giving more extensive coverage of the subject. Homer E. Newell & John E. Naugle (of NASA) in 6 *Astro. & Aero.* 78 (Feb. 1968): "Suitable for Space Applications: Geodesy, World Geodetic Reference System, Define Gravity Field; Communications and Navigation-Point-to-Point Intercontinental, Small Terminal Multiple Access, Navigation-Traffic Control, Data Relay, Earth-Lunar-Planetary, Voice Broadcast, Community Television, Television Broadcast; Meteorology, Observe Day and Night Cloud Cover, Continuous Observations, Define Atmospheric Structure for Long Range Forecast, Earth Resources Survey, Geography and Cartography, Geology and Minerology, Agriculture and Forestry, Water Resources and Pollution

Control, Oceanography." The listed items are examples of the use of space itself as a natural resource in communications and in collecting information about the earth.

R. J. Helberg, Ass't Division Manager, Space Division, The Boeing Co., in a paper, "Lunar Orbiter," given at Stanford University at a conference (mimeo., Aug. 16–18, 1967), gives a number of examples of intelligence gathered from space used for the economic benefit of mankind. Fault structures extending from Swedish iron ore deposits into Finland and Norway were identified from about 1,000 miles up and are being explored for iron deposits. Photographs taken from about 125 miles up have assisted in Australian oil exploration. Much of the equipment utilized for gathering information about the moon is equally useful for earth. Work has been divided into the field of agriculture/forestry resources, geology/hydrology (mineral and water resources), geography (cultural resources), and oceanography (marine resources). References to these programs are scattered throughout the NASA authorizations for Fiscal Year 1967 and *Hearings before the Senate Committee on Aeronautical and Space Sciences,* 89th Cong., 2d Sess. (1966). See pp. 338, 352, 378, 387 (meteorological satellite program), 376, 637, 659 (geodetic program), 377 (weather services), 290, 321 (navigational aids), 146, 154–57, 260, 636–37 and 660 (manned orbiting laboratory) as examples of the types of space activity aimed at acquiring information about the earth or providing improved facilities for activities on earth. See *Time,* Mar. 15, 1966, at 88 for an article noting the location of fresh water through the use of air-borne infrared sensors, and the plans to use EROS (Earth Resources Observation Satellites) for world-wide fresh-water studies by 1969. Christol, *supra* note 4, at 277, gives a brief discussion of observational activities. According to the *New York Times,* Dec. 29, 1965, disease patterns in timber can be detected from aerial or space reconnaissance as much as three years before difficulty can be observed from the ground. If extensive materials in this area are desired, see the AIAA International Aerospace Abstracts index and the NASA index of abstracts and articles, both of which over the past several years have listed a substantial number of papers given at the numerous technical conferences held throughout the world.

[27] In time of war or international tension, nations with the

pouse a right to complete secrecy of all events within their borders,[28] but since 1964 they have said comparatively little about this aspect of activity in space.[29] The changed emphasis possibly reflects a growing realization on the part of the Soviets that such a policy would severely restrict their own space activities and would be extremely difficult to implement without seriously hampering all space activity.[30] If the Russian claim to the

right of secrecy within its borders is being de facto modified as far as observation from space is concerned due to the advent of activities in space, additional relaxations may slowly follow but only as a part of a general easing of tensions between East and West and not because of activities in space.

There is no question that space vehicles passing above the earth at varying altitudes above the claimed sovereignty of the subjacent state have created difficult new factual situations to which rules of conduct of nations must be applied.[31]

No formal protests have been made even about satellites engaged in military reconnaissance, and it presently seems doubtful that protests will be made as a result of economic and commercial information-collection space activities. If this proves so, then international law appears to be developing in such a way as to allow the acquiring nation to utilize information gathered for its own economic and commercial purposes. Basic scientific information, when not in a security-suffused field, tends to be widely shared by most nations,[32] but there is no equivalent sharing of strategically or economically valuable information. In the absence of agreements requiring the sharing of commercial and economic information obtained through reconnaissance from space, it is doubtful that any legal obligation to share exists. The moral issue is entirely subjective. If this interpretation is correct, the space powers have in their possession a marked potential advantage in the exploitation of the natural resources of the earth and sea and in the planning

power to do so are prone to declare defensive zones from which foreign observers are excluded by force regardless of legal protests. McDougal *et al., supra* note 4, at 283 ff. discuss the potential for intelligence-gathering by spacecraft and note the activities likely to provoke controversy. Johnson, then General Counsel of NASA, noted that "The disturbing or threatening nature of an activity in outer space does not depend upon its being directly over the nation affected." NASA News Release, Aug. 4, 1962, of an address before the ABA Section on International and Comparative Law, San Francisco, Cal. See to the same effect, Mankiewicz, "The Regulation of Activities in Extra-Aeronautical Space, and Some Related Problems," 8 *McGill L.J.* 193–95 (1961–62). Christol, *supra* note 4, at 95–103, 271, 274–75, 277–95, 368 (1962) discusses the subject and notes the problems of an open versus a closed society in relation to the United States and Russia.

[28] Rusk, "U.S. Again Calls for Action on Drafting Disarmament Treaty," 47 *Dept. of State Bull.* 245 (1962); Rusk, "Basic Issues Underlying the Present Crisis," 47 *Dept. of State Bull.* 870 (1962). Kislov & Krylov, "State Sovereignty in Airspace," *Int'l Aff.* 34 (Moscow, Mar. 1956); *Legal Problems of Space Exploration, A Symposium*, Senate Document 26, 87th Cong., 1st Sess., 1037 (1961); Lissitzyn, "Some Legal Implications of the U-2 and RB-47 Incidents," 56 *Am. J. Int'l L.* 136 (1962); Wright, "Legal Aspects of the U-2 Incident," 54 *Am. J. Int'l L.* 836 (1960). Soviet drafts: "The use of artificial satellites for the collection of intelligence information in the territory of a foreign state is incompatible with the objectives of mankind in its conquest of outer space." U.N. Doc. A/AC.105/12, Annex 1, 2 (1963). "Space vehicles abroad on which devices have been discovered for the collection of intelligence information in the territory of another state shall not be returned." U.N. Doc. A/AC.105/12, Annex 1, 4 (1963). However, see the Agreement on the Rescue of Astronauts, and the Return of Objects Launched into Outer Space (both reproduced in Appendix E) which makes no reference to the limitation proposed by the Soviets.

[29] See *Staff of Senate Committee on Aeronautical and Space Sciences*, 89th Cong., 2d Sess., Space Treaty Proposals by the United States and USSR 12ff. (Comm. Print 1966); Soviet Draft which makes no specific reference to observational activities from space. U.N. Doc. A/6352 (June 16, 1966). The general treaty on space activities makes no reference to observational activities but has the general requirement of peaceful purposes.

[30] Photographs of clouds for weather forecasting purposes might include views of the surface of the earth. Magnetic surveys for navigational purposes might indicate the presence

of ore deposits. Infrared surveys intended to study volcanic activity might reveal concentrations of industry, etc. Even if the technical aspects of the problem of avoiding surveillance as a by-product of other activities could be surmounted, mutual inspection of facilities would be needed to insure compliance. "According to published reports, the Soviets developed their own reconnaissance satellite capacity early in 1964. Shortly after this, Soviet propaganda attacks on United States reconnaissance satellites ceased and the public concessions reflected in the most recent United Nations documents indicate that the Soviets no longer object to this activity." (Paper delivered by Morenoff, "Communications in Orbit: A Prognosis for World Peace," *Ninth Colloquium on the Law of Outer Space* 11 [Madrid, Oct. 1966].) Morenoff's book, *World Peace through Space Law* (1967), is devoted almost entirely to the problems of surveillance by satellite.

[31] Chap. 4 *supra* discusses the problem. See, as an example of the efforts to formulate rules, "Space Treaty Proposals by the U.S. and the USSR." U.N. Docs. A/AC.105/32 (June 17, 1966) and A/652 (June 16, 1966).

[32] See Frutkin, *International Cooperation in Space, passim* (1965).

of their own economies based on a knowledge of what is available and what is being done in other countries.[33] Good neighborliness, altruism, and the tradition of scientific cooperation, some of which has been organized internationally for many years, as in WMO and WHO, and some of which may be organized on the basis of satellite-acquired information, as, perhaps, with storm control in the future, may result in a sharing of information, particularly where it may assist in averting damage from natural forces such as hurricanes, volcanoes, tidal waves, and the like. Lacking formal international undertakings, it might be argued that a moral, rather than a legal, obligation exists to make such information generally available.[34]

In those situations where the acquired information related to the existence of natural resources on land masses, the observing state would ordinarily be unable to exploit them except by entering into an agreement with the observed state on mutually acceptable terms or by acquiring the territory. Despite the intimation to the contrary by McDougal, Lasswell, and Vlasic it would appear that the observing state would be subject to no enforceable obligation to share its knowledge in order that the nations could bargain on an equal basis, for the law concerning taking unfair economic advantage of one state by another remains at best embryonic.

As technology advances and economically valuable information is routinely available from activities in space, nonspace powers will almost certainly clamor for sharing. Based on precedent alone, the prospects are poor, particularly for the underdeveloped nations, but there are possibilities that the space powers will share their knowledge either for altruistic reasons or for reasons of international prestige. Nonspace powers may find it helpful to enter into advance cost-sharing agreements with one of the space powers, or consortiums may find it possible to develop cooperatively their own satellite systems for collecting economic information. Another pos-

sibility is to have information gathered by internationally controlled satellites, and then have it made available to all nations or to the specific nations concerned. These suggestions for internationalization require far more cooperative effort and sharing than states have thus far proven willing to undertake, but consideration of them before national interests become vested in the fruits of the new technology appears highly desirable.

The legal questions relating to injury and damages resulting from the modification of weather through the use of space-going capabilities to the detriment of a neighboring state are even less clear. This situation is not specifically covered by the treaties which have been approved to date, or by the most recent drafts of the proposed liability treaty. Consequently, it is suggested that customary rules of international law, probably influenced by the terms of the Treaty on Principles, could well be interpreted as imposing absolute liability, for intentional acts at least, providing that the major hurdle of proof of causation could be overcome. Other space activities resulting in physical damage to a foreign state would presumably follow this pattern. It might be noted that claims resulting from nuclear tests which involved airspace have been made and that damages have been reimbursed, but without admission of liability.[35] Liability under such circumstances would be consistent with concepts of fairness and with the provisions of the space treaties, but problems of evidence and proof present major difficulties beyond the answers technology can now provide with certainty.

A space power now has no legal obligation to collect and disseminate weather information, although the United States does so now; to position navigational satellites; to provide ocean current information; or to provide any general information of great value to other nations. If the space power does make such information available and it proves to be erroneous, is that power liable for losses suffered as a result of reliance on the information? Treaty provisions to date do not cover this situation, and the very practical aspects of it must be taken into consideration. In all probability, the nation using the information provided by the space power will be on notice that accuracy is limited by the technology and will proceed at his own risk. The space power might not make the information available if it thought there would be claims for errors beyond prevention by the technology. This reasoning leads to the conclusion that

---

[33] Obviously, this advantage will depend on the amount of worthwhile information collected and collectible only through activities in space. G. Bylinski, "From a High-flying Technology, a Fresh View of Earth," 87 *Fortune* 100 (June 1, 1968). (Remote sensors in planes and satellites are bringing a big new market into focus).

[34] If there is an obligation on the space power to make such information available, then the benefitting nation would surely be under a reciprocal obligation to participate in the cost of the space activity on a ratio based on relative use of the information tempered perhaps by ability to pay, as it is done in the United Nations.

[35] See chapter 6 *supra* for further discussion.

there should be no liability for information sharing in the absence of evidence of deliberate efforts to mislead.

Pollution

Pollution or contamination constitutes a special aspect of the conservation and, to a lesser extent the allocation, of resources of outer space. Present concern is partly practical but primarily scientific, although it is theoretically possible that pollution of earth from space might result in disaster to the human race.[36] Pollution from earth might also be disastrous to life on a celestial body, if any exists. Note that it is now considered doubtful that intelligent life exists anywhere else within the solar system than on earth.

Contamination may result from the introduction of living organisms, radioactive materials, fuel residues, or debris left in space or on celestial bodies as a consequence of man's activities in space. The dangers of pollution have received a considerable amount of attention from nongovernmental agencies[37] as well as from governments and the United Nations.[38]

As we have noted earlier, the United States West Ford Project, involving tiny orbiting copper dipoles for use in communications and other experiments, caused scientific concern which was heavily augmented by Soviet propaganda efforts and contributed to the adoption of a provision in a U.N. resolution calling for international consultations prior to space activities or experiments which could cause potentially harmful interference.[39] High-altitude nuclear tests by Russia and the United States caused controversy, not only because of the threat to peace but also because of the creation of radiation belts which interfered with all types of radio communications.[40] In fact, some months after the explosions the interference was sufficiently high to be of concern to radio astronomy.[41] The Nuclear Test Ban Treaty[42] should prevent further contamination of space from this kind of activity by Treaty members, but it will not prevent other contaminants from being introduced into space.[43]

The COSPAR Consultative Group has also concerned

---

[36] In a meeting with NASA, representatives of the Dept. of Agriculture warned that without precautions insects, diseases, and other plagues from outer space could conceivably be brought to earth on returning spacecraft and multiply in an atmosphere that could not control them. *New York Times,* Jan. 9, 1966, at 58.

[37] The Ad Hoc Committee on Contamination by Extraterrestrial Exploration (CETEX) was organized by the International Council of Scientific Unions (ICSU) at a meeting held in 1958 and ceased to exist after making a report in 1959. See John A. Johnson, "Pollution and Contamination in Space," *Law and Politics in Space* 39 (First McGill Conference on the Law of Outer Space, Law, and Politics in Space, Cohen ed. 1964). CETEX proposed general principles as follows: (1) freedom of action for experimentation and limitations of this freedom for compelling reasons; (2) the Committee on Space Research (COSPAR), established by ICSU in 1958, should be informed at the earliest possible date of any proposed experiments in outer space so that the committee could study such plans for any possible conflicts and make recommendations for minimizing any possible harmful effects; (3) experiments in space should be carried out only if capable of gathering useful scientific data.

The committee also recommended that no "soft" landings requiring the use of large quantities of gas be made on the moon prior to the completion of extensive studies of the nature and composition of the moon's atmosphere and that no nuclear explosions be set off near the surface of the moon or planets, and that great care be taken through sterilization to prevent the introduction of living organisms from earth to the other planets.

[38] The U.N. Ad Hoc Committee on Peaceful Uses of Outer

Space (June 1959) urged further study in the preservation of the existing environment of the moon and planets. U.N. Res. 1962 (XVIII), para. 6 (Dec. 13, 1963). U.N. Res. 1963 (XVIII), Art. II, para. 1 (Dec. 13, 1963). U.N. Doc. A/5785 para. B32 (Nov. 13, 1964). See "International Cooperation and Organization for Outer Space," *Staff Report for the Committee on Aeronautical and Space Sciences,* U.S. Senate, 89th Cong., 1st Sess., at 229, 231, 233, 238, 239, 248–49, 322, 351, 390–99, 401, 407 (1965) [hereinafter cited as *Staff Report*]. Most books on space law or space activities contain some references to pollution caused by space activities. See, e.g., McDougal *et al., supra* note 4, at 285, 531, 534–36, 539 note, 625–32, 652 note, 653, 655, 704, 734. Haley, *Space Law and Government* 142, 150, 269, 277, 281–93, 314 (1963).

[39] A/Res/1962 (XVIII), para. 6 (Dec. 24, 1963). See also Space Science Board, *U.S. Space Science Program: Report to COSPAR* 153–54 (1964).

[40] H. J. Taubenfeld, "Nuclear Testing and International Law," 16 *Sw. L.J.* 365, 397 (1962). Nuclear propulsion may also be a source of contamination; 2.2 lbs. of plutonium 238 on board a satellite as fuel was vaporized on reentry into the earth's atmosphere. *Washington Post,* May 24, 1964, at 8.

[41] Sir H. Massey, *Space Physics* 208 (1964).

[42] 14 *U.S.T.* 1313; *T.I.A.S.* 5433.

[43] See, e.g., the story in the *Washington Post,* Jan. 18, 1966, at 6, col. 6, relative to colored vapor clouds ejected by Nike Apache rockets at elevations up to 125 miles over Wallops Island, Va. The Soviet Union has been criticized for inadequate sterilization of the space vehicle claimed to have landed on Venus. See *Dallas News,* Mar. 6, 1966, at 18, col. 2. The Soviets say they have observed careful sterilization procedures utilizing a powerful disinfectant gas. *New York Times,* May 12, 1966, at 22, col. 3.

itself with the general question of contamination or pollution of outer space, the upper atmosphere, the moon, and planets.[44] It has proposed classifying effects in the upper atmosphere which seem equally appropriate for the lower reaches of outer space.[45] The classes of effect are:

1. Harmless, short-term, and observable localized changes.
2. Noninterfering, long-term, and world-wide changes that can be identified.
3. Changes causing extensive interference with experiments or other human activities.
4. Changes in the atmosphere that may change man's environment.

The first two classes are of limited concern and are characteristic of many space activities.[46] The third group is well represented by high-altitude nuclear explosions[47] which, in addition to interfering with communications, have also interfered with studies of upper atmospheric regions and for several hundred miles above the earth. The Consultative Group on Potentially Harmful Effects of Space reported that it found no indication of changes of the fourth variety. It may be too early to ascertain if this is correct, since changes resulting from nuclear explosions, for example, may be very subtle and slow in manifestation.

The COSPAR Consultative Group and others have also considered other phenomena such as the exchange rates of the upper atmosphere, the effects of rocket contamination, possible catalytic effects which might trigger chemical and photochemical processes, and radiation imbalances.[48] Such phenomena may also be classed as or involve potential pollutants. The possible consequences of nuclear power in space activities, high-flying supersonic aircraft, and the extensive use of completely disintegrating meteorological rockets have also been the subject of concern, but no detailed rules have been formulated by the states. A related problem is the increasing amount of useless debris continuing in orbit as a result of various activities in space.[49] Extensive consideration has been given to sterilization of spacecraft which might approach celestial bodies, such as the moon, Mars, or Venus, with a suggestion that there be only flyby missions until more extensive studies have been made[50] and general standards for sterilization of spacecraft have been suggested. The recommendations of the consultative group were adopted by COSPAR,[51] but have essentially moral rather than legal force.

The Treaty on Principles provides that space activities are to be conducted "with due regard to the corresponding interests of all other States . . . and conduct explora-

---

44 See *Staff Report, supra* note 38, at 391. At a 1964 session of COSPAR, a resolution was adopted to the effect that no spacecraft should be landed on Mars if there were more than one chance in 10,000 that it was carrying earthly micro-organisms that could contaminate. 2 *Astro. & Aero.* 185 (May 1964).

45 No attempt is made here to draw a line of demarcation between airspace and outer space. For a discussion of this problem see pp. 36–55.

46 Perhaps the continued transmission of radio signals by a space craft should be considered in this category. Vanguard I, launched on Mar. 17, 1968, continued transmitting until at least May 1964; 3 *Astro. & Aero.* 99 (Apr. 1965). Devices to shut off such signals should be included routinely.

47 See *Staff Report, supra* note 38, at 391.

48 There is no possibility of a soft landing on any celestial body without contaminating it with the exhaust of retro-rockets. See article, "Moon's Air Called Foul by Scientist," *Dallas News,* May 24, 1966, at A10, col. 4. G.J.F. MacDonald, U.C.L.A.,

planetary and space physicist, suggests supersonic aircraft and spacecraft may leave enough hydrocarbons in the atmosphere to result in a substantial increase of temperature of the earth. Getze, *Los Angeles Times,* Apr. 18, 1966, at 3.

49 Various speculative solutions have been proposed, such as using a manned space vehicle to "sweep the skies" by gathering in the derelicts of space. Considering the limited maneuverability of space vehicles in orbit, none of the proposals put forward is presently practical.

Lipson & Katzenbach, *Space Law,* note at 29 (1961) suggests that, "There is scientific opinion to the effect that a state with space capabilities could propel into orbit a large quantity of 'junk' (for example, radioactive waste), the effect of which would be to preclude much further scientific experimentation and increase the hazards of space travel and the possibility of surprise missile attack. Such a program would overload tracking facilities and could distort communications. Presumably an effort would be made to justify it as a measure of self-defense. Steps to limit the number of satellites that can be put into orbit and to furnish some assurances that each serves a useful function would be constructive contributions to the law of space . . . "

50 *Supra* note 44; *Staff Report, supra* note 38, at 397–98. See Opfell, Miller, Kovar, Natôn, & Allen, *Sterilization Handbook: Final Report* (Dynamic Science Corp. IN-65-24296, Aug. 1964) containing a substantial amount of technical material on methods of sterilization. Numerous press articles have been published: e.g., Lederberg, *Washington Post,* Aug. 7, 1966, comments that an American flag bootlegged aboard Surveyor I, which soft-landed on the moon, was a violation of international space policy. See also Haggerty, *J. Armed Forces,* Apr. 9, 1966, at 9 discussing some of the problems of sterilization.

51 *Staff Report, supra* note 38, at 391.

tion of them [celestial bodies] so as to avoid their harmful contamination and also adverse changes in the environment of the Earth resulting from the introduction of extraterrestrial matter and, where necessary, shall adopt appropriate measures for this purpose."[52] The article continues with provisions for international consultations where "potentially harmful interference with activities in the peaceful exploration and use" is feared. This language is very general and subject to varied interpretations, but it is surely not much less definite than the "general welfare" clause of the United States Constitution.[53] It is interesting to note that the provisions for consultation relate to "interference . . . in the peaceful exploration and use of outer space" but do not technically apply to potential contamination of the earth from extraterrestrial matter.[54] If the state engaging in an activity in space does not initiate consultations, any other state party to the treaty "which has reason to believe that an activity or experiment . . . would cause potentially harmful interference . . . may request consultation concerning the activity or experiment." This language is a compromise, for the Soviets had wished to make consultation mandatory prior to initiation of a space activity, whereas the United States had feared that a mandatory provision might be used as a veto.

The numerous conventions relating to pollution of the sea[55] give useful examples of the types of treaties which

can be negotiated if developing technology provides the need. It would be useful to keep under continuing consideration the kinds of arrangements which will be needed as technology advances. The policy suggested in the U.N. resolutions and discussions and in the Treaty on Principles seems to require a showing that a particular activity will be harmful before it is appropriate to bar it. This is clearly the situation relative to the high seas where disparate theories of scientists are seldom accepted without practical proof of harm. In the 1960s, the necessity for extensive modification of the rules relating to pollution of the seas demonstrates that advancing technology and increasing and changing use will probably require frequent updating of rules relative to contamination of space.

Natural Resources: Summary

The allocation, control, conservation, and protection of resources and the prevention of pollution are the subject of general regulation by the terms of treaties and the recommendations of the United Nations resolutions. These controls are a beginning and may be as specific as can be devised until additional technical knowledge is acquired, and, with luck and good will on the part of the space powers, they should provide a substantial amount of protection to earth from extraterrestrial contamination and should also prevent space and celestial bodies from becoming seriously contaminated with living organisms from earth. The Nuclear Test Ban Treaty, which is specific in its prohibitions, gives some protection against nuclear contamination of earth, airspace, space, and celestial bodies, but a number of nations including France, Communist China, and Cuba are not parties to that agreement. As technology progresses and additional knowledge is acquired, it can be hoped that self-interest of nations will be persuasive enough to cause them to agree on additional details of regulations and possibly of enforcement.

The space powers have unilaterally, by treaty and by United Nations resolution, indicated their willingness and intent to conduct their activities in space in such a manner as to avoid interference with others seeking to investigate and possibly to exploit the resources of space and to utilize space in exploiting the resources of earth. Continuing and determined efforts must be made to negotiate detailed agreements as rapidly as the problems and satisfactory solutions can be identified, but it would be injudicious to negotiate additional details of agreements based only on surmise instead of facts. It must

---

[52] Art. IX, U.N. Res. 1962 (XVIII) (Dec. 13, 1965) contains almost identical language. The resolution is, of course, only a recommendation, whereas the treaty is binding on the parties to it.

[53] Art. I, sec. 8, "The Congress shall have power to levy and collect taxes, duties, imposts, and excises to pay the debts and provide for the common defense and general welfare of the United States."

[54] It is probably not safe to assume that this distinction represents a carefully considered opinion that dangers on earth from extraterrestrial contamination are nonexistent, but as evidence mounts against the probability of extraterrestrial life in the solar system, the danger of contamination of earth seems less.

[55] See the collection of treaties contained in *Treaties and Other International Agreements Containing Provisions on Commercial Fisheries, Marine Resources, Sport Fisheries, and Wildlife to Which the United States Is Party*, prepared for the use of the Senate Committee on Commerce, 89th Cong., 1st Sess. (Comm. Print, Jan. 1965) by the Legislative Reference Service, the Library of Congress. See particularly at 327, Amendments of the International Convention for the Prevention of Pollution of the Sea by Oil, 1954; adopted at London Apr. 11, 1962, 88th Cong., 1st Sess., Senate Exec. Comm., for detailed rules relating to the discharge of oily substances at sea.

be kept in mind that international law relating to space is but one part of international law, and it is not likely that a space law regime substantially at variance from other areas of international law will gain wide acceptance among nations.

Nations will almost certainly continue to acquire information about all areas of the earth by all means at their disposal, including observation from satellites. Nonspace powers are at a substantial disadvantage, but no agreement limiting the right of information acquisition could be enforced now except by placing all space activities under the control of an international organization or by granting unlimited rights of inspection at all installations having to do with space activities. Neither is probable until a world full of distrustful nations is ready to accept a form of world government, a prospect that does not seem the least bit imminent.

Conclusions

This study of that part of public international law which relates to the activities of man in space shows that even in areas where the major space powers might be expected to disagree, there has been a worthwhile and even rapid development of a law specifically directed to new problems and to old problems carried over into this new milieu. Moreover, it is now the consensus that traditional international law applies, in all appropriate contexts, to man's activities in space. Questions involving economic, political and strategic interests of the United States, the Soviet Union, and other nations, such as the extent of air space, the right of surveillance of earth from space, and the use and sharing of radio frequencies, remain unresolved and it is unlikely that comprehensive and detailed solutions of these most difficult issues will be forthcoming in the near future. Yet, there are already numerous examples of fruitful cooperation in lawmaking and in functional cooperation. Future arrangements may well be along such functional lines as well as with "spatial" concepts of less importance. The fact that control over superjacent outer space would give little additional security protection to a subjacent state provides a strong practical argument in favor of agreements and controls of this functional type. Practical problems of identifying and protecting "national" blocks of space add to the attractiveness of functional controls and guidelines.

The answers to such questions as the legal status of space ownership and control of the celestial bodies and space craft, and of the duties owed to astronauts have been developed along broad policy lines which leave many more details to be resolved when more adequate knowledge is acquired and when and if specific problems arise. Generally speaking, nations have insisted on retention of control and jurisdiction over their own space vehicles and astronauts. Other states have acquiesced and have also accepted an affimative duty to give appropriate assistance in the event of difficulties.

Of substantial importance is the now widely accepted rule that no state may require sovereignty over a celestial body or block of space beyond its superjacent air space by any means whatever. This is, to date, a self-policed, self-denying rule. No international machinery for regulation or control exists. Under this present regime, nations have retained almost total control over their own space activities and are entitled to any benefits which may arise from their exploitation of resources of space and celestial bodies. While numerous suggestions have been made by writers and even some government spokesmen that the exploration and exploitation of space and celestial bodies should be by or under the control of the United Nations or some other international institution functioning for the benefit of all nations, there is little basis to believe that nations having the ability to explore and exploit space and celestial bodies are now or will soon be prepared to subject their activities to international control.

The criteria for a "just" allocation of and control over activities in space and of resources of space and the celestial bodies, including the use of space for communications vehicles and for the orbiting and maneuvering of space vehicles of all varieties for all purposes, have to date been established on the basis of political policy considerations as seen by the space powers and other nations. This pattern seems likely to persist. In the event that broad international agreement on the appropriate criteria can eventually be reached, international institutions, existing or new, can readily be devised to interpret and apply the criteria for the allocation and control of activities in space and resources of space on agreed standards. Adequate technological information about the nature, extent, and exploitability of these resources is just beginning to become available and may not be fully developed for many years. Even such comparatively advanced utilizations of space, as for communications and information gathering about the earth, are as yet technological infants. The international institutions established to administer commercial communications utilizing space are not yet stabilized and the agreements which established Intelsat, the international telecommunications consortium, are already being renegotiated and will probably require review every few years if the international managerial structure is to be kept responsive to economic, political, and technological conditions. The overall effects of the reported Soviet proposal to form an international communications consortium on the basis of one state, one vote, for example, cannot now be determined.

There do not exist supranational international institutions with authority to control any of man's activities in space, but the United Nations, the International Telecommunications Union, and other similar organizations have proven valuable and effective as forums for the exchange of ideas and for the development of understanding. Numerous General Assembly resolutions and the negotiation within the halls of the U.N. of formal treaties enunciating general and specific rules relating to activities of man in space give witness to this fact. The extent to which either resolutions or treaties may be legally binding on non-members of the United Nations and/or non-parties to treaties is a facet of the overall interpretation and application of international law and depends in part on the extent to which the resolution or treaty represents a restatement of customary international law. These problems are no different at base than

they are for other critical areas of international concern in such fields as the law of war, disarmament, fisheries, or air traffic control and regulation.

Years ago at least a few authors and government spokesmen suggested, perhaps for dramatic emphasis, that an international legal vacuum existed with respect to man's activities in outer space. As this study makes clear, there has never been a legal vacuum; international law as developed to date is no less applicable to the activities of states in outer space and on the celestial bodies than to their actions in more familiar spheres.

This existing regime has been increased in the space age by numerous United Nations resolutions relating to activities in space. In addition, there are presently in force the 1967 General Treaty of Principles Governing the Activities of States in the Exploration and Use of Outer Space, including the Moon and other Celestial Bodies; the 1963 Treaty Banning Nuclear Weapon Tests in the Atmosphere, in Outer Space, and Underwater; the Agreement Establishing Interim Arrangements for a Global Commercial Communications Satellite System and the two subordinate agreements relating to satellite communications. In 1968, an Agreement on the Rescue of Astronauts, the Return of Astronauts, and the Return of Objects Launched into Outer Space was signed by all the major space powers and most other nations. There are also perhaps two hundred minor bilateral agreements to which the United States is a party, relating to a great variety of cooperative activities in the exploration of space. There are treaties for Western European and for Communist bloc cooperative activities. Even on the question of liability, where a specific Treaty for Liability for Damages Caused by Objects Launched into Outer Space is in the draft stage at the moment of this writing, the Treaty on Principles contains as part of its general terms provisions for absolute state liability for all activities in space. Peripherally, it should also be noted that all major states, including the United States and the Soviet Union, and apparently many smaller states have enacted legislation governing their domestic and international space activities. If as the French are fond of pointing out *c'est le premier pas qui coûte,* the space powers, with most nations joining, have already taken steps forward, indeed several lengthy strides, toward the mutual accommodation of their claims to the use of outer space.

In time there will probably be a need to develop international institutions to complement the self-policed, self-denying approach of present treaties and U.N. resolutions to ownership and control over space resources and to conflicts over those resources. Negotiation of detailed agreements concerning most space activities will become necessary as adequate technical knowledge becomes available in order to assure the peaceful, orderly exploration and utilization of space. Detailed regulations remain to be worked out which will be consistent with the broad general rules of already developed international law and the patterns already accepted for outer space activities. Revisions will be required to keep the law abreast of technological advances and major political power changes, just as in all other fields.

Man's ability to use outer space is of recent origin and the valuable activities and resources which may lie there are still unallocated among the states. Clearly, to the extent that space activities and resources prove politically, strategically, and economically important, a great challenge exists to develop political policy strategies to govern and regulate these new capabilities in order to minimize the conflicts between nations which may arise. The techniques adopted may even provide relevant precedent and experience for the settlement of similar types of distributive disputes arising from man's activities in the air, on the surface of the earth, and on and under the surface of the seas. To recall President Kennedy's words, space must be "a sea of peace" and not a "new terrifying theater of war." If we achieve this mission, space may also become an important classroom for peaceful international conflict adjustment in other theaters of contest, contributing significant precedent, experience, and good will to the larger task.

Appendixes

United States Military Space Programs

The names used are informal; the Department of Defense now uses code numbers.

Despite its length, this listing is indicative, rather than complete.

Advanced Research Projects Agency (ARPA)

BAMBI—An approach to the development of a ballistic-missile interception system using satellite-based spacecraft to intercept and destroy enemy missiles during the boost phase of flight.

ARENTS-ARPA—Environmental test satellite to investigate space conditions in 22,000-mile-high orbits, where it might be advantageous to place communications and other satellites.

VELA—A research and development project aimed at devising a satellite system for detecting nuclear explosions in space.

PRESS—Pacific Range Electromagnetic Signature Study for an advanced radar system to detect approaching ICBM warheads.

RBS—Random Barrage System. A study of the feasibility of placing armed satellites into random orbits as a defensive measure against the ICBM.

Army

SECOR—Sequential Collation of Range. Project to produce a satellite device for geodetic measurements of high accuracy.

NIKE-ZEUS—An antimissile missile designed to destroy ICBM warheads in the terminal phase of flight.

LAMP—Lunar Analysis and Mapping Program. A lunar topographical map produced by using photographs obtained by lunar probes in the scientific space program.

Navy

TRANSIT—A navigational system designed to enable Polaris submarines and other craft to fix their positions with great accuracy, regardless of weather.

YO-YO—Study for a photoreconnaissance satellite to be launched at sea, to make one orbit, and to be recovered.

Department of Defense (Joint Projects)

COMMUNICATIONS SYSTEMS—the Air Force is responsible for the development, production, and launch of these systems, whereas the Army is to develop the required ground communications systems, and the Navy to provide ship-borne communications stations.

ANNA (joint with NASA)—A geodetic satellite for intercontinental surveying.

SPADATS, SPASUR, AND BMEWS—Surveillance of space is undertaken through the Air Force-operated Space Detection and Tracking System (SPADATS) and the Navy-operated Space Surveillance Facility (SPA-SUR). The United States maintains a log to help determine the paths of known satellites. These systems are tied to the Ballistic Missile Early Warning System (BMEWS), which uses radar to detect and determine the orbits of space objects over the United States at altitudes of up to 1,000 miles. The surveillance network is being extended to the moon by an intensive examination of space between the earth and the moon or any other natural satellites astronomers may have missed, thus inventorying everything in orbit in earth-moon space so the surveillance system can tell when something is added.

Air Force

AEROSPACE PLANE (ASP)—Research program to develop a manned spacecraft able to take off and land like an aircraft.

DISCOVERER—Designed to probe space conditions, develop means of recovering satellite payloads, and provide a test-bed for satellite research programs such as Midas and Samos.

X-20 (DYNA-SOAR)—Research and development effort to produce a manned orbital "boost-glide" spacecraft with wings. A primary aim is to develop controlled reentry as opposed to the Project Mercury ballistic-type return and to investigate the feasibility of a spacecraft for orbital reconnaissance and defense and offense. Now cancelled.

ORION—Engineering study for a space booster launched by a series of atomic explosions.

SAINT—Satellite Inspector. Research and development program for a spacecraft to inspect unidentified satellites. The name was slightly altered in view of protests by religious groups.

MIDAS—Missile Defense Alarm System of early-warning satellites equipped with infrared sensors to detect ICBM launches.

SAMOS—Surveillance and Missile Observation Satellite. Polar-orbiting satellite equipped with high-resolution cameras.

ALOMAR—Space Logistics, Maintenance, and Rescue craft. Such a vehicle would be needed to support military space operations.

GLOBAL SURVEILLANCE SYSTEM—A study for a manned reconnaissance-strike spacecraft.

ORBITAL WEAPONS SYSTEM—Studies of orbital bombing systems. Note that the U.S. is now pledged not to place weapons of mass destruction in orbit.

B

Jurisdiction of the United States over "Crimes" and Certain Other Acts in Outer Space*

We have noted in chapter 3 that the Uniform Code of Military Justice (10 U.S.C., chap. 47 [secs. 801–940], 70 A. Stat. 37 ff.) is believed to be clearly applicable to all "members of a regular component of the armed forces" (Art. 2, 10 U.S.C. sec. 802) "in all places" (Art. 5, 10 U.S.C. sec. 805). This would appear to cover all usual "crimes" in outer space, in a spacecraft, or on a celestial body if perpetrated by a member of the United States armed forces. Whatever the status of U.S. military personnel, a series of Supreme Court decisions has made it clear that civilians, wherever they may be, cannot, at least in peacetime, constitutionally be subjected to United States military court-martial so as to deprive them of the right to trial by jury and other procedural rights guaranteed by the Constitution.[1] Their

effect has been largely to nullify the applicability of the Uniform Code to civilians at least for important crimes. Since these cases involved civilians actually employed by or accompanying as dependents United States military forces at United States bases abroad, the situation of United States civilians who are neither employed by, accompanying, nor having any dependent relation with the military, would be even stronger. Whereas the first group of NASA astronauts was selected from military personnel, this is no longer entirely the case.

Another, more general, approach—at least to criminal activities—over which Congress has desired to assert control is used for acts falling within what is called the "special maritime and territorial jurisdiction of the United States."[2] The areas involved include American ships in interstate state or foreign waters, or on the high seas; federal lands within the several states; guano islands appertaining to the United States; and, most recently, American aircraft over interstate or foreign waters, or over the high seas. And, of course, Congress regularly legislates for territories and possessions of the United States, over which the United States claims sovereignty, and for such interesting hybrids as the Trust Territories

---

* This appendix owes much to the study by Richard Bilder, "Control of Criminal Conduct in Antarctica," 52 *Va. L. Rev.* 231 ff. (1966). See also Haughley, "Criminal Responsibility in Outer Space," in *Proceedings of the Conference on Space Science and Space Law,* at 146 ff. (Schwartz ed. 1964).

[1] See Reid v. Covert, 354 U.S. 1 (1957) (capital offense by civilian dependent); Kinsella v. Singleton, 361 U.S. 234 (1960) (other capital offense by dependent); Grisham v. Hagan, 361 U.S. 278 (1960) (capital offense by civilian employee); McElroy v. Guagliardo, 361 U.S. 281 (1960) (other than capital offense by employee); Toth v. Quarles 350 U.S. 11 (1955) (offense while in service by since-discharged ex-serviceman). While these cases have involved only Articles 2(11) and 3(a), the reasoning would probably apply to Art. 2(12) as well. The decisions do not reach "petty offenses," although it is understood that the armed services have refrained from trying civilians for

such offenses. See articles in 13 *Stan. L. Rev.* (May 1961); 46 *Va. L. Rev.* 576 (Apr. 1960); 28 *Geo. Wash. L. Rev.* 913 (June 1960); 49 *Geo. L.J.* 139 (Fall 1960); 1960 *Duke L.J.* (Summer 1960); 71 *Harv. L. Rev.* 712 (1957); Falk, 32 *Temp. L.Q.* 295 (Spring 1959).

[2] See 18 U.S.C. sec. 7, June 25, 1948, 62 Stat. 685.

of the Pacific over which the United States exercises complete control, but with no claim of sovereignty at all.[3]

After defining the "special maritime and territorial jurisdiction of the United States," Title 18 in other sections provides that certain types of conduct, when committed within this "special jurisdiction," constitute federal crimes. The proscribed conduct includes arson, assault, maiming, embezzlement, theft, receiving stolen property, false pretenses, murder, manslaughter, attempts to commit murder or manslaughter, malicious mischief, rape, and robbery.[4] Other federal statutes vest the United States District Courts with jurisdiction over offenses against the United States,[5] and provide that the trial of all offenses begun or committed upon the high seas, or elsewhere, out of the jurisdiction of any particular state or district shall be in the district where the offender is arrested or first brought.[6]

This is not to say that outer space itself or the celestial bodies are within this special jurisdiction nor that spacecraft are within the terms "vessel" or "aircraft" used in the statute. Moreover, the courts have construed Title 18, sec. 7, strictly. As enacted in 1948, the section did not mention aircraft. In 1950, a case arose involving an assault by a passenger on other passengers and members of the crew of a United States flag aircraft which was in

flight over the Atlantic Ocean between San Juan, Puerto Rico, and New York. In *United States v. Cordova,*[7] the New York Federal District Court dismissed the case for want of jurisdiction. Although finding that the accused had in fact committed the assault, the court held that the offense was neither committed on board an American "vessel" nor on the "high seas" within the meaning of the statute predecessor to 18 U.S.C. sec. 7, and that there was consequently no federal court jurisdiction to punish the act.[8] This decision led directly to a 1952 amendment of 18 U.S.C. sec. 7 adding a new paragraph (5) specifically including within the special jurisdiction aircraft in flight over the high seas.[9] Congress could and may, in time, extend this special jurisdiction.

To cover flights in outer space, Congress might well vest plenary authority in the Executive over activities on the moon and the celestial bodies similar to authority vested in the President over the trust territories and Palmyra, Midway, and Wake Island. This would permit, in the name of the President, formulation of regulations governing both civil and criminal acts, while regulations would probably be effective upon publication in the *Federal Register.* No claim to sovereignty would be involved.

There are, in addition, already numerous federal criminal statutes apparently designed to deal with certain activities wherever conducted. These include statutes punishing such conduct as treason, espionage, fraud against the government, draft and income tax evasion, counterfeiting and perjury, even when committed extraterritorially.[10] These presumably are

---

[3] Art. IV, cl. 2, of the Constitution empowers Congress "to make all needful rules and regulations respecting the territory or other property belonging to the United States." This power applies where the U.S. has exclusive jurisdiction. Vermilya-Brown v. Coward, *supra* at 381. For legislation as to Trust Territories of the Pacific, see 48 U.S.C. 1681 and Executive Orders 9875, 10265, 10408 and 10470. For Guam, see 38 U.S.C. 1421, Pugh v. U.S. 212 F. 2d 761 (1954). Hatchett v. Government of Guam, 212 F. 2d 767 (1954), American Pacific Dairy Products v. Siciliano 235 F. 2d 74 (1956). For the guano islands, see 48 U.S.C. 1411–19; 1 Moore, *International Law,* secs. 112–15 (1906); 1 Hackworth *Digest of International Law,* sec. 177 (1940), Jones v. U.S., 137 U.S. 202 (1890), Smith v. U.S., 137 U.S. 224, Biddle v. U.S., 156 F. 759 (1907). For Canton and Enderbury Islands, see 1 Hackworth 509–10 (1940). O.L. 72 May 24, 1949 (63 Stat. 89) extends the jurisdiction of the District Court of Hawaii to Canton and Enderbury with a proviso that such extension shall not be construed as prejudicial to U.K. claims to the islands. They are a present U.S.–U.K. condominium. P.L. 553 of June 15, 1950 (64 Stat. 2[7]) extends to Canton and Enderbury the laws of the U.S. relating to acts or offenses consummated or committed on the high seas on board a vessel belonging to the U.S.

[4] The Code references are respectively 18 U.S.C. sec. 81, 113, 114, 661, 662, 1025, 1111(b), 1113, 1363, 2031, and 2111.

[5] 18 U.S.C. sec. 3231.

[6] 18 U.S.C. sec. 3238.

[7] 89 F. Supp. 298 (E.D.N.Y. 1950).

[8] For other cases of narrow construction, see U.S. v. Wittberger, 5 Wheat. 76 (1820), and U.S. v. Tully, 140 Fed. 899 (C.C.D. Montana) (1905).

[9] Act of July 12, 1952, 66 Stat. 589. For Reports, see Sen. Report No. 1155 and H.R. No. 2257 (82d Cong., 2d Sess. 1952); U.S. Code Cong. & Admin. News, 82d Cong., 2d Sess. 1052 p. 2101. See also 80th Cong., H. Rep. No. 304. On the general problem of crimes on board aircraft, see also Hilbert, "Jurisdiction in High Seas Criminal Cases," 18 *J. Air L. & Comm.* 427 (Autumn 1951); 19 *J. Air L. & Comm.* 25 (Winter 1952); articles in 36 *Cornell L.Q.* 374 (Winter 1951); 99 *U. Pa. L. Rev.* 1083 (Oct. 1961); 41 *Cornell L.Q.* 243 (1956); 26 *J. Air L. & Commerce* 285 (1959); 5 *Int'l & Comp. L.Q.* 601 (1956); Braun, "Jurisdiction of U.S. Courts Over Crimes in Aircraft," 16 *Stan. L. Rev.* 45 (Dec. 1962). And see for U.K. experience: Regina v. Martin (1956) 2 All E. R. 86.

[10] See, e.g., 18 U.S.C. 2381 (treason "within the United States or elsewhere"); 18 U.S.C. 953 (private correspondence with foreign governments by any citizen "wherever he may be");

not near-run problems with respect to outer space activities.

Certain obvious problems arise. If one behaves obnoxiously in outer space, but no specific criminal law is applicable, can he be "arrested" or detained? Is this false arrest or assault? Is there a deprivation of liberty without due process of law?[11] There is available, of course, the analogy of the ship's captain's obligation to restrain one who endangers the ship or life on board, yet this does not resolve all the questions.

This leads to the further questions, too, of what law governs more ordinary "transactions," tortious and contractual, in areas not under the jurisdiction of the United States. In traditional practice, for example, courts in the United States normally apply the law of the place where a tort occurs but, where that place has no law, they apply the law of the forum.[12] Speculation on these points seems of little point here for two reasons: their relative remoteness from short-run reality and their excellent treatment in depth in the general coverage of tort and contract problems in McDougal, Lasswell, and Vlasic, *Law and Public Order in Space* (1963).

It can also be noted that, to the extent that U.S. law covers the actions of U.S. citizens and nationals in remote areas, it covers nonprivileged foreign nationals as well. For example, foreign nationals who are members of the U.S. armed forces or who commit acts within the special maritime and territorial jurisdiction appear to be covered by U.S. law.[13] They would, equally, benefit from limitations imposed by the Constitution, e.g., as civilians accompanying the armed forces. Of course, political considerations might make the United States reluctant to act against a foreign national even if the right to act was asserted. Furthermore, just as the Antarctic Treaty of 1959 provides in Article 8:

In order to facilitate the exercise of their functions under the present treaty, and without prejudice to the respective positions of the contracting parties relating to jurisdiction over all other persons in Antarctica, observers . . . and scientific personnel exchanged under . . . the treaty, and members of the staffs accompanying any such persons, shall be subject only to the jurisdiction of the contracting party of which they are nationals in respect of all acts or omissions occuring while they are in Antarctica for the purpose of exercising their functions.

The nations now engaged in outer space activities have indicated that the country of nationality would normally have sole jurisdiction over its astronauts.

It seems clear that, if the matter arose, the United States would be unwilling to admit that any U.S. citizen or national was normally subject to the jurisdiction of *another* state for acts taking place in outer space. The nationality principle would be inapplicable on its face; the United States would deny any other state's claim based on "territory" for reasons developed in the text. As was said at the hearings on the Antarctic Treaty: "By virtue of recognizing that there is no sovereignty over Antarctica we retain jurisdiction over our own citizens and would deny the right of other claimants to try that citizen."[14] A substitution of the term "outer space" for "Antarctica" would be appropriate in this context.

Absent a treaty or rule of customary law, jurisdiction might rest in a foreign state if an American's act occurred in a foreign craft or possibly at a foreign base, or was directly detrimental to a foreign state's important interests (the "protective" principle), or constituted a crime against all mankind (piracy, or the like). These problems are also noted in the text and do not relate uniquely to the United States. And to some of these questions, the space treaty, signed in January, 1967, begins to provide some answers for parties in providing, as did Resolution 1962 (XVIII), Article 8, that: "A State party to the treaty on whose registry an object launched into outer space is carried shall retain jurisdiction and control over such object, and over any personnel thereof, while in outer space or on a celestial body."[15] Moreover, Article

---

and secs. 911 and 2001 of the Internal Revenue Code. Under the rule of U.S. v. Bowman, 260 U.S. 94 (1922), a number of provisions of the Criminal Code would probably be applicable to conduct abroad which affects important U.S. government interests, e.g., bribery and graft of government officers and officials (18 U.S.C. 201–223), offenses involving coins and currency (18 U.S.C. 331–32 and 336), and conspiracy to defraud the U.S. (18 U.S.C. 371–72).

[11] In Reid v. Covert, *supra* note 1, at 4, the Supreme Court said that "at the beginning we reject the idea that when the United States acts against citizens abroad it can do so free of the Bill of Rights."

[12] See Goodrich, *Conflict of Laws* sec. 92 (1964); Cuba R.R. v. Crosby, 222 U.S. 473, 478 (1912).

[13] See, e.g., Restatement of the For. Rel. Law of the U.S., sec. 31(b). Note the case of Regina v. Anderson [1868] Cox, Crim. Cases 198 (U.K.). See also 13 *Stan. L.R.* 155 (Dec. 1960); 45 *Cal. L. Rev.* 199 (May 1957).

[14] Statement by Phleger, head of the U.S. Delegation, *Hearings on the Antarctica Treaty* at 62 (1959). The President has a statutory duty to take action to protect Americans imprisoned or detained abroad (22 U.S.C. 1732).

[15] Resolution 1962 (XVIII) provides:
"7. The State on whose registry an object launched into outer space is carried shall retain jurisdiction and control

5 provides in part that astronauts who have made a forced landing shall "be safely and promptly returned to the State of registry of their space vehicle." Under the treaty, it is thus the "flag" state (the state of registry) which is of prime importance for jurisdiction, not the state of the astronaut's nationality, although for the foreseeable future these are apt to be identical. Spacecraft manned by crews of mixed nationalities are nevertheless within the realm of possibility.[16] There is further discussion of some of these issues of jurisdiction in Appendix D.

---

over such object, *and any personnel thereon,* while in outer space." [italics added]

"9. States shall regard astronauts as envoys of mankind in outer space, and shall render to them all possible assistance in the event of accident, distress, or emergency landing on the territory of a foreign State or on the high seas. Astronauts who make such a landing shall be safely and promptly returned *to the State of registry of their space vehicle."* [italics added]

[16] Compare the recent Crimes Aboard Aircraft Convention.

C Domestic Use of Communications Satellites

Domestic aspects of communications utilizing satellites (see chap. 5) are and will long continue to be matters of substantial controversy and concern. The Communications Satellite Corporation (ComSat) has been established as a privately owned juridical entity, but it is so closely controlled and regulated as to be a quasi-private or quasi-public corporation.[1]

ComSat has three closely related areas of activity:[2] first, as a domestic communications carrier; second, as the United States participant in Intelsat, the International Telecommunications Satellite Consortium for global communications by satellite; and third, as the manager of Intelsat. The distinctions between these functions have not always been kept in mind by the Federal Communications Commission (FCC) and other agencies of the government with the result that the FCC may have at times exercised regulatory or adjudicatory authority over what would appear to have been Intelsat business.[3] This problem is discussed briefly in chapter 5.

---

[1] Communications Satellite Act of 1962 (ComSat Act) P.L. 87–624, 87th Cong. 2d. Sess., approved Aug. 31, 1962; 47 N.S.C. 701–44 (1962).

[2] Established by the Agreement Establishing Interim Arrangements for a Global Commerical Communications Satellite System (Interim Agreement) T.I.A.S. 5646. The triple role is the source of many of the difficulties as it hardly is possible to distinguish technically and legally where one rule ends and another begins. ComSat as a domestic communications carrier is fully subject to the laws and regulations of the United States. It fulfills a quasi-governmental function as the U.S. designed entity in Intelsat and as such is subject to U.S. laws and regulations in discharging its heavy responsibility in the international field. As manager of Intelsat, it is responsible to its members. See 32 *Telecommunications Reports* 28, 29, 30 (June 20, 1966) [hereinafter cited as *T.R.*] for an account of a meeting of the Inst. of Elect. Eng. in Philadephia, Pa., June 15–17, 1966, during which these subjects were discussed. The progress made in a new field of technology and the amount of cooperation achieved is very great, but the way has not been nor will it be smooth in the future.

[3] The confusion which exists in allocation and assignment of frequencies domestically is set forth in some detail in Metzger & Burrus, "Radio Frequency Allocation in the Public Interest: Federal Government and Civilian Use," 4 *Duquesne L. Rev.* 1 (1965–66). The article emphasizes the division of responsibility between the FCC and DTM-IRAC and the subservience of the FCC: "[T]he present system of dual control is deficient in its failure to afford the means for any coherent policy planning with respect to allocation needs and usages in the future." The President's Communications Policy Board, *Telecommunications, a Program for Progress,* note 4, at 46–50 (1951) said among other things: "The present telecommunications legislation and organization have failed to produce adequate direction, leadership, administration, and control and have fostered dissension between the federal government and industry. Many of these shortcomings could have been mitigated if not avoided." Few independent writers have praise for the existing format of U.S. government controls and regulations for domestic and international telecommunications. While not in quite this category, the FCC "authorized" ComSat to make available to Canada units of satellite utilization via the Andover, Me., earth station. "Authorization" implies the right to "deny," a situation almost certain to encourage Canada to develop its own earth stations even if technologically not needed. 33 *T.R.* 14 (Jan. 23, 1967).

ComSat was incorporated and capitalized at $200 million on the assumption that the cost of establishing a global communications satellite system could be considerably greater than has thus far proven to be the case.[4]

It was also not known to what extent other nations would participate in the costs of developing the Intelsat system and if they would provide their own earth stations. About sixty nations have joined Intelsat, and as a result, the United States ComSat now has only slightly more than a half-interest in Intelsat and may have difficulty retaining even this amount of ownership after the new negotiations which are supposed to be completed by the end of 1970 in accordance with the terms of the Interim Arrangement (see pp. 264–73). The United States will most certainly continue to be the heaviest single user of Intelsat facilities even without including domestic use. Other participating nations have provided or indicate an intent to provide their own earth station facilities, either individually or in groups.[5] These happy developments in international cooperation have reduced the investment required of ComSat.

Also, at the time it was incorporated and capitalized, it was thought that ComSat might furnish the United States Department of Defense all its communications satellite requirements, but a separate military system has been established and some supplemental circuits have been procured through conventional communications carriers. The military system is orbiting satellites at slightly less than 21,000 miles high, which makes the satellites appear to drift slowly eastward. In mid-1967 there were about twenty satellites in this system and more may possibly be added.[6] The military system has

---

See also "Electromagnetic Spectrum Utilization: The Silent Crisis," *A Report on Telecommunication Science and the Federal Government* by the *Telecommunication Science Panel of the Commerce Technical Advisory Board,* U.S. Dept. of Commerce, *passim* (Oct. 1966).

[4] See 2 *International Legal Materials* 395 (Mar. 1963) for ComSat's Articles of Incorporation dated Feb. 1, 1963. ComSat's prospectus of June 3, 1964, for sale of stock indicates it had not then been finally determined that synchronous orbits at 22,300 miles' elevation rather than nonsynchronous controlled or uncontrolled orbits at lower elevations would be used. The lower orbits require more satellites and even more sophisticated ground equipment, which add substantially to the cost of a system. *Communications Satellite Systems Technology* (Marsten ed. Dec. 1966) provides ready access to a collection of technical papers on communications satellites and the systems which have been established under U.S. aegis. See also Silberman, "The Little Bird That Casts a Big Shadow," 75 *Fortune* 108 (Feb. 1967) which suggests that ComSat was overcapitalized because of the expectation that nonsynchronous orbits would be used. "Communications Satellites: Technical, Economic and International Developments," *Staff Report of Senate Committee on Aeronautical and Space Sciences,* 87th Cong. 2d. Sess., at 3 (Feb. 25, 1962) states without clarification: "There appears to be general agreement on the ultimate desirability of a synchronous satellite system, i.e., one situated over the equator and having an orbit corresponding to the period of rotation of the earth, thus making the satellite appear to hang stationary. It is easier to launch a satellite into a lower orbit than into a synchronous orbit. This makes it desirable to use a lower orbit system, particularly in the interim until a synchronous system is available." ComSat has, in fact, used the synchronous system only, except for experimental work. Numerous Congressional and other documents indicate many unresolved technological problems which may have a bearing on the ultimate cost of communications satellite systems. See also ComSat's *Report to the President and the Congress for the Calendar Year 1966,* at 5: "[T]he Interim Communications Satellite Committee agreed formally in early 1966 to provide basic coverage with synchronous satellites. This significant step forward substantially reduced the potential cost of earth stations for the coming system, for earlier concepts of a global system required a number of satellites in a random orbiting or a medium altitude pattern with tracking antennas at the earth stations. . . . Since three such [synchronous] satellites can virtually cover the earth, the cost of spacecraft for a synchronous global system as well as the cost of earth stations could be substantially reduced." At the May 10, 1967, annual meeting ComSat's chairman reported that on May 2, 1967, ComSat had $158,000,000 invested in various securities. ComSat representatives have acknowledged at least a temporary overcapitalization but insist ultimate requirements will equal or exceed available capital. 32 *T.R.* 15 (Oct. 10, 1966) quoting

---

ComSat financial vice-president and treasurer Mathews. Report filed with the FCC in Nov. 1966 indicated an average net investment in the communications system in 1971 of only $102,268,000. 32 *T.R.* 22 (Nov. 14, 1966); *id.* at 7 (Dec. 5, 1966); 33 *T.R.* 3 (Jan. 9, 1967); *id.* at 18 (Jan. 23, 1967); *id.* at 12 (Feb. 27, 1967). These are ComSat estimates and are probably too high by several million dollars. The reports all indicate indecision on the part of the FCC over what rules to apply in accounting requirements and for capital expenditures. Much of the indecision is based on lack of experience with communications satellites, the rapidly developing technology, lack of adequate legislative guidelines and political pressures from various communications entities, frequently through Congress.

[5] In some instances financing has been arranged through the Export-Import Bank, 33 *T.R.* 40 (Apr. 10, 1967). AID, contractor financing, and other borrowing sources have also been utilized.

[6] *Chicago Tribune,* Jan. 18, 1967, at 9, and Jan. 19, 1967, sec. 1, at 22; *Washington Post,* Jan. 19, 1967, at A7. See *Hearings before Senate Comm. on Aeronautical and Space Science,* 89th Cong., 2d Sess. (Jan. 25, 26, 1966), for a description of the military program. See also 32 *T.R.* 9 (June

comparatively small capacity per satellite and at times necessarily has to use shipboard, portable, or other small earth stations. Other government agencies will use the military system under some circumstances.[7] The Department of Defense considered the program necessary because of "problems associated with international control of the commercial system," the "added survivability" of a Defense Communications Satellite System with "multiple uncontrolled satellites," and the requirement for "critical circuitry to remote areas which would not logically be served by other high quality means." Total cost of the initial Defense Satellite Communications System through the Research and Development portion was given at about $140 million in the 1966 Congressional Hearings (see p. 129). Of this, about $55 million relates to the space-borne segment. The same source indicates that total government expenditures for communications research and development is about $500 million to the end of fiscal year 1966.[8]

Establishment of the Military Satellite Communications System has presented comparatively minor domestic legal problems,[9] although numerous policy questions relating to government contracts for satellite channels remain the subject of controversies which may finally be resolved in the United States Supreme Court or by further congressional action.[10] Internationally, the

military system's existence can be pointed to as justification for other national systems not part of Intelsat, and domestically it means that a substantial amount of long-distance communications traffic is taken out of the private business sector.

The availability of unused capital funds, for the reasons noted above, undoubtedly has a bearing on the position taken by ComSat in connection with earth-station ownership, other national satellite communication systems, and generally any question relating to domestic investments in long-distance communications. These unresolved questions have great economic and political significance, especially since invested capital is an important criterion in determining the amount of return a regulated industry may have.[11]

ComSat, in common with all communications carriers and because of the terms of the ComSat Act, is subject to extremely detailed control and regulation by various United States government agencies (particularly the FCC[12]), and is in vigorous competition with conventional communications common carriers, which own approximately half interest in it[13] and, with representa-

---

20, 1966) for a description of the initial launch specifically for this system.

[7] Capacity could be greatly increased by using larger and more powerful earth stations.

[8] See *Hearings, supra* note 6, at 76. AT&T reports it has spent $78,000,000 in work on satellite communications since 1959 and has spent $2 billion on communications research and development since World War II. Much of this effort has contributed to satellite communications technology. 32 *T.R.* 27 (Sept. 19, 1967) quoting AT&T Vice-president Hough's letter to Senate Commerce Communications Subcommittee.

[9] It is authorized by the ComSat Act, Art. 201 (a) (6). See "Government Use of Satellite Systems," *43d Report by the Committee on Government Operations,* 89th Cong., 2d Sess., at 23 (Oct. 19, 1966), for a discussion of the various statutes and policies relative to procurement of satellite services. The FCC has very little control over government communications. See Metzger & Burrus, *supra* note 3.

[10] The Dept. of Defense initially gave ComSat a contract for 30 channels but under FCC and Congressional pressure the contract was reassigned to the conventional common carriers which purchase satellite channels from ComSat and resell them at a profit. Although little information is available, it is difficult to avoid wondering how much pressure the members of ComSat's Board of Directors elected by AT&T, IT&T, etc., applied internally. See letter from President's Special Ass't for

Telecommunications, Gen. James D. O'Connell, June 28, 1966, reprinted in *Hearings on Government Use of Satellite Communications before the Military Operations Subcommittee of the House Committee on Government Operations,* 89th Cong., 2d Sess., at 304–5 (1966). H.R. Report 231–38, "Gov't Use of Communications Satellites," 89th Cong., 2d Sess., at 7, 49–56 (1966). FCC 67–163, at 2, 3 (Feb. 3, 1967). The matter has been referred to as a "flap," as intergovernmental agency bickering, etc., and is extensively reported in *Telecommunications Reports.* See for part of the coverage 32 *T.R.* 18–26 (Oct. 10, 1966); 32 *T.R.* 13 (Oct. 3, 1966); 33 *T.R.* 26 (Dec. 12, 1966).

ComSat does furnish service direct to NASA, apparently without particular objection from common carriers, 32 *T.R.* 1 (July 11, 1966). The very heavy NASA communications requirements are in connection with space exploration.

[11] See 33 *T.R.* 1 ff. (Apr. 10, 1967) for a discussion of some aspects of rate-making. After extensive hearings which received considerable public attention the FCC set 7–7½ percent as a rate of return for AT&T. Rate and rate base are both highly controversial and numerous appeals should be expected. The FCC's handling of the matter has, since the hearings were announced, kept AT&T stock prices unstable because of uncertainty over future dividend rates (*Wall Street Journal,* July 6, 1967, at 3).

[12] See ComSat Act as a whole and esp. secs. 201, 302, 304, 401, 403, and 404, reproduced in Appendix E as item 7.

[13] Communications Common Carriers elect 6 directors, the public stockholders elect 6, and the United States appoints 3 directors. ComSat Act sec. 303. ComSat dissatisfaction with this arrangement came into the open at the May, 1967, annual meeting, at which time its officers reported that ComSat was

tion on the board, have access to all of its business plans.

Several domestic questions await policy decisions which cumulatively may have a substantial impact not only on the communications industry but also on the entire economy and social structure of the United States. Neither the FCC nor any other federal agency has displayed the capability of providing and enforcing authoritative answers.[14]

Another basic policy question is whether or not Congress intended, aside from possible government systems, that ComSat should have a complete domestic as well as international monopoly on ownership and operation of communications satellites. The American Broadcasting Company filed an application with the FCC[15] requesting its own satellite system. ABC's proposal suggested the system should be open to all networks on a shared cost basis. No solution has been found, although numerous interested parties have filed briefs with the FCC[16] in response to its Notice of Inquiry and Supplemental Notice of Inquiry. The inquiry and controversy goes far beyond ABC's request and covers the entire area of domestic communications satellites, educational television, direct broadcast to homes, etc. The uncertainties in the law and the difficulties in establishing approved public policies on the political, economic, and educational aspects of ownership, operation, and control are contributing to delay in the utilization of communications satellites for domestic purposes in the United States. It is unquestionably technically feasible, but to what extent technical factors makes it desirable to delay or move slowly is difficult to determine. Possibly, with the use of higher and higher frequencies, with congestion of the electromagnetic frequencies, and with the construction of ever greater numbers of high-rise buildings to interfere, there will be increased use of community-type antennae to avoid problems of reflected signals and interference. What impact lasers and masers will have on communications is presently unknown. Cables may be used increasingly; this would alleviate to some extent the problems of reflection and congestion, although the volume of commercial traffic continues to increase at a rapid rate. The FCC is asking everyone for suggestions but does not appear to be providing much leadership in

considering asking Congress for a change in legislation to remove some carrier representation from the ComSat board if carrier ownership of stock fell below 45 percent (*Wall Street Journal,* May 10, 1967, at 15). Carriers would continue to have access to all of ComSat's business plans, but carrier influence on ComSat decisions would be lessened to some extent. The conflict of interest is patent but was specifically provided for in the Congressional action authorizing ComSat.

14 James D. O'Connell, Director of Telecommunications Management and Special Assistant to the President for Telecommunications, stated: "the nation's telecommunications structure lacks strong central authority to meet complex problems, and cannot reach 'must' goals with present arrangements." He went on to declare the need for a Department of Communications. 33 *T.R.* 1 (Mar. 13, 1967). Seventeen government departments and agencies are involved in various aspects of telecommunications decisions, and the FCC responds to first one pressure and then another. In many, if not most instances, decisions are just compromises attempting to give all competing parties enough to gain acceptance if not approval. Congress, also susceptible to political pressures, has been unable to provide adequate guidelines and has fragmented authority and reponsibility. Uncertainties on requirements for FCC approvals where Intelsat is involved are numerous. See, e.g., 32 *T.R.* 3, 4, 5 (June 27, 1966); 32 *T.R.* 23 (June 6, 1966), quoting ComSat chairman McCormack as saying some members of Intelsat "are dubious about ComSat's continuing ability as the consortium's manager to spend their money in their interests while being subject to the detailed regulations" of the FCC. Previously, ComSat had requested the FCC to modify rules which, "if literally construed . . . have the effect of imposing United States regulatory requirements upon public and private entities wholly outside the jurisdiction of the United States. . . ." 32 *T.R.* 28 (Mar. 28, 1966).

See also 32 *T.R.* 18 (June 13, 1966) with reference to ownership of earth stations. The confusion in U.S. policy has been recognized by the President who has appointed a task force to review federal communications policy, including the possibility of a merger of all international operations of AT&T, IT&T, RCA, and Western Union. *Newsweek,* Aug. 28, 1967, at 59. Vested interests are powerful enough that little is likely to be accomplished for a long time.

15 See *New York Times,* May 14, 1965, at 1. Application filed with the FCC Sept. 21, 1965. See *Wall Street Journal,* Sept. 22, 1965, at 2, for an excellent summary of the application which, if granted, would authorize sychronous satellite at 100° west longitude, two transmitting earth stations, and about 200 receiving stations or antennas. Annual cost was estimated at $0.9 million compared with $11.9 million paid by ABC to AT&T for the lease of land-transmission facilities for 14 hours a day. This system would provide 5 TV channels on a 24-hour-a-day basis, one channel to be made available without charge to National Educational Television and its affiliated stations. Subsequently ABC indicated it thought radio programs should be included. See *Washington Post,* Oct. 21, 1965.

16 In addition to ABC, these include CBS, NBC, AT&T, ComSat, the Ford Foundation, Western Union Telegraph, Western Union International, IT&T, World Communications, National Association of Educational Broadcasters, the NAM, Dow Jones, American Petroleum Institute, American Trucking Association, Carnegie Commission on Educational Television, GT&E Service Corp., Hawaiian Telephone Co., HEW, the JFD Electronics Corp., and many others.

the matter.[17] The political and economic indecision of the United States government may well be preventing Americans from enjoying domestically all the advantages of satellite communications, but it is only fair to note that the technological uncertainties and the problems of ascertaining a satisfactory format for a domestic system do justify a considerable amount of caution. It has not been possible to ascertain if any international commitments have had a bearing on these delays. Through 1966 and 1967 additional proposals with extensive briefs were filed with the FCC by the Ford Foundation, the Carnegie Foundation, and many others affirming and denying the FCC's right to authorize any entity other than ComSat to operate a communications satellite system for domestic needs, and also arguing that a noncommercial educational and cultural television system should be provided. A name suggested for an educational TV system was Broadcasters' Nonprofit Satellite Service. The Ford Foundation justified financing by the telecommunications industry as a "people's dividend" from the vast amounts the government has spent on space research and development[18] and proposed that control be vested in a public but nongovernmental board. The proposal suggested from four to six synchronous satellites with capital costs from $80 million to $92 million and annual operating costs from $19.3 million to $22.2 million. Subsequent proposals would increase the size and cost of the system.[19]

ComSat announced a willingness to construct and operate a domestic system with special charges on all commercial users to finance noncommercial broadcasting and filed extensive documents with the FCC describing in some detail its proposal. The Ford Foundation objected vigorously to ComSat's ownership of such a system.[20] ComSat argues that, "as a matter of law, the Commission [FCC] is without power to authorize any nongovernment entity other than ComSat to operate communications satellites,"[21] and "no legislation seeking such power should be proposed." An opposite view is taken by a number of other submissions to the FCC of which Ford's statement is fairly typical: "The legislative history of Section 102(d) [ComSat Act] shows that Congress considered and rejected the position that further legislation is a prerequisite to FCC authorization of additional domestic communications—satellite facilities."[22] The FCC initially authorized ComSat to take title to all earth stations for two years.[23] ComSat undertook to acquire existing earth stations and commenced

---

[17] FCC Chairman Hyde, in a speech to state regulatory commissions, said making satellite service available domestically was "among the most profound matters to face FCC" and asked for suggestions but offered no guidance. This is rather typical. The FCC refused a Western Union request for earth stations saying the question was premature. 33 *T.R.* 8 (Jan. 9, 1967).

[18] The proposals received extensive press coverage. For examples see: *Washington Post*, Aug. 7, 1966, at E4; *New York Times*, Aug. 7, 1966, sec. 4, at E4, E7; *Newsweek*, Aug. 15, 1966, at 76–77; *Wall Street Journal*, Sept. 12, 1966, at 11; *Barron's National Business and Financial Weekly*, Oct. 3, 1966, at 1. As should be anticipated, opinion varies from strong support to bitter opposition. D. W. Smythe, "Freedom of Information: Some Analysis and a Proposal for Satellite Broadcasting," 6 *Q. Rev. Econ. & Bus.* 7 (1966), criticizes sharply the entire concept of ComSat and Intelsat and recommends a U.N.-owned controlled system financed the same way as the U.N. and controlled by a board similar to that of the BBC. See 33 *T.R.* 1–5, 30–36 (Jan. 30, 1967), for a considerable discussion of the Carnegie report on ETV which offered a plan without definitive suggestions for the FCC's domestic satellite inquiry.

[19] See *Washington Post*, Dec. 12, 1966, at A1; *Wall Street Journal*, Dec. 13, 1966, at 24.

[20] *New York Times*, Aug. 29, 1966, at 1; *Wall Street Journal*, Aug. 30, 1966, at 24. See also *Chicago Tribune*, Apr. 3, 1967, sec. 1, at 6, reporting a ComSat offer to the FCC to set up an experimental domestic satellite system with free-channel service for demonstrations of educational television; and the *Wall Street Journal*, Apr. 3, 1967, at 3, for Ford's contrary position asking the FCC to "delay for one year final authorization of any domestic service" to permit "adequate Congressional consideration" and to avoid giving ComSat "unprecedented control over the development of an emerging technology." See ComSat filings with the FCC dated Aug. 1966; Dec. 16, 1966; Mar. 1967, etc.

[21] Letter dated Dec. 16, 1966, from McCormack of ComSat to Hyde, Chairman of FCC, transmitting and summarizing brief prepared by ComSat.

[22] Legal Brief and Comments of the Ford Foundation in Response to Paragraphs 4(a) and 4(b) of the FCC's Notice of Inquiry of Mar. 2, 1966, In the Matter of Establishment of Domestic Non-Common Carrier Communications-Satellite Facilities by Non-Governmental Entities. Docket No. 1649, at 2. Ford's submission is in several parts and the full arguments are developed therein. See FCC Docket 16495 Public Interest Issues; Supp. Legal Brief, Ford Foundation, Vols. 1 & 2 dated Apr. 3, 1967, and earlier submissions. Numerous other organizations and institutions also filed comments with proposals. The Carnegie Institution has made a substantial study of educational television and related subjects. The National Science Foundation and the National Foundation on the Arts and Humanities, both government agencies, endorsed use of satellites for public information and ETV (32 *T.R.* 38 [Dec. 5, 1966]).

[23] FCC 66–677 86505 Docket No. 16058, July 21, 1966, para. 37.

planning and construction of additional stations. As the end of the two-year period approached, the FCC suggested at least informally that ComSat and other communications carriers resolve the question of ownership of earth stations by agreement. This failed, as should have been anticipated because of the conflicting economic interests and the desires for rate-base investments, and the FCC, for want of a better solution, ordered ownership of the earth stations to be divided on the basis of use, following a theory previously set forth in decisions relating to cables and justified by the language "public convenience, interest, or necessity."[24]

In theory, at least, the same concept could be applied to ComSat's interest in the space segment. The present arrangement is to be reviewed in 1969.[25] ComSat is to be manager of the earth stations, subject to overall control and guidance by a committee of all owners to be established by agreement, subject to FCC approval. Rates which had previously been computed and approved by the FCC on the basis of ownership by ComSat alone had to be recomputed and approved by the FCC on the basis of divided ownership.[26] This follows the

pattern of ownership of Intelsat, so that in fact the FCC ruling gives the communications carriers other than ComSat a three-quarters ownership of the earth stations, one-half directly and one-fourth stemming from their approximately half-ownership of ComSat. There is no assurance that the FCC will not take another step in 1969 and exclude ComSat entirely from ownership of the earth stations—or restore it to full ownership.

Additional questions might be raised about ownership of the terrestrial communications links tying the earth stations to the regular domestic communications system. Under the arrangements adopted thus far there is little doubt that this link will continue to be owned and operated by the conventional terrestrial communications carriers rather than by ComSat. The ownership of the link may be divided among the carriers according to usage or a single carrier may own a particular line.

Although the action taken by the FCC may be defensible and is not contrary to law, it is difficult to envisage how ComSat can be properly managed and operated if the basic rules under which it operates are to be radically changed every two or three years. It is recognized that the FCC is establishing rules for novel circumstances, but it is difficult to avoid wondering if

[24] ComSat Act, sec. 217(c)(7). The Supreme Court has upheld similar language as being as "concrete as the complicated factors for judgment in such a field of delegated authority permit." FCC v. Pottsville Broadcasting Co, 309 U.S. 134, (1940), but as Davis, *Administrative Law* 46 (1951) noted, it is no real standard and amounts to saying, "Here is a problem, deal with it." The specific language involved in the Pottsville case was "public convenience, interest or necessity."

[25] FCC 66-1133 91927 Docket No. 15735, Dec. 8, 1966. Intelsat agreements will also be under review. ComSat was given the right to 50 percent ownership, and the remaining ownership was divided among various American carriers in accordance with anticipated usage. Among the carriers involved are AT&T, Hawaiian Tel., ITTPR-ITTVI, RCAC, and WUI.

[26] Computation of rates is a very inexact science with many factors to be taken into consideration. The FCC has not spelled out in detail how rates are to be computed, but in a recent telephone rate case involving AT&T, the FCC listed a number of items to be considered: (*a*) book costs of interexchange circuit plant; (*b*) time, worth, value, nationwide average, or individual area studies; (*c*) nature and degree of risk from competition, technological change, demand for services, unit changes in costs and revenues; (*d*) comparative risks of other regulated utilities; (*e*) authorized rates of return below those requested; (*f*) comparative rate of return on equity investments; (*g*) comparative rate of return based on debt structure; (*h*) whether rate structure should be based on imputed debt structure of current 32 percent or on the 40 percent ratio given as objective; (*i*) what estimated annual rate of growth in capital investment should be assumed; (*j*) what effect the adoption of liberalized depreciation for tax purposes would

have. See 33 *T.R.* 2, 3 (Apr. 10, 1967). A firm philosophy for a ComSat rate structure has not yet been developed, but it would seem that capital investment in the communications system would be an important element. Earlier, ComSat had stated a need for a 12 percent rate of return in projecting requirements over a five-year period, citing high risk involved in the operation of a satellite system. 32 *T.R.* 1 (July 11, 1966). ComSat has filed extensive documentation with the FCC and has also suggested that possibly earnings could be based on volume of business rather than on rate base which would eliminate a major cause of controversy over ownership of earth stations. The rate discussions will be more or less continuous. See 32 *T.R.* 22 (Nov. 14, 1966).

The matter has been considered of such significance that the FCC has permitted NASA to intervene in the rate hearings. 33 *T.R.* 4 (Mar. 20, 1967). Distinctions between ComSat and Intelsat rates have not always been clear. ComSat files monthly financial reports with the FCC, similar to those submitted by other common carriers. 32 *T.R.* 14 (May 23, 1966). A member of its board only "half-facetiously" suggested that ComSat acquire the cables from record carriers who complained that ComSat prevented them from expansion. 32 *T.R.* 20 (Mar. 14, 1966). A Western Union request to build earth stations to provide satellite service was dismissed as premature (33 *T.R.* 27, 28 [Dec. 12, 1966]), since no domestic system was available. 33 *T.R.* 8 (Jan. 9, 1967). In July 1967 the FCC held AT&T was entitled to a 7½ percent return but it is quite unclear as to exactly what is included in the base. *Wall Street Journal*, July 6, 1967, at 3 and July 7, 1967, at 3.

the FCC as well as Congress is not succumbing to political pressures of economic interests where the best interests of the public might suggest a different result. The division of authority between the FCC and the Executive branch discussed by Metzger and Burrus[27] is doubtless a contributing factor in the FCC's inability to resolve pressing problems.

The identification of "authorized user,"[28] i.e., to what entities may ComSat make satellite circuits directly available has been a subject of considerable controversy, with most of the carriers arguing against direct service to communications users. However, the FCC has found that:

(a) ComSat may, as a matter of law, be authorized to provide service directly to noncarrier entities; (b) ComSat is to be primarily a carrier's carrier and in ordinary circumstances users of satellite facilities should be served by the terrestrial carriers; and (c) in unique and exceptional circumstances ComSat may be authorized to provide services directly to noncarrier users. Therefore, the authorization to ComSat to provide services directly is dependent upon the nature of the service, i.e., unique or exceptional, rather than the identity of the user. The FCC policy recognizes that the United States Government has a special position and that ComSat may be authorized to provide service directly to the government, "if such service is required to meet unique government needs or is otherwise required in the national interest, in circumstances where the Government's needs cannot be effectively met under the carrier's carrier approach."[29]

In February 1967 the FCC stated that it would look to the Director of Telecommunications Management for a representation as to whether any services in question are required in the national interest.[30] ComSat, the Department of Defense, and the General Services Administration had taken a position before the FCC that the Executive branch of the government, at its discretion, had the authority under the ComSat Act to obtain satellite services directly from ComSat.[31] But this position seems to have been modified to some extent. A general pattern of rulings is not yet available, but apparently the FCC position limits the situations in which ComSat can make communications satellite circuits available directly to a noncarrier, even if the noncarrier is a United States government agency and ComSat would make the service available directly at appreciably less cost than similar service through a carrier. The FCC's known attitude on this point may have contributed to the decision of the Department of Defense to establish its own communications satellite system.

A closely related problem involves another aspect of rates.[32] ComSat wants separate rates to be established for circuits utilizing satellites, whereas the terrestrial carriers wish to use composite rates. ComSat wants to encourage the use of satellites and to make clear the economies of the satellite system, whereas the terrestrial carriers do not think it proper to give all the benefit to those customers who are fortunate enough to be able to utilize the satellites and want to spread the savings to all their customers. The terrestrial carriers also want to protect their existing investments and have shown no enthusiasm for expediting the use of satellites for communications since ComSat was established. The FCC adopted the position of the terrestrial carriers on the theory that the satellites should be for the benefit of all.[33] If satellite circuits took business from conventional circuits it is argued that the remaining communications over conventional circuits would be required to pay increased rates and some of the conventional carriers might be forced out of business entirely. To the extent that it is strategically necessary or desirable to have both satellite and conventional communications facilities available and to maintain adequate communications everywhere, the FCC position is justified. But the FCC has not shown a willingness to make decisions which would leave the terrestrial communications carriers excessively unhappy. FCC Chairman Hyde has stated, "It is national policy in the communications field to promote the maintenance of a diversity of facilities.

---

[27] See *supra,* note 3.

[28] ComSat Act, sec. 305.

[29] FCC Public Notice: C87035 of July 21, 1966, and FCC 66–677 86505 Docket No. 16058 of July 21, 1966.

[30] FCC 67–94725 Docket No. 16058 Feb. 3, 1967. See also E.O. 11191 assigning certain responsibilities to the Director of Telecommunications Management. This situation is another major example of divided authority and dominance of the DTM over the FCC in certain areas. The FCC indicated clearly that the DTM and not ComSat would advise the FCC on questions of national interest with regard to applications for authority to provide service directly to government agencies. 33 *T.R.* 3 (Feb. 6, 1967).

[31] ComSat Report to the President, *supra* note 4, at 13.

[32] See *supra* note 26.

[33] FCC 66–677 86505 Docket No. 16058 of July 21, 1966, paras. 31–36 and 37 (d). See also 32 *T.R.* 24 (Oct. 17, 1966) in which ComSat's concern is expressed over the FCC's "seeming adoption" of fixed views to be applied in determining rates for space services, with a resultant decline in incentive to use satellites for communications.

Accordingly, in the next several years, it will have to be determined under what circumstances the laying of additional submarine cables will be economically justified and supportable consistent with maintaining viable international operations of both the ComSat and the international cable carriers."[34] To the extent that the FCC position is based on protection of investments in a communications system rendered uneconomic by technological advances, it is difficult if not impossible to justify. The true rationale of the FCC position cannot be easily ascertained. The FCC position was unchanged in a reconsideration which emphasized its responsibility to see that no overall deterioration in communications services occurs in a situation where ComSat has "a favored position with respect to a more economical medium [than] have conventional carriers which are at a disadvantage in not being able to acquire such a favored position."[35] Final determinations of these problems will be worked out on broad policy grounds utilizing political, economic, military, and social factors rather than narrow legal arguments.

There is yet another fundamental decision which must be made within the next few years involving whether or not to permit direct radio and television broadcasting from satellite to home receivers.[36] The potential here, both domestically and internationally, is enormous. When and if such systems are developed, one or two television and one or two radio stations could easily blanket the nation—or the world. There would technically be no need for any local radio or television broadcast stations. How these problems are to be handled will require the greatest possible consideration, and large numbers of people are already deeply concerned

and are taking steps to force not only government officials but also the public to recognize the possible consequences. Educational television, for which there have been a number of proposals, with its great potential for influencing thought has become intertwined with the problems of direct transmission from satellites to home receivers. The President has called the dual problem to the attention of Congress in a message which indicates ETV should be free of government control, but he does not purport to set forth any details of operational control or financing.[37] Although no emphasis is being placed on development of direct broadcast, need for policy decisions has acquired some degree of urgency. Short-wave radio transmission from a single station has long been available over a wide area of the earth and presents essentially the same problem, although not so acutely. The only practical international control has been by jamming. A few nations may have or may develop the ability to silence satellites by knocking them out of the sky. Decisions will be based on political and economic rather than legal considerations[38] (see chap. 5).

The functions and extent of regulatory authority held by the FCC and by the Director of Telecommunications Management and associated offices and the division of authority and responsibility should be extensively reevaluated. The rapidly developing communications satellite technology and the ambiguities of the ComSat Act and the FCC acts have permitted or almost forced the FCC to attempt to exercise authority over ComSat's every action and over its relationships with communica-

---

34 Quoted in 33 *T.R.* 15 (Mar. 20, 1967) from testimony before House Interstate and Foreign Commerce Committee, Mar. 14, 1967.

35 FCC 67–164 94725 Docket No. 16058 Feb. 3, 1967, paras. 7 and 8. It is impossible to ascertain how much the FCC was influenced by a desire to protect investments in the existing communications systems. The fundamental question of who may own communications satellites has been referred to *supra* at 208–9.

36 In the *Hearings before the Committee on Aeronautical and Space Sciences, supra* note 6, at 80, it is said that direct TV reception may be possible by the late 1970s or earlier. Direct radio reception to home receivers could be ready in three years. More recent estimates reduce considerably the length of time required, but some developments could possibly result in others, such as community antennas. The problems of reflection of high-frequency transmissions from natural and manmade structures is practically an unexplored factor.

37 See *New York Times,* Mar. 1, 1967, at 1. *Washington Post,* Mar. 1, 1967, at 1. The Ford Foundation, ComSat, and a large number of other organizations have submitted various proposals to the FCC starting in August 1966 or earlier. *Wall Street Journal,* Apr. 13, 1967, at 6, carries an article indicating the political complexity of ETV control and financing and suggests any miscue may defeat proposed legislation. The President's message "was not definitive neither as to financing nor as to the means for providing network service." 33 *T.R.* 17 (Mar. 6, 1967). The message requested $9,000,000 for the first year of operation of the proposed Corporation for Public Television. Western Union Vice-President Hilburn suggests use of NASA's ATA satellite as an interim approach for providing satellite service for ETV (33 *T.R.* 29–31 [May 1, 1967]).

38 Doyle, "Communications Satellites: International Organization for Development and Control," 55 *Cal. L. Rev.* 431, 445–48 (May 1967), takes the position that the problem is new and peculiar to communications satellites. Preventive actions have been mentioned: "jamming, destruction of satellites, independent economic or political sanctions, and counter broadcasts are means which might be considered by the offended states."

tions carriers and users. Some of these decisions, which may have practical life-and-death consequences on some of the major communications entities or result in a radical restructuring of the entire communications industry of the United States, are so important that they should be made by Congress. Whether or not Congress has the capacity to resolve the problems without allowing political pressures to exercise excessive influence in areas which should be resolved on the basis of economic and social welfare of the United States is open to doubt.

D International Organizations and Outer Space Activities

Throughout this study, the role of those international organizations that have already contributed to the emerging law concerned with man's activities in outer space has been developed in some detail. Chief among these are the General Assembly of the United Nations and the International Telecommunications Union (ITU). This appendix is designed therefore (1) to provide a very brief overview of the role of *other* international governmental and nongovernmental organizations as background for the study of the legal problems with which we are concerned; and (2) to provide more historically complete and systematic treatment of the past and present role of the United Nations as a form of case study of the prospects and possibilities of international supervision, control, and operations in this field. We exclude here consideration of the ITU, which is covered in chapter 5. The problem of the return of downed space vehicles and astronauts is used in this context as a special case study. The United Nations materials are presented first.

It is possible to call on a number of excellent recent studies of the development of outer space activities among governments and in intergovernmental and nongovernmental international organizations.[1] With the

exception of the United Nations system, these arrangements are not for the most part concerned with general legal regimes or with the creation of norms in any way. They do form the background against which the law concerning outer space activities has developed, but the existence of the studies noted above relieves us of doing more than identifying these agencies and arrangements in most cases.

(1965); Haley, *Space Law and Government* (1963); "United States International Space Programs: Texts of Executive Agreements, Memoranda of Understanding, and Other International Arrangements, 1959–1965," *Staff Report Prepared for the Senate Committee on Aeronautical and Space Sciences,* 89th Cong., 1st Sess., Doc. No. 44 (July 30, 1965) [hereinafter cited as *Texts*]; Christol, *The International Law of Outer Space,* chaps. 3–6, *passim* (1966); Van Dyke, *Pride and Power,* chap. 14 (1964); Lipson, "Space Technology and the Law of International Organization," *Report of the Space Law Committee of the Int'l Law Ass'n,* Annex II (Tokyo, 1964); Kash, *The Politics of Space Cooperation* (1967).

For suggestions on the need and utility of international cooperation, see also Ambassador Goldberg, "International Cooperation in Outer Space," 54 *Dept. St. Bull.* 163–67 (Jan. 31, 1966); Subcomm. on Int'l Orgs. and Movements, Comm. on For. Aff., 89th Cong., 2d Sess., at 35–40; *Report on Activities of the International Cooperation Years* (June 1966); Bloomfield, "Outer Space and International Cooperation," 19 *Int'l Org.* 603 (1965); Bourley, "International Organizations for Cooperation in Space and the Problem of Liability for Space Activities," *Proceedings, Eighth Colloq.* 1–9 (1965); Lipson, *supra,* at 702–9.

---

[1] See "International Cooperation and Organization for Outer Space," *Staff Report Prepared for the Senate Committee on Aeronautical and Space Sciences,* 89th Cong., 1st Sess., Doc. No. 56 (Galloway ed., Aug. 12, 1965) [hereinafter cited as *Staff Report*]; Frutkin, *International Cooperation in Space*

The United Nations System and Outer Space Activities

It is interesting and undoubtedly significant that the potentials and threats of outer space activities were first formally brought to international attention in the course of international disarmament discussions.[2] In 1957, President Eisenhower noted the dangers inherent in the development of outer space weapons and stated that the United States was willing "to enter into any reliable agreement which would . . . mutually control the outer space missile and satellite development."[3] A memorandum of January 12, 1957, to the First Committee of the General Assembly next called the world's attention to the need for international inspection and participation in testing earth satellites, long-range unmanned weapons, intercontinental missiles, and space platforms.[4] This theme was reiterated by Secretary of State Dulles in July 1957, and it was formalized as one element of a ten-point program submitted to the U.N.'s Disarmament Subcommittee, meeting in London in late August 1957.[5] This entire disarmament proposal was rejected by the Soviet Union.

On October 4, 1957, Sputnik I achieved orbit. Thereafter, in October and November, the General Assembly discussed disarmament and, on November 14, 1957, a resolution was adopted which urged that an agreement, including provision for the joint study of "an inspection system designed to ensure that the sending of objects through outer space shall be exclusively for peaceful and scientific purposes," be concluded as a matter of priority.[6] The need for control of outer space techniques "this time, and in time" was also stressed in letters from President Eisenhower to Premier Bulganin in January and February 1958, but the Soviet Union proved unwilling to discuss the question outside the context of general disarmament.[7] Outer space continued to be a factor in disarmament discussions both in and out of the United Nations but, in view of the lack of progress and hence the lack of direct relevance to this study, we will not further discuss the proceedings here, although we return to the disarmament question briefly hereafter in connection with the events of 1963.[8]

After the failure to make progress in the disarmament exchange in the winter of 1957–58, and the successful orbiting on January 31, 1958, of the United States' Explorer I, the Soviet Union submitted on March 15, 1958, a proposed agenda item for consideration at the thirteenth regular meeting of the General Assembly. In this agenda item, the "banning of the use of cosmic space for military purposes, the elimination of foreign bases on the territories of other countries, and international co-operation in the study of cosmic space" were linked. States were to launch rockets into cosmic space only under an agreed international program, and a United Nations agency for international cooperation in the study of cosmic space was proposed:

To work out an agreed international programme for

---

[2] In addition to the official documents the matters covered in this section are also reported and/or analyzed in varying degrees in, among many: Jessup & Taubenfeld, *Controls for Outer Space and the Antarctic Analogy*, 252–65 (1959); *Staff Report, supra* note 1, at 163–552; Jessup & Taubenfeld, "The United Nations Ad Hoc Committee on the Peaceful Uses of Outer Space," 53 *Am. J. Int'l L.* 877–81 (1959) [hereinafter cited as "U.N. Ad Hoc Committee . . ."]; Taubenfeld, "Considerations at the United Nations of the Status of Outer Space," 53 *Am. J. Int'l L.* 400–405 (1959); Frutkin, *supra* note 1, at 141–85; Haley, *supra* note 1, at 298–328; Cooper, "Aerospace Law: Progress in the UN," 2 *Astro. & Aero.* 42–66 (May 1964); Zemanek, "The United Nations and the Law of Outer Space," *1965 Yrbk. World Affairs* 199–222. [hereinafter cited as Zemanek]; Simsarian, "Outer Space Co-operation in the United Nations," 57 *Am. J. Int'l L.* 854–67 (1963); Dembling & Arons, "Space Law and the United Nations: The Work of the Legal Subcommittee of the United Nations Committee on the Peaceful Uses of Outer Space," 32 *J. Air L. & Commerce* 329–86 (1966) [hereinafter cited as "Space Law . . ."]; Dembling & Arons, "The United Nations Celestial Bodies Convention," 32 *J. Air L. & Commerce* 535–50 (1966) [hereinafter cited as "Celestial Bodies . . ."]; Dembling & Arons, "The Evolution of the Outer Space Treaty," 33 *J. Air L. & Commerce* 419–56 (1967); and Dembling & Arons, "The Treaty on Rescue and Return of Astronauts and Space Objects," 9 *Wm. & Mary L. Rev.* 630–63 (1968) [hereinafter cited as "Treaty . . ."]; Bloomfield, *supra* note 1, at 603–21.

[3] 36 *Dept. State Bull.* 124 (1957).

[4] See *Documents on Disarmament, 1945–1949,* 33 (Dept. of State Pub. 7009, 1960), and, for Ambassador Lodge's statement, 36 *Dept. State Bull.* 227 (1957).

[5] See *Documents on Disarmament, supra* note 4, at 832, 871; 37 *Dept. State. Bull.* 271, 453 (1957).

[6] General Assembly Resolution 1148 (XII) (Nov. 14, 1957).

[7] See *Documents on Disarmament, supra* note 4, at 938–40, 1047; 38 *Dept. State Bull.* 126 (1958); *Background of Heads of Government Conference (1960): Principal Documents, 1955–59,* 159, 163 (Dept. State Pub. 6972).

[8] For an account of the disarmament discussions from 1957 to 1964 with respect to outer space activities, see *Staff Report, supra* note 1, at 163–83.

launching intercontinental and space rockets with the aim of studying cosmic space, and supervise the implementation of this programme;

To continue on a permanent basis the cosmic space research now being carried on within the framework of the International Geophysical Year;

To serve as a world center for the collection, mutual exchange and dissemination of information on cosmic research;

To coordinate national research programmes for the study of cosmic space and render assistance and help in every way towards their realization.[9]

On September 2, 1958, the United States also proposed that a "programme for international cooperation in the field of outer space" be included in the Assembly's agenda.[10] On September 22 the General Assembly combined these requested items into a single "Question of Peaceful Use of Outer Space" and included the question in its agenda, referring it to the First Committee (Political and Security) for consideration and report.

On November 13 twenty nations, including the United States, submitted a different draft resolution calling only for the establishment by the General Assembly of an ad hoc committee on the peaceful uses of outer space to report to the Fourteenth General Assembly on:

(a) the activities and resources of the United Nations, its specialized agencies, and of other international bodies relating to the peaceful uses of outer space;

(b) the area of international co-operation and programmes in the peaceful uses of outer space which could appropriately be undertaken under United Nations auspices to the benefit of states irrespective of the stage of their economics or scientific development;

(c) the future United Nations organizational arrangements to facilitate international co-operation in this field;

(d) the nature of legal problems which may arise in carrying out of programmes to explore outer space.[11]

On November 18 the Soviet Union submitted a drastically revised version of its earlier resolution, which did not mention a United Nations agency and the elimination of military bases but suggested instead the establishment of a United Nations committee for co-operation in the study of cosmic space and of a preparatory group to draft a program for that committee.[12] Members of the twenty-nation group objected particularly to the inclusion of several Soviet satellite nations and "unfriendly" "neutral" nations in the preparatory group, and countered with a revised draft of their own resolution. It named as members of the proposed ad hoc committee Argentina, Australia, Belgium, Brazil, Canada, Czechoslovakia, France, India, Iran, Italy, Japan, Mexico, Poland, Sweden, USSR, U.A.R., U.K., and the U.S.A.[13] In addition, minor changes were made to indicate the interest of small nations in outer space activities.

Compromise on the states to be included and on the Soviet desire to establish a more permanent body at once proved impossible, and the Soviet Union withdrew its draft resolution since no "unanimous" decision was in sight and unanimity, they argued, was essential. The revised twenty-power draft was then adopted as a whole by the First Committee by fifty-four votes to nine (Soviet bloc), with eighteen abstentions (Arab-Asian group plus Austria, Yugoslavia, Ethiopia, Finland, and Israel). The Soviet Union, Poland, and Czechoslovakia immediately announced that they would not cooperate in the ad hoc committee's work, however.[14] As a consequence, two "neutral" nations, India and the U.A.R. also did not participate, arguing that, without the Soviet Union's presence, no sound action could be taken.

In addition to the "action" paragraph already noted, the resolution recommended by the First Committee recognized "the common interest of mankind in outer space and that it is the common aim that it should be used for peaceful purposes only," and sought "to avoid the extension of present national rivalries into this new field." In the First Committee, a perhaps surprising number of representatives took stands, in the course of discussing these draft resolutions, on one or more of the "legal" issues involved, some of which were noted in chapter 4.

On the broadest aspects of the use of outer space, there was universal agreement on limiting its use to "peaceful" purposes, a concept which had already been expressed in General Assembly Resolution 1148 (XII) and in the U.S. National Aeronautics and Space Act of

---

9 A/3818, Mar. 17, 1958.

10 A/3902, Sept. 2, 1958.

11 A/C.1/L.220. Other countries were Australia, Belgium, Bolivia, Canada, Denmark, France, Guatemala, Ireland, Italy, Japan, Nepal, The Netherlands, New Zealand, Sweden, Turkey, Union of South Africa, United Kingdom, Uruguay, and Venezuela.

---

12 U.N. Doc. A/C.1/L.219/Rev. 1, Nov. 18, 1958.

13 U.N. Doc. A/C.1/L.220/Rev. 1, Nov. 21, 1958.

14 See A/C.1/SR.955, at 15 (Nov. 24, 1958), and see, generally, *Report of the First Committee*, A/4009, Nov. 28, 1958.

1958 and which was reaffirmed in the resolution as adopted. Several representatives felt that as yet no legal norms existed to govern occurrences in outer space and that outer space was a "judicial vacuum"; but the Netherlander, Schurmann, argued that "the general principles of law recognized by civilized nations" must be applicable to relations between nations in space. Those speaking to the point at least generally agreed that the rules of the Paris Convention of 1919 and of the Chicago Convention of 1944 related only to "airspace," in the sense of the term *"espace atmosphérique"* as used in the Paris Convention, but only a few attempted to indicate where "outer space" began. The concept of *"usque ad coelum"* was characterized as "absurd" with respect to "ownership" of outer space.[15]

It was said that space, unlike the seas, which are finite in nature, is "indivisible" and hence not subject to the extension of national sovereignty. Representatives of several small nations cited the lack of protests at the passage overhead of Russian and American orbiting satellites as "proof" of the nonexistence of national sovereignty at these altitudes. The concept that space is *res nullius* and therefore subject to acquisition was rejected by several spokesmen of smaller nations, who termed the "appropriation" of space or of heavenly bodies "impossible" or at least "improper." Others stated that "space"—the moon, the planets, etc.—was "owned" or "belonged" to or was the "common domain" or the "common property" of the "world" or all nations or all peoples. The Italian representative generously added to this assertion that outer space "belonged" to all states of the world, that it was equally the property of "all other communities of thinking and organized beings living on other planets."

Equality of access to and the enjoyment of the benefits to be obtained from use of outer space were stated by representatives of several small powers, some of whom formally termed outer space as a *res communis omnium* or *res extra commercium,* to be existent rights, or at least essential rules, for man's development of space. Only a few seemed to insist on an unlimited, free, and equal right to "use" outer space, for most of those who discussed this point noted that rights of free use by all would be feasible only under international control,

owing to the danger to the rest of the world of abuses of such rights.[16]

Although the representatives of both the United States and the Soviet Union agreed to the need for the peaceful exploitation of man's new capabilities in outer space for the benefit of all mankind, neither at that time took a position on the potential legal status of space and neither country stated a position which would estop future claims from being made. Neither talked in the narrower terminology of rights and obligations employed by many of the representatives of States not having the ability to penetrate into space. All this indicated, as the Canadian and New Zealand representatives pointed out, that "in the last resort, the choice between various possible legal arrangements for outer space [will be] a political decision,"[17] an observation which is no less valid today.

A resolution setting up the ad hoc committee was adopted by the General Assembly on December 13, 1958, as Resolution 1348 (XIII), but the Soviet position of noncooperation remained unchanged. The Ad Hoc Committee operated through the Technical Subcommittee and the Legal Subcommittee. By mid-June these two Committees had completed their reports and the Secretariat had also prepared one on "the activities and resources of the United Nations, of its specialized agencies and of other international bodies related to the peaceful uses of outer space." These reports set much of the tone of all that has followed in the United Nations and are worthy of brief note even at this date.

The Technical Subcommittee concluded, in general, that the exploration of space was "a task vast enough to enlist the talents of scientists of all nations." Just as there was no way to limit the definition of "atmosphere" for WMO's weather purposes, there was general agreement that outer space was scientifically indivisible. The usefulness of participation in space efforts by nations lacking launching capabilities, particularly through such voluntary cooperative scientific arrangements as the IGY's successor in this field, COSPAR, was emphasized, and the United States was complimented several times on its offers to permit scientists from other nations to design experiments to be carried out by US-launched

---

[15] Compare the comment of the Supreme Court of the United States that, with respect to private claims in *airspace,* this "doctrine has no place in the modern world." United States v. Causby, 328 U.S. 256, 260–61 (1946).

[16] For the position of the various delegations, see A/C.1/SR.982–90 and Taubenfeld, *supra* note 2, at 400, 402–405. On the first few years of discussion at the U.N., see also *Staff Report, supra,* note 1, at 183–203; Zemanek, *supra* note 2, at 199–204.

[17] A/C.1/SR.986, at 9, and A/C.1/SR.988, at 9.

satellites. The stress was on cooperative efforts of the COSPAR type, although it was generally agreed that when the research stage was passed, functional intergovernmental arrangements of the WMO, ITU type were probably essential. The possibility of international launching sites was also raised.[18]

The Technical Subcommittee's report emphasized these points in stating that to make best use of all available talent and in some cases owing to the costs involved, "space activities, scientific and technological . . . even more than . . . astronomy . . . inherently ignore national boundaries. Space activities must to a large extent be an effort of Planet Earth as a whole." The connection between military activities and space research with its hampering effect on exchange of information was also noted, but it was concluded that the development of space vehicles had reached the point in several countries where it was a question of engineering only, not of science. Some of the potentially useful scientific studies were outlined, as were the techniques available for use and the possibilities for application of new knowledge to improvement in weather forecasting, radio communications, mapping, and navigation. International cooperation was felt to be scientifically desirable or even essential for such matters as orderly use of radio frequencies, registration of orbital elements at a central point, removal of spent satellites, termination of transmissions, reentry, recovery, and return of equipment, identification of origin of contamination both of outer space and of earth on return. The allocation of radio frequencies for space activities was here suggested as "the first technical area in which immediate international action is required." The ITU was urged to act on the radio problem, and stress was laid on the usefulness of COSPAR, the World Data Centers, and WMO in promoting international cooperation. A need was felt for a suitable center related to the United Nations to act as a focal point for cooperative efforts in outer space. It was suggested that the United Nations Secretariat might include a small section to keep cooperation under review, or a new UN body might be created to do that job. There was, however, no need yet for "an international agency for outer space."

The Legal Subcommittee, which, even without Soviet participation, had a more difficult time in achieving consensus, observed that the provisions of the United Nations Charter and of the Statute of the International Court of Justice were, as a matter of principle, not limited in their operation to the confines of the earth. It was generally agreed that not enough was known about the actual and prospective uses of outer space to make a comprehensive code practicable or desirable, but that it was necessary to take "timely, constructive action and to make the law of space responsive to the facts of space."[19] "It was unanimously recognized that the principles and procedures developed . . . to govern the use of such areas as the airspace and the sea deserved attentive study for possibly fruitful analogies . . . [though] outer space activities were distinguished by many specific factual conditions . . . that would render many of its legal problems unique."

It was suggested that among legal problems susceptible to priority treatment was the broad problem of freedom of outer space for exploration and use. The Legal Committee, in mentioning the flight of space vehicles "over" countries during the IGY, suggested that "with this practice, there may have been initiated the recognition or establishment of a generally accepted rule to the effect that, in principle, outer space is, on conditions of equality, freely available for exploration and use by all in accordance with existing or future international law or agreements."

Other priority problems noted by the Committee were liability for injury or damage caused by space vehicles, including the need for machinery to determine liability and ensure payment of compensation. Here, the committee suggested the compulsory submission to the International Court of Justice of disputes between states over liability and considered relevant ICAO's experience with respect to the 1952 Convention on Damage Caused by Foreign Aircraft to Third Parties on the Surface.[20] Allocation of radio frequencies, termination of transmissions, avoidance of interference between space vehicles and aircraft, identification and registration of vehicles through markings, call signs and orbit and transit characteristics, registration and coordination of launchings, and reentry and landing problems were also considered of current importance.

Problems the Committee felt could be ignored for the present because they were too remote from the point of view of technological development or because activities could be conducted without their resolution included the

---

[18] The Technical Committee's Report is A/AC.98/3.

[19] The Legal Committee's Report is A/AC.98/2.

[20] See S. Latchford, "The Bearing of International Air Navigation Conventions on the Use of Outer Space," 53 *Am. J. Int'l L.* 405 ff. (1959).

determination of precise limits between airspace and outer space, the provision of regulations against contamination of outer space or from outer space, the promulgation of rules covering sovereignty, exploration, settlement, and exploitation of celestial bodies, and rules for the avoidance of interference among space vehicles.[21] Some of these have by now already become more pressing. It was obvious that the Committee was perhaps overly cautious about several problems, which many then felt were more imminent than the committee was willing to acknowledge.

The general conclusions of the Ad Hoc Committee may be briefly summarized:[22] no autonomous intergovernmental agency should be created at this time nor should any such existing agency be asked to undertake overall responsibility for space matters; a small unit in the Secretariat might serve as a focal point for cooperation and a small committee there would advise the Secretary-General; a special committee of the General Assembly could be set up (although the criteria for its composition could not then be agreed upon):[23]

(a) To provide a focal point for facilitating international co-operation with respect to outer space activities undertaken by governments, specialized agencies, and international scientific organizations;
(b) To study practial and feasible measures for facilitating international co-operation, including those indicated by the Ad Hoc Committee in its report . . .;
(c) To consider means, as appropriate, for studying and resolving legal problems which may arise in the carrying out of programs for the exploration of outer space;
(d) To review, as appropriate, the subject matter entrusted by the General Assembly to the Ad Hoc Committee.

Thus, the Committee stressed for the United Nations a role of coordinator or promoter of cooperation, although the Swedish representative feared an increasing gap between the great forward surge of space activities and the efforts of the United Nations to promote the use of space for the benefit of all mankind, unless immediate action was taken within the United Nations.[24] Others, including the United States, insisted on "modest proposals" to meet only the most pressing needs.[25]

At the fall meeting of the General Assembly, the Ad Hoc Committee was transformed into a twenty-four-member permanent committee, the Committee on the Peaceful Uses of Outer Space.[26] This Outer Space Committee had five "neutral" states and seven Eastern European states, thus giving the Soviet Union the "soft" parity it had sought.

The Committee was charged anew with the task of studying "means . . . for giving effect to programmes in the peaceful uses of outer space which could appropriately be undertaken under United Nations auspices," and with studying the legal problems involved in space exploration. It was also to plan a world scientific conference on the peaceful uses of outer space to be held in 1960 or 1961.

The Committee was unable to meet at all in 1960 or 1961 because of conflict between the United States and the Soviet Union over unanimous versus majority voting, over the designation of the committee's officers, and over the mechanics of planning the proposed space conference.[27] The Soviet Union firmly insisted on a special arrangements subcommittee with equal representation for East and West. The United States, fearing the creation of a "hard" parity precedent, was unwilling to yield on this issue. Neither country wanted the space committee to meet until this issue was resolved.

Despite this major problem, in an effort to make progress, at the meeting of the United Nations in the fall of 1961, the United States, Italy, Canada, and Australia jointly sponsored a resolution in the First Committee, which for the first time formally suggested principles to govern the exploration and use of outer space. It also focused attention on advances and problems in the fields of meteorology and telecommunications, provided for a registry in the Secretariat of outer space launchings, continued and added members to the Outer Space Committee, and requested that Committee "to meet early in 1962."[28]

---

[21] The United States has also suggested that the problem of relations with extraterritorial life had a very low priority. U.N. Doc. A/AC/98/L.7.

[22] The *Report of the Ad Hoc Committee,* submitted to the General Assembly on June 25, 1959, is A/4141. On the committee's work, see Jessup & Taubenfeld, "U.N. Ad Hoc Committee . . . ," *supra* note 2, at 877 ff.; *Staff Report, supra* note 1, at 186–93.

[23] The Australian representative suggested that not only geographical distribution but the present distribution of capabilities and active interest in outer space also be considered. A/AC.98/SR.5 (Prov.), at 4.

[24] A/C.98/SR.4 (Prov.), at 6.

[25] See, e.g., *id.* at 4–5.

[26] Res. 1472 (XIV), Dec. 12, 1959.

[27] On the committee from 1959–62, see *Staff Report, supra* note 1, at 194–227.

[28] See A/C.1/L.301 (Dec. 2, 1961).

In the course of the First Committee's consideration, certain changes were made. The role of the Secretary-General was deemphasized; Chad, Mongolia, Morocco, and Sierra Leone were added to the space committee rather than Nigeria and Chad alone; and a firm date for a Committee meeting ("not later than 31 March 1962") was set. A compromise on voting was achieved; the Committee was to try to move by consensus; if it failed, majority voting would be used. The statement of principles and the general tenor of the resolution, as adopted by the General Assembly on December 20, 1961, as Resolution 1721 (XVI) including the votes of the United States and Russia, were along the lines suggested by the United States and constituted an interesting success for American diplomacy in this area.

In the first part of the resolution, the General Assembly recognized "the common interest of mankind in furthering the peaceful uses of outer space and the urgent need to strengthen international cooperation in this important field," and commended to states the principles that: "(a) International law, including the Charter of the United Nations, applies to outer space and celestial bodies; (b) Outer space and celestial bodies are free for exploration and use by all States in conformity with international law and are not subject to national appropriation." This has been discussed in general in the text in chapters 3 and 4. Other parts of the resolution dealt with the problems of organizing to further the study of meteorological phenomena and to provide better weather forecasting, of continuing and intensifying the international approach to the problems and potentials of communications satellites, and, as noted above, of formulating the future efforts and responsibilities of the Outer Space Committee. In addition the Secretary-General was requested to maintain the public registry of launchings "into orbit or beyond" through information supplied by states, a matter discussed in chapter 4.[29]

By the spring of 1962 various factors including, in all probability, the orbital flight of Col. Glenn, led both to bilateral meetings on space science between the United States and the USSR and to a real beginning of the work of the Outer Space Committee. That Committee met eight times in March 1962 under an agreed formula by which work was to be done "in such a way that the Committee will be able to reach agreement . . . without need for voting."[30] Discussion in March was focused on

the role of the U.N.'s Secretary-General and the Secretariat, while the U.S. pressed for at least a limited role as a "clearinghouse" for space information and the Soviet Union insisted that no operating role, even to that extent, was appropriate.[31] Two sub-committees of the whole were also established, one on scientific and technical matters, the other on legal problems.

At these meetings, in considering the prospective work for the Legal Subcommittee, the United States representative suggested that early attention be given to state responsibility for accidents and to "return-to-earth" arrangements. The Soviet representative offered as priority items the problems of harmful space experiments, a limitation of space use to "responsible governments, and return arrangements."[32] As we have noted, suggestions from other representatives ranged anew over the field of the law of space activities. Bernard of France wanted an examination of the definition of outer space and its relation to airspace, an investigation of just which rules of international law were applicable to outer space activities, and an immediate effort to create rules on contamination.[33] Others favored one or another of these items as of prime importance.[34] There was also wide agreement on the general utility of having the parent group, the Committee on the Peaceful Uses of Outer Space, serve as a coordinator of space activities already being performed by other agencies and organizations including, especially, the WMO, ITU, and COSPAR.[35]

The Scientific and Technical Subcommittees thereafter began a series of relatively successful periodic meetings

---

[29] For other brief comments, see *Staff Report, supra* note 1, at 260–66.

[30] A/AC.105/SR.2, at 5 (Mar. 19, 1962). This "decision" was itself taken by the technique of having the chairman (Matsch) state it, without objection, thus avoiding a vote. On this period, see *Staff Report, supra* note 1, at 203–8; *1962 U.N. Yearbook* at 37–55.

[31] See, e.g., A/AC.105/PV.8, at 41–42, 49–50 (8th meeting, Mar. 27, 1962) (May 15, 1962) and PV.9, at 3, 4 (9th meeting, Mar. 29, 1962) (May 9, 1962).

[32] See, e.g., A/AC.105/PV.8, at 34–41 (8th meeting, Mar. 29, 1962) (May 15, 1962) (U.S.); *id.* at PV.3 at 23–35 (3d meeting, Mar. 20, 1962) (May 7, 1962) (USSR). On the work of the First Session of the Legal Subcommittee, see Dembling & Arons, "Space Law . . . ," *supra* note 2, at 331–33.

[33] A/AC.105/PV/3 (3d meeting, Mar. 20, 1962), 23–27 (May 7, 1962).

[34] See, e.g., A/AC.105/PV/4, at 23–37 (4th meeting, Mar. 21, 1962) (May 7, 1962) (Canada); *id.* at PV/5, at 12–17, 32, 38–40 (5th meeting, Mar. 22, 1962) (May 7, 1962) (Australia) (Iran); *id.* at PV/6 (6th meeting, Mar. 23, 1962) (May 7, 1962) (Poland).

[35] A/AC.105/L.1, at 3 (Mar. 29, 1962).

which still continue but are not chronicled here largely because studies of these meetings are available in other sources.[36] Moreover, their subject matter, while involving political considerations, is generally less controversial than that with which the Legal Subcommittee had to deal. As van de Hulst put it in describing the work of COSPAR:

Scientists among themselves have fewer problems than perhaps the Governments have among themselves, and generally are facing very well-defined common [objectives] in the pursuit of research, and this introduces a natural point of convergence, namely the correct result. Although occasionally rivalries occur and different methods or schools of thought may prevail in a certain scientific approach, this has never cut very deep, and they can exist as well within one country as within different countries. There is no correspondence at all to the political situation there.[37]

As the Soviet representative Morozov commented: "Let us say that in science we can cooperate, but in law we cannot."[38]

At the meeting of the Legal Subcommittee in the spring of 1962 the political overtones of the space race were again evident. The United States was formally attacked by the Soviet Government for conducting high-altitude nuclear tests, for example.[39] Nevertheless, some progress was made in considering the problems of assistance to and return of space personnel and vehicles, of liability for space vehicle accidents, and of the nature of a draft declaration of basic principles. Attention was centered on proposals advanced by the two space powers.[40]

At this time, the Soviet proposal included several items unacceptable to the United States, including a requirement for advance consent by "concerned" countries to any use of space that might prove harmful, a limitation of space use to states alone (thus presumably barring companies and international organizations), a prohibition on intelligence-gathering, and a proposal permitting non-return of spacecraft used for intelligence activities. The United States in turn offered draft resolutions which it considered more suitable.[41]

The other states present sought to find some common ground between the two chief rivals, but at this time no formula could be found. At most the chairman was left to report that "the meetings offered the possibility for a most useful exchange of views."[42]

The full Committee on the Peaceful Uses of Outer Space met in September 1962, with further U.S.–USSR charges and countercharges concerning high-altitude nuclear tests and secrecy in launching vehicles into space.[43] At the time, the Soviet Union appeared reluctant to give up any of the points noted above, and no further progress was made toward agreement on legal issues. Perhaps the most interesting single session was that in which the United States produced a part of a Soviet vehicle which had fallen, without injuring anyone, on Manitowoc, Wis., on September 5, 1962.[44] The proposals made by the major space powers and a draft code prepared by the U.A.R. were simply attached to the committee's report to the assembly.[45]

In the First Committee in December further draft declarations were submitted by the United Kingdom and the United States.[46] The British statement was brief and included a provision giving each state and its nationals equal rights in the exploration and use of outer space. The United States continued to press for a resolution, while the Soviet Union urged more formal treaty arrangements.[47] There was an extended debate on surveillance from space, the Communist countries arguing, as we have noted before, that such information-gathering is espionage and hence illegal. The United States, however, has uniformly insisted that observation from space,

---

[36] See, e.g., on the meetings in May–June 1962, *Staff Report, supra* note 1, at 208–10.

[37] A/AC.105/PV.14, at 32 (Sept. 13, 1962) cited in *Staff Report, supra* note 1, at 208.

[38] A/AC.105/PV.12, at 52 (Sept. 12, 1962).

[39] See A/AC.105/C.1/1; A/AC/105/C.2/1, at 1 (June 5, 1962). For the U.S. response, see A/AC.105/C.2/SR. 4 at 8 (4th meeting, June 4, 1962). The U.S. later noted that the Soviet Union had also conducted such tests. See A/AC.105/PV.11 at 7–10 (Sept. 11, 1962) and see statement of Pres. Kennedy, Mar. 2, 1962, *Dept. State Bull.* 445 (Mar. 19, 1962) and AEC press releases of Oct. 23, 29, and Nov. 1, 1962, Nos. E–384, E–394, and E–446.

[40] See *Report of the Legal Subcommittee,* A/AC.105/6 (July 9, 1962). For the May-June, 1962, meetings see also *Staff Report supra* note 1, at 211–16.

[41] See A/AC.105/C.A/SR.7 (7th meeting, June 7, 1962) (Aug. 21, 1962).

[42] See *Report of the Legal Subcommittee, supra* note 40, at 9.

[43] On the meetings, see *Staff Report supra* note 1, at 216–21.

[44] For an account, see A/AC.105/PV.15, at 56–61, and *Washington Post,* Jan. 8, 1963, at 1.

[45] A/5181 (Sept. 27, 1962).

[46] See A/C. 1/879 (Dec. 4, 1962) (U.K.) and A/C.1/881 (Dec. 8, 1962) (U.S.A.).

[47] See, e.g., A/C.1/PV.1289, at 12 (Dec. 3, 1962) (U.S.A.); *id.* at 58–60 (U.S.S.R.); and A/C.1/PV.1296, at 3–12 (Dec. 10, 1962) (U.S.A.).

of all types, "is consistent with international law."[48] Many other representatives supported the position of the United States.[49] As at other times, the progress in scientific cooperation was more notable.

By the end of 1962, the United Nations thus had before it seven proposals concerned with the legal problems of outer space activities. These included: (1) a USSR proposal containing a draft declaration of basic principles governing the activities of states pertaining to the exploration and use of outer space; (2) a USSR proposal containing a draft international agreement on the rescue of astronauts and spaceships making emergency landings; (3) a United States draft proposal on assistance to, and return of, space vehicles and personnel; (4) a United States draft proposal on liability for space vehicle accidents; (5) a proposal by the United Arab Republic containing a draft code for international cooperation in the peaceful uses of outer space; (6) a proposal by the United Kingdom containing a draft declaration of basic principles governing the activities of states pertaining to the exploration and use of outer space; (7) a United States proposal containing a draft declaration of principles relating to the exploration and use of outer space. In Resolution 1802 (XVII) of December 14, 1962, the General Assembly stressed the need for the progressive development of law for outer space and requested the Committee on the Peaceful Uses of Outer Space to continue urgently its work on the further elaboration of basic legal principles governing these matters.

The Legal Subcommittee met in April and May of 1963 and made little formal progress, though differences were to some extent narrowed.[50] Agreement was reached, for example, that the form of U.N. statement on the general principles governing state activities should be that of a declaration, but no consensus existed as to the legal form of the instrument in which the principles were to be embodied. The Communist bloc representatives urged that the declaration of general principles should be adopted in the form of an international treaty. Others, including the representatives of Argentina, Australia, India, Japan, Lebanon, and the United States, took the view that a General Assembly resolution would be the most appropriate instrument for the declaration at that time, and that later an international treaty based on such a declaration might be elaborated.

Australia observed that a survey of the proposals on general principles set forth in General Assembly Resolution 1802 (XVII) disclosed a substantial area of agreement, and felt that the quick way to break away from the stalemate in which the subcommittee's first session had ended in 1962 was to accept the fact of certain disagreements and adopt a text embodying the elements on which agreement existed.

The representative of Belgium argued again that the sphere of application of space law should not be based on a demarcation between outer space and airspace, but rather on the means employed—the space vehicle—and that therefore space law should be applicable in both atmospheric and outer space whenever the activities of space vehicles or the consequences of their activities were concerned. In his view, an internationally agreed upon legal definition of space vehicles should be included in any settlement of specific problems, such as liability for damage or assistance to astronauts, and also in any general statement of principles.

Several representatives, including those of Czechoslovakia, Hungary, Mongolia, Rumania, and the USSR pointed out that agreement on the general principles governing the outer space activities of states was an essential prerequisite for the preparation of detailed international agreements on assistance to and return of astronauts and space vehicles and on liability for space vehicle accidents. In all, the chairman could at most report that there had been a "certain rapprochement and clarification of ideas."[51]

The outer space committee itself made little progress in its September meeting,[52] but the U.S.–USSR thaw had already resulted in the Nuclear Test Ban Treaty of

---

48 See statement of Senator Gore, A/C.1/PV.1289, at 13 (Dec. 3, 1962). For a Soviet comment, see *id.* at 57.

49 See, e.g., statement of Belaunde (Peru), U.N. Doc. A/C.1/PV.1290, at 58 (Dec. 4, 1962).

50 The Outer Space Committee proper met in Feb.–Mar. 1, 1963, but devoted most of its time to deciding on meeting places for its Subcommittees. This, too, involved arguments over a Soviet "veto" on proceedings. After much argument, the Legal Subcommittee met in New York; the Scientific Committee met in Geneva. See *Staff Report, supra* note 1, at 227–28. On the work of the Second Session of the Legal Subcommittee, see Dembling & Arons, "Space Law . . . ," *supra* note 2, at 333–36.

51 See *Report of Legal Subcommittee on Work of Its Second Session,* Apr. 16, May 3, 1963, A/AC.105/12. For a summary, see *Staff Report supra,* note 1, at 229–31. For the views of U.S. Representative Meeker see 8 *Dept. State Bull.* 923–25 (June 10, 1963).

52 See *Report,* A/5549 (Sept. 24, 1963).

August 1963.[53] Then, while discussions were continuing over a statement of legal principles, the General Assembly, on October 17, 1963, adopted Resolution 1884 (XVIII) (noted in chaps. 3 and 4), which recorded the understanding achieved during the Geneva disarmament negotiations between the United States and the Soviet Union, not to station nuclear or other weapons of mass destruction in outer space. The nations were solemnly called upon to abide by this principle. Ambassador Stevenson, for the United States, said that this policy had already been adopted by the United States and pointed out that it would certainly "seem easier not to arm an environment that has never been armed than to agree to disarm areas which have been armed."[54] The resolution was adopted unanimously. The probable reasons for this rapid progress are noted in this study.

Members of the Outer Space Committee met informally during the fall U.N. session and, on November 22, 1963, the committee met rather hastily to consider a nine-point draft declaration of legal principles prepared by the members.[55] The Committee agreed unanimously to submit this draft to the General Assembly, stating that it represented the maximum area of agreement possible at the time.[56]

In the full Outer Space Committee and in the First Committee in the late fall, discussions were renewed; we have drawn on some of these statements in this study.[57] Bulgaria, Hungary, Italy, the United Kingdom, and Yugoslavia, among others, considered that the legal principles contained in the draft declaration could serve as a basis for the development of the law of outer space. Italy, the USSR, the United Kingdom, and the United States were among those declaring their intent to conduct their activities in outer space in conformity with the principles of the declaration.

The representative of France, however, called the draft declaration only a declaration of intention and stressed that a General Assembly resolution, even though adopted unanimously, could not create juridical obligations incumbent upon member states.[58] He and the delegations of Hungary, India, Japan, Poland, USSR, and Yugoslavia, all expressed the opinion that certain provisions of the declaration would have to be further developed in the form of international agreements. The view was also expressed that the draft declaration should not be regarded as a comprehensive and final list of legal principles covering all the problems created by the exploration and use of outer space, but rather, as Japan expressed it, as a starting point for further work of expansion and elaboration.

Voicing reservations about the draft declaration, both in substance and in form, the USSR representative emphasized that his government still considered that the declaration of principles should be set out in a form similar to a treaty containing firm legal obligations on the part of states.

The representatives of Belgium and Rumania emphasized the importance of a clear-cut definition of the terms and concepts to be used in the legal principles relating to space law, while the representative of the United Kingdom stressed the need for defining the concept of registry as used in the draft declaration.

Brazil suggested that the declaration should incorporate a ban on the utilization of a communications system based on satellites for purposes of encouraging national, racial, or class rivalries and also as a reference to international scrutiny of global satellite communication. The representatives of Australia, Austria, Brazil, India, Pakistan, and the United Arab Republic expressed regret that the draft declaration did not contain a legal principle designed to preclude the placing in orbit of weapons of mass destruction on the lines formulated in assembly Resolution 1884 (XVIII). The representative of Japan said that the agreement to refrain from stationing weapons of mass destruction in outer space should be embodied in a binding international instrument, including provisions for verification as soon as possible.

In the course of discussion, the U.A.R. representative referred to the Antarctic Treaty of 1959 as an appropriate analogy. It proclaimed that Antarctica could be used only for peaceful purposes and prohibited all measures of a military nature on that continent. Commenting on this analogy, the representative of Canada

---

[53] For a discussion of this period, see *Staff Report, supra* note 1, at 231–33.

[54] *U.S. Arms Control and Disarmament Agency, Docs. on Disarmament, 1963*, 535–37 (Pub. No. 24, Oct. 1964).

[55] The chairman introduced the draft, which was not formally sponsored by any state.

[56] See the additional *Report of the Committee on the Peaceful Uses of Outer Space*, A/5549/Add. 1 (Nov. 27, 1963). See also *Staff Report, supra* note 1, at 233–35.

[57] See First Committee meeting 1342–46; draft declaration, A/C.1/L. 331; Report of First Committee, A/5656. See also *Report of the Committee* A/5549 and Add. 1 See also *Staff Report, supra* note 1, at 235–37.

[58] For a full discussion of the legal effect of the resolutions, see *supra,* chap. 4.

urged that the present situation concerning outer space differed from the situation which existed when the treaty was negotiated making Antarctica an arms-free area. At that time, no states had weapons systems which could have involved Antarctica in case of war. Now, however, intercontinental ballistic missiles, which represent the primary strategic weapon, could presumably pass through outer space on their way to a target. His government felt that Resolution 1884 (XVIII), together with the Moscow Treaty, constituted one of the most important disarmament measures for limiting the means of using outer space for military purposes. Insofar as intercontinental ballistic missiles were concerned, it felt the problem was not to prohibit their use in outer space but to negotiate an agreement reserving outer space for peaceful uses only.

The representative of India cited General Assembly Resolution 1884 (XVIII), which prohibited the stationing in outer space of weapons of mass destruction but did not make specific provision for verification, as in other disarmament proposals. He maintained that a legal principle on the same lines which forbade military uses of outer space and which did not provide for verification measures would not entail any added risk.

The representatives of France, Brazil, and the United Arab Republic expressed doubts concerning an unqualified extension to outer space of international law and the United Nations Charter. The representative of France noted that traditional international law, whose principles in matters relating to land, sea, and air were well established, could not be applied as it stood with regard to outer space. The representatives of Brazil and the United Arab Republic suggested that a study should be made to determine precisely what rules of international law or practice were applicable to outer space.

Application of the declaration of legal principles to international organizations taking part in activities in outer space was also discussed. In the opinion of Australia, Nigeria, and the United Kingdom, the omission from all paragraphs of the declaration, except the fifth, of any reference to international organizations conducting activities in outer space was not to be regarded as excluding such organizations from the scope of the declaration or as prejudicing their position in any way.

Concerning the stipulations providing for consultations about potentially harmful experiments in outer space, the representatives of Australia, Brazil, Canada, India, and Nigeria, among others, considered that the system of consultations should be made more precise and more binding. Australia, Brazil, and India suggested that

the system could be explicitly linked with presently existing international forums, such as the Consultative Group on Potentially Harmful Effects of Space Experiments established by the Committee on Space Research (COSPAR) of the International Council of Scientific Unions. On the other hand, the representative of the United States, although considering the consultative group of COSPAR as an appropriate forum, said that it would be inappropriate to specify one particular mode of conducting international consultations exclusively and for all time.

The representative of Japan considered that the provision of the draft declaration providing for the return of space devices found outside the state of registry and for furnishing identifying data upon request prior to return was ambiguous and legally untenable. The obligation to return space devices, he felt, should be conditional upon a corresponding obligation on the part of launching states to provide in advance adequate information concerning these devices. The views expressed by the Japanese representative were supported by the representatives of Nigeria, Pakistan, and the United Arab Republic. The United States representative emphasized that the provision in question did not seek to cover every conceivable situation and did not contain details for precise application. In his opinion, such matters would need further elaboration in subsequent instruments.

Referring to the provision of the draft declaration which dealt with the question of liability for damage, the United Kingdom's spokesman said the terms were so broad that application might well give rise to difficulties and, consequently, considerable amplification would be needed when a detailed agreement concerning liability for space vehicle accidents came to be drafted. The representatives of both France and the United Kingdom stressed that further and more detailed provisions would be needed relating to liability of international organizations, particularly for the purpose of confirming what was already implicit in the draft declaration, namely, that international organizations as well as their constituent states could be internationally liable for damages resulting from outer space activities.

It was in these debates, too, that the United States representative called for greater international cooperation while stating that "these legal principles reflect international law as it is accepted by the Members of the United Nations."[59] It should be noted that the Soviet Union had now agreed to omit certain items for which

---

[59] See A/C.1/PV.1342, at 12 (Dec. 2, 1963).

it had long argued: there was no "veto" of experiments by any nation; there was no limitation of space activities to states; the question of information-gathering satellites was ignored, both as to their legality and their return to a launching state.

On December 5 the draft declaration of legal principles was unanimously approved by the First Committee, and on December 13 it was unanimously adopted by the General Assembly as Resolution 1962 (XVIII), which has been discussed at length earlier in this study. On December 13 the Assembly also unanimously adopted a five-part Resolution 1963 (XVIII) on international cooperation in the peaceful uses of outer space. This resolution had been recommended by the First Committee, which had approved it by acclamation on December 5 on the proposal of twenty-seven of the twenty-eight members of the Committee on the Peaceful Uses of Outer Space.[60]

In the first part of Resolution 1963 (XVIII) the General Assembly recommended that consideration be given to the future incorporation in international agreement form of appropriate legal principles governing the activities of states in the exploration and use of outer space. It requested the Committee to continue to study and report on legal problems which might arise in the exploration and use of outer space, and in particular to arrange for the prompt preparation of draft international agreements on liability for damage caused by objects launched in outer space and on assistance to, and return of, astronauts and space vehicles. Other parts of the resolution:

(1) endorsed the recommendations contained in the report of the Committee on the Peaceful Uses of Outer Space concerning exchange of information, encouragement of international programmes, international sounding rocket facilities, education and training and potentially harmful effects of space experiments: (2) welcomed the decision of the Committee on the Peaceful Uses of Outer Space to undertake, in cooperation with the Secretary General: (a) the preparation of a working paper on the activities and resources of the United Nations, the specialized agencies, and other competent international bodies relating to the peaceful uses of outer space; (b) the preparation of a summary of national and of cooperative international space activities; (c) the preparation of a list of available bibliographic and abstracting services covering scientific and technical results and publications in space and space-related areas; (d) the compilation, in cooperation with the United Nations Educational, Scientific and Cultural Organization, of reviews of information on facilities for education and train-

ing in basic subjects related to the peaceful uses of outer space; and (e) the establishment, at the request of the Government of India, of a group of six scientists to visit the sounding rocket launching facility at Thumba and advise on its eligibility for United Nations sponsorship; (3) noted that the Secretary-General was maintaining a public registry of objects launched into orbit or beyond on the basis of information being furnished by Member States of the United Nations; (4) noted that certain Member States had, on a voluntary basis, provided information on their national space programmes and invited other Member States to do so,[61] (5) invited Member States to give favorable consideration to requests of countries desirous of participating in the peaceful exploration of outer space for appropriate training and technical assistance; (6) noted the considerable measure of cooperation in the peaceful exploration and use of outer space under way among Member States; (7) noted that the USSR and the United States have reached an agreement looking towards cooperation in the fields of satellite meteorology, communications, and magnetic field mapping; (8) encouraged Member States to continue and extend cooperative arrangements so that all Members could benefit from the peaceful exploration and use of outer space; and (9) expressed the belief that international cooperation could be beneficial in furthering the exploration of the solar system.

In part V, the General Assembly requested the Committee on the Peaceful Uses of Outer Space to continue its work.[62]

The problem of liability for space vehicle accidents was also discussed at length in 1963 (see chap. 6). As suggested above, the issue of assistance to and return of astronauts and space vehicles was also considered. Both the U.S. and the USSR agreed that action was now necessary and that, later on, a treaty would be. In Resolution 1963 (XVIII) the General Assembly requested that this problem be given prompt treatment.

Meeting in March 1964 the Legal Subcommittee devoted its time to new or revised proposals concerning assistance and return of astronauts and of space vehicles and liability.[63] Neither at the spring nor at the fall meet-

---

[60] See U.N. Doc. A/C.1/L.332 and Rev. 1.

[61] In 1963 there were 30 U.S. and USSR notifications concerning 52 successful launchings. See A/AC.105/INF. 25–AC.105/INF.55.

[62] As noted previously, the important work of scientific and technical coordination is not surveyed herein. See *U.N. Yearbook, 1963, passim,* and sources and documents cited therein.

[63] On assistance and return, see: A/AC.105/C.2/Revs. 1 and 2 (Soviet drafts); A/AC.105/C.2/L.9 (U.S. draft); W.G.I/17 and Rev. 1 and W.C.I/30 (Australian and Canadian proposals).

On liability, see A/AC.105/C.2/L.8 and Revs. 1 and 2

ings in 1964 were full drafts of either agreement completed[64] nor, in fact, despite the friendlier climate for a period after mid-1963, was the work finished when in 1965 the Vietnam crisis again exacerbated relations between the major powers.

The March 1964 meeting opened with a new request by the Soviet Union for further study of "general principles" as well as of conventions covering liability and return, but this proposal received little non-Soviet-bloc support. Two working groups, each open to the full membership of the Legal Subcommittee, were established to deal with the two proposed treaty areas.

On the draft treaty for the return of space vehicles and astronauts, there was general agreement on the humanitarian concern for the plight of astronauts who missed their proper landing place and on the scientific utility of returning to the appropriate state a fallen spacecraft or its parts. In the 1964 meetings, the United States suggested[65] that the state of registry or the international organization responsible for a launching should have prime responsibility but that all parties should take "all possible steps to assist or rescue promptly the personnel of spacecraft who are the subject of accident or experience conditions of distress or who may make emergency landing by reason of accident, distress, or mistake." It was also suggested that each party should permit, subject to control by its own authorities, the launching authorities to provide such measures of assistance as might be necessitated by the circumstances (based on Article 25 of the Chicago Convention on Civil Aviation). In addition, it was proposed simply: "Upon request by the State of registry or international organiza-

tion responsible for launching, a Contracting Party shall return to that State or international organization an object launched into outer space or parts thereof that have returned to Earth. Such State or international organization shall, upon request, furnish identifying data."

A reading of these March 1964 discussions leads then to certain conclusions:

1. The major space powers were in agreement[66] that a party should be under a mandatory obligation to request the launching authority's assistance on its own territory if it proved unable to carry out necessary rescue operations.

2. Non-launching states were concerned with provisions regarding assistance on the high seas or elsewhere beyond territory under national jurisdiction or control, lest a launching authority claim an *exclusive* right to conduct rescue operations on the high seas.

3. There was a split over whether or not an astronaut was to be returned promptly to the launching state or whether, simply, his departure was not to be opposed in normal cases.

4. There was a split over whether or not a vehicle would be returned in *all* circumstances (U.S. view), only if there were prior compliance with some rules (e.g., announcement of the launching, USSR–Japanese view), or if the purpose of the mission were "peaceful" and, especially, if it were not engaged in "espionage" activities (USSR view).

5. There was near universal agreement that expenses incurred in recovering a space object should be reimbursed by the launching state, but that there should be no reimbursement for expenses incurred in fulfilling the humanitarian duty of rescuing astronauts, although India and certain states seemed to suggest otherwise.

6. Suggestions for peaceful settlement of disputes under the proposed treaty ranged from use of the International Court of Justice for all disputes (U.S.), or only after other means failed (U.K.) or only by special agreement of the parties (USSR). The USSR's position is of course entirely consistent with its overall lack of trust in international adjudication.

7. The problem of the "cold war" was again evident in the discussion of potential parties to the treaty. The United States proposed that member states of the United Nations family and any other state invited by the Gen-

---

(U.S. drafts); A/AC.105/C.2/L.10 (Hungarian draft); A/AC.105/C.2/L.7 and Revs. 1 and 2 (Belgian working paper).

[64] See *Reports of the Legal Subcommittee,* A/AC.105/19 (covering Mar. 9–26, 1964), A/AC.105/21 (covering October 5–23, 1964) and Adds. and the Report of the Full Committee, A/5785, Nov. 13, 1964. This latter report and U.S. drafts on assistance (A/AC.105/21/Add. 1, Oct. 27, 1964) and liability (A/AC.105/C.2/L.8/Rev. 2, Oct. 20, 1964), a Soviet draft on rescue (A/AC.105/21, Annex I, at 2–6 (Oct. 23, 1964), and a Hungarian draft on liability (A/AC.105/21, Annex II, at 2–6 [Oct. 23, 1964]) are conveniently reproduced in *Staff Report supra* note 1, at 241–60. On the Mar. 1964 meeting, see Dembling, "Status of the Law of Outer Space in the United Nations," paper presented at the 1964 Annual Convention, Federal Bar Ass'n (mimeo., Sept. 11, 1964). On the Third and Fourth Sessions of the Legal Subcommittee, see Dembling & Arons, "Space Law . . . ," *supra* note 2, at 336–71.

[65] A/AC.105/C.2/L.9.

---

[66] See Soviet draft A/AC.105/C.2/L.2/Rev. 2 and Australia-Canada proposal WG.I/17.

eral Assembly should be entitled to become a party to the agreement. The USSR felt that "all States" should be eligible, its usual formula.

Revised versions of the various proposals were discussed at the second part of the third session in the fall of 1964,[67] and agreement was reached on a preamble and three articles on assistance and return.[68] It is interesting to note in these negotiations the multiple, shifting conflicts of interest and points of view over the issue; while the Soviet-U.S. confrontation has led to some of the disagreements, other controversies have distinctly involved the "rich" against the "poor," and some saw the United States opposed by its European friends and allies. The United States and Russia seemed in general agreement, however, on such issues as: a universal duty to rescue astronauts; a duty to notify the state of "launching" or "registry" of the retrieval of astronauts or a vehicle; and a mandatory obligation on a state unable to render proper assistance to request assistance and the obligation of others to respond.

There was nevertheless general disagreement over the following:

1. In the matter of rescue on the high seas, most states felt that a joint search would be appropriate. The Soviet Union urged, initially, an exclusive right in the launching state to effect or control the rescue, thus excluding all other states, presumably for security reasons.[69] This arrogation of an exclusive jurisdiction on the seas was resisted by the United States and by the other non-Communist members. It was later somewhat modified, as we will see, to a concept of "direction" of the operations.

2. The Soviet Union sought to limit the duty to return space vehicles, etc., to those launched with prior announcement. The Japanese suggested a return only of objects registered with the United Nations.[70] The United States objected to any need for prior registration, etc., as a precondition to return.

3. The Soviet Union sought to limit the return to objects (and astronauts) launched for "peaceful" purposes, presumably as determined by the rescuing state; the United States opposed any such limitation. This is

perhaps the clearest continuation of a pre-1963 argument—that concerning observation satellites. The Soviet Union later proposed a return only if the launching was for purposes in accord with the 1963 Declaration of Legal Principles, but this was also considered too uncertain by the United States and others, since determination would again presumably be made by the rescuing state.

4. There was also disagreement over the use of the International Court of Justice. The United States suggested a general use, whereas the Soviet Union insisted that it be only with the consent of all parties. Russia also insisted that "all states" be eligible parties to the proposed treaty; the United States desired to limit treaty membership to members of the United Nations or states invited by the U.N. General Assembly, thus seeking to exclude Communist China.

5. There was also an "East-West" split over the question of whether international organizations should be permitted to possess rights and duties under the convention independent of the states comprising such organizations.

Among other objections raised by the nonspace powers were: a demand for right to refuse entry to security-important areas to officials of launching states;[71] a demand for a right to hold an astronaut if he committed a crime after landing;[72] a demand that, prior to a return, the launching state accept the obligation to compensate for damage done;[73] a demand for *full* reimbursement for costs incurred in rescuing vehicles and personnel (the major powers and most other states had earlier seemed to agree that assistance to astronauts was a humanitarian duty and should not require reimbursement). Some states now argued that the expenses of locating astronauts should be fully reimbursed since, unlike rescues at sea where all seafaring nations may have personnel in distress, the rescue of astronauts would be for the benefit of only a few states.

Despite major disagreements, by the end of the third session a preamble, one partial and two complete articles were approved by Working Group I. Article 2 of the agreed draft required a state learning of an accident or of

---

[67] See revised Soviet draft, A/AC.105/C.2/L.2/Rev. 2, and the revised Australia-Canada draft, W.G.I/30.

[68] The agreed draft appears as Annex III, *Report of the Legal Subcommittee*, U.N. Doc. A/AC.105/21.

[69] For criticism of this view on humanitarian grounds, see the statement of the Italian delegate, SR.29–37, at 56.

[70] See W.G.I/9.

[71] Sweden, SR.29–37, at 56. Note the delicate position caused by Sweden's geographic proximity to the USSR.

[72] France, WG.I/17.

[73] Japan, WG.I/23. Other proposals sought to achieve the same end by linking the rescue and return convention to the proposed liability convention. The Soviet Union insisted that claims should not lead to sequestration of space vehicles.

the distress of space personnel of another state to notify immediately both the state which announced the launching and the Secretary-General of the United Nations. Article 3 provided that where space personnel made an emergency landing in territory under the jurisdiction of a contracting party, "it shall immediately take all possible steps, within the limits of the means at its disposal, to rescue the personnel and render them the necessary assistance." The assistance was to be that which would be furnished to its own personnel; and the state rendering it could request technical assistance from the state announcing the launching, as long as it remained "under the direction and control" of the rendering party.

Article 6 concerned return of space objects, as distinguished from assistance to personnel, and covered landings which take place within the territory or jurisdiction of a contracting party, on the high seas, and elsewhere. As in Article 2, the same duties of notification were put upon the party learning that such a landing had taken place. The state announcing the launching was obligated upon notice to take "prompt and effective steps" to remove or render harmless a space object or component thereof which is of a "hazardous and deleterious nature." In addition, if the state announcing the launching knows that a space object which has landed on the territory of a contracting party is hazardous, it must immediately notify the contracting party and, upon request, remove the object or render it harmless. The party recovering the space object was to request the technical assistance of the state announcing the launching, which in turn was to furnish identifying data upon request.

There remained, at this time, disagreement on the Soviet proposal which conditioned the return of space objects upon whether the launching was for purposes in accord with the Declaration of Legal Principles.

The fourth session of the Legal Subcommittee was not held until September 20–October 1, 1965. The working group procedure, which had not apparently expedited matters much, was abandoned in favor of formal sessions. At this session, some further consensus was achieved on the rendering of assistance to the crews of spaceships,[74] but no broad progress was visible. The key issue of national security was clearly involved as a limiting factor and, doubtless, international tension over

Vietnam made agreement on any problem more difficult to achieve.

These sessions threw additional light on the meaning of and outlook for the principles stated in Resolution 1962. Over the years, for example, the Soviet Union shifted from an insistence that only space objects launched for "peaceful" purposes need be returned, to a return only of objects "launched in accordance with the Declaration of Legal Principles Governing the Activities of States in the Exploration and Use of Outer Space."[75] It was still suggested by Communist representatives that this meant for "peaceful" purposes[76] and was resisted by the United States[77] which suggested as a maximum requirement that the responsible state furnish identifying data if requested. Other representatives noted, too, the problem involved in permitting the state holding the vehicle to decide unilaterally as to the compliance of the launch,[78] but mediating suggestions were insufficient to achieve an agreement in 1965.[79]

Soviet proposals[80] for the return of astronauts also referred to launchings in accordance with the same principles. The duty to return persons and objects made by the West was not so limited.[81] Several representatives again objected to placing in any state's hands the unilateral right to make such a determination of propriety as a condition of return and they argued that paragraph 9 of the declaration itself imposed an unconditional duty to return astronauts landing in distress.[82]

In this context, the Canadian representative stated that the declaration was intended to constitute "a set of guidelines, to be taken into account in the drafting of rules on specific matters, but not having themselves the character of treaty provisions."[83] On the other hand, the Communist representatives argued that launchings which did not comply with the declaration (presumably as interpreted by them) were hostile and could be dealt

---

[74] See, e.g., statements of various delegates SR.42, at 8 (France), SR.42, at 9 (Rumania), SR.43, at 4 (Argentina), SR.42, at 7 and SR.43, at 3 (Mexico).

[75] See A/AC.105/C.2/L. 2/Rev. 2 (Soviet draft).

[76] SR.44, at 8 (Hungary).

[77] SR.44, at 3.

[78] SR.43, at 3 (Mexico).

[79] See comments of Mexico, SR.43, at 3, SR.44, at 5; Rumania and Austria, SR.44, at 4–5.

[80] See U.N. Doc. A/AC.105/C.2/L.2/Rev.2.

[81] See U.N. Docs. A/AC.105/C.2/L.9 (US draft) and WG.1/30 (Australia-Canada Working Group draft).

[82] SR.46, at 3–4 (U.S.); SR.47, at 3(Canada); SR.47, at 6–7 (Australia).

[83] SR.47, at 3.

with as such.[84] Again, no easy solution was then at hand for the divergent points of view.[85]

The contention over control of the seas was equally difficult.[86] The Soviet Union continued to insist that the launching authority should at least direct the operations if it did not fully control them;[87] the West argued that the state with closest facilities for rescue was the one best suited to take prompt measures and that, while cooperation with the launching state was appropriate, no state should be bound by orders from another.[88] Russia did finally offer a compromise by which the launching state would "undertake general coordination of the rescue operations" while other states, if any, carrying out the operations would do so "in accordance with the recommendations and technical advice" of the launching state.[89] No further agreement was reached at that time, however, and the language suggested left much room for interpretation.[90]

In May 1966, in a dramatic advance, both the United States and the Soviet Union pressed new initiatives toward an outer space treaty in the United Nations. On May 7th, President Johnson proposed that the U.N. Committee for the Peaceful Uses of Outer Space consider a treaty for the moon and the celestial bodies similar to the "open" regime agreed to for Antarctica in 1959.[91] Two days later, the U.S. asked consideration of a treaty by the Legal Subcommittee of the U.N. Outer Space Committee.[92] On May 30 the Soviet Union, by letter to the Secretary-General, proposed that the agenda of the twenty-first session of the General Assembly include the question of concluding a treaty covering legal principles governing space exploration.[93] While the basic proposals were similar to those of the United States, the Soviet initiative was different in proposing to make rules for all space activities through initial work in the General Assembly while the United States proposed dealing only with the celestial bodies, using the Outer Space Committee. In a letter of June 16th, the United States sent a draft treaty to the Outer Space Committee and asked for a meeting of the Legal Subcommittee on July 12.[94] By letter of that same date, the Soviet Union submitted its proposed treaty to the Secretary-General for circulation.[95] The Soviet Union proved amenable to consideration of the drafts by the Outer Space Committee and meetings of that Committee's Legal Subcommittee in fact were held in Geneva in July 1966.

At these meetings, the United States accepted the idea of a broader treaty applicable to space activities in general.[96] All twenty-eight members accepted some nine draft proposals along the lines of the U.N. resolutions of 1961 and 1963 to the effect that: exploration should be carried out in accordance with international law and the U.N. Charter; no state can claim sovereignty over outer space or the celestial bodies by any means; weapons of mass destruction should not be orbited or placed on celestial bodies; space powers are internationally liable for damage caused other states by objects launched into outer space; military activities and bases on the celestial bodies were barred.

At the close of the Geneva session, the Committee agreed to meet just before the General Assembly in September. Major unresolved disagreements were the anticipated ones: the United States proposed to have full reports on all activities on the celestial bodies presented by the space explorers; the Soviet Union said that reporting should be on a "voluntary basis"; the United States suggested that all bases on celestial bodies should

---

[84] This was the view expressed by the Soviet (SR.46, at 3), Bulgarian (SR.46, at 4), and Rumanian (SR.47, at 5–6) delegates.

[85] For other suggestions, see the Mexican statements, SR.45, at 8 and SR.46, at 5.

[86] The fourth session had three drafts before it: Art. 4 of the Soviet draft (U.N. Doc. A/AC.105/C.2/L.2/Rev. 2), Art. 2 of the U.S. draft (U.N. Doc. A/AC.105/C.2/L.9), and Art. 4 of the Australia-Canada draft (WG.I/30).

[87] See SR.45, at 3, 4, 7–8.

[88] See the statements by the delegates of France (SR.45, at 9) and of the United States (SR.45, at 5).

[89] SR.45, at 3.

[90] *The Report of the Legal Subcommittee on the Work of Its Fourth Session* is A/AC.105/29 (1 Oct. 1965).

[91] For text of the speech, see 54 *Dept. State Bull.* 900 (1966) or *New York Times,* May 8, 1966, at 66. This had been foreshadowed by speeches of Ambassador Goldberg at the U.N. on Sept. 23 and Oct. 18, 1965. See, e.g., *Washington Post,* Dec. 20, 1965, at A15.

[92] See 54 *Dept. State Bull.* 900 (1966) or *New York Times,* June 17, 1966.

[93] For text, see A/6341 (1966) and *New York Times,* June 1, 1966, at 27. For comment, see *Washington Post,* June 1, 1966, at A1; *New York Times,* June 3, 1966, editorial.

[94] See A/AC.105/32(June 17, 1966).

[95] See A/6352 (June 16, 1966).

[96] On the Geneva meetings, the documentation for which is difficult to obtain, see the detailed account in Dembling and Arons, "Celestial Bodies . . . ," *supra* note 2, at 535, 538–48. See also, for newspaper accounts, e.g., *New York Times,* July 22, 1966, July 31, 1966. For Ambassador Goldberg's opening statement, see 54 *Dept. State Bull.* 249–52 (Aug. 15, 1966).

always be open to visits; the Soviets proposed that visits should be by prior agreement; the United States wanted disputes to be referrable ultimately to the International Court of Justice; Russia suggested negotiation; the United States wanted to limit signatories to U.N. members and nonmembers invited by the General Assembly; Russia wanted the treaty available to "all nations," with Communist China perhaps in mind. There were also the questions of whether "military" equipment could be used for space exploration; whether a provision requiring cooperative use of tracking facilities should be included; whether a United Kingdom proposal on international organizations should be adopted.

The Legal Subcommittee met again in New York beginning on September 12.[97] Some differences proved amenable to reasonably rapid resolution: the United States, for example, stated that it would not insist that space stations and vehicles be "open at all times for inspection" but agreed that visits be made "on a basis of reciprocity" with "reasonable advance notice" to host governments, and that reports be submitted by governments only "to the extent feasible and practicable."[98] The Soviet Union, which had insisted that states granting tracking facilities to any space power make them equally available to all powers, continued to press for this privilege but now agreed to meet expenses incurred in tracking. The U.S. and most other states continued to insist that compulsory access was unacceptable.[99] A revised Soviet draft in early October accepted the U.S. revisions about information and access to bases and also now agreed that equal access to tracking facilities should be arranged by bilateral negotiations.[100] In early December President Johnson was able to announce that agreement had been reached on the final form of a treaty.[101] This treaty was approved by the United Nations on December 19, 1966,[102] and, as we have noted in chapters 3 and 4, was signed by more than sixty nations in January 1967. Its meaning has been discussed extensively in this study.

In the rush to prepare the 1967 treaty, the U.N. Outer Space Committee could give no further attention to the drafts on rescue and return and on liability. The General Assembly expressly requested further work on these subjects.[103] At its sixth session, held in Geneva between June 19 and July 14, 1967, the Legal Subcommittee resumed its work on the basis of the draft treaty proposed earlier by the U.S. (as noted above herein), a revised Australian-Canada working paper,[104] and a revised Soviet draft,[105] which still omitted coverage of the *return* of astronauts and space objects. This basic divergence in views prevented further progress at that time.

In the fall of 1967 the Soviet Union dramatically shifted its position and stated that it had no objection to including provisions on return.[106] By the end of 1967 a Treaty on Rescue and Return was a reality.[107]

That Treaty has been reviewed as to most of its substance in chapter 4. Briefly, it will be recalled that it provides for the notification of accidents; the rescue of astronauts on the territory of a party and the high seas or anywhere else not under the jurisdiction of any state; the return of astronauts without any qualifications; the recovery and return of space objects; identification and assisting in the expenses of recovery; and definition of "launching authority" which for the first time expressly covers international organizations as well as states.[108] Two additional points, one now fairly typical: It was agreed by the parties, in order to reach agreement overall, that no express provision would be included for the settlement of disputes arising from the Agreement.[109] This was also true of the Outer Space Treaty of 1967. The solution of disputes is thus left to normal diplomatic procedures or by other applicable international agreements. Second, the Treaty is open to signature by "all states" to carry out its humanitarian purposes. As the U.S. carefully pointed out, acceptance of the Treaty by

---

[97] See Dembling & Arons, *supra* note 2, at 548–50; *New York Times,* Sept. 14, 1966.

[98] See *New York Times, id.*

[99] See *New York Times,* Sept. 17, 1966; Sept. 23, 1966. The U.S. offered to make tracking facilities of the U.S. available to the USSR by means of a "mutually beneficial agreement."

[100] See *New York Times,* Oct. 6, 1966.

[101] See *New York Times,* Dec. 9, 1966; Pres. Doc. 178–82 (Dec. 12, 1966).

[102] See also *New York Times,* Dec. 20, 1966.

[103] Gen. Assembly Resolution 2222 (XXI) January 25, 1967.

[104] A/AC.105/C.2/L.20 (1967). On developments in 1967–68, see *supra,* chaps. 3 and 4, *passim,* and Dembling & Arons, "Treaty . . . ," *supra* note 2, at 630–63.

[105] A/AC.105/C.2/L.18 (1967).

[106] See statement of Ambassador Morozov, A/AC.105/ PV.49 at 61 (1967).

[107] See Dembling & Arons, "Treaty . . . ," *supra* note 2, at 639–41.

[108] On the meaning of the treaty, see *supra,* chap. 4, *passim,* and Dembling & Arons, *id.* at 641 ff.

[109] The U.S. drafts included recourse to the International Court of Justice; the Soviet Union suggested a limit to consultation between the parties.

the governments of East Germany or Communist China would of course not constitute formal recognition by other parties.[110]

The United Nations has thus already served as an official focus for the discussion of basic issues of outer space activity and has played a major part in the creation of the emerging law relevant to such activity. It has nevertheless itself been given only a small role in the actual conducting and control of outer space operations. The field of outer space is so intimately connected with national power and prestige that nations have been unwilling to consider international operations or controls. As with other areas, we have even today basically only the assurance of states that outer space will in fact be used for the benefit of all men.

The Specialized Agencies

In addition to the contributions to the development of the law of outer space activities made by the General Assembly, the U.N.'s specialized agencies have also played some role in the field.[111] We have already noted, in chapter 5, the activities of the International Telecommunications Union (ITU) and its subsidiary bodies in assigning radio channels for space activities, space communications, and radio astronomy.[112]

The International Civil Aviation Organization (ICAO) with over 110 members, already exercises responsibilities which may prove relevant to space operations.[113] The organization now coordinates planning of technical programs for improving air navigation facilities; it promulgates international standards and recommends practices (the ICAO Annexes) which parties are generally bound to observe; it has established jointly supported ocean weather stations; it administers (with the U.N.) a large technical assistance program. In important matters, ICAO is a lawmaking body; none of its Annexes or Amendments has ever been disapproved by a majority or even by a large number of states.

We have noted earlier both that ICAO's regime is limited to airspace[114] and that the Soviet Union is not a member of the ICAO. Until recently, the organization had been reluctant to attempt to assume a larger role in space activities,[115] although several commentators have at times suggested such an expansion.[116] Moreover, certain space developments—satellite communications systems, for example—may well affect civil aviation. It is also clear that the status of space vehicles and their relationship to ICAO's concerns *while in airspace* on ascent or descent may in time require clarification.

ICAO has sporadically considered the problems of outer space activities since 1956, particularly in its Legal Committee.[117] The United States, joined by other countries including the United Kingdom, have nevertheless been firm in arguing that ICAO should not attempt any general approach to outer space through broad legal and technical studies, that it should deal with specific problems only as they arise, and that the question of the upper limit of airspace is a political rather than a legal question.[118] Other states' representatives urged a more active role, at least where space activities impinged on airspace activities, as in the problem of liability.[119]

In 1965, in a change of pace, the ICAO Assembly resolved to move beyond its passive role and to begin the study of the aspects of space activities which will affect civil aviation.[120] In fact, in the fields of telecommunications and meteorology, ICAO has become active to a limited extent since arrangements in these fields are

[110] See statement of Ambassador Goldberg, Dec. 16, 1967, U.S./U.N. Press Release 246 (Dec. 16, 1967).

[111] See generally, Jessup & Taubenfeld, *Controls . . . , supra* note 2, at 87–92; *Staff Report, supra* note 1, at 263–784; Haley, *supra* note 1, at 304–12; U.N., *Review* (by the Secretariat) of the activities and resources of the U.N. and its specialized agencies, A/AC.105/L.29 (1966).

[112] See also *Staff Report, supra* note 1, at 263–84. For U.N. information on the ITU and space activities, see, e.g., A/AC.105/L.12, A/AC.105/L.16, E/4037/Add. 1, A/AC.105/L.24 (Fifth Report, 1966).

[113] See *Staff Report, supra* note 1, at 331–48; Schenkman, *The International Civil Aviation Organization* (Geneva, 1955); Billyou, *Air Law* 263–66 and sources cited (2d ed. 1964); Jessup & Taubenfeld, *Controls . . . ,* at 87–89.

[114] See *supra,* chap. 3 for a relevant discussion. ICAO Annexes, it will be recalled, define an aircraft as "Any machine that can derive support in the atmosphere from the reactions of the air" (Annex 6). *Present* space vehicles, at least, seem to be excluded.

[115] See, e.g., ICAO, Legal Committee, 12th Sess., Doc. 8111-LC/146–2, at 204 (1960).

[116] See, e.g., *Staff Report, supra* note 1 at 340 and sources cited, esp. in notes 1–3.

[117] See *id.* at 340–47.

[118] See *Report and Minutes of the Legal Commission,* Twelfth Session of the ICAO Assembly, ICAO Doc. 8010, A12-LE/1, at 26, 32.

[119] See *id.* at 30 (France, Mexico).

[120] See, e.g., A/AC.105/PV.40, at 105–7 (statement of Mr. Heierman of ICAO) (Oct. 7, 1965).

directly important to air transport.[121] Other roles for ICAO—administration of a navigational satellite system for the benefit of aircraft,[122] regulation of the aeronautical use of communications satellites, the creation of workable definitions for "aircraft, airspace," etc.— have all been suggested.[123] All would raise political problems and legal issues as well. Of course, the existing organization is not designed to undertake direct exploration, exploitation, or control of a new area; it is a device for the orderly use of existing opportunities in a commercial field. As an entity, ICAO has continued to move most cautiously in this new field.

Although several other agencies have a direct interest in space activities, they are not themselves primarily operating entities and, hence, their effect on the law is necessarily indirect. The World Meteorological Organization (WMO) for example, with some 127 members in early 1966, essentially coordinates and promotes cooperation among national weather services. The WMO has concerned itself with space technology since 1958 through studies, the creation of a panel of experts, reports on space activities of special significance for meteorology, the preparation of a World Weather Watch (a cooperative global observing and prediction system), etc.[124]

It has participated in the International Geophysical Year (IGY), the Years of the Quiet Sun, and the work of the U.N. Outer Space Committee.

UNESCO and the World Health Organization (WHO) have played some similar part. UNESCO[125] was mentioned in the 1959 Ad Hoc Committee Report and has undertaken to assist in the coordination of basic research by giving financial support to international scientific organizations interested in space, by helping to organize international meetings, and by organizing training courses in science. It has also urged and encouraged an interest in space communications as a technique for mass global communications, a subject discussed elsewhere in this study.

WHO has also been represented at meetings of the U.N. Outer Space Committee.[126] It is interested in the effects of space flight on health, on contamination and so forth. It has not yet had an active program connected with outer space activities but could play a larger role in time.

In addition, the International Atomic Energy Agency (IAEA) has evinced some interest in technological problems of space activities (propulsion, other energy requirements, shielding, contamination, etc.) and in some biological aspects (effects of radiation, etc.).[127] It has assisted to a limited degree in organizing meetings and has prepared some research papers. The idea of

---

[121] See *Staff Report, supra* note 1, at 342–44.

[122] For a comment on a joint approach by ICAO and the Inter-Govermental Maritime Consultative Organization (IMCO) to the problems of navigation satellites, see A/AC.105/PV.37, at 15.

[123] See Staff Report, *supra* note 1, at 344–47. In general, see also J. H. Heierman, "The International Civil Aviation Organization and Outer Space," 2 *ICAO Bull.,* 3–5 (1966); Larsen, "Space Activities and Their Effect on International Civil Aviation" (mimeo., paper prepared for the *Tenth Colloquium of the IISL,* 1967).

[124] See WMO, *First Report on the Advancement of Atmospheric Sciences and Their Application in the Light of Developments in Outer Space* (Geneva, Secretariat of the WMO, June, 1962). See also *Second* (1963), *Third* (1964), etc. *Reports.* For a summary, see *Staff Report, supra* note 2, at 284–308. See also *Reports of WMO to the Outer Space Committee,* e.g., A/AC.105/PV., at 63–68 (6 Oct. 6, 1965), and A/AC.105/L.31 (*Fifth Report*). For President Johnson's statement on the WMO and the World Weather Watch, see *Pres. Doc.* 439 (Mar. 25, 1966).

In considering the need for international cooperation in scientific affairs, Harlan Cleveland, then Assistant Secretary of State for International Organization Affairs, said, in 1964: "The technological imperative—the impulse to build worldwide technical agencies—comes of course from the headlong pace of scientific discovery. A world technical community is in the making because international communications, international transport, and international economics demand international

organizations—and because you can't deal with world health or world weather or radio frequencies and a lot of other things except on a world basis . . . ."

"Taken together, three new kinds of technology—weather satellites, communications satellites, computer technology— now make it technically possible to work out a global weather reporting and forecasting system, a prospect too valuable to all nations to leave unexploited. The United States is now engaged in a very large program of research and development in this field that will involve the cooperation of more than 100 other countries. This, together with what other countries are doing, will fit into an overall plan for a World Meteorological Organization, a specialized agency of the U.N.

"In just two years our first Tiros satellites discovered 20 hurricanes, typhoons, and tropical storms and observed the behavior of 62 others. And world data centers to process these and other reports and issue warnings have been established in Washington and Moscow." See *Cong. Rec.* 5462–64 (Mar. 18, 1964); *Astronautics & Aeronautics,* 1964, 83–84 (NASA, 1965).

[125] See *Staff Report, supra* note 1, at 308–19.

[126] See, e.g., A/AC.105/C.2/SR. (Aug. 21, 1962).

[127] See *Staff Report, supra* note 1, at 319–31 and e.g., statement by the IAEA representative, A/AC.105/L.21 (Oct. 8, 1965).

using the IAEA as an analogy for the regulation of at least certain outer space activities has also been broached in the literature.[128]

In all, despite the potential inherent in each of these organizations, they have to date played little or no part in space developments; at most they have helped fill the need for the exchange of information, the coordination of programs, and the creation of prospective programs. The nations have been as unwilling to give these agencies any operating role (except inevitably for the essential but limited functions of the ITU) as they have been unwilling to give the United Nations itself any major part in the conduct of space activities.

Other International Arrangements

Bilateral

One of the most striking aspects of the movement of the major powers into outer space activities is the extent to which other nations have, by one program or another, been brought into formal legal arrangements with a launching state, to date almost exclusively with the United States. In addition to the general treaties discussed at length in the text of earlier chapters, agreements made by the United States have taken the form of executive agreements and memoranda of understanding.[129] Under section 205 of the National Aeronautics and Space Act of 1958, as amended,[130] the administration was encouraged to engage in a "program of international cooperation" and by mid-1967 NASA had developed formal contacts with some eighty-four countries or separate jurisdictions.[131] Intergovernmental executive arrangements have been negotiated by the Department of State on behalf of and with the assistance of NASA, while NASA has entered into memoranda of understanding and letter agreements with cooperating foreign agencies after consultation and concurrence by

the Department of State.[132] Other relevant arrangements have been made by the Smithsonian Institute's Astrophysical Observatory.

Among the areas covered, the United States had entered into bilateral tracking and data acquisition agreements with Australia, Canada, Chile, Ecuador, Malagasy, Mexico, Nigeria, South Africa, Spain, and the United Kingdom.[133] Experimental communications satellite testing agreements were in effect with Brazil, Canada, France, the Federal Republic of Germany, India, Italy, Japan, the Scandinavian countries, Spain, and the United Kingdom.[134] Cooperative project agreements, including some fourteen for jointly created satellites and the launching of satellites prepared in other countries, were in existence with Argentina, Australia, Brazil, Canada, Denmark, France, the Federal Republic of Germany, India, Italy, Japan, Mexico, the Netherlands, New Zealand, Norway, Pakistan, Sweden, the United Kingdom, the Soviet Union, and with the European Space Research Organization (ESRO) as an entity.[135] The Smithsonian Institute has also made certain space-related arrangements with Argentina, Australia, India, the Netherland Antilles, Peru, Spain, and South Africa.[136] There are now several score of stations throughout the world engaged in reading out pictures from U.S. weather satellites;[137] many Resident Research Associates from dozens of countries working at NASA centers; International Fellows from numerous countries

---

[128] See remarks of Secretary of State Dulles, 1959; 2 *Documents on Disarmament, 1945–59,* 942 (Dept. of State 7008; 1960). For detailed comments, see *Staff Report, supra* note 1, at 323–30.

[129] *Texts, supra* note 1, *passim.* See generally Frutkin, *supra* note 1, at chap. 2, and A/AC.105/L.25 (National and Cooperative International Space Activities).

[130] *Public Law* 85–568, 72 Stat. 426. For national arrangements *within* other states, see *Staff Report, supra* note 1, at 63–101, which covers space program in 39 other countries.

[131] See, e.g., NASA Report of Apr. 28, 1966; *New York Times,* Apr. 28, and Apr. 29, 1966; speech of Meeker, Aug. 17, 1967, at 9–10 (mimeo.).

[132] *Texts, supra* note 1, at 3.

[133] These are reproduced in *Texts, supra* note 1, at 9–227. In general, see also NASA, "NASA International Activities Summary," *NASA International Programs* 16–17 (1966).

[134] These are reproduced in *Texts, supra* note 1, at 229–79. This section does not include discussion of commercial communications arrangements developed through ComSat Corp. See chap. 5.

[135] See *Texts, supra* note 1, at 281–427. On the Soviet-U.S. arrangements, see also *id.* at 5–6. On European–U.S. cooperation in deep space research, see remarks of then-Chancellor Erhard, Dec. 1965, *Washington Post,* Dec. 21, 1965, at A1.

The NASA–ESRO arrangement affirms "a mutual desire to understand a cooperative program of space research by means of satellites" and a willingness to make the results "freely available to the world scientific community."

On joint U.S., U.K., French, Dutch, and private company experiments in OGO V, see *New York Times,* March 5, 1968, at 17.

[136] See *Texts, supra* note 1, at 509–25.

[137] On the 80 stations in 24 countries which received pictures directly from ESSA II, see *New York Times,* March 1, 1966, at 15.

study at American universities. In addition, many technical trainees from other countries were in training in the United States as part of NASA's cooperative projects. By mid-1967 the United States had cooperative agreements with thirty-four countries and ESRO, and had space agreements of one sort or another with eighty-four nations.[138] There were, in addition, the special U.S.–USSR arrangements in the fields of meteorology and communications which we have described earlier.[139]

Typically, executive agreements concerning cooperative projects outline the basic nature of the experiment, list the specific responsibilities for each party for providing equipment and technicians, and call for the exchange of scientific data recovered from the experiment. The cooperating country usually provides part or all of the scientific payload. There is ordinarily no exchange of funds and each party finances its part of the activity. In almost all instances the United States provides the rockets which may be launched by NASA or by a cooperating country from a United States range or from a range of a cooperating country. Ownership of a rocket may be retained by the United States, or it may be transferred on the basis of grant or purchase. Launching and tracking equipment is frequently made available on a loan basis. Technicians may be either American, or from the cooperating country, or both, and U.S. training of personnel may be included.

Only a few agreements make any reference to liability in the event of an accident resulting in damages, and in those cases the initiative for such provisions seems to have come from the cooperating country rather than from the United States. Most tracking station agreements—the second most numerous category—include a clause providing that "all costs of constructing, installing, equipping and operating the station will be borne by the Government of the United States . . ."[140] which is probably broad enough to include damages. However, a few agreements do contain specific liability provisions.[141] Agreements relating to communications

satellite experiments include no reference to liability. Such agreements usually provide for experimental use of a satellite for communication, with each party providing its own transmitting and receiving equipment, personnel, and an exchange of data.

The cooperative project agreements, fairly similar in form regardless of the nature of the particular activity they seek to implement, are frequently reached in two steps: an exchange of formal diplomatic notes between governments—represented by their respective foreign offices[142]—and memoranda of understanding or letters of agreement between agencies of governments. The diplomatic notes may serve as an umbrella agreement for several cooperative space activities. They are usually general in nature and express an intent to achieve further cooperation by making possible joint projects, which may not be further specified or are named without explanatory detail. The exchange of diplomatic notes is usually supplemented by memoranda of understanding about each specific project entered into by the cooperating agencies of the states which were parties to the exchange of notes.

NASA has stated[143] that in developing its international activities it has observed the following guidelines:

1. Designation by each participating government of a central civilian agency for the negotiation and supervision of joint efforts
2. Agreement upon specific projects rather than generalized programs
3. Acceptance of financial responsibility by each participating country for its own contributions to joint projects
4. Projects of scientific validity and mutual interest
5. General publication of scientific results

Leaving the details of specific activities for coverage in memoranda of understanding or letters of agreement between NASA and the foreign cooperating agency provides flexibility and ease of modification which would not exist if changes could be effected only by the exchange of formal diplomatic notes. However, in some

---

[138] See generally speech of Meeker, *supra* note 131, at 9–10.

[139] For an account and documents, see also *Staff Report, supra* note 1, at 134–61; *Frutkin, supra* note 1, at chap. 3; *Space Bus. Daily,* March 20, 1968, at 109 (on the first meteorological pictures received by ESSA from Cosmos CCVI).

[140] Agreement with Spain on Tracking Stations, Jan. 29, 1964, 15 *U.S.T.* 153, *T.I.A.S.* No. 5533.

[141] Cooperative Agency Agreement with DOS (Dept. of Supply, Australia) for the Establishment of a NASA Deep Space Radio Tracking Facility near Canberra, Australia, June 10, 1963.

---

[142] For the United States, the Department of State. One or the other of the parties is customarily represented by an ambassador or other senior official who may have been visiting in the country at the time. Thus, then Vice-president Johnson while on a visit to Italy signed a U.S.-Italian exchange of notes entitled Outer Space Cooperation; Space Science Research Programs (Sept. 5, 1962) *T.I.A.S.* 5172; 13 *U.S.T.* 2120. Occasionally a prime minister may elect to sign such an agreement as with a tracking station agreement with Nigeria.

[143] NASA, *NASA International Programs* 1 (1965).

instances it appears that the entire arrangements may be included in the formal notes; in other instances the formal notes have been dispensed with entirely, although there is no clear pattern of situations in which this has been done.[144] Presumably the constitutional and policy requirements of the cooperating countries account in part for the differences. It might be observed that a diplomatic note exists in every instance where the United States is authorized to build or utilize facilities on foreign soil. Sometimes a letter of agreement between an official of NASA and a counterpart in the co-operating state has been used rather than a memorandum of understanding. Letters have been used for agreements to include some non-U.S. experiments with an American launching.[145] Sometimes, too, letters of agreement are used for a project proposed at the last minute, and there is not time to permit the preparation of the slightly more formal memorandum of understanding.[146]

The convenience and practical common sense of using the simplest form of executive agreements to cover temporary arrangements for single and perhaps only minor space experiments is obvious. Formal treaties might be out of date by the time they are ratified without ever having been utilized. Government-to-government exchanges are occasionally used to confirm agency-to-agency agreements already made and, in some instances,

already carried through to completion of the experiment. Whether confirmation occurs before or after completion of the experiment is apparently based on the problems of the moment rather than on narrow policy or legal rules. In other instances agency-to-agency agreements contain no reference to governmental approvals.[147] Even the NASA–Soviet Academy of Sciences Memorandum of Understanding for Cooperation in Space of June 8, 1962, stated no requirement for confirmation of the exchange, but on August 29, 1962, an exchange of diplomatic notes was accomplished.[148]

The procedures and policies being used in connection with agreements for cooperative activities in space present no significant departures from those of the past used by the United States in connection with treaties and executive agreements. Congress authorized and directed NASA to engage in cooperative activities in space, and the legislative history of the Act creating NASA indicates an anticipation that executive agreements would be used extensively.[149] These usually do not call for an exchange of funds, as each agency is usually responsible for its own costs, although in a number of instances there have been provisions for a loan of equipment. A few observers and technicians may be temporarily in the country where the launching takes place, but numbers are small, visas are handled routinely, and no special arrangements are

---

[144] NASA-Argentine Comision Nacional de Investigaciones Espaciales, "Memorandum of Understanding" (June 14, 1961) covering cooperation in launching upper atmosphere probes and a similar agreement, also with Argentina, dated May 18, 1965, make no reference to being based on an exchange of diplomatic notes. NASA-Brazilian Comissão Nacional de Atividades Espaciais, "Memorandum of Understanding" (Mar. 14, 1963, and July 1, 1965) covering probes of the upper atmosphere make no reference to an exchange of diplomatic notes. Similar activities with Australia are provided for by memoranda of understanding, each of which refers to an underlying diplomatic note.

[145] A number of letters from Dryden and Frutkin, both from NASA, to various research institutions in Europe, especially England, testify to the popularity of this method of agreeing on the inclusion of foreign experiments in U.S. launchings.

[146] As an example, India indicated an interest in participating in communications experiments to be conducted on a U.S. satellite then almost ready for launching. NASA suggested a "simple exchange of letters, thereby dispensing with the more formal memo of understanding which calls for confirmation by an exchange of diplomatic notes." Letter from Frutkin, Assistant Administrator for International Programs for NASA, to Shroff, Deputy Secretary of the Department of Atomic Energy of India (Oct. 23, 1964).

[147] Memoranda of Understanding between NASA and Argentina, *supra* note 144; Memoranda of Understanding between NASA and Brazil, *supra* note 144; and Memorandum of Understanding between NASA and Department of Atomic Energy of Dec. 31, 1963. "Memorandum of Understanding," NASA-Scandinavian Commission for Satellite Telecommunications (May 22, 1963); "Memorandum of Understanding" between Dept. of Posts and Telego Communications of the U.S. of Brazil and NASA (July 13, 1961); and Agreement between NASA and Japanese Ministry of Posts and Telecommunications (Nov. 6, 1962) and others.

[148] 52 *Dept. of State Bull.* 964–65 (Dec. 24, 1962).

[149] President Eisenhower, on signing the bill into law on July 29, 1958, took note of the fact that sec. 205 of the Act says that the new agency "may" enter into cooperative agreements with the advice and consent of the Senate; this he said was a permissive provision, allowing the space agency to seek Senate advice and consent where this was appropriate but not precluding executive agreements without recourse to the Senate. Eisenhower indicated that to interpret sec. 205 otherwise would be to raise serious constitutional questions. See *Documents on International Aspects of the Exploration and Use of Outer Space* (1954–62); *Staff Report of the Senate Committee on Aeronautical and Space Sciences*, 88th Cong., 1st Sess., Doc. No. 18 (May 9, 1963). See also Frutkin, *supra* note 1, at 28–35.

necessary for them. The limited number of personnel involved is unlikely to create any incidents or have any impact on the local community. The only exceptions are a few of the tracking stations. In those instances where construction of facilities and stationing of personnel are involved, considerably more detail is included since acquiring the use of land and stationing personnel in the host country is involved. Free and full exchange of scientific information acquired through cooperative endeavors is called for in almost every instance.

Note: Bilateral Space Agreements Involving the Soviet Union

In addition to U.S.–USSR agreements involving communications and meteorological links,[150] Russia has also entered into arrangements with other states for cooperative space activities. In June 1966 a ten-year arrangement involving common experiments was made with France, for example.[151] Russia has also established stations in the United Arab Republic and in Mali to be jointly operated to photograph artificial satellites[152] and has agreed to aid Cuba's meteorological service and hurricane detection system.[153] No doubt other specific agreements exist; in late 1965 Radio Prague disclosed that, at a meeting of Soviet-bloc countries in Moscow in November 1965, Russia had agreed to launch Communist nations' artificial satellites, sounding rockets, and probes for scientific research.[154] Although very small in comparison with American cooperative programs to date, there is ample evidence that the Soviet Union has also moved in the field of bilateral arrangements.

Other Multilateral Space Agreements

At least in Western Europe a determined effort to move collectively into the field of space activities has developed.[155] France, the United Kingdom, the Netherlands, Switzerland, West Germany, Belgium, Sweden, Denmark, Spain, and Italy have joined forces in the European Space Research Organization (ESRO), which aims at the development and construction of space vehicle launchers and their equipment. Initially, work involved vehicles and satellites contributed by Britain, France, West Germany, and Italy, while the Netherlands and Belgium furnished radio and other equipment and Australia was responsible for some of the range and support facilities.

ESRO is designed to promote the training of European experts in space technology, to help with the exchange of scientific and technical information, and to assure national research groups of launching arrangements. Sounding rocket experiments began in July 1964, and the first ESRO satellites were set for NASA launching in 1967–68.[156] Also planned are a European Space Technology Center (ESTEC), a computing center at Darmstadt, and an institute in Italy to do research on physical and chemical processes in outer space.

In the spring and summer of 1966 certain dissatisfaction was evident with respect to cost-sharing as costs rose steadily. Britain, in particular, threatened to with-

---

[150] For more recent reports on the meteorological exchange, see *New York Times*, Sept. 27, 1966; *Av. Wk.*, Sept. 26, 1966, at 26–27; *Space Bus. Daily*, Mar. 20, 1968, at 109. In Aug. 1966 the USSR transmitted to the U.S. for the first time information obtained from its own known meteorological satellite, Cosmos CXXII, launched June 25. Previously, the USSR had relayed only conventional observations from land stations, ships, and balloons. Direct telecommunications channels between Moscow and Washington, D.C., were established after the Mar. 1963 signing of a bilateral agreement for the exchange of meteorological satellite data under a June 1962 space cooperation accord. See *New York Times*, Aug. 20, 1966. On possible Soviet–U.S. relations, see also Frutkin, 4 *Astro & Aero*. 20 (Feb. 1966).

[151] See, e.g., 4 *Astro. & Aero*. 15–16 (Aug. 1966); *Space Bus. Daily*, June 28, 1966, at 344; *New York Times*, Dec. 6, 1966; Dec. 10, 1966. For more recent developments, see *New York Times*, Oct. 4, 1967, at 3 and Jan. 18, 1968, at 52; *Av. Wk.*, Oct. 30, 1967, at 13.

[152] See *New York Times*, Apr. 16, 1966.

[153] *New York Times*, May 19, 1966.

[154] *New York Times*, Dec. 12, 1965. On joint Soviet Blue program, see also *New York Times*, Dec. 14, 1967, at 26C.

[155] For brief accounts of the European activities, see *Staff Report*, *supra* note 1, at 103–32; Frutkin, *supra* note 1, at 132–41. The ESRO and ELDO Conventions are reprinted in *Staff Report*, *supra* note 1, at 509–41. On Europe's interest in space technology, see also *New York Times*, July 13, 1966. For more recent comments on and studies of ESRO and ELDO, see also Walsh, *Science and International Public Affairs*, *passim* (1967); Walsh, "Space Sciences Research in Europe Suffers Growing Pains," 158 *Science* 242 (Oct. 13, 1967); *Av. Wk.*, Aug. 28, 1967, at 29.

[156] In Dec. 1966 NASA and ESRO signed the first agreement under which a foreign country or organization would obtain satellite launchings from the U.S. on a reimbursable basis. See NASA Release 66–3322 (Dec. 30, 1966). See also Stubbs, "ESRO's First Satellite," 33 *New Scientist* 10–11 (Jan. 5, 1967). On reported fears that prospective launching of rockets in northern Europe might cause injury among the Lapp population of Sweden, see *New York Times*, Oct. 21, 1964.

draw, but the matter was at least temporarily resolved by late summer.[157]

Regional European cooperation in the field of communications satellites is effected through the European Conference on Satellite Communications. There is also some machinery available in NATO[158] and a special Scandinavian Committee for Satellite Telecommunication.

In addition to the European governments, space efforts are supported as well by Eurospace, a combination of over a hundred commercial firms seeking to participate in the new space technology.[159] In Britain space industries have formed a British Space Development Company (BSDC), a consortium of interested companies which has, among other things, advocated (at least at one time) a Commonwealth satellite communications system.[160]

In the Western hemisphere an Inter-American Committee on Space Research was established in November 1960. It was designed to encourage and coordinate space-related research and activities in Latin America, but it is still apparently in the planning stage.[161]

Nongovernmental Space Agreements

A number of nongovernmental (using the term formally in some cases) arrangements and organizations have played and are playing an important role in outer space research. Despite their importance, here we note them only briefly; some have been extensively reported on elsewhere, while others have little or no *direct* role in the creation of the law governing space activities.

Those familiar with space achievements to date will readily recall that the space age was begun in the period known as the International Geophysical Year (1957–58). That remarkable, quasi-governmental, cooperative achievement by scientists from sixty-six countries provided the means for coordinating nationally prepared scientific programs, especially for the Antarctic and outer space. The IGY has been thoroughly chronicled,[162] and its impetus with respect to space research and to a feeling of a shared world interest in outer space developments is apparent. Yet of all the IGY programs, that for space achieved the poorest record for the exchange of information, a tribute to the delicacy of the interconnection between scientific and military prestige considerations in this new arena.[163] The influence of the IGY on the development of a regime for space activities was discussed in chapter 4.

The coordinating function for national space programs partially achieved by the IGY was continued in the Committee on Space Research (COSPAR).[164] COSPAR was at first composed of representatives from countries engaged in launching rockets or satellites (Australia, Canada, France, Japan, the USSR, the U.K., and the U.S.A.) together with three from states engaged in tracking space vehicles, chosen on a rotational basis, plus representatives from the nine international scientific unions interested in space research. Here, too, the political realities of space progress required changes; the Soviet Union, within the first year, demanded a form of "veto" in this formally nongovernmental organization and, under the threat of a Soviet boycott, the arrangements were changed to permit, in fact, either great space power to "veto"[165] proposed activities of the organiza-

---

[157] See, e.g., *New York Times*, Apr. 28, 1966, Apr. 29, 1966; June 10, 1966; *Tech. Wk.*, July 18, 1966, at 20; 4 *Astro. & Aero.* 23–25 (Sept. 1966); *Av. Wk.*, Sept. 5, 1966, at 21, 29. See also, U.K. Embassy, *Inform. Bull.* 195/66 (June 1966) and Note, "A Space Policy for Britain," 10 *Spaceflight* 56 (Feb. 1968).

[158] See *Staff Report, supra* note 1, at 120–22.

[159] See *Staff Report, supra* note 1, at 12–28.

[160] See Fennessy, "The British Space Development Co.," *Interavia* 765 (1965).

[161] See *Staff Report, supra* note 1, at 133–140.

[162] See, e.g., Sullivan, *Assault on the Unknown: The International Geophysical Year* (1961); Jessup & Taubenfeld, *Controls. . . . , supra* note 2, at 110–16, 228–32; *Staff Report, supra* note 1, at 353–73; Christol, *supra* note 1, at 127–35; Wilson, *I.G.Y.: The Year of the New Moons* (1961); McDougal, Lasswell, & Vlasic, *Law and Public Order in Space* 202–206 (1963); see generally Schwartz, *International Organizations and Space Cooperation* (1962). The Statutes and Rules of the International Council of Scientific Unions (ICSU), the "father" of the IGY, are conveniently reprinted in *Staff Report, supra* note 1, at 478 ff. That report also reprints (at 493 ff.) the constitution of the Committee on Space Research (COSPAR), the constitution of the International Astronautical Federation, the Statutes of the International Institute of Space Law, and the International Academy of Astronautics, and the ESRO and ELDO conventions. For an earlier report on the IGY, see "The International Geophysical Year and Space Research," *Staff Report of the House Select Committee on Astronautics and Space Exploration*, 86th Cong., 1st Sess., House Doc. No. 88 (1959).

[163] See Jessup & Taubenfeld 229.

[164] See *Staff Report* 378–400; Jessup & Taubenfeld, *Controls . . . , supra* note 2, at 231–32; Christol, *supra* note 1, at 136 ff.

[165] See articles in *New York Times*, Apr. 28, 1959, at 8 (Hamilton) and at 28 (Sullivan).

tion. Thus, each in effect controls the election of three of the seven members of COSPAR's Bureau of the Executive Council, and a vote of two-thirds of this bureau is necessary to confirm decisions made by the Executive Council.[166] Despite this perhaps inevitable handicap, COSPAR has been active in arranging for the exchange of information and in reporting national space activities. Both major powers have been actively concerned with the questions of radio frequencies for space research and operations, of potentially harmful space experiments, and of the sterilization of space vehicles. Annual meetings are held with an' increasingly large attendance of scientists from several dozen nations.[167]

Coordinated scientific programs patterned on the IGY have also been continued through International Geophysical Cooperation 1959 (IGY–1959) and the International Years of the Quiet Sun (IQSY).[168] The latter took place in 1964–65, and a special "watch on the sun" was kept by scientists around the world.

The International Astronautical Federation (IAF) is a federation of national societies interested in space exploration and rocketry. It was actually founded seven years before Sputnik I. It enjoys consultative status with UNESCO. In 1960, it in turn founded the International Institute of Space Law (IISL), a group of legal scholars interested in legal and governmental problems created by space activities, and the International Academy of Astronautics (IAA), a distinguished group of individuals drawn from the basic, engineering, and life sciences, with special interests and expertise in the space field.[169]

These organizations, together with national groups, are important for the exchange of information and for the generation of ideas; being nongovernmental, they do not create international norms directly, although in some cases their studies and activities may be highly relevant to the positions assumed by governments.[170]

potentially disruptive space activities conducted by other nations, e.g., the United States suggested the utility of discussion in COSPAR's Consultative Group on Potentially Harmful Effects of Space Experiments. That group has in fact reported on Project West Ford, on upper atmospheric pollution and on contamination of planets. See, e.g., *Staff Report, supra* note 1, at 390–99.

---

[166] See *Staff Report, supra* note 1, at 380–81.

[167] See generally *id.* at 378–400 and Peavey, "International Cooperation in Space Science," in *Proceedings of the Conference on Space Science and Space Law,* at 89–101 (Schwartz ed. 1964). For a recent report by COSPAR on training and education, see A/AC.105/L.27 (1966).

[168] See *Staff Report, supra* note 1, at 373–78 and sources cited.

[169] On the IAF, the IISL and the IAA, see Haley, *supra* note 1, at chap. 2 (1963); *Staff Report, supra* note 1, at 410–19. Haley was actively concerned in the organizations from their beginning.

[170] In resisting Soviet demands for a national "veto" over

E

Treaties, Statutes, and Other Legal Documents

This Appendix includes several of the more significant documents relating to man's activities in space. Many additional documents are not included to avoid unnecessary duplication. The Senate Committee on Aeronautical and Space Sciences has issued a number of publications, most of which are listed in the bibliography reproducing practically all agreements relating to space activities between the United States and other countries. The Senate publications also include most significant United Nations documents and many United States documents relating to activities in space. The United States Senate will undoubtedly continue publishing significant documents as they become available, and this source should always be examined for current documents.

The documents included in this Appendix are as follows:

1. The National Aeronautics and Space Act of 1958, approved July 29, 1958.
2. Treaty on Principles Governing the Activities of States in the Exploration and Use of Outer Space, Including the Moon and Other Celestial Bodies, signed January 27, 1967.
3. United Nations General Assembly Resolution 1721 (XVI) of December 20, 1961, on the Peaceful Uses of Outer Space.
4. United Nations Resolution of the General Assembly 1884 (XVIII), dated October 17, 1963, on the Question of General and Complete Disarmament.
5. United Nations Resolution of the General Assembly 1962 (XVIII), dated December 13, 1963, on the Declaration of Legal Principles Governing Activities of States in the Exploration and Use of Outer Space.
6. United Nations Resolution of the General Assembly 1963 (XVIII), dated December 13, 1963, on International Cooperation in the Peaceful Uses of Outer Space.
7. Treaty Banning Nuclear Weapons Tests in the Atmosphere, in Outer Space, and under Water, entered into force October 10, 1963.
8. Communications-Satellite Act of 1962, approved August 31, 1962.
9. Agreement Establishing Interim Arrangements for a Global Commercial Communications Satellite System, entered into force August 20, 1964.
10. Special Agreement, entered into force August 20, 1964. This agreement relates to the establishment of a Global Commercial Communications Satellite System.
11. Communications Satellite System Arbitration Agreement, entered into force November 21, 1966.
12. Executive Order 11277, dated April 30, 1966, Designating the International Telecommunications Satellite Consortium as an International Organization Entitled To Enjoy Certain Privileges, Exemptions and Immunities.
13. United Nations Document A/AC.105/C.2/W.2/Rev. 3, dated 24 September 1965, constituting a Comparative Table of Provisions Contained in the Proposals for a Treaty for Liability for Damage Caused by Objects Launched into Outer Space.
14. Annex to Resolution 2345 (XXII), December 19, 1968, of the United Nations General Assembly, being an Agreement on the Rescue of Astronauts, the

Return of Astronauts and the Return of Objects Launched into Outer Space.

15. Executive Agreement of 23 January 1967 between the United States and the United Kingdom providing for the Establishment of a Station for Space Vehicle Tracking and Communication on Antigua, British West Indies. (It should be noted that this agreement is considerably more detailed than other agreements for similar purposes.)

16. Agreement with European Space Research Organization (ESRO), dated 28 November 1966, providing for the establishment of an ESRO Telemetry/ Telecommand Station near Fairbanks, Alaska, for use in connection with space activities of ESRO. (This is one of the very few agreements providing for establishment of a space station on United States territory and with an international organization. It contains more detail than most agreements permitting the United States to establish stations on the territory of other nations.)

17. Executive Order 11227, dated June 2, 1965, Designating the Interim Communications Satellite Committee as a Public International Organization Entitled To Enjoy Certain Privileges, Exemptions, and Immunities.

18. Agreement between the Government of the Union of Soviet Socialist Republics and the Government of France Concerning Cooperation in the Study and Exploration of Outer Space for Peaceful Purposes.

19. Executive Order 11191, dated January 4, 1965, Providing for the Carrying Out of Certain Provisions of the Communications Satellite Act of 1962.

Copies of the documents follow in the order listed.

National Aeronautics and Space Act, July 29, 1958[1]

AN ACT To provide for research into problems of flight within and outside the earth's atmosphere, and for other purposes.

Be it enacted by the Senate and House of Representatives of the United States of America in Congress assembled,

Title I—Short Title, Declaration of Policy, and Definitions

SHORT TITLE

SEC. 101. This Act may be cited as the "National Aeronautics and Space Act of 1958".

DECLARATION OF POLICY AND PURPOSE

SEC. 102. (a) The Congress hereby declares that it is the policy of the United States that activities in space should be devoted to peaceful purposes for the benefit of all mankind.

(b) The Congress declares that the general welfare and security of the United States require that adequate provision be made for aeronautical and space activities. The Congress further declares that such activities shall be the responsibility of, and shall be directed by, a civilian agency exercising control over aeronautical and space activities sponsored by the United States, except that activities peculiar to or primarily associated with the development of weapons systems, military operations, or the defense of the United States (including the research and development necessary to make effective provision for the defense of the United States) shall be the responsibility of, and shall be directed by, the Department of Defense; and that determination as to which such agency has responsibility for and direction of any such activity shall be made by the President in conformity with section 201(e).

(c) The aeronautical and space activities of the United States shall be conducted so as to contribute materially to one or more of the following objectives:

(1) The expansion of human knowledge of phenomena in the atmosphere and space;

(2) The improvement of the usefulness, performance, speed, safety, and efficiency of aeronautical and space vehicles;

(3) The development and operation of vehicles capable of carrying instruments, equipment, supplies, and living organisms through space;

(4) The establishment of long-range studies of the potential benefits to be gained from, the opportunities for, and the problems involved in the utilization of aeronautical and space activities for peaceful and scientific purposes;

(5) The preservation of the role of the United States as a leader in aeronautical and space science and technology and in the application thereof to the conduct of peaceful activities within and outside the atmosphere;

(6) The making available to agencies directly concerned with national defense of discoveries that have military value or significance, and the furnishing by such agencies, to the civilian agency established to direct and control nonmilitary aeronautical and space activities, of information as to discoveries which have value or significance to that agency;

(7) Cooperation by the United States with

---

[1] Public Law 85–568, 85th Cong., H.R. 12575 (72 Stat. 426).

other nations and groups of nations in work done pursuant to this Act and in the peaceful application of the results thereof; and

(8) The most effective utilization of the scientific and engineering resources of the United States, with close cooperation among all interested agencies of the United States in order to avoid unnecessary duplication of effort, facilities, and equipment.

(d) It is the purpose of this Act to carry out and effectuate the policies declared in subsections (a), (b), and (c).

DEFINITIONS

SEC. 103. As used in this Act—

(1) the term "aeronautical and space activities" means (A) research into, and the solution of, problems of flight within and outside the earth's atmosphere, (B) the development, construction, testing, and operation for research purposes of aeronautical and space vehicles, and (C) such other activities as may be required for the exploration of space; and

(2) the term "aeronautical and space vehicles" means aircraft, missiles, satellites, and other space vehicles, manned and unmanned, together with related equipment, devices, components, and parts.

Title II—Coordination of Aeronautical and Space Activities

NATIONAL AERONAUTICS AND SPACE COUNCIL

SEC. 201. (a) There is hereby established the National Aeronautics and Space Council (hereinafter called the "Council") which shall be composed of—

(1) The President (who shall preside over meetings of the Council);

(2) the Secretary of State;

(3) the Secretary of Defense;

(4) the Administrator of the National Aeronautics and Space Administration;

(5) the Chairman of the Atomic Energy Commission;

(6) not more than one additional member appointed by the President from the departments and agencies of the Federal Government; and

(7) not more than three other members appointed by the President, solely on the basis of established records of distinguished achievement, from among individuals in private life who are eminent in science, engineering, technology, education, administration, or public affairs.

(b) Each member of the Council from a department or agency of the Federal Government may designate another officer of his department or agency to serve on the Council as his alternate in his unavoidable absence.

(c) Each member of the Council appointed or designated under paragraphs (6) and (7) of subsection (a), and each alternate member designated under subsection (b), shall be appointed or designated to serve as such by and with the advice and consent of the Senate, unless at the time of such appointment or designation he holds an office in the Federal Government to which he was appointed by and with the advice and consent of the Senate.

(d) It shall be the function of the Council to advise the President with respect to the performance of the duties prescribed in subsection (e) of this section.

(e) In conformity with the provisions of section 102 of this Act, it shall be the duty of the President to—

(1) survey all significant aeronautical and space activities, including the policies, plans, programs, and accomplishments of all agencies of the United States engaged in such activities;

(2) develop a comprehensive program of aeronautical and space activities to be conducted by agencies of the United States;

(3) designate and fix responsibility for the direction of major aeronautical and space activities;

(4) provide for effective cooperation between the National Aeronautics and Space Administration and the Department of Defense in all such activities, and specify which of such activities may be carried on concurrently by both such agencies notwithstanding the assignment of primary responsibility therefor to one or the other of such agencies; and

(5) resolve differences arising among departments and agencies of the United States with respect to aeronautical and space activities under this Act, including differences as to whether a particular project is an aeronautical and space activity.

(f) The Council may employ a staff to be headed by a civilian executive secretary who shall be appointed by the President by and with the advice and consent of the Senate and shall receive compensation at the rate of $20,000 a year. The executive secretary, subject to the direction of the Council, is authorized to appoint and fix the compensation of such personnel, including not more than three persons who may be appointed without regard to the civil service laws or the Classification Act of 1949² and compensated at the rate of not more than $19,000 a year, as may be necessary to perform such duties as may be prescribed by the Council in connection with the performance of its functions. Each appointment under this subsection shall be subject to the same security requirements as those established for personnel of the National Aeronautics and Space Administration appointed under section 203(b) (2) of this Act.

(g) Members of the Council appointed from private life under subsection (a) (7) may be compensated at a rate not to exceed $100 per diem, and may be paid travel expenses and per diem in lieu of subsistence in accordance with the provisions of section 5 of the Administrative Expenses Act of 1946 (5 U.S.C. 73b–2)³ relating to persons serving without compensation.

NATIONAL AERONAUTICS AND SPACE ADMINISTRATION

SEC. 202. (a) There is hereby established the National Aeronautics and Space Administration (hereinafter called the "Administration"). The Administration shall be headed by an Administrator, who shall be appointed from civilian life by the President by and with the advice and consent of the Senate, and shall receive compensation at the rate of $22,500 per annum. Under the supervision and direction of the President, the Administrator shall be responsible for the exercise of all powers and the discharge of all duties of the Administration, and shall have authority and control over all personnel and activities thereof.

(b) There shall be in the Administration a Deputy Administrator, who shall be appointed from civilian life by the President by and with the advice and consent of the Senate, shall receive compensation at the rate of $21,500 per annum, and shall perform such duties and exercise such powers as the Administrator may prescribe. The Deputy Administrator shall act for, and exercise the powers of, the Administrator during his absence or disability.

(c) The Administrator and the Deputy Administrator shall not engage in any other business, vocation, or employment while serving as such.

FUNCTIONS OF THE ADMINISTRATION

SEC. 203. (a) The Administration, in order to carry out the purpose of this Act, shall—

(1) plan, direct, and conduct aeronautical and space activities;

(2) arrange for participation by the scientific community in planning scientific measurements and observations to be made through the use of aeronautical and space vehicles, and conduct or arrange for the conduct of such measurements and observations; and

(3) provide for the widest practicable and appropriate dissemination of information concerning its activities and the results thereof.

(b) In the performance of its functions the Administration is authorized—

(1) to make, promulgate, issue, rescind, and amend rules and regulations governing the manner of its operations and the exercise of the powers vested in it by law;

(2) to appoint and fix the compensation of such officers and employees as may be necessary to carry out such functions. Such officers and employees shall be appointed in accordance with the civil-service laws and their compensation fixed in accordance with the Classification Act of 1949, except that (A) to the extent the Administrator deems such action necessary to the discharge of his responsibilities, he may appoint and fix the compensation (up to a limit of $19,000 a year, or up to a limit of $21,000 a year for a maximum of ten positions) of not more than two hundred and sixty of the scientific, engineering, and administrative personnel of the Administration without regard to such laws, and (B) to the extent the Administrator deems such action necessary to recruit specially qualified scientific and engineering talent, he may establish the entrance grade for scientific and engineering personnel without previous service in the Federal Government at a level up to two grades higher than the grade provided for such personnel under the General Schedule established by the Classification Act of 1949, and fix their compensation accordingly;

(3) to acquire (by purchase, lease, condemnation, or otherwise), construct, improve, repair, operate, and maintain laboratories, research and testing sites and facilities, aeronautical and space vehicles, quarters and related accommodations for employees and dependents of employees of the Administration, and such other real and personal property (including patents), or any interest therein as the Administration deems necessary within and outside the continental United States; to lease to others such real and personal property; to sell and

---

² 63 Stat. 954; 5 U.S.C. 1071 note.
³ 60 Stat. 394.

otherwise dispose of real and personal property (including patents and rights thereunder) in accordance with the provisions of the Federal Property and Administrative Services Act of 1949, as amended (40 U.S.C. 471 et seq.);[4] and to provide by contract or otherwise for cafeterias and other necessary facilities for the welfare of employees of the Administration at its installations and purchase and maintain equipment therefor;

(4) to accept unconditional gifts or donations of services, money, or property, real, personal, or mixed, tangible or intangible;

(5) without regard to section 3648 of the Revised Statutes, as amended (31 U.S.C. 529),[5] to enter into and perform such contracts, leases, cooperative agreements, or other transactions as may be necessary in the conduct of its work and on such terms as it may deem appropriate, with any agency or instrumentality of the United States, or with any State, Territory, or possession, or with any political subdivision thereof, or with any person, firm, association, corporation, or educational institution. To the maximum extent practicable and consistent with the accomplishment of the purpose of this Act, such contracts, leases, agreements, and other transactions shall be allocated by the Administrator in a manner which will enable small-business concerns to participate equitably and proportionately in the conduct of the work of the Administration;

(6) to use, with their consent the services, equipment, personnel, and facilities of Federal and other agencies with or without reimbursement, and on a similar basis to cooperate with other public and private agencies and instrumentalities in the use of services, equipment, and facilities. Each department and agency of the Federal Government shall cooperate fully with the Administration in making its services, equipment, personnel, and facilities available to the Administration, and any such department or agency is authorized, notwithstanding any other provision of law, to transfer to or to receive and the Administration, without reimbursement, aeronautical and space vehicles, and supplies and equipment other than administrative supplies or equipment;

(7) to appoint such advisory committees as may be appropriate for purposes of consultation and advice to the Administration in the performance of its functions;

(8) to establish within the Administration such offices and procedures as may be appropriate to provide for the greatest possible coordination of its activities under this Act with related scientific and other activities being carried on by other public and private agencies and organizations;

(9) to obtain services as authorized by section 15 of the Act of August 2, 1946 (5 U.S.C. 55a),[6] at rates not to exceed $100 per diem for individuals;

(10) when determined by the Administrator to be necessary, and subject to such security investigations as he may determine to be appropriate, to employ aliens without regard to statutory provisions prohibiting payment of compensation to aliens:

(11) to employ retired commissioned officers of the armed forces of the United States and compensate them at the rate established for the positions occupied by them within the Administration, subject only to the limitations in pay set forth in section 212 of the Act of June 30, 1932, as amended (5 U.S.C. 59a);[7]

(12) with the approval of the President, to enter into cooperative agreements under which members of the Army, Navy, Air Force, and Marine Corps may be detailed by the appropriate Secretary for services in the performance of functions under this Act to the same extent as that to which they might be lawfully assigned in the Department of Defense; and

(13) (A) to consider, ascertain, adjust, determine, settle, and pay, on behalf of the United States, in full satisfaction thereof, any claim for $5,000 or less against the United States for bodily injury, death, or damage to or loss of real or personal property resulting from the conduct of the Administration's functions as specified in subsection (a) of this section, where such claim is presented to the Administration in writing within two years after the accident or incident out of which the claim arises; and

(B) if the Administration considers that a claim in excess of $5,000 is meritorious and would otherwise be covered by this paragraph, to report the facts and circumstances thereof to the Congress for its consideration.

[4] 63 Stat. 377.
[5] 60 Stat. 809.
[6] 60 Stat. 810.
[7] 68 Stat. 18.

CIVILIAN-MILITARY LIAISON COMMITTEE

SEC. 204. (a) There shall be a Civilian-Military Liaison Committee consisting of—

(1) a Chairman, who shall be the head thereof and who shall be appointed by the President, shall serve at the pleasure of the President, and shall receive compensation (in the manner provided in subsection (d)) at the rate of $20,000 per annum;

(2) one or more representatives from the Department of Defense, and one or more representatives from each of the Departments of the Army, Navy, and Air Force, to be assigned by the Secretary of Defense to serve on the Committee without additional compensation; and

(3) representatives from the Administration, to be assigned by the Administrator to serve on the Committee without additional compensation, equal in number to the number of representatives assigned to serve on the Committee under paragraph (2).

(b) The Administration and the Department of Defense, through the Liaison Committee, shall advise and consult with each other on all matters within their respective jurisdictions relating to aeronautical and space activities and shall keep each other fully and currently informed with respect to such activities.

(c) If the Secretary of Defense concludes that any request, action, proposed action, or failure to act on the part of the Administrator is adverse to the responsibilities of the Department of Defense, or the Administrator concludes that any request, action, proposed action, or failure to act on the part of the Department of Defense is adverse to the responsibilities of the Administration, and the Administrator and the Secretary of Defense are unable to reach an agreement with respect thereto, either the Administrator or the Secretary of Defense may refer the matter to the President for his decision (which shall be final) as provided in section 201(c).

(d) Notwithstanding the provisions of any other law, any active or retired officer of the Army, Navy, or Air Force may serve as Chairman of the Liaison Committee without prejudice to his active or retired status as such officer. The compensation received by any such officer for his service as Chairman of the Liaison Committee shall be equal to the amount (if any) by which the compensation fixed by subsection (a) (1) for such Chairman exceeds his pay and allowances (including special and incentive pays) as an active officer, or his retired pay.

INTERNATIONAL COOPERATION

SEC. 205. The Administration, under the foreign policy guidance of the President, may engage in a program of international cooperation in work done pursuant to this Act, and in the peaceful application of the results thereof, pursuant to agreements made by the President with the advice and consent of the Senate.

REPORTS TO THE CONGRESS

SEC. 203. (a) The Administration shall submit to the President for transmittal to the Congress, semiannually and at such other times as it deems desirable, a report of its activities and accomplishments.

(b) The President shall transmit to the Congress in January of each year a report, which shall include (1) a comprehensive description of the programed activities and the accomplishments of all agencies of the United States in the field of aeronautics and space activities during the preceding calendar year, and (2) an evaluation of such activities and accomplishments in terms of the attainment of, or the failure to attain, the objectives described in section 102(c) of this Act.

(c) Any report made under this section shall contain such recommendations for additional legislation as the Administrator or the President may consider necessary or desirable for the attainment of the objectives described in section 102(c) of this Act.

(d) No information which has been classified for reasons of national security shall be included in any report made under this section, unless such information has been declassified by, or pursuant to authorization given by, the President.

Title III—Miscellaneous

NATIONAL ADVISORY COMMITTEE FOR AERONAUTICS

SEC. 301. (a) The National Advisory Committee for Aeronautics, on the effective date of this section, shall cease to exist. On such date all functions, powers, duties, and obligations, and all real and personal property, personnel (other than members of the Committee), funds, and records of that organization, shall be transferred to the Administration.

(b) Section 2302 of title 10 of the United States Code[8] is amended by striking out "or the Executive Secretary of the National Advisory Committee for Aeronautics." and inserting in lieu thereof "or the Administrator of the National Aeronautics and Space

---

[8] 70A Stat. 127.

Administration."; and section 2303 of such title 10 is amended by striking out "The National Advisory Committee for Aeronautics." and inserting in lieu thereof "The National Aeronautics and Space Administration."

(c) The first section of the Act of August 26, 1950 (5 U.S.C. 22–1), is amended by striking out "the Director, National Advisory Committee for Astronautics" and inserting in lieu thereof "the Administrator of the National Aeronautics and Space Administration", and by striking out "or National Advisory Committee for Aeronautics" and inserting in lieu thereof "or National Aeronautics and Space Administration".

(d) The Unitary Wind Tunnel Plan Act of 1949 (50 U.S.C. 511–515)[9] is amended (1) by striking out "The National Advisory Committee for Aeronautics (hereinafter referred to as the 'Committee')" and inserting in lieu thereof "The Administrator of the National Aeronautics and Space Administration (hereinafter referred to as the 'Administrator')"; (2) by striking out "Committee" or "Committee's" wherever they appear and inserting in lieu thereof "Administrator" and "Administrator's", respectively; and (3) by striking out "its" wherever it appears and inserting in lieu thereof "his".

(e) This section shall take effect ninety days after the date of the enactment of this Act, or on any earlier date on which the Administrator shall determine, and announce by proclamation published in the Federal Register, that the Administration has been organized and is prepared to discharge the duties and exercise the powers conferred upon it by this Act.

TRANSFER OF RELATED FUNCTIONS

Sec. 302. (a) Subject to the provisions of this section, the President, for a period of four years after the date of enactment of this Act, may transfer to the Administration any functions (including powers, duties, activities, facilities, and parts of functions) of any other department or agency of the United States, or of any officer or organizational entity thereof, which relate primarily to the functions, powers, and duties of the Administration as prescribed by section 203 of this Act. In connection with any such transfer, the President may, under this section or other applicable authority, provide for appropriate transfers of records, property, civilian personnel, and funds.

(b) Whenever any such transfer is made before January 1, 1959, the President shall transmit to the Speaker of the House of Representatives and the Presi-

dent pro tempore of the Senate a full and complete report concerning the nature and effect of such transfer.

(c) After December 31, 1958, no transfer shall be made under this section until (1) a full and complete report concerning the nature and effect of such proposed transfer has been transmitted by the President to the Congress, and (2) the first period of sixty calendar days of regular session of the Congress following the date of receipt of such report by the Congress has expired without the adoption by the Congress of a concurrent resolution stating that the Congress does not favor such transfer.

ACCESS TO INFORMATION

Sec. 303. Information obtained or developed by the Administrator in the performance of his functions under this Act shall be made available for public inspection, except (A) information authorized or required by Federal statute to be withheld, and (B) information classified to protect the national security: *Provided,* That nothing in this Act shall authorize the withholding of information by the Administrator from the duly authorized committees of the Congress.

SECURITY

Sec. 304. (a) The Administrator shall establish such security requirements, restrictions, and safeguards as he deems necessary in the interest of the national security. The Administrator may arrange with the Civil Service Commission for the conduct of such security or other personnel investigations of the Administration's officers, employees, and consultants, and its contractors and subcontractors and their officers and employees, actual or prospective, as he deems appropriate; and if any such investigation develops any data reflecting that the individual who is the subject thereof is of questionable loyalty the matter shall be referred to the Federal Bureau of Investigation for the conduct of a full field investigation, the results of which shall be furnished to the Administrator.

(b) The Atomic Energy Commission may authorize any of its employees, or employees of any contractor, prospective contractor, licensee, or prospective licensee of the Atomic Energy Commission or any other person authorized to have access to Restricted Data by the Atomic Energy Commission under subsection 145b. of the Atomic Energy Act of 1954 (42 U.S.C. 2165 (b)),[10] to permit any member, officer, or employee of the Council, or the Administrator, or any officer, employee,

[9] 63 Stat. 986.

[10] 68 Stat. 942.

member of an advisory committee, contractor, subcontractor, or officer or employee of a contractor or subcontractor of the Administration, to have access to Restricted Data relating to aeronautical and space activities which is required in the performance of his duties and so certified by the Council or the Administrator, as the case may be, but only if (1) the Council or Administrator or designee thereof has determined, in accordance with the established personnel security procedures and standards of the Council or Administration, that permitting such individual to have access to such Restricted Data will not endanger the common defense and security, and (2) the Council or Administrator or designee thereof finds that the established personnel and other security procedures and standards of the Council or Administration are adequate and in reasonable conformity to the standards established by the Atomic Energy Commission under section 145 of the Atomic Energy Act of 1954 (42 U.S.C. 2165). Any individual granted access to such Restricted Data pursuant to this subsection may exchange such Data with any individual who (A) is an officer or employee of the Department of Defense, or any department or agency thereof, or a member of the armed forces, or a contractor or subcontractor of any such department, agency, or armed force, or an officer or employee of any such contractor or subcontractor, and (B) has been authorized to have access to Restricted Data under the provisions of section 143 of the Atomic Energy Act of 1954 (42 U.S.C. 2163).

(c) Chapter 37 of title 18 of the United States Code (entitled Espionage and Censorship)[11] is amended by—

    (1) adding at the end thereof the following new section: §799. Violation of regulations of National Aeronautics and Space Administration

"Whoever willfully shall violate, attempt to violate, or conspire to violate any regulation or order promulgated by the Administrator of the National Aeronautics and Space Administration for the protection or security of any laboratory, station, base or other facility, or part thereof, or any aircraft, missile, spacecraft, or similar vehicle, or part thereof, or other property or equipment in the custody of the Administration, or any real or personal property or equipment in the custody of any contractor under any contract with the Administration or any subcontractor of any such contractor, shall be fined not more than $5,000, or imprisoned not more than one year, or both."

    (2) adding at the end of the sectional analysis thereof the following new item: "799. Violation of regulations of National Aeronautics and Space Administration."

(d) Section 1114 of title 18 of the United States Code[12] is amended by inserting immediately before "while engaged in the performance of his official duties" the following: "or any officer or employee of the National Aeronautics and Space Administration directed to guard and protect property of the United States under the administration and control of the National Aeronautics and Space Administration,".

(e) The Administrator may direct such of the officers and employees of the Administration as he deems necessary in the public interest to carry firearms while in the conduct of their official duties. The Administrator may also authorize such of those employees of the contractors and subcontractors of the Administration engaged in the protection of property owned by the United States and located at facilities owned by or contracted to the United States as he deems necessary in the public interest, to carry firearms while in the conduct of their official duties.

PROPERTY RIGHTS IN INVENTIONS

SEC. 305. (a) Whenever any invention is made in the performance of any work under any contract of the Administration, and the Administrator determines that—

    (1) the person who made the invention was employed or assigned to perform research, development, or exploration work and the invention is related to the work he was employed or assigned to perform, or that it was within the scope of his employment duties, whether or not it was made during working hours, or with a contribution by the Government of the use of Government facilities, equipment, materials, allocated funds, information proprietary to the Government, or services of Government employees during working hours; or

    (2) the person who made the invention was not employed or assigned to perform research, development, or exploration work, but the invention is nevertheless related to the contract, or to the work or duties he was employed or assigned to perform, and was made during working hours, or with a contribution from the Government of the sort referred to in clause (1),

such invention shall be exclusive property of the United

---

[11] 62 Stat. 736–738; 65 Stat. 719; 18 U.S.C. 791–793.

[12] 62 Stat. 756.

States and if such invention is patentable a patent therefor shall be issued to the United States upon application made by the Administrator, unless the Administrator waives all or any part of the rights of the United States to such invention in conformity with the provisions of subsection (f) of this section.

(b) Each contract entered into by the Administrator with any party for the performance of any work shall contain effective provisions under which such party shall furnish promptly to the Administrator a written report containing full and complete technical information concerning any invention, discovery, improvement, or innovation which may be made in the performance of any such work.

(c) No patent may be issued to any applicant other than the Administrator for any invention which appears to the Commissioner of Patents to have significant utility in the conduct of aeronautical and space activities unless the applicant files with the Commissioner, with the application or within thirty days after request therefor by the Commissioner, a written statement executed under oath setting forth the full facts concerning the circumstances under which such invention was made and stating the relationship (if any) of such invention to the performance of any work under any contract of the Administration. Copies of each such statement and the application to which it relates shall be transmitted forthwith by the Commissioner to the Administrator.

(d) Upon any application as to which any such statement has been transmitted to the Administrator, the Commissioner may, if the invention is patentable, issue a patent to the applicant unless the Administrator, within ninety days after receipt of such application and statement, requests that such patent be issued to him on behalf of the United States. If, within such time, the Administrator files such a request with the Commissioner, the Commissioner shall transmit notice thereof to the applicant, and shall issue such patent to the Administrator unless the applicant within thirty days after receipt of such notice requests a hearing before a Board of Patent Interferences on the question whether the Administrator is entitled under this section to receive such patent. The Board may hear and determine, in accordance with rules and procedures established for interference cases, the question so presented, and its determination shall be subject to appeal by the applicant or by the Administrator to the Court of Customs and Patent Appeals in accordance with procedures governing appeals from decisions of the Board of Patent Interferences in other proceedings.

(e) Whenever any patent has been issued to any applicant in conformity with subsection (d), and the Administrator thereafter has reason to believe that the statement filed by the applicant in connection therewith contained any false representation of any material fact, the Administrator within five years after the date of issuance of such patent may file with the Commissioner a request for the transfer to the Administrator of title to such patent on the records of the Commissioner. Notice of any such request shall be transmitted by the Commissioner to the owner of record of such patent, and title to such patent shall be so transferred to the Administrator unless within thirty days after receipt of such notice such owner of record requests a hearing before a Board of Patent Interferences on the question whether any such false representation was contained in such statement. Such question shall be heard and determined, and determination thereof shall be subject to review, in the manner prescribed by subsection (d) for questions arising thereunder. No request made by the Administrator under this subsection for the transfer of title to any patent, and no prosecution for the violation of any criminal statute, shall be barred by any failure of the Administrator to make a request under subsection (d) for the issuance of such patent to him, or by any notice previously given by the Administrator stating that he had no objection to the issuance of such patent to the applicant therefor.

(f) Under such regulations in conformity with this subsection as the Administrator shall prescribe, he may waive all or any part of the rights of the United States under this section with respect to any invention or class of inventions made or which may be made by any person or class of persons in the performance of any work required by any contract of the Administration of the Administrator determines that the interests of the United States will be served thereby. Any such waiver may be made upon such terms and under such conditions as the Administrator shall determine to be required for the protection of the interests of the United States. Each such waiver made with respect to any invention shall be subject to the reservation by the Administrator of an irrevocable, nonexclusive, nontransferrable, royalty-free license for the practice of such invention throughout the world by or on behalf of the United States or any foreign government pursuant to any treaty or agreement with the United States. Each proposal for any waiver under this subsection shall be referred to an Inventions and Contributions Board which shall be established by the Administrator wthin the Administration. Such Board shall accord to each interested party an opportunity for hearing, and shall transmit to the Administrator its findings of fact with respect to such proposal and its recommendations for action to be taken with respect thereto.

(g) The Administrator shall determine, and promulgate regulations specifying, the terms and conditions upon which licenses will be granted by the Administration for the practice by any person (other than an agency of the United States) of any invention for which the Administrator holds a patent on behalf of the United States.

(h) The Administrator is authorized to take all suitable and necessary steps to protect any invention or discovery to which he has title, and to require that contractors or persons who retain title to inventions or discoveries under this section protect the inventions or discoveries to which the Administration has or may acquire a license of use.

(i) The Administration shall be considered a defense agency of the United States for the purpose of chapter 17 of title 35 of the United States Code.[13]

(j) As used in this section—

(1) the term "person" means any individual, partnership, corporation, association, institution, or other entity;

(2) the term "contract" means any actual or proposed contract, agreement, understanding, or other arrangement, and includes any assignment, substitution of parties or subcontract executed or entered into thereunder; and

(3) the term "made", when used in relation to any invention, means the conception or first actual reduction to practice of such invention.

CONTRIBUTIONS AWARDS

SEC. 306. (a) Subject to the provisions of this section, the Administrator is authorized, upon his own initiative or upon application of any person, to make a monetary award, in such amount and upon such terms as he shall determine to be warranted, to any person (as defined by section 305) for any scientific or technical contribution to the Administration which is determined by the Administrator to have significant value in the conduct of aeronautical and space activities. Each application made for any such award shall be referred to the Inventions and Contributions Board established under section 305 of this Act. Such Board shall accord to each such applicant an opportunity for hearing upon such application,

[13] 66 Stat. 805–808.

and shall transmit to the Administrator its recommendation as to the terms of the award, if any, to be made to such applicant for such contribution. In determining the terms and conditions of any award the Administrator shall take into account—

(1) the value of the contribution to the United States;

(2) the aggregate amount of any sums which have been expended by the applicant for the development of such contribution;

(3) the amount of any compensation (other than salary received for services rendered as an officer or employee of the Government) previously received by the applicant for or on account of the use of such contribution by the United States; and

(4) such other factors as the Administrator shall determine to be material.

(b) If more than one applicant under subsection (a) claims an interest in the same contribution, the Administrator shall ascertain and determine the respective interests of such applicants, and shall apportion any award to be made with respect to such contribution among such applicants in such proportions as he shall determine to be equitable. No award may be made under subsection (a) with respect to any contribution—

(1) unless the applicant surrenders, by such means as the Administrator shall determine to be effective, all claims which such applicant may have to receive any compensation (other than the award made under this section) for the use of such contribution or any element thereof at any time by or on behalf of the United States, or by or on behalf of any foreign government pursuant to any treaty or agreement with the United States, within the United States or at any other place;

(2) in any amount exceeding $100,000, unless the Administrator has transmitted to the appropriate committees of the Congress a full and complete report concerning the amount and terms of, and the basis for, such proposed award, and thirty calendar days of regular session of the Congress have expired after receipt of such report by such committees.

APPROPRIATIONS

SEC. 307. (a) There are hereby authorized to be appropriated such sums as may be necessary to carry out this Act, except that nothing in this Act shall authorize the appropriation of any amount for (1) the acquisition or condemnation of any real property, or (2) any other item of a capital nature (such as plant or facility acquisition, construction, or expansion) which exceeds $250,000. Sums appropriated pursuant to this subsection for the construction of facilities, or for research and development activities, shall remain available until expended.

(b) Any funds appropriated for the construction of facilities may be used for emergency repairs of existing facilities when such existing facilities are made inoperative by major breakdown, accident, or other circumstances and such repairs are deemed by the Administrator to be of greater urgency than the construction of new facilities.

Approved July 29, 1958.

Statement by President Eisenhower upon Signing the National Aeronautics and Space Act, July 29, 1958[1]

I have today signed H.R. 12575, the National Aeronautics and Space Act of 1958.[2]

The enactment of this legislation is an historic step, further equipping the United States for leadership in the space age. I wish to commend the Congress for the promptness with which it has created the organization and provided the authority needed for an effective national effort in the fields of aeronautics and space exploration.

The new Act contains one provision that requires comment. Section 205 authorizes cooperation with other nations and groups of nations in work done pursuant to the Act and in the peaceful application of the results of such work, pursuant to international agreements entered into by the President with the advice and consent of the Senate. I regard this section merely as recognizing that international treaties may be made in this field, and as not precluding, in appropriate cases, less formal arrangements for cooperation. To construe the section otherwise would raise substantial constitutional questions.

The present National Advisory Committee for Aeronautics (NACA), with its large and competent staff and well-equipped laboratories, will provide the nucleus for the NASA. The NACA has an established record of research performance and of cooperation with the Armed Services. The combination of space exploration responsibilities with the NACA's traditional aeronautical research functions is a natural evolution.

The enactment of the law establishing the NACA in 1915 proved a decisive step in the advancement of our civil and military aviation. The Aeronautics and Space Act of 1958 should have an even greater impact on our future.

President Johnson Hails U.N. Accord on Treaty Governing Exploration of Outer Space

Statement by President Johnson[1]

I am glad to confirm on the basis of Ambassador Goldberg's [Arthur J. Goldberg, U.S. Representative to the United Nations] report to me this morning that agreement has been reached at the United Nations among members of the Outer Space Committee, including the United States, on a draft text of a treaty governing the exploration of outer space, including the moon and other celestial bodies.

In accordance with U.N. procedures, it is expected that a resolution endorsing the treaty will be submitted formally early next week, with broad cosponsorship, along with the agreed text of the Outer Space Treaty. We look forward to early action by the Assembly on this matter.

Progress toward such a treaty commenced on May 7 of this year when I requested Ambassador Goldberg to initiate consultations for a treaty in the appropriate U.N. body.[2] After businesslike negotiations within the U.N. Outer Space Committee in Geneva and at the United Nations in New York,[3] this important step toward peace has been achieved.

It is the most important arms control development since the limited test ban treaty of 1963.[4] It puts in treaty form the "no bombs in orbit" resolution of the United Nations.[5] It guarantees free access to all areas and installations on celestial bodies. This openness, taken with other provisions of the treaty, should prevent warlike

---

[1] *Public Papers of the Presidents: Dwight D. Eisenhower, 1958,* p. 573.

[2] *Supra.*

[1] Read by Acting Press Secretary George Christian at a news conference at Austin, Tex., on Dec. 8; the text also was released at the United States Mission to the United Nations at New York, N.Y., on Dec. 8 (U.S./U.N. press release 5011).

[2] For background, see BULLETIN of June 6, 1966, p. 900; for a letter from Ambassador Goldberg to the chairman of the U.N. Committee on the Peaceful Uses of Outer Space on June 16 and text of the U.S. draft treaty, see *ibid.,* July 11, 1966, p. 60.

[3] For background, see *ibid.,* Aug. 15, 1966, p. 249; Aug. 29, 1966, p. 321; and Oct. 17, 1966, p. 605.

[4] For text, see *ibid.,* Aug. 12, 1963, p. 239.

[5] For text of U.N. General Assembly Resolution 1884 (XVIII), see *ibid.,* Nov. 11, 1963, p. 754.

preparations on the moon and other celestial bodies.

This treaty has historic significance for the new age of space exploration. I salute and commend all members of the United Nations who contributed to this significant agreement.

In the expectation that formal U.N. action will have been completed at an early date, I plan to present the treaty to the Senate for advice and consent at the next session of Congress, and I hope that the United States will be one of the first countries to ratify it.

Text of Treaty

TREATY ON PRINCIPLES GOVERNING THE ACTIVITIES OF STATES IN THE EXPLORATION AND USE OF OUTER SPACE, INCLUDING THE MOON AND OTHER CELESTIAL BODIES

The States Parties to this Treaty,

Inspired by the great prospects opening up before mankind as a result of man's entry into outer space,

Recognizing the common interest of all mankind in the progress of the exploration and use of outer space for peaceful purposes,

Believing that the exploration and use of outer space should be carried on for the benefit of all peoples irrespective of the degree of their economic or scientific development,

Desiring to contribute to broad international co-operation in the scientific as well as the legal aspects of the exploration and use of outer space for peaceful purposes,

Believing that such co-operation will contribute to the development of mutual understanding and to the strengthening of friendly relations between States and peoples,

Recalling resolution 1962 (XVIII), entitled "Declaration of Legal Principles Governing the Activities of States in the Exploration and Use of Outer Space", which was adopted unanimously by the United Nations General Assembly on 13 December 1963,

Recalling resolution 1884 (XVIII), calling upon States to refrain from placing in orbit around the earth any objects carrying nuclear weapons or any other kinds of weapons of mass destruction or from installing such weapons on celestial bodies, which was adopted unanimously by the United Nations General Assembly on 17 October 1963,

Taking account of United Nations General Assembly resolution 110 (II) of 3 November 1947, which condemned propaganda designed or likely to provoke or en-

courage any threat to the peace, breach of the peace or act of aggression, and considering that the aforementioned resolution is applicable to outer space,

Convinced that a Treaty on Principles Governing the Activities of States in the Exploration and Use of Outer Space, including the Moon and Other Celestial Bodies, will further the Purposes and Principles of the Charter of the United Nations,

Have agreed on the following:

ARTICLE I

The exploration and use of outer space, including the moon and other celestial bodies, shall be carried out for the benefit and in the interests of all countries, irrespective of their degree of economic or scientific development, and shall be the province of all mankind.

Outer space, including the moon and other celestial bodies, shall be free for exploration and use by all States without discrimination of any kind, on a basis of equality and in accordance with international law, and there shall be free access to all areas of celestial bodies.

There shall be freedom of scientific investigation in outer space, including the moon and other celestial bodies, and States shall facilitate and encourage international co-operation in such investigation.

ARTICLE II

Outer space, including the moon and other celestial bodies, is not subject to national appropriation by claim of sovereignty, by means of use or occupation, or by any other means.

ARTICLE III

States Parties to the Treaty shall carry on activities in the exploration and use of outer space, including the moon and other celestial bodies, in accordance with international law, including the Charter of the United Nations, in the interest of maintaining international peace and security and promoting international co-operation and understanding.

ARTICLE IV

States Parties to the Treaty undertake not to place in orbit around the earth any objects carrying nuclear weapons or any other kinds of weapons of mass destruction, install such weapons on celestial bodies, or station such weapons in outer space in any other manner.

The moon and other celestial bodies shall be used by all States Parties to the Treaty exclusively for peaceful purposes. The establishment of military bases, installations and fortifications, the testing of any type of weapons and the conduct of military manoeuvres on celestial bodies shall be forbidden. The use of military personnel for scientific research or for any other peaceful purposes shall not be prohibited. The use of any equipment or facility necessary for peaceful exploration of the moon and other celestial bodies shall also not be prohibited.

ARTICLE V

States Parties to the Treaty shall regard astronauts as envoys of mankind in outer space and shall render to them all possible assistance in the event of accident, distress, or emergency landing on the territory of another State Party or on the high seas. When astronauts make such a landing, they shall be safely and promptly returned to the State of registry of their space vehicle.

In carrying on activities in outer space and on celestial bodies, the astronauts of one State Party shall render all possible assistance to the astronauts of other States Parties.

States Parties to the Treaty shall immediately inform the other State Parties to the Treaty or the Secretary-General of the United Nations of any phenomena they discover in outer space, including the moon and other celestial bodies, which could constitute a danger to the life or health of astronauts.

ARTICLE VI

States Parties to the Treaty shall bear international responsibility for national activities in outer space, including the moon and other celestial bodies, whether such activities are carried on by governmental agencies or by non-governmental entities, and for assuring that national activities are carried out in conformity with the provisions set forth in the present Treaty. The activities of non-governmental entities in outer space, including the moon and other celestial bodies, shall require authorization and continuing supervision by the State concerned. When activities are carried on in outer space, including the moon and other celestial bodies, by an international organization, responsibility for compliance with this Treaty shall be borne both by the international organization and by the States Parties to the Treaty participating in such organization.

ARTICLE VII

Each State Party to the Treaty that launches or procures the launching of an object into outer space, including the moon, and other celestial bodies, and each State Party from whose territory or facility an object is launched, is internationally liable for damage to another State Party to the Treaty or to its natural or juridical per-

sons by such object or its component parts on the Earth, in air space or in outer space, including the moon and other celestial bodies.

ARTICLE VIII

A State Party to the Treaty on whose registry an object launched into outer space is carried shall retain jurisdiction and control over such object, and over any personnel therefor, while in outer space or on a celestial body. Ownership of objects launched into outer space, including objects landed or constructed on a celestial body, and of their component parts, is not affected by their presence in outer space or on a celestial body or by their return to the Earth. Such objects or component parts found beyond the limits of the State Party to the Treaty on whose registry they are carried shall be returned to that State, which shall, upon request, furnish identifying data prior to their return.

ARTICLE IX

In the exploration and use of outer space, including the moon and other celestial bodies, States Parties to the Treaty shall be guided by the principle of co-operation and mutual assistance and shall conduct all their activities in outer space, including the moon and other celestial bodies, with due regard to the corresponding interests of all other States Parties to the Treaty. States Parties to the Treaty shall pursue studies of outer space, including the moon and other celestial bodies, and conduct exploration of them so as to avoid their harmful contamination and also adverse changes in the environment of the Earth resulting from the introduction of extraterrestrial matter and, where necessary, shall adopt appropriate measures for this purpose. If a State Party to the Treaty has reason to believe that an activity or experiment planned by it or its nationals in outer space, including the moon and other celestial bodies, would cause potentially harmful interference with activities of other States Parties in the peaceful exploration and use of outer space, including the moon and other celestial bodies, it shall undertake appropriate international consultations before proceeding with any such activity or experiment. A State Party to the Treaty which has reason to believe that an activity or experiment planned by another State Party in outer space, including the moon and other celestial bodies, would cause potentially harmful interference with activities in the peaceful exploration and use of outer space, including the moon and other celestial bodies, may request consultation concerning the activity or experiment.

ARTICLE X

In order to promote international co-operation in the exploration and use of outer space, including the moon and other celestial bodies, in conformity with the purposes of this Treaty, the States Parties to the Treaty shall consider on a basis of equality any requests by other States Parties to the Treaty to be afforded an opportunity to observe the flight of space objects launched by those States.

The nature of such an opportunity for observation and the conditions under which it could be afforded shall be determined by agreement between the States concerned.

ARTICLE XI

In order to promote international co-operation in the peaceful exploration and use of outer space, States Parties to the Treaty conducting activities in outer space, including the moon and other celestial bodies, agree to inform the Secretary-General of the United Nations as well as the public and the international scientific community, to the greatest extent feasible and practicable, of the nature, conduct, locations and results of such activities. On receiving the said information, the Secretary-General of the United Nations should be prepared to disseminate it immediately and effectively.

ARTICLE XII

All stations, installations, equipment and space vehicles on the moon and other celestial bodies shall be open to representatives of other States Parties to the Treaty on a basis of reciprocity. Such representatives shall give reasonable advance notice of a projected visit, in order that appropriate consultations may be held and that maximum precautions may be taken to assure safety and to avoid interference with normal operations in the facility to be visited.

ARTICLE XIII

The provisions of this Treaty shall apply to the activities of States Parties to the Treaty in the exploration and use of outer space, including the moon and other celestial bodies, whether such activities are carried on by a single State Party to the Treaty or jointly with other States, including cases where they are carried on within the framework of international inter-governmental organizations.

Any practical questions arising in connexion with activities carried on by international inter-governmental organizations in the exploration and use of outer space, including the moon and other celestial bodies, shall be resolved by the States Parties to the Treaty either with the appropriate international organization or with one or more States members of that international organization, which are Parties to this Treaty.

ARTICLE XIV

1. This Treaty shall be open to all States for signature. Any State which does not sign this Treaty before its entry into force in accordance with paragraph 3 of this article may accede to it at any time.

2. This Treaty shall be subject to ratification by signatory States. Instruments of ratification and instruments of accession shall be deposited with the Governments of the Union of Soviet Socialist Republics, the United Kingdom of Great Britain and Northern Ireland and the United States of America, which are hereby designated the Depositary Governments.

3. This Treaty shall enter into force upon the deposit of instruments of ratification by five Governments including the Governments designated as Depositary Governments under this Treaty.

4. For States whose instruments of ratification or accession are deposited subsequent to the entry into force of this Treaty, it shall enter into force on the date of the deposit of their instruments of ratification or accession.

5. The Depositary Governments shall promptly inform all signatory and acceding States of the date of each signature, the date of deposit of each instrument of ratification of and accession to this Treaty, the date of its entry into force and other notices.

6. This Treaty shall be registered by the Depositary Governments pursuant to Article 102 of the Charter of the United Nations.

ARTICLE XV

Any State Party to the Treaty may propose amendments to this Treaty. Amendments shall enter into force for each State Party to the Treaty accepting the amendments upon their acceptance by a majority of the States Parties to the Treaty and thereafter for each remaining State Party to the Treaty on the date of acceptance by it.

ARTICLE XVI

Any State Party to the Treaty may give notice of its withdrawal from the Treaty one year after its entry into force by written notification to the Depositary Governments. Such withdrawal shall take effect one year from the date of receipt of this notification.

ARTICLE XVII

This Treaty, of which the Chinese, English, French, Russian and Spanish texts are equally authentic, shall be deposited in the archives of the Depositary Governments. Duly certified copies of this Treaty shall be transmitted by the Depositary Governments to the Governments of the signatory and acceding States.

IN WITNESS WHEREOF the undersigned, duly authorized, have signed this Treaty.

DONE in _____, at the cities of London, Moscow and Washington, the _____ day of _____ one thousand nine hundred and _____.
[Signed 27 January 1967.]

United Nations Resolution on The Peaceful Uses of Outer Space

The text of the General Assembly Resolution 1721 (XVI) of December 20, 1961, appears below and particular attention is called to the first section which commends to States the guiding principles of freedom for outer space and celestial bodies, and the extension of international law and the provisions of the United Nations Charter to the new space environment.

A

The General Assembly,

Recognizing the common interest of mankind in furthering the peaceful uses of outer space and the urgent need to strengthen international co-operation in this important field,

Believing that the exploration and use of outer space should be only for the betterment of mankind and to the benefit of States irrespective of the stage of their economic or scientific development,

1. *Commends* to States for their guidance in the exploration and use of outer space the following principles:

(a) International law, including the Charter of the United Nations, applies to outer space and celestial bodies:

(b) Outer space and celestial bodies are free for exploration and use by all States in conformity with international law and are not subject to national appropriation;

2. *Invites* the Committee on the Peaceful Uses of Outer Space to study and report on the legal problems which may arise from the exploration and use of outer space.

B

The General Assembly,

Believing that the United Nations should provide a focal point for international co-operation in the peaceful exploration and use of outer space,

1. *Calls upon* States launching objects into orbit or

beyond to furnish information promptly to the Committee on the Peaceful Uses of Outer Space, through the Secretary-General, for the registration of launchings;

2. *Requests* the Secretary-General to maintain a public registry of the information furnished in accordance with paragraph 1 above;

3. *Requests* the Committee on the Peaceful Uses of Outer Space, in co-operation with the Secretary-General and making full use of the functions and resources of the Secretariat:

(a) To maintain close contact with governmental and non-governmental organizations concerned with outer space matters;

(b) To provide for the exchange of such information relating to outer space activities as Governments may supply on a voluntary basis, supplementing but not duplicating existing technical and scientific exchanges;

(c) To assist in the study of measures for the promotion of international co-operation in outer space activities;

4. *Further requests* the Committee on the Peaceful Uses of Outer Space to report to the General Assembly on the arrangements undertaken for the performance of those functions and on such developments relating to the peaceful uses of outer space as it considers significant.

C

The General Assembly,

Noting with gratification the marked progress for meteorological science and technology opened up by the advances in outer space,

Convinced of the world-wide benefits to be derived from international co-operation in weather research and analysis,

1. *Recommends* to all Member States and to the World Meteorological Organization and other appropriate specialized agencies the early and comprehensive study, in the light of developments in outer space, of measures:

(a) To advance the state of atmospheric science and technology so as to provide greater knowledge of basic physical forces affecting climate and the possibility of large-scale weather modification;

(b) To develop existing weather forecasting capabilities and to help Member States to make effective use of such capabilities through regional meteorological centres;

2. *Requests* the World Meteorological Organization, consulting as appropriate with the United Nations Educational Scientific and Cultural Organization and other

specialized agencies and governmental and non-governmental organizations, such as the International Council of Scientific Unions, to submit a report to its member Governments and to the Economic and Social Council at its thirty-fourth session regarding appropriate organizational and financial arrangements to achieve those ends, with a view to their further consideration by the General Assembly at its seventeenth session;

3. *Requests* the Committee on the Peaceful Uses of Outer Space, as it deems appropriate, to review that report and submit its comments and recommendations to the Economic and Social Council and to the General Assembly.

D

The General Assembly,

Believing that communication by means of satellites should be available to the nations of the world as soon as practicable on a global and non-discriminatory basis,

Convinced of the need to prepare the way for the establishment of effective operational satellite communications,

1. *Notes with satisfaction* that the International Telecommunication Union plans to call a special conference in 1963 to make allocations of radio frequency bands for outer space activities;

2. *Recommends* that the International Telecommunication Union consider at that conference those aspects of space communication in which international co-operation will be required;

3. *Notes* the potential importance of communication satellites for use by the United Nations and its principal organs and specialized agencies for both operational and informational requirements;

4. *Invites* the *Special Fund and the Expanded Programme of Technical Assistance,* in consultation with the International Telecommunication Union, to give sympathetic consideration to requests from Member States for technical and other assistance for the survey of their communication needs and for the development of their domestic communication facilities so that they may make effective use of space communication;

5. *Requests* the International Telecommunication Union, consulting as appropriate with Member States, the United Nations Educational, Scientific and Cultural Organization and other specialized agencies and governmental and non-governmental organizations, such as the Committee on Space Research of the International Council of Scientific Unions, to submit a report on the implementation of those proposals to the Economic and

Social Council at its thirty-fourth session and to the General Assembly at its seventeenth session;

6. *Requests* the Committee on the Peaceful Uses of Outer Space, as it deems appropriate, to review that report and submit its comments and recommendations to the Economic and Social Council and to the General Assembly.

E

The General Assembly,

Recalling its resolution 1472(XIV) of 12 December 1959,

Noting that the terms of office of the members of the Committee on the Peaceful Uses of Outer Space expire at the end of 1961,

Noting the report of the Committee on the Peaceful Uses of Outer Space, [U.N.doc.A/4987.]

1. *Decides* to continue the membership of the Committee on the Peaceful Uses of Outer Space as set forth in General Assembly resolution 1472(XIV) and to add Chad, Mongolia, Morocco and Sierra Leone to its membership in recognition of the increased membership of the United Nations since the Committee was established;

2. *Requests* the Committee to meet not later than 31 March 1962 to carry out its mandate as contained in General Assembly resolution 1472(XIV), to review the activities provided for in the present resolution and to make such reports as it may consider appropriate.

Resolution Adopted by the General Assembly [on the Report of the First Committee (A/5571)] 1884 (XVIII) Question of General and Complete Disarmament

The General Assembly,

Recalling its resolution 1721 A (XVI) of 20 December 1961, in which it expressed the belief that the exploration and use of outer space should be only for the betterment of mankind,

Determined to take steps to prevent the spread of the arms race to outer space,

1. *Welcomes* the expressions by the Union of Soviet Socialist Republics and the United States of America of their intention not to station in outer space any objects carrying nuclear weapons or other kinds of weapons of mass destruction;

2. *Solemnly calls upon* all States:

(*a*) To refrain from placing in orbit around the earth any objects carrying nuclear weapons or any other kinds of weapons of mass destruction, installing such weapons on celestial bodies, or stationing such weapons in outer space in any other manner;

(*b*) To refrain from causing, encouraging or in any way participating in the conduct of the foregoing activities.

1244th plenary meeting,
17 October 1963.

United Nations Resolution 1962 (XVIII), December 13, 1963

Declaration of Legal Principles Governing Activities of States in the Exploration and Use of Outer Space

The General Assembly,

Inspired by the great prospects opening up before mankind as a result of man's entry into outer space,

Recognizing the common interest of all mankind in the progress of the exploration and use of outer space for peaceful purposes,

Believing that the exploration and use of outer space should be for the betterment of mankind and for the benefit of States irrespective of their degree of economic or scientific development,

Desiring to contribute to broad international cooperation in the scientific as well as in the legal aspects of exploration and use of outer space for peaceful purposes,

Believing that such co-operation will contribute to the development of mutual understanding and to the strengthening of friendly relations between nations and peoples,

Recalling General Assembly resolution 110 (II) of 3 November 1947, which condemned propaganda designed or likely to provoke or encourage any threat to the peace, breach of the peace, or act of aggression, and considering that the aforementioned resolution is applicable to outer space,

Taking into consideration General Assembly resolutions 1721 (XVI) of 20 December 1961 and 1802 (XVII) of 14 December 1962, approved unanimously by the States Members of the United Nations,

Solemnly declares that in the exploration and use of outer space States should be guided by the following principles:

1. The exploration and use of outer space shall be carried on for the benefit and in the interests of all mankind.

2. Outer space and celestial bodies are free for exploration and use by all States on a basis of equality and in accordance with international law.

3. Outer space and celestial bodies are not subject to national appropriation by claim of sovereignty, by means of use or occupation, or by any other means.

4. The activities of States in the exploration and use of outer space shall be carried on in accordance with international law including the Charter of the United Nations, in the interest of maintaining international peace and security and promoting international co-operation and understanding.

5. States bear international responsibility for national activities in outer space, whether carried on by governmental agencies or by non-governmental entities, and for assuring that national activities are carried on in conformity with the principles set forth in this Declaration. The activities of non-governmental entities in outer space shall require authorization and continuing supervision by the State concerned. When activities are carried on in outer space by an international organization, responsibility for compliance with the principles set forth in this Declaration shall be borne by the international organization and by the States participating in it.

6. In the exploration and use of outer space, States shall be guided by the principle of co-operation and mutual assistance and shall conduct all their activities in outer space with due regard for the corresponding interests of other States. If a State has reason to believe that an outer space activity or experiment planned by it or its nationals would cause potentially harmful interference with activities of other States in the peaceful exploration and use of outer space, it shall undertake appropriate international consultations before proceeding with any such activity or experiment. A State which has reason to believe that an outer space activity or experiment planned by another State would cause potentially harmful interference with activities in the peaceful exploration and use of outer space may request consultation concerning the activity or experiment.

7. The State on whose registry an object launched into outer space is carried shall retain jurisdiction and control over such object, and any personnel thereon, while in outer space. Ownership of objects launched into outer space, and of their component parts, is not affected by their passage through outer space or by their return to the earth. Such objects or component parts found beyond the limits of the State of registry shall be returned to that State, which shall furnish identifying data upon request prior to return.

8. Each State which launches or procures the launching on an object into outer space, and each State from

whose territory or facility an object is launched, is internationally liable for damage to a foreign State or to its natural or juridical persons by such object or its component parts on the earth, in air space, or in outer space.

9. States shall regard astronauts as envoys of mankind in outer space, and shall render to them all possible assistance in the event of accident, distress, or emergency landing on the territory of a foreign State or on the high seas. Astronauts who make such a landing shall be safely and promptly returned to the State of registry of their space vehicle.

United Nations Resolution 1963 (XVIII), December 13, 1963 International Cooperation in the Peaceful Uses of Outer Space

The General Assembly,

Recalling its resolutions 1721 (XVI) of 20 December 1961 and 1802 (XVII) of 14 December 1962, on international co-operation in the peaceful uses of outer space,

Having considered the Report (A/5549 and A/5549 /Add. 1) submitted by the Committee on the Peaceful Uses of Outer Space,

Mindful of the benefits which all Member States would enjoy by participation in international programmes of co-operation in this field,

I

1. *Recommends* that consideration should be given to incorporating in international agreement form, in the future as appropriate, legal principles governing the activities of the States in the exploration and use of outer space;

2. *Requests* the Committee on the Peaceful Uses of Outer Space to continue to study and report on legal problems which may arise in the exploration and use of outer space, and in particular to arrange for the prompt preparation of draft international agreements on liability for damage caused by objects launched into outer space and on assistance to and return of astronauts and space vehicles;

3. *Further requests* the Committee on the Peaceful Uses of Outer Space to report to the General Assembly at its nineteenth session on the results achieved in preparing these two agreements;

II

1. *Endorses* the recommendations of the Report of the Committee on the Peaceful Uses of Outer Space concerning exchange of information, encouragement of international programmes, international sounding rocket facilities, education and training and potentially harmful effects of space experiments;

2. *Welcomes* the decision of the Committee, in co-operation with the Secretary-General and making full use of the functions and resources of the Secretariat, to undertake the following:

(a) Preparation of a working paper on the activities and resources of the United Nations, of its specialized agencies, and of other competent international bodies relating to the peaceful uses of outer space;

(b) Preparation of a summary of national and of co-operative international space activities;

(c) Preparation of a list of available bibliographic and abstracting services covering the scientific and technical results and publications in space and space-related areas;

(d) Compilation in co-operation with UNESCO [United Nations Educational, Scientific and Cultural Organization] of reviews of information on facilities for education and training in basic subjects related to the peaceful uses of outer space in universities and other places of learning;

(e) Establishment, at the request of the Government of India, of a group of six scientists to visit the sounding rocket launching facility at Thumba and to advise the Committee on its eligibility for United Nations sponsorship in accordance with the basic principles endorsed by the General Assembly in resoluton 1802 (XVII).

3. *Notes with appreciation* that, in accordance with General Assembly resolution 1721 (XVI), the Secretary-General is maintaining a public registry of objects launched into orbit or beyond on the basis of information being furnished by States Members of the United Nations;

4. *Notes with appreciation* that certain Member States have, on a voluntary basis, provided information on their national space programmes and invites other Member States to do so;

5. *Invites* Member States to give favourable consideration to requests of countries desirous of participating in the peaceful exploration of outer space for appropriate training and technical assistance on a bilateral basis or on any other basis they see fit;

6. *Notes* the considerable measure of co-operation in the peaceful exploration and use of outer space under way among Member States;

7. *Notes* that the United States and the Soviet Union have reached an agreement looking toward co-operation in the fields of satellite meteorology, communications and magnetic field mapping;

8. *Encourages* Member States to continue and extend co-operative arrangements so that all Members can benefit from the peaceful exploration and use of outer space;

9. *Believes* that international co-operation can be beneficial in furthering the exploration of the solar system;

III

1. *Notes with appreciation* (a) the Second Report of the World Meteorological Organization on the advancement of atmospheric sciences and their application in the light of developments in outer space and (b) the organizational and financial steps taken by the Fourth Congress of the World Meteorological Organization in response to resolutions 1721 C (XVI) and 1802 III (XVII);

2. *Endorses* efforts toward the establishment of a World Weather Watch under the auspices of the World Meteorological Organization to include the use of satellite as well as conventional data with data centres to facilitate the effectiveness of the system;

3. *Urges* that Member States (a) extend their national and regional meteorological efforts to implement the expanded programme of the World Meteorological Organization, (b) co-operate in the establishment of the World Weather Watch, and (c) increase research and training in the atmospheric sciences;

4. *Invites* the World Meteorological Organization to make a progress report to the Committee on the Peaceful Uses of Outer Space in 1964 relating to its activities in this field;

IV

1. *Notes with appreciation* the Second Report of the International Telecommunication Union on Telecommunication and the Peaceful Uses of Outer Space;

2. *Welcomes* the decisions of the October-November 1963 Extraordinary Administrative Radio Conference convened by the International Telecommunication Union on the allocation of frequency bands for space communication and procedures for their use as a step in the development of space radio communications;

3. *Invites* the International Telecommunication Union to make a progress report to the Committee on the Peaceful Uses of Outer Space in 1964 relating to its activities in this field;

4. *Recognizes* the potential contribution of communications satellites in the expansion of global telecommunications facilities and the possibilities this offers for increasing the flow of information and for furthering the objectives of the United Nations and its agencies;

V

Requests the Committee on the Peaceful Uses of Outer Space to continue its work as set forth in General Assembly resolutions 1472 (XIV), 1721 (XVI), 1802 (XVII), and in this resolution, and to report to the General Assembly at its nineteenth session on the activities of the Committee.

Treaty Banning Nuclear Weapon Tests in the Atmosphere, In Outer Space, and Under Water

[President Kennedy transmitted the treaty to the Senate on August 8, 1963, and after an extensive investigation and debate of the subject, the Senate approved ratification on September 24. Ratified by the President on October 7, the treaty entered into force on October 10. By December 31, 1963, 106 countries had signed or acceded to the treaty.]

The Governments of the United States of America, the United Kingdom of Great Britain, and Northern Ireland, and the Union of Soviet Socialist Republics, hereinafter referred to as the "Original Parties",

Proclaiming as their principal aim the speediest possible achievement of an agreement on general and complete disarmament under strict international control in accordance with the objectives of the United Nations which would put an end to the armaments race and eliminate the incentive to the production and testing of all kinds of weapons, including nuclear weapons,

Seeking to achieve the discontinuance of all test explosions of nuclear weapons for all time, determined to continue negotiations to this end, and desiring to put an end to the contamination of man's environment by radioactive substances,

Have agreed as follows:

ARTICLE I

1. Each of the Parties to this Treaty undertakes to prohibit, to prevent, and not to carry out any nuclear weapon test explosion, or any other nuclear explosion, at any place under its jurisdiction or control:

(a) in the atmosphere; beyond its limits, including outer space; or underwater, including territorial waters or high seas; or

(b) in any other environment if such explosion causes radioactive debris to be present outside the territorial limits of the State under whose jurisdiction or control such explosion is conducted. It is understood in this connection that the provisions of this subparagraph are without prejudice to the conclusion of a treaty resulting in the permanent banning of all nuclear test explosions, including all such explosions underground, the conclusion of which, as the Parties have stated in the Preamble to this Treaty, they seek to achieve.

2. Each of the Parties to this Treaty undertakes furthermore to refrain from causing, encouraging, or in any way participating in, the carrying out of any nuclear weapon test explosion, or any other nuclear explosion, anywhere which would take place in any of the environments described, or have the effect referred to, in paragraph 1 of this Article.

ARTICLE II

1. Any Party may propose amendments to this Treaty. The text of any proposed amendment shall be submitted to the Depositary Governments which shall circulate it to all Parties to this Treaty. Thereafter, if requested to do so by one-third or more of the Parties, the Depositary Governments shall convene a conference, to which they shall invite all the Parties, to consider such amendment.

2. Any amendment to this Treaty must be approved by a majority of the votes of all the Parties to this Treaty, including the votes of all of the Original Parties. The amendment shall enter into force for all Parties upon the deposit of instruments of ratification by a majority of all the Parties, including the instruments of ratification of all of the Original Parties.

ARTICLE III

1. This Treaty shall be open to all States for signature. Any State which does not sign this Treaty before its entry into force in accordance with paragraph 3 of this Article may accede to it at any time.

2. This Treaty shall be subject to ratification by signatory States. Instruments of ratification and instruments of accession shall be deposited with the Governments of the Original Parties—the United States of America, the United Kingdom of Great Britain and Northern Ireland, and the Union of Soviet Socialist Republics—which are hereby designated the Depositary Governments.

3. This Treaty shall enter into force after its ratification by all the Original Parties and the deposit of their instruments of ratification.

4. For States whose instruments of ratification or accession are deposited subsequent to the entry into force of this Treaty, it shall enter into force on the date of the deposit of their instruments of ratification or accession.

5. The Depositary Governments shall promptly inform all signatory and acceding States of the date of each

signature, the date of deposit of each instrument of ratification of and accession to this Treaty, the date of its entry into force, and the date of receipt of any requests for conferences or other notices.

6. This Treaty shall be registered by the Depositary Governments pursuant to Article 102 of the Charter of the United Nations.

ARTICLE IV

This Treaty shall be of unlimited duration.

Each Party shall in exercising its national sovereignty have the right to withdraw from the Treaty if it decides that extraordinary events, related to the subject matter of this Treaty, have jeopardized the supreme interests of its country. It shall give notice of such withdrawal to all other Parties to the Treaty three months in advance.

ARTICLE V

This Treaty of which the English and Russian texts are equally authentic, shall be deposited in the archives of the Depositary Governments. Duly certified copies of this Treaty shall be transmitted by the Depositary Governments to the Governments of the signatory and acceding States.

IN WITNESS WHEREOF, the undersigned, duly authorized, have signed this Treaty.

DONE in triplicate at the city of Moscow the fifth day of August, one thousand nine hundred and sixty-three.

For the Government of the United States of America

For the Government of the United Kingdom of Great Britain and Northern Ireland

For the Government of the Union of Soviet Socialist Republics

Communications-Satellite Act, Approved August 31, 1962[1]

AN ACT To provide for the establishment, ownership, operation, and regulation of a commercial communications satellite system, and for other purposes.

Be it enacted by the Senate and House of Representatives of the United States of America in Congress assembled,

Title I—Short Title, Declaration of Policy and Definitions

SHORT TITLE

SEC. 101. This Act may be cited as the "Communications Satellite Act of 1962."

---

[1] Public Law ST–624, 87th Cong., H.R. 11040, Aug. 31, 1962 (76 Stat. 419).

DECLARATION OF POLICY AND PURPOSE

SEC. 102. (a) The Congress hereby declares that it is the policy of the United States to establish, in conjunction and in cooperation with other countries, as expeditiously as practicable a commercial communications satellite system, as part of an improved global communications network, which will be responsive to public needs and national objectives, which will serve the communcation needs of the United States and other countries, and which will contribute to world peace and understanding.

(b) The new and expanded telecommunication services are to be made available as promptly as possible and are to be extended to provide global coverage at the earliest practicable date. In effectuating this program, care and attention will be directed toward providing such services to economically less developed countries and areas as well as those more highly developed, toward efficient and economical use of the electromagnetic frequency spectrum, and toward the reflection of the benefits of this new technology in both quality of services and charges for such services.

(c) In order to facilitate this development and to provide for the widest possible participation by private enterprise, United States participation in the global system shall be in the form of a private corporation, subject to appropriate governmental regulation. It is the intent of Congress that all authorized users shall have nondiscriminatory access to the system; that maximum competition be maintained in the provision of equipment and services utilized by the system; that the corporation created under this Act be so organized and operated as to maintain and strengthen competition in the provision of communications services to the public; and that the activities of the corporation created under this Act and of the persons or companies participating in the ownership of the corporation shall be consistent with the Federal antitrust laws.

(d) It is not the intent of Congress by this Act to preclude the use of the communications satellite system for domestic communication services where consistent with the provisions of this Act nor to preclude the creation of additional communications satellite systems, if required to meet unique governmental needs or if otherwise required in the national interest.

DEFINITIONS

SEC. 103. As used in this Act, and unless the context otherwise requires—

(1) the term "communications satellite system" refers to a system of communications satellites in space whose purpose is to relay telecommunication information between satellite terminal stations, together with such associated equipment and facilities for tracking, guidance, control, and command functions as are not part of the generalized launching, tracking, control, and command facilities for all space purposes.

(2) the term "satellite terminal station" refers to a complex of communication equipment located on the earth's surface, operationally connected with one or more terrestrial communication systems, and capable of transmitting telecommunications to or receiving telecommunications from a communications satellite system.

(3) the term "communications satellite" means an earth satellite which is intentionally used to relay telecommunication information;

(4) the term "associated equipment and facilities" refers to facilities other than satellite terminal stations and communications satellites, to be constructed and operated for the primary purpose of a communications satellite system, whether for administration and management, for research and development, or for direct support of space operations;

(5) the term "research and development" refers to the conception, design, and first creation of experimental or prototype operational devices for the operation of a communications satellite system, including the assembly of separate components into a working whole, as distinguished from the term "production," which relates to the construction of such devices to fixed specifications compatible with repetitive duplication for operational applications; and

(6) the term "telecommunication" means any transmission, emission or reception of signs, signals, writings, images, and sounds or intelligence of any nature by wire, radio, optical, or other electromagnetic systems.

(7) the term "communications common carrier" has the same meaning as the term "common carrier" has when used in the Communications Act of 1934, as amended, and in addition includes, but only for purposes of sections 303 and 304, any individual, partnership, association, joint-stock company, trust, corporation, or other entity which owns or controls, directly or indirectly, or is under direct or indirect common control with, any such carrier;

and the term "authorized carrier", except as otherwise provided for purposes of section 304 by section 304(b) (1), means a communications common carrier which has been authorized by the Federal Communications Commission under the Communications Act of 1934, as amended, to provide services by means of communications satellites;

(8) the term "corporation" means the corporation authorized by title III of this Act.

(9) the term "Administration" means the National Aeronautics and Space Administration; and

(10) the term "Commission" means the Federal Communications Commission.

Title II—Federal Coordination, Planning, and Regulation

IMPLEMENTATION OF POLICY

SEC. 201. In order to achieve the objectives and to carry out the purposes of this Act—

(a) the President shall—

(1) aid in the planning and development and foster the execution of a national program for the establishment and operation, as expeditiously as possible, of a commercial communications satellite system;

(2) provide for continuous review of all phases of the development and operation of such a system, including the activities of a communications satellite corporation authorized under title III of this Act;

(3) coordinate the activities of governmental agencies with responsibilities in the field of telecommunication, so as to insure that there is full and effective compliance at all times with the policies set forth in this Act;

(4) exercise such supervision over relationships of the corporation with foreign governments or entities or with international bodies as may be appropriate to assure that such relationships shall be consistent with the national interest and foreign policy of the United States;

(5) insure that timely arrangements are made under which there can be foreign participation in the establishment and use of a communications satellite system;

(6) take all necessary steps to insure the availability and appropriate utilization of the communications satellite system for general governmental purposes except where a separate communications satellite system is required to meet unique governmental needs, or is otherwise required in the national interest; and

(7) so exercise his authority as to help attain coordinated and efficient use of the electromagnetic spectrum and the technical compatibility of the system with existing communications facilities both in the United States and abroad.

(b) the National Aeronautics and Space Administration shall—

(1) advise the Commission on technical characteristics of the communications satellite system;

(2) cooperate with the corporation in research and development to the extent deemed appropriate by the Administration in the public interest;

(3) assist the corporation in the conduct of its research and development program by furnishing to the corporation, when requested, on a reimbursable basis, such satellite launching and associated services as the Administration deems necessary for the most expeditious and economical development of the communications satellite system;

(4) consult with the corporation with respect to the technical characteristics of the communications satellite system;

(5) furnish to the corporation, on request and on a reimbursable basis, satellite launching and associated services required for the establishment, operation, and maintenance of the communications satellite system approved by the Commission; and

(6) to the extent feasible, furnish other services, on a reimbursable basis, to the corporation in connection with the establishment and operation of the system.

(c) the Federal Communications Commission, in its administration of the provisions of the Communications Act of 1934, as amended, and as supplemented by this Act, shall—

(1) insure effective competition, including the use of competitive bidding where appropriate, in the procurement by the corporation and communications common carriers of apparatus, equipment, and services required for the establishment and operation of the communications satellite system and satellite terminal stations; and the Commission shall consult with the Small Business Administration and solicit its recommendations on measures and procedures which will insure that small business concerns are given an equitable

opportunity to share in the procurement program of the corporation for property and services, including but not limited to research, development, construction, maintenance, and repair.

(2) insure that all present and future authorized carriers shall have nondiscriminatory use of, and equitable access to, the communications satellite system and satellite terminal stations under just and reasonable charges, classifications, practices, regulations, and other terms and conditions and regulate the manner in which available facilities of the system and stations are allocated among such users thereof;

(3) in any case where the Secretary of State, after obtaining the advice of the Administration as to technical feasibility, has advised that commercial communication to a particular foreign point by means of the communications satellite system and satellite terminal stations should be established in the national interest, institute forthwith appropriate proceedings under section 214(d) of the Communications Act of 1934, as amended, to require the establishment of such communication by the corporation and the appropriate common carrier or carriers;

(4) insure that facilities of the communications satellite system and satellite terminal stations are technically compatible and interconnected operationally with each other and with existing communications facilities;

(5) prescribe such accounting regulations and systems and engage in such ratemaking procedures as will insure that any economies made possible by a communications satellite system are appropriately reflected in rates for public communication services;

(6) approve technical characteristics of the operational communications satellite system to be employed by the corporation and of the satellite terminal stations; and

(7) grant appropriate authorizations for the construction and operation of each satellite terminal station, either to the corporation or to one or more authorized carriers or to the corporation and one or more such carriers jointly, as will best serve the public interest, convenience, and necessity. In determining the public interest, convenience, and necessity the Commission shall authorize the construction and operation of such stations by com-

munications common carriers or the corporation, without preference to either;

(8) authorize the corporation to issue any shares of capital stock, except the initial issue of capital stock referred to in section 304(a), or to borrow any moneys, or to assume any obligation in respect of the securities of any other person, upon a finding that such issuance, borrowing, or assumption is compatible with the public interest, convenience, and necessity and is necessary or appropriate for or consistent with carrying out the purposes and objectives of this Act by the corporation;

(9) insure that no substantial additions are made by the corporation or carriers with respect to facilities of the system or satellite terminal stations unless such additions are required by the public interest, convenience, and necessity;

(10) require, in accordance with the procedural requirements of section 214 of the Communications Act of 1934, as amended, that additions be made by the corporation or carriers with respect to facilities of the system or satellite terminal stations where such additions would serve the public interest, convenience, and necessity; and

(11) make rules and regulations to carry out the provisions of this Act.

Title III—Creation of a Communications Satellite Corporation

CREATION OF CORPORATION

SEC. 301. There is hereby authorized to be created a communications satellite corporation for profit which will not be an agency or establishment of the United States Government. The corporation shall be subject to the provisions of this Act, to the extent consistent with this Act, to the District of Columbia Business Corporation Act. The right to repeal, alter, or amend this Act at any time is expressly reserved.

PROCESS OF ORGANIZATION

SEC. 302. The President of the United States shall appoint incorporators, by and with the advice and consent of the Senate, who shall serve as the initial board of directors until the first annual meeting of stockholders or until their successors are elected and qualified. Such incorporators shall arrange for any initial stock offering and take whatever other actions are necessary to establish the corporation, including the filing of articles of incorporation, as approved by the President.

DIRECTORS AND OFFICERS

SEC. 303. (a) The corporation shall have a board of directors consisting of individuals who are citizens of the United States, of whom one shall be elected annually by the board to serve as chairman. Three members of the board shall be appointed by the President of the United States, by and with the advice and consent of the Senate, effective the date on which the other members are elected, and for terms of three years or until their successors have been appointed and qualified, except that the first three members of the board so appointed shall continue in office for terms of one, two, and three years, respectively, and any member so appointed to fill a vacancy shall be appointed only for the unexpired term of the director whom he succeeds. Six members of the board shall be elected annually by those stockholders who are communications common carriers and six shall be elected annually by the other stockholders of the corporation. No stockholder who is a communications common carrier and no trustee for such a stockholder shall vote, either directly or indirectly, through the votes of subsidiaries or affiliated companies, nominees, or any persons subject to his direction or control, for more than three candidates for membership on the board. Subject to such limitation, the articles of incorporation to be filed by the incorporators designated under section 302 shall provide for cumulative voting under section 27(d) of the District of Columbia Business Corporation Act (D.C. Code, sec. 29–911 (d)).

(b) The corporation shall have a president, and such other officers as may be named and appointed by the board, at rates of compensation fixed by the board, and serving at the pleasure of the board. No individual other than a citizen of the United States may be an officer of the corporation. No officer of the corporation shall receive any salary from any source other than the corporation during the period of his employment by the corporation.

FINANCING OF THE CORPORATION

SEC. 304. (a) The corporation is authorized to issue and have outstanding, in such amounts as it shall determine, shares of capital stock, without par value, which shall carry voting rights and be eligible for dividends. The shares of such stock initially offered shall be sold at a price not in excess of $100 for each share and in a manner to encourage the widest distribution to the

American public. Subject to the provisions of subsections (b) and (d) of this section, shares of stock offered under this subsection may be issued to and held by any person.

(b) (1) For the purposes of this section the term "authorized carrier" shall mean a communications common carrier which is specifically authorized or which is a member of a class of carriers authorized by the Commission to own shares of stock in the corporation upon a finding that such ownership will be consistent with the public interest, convenience, and necessity.

(2) Only those communications common carriers which are authorized carriers shall own shares of stock in the corporation at any time, and no other communications common carrier shall own shares either directly or indirectly through subsidiaries or affiliated companies, nominees, or any persons subject to its direction or control. Fifty per centum of the shares of stock authorized for issuance at any time by the corporation shall be reserved for purchase by authorized carriers and such carriers shall in the aggregate be entitled to make purchases of the reserved shares in a total number not exceeding the total number of the nonreserved shares of any issue purchased by other persons. At no time after the initial issue is completed shall the aggregate of the shares of voting stock of the corporation owned by authorized carriers directly or indirectly through subsidiaries or affiliated companies, nominees, or any persons subject to their direction or control exceed 50 per centum of such shares issued and outstanding.

(3) At no time shall any stockholder who is not an authorized carrier, or any syndicate or affiliated group of such stockholders, own more than 10 per centum of the shares of voting stock of the corporation issued and outstanding.

(c) The corporation is authorized to issue, in addition to the stock authorized by subsection (a) of this section, nonvoting securities, bonds, debentures, and other certificates of indebtedness as it may determine. Such nonvoting securities, bonds, debentures, or other certificates of indebtedness of the corporation as a communications common carrier may own shall be eligible for inclusion in the rate base of the carrier to the extent allowed by the Commission. The voting stock of the corporation shall not be eligible for inclusion in the rate base of the carrier.

(d) Not more than an aggregate of 20 per centum of the shares of stock of the corporation authorized by subsection (a) of this section which are held by holders other than authorized carriers may be held by persons of the classes described in paragraphs (1), (2), (3), (4), and (5) of section 310(a) of the Communications Act of 1934, as amended (47 U.S.C. 310).

(c) The requirement of section 45 (b) of the District of Columbia Business Corporation Act (D.C. Code, sec. 29–920(b)) as to the percentage of stock which a stockholder must hold in order to have the rights of inspection and copying set forth in that subsection shall not be applicable in the case of holders of the stock of the corporation and they may exercise such rights without regard to the percentage of stock they hold.

(f) Upon application to the Commission by any authorized carrier and after notice and hearing, the Commission may compel any other authorized carrier which owns shares of stock in the corporation to transfer to the applicant, for a fair and reasonable consideration, a number of such shares as the Commission determines will advance the public interest and the purposes of this Act. In its determination with respect to ownership of shares of stock in the corporation, the Commission, whenever consistent with the public interest, shall promote the widest possible distribution of stock among the authorized carriers.

PURPOSES AND POWERS OF THE CORPORATION

Sec. 305. (a) In order to achieve the objectives and to carry out the purposes of this Act, the corporation is authorized to—

(1) plan, initiate, construct, own, manage, and operate itself or in conjunction with foreign governments or business entities a commercial communications satellite system;

(2) furnish, for hire, channels of communication to United States communications common carriers and to other authorized entities, foreign and domestic; and

(3) own and operate satellite terminal stations when licensed by the Commission under section 201(c) (7).

(b) Included in the activities authorized to the corporation for accomplishment of the purposes indicated in subsection (a) of this section, are, among others not specifically named—

(1) to conduct or contract for research and development related to its mission;

(2) to acquire the physical facilities, equipment and devices necessary to its operations, including communications satellites and associated equipment and facilities, whether by construction, purchase, or gift;

(3) to purchase satellite launching and related services from the United States Government;

(4) to contract with authorized users, including the United States Government, for the services of the communications satellite system; and

(5) to develop plans for the technical specifications of all elements of the communications satellite system.

(c) To carry out the foregoing purposes, the corporation shall have the usual powers conferred upon a stock corporation by the District of Columbia Business Corporation Act.

Title IV—Miscellaneous

APPLICABILITY OF COMMUNICATIONS ACT OF 1934

Sec. 401. The corporation shall be deemed to be a common carrier within the meaning of section 3(h) of the Communications Act of 1934, as amended, and as such shall be fully subject to the provisions of title II and title III of that Act. The provision of satellite terminal station facilities by one communication common carrier to one or more other communications common carriers shall be deemed to be a common carrier activity fully subject to the Communications Act. Whenever the application of the provisions of this Act shall be inconsistent with the application of the provisions of the Communications Act, the provisions of this Act shall govern.

NOTICE OF FOREIGN BUSINESS NEGOTIATIONS

Sec. 402. Whenever the corporation shall enter into business negotiations with respect to facilities, operations, or services authorized by this Act with any international or foreign entity, it shall notify the Department of State of the negotiations, and the Department of State shall advise the corporation of relevant foreign policy considerations. Throughout such negotiations the corporation shall keep the Department of State informed with respect to such considerations. The corporation may request the Department of State to assist in the negotiations, and that Department shall render such assistance as may be appropriate.

SANCTIONS

Sec. 403. (a) If the corporation created pursuant to this Act shall engage in or adhere to any action, practices, or policies inconsistent with the policy and purposes declared in section 102 of this Act, or if the corporation or any other person shall violate any provision of this Act, or shall obstruct or interfere with any activities authorized by this Act, or shall refuse, fail, or neglect to discharge his duties and responsibilities under this Act, or shall threaten any such violation, obstruction, interference, refusal, failure, or neglect, the district court of the United States for any district in which such corporation or other person resides or may be found shall have jurisdiction, except as otherwise prohibited by law, upon petition of the Attorney General of the United States, to grant such equitable relief as may be necessary or appropriate to prevent or terminate such conduct or threat.

(b) Nothing contained in this section shall be construed as relieving any person of any punishment, liability, or sanction which may be imposed otherwise than under this Act.

(c) It shall be the duty of the corporation and all communications common carriers to comply, insofar as applicable, with all provisions of this Act and all rules and regulations promulgated thereunder.

REPORTS TO THE CONGRESS

Sec. 404. (a) The President shall transmit to the Congress in January of each year a report which shall include a comprehensive description of the activities and accomplishments during the preceding calendar year under the national program referred to in section 201(a)(1), together with an evaluation of such activities and accomplishments in terms of the attainment of the objectives of this Act and any recommendations for additional legislative or other action which the President may consider necessary or desirable for the attainment of such objectives.

(b) The corporation shall transmit to the President and the Congress, annually and at such other times as it deems desirable, a comprehensive and detailed report of its operations, activities, and accomplishments under this Act.

(c) The Commission shall transmit to the Congress, annually and at such other times as it deems desirable, (i) a report of its activities and actions on anticompetitive practices as they apply to the communications satellite programs; (ii) an evaluation of such activities and actions taken by it within the scope of its authority with a view to recommending such additional legislation which the Commission may consider necessary in the public interest; and (iii) an evaluation of the capital structure of the corporation so as to assure the Congress that such structure is consistent with the most efficient and economical operation of the corporation.

Approved August 31, 1962, 9:51 a.m.

Multilateral Communications Satellite System (ComSat)

Agreement establishing interim arrangements for a global commercial communications satellite system and special agreement.
Done at Washington August 20, 1964;
Entered into force August 20, 1964.

AGREEMENT ESTABLISHING INTERIM ARRANGEMENTS FOR A GLOBAL COMMERCIAL COMMUNICATIONS SATELLITE SYSTEM

The Governments signatory to this Agreement,

Recalling the principle set forth in Resolution No. 1721 (XVI) of the General Assembly of the United Nations that communications by means of satellites should be available to the nations of the world as soon as practicable on a global and non-discriminatory basis;

Desiring to establish a single global commercial communications satellite system as part of an improved global communications network which will provide expanded telecommunications services to all areas of the world and which will contribute to world peace and understanding;

Determined, to this end, to provide, through the most advanced technology available, for the benefit of all nations of the world, the most efficient and economical service possible consistent with the best and most equitable use of the radio medium;

Believing that satellite communications should be organized in such a way as to permit all States to have access to the global system and those States so wishing to invest in the system with consequent participation in the design, development, construction (including the provision of equipment), establishment, maintenance, operation and ownership of the system;

Believing that it is desirable to conclude interim arrangements providing for the establishment of a single global commercial communications satellite system at the earliest practicable date, pending the working out of definitive arrangements for the organization of such a system;

Agree as follows:

ARTICLE I

(a) The Parties to this Agreement shall co-operate to provide, in accordance with the principles set forth in the Preamble to this Agreement, for the design, development, construction, establishment, maintenance and operation of the space segment of the global commercial communications satellite system, to include

(i) an experimental and operational phase in which it is proposed to use one or more satellites to be placed in synchronous orbit in 1965;

(ii) succeeding phases employing satellites of types to be determined, with the objective of achieving basic global coverage in the latter part of 1967; and

(iii) such improvements and extensions thereof as the Committee established by Article IV of this Agreement may decide subject to the provisions of Article VI of this Agreement.

(b) In this Agreement,

(i) the term "space segment" comprises the communications satellites and the tracking, control, command and related facilities and equipment required to support the operation of the communications satellites;

(ii) the terms "design" and "development" include research.

ARTICLE II

(a) Each Party either shall sign or shall designate a communications entity, public or private, to sign the Special Agreement which is to be concluded further to this Agreement and which is to be opened for signature at the same time as this Agreement. Relations between any such designated entity and the Party which has designated it shall be governed by the applicable domestic law.

(b) The Parties to this Agreement contemplate that administrations and communications carriers will, subject to the requirements of their applicable domestic law, negotiate and enter directly into such traffic agreements as may be appropriate with respect to their use of channels of communication provided by the system to be established under this Agreement, services to be furnished to the public, facilities, divisions of revenues and related business arrangements.

ARTICLE III

The space segment shall be owned in undivided shares by the signatories to the Special Agreement in proportion to their respective contributions to the costs of the design, development, construction and establishment of the space segment.

ARTICLE IV

(a) An Interim Communications Satellite Committee, hereinafter referred to as "the Committee", is hereby established to give effect to the co-operation provided for by Article I of this Agreement. The Committee shall have responsibility for the design, development, construction, establishment, maintenance and operation of the space segment of the system and, in particular, shall exercise the functions and have the powers set forth in this Agreement and in the Special Agreement.

(b) The Committee shall be composed as follows: one representative from each of the signatories to the Special Agreement whose quota is not less than 1.5%, and one representative from any two or more signatories to the Special Agreement whose combined quotas total not less than 1.5% and which have agreed to be so represented.

(c) In the performance of its financial functions under this Agreement and under the Special Agreement the Committee shall be assisted by an advisory sub-committee on finance. This sub-committee shall be established by the Committee as soon as the Committee becomes operative.

(d) The Committee may establish such other advisory sub-committees as it thinks fit.

(e) No signatory or group of signatories to the Special Agreement shall be deprived of representation on the Committee because of any reduction pursuant to Article XII (c) of this Agreement.

(f) In this Agreement, the term "quota", in relation to a signatory to the Special Agreement, means the percentage set forth opposite its name in the Annex to the Special Agreement as modified pursuant to this Agreement and the Special Agreement.

ARTICLE V

(a) Each signatory to the Special Agreement or group of signatories to the Special Agreement represented on the Committee shall have a number of votes equal to its quota, or to their combined quotas, as the case may be.

(b) A quorum for any meeting of the Committee shall consist of representatives having, in total, a number of votes exceeding the vote of the representative with the largest vote by not less than 8.5.

(c) The Committee shall endeavor to act unanimously; however, if it fails to reach agreement it shall take decisions by a majority of the votes cast, except that, with respect to the following matters, and subject to paragraphs (d) and (e) of this Article any decision must have the concurrence of representatives whose total votes exceed the vote of the representative with the largest vote by not less than 12.5:

(i) choice of type or types of space segment to be established;

(ii) establishment of general standards for approval of earth stations for access to the space segment;

(iii) approval of budgets by major categories;

(iv) adjustments of accounts pursuant to Article 4 (c) of the Special Agreement;

(v) establishment of the rate of charge per unit of satellite utilization pursuant to Article 9 (a) of the Special Agreement;

(vi) decisions on additional contributions pursuant to Article VI (b) of this Agreement;

(vii) approval of the placing of contracts pursuant to Article 10 (c) of the Special Agreement;

(viii) approval of matters relating to satellite launchings pursuant to Article 10 (d) of the Special Agreement;

(ix) approval of quotas pursuant to Article XII (a) (ii) of this Agreement;

(x) determination of financial conditions of accession pursuant to Article XII (b) of this Agreement;

(xi) decisions relating to withdrawal pursuant to Article XI (a) and (b) of this Agreement and Article 4 (d) of the Special Agreement;

(xii) recommendation of amendments pursuant to Article 15 of the Special Agreement;

(xiii) adoption of the rules of procedure of the Committee and the advisory sub-committees;

(xiv) approval of appropriate compensation to the Corporation for its performance of services as manager pursuant to Articles 5 (c) and 9 (b) of the Special Agreement.

(d) If the Committee, upon the expiration of sixty days following the date when such matter has been proposed for decision, shall not have taken a decision pursuant to paragraph (c) (i) of this Article on the type of space segment to be established to achieve the objective stated in paragraph (a) (ii) of Article I of this Agreement, a decision on such matter may thereafter be taken by the concurring votes of representatives whose total votes exceed the vote of the representative with the largest vote by not less than 8.5.

(e) If the Committee, upon the expiration of sixty days following the date when such matter has been proposed for decision, shall not have approved

(i) any particular budget category, pursuant to paragraph (c) (iii) of this Article,

(ii) the placing of any particular contract, pursuant to paragraph (c) (vii) of this Article, or

(iii) any particular matter relating to satellite launchings, pursuant to paragraph (c) (viii) of this Article,

relating to achievement of the objectives stated in paragraphs (a) (i) and (a) (ii) of Article I of this Agreement, a decision on such matter may thereafter be taken by the concurring votes of the representatives whose total votes exceed the vote of the representative with the largest vote by not less than 8.5.

ARTICLE VI

(a) The contributions of the signatories to the Special Agreement towards the costs of the design, development, construction and establishment of the space segment during the interim arrangements shall be based upon an estimate of U.S. $200,000,000 for such costs. Each signatory to the Special Agreement shall pay its quota of such costs in accordance with the provisions of the Special Agreement.

(b) The Committee shall determine whether contributions are required during the interim arrangements in excess of the above $200,000,000 estimate and, if so, in what amounts. If any additional contributions required during the interim arrangements were to result in total contributions exceeding U.S. $300,000,000, a special conference of the signatories to the Special Agreement shall be convened to consider the matter and recommend appropriate action before decisions are taken by the Committee. The conference shall determine its own procedure.

(c) Each signatory to the Special Agreement may assume the obligation to pay all or part of its quota of any such additional contributions, but no signatory to the Special Agreement shall be required to do so. To the extent that such obligation is not assumed by any signatory to the Special Agreement, it may be assumed by the remaining signatories to the Special Agreement in the proportion that their respective quotas bear to each other or as they may otherwise agree. However, if a signatory to the Special Agreement, which is a member of a group of signatories formed in order to appoint jointly a representative on the Committee pursuant to Article IV (b) of this Agreement, does not assume the obligation to pay such additional contributions, the remaining signatories of that group may assume that obligation in whole or in part to the extent that these remaining signatories may agree. The quotas of the signatories to the Special Agreement shall be adjusted accordingly.

ARTICLE VII

In order to ensure the most effective utilization of the space segment in accordance with the principles set forth in the Preamble to this Agreement, no earth station shall be permitted to utilize the space segment unless it has been approved by the committee pursuant to Article 7 of the Special Agreement.

ARTICLE VIII

The Communications Satellite Corporation, incorporated under the laws of the District of Columbia, herein referred to as "the Corporation", shall, pursuant to general policies of the Committee and in accordance with specific determinations which may be made by the Committee, act as the manager in the design, development, construction, establishment, operation and maintenance of the space segment.

ARTICLE IX

(a) Having regard to the program outlined in Article I of this Agreement, within one year after the initial global system becomes operational and in any case not later than 1st January 1969, the Committee shall render a report to each Party to this Agreement containing the Committee's recommendations concerning the definitive arrangements for an international global system which shall supersede the interim arrangements established by this Agreement. This report, which shall be fully representative of all shades of opinion, shall consider, among other things, whether the interim arrangements should be continued on a permanent basis or whether a permanent international organization of a General Conference and an international administrative and technical staff should be established.

(b) Regardless of the form of the definitive arrangements,

(i) their aims shall be consonant with the principles set forth in the Preamble to this Agreement;

(ii) they shall, like this Agreement, be open to all States members of the International Telecommunication Union or their designated entities;

(iii) they shall safeguard the investment made

by signatories to the Special Agreement; and

(iv) they shall be such that all parties to the definitive arrangements may have an opportunity of contributing to the determination of general policy.

(c) The report of the Committee shall be considered at an international conference, at which duly designated communications entities may also participate, to be convened by the Government of the United States of America for that purpose within three months following submission of the report. The Parties to this Agreement shall seek to ensure that the definitive arrangements will be established at the earliest practicable date, with a view to their entry into force by 1st January 1970.

ARTICLE X

In considering contracts and in exercising their other responsibilities, the Committee and the Corporation as manager shall be guided by the need to design, develop and procure the best equipment and services at the best price for the most efficient conduct and operation of the space segment. When proposals or tenders are determined to be comparable in terms of quality, c.i.f. price and timely performance, the Committee and the Corporation as manager shall also seek to ensure that contracts are so distributed that equipment is designed, developed and procured in the States whose Governments are Parties to this Agreement in approximate proportion to the respective quotas of their corresponding signatories to the Special Agreement; provided that such design, development and procurement are not contrary to the joint interests of the Parties to this Agreement and the signatories to the Special Agreement. The Committee and the Corporation as manager shall also seek to ensure that the foregoing principles are applied with respect to major sub-contracts to the extent that this can be accomplished without impairing the responsibility of the prime contractor for the performance of work under the contract.

ARTICLE XI

(a) Any Party may withdraw from this Agreement, and this Agreement shall cease to be in force for that Party three months after that Party shall have notified the Government of the United States of America of its intention to withdraw and the latter shall inform the other Parties accordingly. In the event of such withdrawal, the corresponding signatory to the Special Agreement shall pay all sums due under the Special

Agreement, together with a sum which shall be agreed between that signatory and the Committee in respect of costs which will result in the future from contracts concluded prior to notification of withdrawal. If agreement has not been reached within three months after notification of withdrawal, the Committee shall make a final determination of the sums which shall be paid by that signatory.

(b) Not less than three months after the rights of a signatory to the Special Agreement have been suspended pursuant to Article 4 (d) of the Special Agreement, and if that signatory has not meanwhile paid all sums due, the Committee, having taken into account any statement by that signatory or the corresponding Party, may decide that the Party in question is deemed to have withdrawn from this Agreement; this Agreement shall thereupon cease to be in force for that Party.

(c) Withdrawal by a Party from this Agreement shall automatically effect withdrawal from the Special Agreement by the corresponding signatory to the Special Agreement, but the obligation to make payments under paragraph (a) of this Article or under Article 4 (d) of the Special Agreement shall not be affected by such withdrawal.

(d) Upon any withdrawal under paragraph (a) or (b) of this Article, the Committee, to the extent required to account for the quota of the withdrawing signatory to the Special Agreement, shall increase the quotas of the remaining signatories to the Special Agreement in proportion to their respective quotas or as they may otherwise agree. However, if the signatory to the Special Agreement corresponding to the withdrawing Party was at the time of withdrawal a member of a group of signatories formed in order to appoint jointly a representative on the Committee pursuant to Article IV (b) of this Agreement, the quota of the signatory in question shall be distributed by increasing the quotas of the remaining signatories of that group to the extent that those remaining signatories may agree.

(e) Withdrawal by any Party may also take place if, at the request of the Party concerned, the Committee approves the transfer of the rights and obligations of that Party and the corresponding signatory to the Special Agreement under this Agreement and the Special Agreement to another Party and its corresponding signatory to the Special Agreement. Such transferee or transferees need not have been Parties to the Agreement or signatories to the Special Agreement prior to the time of such transfer.

ARTICLE XII

(a) This Agreement shall be open at Washington for six months from 20th August 1964 for signature:

(i) by the Government of any State which is listed by name in the Annex to the Special Agreement when it is first opened for signature, and

(ii) by the Government of any other State which is a member of the International Telecommunication Union, subject to approval by the Committee of the quota of that Government or its designated communications entity, public or private. On such approval and entry into force or provisional application, the name of that State and the name of its corresponding signatory to the Special Agreement, and its quota are deemed to be inserted in the Annex to the Special Agreement.

(b) The Government of any State which is a member of the International Telecommunication Union may accede to this Agreement after it is closed for signature upon such financial conditions as the Committee shall determine. On such accession, the name of that State and the name of its corresponding signatory to the Special Agreement, and its quota are deemed to be inserted in the Annex to the Special Agreement.

(c) The quotas of the signatories to the Special Agreement shall be reduced pro rata as necessary to accommodate additional signatories to the Special Agreement, provided that the combined original quotas of all signatories to the Special Agreement other than the signatories listed in the Annex to the Special Agreement when this Agreement is first opened for signature shall not exceed 17%.

(d) This Agreement shall enter into force on the date upon which it has been signed without reservation as to approval, or has been approved after such reservation, by two or more Governments. Subsequently it shall enter into force in respect of each signatory Government on signature or, if it signs subject to a reservation as to approval, on approval by it.

(e) Any Government which signs this Agreement subject to a reservation as to approval may, so long as this Agreement is open for signature, declare that it applies this Agreement provisionally and shall thereupon be considered a Party to this Agreement. Such provisional application shall terminate

(i) upon approval of this Agreement by that Government, or

(ii) upon withdrawal by that Government in accordance with Article XI of this Agreement.

(f) Notwithstanding anything contained in this Article, this Agreement shall not enter into force for any Government nor be applied provisionally by any Government until that Government or its corresponding signatory shall have signed the Special Agreement.

(g) If at the expiration of a period of nine months from the date when it is first opened for signature this Agreement has not entered into force for or has not been provisionally applied by the Government of a State which has signed it in accordance with paragraph (a) (i) of this Article, the signature shall be considered of no effect and the name of that State and of its corresponding signatory to the Special Agreement, and its quota shall be deemed to be deleted from the Annex to the Special Agreement; the quotas of the signatories to the Special Agreement shall accordingly be increased pro rata. If this Agreement has not entered into force for or has not been provisionally applied by the Government of a State which has signed it in accordance with paragraph (a) (ii) of this Article within a period of nine months from the date when it is first opened for signature, the signature shall be considered of no effect.

(h) The corresponding signatory to the Special Agreement of any Government which has signed this Agreement subject to a reservation as to approval, and which has not provisionally applied it, may appoint an observer to the Committee in the same manner as that signatory could have been represented in accordance with Article IV (b) of this Agreement if that Government had approved this Agreement. Any such observer, who shall have the right to speak but not to vote, may attend the Committee only during a period of nine months from the date when this Agreement is first opened for signature.

(i) No reservation may be made to this Agreement except as provided in this Article.

ARTICLE XIII

(a) Notifications of approval or of provisional application and instruments of accession shall be deposited with the Government of the United States of America.

(b) The Government of the United States of America shall notify all signatory and acceding States of signatures, reservations of approval, deposits of notifications of approval or of provisional application, deposits of instruments of accession and notifications of withdrawals from this Agreement.

ARTICLE XIV

Upon entry into force of this Agreement, the Government of the United States of America shall register it with the Secretary-General of the United Nations in accordance with Article 102 of the Charter of the United Nations.

ARTICLE XV

This Agreement shall remain in effect until the entry into force of the definitive arrangements referred to in Article IX of this Agreement.

Special Agreement

Whereas certain Governments have become Parties to an Agreement Establishing Interim Arrangements for a Global Commercial Communications Satellite System; and

Whereas those Governments have undertaken therein to sign or to designate a communications entity to sign this Special Agreement;

The signatories to this Special Agreement hereby agree as follows:

ARTICLE 1

In this Special Agreement:

(a) "The Agreement" means the Agreement Establishing Interim Arrangements for a Global Commercial Communications Satellite System opened for signature on August 20, 1964, at Washington;

(b) "The Committee" means the Interim Communications Satellite Committee established by Article IV of the Agreement;

(c) "The Corporation" means the Communications Satellite Corporation incorporated under the laws of the District of Columbia pursuant to the Communications Satellite Act of 1962[1] of the United States of America;

(d) "Design" and "development" include research;

(e) "Quota", in relation to a signatory, means the percentage set forth opposite its name in the Annex to this Special Agreement as modified pursuant to the Agreement and this Special Agreement;

(f) "Signatory" means a Government or a communications entity which has signed this Special Agreement and in respect of which it is in force;

(g) "The space segment" means the space segment defined in Article I (b) (i) of the Agreement.

---

[1] 76 Stat. 423; 47 U.S.C. §§ 731–735.

ARTICLE 2

Each signatory undertakes to fulfill the obligations placed upon it by the Agreement and thereby obtains the rights provided therein.

ARTICLE 3

Each signatory undertakes to contribute a percentage of the costs of the design, development, construction and establishment of the space segment equal to its quota.

ARTICLE 4

(a) During a period of nine months from the date when the Agreement is first opened for signature, each signatory shall, within four weeks from the date of entry into force of this Special Agreement for that signatory, make a payment on account to the Corporation, in United States dollars, or in currency freely convertible into United States dollars, of a percentage equal to its quota of the expenditure which the Corporation has incurred for the design, development, construction and establishment of the space segment prior to the date when the Agreement is first opened for signature, and, according to estimates established by the Corporation at that date, is to incur for those purposes within six months after that date, together with its proportionate share of any additional contribution required pursuant to paragraph (b) of this Article, and appropriate interest on all such amounts. Each signatory shall pay the remainder of its contribution pursuant to Article 3 of this Special Agreement in accordance with paragraph (b) of this Article.

(b) The Corporation shall submit to the Committee estimates of the time phasing of payments required pursuant to Article 3 of this Special Agreement. The Committee shall call on the signatories to make their respective proportionate payments in order to enable obligations to be met as they become due. Payments shall be made to the Corporation by each signatory in United States dollars, or in currency freely convertible into United States dollars, and in such amounts that, accounting on a cumulative basis, the sums paid by the signatories are in proportion to their respective quotas. Where a signatory other than the Corporation incurs obligations pursuant to authorization by the Committee, the Committee shall cause payments to be made to that signatory.

(c) Accounts for expenditure referred to in paragraphs (a) and (b) of this Article shall be subject to review by the Committee and shall be subject to such adjustment as the Committee may decide.

(d) Each signatory shall pay the amount due from it under paragraph (b) of this Article on the date designated by the committee. Interest at the rate of six per cent per annum shall be added to any amount unpaid after that date. If the signatory has not made a payment within three months of its becoming due, the rights of the signatory under the Agreement and this Special Agreement shall be suspended. If, after such suspension, the Committee decides, pursuant to Article XI (b) of the Agreement, that the defaulting signatory is deemed to have withdrawn from this Special Agreement, the Committee shall then make a binding determination of the sums already due together with a sum to be paid in respect of the costs which will result in the future from contracts concluded while that signatory was a party. Such withdrawal shall not, however, affect the obligation of the signatory concerned to pay sums due under this Special Agreement, whether falling due before it ceased to be a party or payable in accordance with the aforesaid determination of the Committee.

ARTICLE 5

The following shall be included as part of the costs of the design, development, construction and establishment of the space segment to be shared by the signatories in proportion to their respective quotas:

(a) The direct and indirect costs for the design, development, construction and establishment of the space segment incurred by the Corporation prior to the date when the Agreement is first opened for signature;

(b) All direct and indirect costs for the design, development, construction and establishment of the space segment incurred by the Corporation or pursuant to authorization by the Committee by any other signatory on behalf of the signatories to this Special agreement subsequent to the date when the Agreement is first opened for signature;

(c) All direct and indirect costs incurred by the Corporation which are allocable to its performance of services as manager in the design, development, construction and establishment of the space segment and appropriate compensation to the Corporation, as may be agreed between the Corporation and the Committee, for such services.

ARTICLE 6

The following shall not form part of the costs to be shared by the signatories:

(a) Taxes on the net income of any of the signatories;

(b) Design and development expenditure on launchers and launching facilities except expenditure incurred for the adaptation of launchers and launching facilities in connection with the design, development, construction and establishment of the space segment;

(c) The costs of the representatives of the signatories on the Committee and on its advisory sub-committees and the staffs of those representatives except insofar as the Committee may otherwise determine.

ARTICLE 7

(a) In considering whether an earth station should be permitted to utilize the space segment, the Committee shall take into account the technical characteristics of the station, the technical limitations on multiple access to satellites due to the existing state of the art, the effect of geographical distribution of earth stations on the efficiency of the services to be provided by the system, the recommended standards of the International Telegraph and Telephone Consultative Committee and the International Radio Consultative Committee of the International Telecommunication Union, and such general standards as the Committee may establish. Failure by the Committee to establish general standards shall not of itself preclude the Committee from considering or acting upon any application for approval of an earth station to utilize the space segment.

(b) Any application for approval of an earth station to utilize the space segment shall be submitted to the Committee by the signatory to this Special Agreement in whose area the earth station is or will be located or, with respect to other areas, by a duly authorized communications entity. Each such application shall be submitted either individually or jointly on behalf of all signatories and duly authorized communications entities intending to utilize the space segment by means of the earth station which is the subject of the application.

(c) Any application for approval of an earth station located in the territory of a State whose Government is party to the Agreement which is to be owned or operated by an organization or organizations other than the corresponding signatory shall be made by that signatory.

ARTICLE 8

(a) Each applicant for approval of an earth station pursuant to Article 7 of this Special Agreement shall be responsible for making equitable and non-discriminatory arrangements for the use of the earth station by all signatories or duly authorized communications entities intended to be served by the earth station individually or jointly with other earth stations.

(b) To the extent feasible the Committee shall allot to the respective signatory or duly authorized communications entity, for use by each earth station which has been approved pursuant to Article 7 of this Special Agreement, an amount of satellite utilization appropriate to satisfy the total communications capability requested on behalf of all signatories and duly authorized communications entities to be served by such earth station.

(c) In making allotments of satellite utilization the Committee shall give due consideration to the quotas of the signatories to be served by each earth station.

ARTICLE 9

(a) The Committee shall specify the unit of satellite utilization and from time to time shall establish the rate of charge per unit at a level which, as a general rule, shall be sufficient, on the basis of the estimated total use of the space segment, to cover amortization of the capital cost of the space segment, an adequate compensation for use of capital, and the estimated operating, maintenance and administration costs of the space segment.

(b) In establishing the unit rate of charge pursuant to paragraph (a) of this Article, the Committee shall include in the estimated operating, maintenance and administration costs of the space segment the estimated direct and indirect costs of the Corporation which are allocable to its performance of services as manager in the operation and maintenance of the space segment and appropriate compensation to the Corporation, it may be agreed between the Corporation and the Committee, for such services.

(c) The Committee shall arrange for the payment of charges for allotments of satellite utilization to be made quarterly to the Corporation. The charges shall be computed in United States dollars and paid in United States dollars or in currency freely convertible into United States dollars.

(d) The components of the unit rate of charge representing amortization and compensation for the use of capital shall be credited to the signatories in proportion to their respective quotas. In the interests of avoiding unnecessary transfers of funds between signatories, and of keeping to a minimum the funds held by the Corporation on behalf of the signatories, the Committee shall make suitable arrangements for funds representing these components to be retained by signatories where appropriate or, if collected, to be distributed among the signatories in such a way that the credits established for signatories are discharged.

(e) The other components of the unit rate of charge shall be applied to meet all operating, maintenance, and administration costs, and to establish such reserves as the Committee may determine to be necessary. After providing for such costs and reserves, any balance remaining shall be distributed by the Corporation, in United States dollars, or in currency freely convertible into United States dollars, among the signatories in proportion to their respective quotas; but if insufficient funds remain to meet the operating, maintenance and administration costs, the signatories shall pay to the Corporation, in proportion to their respective quotas, such amounts as may be determined by the Committee to be required to meet the deficiency.

(f) The Committee shall institute appropriate sanctions in cases where payments pursuant to this Article shall have been in default for three months or longer.

ARTICLE 10

(a) All contracts placed by the Corporation or by any other signatory pursuant to authorization by the Committee relating to design, development and procurement of equipment for the space segment shall, except as otherwise provided by the Committee, be based on responses to appropriate requests for quotations or invitations to tender from among persons and organizations qualified to perform the work under the proposed contract whose terms are furnished to the Committee by the signatories.

(b) For contracts which exceed U.S. $125,000 the issue by the Corporation of requests for quotations or invitations to tender shall be in accordance with such conditions as the Committee may determine. The Corporation shall keep the Committee fully informed of decisions taken relating to such contracts.

(c) The Corporation shall consult the Committee before issuing requests for proposals and invitations to tender for contracts for design, development and procurement of equipment for the space segment which are expected to exceed U.S. $500,000. If, as a result of its evaluation of responses to such requests or invitations, the Corporation desires that a contract be placed which exceeds U.S. $500,000, it shall submit its valuation and recommendations to the Committee. The approval of the Committee shall be required before each such contract is placed either by the Corporation as manager or by any other signatory pursuant to authorization by the Committee.

(d) The Committee shall approve the program for the launching of satellites and for associated services, the launch source and the contracting arrangements.

(e) Except as otherwise directed by the Committee, and subject to paragraphs (c) and (d) of this Article, all contractors shall be selected by the Corporation and all contracts shall be in the name of and be executed and administered by the Corporation as manager.

(f) Except as otherwise determined by the Committee, all contracts and sub-contracts placed for design, development and procurement of equipment for the space segment shall contain appropriate provisions to the effect that all inventions, technical data and information arising directly from any work performed under such contracts (except inventions, technical data and information pertaining to launchers and launchings) shall be disclosed to the Committee and may be used only in the design, development, manufacture and use of equipment and components for the space segment established under the present interim arrangements or under any definitive arrangements which may succeed these interim arrangements, without payment of royalties, by each signatory or any person in the jurisdiction of a signatory or the Government which has designated that signatory.

(g) Except as it may otherwise determine, the Committee shall endeavor to have included in all contracts placed for design and development appropriate provisions which will ensure that inventions, technical data and information owned by the contractor and its subcontractors which are directly incorporated in work performed under such contracts, may be used on fair and reasonable terms by each signatory or any person in the jurisdiction of a signatory or the Government which has designated that signatory, provided that such use is necessary, and to the extent that it is necessary to use such inventions, technical data and information for the exercise of the right to use under paragraph (f) of this Article.

(h) The provisions of this Article shall not be held to apply to contracts for design, development, construction and establishment of the space segment to which the Corporation is a party on the date when the Agreement is first opened for signature. Subject to the provisions of Article 4 (c) of this Agreement, all such contracts shall be recognized by the Committee as continuing obligations for budgetary purposes.

ARTICLE 11

Each signatory shall keep such books, records, vouchers and accounts of all costs for which it is authorized to be reimbursed under this Special Agreement with respect to the design, development, construction, establishment, maintenance and separation of the space segment as may be appropriate and shall at all reasonable times make them available for inspection by members of the Committee.

ARTICLE 12

In addition to functions stated elsewhere in this Special Agreement, the Corporation, as manager pursuant to Article VIII of the Agreement, shall:

(a) prepare and submit to the Committee the annual programs and budgets;

(b) recommend to the Committee the type or types of space segment to be established;

(c) plan, conduct, arrange for and co-operate in studies, design work and development for improvement of the space segment;

(d) operate and maintain the space segment;

(e) furnish to the Committee such information as may be required by any representative on the Committee to enable him to discharge his responsibilities as a representative;

(f) arrange for technicians, selected by the Committee with the concurrence of the Corporation from among persons nominated by signatories, to participate in the assessment of designs and of specifications for equipment for the space segment;

(g) use its best efforts to arrange for inventions, technical data and information arising directly from any jointly financed work performed under contracts placed before the date on which the Agreement is opened for signature to be disclosed to each signatory and to be made available for use free of charge in the design, development, manufacture and use of equipment and components for the space segment by each signatory or any person in the jurisdiction of the signatory or the Government which has designated that signatory.

ARTICLE 13

Neither the Corporation as signatory or manager, nor any other signatory as such, shall be liable to any other signatory for loss or damage sustained by reason of a failure or breakdown of a satellite at or after launching or a failure or breakdown of any other portion of the space segment.

ARTICLE 14

Arrangements shall be made whereby all legal disputes arising in connection with this Special Agreement or in connection with the rights and obligations of signatories can, if not otherwise settled, be submitted to the decision of an impartial tribunal, to be established in accordance with such arrangements, which would decide such questions in accordance with general principles of law. To this end, a group of legal experts appointed by the signatories and by the prospective signatories listed in the Annex to this Agreement when it is first opened for signature shall recommend a draft of a Supplementary Agreement containing such arrangements; the signatories shall, after considering that draft, conclude a Supplementary Agreement for such arrangements within a period of three months from the date when the Agreement is first opened for signature. The Supplementary Agreement shall be binding on all those who subsequently become signatories to this Special Agreement.

ARTICLE 15

Any proposed amendment to this Special Agreement shall first be submitted to the Committee. If recommended by the committee for adoption, it shall enter into force for all signatories when notifications of approval have been deposited with the Government of the United States of America by two-thirds of the signatories, provided that no amendment may impose upon any signatory any additional financial obligation without its consent.

ARTICLE 16

This Special Agreement shall enter into force for each signatory on the day of signature, provided that the Agreement shall have entered into force for or shall have been provisionally applied by the Government which is or has designated the signatory in question; it shall continue in force for as long as the Agreement continues in force.

[Entered into force August 20, 1964.]

Communications Satellite System Arbitration Agreement

[Opened for signature at Washington, June 4, 1965.]
[Entered into force November 21, 1966.]

Supplementary Agreement on Arbitration

Whereas Article 14 of the Special Agreement signed pursuant to Article II of the Agreement Establishing Interim Arrangements for a Global Commercial Communications Satellite System opened for signature on 20 August, 1964, at Washington provides for arrangements to be made by a Supplementary Agreement whereby legal disputes may, if not otherwise settled, be submitted to the decision of an impartial tribunal;

It is hereby agreed as follows:

ARTICLE 1

In this Supplementary Agreement:

(a) "The Agreement" means the Agreement Establishing Interim Arrangements for a Global Commercial Communications Satellite System opened for signature on 20 August, 1964, at Washington;

(b) "The Special Agreement" means the Special Agreement signed pursuant to Article II of the Agreement;

(c) "The Committee" means the Interim Communications Satellite Committee established by Article IV of the Agreement;

(d) "Signatory" means, as in the Special Agreement, a Government or communications entity which has signed the Special Agreement and in respect of which it is in force.

ARTICLE 2

(a) An arbitral tribunal constituted under this Supplementary Agreement is competent to give a decision in any legal dispute over the following matter: whether an action or a failure to act by the Committee or by any signatory or signatories is authorized by or is in compliance with the Agreement and the Special Agreement.

(b) An arbitral tribunal constituted in accordance with this Supplementary Agreement shall also be competent to give a decision on any legal dispute arising in connection with any other agreement relating to the arrangements established by the Agreement and the Special Agreement where the signatories which are parties to that other agreement have agreed to confer such a competence. A tribunal in exercising such competence shall act in accordance with the agreement which confers competence on it.

(c) Only the following may be parties in arbitration proceedings instituted under this Supplementary Agreement:

  (i) Any signatory,
  (ii) The Committee.

ARTICLE 3

(a) Within 30 days of the entry into force of this Supplementary Agreement and every two years thereafter, each signatory shall submit to the Committee the name of a legal expert of generally recognized ability who will be available for the succeeding two years to serve as president of tribunals constituted under this Supplementary Agreement. From such nominees the Committee shall appoint seven individuals to a panel from which presidents of tribunals shall be selected.

(b) The members of the panel shall be appointed by the unanimous agreement of the members of the Com-

mittee or, if not so appointed within three months from the entry into force of this Supplementary Agreement and every two years thereafter, by a decision of the Committee taken in the same manner mentioned in Article V (c) of the Agreement in respect of the matters listed in subparagraphs (i) to (xiv) of that paragraph. The members of the panel shall be appointed for a term of two years, and may be reappointed.

(c) For the purpose of designating a chairman, the panel shall be convened to meet by the chairman of the Committee as soon as possible after the panel has been appointed. The quorum for a meeting of the panel shall be six members. After discussion among its members, the panel shall designate one of its members as its chairman by a decision taken by the affirmative votes of at least four members, cast in one or, if necessary, more than one secret ballot. The chairman so designated shall hold office as chairman for the rest of his period of office as a member of the panel. The cost of the meeting of the panel shall form part of the costs to be shared by the signatories in accordance with the Special Agreement.

(d) Vacancies on the panel shall be filled by appointment made by the unanimous agreement of the members of the Committee. If the vacancy is not so filled within two months of the date when it arises, the appointment shall be made by decision of the Committee taken in the same manner mentioned in Article V (c) of the Agreement in respect of the matters listed in sub-paragraphs (i) to (xiv) of that paragraph. Vacancies in the office of the chairman of the panel shall be filled by the panel by designation of one of its members in accordance with the procedure set out in paragraph (c) of this Article. A member of the panel appointed to replace a member or designated to replace a chairman whose term of office has not expired shall hold office for the remainder of his predecessor's term.

(e) In appointing the members of the panel the Committee shall seek to ensure that its composition is drawn from the various principal legal systems as they are represented among the signatories.

ARTICLE 4

(a) The party wishing to submit a legal dispute to arbitration shall provide each party and the Committee with a document which contains the following items:

  (i) A list of the parties against which the case is brought;
  (ii) A statement which fully describes the dispute being submitted for arbitration, the reasons why each party is required to par-

ticipate in the arbitration, and the relief being requested;

(iii) A statement which sets forth why the subject matter of the dispute comes within the jurisdiction of a tribunal to be constituted under this Supplementary Agreement, and why the relief being requested can be granted by such tribunal if it finds in the petitioner's favor;

(iv) A statement explaining why the petitioner has been unable to achieve a settlement of the dispute by negotiation or other means short of arbitration;

(v) The name of the individual designated by the petitioner to serve as a member of the tribunal.

(b) Within 21 days from the date copies of the document described in paragraph (a) of this Article have been received by all the parties against which the case is brought, the respondents' side shall designate an individual to serve as a member of the tribunal.

(c) In the event of failure by the respondents' side to make such a designation, the chairman of the panel, within ten days following a request by the applicant's side which shall not be made before the expiration of the 21 day period aforesaid, shall make a designation from among the experts whose names were submitted to the Committee pursuant to Article 3 (a) of this Supplementary Agreement.

(d) Within 15 days after such designation the two members of the tribunal shall agree on a third individual selected from the panel constituted in accordance with Article 3 of this Supplementary Agreement, who shall serve as the president of the tribunal. In the event of failure to reach agreement within such period of time, the chairman of the panel, within ten days after a request from one of the sides, shall designate a member of the panel other than himself to serve as president of the tribunal.

(e) The tribunal shall commence its functions as soon as the president is selected.

(f) Should a vacancy occur in the tribunal for reasons which the president or the remaining members of the tribunal decide are beyond the control of the parties, or are compatible with the proper conduct of the arbitration proceedings, the vacancy shall be filled in accordance with the following provisions:

(i) Should the vacancy occur as a result of the withdrawal of a member appointed by a side to the dispute, then that side shall select a replacement within ten days after the vacancy occurs.

(ii) Should the vacancy occur as a result of the withdrawal of the president of the tribunal or of another member of the tribunal appointed by the chairman, a replacement shall be selected from the panel in the manner described in paragraph (d) or (c) respectively of this Article.

(g) Except as prescribed in this Article, vacancies occurring in the tribunal shall not be filled.

(h) If a vacancy is not filled, the remaining members of the tribunal shall have the power, upon the request of one side, to continue the proceedings and give the tribunal's final decision.

ARTICLE 5

(a) The time and place of the sittings of the tribunal shall be determined by the tribunal.

(b) The proceedings shall be held in private and all material presented to the tribunal shall be treated as confidential, except that the parties to the Agreement whose designated signatories are parties to the dispute shall have the right to be present and shall have access to material presented. When the Committee is a party to the proceedings, all parties to the Agreement and all signatories shall have the right to be present and shall have access to material presented, except where the tribunal shall in exceptional circumstances decide otherwise.

(c) The proceedings shall commence with the presentation of the petitioner's case containing its arguments, related facts supported by evidence and the principles of law relied upon. The petitioner's case shall be followed by the respondent's counter-case. The petitioner may submit a reply to the respondent's counter-case. Additional pleadings shall be submitted only if the tribunal determines they are necessary.

(d) The proceedings shall be conducted in writing, and each side shall have the right to submit written evidence in support of its allegations of fact and law. However, oral arguments and testimony may be given if the tribunal considers it appropriate.

(e) The tribunal may hear and determine counter-claims arising directly out of the subject matter of the dispute provided the counter-claims are within its jurisdiction as defined in Article 2 of this Supplementary Agreement.

(f) At any time during the proceedings, the tribunal

may terminate the proceedings if it decides the dispute is beyond its jurisdiction as defined in Article 2 of this Supplementary Agreement.

(g) The tribunal's deliberations shall be secret and its rulings and decisions must be supported by at least two members.

(h) The tribunal shall support its decision by a written opinion. A member dissenting from the decision may submit a separate written opinion.

(i) The tribunal may adopt additional rules of procedure consistent with those established by this Supplementary Agreement which are necessary for the proceedings.

ARTICLE 6

(a) If one side fails to present its case, the other side may call upon the tribunal to accept its case and to give a decision in its favor. Before doing so, the tribunal shall satisfy itself that it has jurisdiction and that the case is well-founded in fact and in law.

(b) Before giving the decision, the tribunal shall grant a period of grace to the side which has failed to present its case, unless it is satisfied that the party in default does not intend to present its case.

ARTICLE 7

Any signatory, group of signatories, or the Committee, which considers that it has a substantial interest in the decision of the case may petition the tribunal for permission to become a party to the case. If the tribunal determines that the petitioner has a substantial interest in the decision of the case, it shall grant the petition.

ARTICLE 8

Either at the request of a party, or upon its own initiative, the tribunal may appoint such experts as it deems necessary to assist it.

ARTICLE 9

Each of the signatories and the Committee shall provide all information determined by the tribunal, either at the request of a party to the case or upon its own initiative, to be required for the proper handling and determination of the dispute.

ARTICLE 10

During the course of its consideration of the case, the tribunal shall have power, pending the final decision, to make recommendations to the parties with a view to the protection of their respective rights.

ARTICLE 11

(a) The decision of the tribunal shall be based on interpretation of the Agreement, the Special Agreement and this Supplementary Agreement in accordance with generally accepted principles of law.

(b) Should the parties reach an agreement during the proceedings, the agreement shall be recorded in the form of a decision of the tribunal given by the consent of the parties.

(c) The decision of the tribunal shall be binding on all the parties to the dispute and shall be carried out by them in good faith. However, if, in a case in which the Committee is a party, the tribunal decides that a decision of the Committee is null and void as not being authorized by or in compliance with the Agreement and the Special Agreement, the decision of the tribunal shall be binding on all signatories.

ARTICLE 12

Unless the tribunal determines otherwise because of the particular circumstances of the case, the expenses of the tribunal, including the remuneration of the members of the tribunal, shall be borne in equal shares by each side. Where a side consists of more than one party, the share of that side shall be apportioned by the tribunal among the parties on that side.

ARTICLE 13

This Supplementary Agreement shall enter into force when it has been signed by all signatories to the Special Agreement in respect of which the Special Agreement is in force. Thereafter, pursuant to Article 14 of the Special Agreement, it shall enter into force for other signatories on the day on which the Special Agreement enters into force for them. It shall be in force as long as the Special Agreement continues in force.

IN WITNESS WHEREOF the undersigned duly authorized thereto have signed this Agreement.

DONE at Washington this fourth of June, 1965, in the English and French languages, both texts being equally authoritative, in a single original, which shall be deposited in the archives of the Government of the United States of America, which shall transmit a certified copy to each signatory or acceding Government and to the Government of each State which is a member of the International Telecommunication Union.

U.S. Designation of Telecommunications Satellite Consortium as an International Organization*

THE PRESIDENT

EXECUTIVE ORDER 11277

DESIGNATING THE INTERNATIONAL TELECOMMUNICA-
TIONS SATELLITE CONSORTIUM AS AN INTERNATIONAL
ORGANIZATION ENTITLED TO ENJOY CERTAIN PRIVI-
LEGES, EXEMPTIONS, AND IMMUNITIES

By virtue of the authority vested in me by Section 1 of the International Organizations Immunities Act (59 Stat. 669; 22 U.S.C. 288), I hereby designate the International Telecommunications Satellite Consortium, an organization in which the United States participates pursuant to the authority of the Communications Satellite Act of 1962 (76 State. 419; 47 U.S.C. 701–744) and which was established pursuant to the Agreement Establishing Interim Arrangements for a Global Commercial Communications System of August 20, 1964, TIAS 5646 and the Special Agreement signed pursuant thereto, as an international organization, as that term is defined in Section 4(i) of the International Organizations Immunities Act, entitled to enjoy, from and after August 20, 1964, all of the privileges, exemptions, and immunities provided by Section 4(a) of that Act.

The foregoing designation is not intended to abridge in any respect any privileges, exemptions, or immunities which such organization or the Interim Communications Satellite Committee (provided for by the above-mentioned Agreements) may have acquired or may hereafter acquire by treaty, Congressional action, or other Executive order.

LYNDON B. JOHNSON

THE WHITE HOUSE,
April 30, 1966.

---

* [Reproduced from 31 *Federal Register* 6609 (May 4, 1966).]

[F.R. Doc. 66–4899; Filed, May 2, 1966, 1:43 p.m.]

United Nations Committee on the Peaceful Uses of Outer Space

Liability for Damage Caused by Objects Launched into Outer Space

Comparative table of provisions contained in the proposals submitted by Belgium (A/AC.105/C.2/L.7/Rev. 2 and Corr. 1, 2 and 3; and WG.II/27), the United States of America (A/AC.105/C.2/L.8/Rev.3) and Hungary (A/AC.105/C.2/L.10/Rev.1)

	BELGIUM: PROPOSAL (A/AC.105 /C.2/L.7/REV.2 AND CORR. 1, 2 AND 3; WG.II/27) CONVENTION ON THE UNIFICATION OF CERTAIN RULES GOVERNING LIABILITY FOR DAMAGE CAUSED BY SPACE DEVICES	UNITED STATES: PROPOSAL (A/AC.105/C.2/L.8/REV. 3) CONVENTION CONCERNING LIABILITY FOR DAMAGE CAUSED BY THE LAUNCHING OF OBJECTS INTO OUTER SPACE	HUNGARY: PROPOSAL (A/AC.105/C.2/L.10/REV. 1) CONVENTION CONCERNING LIABILITY FOR DAMAGE CAUSED BY THE LAUNCHING OF OBJECTS INTO OUTER SPACE
Preamble	*The Contracting Parties,* *Recalling* the Declaration of Legal Principles Governing the Activities of States in the Exploration and Use of Outer Space adopted by the General Assembly of the United Nations on 13 December 1963 and embodied in resolution 1962 (XVIII), *Recognizing* that activities in the exploration and peaceful uses of outer space may from time to time result in damage, *Recognizing* the need to establish rules governing liability	*The Contracting Parties,* *Recognizing* that activities in the peaceful exploration and use of outer space may on occasion result in damage, *Recalling* General Assembly resolution 1962 (XVIII), entitled "Declaration of Legal Principles Governing Activities of States in the Exploration and Use of Outer Space", *Seeking* to establish a uniform rule of liability and a simple and expeditious procedure governing financial compensation for damage,	*The Contracting States,* *Recognizing* the common interest of mankind in furthering the peaceful exploration and use of outer space, *Recalling* the Declaration of Legal Principles Governing the Activities of States in the Exploration and Use of Outer Space, adopted by the General Assembly on 13 December 1963 as resolution 1962 (XVIII), *Considering* that the States and international organizations involved in the launching of

with a view to ensuring that compensation is paid for damage thus caused,

Have agreed as follows:

Believing that the establishment of such a procedure will contribute to the growth of friendly relations and co-operation among nations,

Agree as follows:

objects into outer space should be internationally liable for damage caused by these objects,

Recognizing the need for establishing international rules and procedures concerning such liability to ensure protection against damage caused by objects launched into outer space,

Believing that the establishment of such rules and procedures would facilitate the taking of the greatest possible precautionary measures by States and international organizations involved in the launching of objects into outer space to protect against damage inflicted by objects launched into outer space,

Have decided to conclude the present Convention:

Definitions ARTICLE 2

"Damage" shall be understood to mean any loss for which compensation may be claimed under the law of the place where the loss is caused. Any damage suffered by a ship, aircraft or space device and by the persons and property carried therein shall be deemed to have been caused in the territory of the flag State or, in the case of a space device and the persons and property carried therein, in the territory of the launching State.

"Launching" shall be understood to mean an attempted launching or a launching operation proper, whether or not it fulfills expectations of those responsible therefor.

"Space device" shall be understood to mean any device intended to move in space and sustained there by means other than the reaction of air, as well as the equipment used for the launching and propulsion of the device.

"Launching State" shall be understood to mean the State or

ARTICLE I

For the purposes of this Convention

(a) "Damage" means loss of life, personal injury, or destruction or loss of, or damage to, property.

(b) The term "launching" includes attempted launchings.

(c) "Launching State" means a Contracting Party, or an international organization which has transmitted a declaration to the Secretary-General under Article III, paragraph 1, of this Convention, which launches or procures the launching of an object into outer space or whose territory or facility is used in such launching, or which exercises control over the orbit or trajectory of an object.

(d) "Presenting State" means a State which is a Contracting Party, or an international organization which has transmitted a declaration to the Secretary-General under Article III, paragraph 1 of this Convention, which presents a claim for

ARTICLE I

1. The provisions of this Convention shall apply to compensation for loss of life, personal injury or other impairment of health, and damage to property (hereinafter called "damage"): . . .

3. For the purpose of this Convention "Space Object" means space ships, satellites, orbital laboratories, containers and any other devices designed for movement in outer space and sustained there otherwise than by the reaction of air, as well as the means of delivery of such objects and any parts thereof.

States which carry out the launching of a space device or whose territory is used for such launching.

"Applicant State" shall be understood to mean the State which has been injured or whose nationals or permanent residents have been injured, and which presents a claim for compensation.

ARTICLE 1

(c) . . . "Wilful misconduct" shall be understood to mean any act or omission perpetrated either with intent to cause damage or rashly and in full knowledge that damage will probably result.

Field of application and exemptions from provisions of agreement

ARTICLE 1

(a) The provisions of this Convention shall apply to compensation for damage caused to persons or property by a space device or space devices. They shall not apply to compensation for damage caused in the territory of the launching State or suffered by its nationals or permanent residents.

State and international organizations

ARTICLE 3

The launching State shall be held liable for compensation for damage caused in the circum-

compensation to a Respondent State.

(e) "Respondent State" means a launching State, or an international organization which has transmitted a declaration to the Secretary-General under Article III, paragraph 1 of this Convention, from which compensation is sought by a Presenting State.

ARTICLE II

4. The compensation which a State shall be liable to pay for damage under this Convention shall be determined in accordance with applicable principles of international law, justice and equity.

ARTICLE II

1. The launching State shall be absolutely liable and undertakes to pay compensation to the Presenting State, in accordance with the provisions of this Convention, for damage on the earth, in air space, or in outer space, which is caused by the launching of an object into outer space, regardless of whether such damage occurs during launching, after the object has gone into orbit, or during the process of re-entry, including damage caused by apparatus or equipment used in such launching.

ARTICLE V

A State shall not be liable under this Convention for damage suffered by its own nationals.

ARTICLE II

1. The launching State shall be absolutely liable . . . .

ARTICLE II

2. A claim for damage may be advanced on the ground of loss of profits and moral damage whenever compensation for such damage is provided for by the law of the State liable for damage in general.

ARTICLE I

1. The provisions of this Convention shall apply to compensation for loss of life, personal injury or other impairment of health, and damage to property (hereinafter called "damage"):

(a) caused by an object launched into outer space, or

(b) caused in outer space, in the atmosphere or on the ground by any manned or unmanned space vehicle or any object after being launched, or conveyed into outer space in any other way, but they shall not apply to nuclear damage resulting from the nuclear reactor of space objects.

2. Liability is also incurred even if, for any reason, the space vehicle or other object has not reached outer space.

ARTICLE VI

1. Liability for damage shall rest with the State or international organization which has

made liable and question of joint liability

stances stated in article 1, as defined in article 2. If several States participate in the launching of a space device, each of them shall be liable for compensation for the whole of the damage, and a claim for compensation may validly be addressed to any one of them.

[ARTICLE 2

"Launching State" shall be understood to mean the State or States which carry out the launching of a space device or whose territory is used for such launching.]

ARTICLE 6

International organizations acceding to this Convention in accordance with the provisions of article 5 shall have the same rights and obligations as States. The States members of the said international organization shall be held jointly liable for the obligations of the latter, in the same manner as provided for in article 3, whether or not such States are parties to the Convention. The accession of an international organization shall be accompanied by a notification of the acceptance by the States members of the organization concerned of the joint obligations so assumed.

The claims referred to in article 4 (a) may, in the case of the international organization, be presented through the Secretary-General of the United Nations.

[ARTICLE I

(c) "Launching State" means a Contracting Party, or an international organization which has transmitted a declaration to the Secretary-General under Article III, paragraph 1, of this Convention, which launches or procures the launching of an object into outer space or whose territory or facility is used in such launching, or which exercises control over the orbit or trajectory of an object.]

ARTICLE II

3. If under this Convention more than one launching State would be liable the Presenting State may proceed against any or all such States individually or jointly for the total amount of damages, and once the amount of liability is agreed upon or otherwise established, each such State proceeded against shall be liable to pay that amount provided that, in no event shall the aggregate of the compensation paid exceed the amount which would be payable under this Convention if only one Respondent State were liable.

ARTICLE III

1. If an international organization which conducts space activities transmits to the Secretary-General of the United Nations a declaration that it accepts and undertakes to comply with the provisions of the present Convention, all the provisions, except Articles X, XI, paragraph 2, XIII, XIV, and XV, shall apply to the organization as they apply to a State which is a Contracting Party.

2. The Contracting Parties to the present Convention undertake to use their best endeavours to insure that any international organization which conducts space activities and of which

launched or attempted to launch the space vehicle or object, or in the case of a common undertaking, with all the States participating in the undertaking or with the State from whose territory or from whose facilities the launching was made, or with the State which owns or possesses the space vehicle or object causing the damage.

2. Where liability may be laid upon more than one State or international organization, their liability towards the claimant shall be joint and several.

ARTICLE VII

If liability for damage rests with an international organization, the financial obligations towards States suffering damage shall be met by the international organization and by its member States jointly and severally.

they are constituent members is authorized to make and will make the declaration referred to in paragraph 1 of this Article.

3. If within one year of the date on which compensation has been agreed upon or otherwise established pursuant to Article VII, an international organization fails to pay such compensation each member of the organization which is a Contracting Party shall, upon service of notice of such default by the Presenting State within three months of such default, be liable for such compensation in the manner and to the extent set forth in Article II, paragraph 3.

Question of absolute liability and exoneration from liability

ARTICLE 1

(b) The occurrence of the event causing the damage shall create a liability for compensation once proof has been given that there is a relationship of cause and effect between the damage, on the one hand, and the launching, motion or descent of all or part of the space device, on the other hand.

(c) Liability for compensation shall cease to exist in the event of wilful misconduct on the part of the applicant State. "Wilful misconduct" shall be understood to mean any act or omission perpetrated either with intent to cause damage or rashly and in full knowledge that damage will probably result.

ARTICLE II

1. The launching State shall be absolutely liable and undertakes to pay compensation to the Presenting State, in accordance with the provisions of this Convention, for damage on the earth, in air space, or in outer space, which is caused by the launching of an object into outer space, regardless of whether such damage occurs during launching, after the object has gone into orbit, or during the process of re-entry, including damage caused by apparatus or equipment used in such launching.

2. If the damage suffered results either wholly or partially from a wilful or reckless act or omission on the part of the Presenting State, or of natural or juridical persons that it represents, the liability of the launching State to pay compensation under paragraph 1 of this article shall, to that extent, be wholly or partially extinguished.

ARTICLE III

Unless otherwise provided in Articles IV and V, exemption from liability may be granted only in so far as the State liable produces evidence that the damage has resulted from natural disaster or from a wilful act or from gross negligence of the party suffering the damage.

ARTICLE IV

1. Whenever damage is done to a space object or to persons and property on board by another space object, no claim shall arise between each other, except in so far as the claimant State produces evidence that the damage has been caused because of the fault of the other State or of a person on behalf of whom the latter State might present a claim [Article VIII].

2. If in the case mentioned in paragraph 1, a claim arises on the part of a third State, liability of the States liable for the space objects shall be joint and several.

ARTICLE V

The State shall assume liability for damage caused on the ground, in the atmosphere or in outer space, if the damage oc-

Limitation of
liability in amount

Payment
of com-
pensation
in con-
vertible
currency

ARTICLE 4

(d) Sums due in compensation for damage shall be fixed and payable either in the currency of the applicant State or in a freely transferable currency.

Presentation of claims by States or international organizations and on behalf of natural or juridical persons

ARTICLE 2

5. "Applicant State" shall be understood to mean the State which has been injured or whose nationals or permanent residents have been injured, and which presents a claim for compensation.

ARTICLE IX

The liability of the launching State shall not exceed $_____ with respect to each launching.

ARTICLE VIII

Payment of compensation shall be made in a currency convertible readily and without loss of value into the currency of or used by the Presenting State.

ARTICLE IV

1. A Contracting Party which suffers damage referred to in Article II, paragraph 1, or whose natural or juridical persons suffer such damage, may present a claim for compensation to a Respondent State.

2. A Contracting Party may also present to a Respondent State a claim of any natural person, other than a person having the nationality of the Respondent State, residing in its territory. However, a claim of any individual claimant may be presented by only one Contracting Party.

ARTICLE III

1. If an international organization which conducts space

curred while exercising an unlawful activity in outer space or the space vehicle or object was launched for unlawful purposes, or if the damage has otherwise resulted from an unlawful activity. In such cases the State liable shall be barred from any exoneration whatsoever.

ARTICLE III

Unless otherwise provided in Articles IV and V, exemption from liability may be granted only in so far as the State liable produces evidence that the damage has resulted from natural disaster or from a wilful act or from gross negligence of the party suffering the damage.

ARTICLE II

1. Liability under this Convention shall not exceed . . . .

ARTICLE VIII

A claim for damage may be made by a State in whose territory damage has occurred or in respect of damage suffered by its citizens or legal entities whether in the territory of that State or abroad.

activities transmits to the Secretary-General of the United Nations a declaration that it accepts and undertakes to comply with the provisions of the present Convention, all the provisions, except Articles X, XI, paragraph 2, XIII, XIV and XV, shall apply to the organization as they apply to a State which is a Contracting Party.

Joinder of actions	ARTICLE 4 (f) There shall be joinder of claims where there is more than one applicant in respect of damage due to the same event or where more than one State is liable and the damage was caused by more than one space device.	ARTICLE VII 2. No increase in the membership of the commission shall take place where two or more Presenting States or Respondent States are joined in any one proceeding before the commission. The Presenting States so joined may collectively appoint one person to serve on the commission in the same manner and subject to the same conditions as would be the case for a single Presenting State. Similarly, where two or more Respondent States are so joined, they may collectively appoint one person to serve on the commission in the same way.	
Presentation of claims for compensation through diplomatic channel	ARTICLE 4 (a) Within two years after the occurrence of the damage, or after the identification of the State liable under article 2, the applicant State shall present through the diplomatic channel, to the State which it holds liable, all claims for compensation concerning itself and its nationals and residents.	ARTICLE IV 3. A claim shall be presented through the diplomatic channel. A Contracting Party may request another State to present its claim and otherwise represent its interest in the event that it does not maintain diplomatic relations with the Respondent State.	ARTICLE X The claim shall be presented through diplomatic channels. The claimant State may request a third State to represent its interests in the event it has no diplomatic relations with the State liable.
Time-limits for presentation of claims	ARTICLE 4 (a) Within two years after the occurrence of the damage, or after the identification of the State liable under article 2, the applicant State shall present through the diplomatic channel, to the State which it holds liable, all claims for compensation concerning itself and its nationals and residents.	ARTICLE IV 4. Notice of a claim must be presented within one year of the date on which the accident occurred or, if the Presenting State could not reasonably be expected to have known of the facts giving rise to the claim, within one year of the date on which these facts became known to the Presenting State.	ARTICLE IX A claim must be presented within one year of the date of occurence of the damage, or of the identification of the State that is liable. If the applicant State could not reasonably be expected to have known of the facts giving rise to the claim, the claim must be presented within one year of the date on which

(e) The periods specified in this article shall not be subject to interruption or suspension.

Pursuit of remedies available in liable State or under other international agreements

ARTICLE 4

(b) If the applicant State or a person represented by it brings an action for compensation before the Courts or administrative organs of the State receiving the claim, it shall not at the same time present a claim for compensation for the same damage under the provisions of this Convention. The said provisions shall not be considered to require, by implication, the prior exhaustion of such remedies as may exist under the rules of ordinary law in the State receiving the claim.

Procedures of settlement of claims for compensation

ARTICLE 4

(c) If the State receiving the claim has not taken, within six months after being approached, a decision considered satisfactory by the applicant State, the latter may have recourse to arbitration.

Within ninety days of the date of the request addressed to it by the applicant State, the State receiving the claim shall appoint one arbitrator, the applicant State shall appoint a second and the President of the International Court of Justice a third. If the State receiving the claim fails to appoint its arbitrator within the prescribed period, the person appointed by the President of the International Court of Justice shall be the sole arbitrator.

The Arbitration Commission shall take its decisions according to law and by majority vote. It shall make an award within six months after the date of its establishment and its decisions shall be binding.

(d) Sums due in compensation for damage shall be fixed and payable either in the cur-

ARTICLE VI

1. The presentation of a claim under this Convention shall not require exhaustion of any remedies in the Respondent State which might otherwise exist.

2. If, however, the Presenting State, or any natural or juridical person whom it might represent, elects to pursue a claim in the administrative agencies or courts of the Respondent State or pursue international remedies outside this Convention, the Presenting State shall not be entitled to pursue such claim under this Convention.

ARTICLE VII

1. If a claim presented under this Convention is not settled within one year from the date on which documentation is completed, the Presenting State may request the establishment of a commission to decide the claim. In such event, the Respondent State and the Presenting State shall each promptly appoint one person to serve on the commission, and a third person, who shall act as chairman, shall be appointed by the President of the International Court of Justice. If the Respondent State fails to appoint its member within three months, the person appointed by the President of the International Court of Justice shall constitute the sole member of the commission.

2. No increase in the membership of the commission shall take place where two or more Presenting States or Respondent States are joined in any one proceeding before the commission. The Presenting States so joined may collectively appoint one person to serve on the commission in the same manner and

these facts officially became known.

ARTICLE XI

1. In case the State liable does not satisfy the claim of the claimant State, the claim for compensation shall be presented to a committee of arbitration set up by the two States on a basis of parity. This Committee will determine its own procedure.

2. Should the committee mentioned in paragraph 1 not arrive at a decision, the States may agree upon an international arbitration procedure or any other method of settlement acceptable to both States.

rency of the applicant State or in a freely transferable currency.

(e) The periods specified in this article shall not be subject to interruption or suspension.

(f) There shall be joinder of claims where there is more than one applicant in respect of damage due to the same event or where more than one State is liable and the damage was caused by more than one space device.

subject to the same conditions as would be the case for a single Presenting State. Similarly, where two or more Respondent States are so joined, they may collectively appoint one person to serve on the commission in the same way.

3. The commission shall determine its own procedure.

4. The commission shall conduct its business and arrive at its decision by majority vote.

5. The decision of the commission shall be rendered expeditiously and shall be binding upon the parties.

6. The expenses incurred in connexion with any proceeding before the commission shall be divided equally between the parties in the proceeding.

Space object not to be subject to sequestration or enforcement measures

Jurisdiction of International Court of Justice

ARTICLE X

Any dispute arising from the interpretation or application of this Convention, which is not previously settled by other peaceful means of their own choice, may be referred by any Contracting Party thereto to the International Court of Justice for decision.

ARTICLE XII

Claim for compensation for damage caused by a space ship of a foreign State shall not constitute ground for sequestration or for the application of enforcement measures to such space ship.

Parties to agreement, signature, accession and ratification

ARTICLE 5

1. This Convention shall be open for signature by States Members of the United Nations or any of the specialized agencies or parties to the Statute of the International Court of Justice, and by any other State or international organization invited by the General Assembly of the United Nations to become a Party to the Convention. Any

ARTICLE XIII

This Convention shall be open for signature by States Members of the United Nations or any of the specialized agencies or Parties to the Statute of the International Court of Justice, and by any other State invited by the General Assembly of the United Nations to become a party. Any such State which does not sign this Convention

ARTICLE XIII

1. This Convention shall be open for signature to all States. It shall be subject to ratification. Instruments of ratification shall be deposited with the Secretary-General of the United Nations.

ARTICLE XIV

After the Convention enters into force it shall be open for accession to other States. Instru-

State or international organization which is invited to do so but does not sign this Convention may accede to it at any time.

2. This Convention shall be subject to ratification or approval by signatory States. Instruments of ratification or approval and instruments of accession shall be deposited with the Secretary-General of the United Nations.

Entry into force

ARTICLE 5

3. This Convention shall enter into force thirty days after the date of the deposit of three instruments of ratification, approval or accession. For each State which deposits its instrument of ratification, approval or accession after the entry into force provided for in the preceding paragraph, this Convention shall enter into force on the date of deposit of such instrument.

Amendments

ARTICLE 8

This Convention may be amended or supplemented at the proposal of one or more Contracting Parties. Such amendments shall take the form of additional protocols which shall be binding on such Contracting Parties as ratify, approve or accede to them. Such protocols shall enter into force when the majority of the Contracting Parties to this Convention have thus accepted them.

Withdrawal from and denunciation of agreement

ARTICLE 7

Each Contracting Party may notify the Secretary-General of the United Nations of its withdrawal from this Convention not less than five years after its

---

may accede to it at any time.

ARTICLE XIV

This Convention shall be subject to ratification or approval by signatory States. Instruments of ratification or approval and instruments of accession shall be deposited with the Secretary-General of the United Nations.

ARTICLE XV

This Convention shall enter into force thirty days following the deposit of the fifth instrument of ratification, approval or accession. It shall enter into force as to a State ratifying, approving, or acceding thereafter upon deposit of its instrument of ratification, approval, or accession.

ARTICLE XI

1. A Contracting Party may propose amendments to this Convention. An amendment shall come into force for each Contracting Party accepting the amendment on acceptance by a majority of the Contracting Parties, and thereafter for each remaining Contracting Party on acceptance by it.

2. After this Convention has been in force five years a revision conference may be called upon the request of a majority of Contracting Parties.

ARTICLE XII

A Contracting Party may give notice of withdrawal from this Convention five years after its entry into force by written notification to the Secretary-General

---

ments of accession shall be deposited with the Secretary-General of the United Nations.

ARTICLE XIII

2. It (the Convention) shall enter into force thirty days after the deposit with the Secretary-General of the United Nations of the fifth instrument of ratification.

ARTICLE XV

With respect to each State which ratifies the Convention or accedes thereto after the deposit of the fifth instrument of ratification, the Convention shall enter into force thirty days after the date of deposit by the State of its instrument of ratification or accession.

ARTICLE XVI

Any Contracting State may denounce this Convention by notification to the Secretary-General of the United Nations. The denunciation shall take ef-

entry into force. Such withdrawal shall take effect one year after receipt of the notice which must be in writing. Such withdrawal shall not relieve the Contracting Party concerned of any obligation or liability arising from damage inflicted before its withdrawal takes effect.

of the United Nations. Such withdrawal shall take effect one year from the date of receipt of the notification by the Secretary-General. A State withdrawing from this Convention shall not thereby be relieved of any obligation or liability with respect to damages arising before withdrawal becomes effective.

fect one year after the date on which the notification has been received by the Secretary-General of the United Nations.

Notifications by Secretary-General

ARTICLE 9

The Secretary-General of the United Nations shall inform signatory States, and those which ratify, approve or accede to this Convention, of signatures, the deposit of instruments of ratification, approval or accession, the entry into force of this Convention, proposals for amendments, notifications of acceptance of additional protocols, and notices of withdrawal.

ARTICLE XVI

The Secretary-General of the United Nations shall inform all States referred to in Article XIII of signatures, deposits of instruments of ratification, approval, or accession, declarations referred to in Article III, paragraph 1, the date of entry into force of this Convention, proposals for amendments, notifications of acceptances of amendments, the date of entry into force of each amendment, requests for the convening of a revision conference, and notices of withdrawal, and shall transmit to those States certified copies of each amendment proposed.

ARTICLE XVII

The Secretary-General of the United Nations shall notify all States concerning:

(a) the signature of this Convention and the deposit of instruments of ratification or accession in accordance with articles XIII and XIV;

(b) the date of entry into force of this Convention in accordance with article XIII;

(c) denunciations received in accordance with article XVI.

Authentic text and deposit of agreement

ARTICLE 10

This Convention, of which the Chinese, English, French, Russian and Spanish texts are equally authentic, shall be deposited with the Secretary-General of the United Nations, who shall send certified true copies to all signatory States and to any State Member of the United Nations which so requests.

ARTICLE XVII

This Convention, of which the Chinese, English, French, Russian and Spanish texts are equally authentic, shall be deposited with the Secretary-General of the United Nations who shall send certified copies to each of the States mentioned in Article XIII.

ARTICLE XVIII

The original of this Convention, of which the texts in Chinese, English, French, Russian and Spanish languages are equally authentic, shall be deposited with the Secretary-General of the United Nations, who shall transmit certified copies thereof to all States.

Annex to Resolution 2345 (XXII)[1]

AGREEMENT ON THE RESCUE OF ASTRONAUTS, THE RETURN OF ASTRONAUTS AND THE RETURN OF OBJECTS LAUNCHED INTO OUTER SPACE

The Contracting Parties,

---

[1] Opened for signature April 22, 1968; entered into force December 3, 1968. TIAS 6599.

Noting the great importance of the Treaty on Principles Governing the Activities of States in the Exploration and Use of Outer Space, including the Moon and Other Celestial Bodies, which calls for the rendering of all possible assistance to astronauts in the event of accident, distress or emergency landing, the prompt and safe return of astronauts, and the return of objects launched into outer space,

Desiring to develop and give further concrete expression to these duties,

Wishing to promote international co-operation in the peaceful exploration and use of outer space,

Prompted by sentiments of humanity,

Have agreed on the following:

Article 1

Each Contracting Party which receives information or discovers that the personnel of a spacecraft have suffered accident or are experiencing conditions of distress or have made an emergency or unintended landing in territory under its jurisdiction or on the high seas or in any other place not under the jurisdiction of any State shall immediately:

(a) Notify the launching authority or, if it cannot identify and immediately communicate with the launching authority, immediately make a public announcement by all appropriate means of communications at its disposal; and

(b) Notify the Secretary-General of the United Nations who should disseminate the information without delay by all appropriate means of communication at his disposal.

Article 2

If, owing to accident, distress, emergency or unintended landing, the personnel of a spacecraft land in territory under the jurisdiction of a Contracting Party, it shall immediately take all possible steps to rescue them and render them all necessary assistance. It shall inform the launching authority and also the Secretary-General of the United Nations of the steps it is taking and of their progress. If assistance by the launching authority would help to effect a prompt rescue, or would contribute substantially to the effectiveness of search and rescue operations, the launching authority shall co-operate with the Contracting Party with a view to the effective conduct of search and rescue operations. Such operations shall be subject to the direction and control of the Contracting Party, which shall act in close and continuing consultation with the launching authority.

Article 3

If information is received or it is discovered that the personnel of a spacecraft have alighted on the high seas or in any other place not under the jurisdiction of any State, those Contracting Parties which are in a position to do so shall, if necessary, extend assistance in search and rescue operations for such personnel to assure their speedy rescue. They shall inform the launching authority and the Secretary-General of the United Nations of the steps they are taking and of their progress.

Article 4

If, owing to accident, distress, emergency or unintended landing, the personnel of a spacecraft land in territory under the jurisdiction of a Contracting Party or have been found on the high seas or in any other place not under the jurisdiction of any State, they shall be safely and promptly returned to representatives of the launching authority.

Article 5

1. Each Contracting Party which receives information or discovers that a space object or its component parts has returned to Earth in territory under its jurisdiction or on the high seas or in any other place not under the jurisdiction of any State, shall notify the launching authority and the Secretary-General of the United Nations.

2. Each Contracting Party having jurisdiction over the territory on which a space object or its component parts has been discovered shall, upon the request of the launching authority and with assistance from that authority if requested, take such steps as it finds practicable to recover the object or component parts.

3. Upon request of the launching authority, objects launched into outer space or their component parts found beyond the territorial limits of the launching authority shall be returned to or held at the disposal of representatives of the launching authority, which shall, upon request, furnish identifying data prior to their return.

4. Notwithstanding paragraphs 2 and 3 of this article, a Contracting Party which has reason to believe that a space object or its component parts discovered in territory under its jurisdiction, or recovered by it elsewhere, is of a hazardous or deleterious nature may so notify the launching authority which shall immediately take effective steps, under the direction and control of the said Contracting Party to eliminate possible danger or harm.

5. Expenses incurred in fulfilling obligations to recover and return a space object or its component parts under paragraphs 2 and 3 of this article shall be borne by the launching authority.

Article 6

For the purposes of this Agreement, the term "launching authority" shall refer to the State responsible for launching, or, where an international intergovernmental organization is responsible for launching, that organization provided that that organization declares its acceptance of the rights and obligations provided for in this Agreement and a majority of the States members of that organization are Contracting Parties to this Agreement and to the Treaty on Principles Governing the Activities of States in the Exploration and Use of Outer Space, Including the Moon and Other Celestial Bodies.

Article 7

1. This Agreement shall be open to all States for signature. Any State which does not sign this Agreement before its entry into force in accordance with paragraph 3 of this article may accede to it at any time.

2. This Agreement shall be subject to ratification by signatory States. Instruments of ratification and instruments of accession shall be deposited with the Governments of the United States of America, the United Kingdom of Great Britain and Northern Ireland and the Union of Soviet Socialist Republics, which are hereby designated the Depositary Governments.

3. This Agreement shall enter into force upon the deposit of instruments of ratification by five Governments including the Governments designated as Depositary Governments under this Agreement.

4. For States whose instruments of ratification or accession are deposited subsequent to the entry into force of this Agreement, it shall enter into force on the date of the deposit of their instruments of ratification or accession.

5. The Depositary Governments shall promptly inform all signatory and acceding States of the date of each signature, the date of deposit of each instrument of ratification of and accession to this Agreement, the date of its entry into force and other notices.

6. This Agreement shall be registered by the Depositary Governments pursuant to Article 102 of the Charter of the United Nations.

Article 8

Any State Party to the Agreement may propose amendments to this Agreement. Amendments shall enter into force for each State Party to the Agreement accepting the amendments upon their acceptance by a majority of the States Parties to the Agreement and thereafter for each remaining State Party to the Agreement on the date of acceptance by it.

Article 9

Any State Party to the Agreement may give notice of its withdrawal from the Agreement one year after its entry into force by written notification to the Depositary Governments. Such withdrawal shall take effect one year from the date of receipt of this notification.

Article 10

This Agreement, of which the English, Russian, French, Spanish and Chinese texts are equally authentic, shall be deposited in the archives of the Depositary Governments. Duly certified copies of this Agreement shall be transmitted by the Depositary Governments to the Governments of the signatory and acceding States.

IN WITNESS WHEREOF the undersigned, duly authorized, have signed this Agreement.

DONE in   copies at

Executive Agreement for Space Tracking and Communications Station on Antigua

British Embassy,
Washington, D.C.
23 January, 1967

The Honourable
  Dean Rusk,
    Secretary of State of the United States of America,
    Washington, D.C.

Sir,

I have the honor to acknowledge the receipt of your Note of the 17th of January, 1967, which reads as follows:

"I have the honor to refer to recent discussions between the representatives of the Government of the United States of America and the Government of the United Kingdom of Great Britain and Northern Ireland concerning the proposed establishment, operation and maintenance by the Government of the United States of a station for space vehicle tracking and communications on Antigua, British West Indies. Such a station would provide required post-launch, pre-insertion, and earth orbital coverage for Project Apollo, which has as its objective a manned landing on the moon. The station would also, in the event of future requirements, support other space projects of a peaceful and scientific character, manned and unmanned.

The discussions revealed that the Government of the United Kingdom (with the concurrence of the Government of Antigua) desires to cooperate with the Government of the United States in a spirit of good-neighborliness in this endeavor and is willing to agree to the establishment, operation and maintenance of such a station on Antigua.

Accordingly, I have the honor to propose an Agreement in the following terms for the establishment, operation and maintenance of the said station:

1. *Definition*
   (a) The term "United States Personnel" means any person who
       (i) is employed by, or under a contract with, the Government of the United States or a United States contractor engaged in works under contracts with that Government, in connection with the establishment, operation and maintenance of the station, and
       (ii) is not ordinarily resident in Antigua and is there solely for the purposes of this Agreement. The term "United States Personnel" also includes dependents of persons referred to in the preceding sentence.
   (b) The term "dependent" means the spouse and children under 21 of a person in relation to whom it is used; and, if they are dependent upon him for their support, the parents and children over 21 of that person.
   (c) The term "United States Contractor" means any person, body or corporation ordinarily resident in the United States of America that is in Antigua for the purposes of this Agreement by virtue of a contract with the Government of the United States or the National Aeronautics and Space Administration (hereinafter referred to as "NASA") and includes a subcontractor.

2. *Land Requirements*
   (a) The station will be located at Dow Hill, near Shirley Heights, on the south side of Antigua. The specific site of the station and the amount of land to be made available, together with rights of access, rights of way and easements as may be necessary for this purpose, shall be as agreed between the appropriate representatives of the two Governments. For the Government of the United States the representative shall be NASA. For the Government of the United Kingdom the representative shall be the Administrator of Antigua until the coming into force of the new Antigua constitution, after which the Government of the United Kingdom will be represented by a permanent secretary of the Antigua Civil Service designated by the Premier of Antigua.
   (b) Except as provided in sub-paragraph (c) of this paragraph, the land areas, rights of way and easements necessary for the station shall be provided free of rent and all other charges for the duration of this Agreement.
   (c) With respect to any privately-owned lands necessary for the station which the Government of Antigua is required to purchase, the conditions of use of such lands shall be as agreed between the appropriate representatives of the two Governments.
   (d) The appropriate representatives of the Government of the United States and of the Government of the United Kingdom are authorized to amend from time to time the arrangements regarding the land areas and rights of access, rights of way and easements.
   (e) As deemed necessary by the Government of the United States, roads shall be constructed or improved at the expense of the Government of the United States to provide suitable connections between the station and other facilities on Antigua. Arrangements with respect to the construction or improvement of such roads shall be agreed upon between the appropriate authorities of the Government of the United States and representatives of the Government of the United Kingdom.

3. *Description of Station*
   The station shall consist chiefly of and include the following: One 30-foot diameter parabolic antenna; transmitting, receiving and servo electronics; recording, data handling, and communications equipment; a power plant with appropriate switch gear and transformers; one 100-foot guyed collimation tower; and the necessary technical and supporting buildings and structures for offices, storage, sanitation and other required purposes. As program requirements develop, additional equipment or changes to existing equipment, consistent with the terms of this Agreement, may be added at the station.

4. *Operation of the Station*
   The station shall be operated by NASA or by United States contractors engaged by NASA. To the maximum extent feasible, qualified local personnel shall be utilized in connection with operation and maintenance of the facility, in addition to essential United States technicians and specialists assigned by NASA or its contractor.

5. *Construction*
   (a) Construction of the station shall be by a United States contractor, who shall, to the maximum extent feasible, employ qualified local sub-

contractors and local labor to perform the required work. Materials and supplies available locally shall be used to the maximum extent feasible consistent with station specifications and standards.

(b) The special electronic and related systems designed for the station are United States equipment and shall be installed by United States technicians.

6. *Costs*

In addition to any costs stated in this Agreement to be borne by the Government of the United States, the costs of construction, installing, equipping, operating and maintaining the station shall be borne by the Government of the United States.

7. *Frequency Authorization and Radio Interference*

(a) Upon the request of the Government of the United States and subject to the provisions of the Radio Regulations of the International Telecommunication Union, the Government of the United Kingdom shall authorize the use of the radio frequencies for the purposes of the station.

(b) Because an essential characteristic of the site to be selected for the station will be its freedom from harmful radio interference, the Government of the United Kingdom shall, insofar as practicable, take such measures to maintain this freedom against the introduction or operation of radio interference-producing devices (such as power lines, industrial facilities, primary highways, aircraft beacons, air-ground communications) within the vicinity of this sensitive radio receiving station and further, in the event it becomes necessary to introduce such devices into the area, the Government of the United Kingdom shall take all precautionary measures possible to minimize or eliminate any harmful interference. The Government of the United Kingdom shall, upon the request of the Government of the United States, investigate any interference to radio reception at the station which may be due to electrical apparatus and shall take all reasonable steps to secure the cessation of the interference.

(c) All telecommunications operations by the station shall be conducted in accordance with applicable provisions of the Radio Regulations of the International Telecommunication Union and telecommunications regulations of the Government of the United Kingdom so as not to cause interference with other authorized telecommunications services.

8. *Entry and Departure of United States Personnel*

The Government of the United Kingdom shall, upon request, take the necessary steps to facilitate the admission into, and departure from, Antigua of such United States personnel as may be assigned to or as may visit Antigua for the purposes of this Agreement.

9. *Importation and Exportation of Materials, Equipment, Supplies, Goods and Other Property*

(a) The Government of the United Kingdom shall, upon request, take the necessary steps to facilitate the admission into Antigua of materials, equipment, supplies, goods or other property of the Government of the United States, or of United States contractors, for the purposes of this Agreement.

(b) The Government of the United States shall retain title and ownership to all materials, equipment, supplies, goods or other property used in connection with the station and shall be entitled to remove the same free of any restrictions at any time.

10. *Fiscal Exemptions*

(a) No taxes or duties of customs shall be imposed upon the importation or exportation of:

(i) materials and equipment imported by or for use of the Government of the United States and United States contractors for the purposes of this Agreement and, if required, certified as such on behalf of the Government of the United States;

(ii) the personal effects and household goods, including privately-owned automobiles, imported by United States personnel on first arrival in Antigua or within six months thereafter and related thereto.

(b) No excise, consumption or other duty shall be levied or charged on any goods or materials purchased locally by or for the use of the Government of the United States for the purposes of this Agreement.

(c) Where the legal incidence of any form of taxation in Antigua depends on residence or domicile, periods during which the United States personnel are in Antigua solely by reason of this Agreement shall not be considered as periods of residence (or as creating a change of residence or domicile) for the purposes of such taxation. United States personnel shall be exempt from taxation in Antigua on the salary and emoluments received by them as such, on any tangible movable property within the station and on the ownership of such property outside the station in Antigua solely by reason of this Agreement.

(d) Nothing in this paragraph shall prevent taxation of United States personnel and United States contractors with respect to any profitable enterprise other than their employment as such in which they may engage in Antigua; and, except as regards salary and emoluments and the tangible movable property referred to in the preceding sub-paragraph, nothing in this paragraph shall prevent taxation to which, even if regarded as resident or domiciled outside Antigua, such persons are liable under the law of Antigua.

(e) Vehicles of the Government of the United States shall be exempted from all fees, taxes and other charges: A list of all such vehicles and their registration numbers shall be furnished to the Government of Antigua. Privately owned automobiles imported by United States personnel (excluding personnel employed by a United States contractor and their dependents) which qualify for exemption under paragraph (a)(ii) above shall also be exempt from Motor Vehicles Tax or any other tax, duty or charge of a similar nature.

(f) The appropriate authorities of the Government of the United States and the Government of Antigua shall collaborate in measures to be taken to prevent abuse of the privileges granted under this paragraph.

11. *Civil Claims*

(a) Claims for damage to property or injury to persons arising from acts or omissions of United States personnel, who are employed by or directly connected with NASA, will be considered and settled in accordance with the provisions of Section 203(b)(13) of the United States National Aeronautics and Space Act (42 U.S.C. section 2473), and as it may be amended.

(b) The Government of the United States may also settle other claims against the United States arising from acts or omissions connected with the station in accordance with applicable provisions of United States law.

12. *Public Services and Facilities*

(a) NASA and its contractors and United States personnel may use the public services and facilities belonging to or controlled or regulated by the Government of the United Kingdom or the Government of Antigua. The terms of use, including charges, shall be no less favorable than those available to other users unless otherwise agreed. No landing charges shall, however, be payable by the United States Government by reason of the use by aircraft, owned or operated by or on behalf of the Government of the United States, of any airport in Antigua. There shall be such contribution by the Government of the United States to the maintenance and operating costs of any airport as may be fair and reasonable, having regard to the use made of it by such aircraft. The amount of such contribution shall be subject to agreement between the appropriate authorities of the Government of the United States and the Government of Antigua.

(b) United States Government vessels using port facilities in Antigua shall not be subject to any toll charges, including lights and harbor dues (except insofar as such charges or dues represent payment for services rendered), nor shall such vessels be subject to compulsory pilotage.

(c) Lights and other aids to navigation of vessels and aircraft placed or established in the station and its vicinity and territorial waters adjacent thereto by the Government of the United States shall conform to the system in use in Antigua. The position and characteristics of any such lights or other aids and any alternations thereof shall be determined in consultation with the appropriate authority of Antigua.

13. *Use of Currency*

(a) The Government of the United States shall collaborate with the Government of Antigua in ensuring compliance with any foreign exchange law in force in Antigua. The Government of the United States and United States contractors may possess and use United States Currency for official purposes, including the payment of personnel, and may purchase and use local currency.

(b) United States personnel may use for internal transactions and export United States currency received from the Government of the United States or United States contractors.

(c) The appropriate authorities shall collaborate in the establishment of facilities to permit the purchase of local currency with United States currency and to prevent unauthorized transactions in either currency.

14. *Driving Permits*

(a) The Government of Antigua shall honor, without driving test or fee, driving permits issued by the United States or a subdivision thereof to United States contractors and to United States personnel, or issue its own driving permits, without test or fee, to such persons who hold such United States permits. United States contractors and United States personnel who do not hold such valid United States driving permits shall be required to obtain licenses in accordance with the law in force in Antigua.

(b) The United States authorities in collaboration with the authorities of Antigua shall issue appropriate instructions to United States contractors and to United States personnel, fully informing them of the traffic laws in force in Antigua and requiring strict compliance therewith.

15. Use of Other United States Facilities in Antigua

(a) *United States Defense Facilities*

NASA and United States contractors engaged by NASA may at any time utilize the logistic support services and other assistance available from United States facilities in Antigua established pursuant to the provisions of the Agreement between the Government of the United States of America and the Government of the Federation of The West Indies concerning United States Defense Areas in the Federation of The West Indies, signed at Port of Spain on February 10, 1961. The provisions of that Agreement shall govern any such services and assistance rendered.

(b) *Post Office and Commissariat Facilities*

NASA and United States contractors engaged by NASA and United States personnel shall have the right of access to and use of the facilities established by the United States military authorities in Antigua pursuant to Articles XIII and XIV of the aforementioned Agreement of February 10, 1961.

16. *Appropriation of Funds*

To the extent that the carrying out of any provisions of this Agreement will depend on funds appropriated by the Congress of the United States, it shall be subject to the availability of such funds.

17. *Supplementary Arrangements*

The appropriate authorities of the Government of the United States and Government of Antigua are authorized to make supplementary arrangements for the implementation of this Agreement in accordance with its purposes.

18. *Discontinuance of Use of Station*

Notwithstanding the provisions of paragraph 19, should changed conditions alter the requirements of the Government of the United States for the station, the Government of the United States shall have the right to discontinue use of the station after suitable advance notice to the Government of the United Kingdom.

19. *Duration*

This Agreement shall enter into force as provided below and shall remain in force initially until December 13, 1974. At any time after June 30, 1974, either Government may give written notice to the other of its intention to terminate the Agreement and the Agreement shall terminate six months after the date of such written notice.

If the foregoing proposals are acceptable to the Government of the United Kingdom of Great Britain and Northern Ireland, I have the honor to suggest that this note and your note in reply to that effect shall constitute an Agreement between our two Governments regarding this matter which shall enter into force on the date of your reply."

I have the honour to inform Your Excellency that the foregoing proposals are acceptable to the Government of the United Kingdom of Great Britain and Northern Ireland, who therefore agree that your Note, together with this reply, shall constitute an Agreement between the two Governments which shall enter into force on this day's date.

I avail myself of this opportunity to renew to you Sir, the assurance of my highest consideration.

(Signed) Patrick Dean

**Organisation Européene des Recherches Spatiales
European Space Research Organization**

Direction Centrale
Headquarters
36, Rue La Perouse
Paris 16ème

G/VII/5–5/DRK/GH/1907   28 November 1966

His Excellency,
Charles E. Bohlen,
Ambassador of the
United States of America
PARIS.

Your Excellency,
I have the honour to acknowledge receipt of your note of today's date, concerning the establishment and operation of a satellite telemetry/telecommand station near Fairbanks, Alaska, in connection with peaceful and scientific space activities to be undertaken by the Organization, which reads as follows:

"Dear Sir:
I have the honor to refer to discussions which have recently taken place between the Government of the United States of America and the European Space Research Organization concerning the establishment and operation of a satellite telemetry/telecommand station near Fairbanks, Alaska, in connection with peaceful and scientific space activities to be undertaken by the Organization.

The Government of the United States (hereinafter referred to as the United States) desires to cooperate with the European Space Research Organization (hereinafter referred to as ESRO) in these activities as part of their actual efforts to foster international cooperation in the peaceful uses of outer space, and agrees to the establishment by ESRO of an earth station on United States territory for space telemetering and telecommand purposes. In furtherance of this objective the United States will use its best efforts to facilitate the necessary local arrangements by ESRO in connection with its activities in Alaska. The United States proposes that this station be established and operated in accordance with the following principles and procedures:

1. *Lease of Land*
   ESRO may acquire by lease an area of land and obtain appropriate easements for the establishment and operation of an earth station for space telemetering and telecommand purposes, to be located in the vicinity of the City of Fairbanks. The United States will seek to facilitate arrangements for the lease of the land and appropriate easements and will help resolve any problem which may arise in connection with the use of such land and such easements.

2. *Construction of the Station*
   ESRO will arrange for the construction of the station which is the subject of this Agreement. The costs of constructing, installing, equipping and operating the station will be borne by ESRO, including the cost of constructing or improving roads and other means of access, except to the extent that contributions may be made by State or local authorities to serve public needs.

3. *Cooperating Agency*
   The National Aeronautics and Space Administration (hereinafter referred to as NASA) is designated by the United States as Cooperating Agency with ESRO on matters pertaining to the implementation of this Agreement.

4. *Description of the Station*
   The ESRO station will consist of installations for:
   Reception and recording of spacecraft telemetry signals (e.g., telemetry and receiving antennae with automatic tracking receivers, pointing gear and radome, telemetry receiving assembly, PCM decommutators and display equipment, coded time generator with decoders and display equipment, graphic and magnetic recorders);
   Transmission of telecommand signals to spacecraft (e.g., transmission antenna and pointing gear, radome, telecommand coder and transmitter);
   Telecommunications with ESRO Control Center (e.g., teleprinter and associated equipment, telephone link);
   Processing of information, maintenance of equipment, scientific and technical measurements on the ground and other tasks ancillary to the above activity (e.g., measuring instruments, antenna command and control desk, calibration tower with antenna and associated equipment);
   Accommodation of staff, equipment and stores; emergency power supply station, transformers, water supply and other services.
   As program requirements develop, additional equipment may be added, or existing equipment changed, at the station, consistent with the terms of this Agreement. ESRO shall notify the United States in advance of any major addition to or change in station equipment.

5. *Telecommunications*
   ESRO will select a contractor who will obtain, in accordance with applicable United States law, appropriate authorizations for the construction and operation of the radio transmission facilities, which authorizations will be granted by the United States subject to compli-

ance by the contractor with applicable United States and international telecommunications regulations.

The United States will act with respect to this station, in all matters concerning the International Telecommunication Union in conformity with the International Telecommunication Convention.

The United States recognizes that an essential characteristic of the station is its need for freedom from harmful radio interference, including interference caused by air-ground communications, and recognizes the importance of measures to maintain this freedom insofar as practicable against the operation of radio interference-producing devices. The United States will take precautionary measures insofar as practicable to eliminate or minimize harmful interference to the extent such devices are subject to the control of or by the United States. In addition, ESRO will seek appropriate arrangements with the State of Alaska insofar as measures for the control of such interference fall within the jurisdiction of the State of Alaska.

The area to be protected from radio interference is that area enclosed by the following points, as determined from U.S. Geological Survey Fairbanks D-1 and D-2, Alaska, 1:63, 360 Scale Topographic Maps:

Latitude 64°55′ 4″N, Longitude 147°32′30″W,
Latitude 64°56′38″N, Longitude 147°32′30″W,
Latitude 64°56′38″N, Longitude 147°31′00″W,
Latitude 64°57′21″N, Longitude 147°31′00″W,
Latitude 64°57′21″N, Longitude 147°27′30″W,
Latitude 64°55′ 4″N, Longitude 147°27′30″W,

6. *Status of ESRO*

ESRO shall, to the extent consistent with the instrument creating it, possess the capacity in the United States to contract, to acquire and dispose of real and personal property, and to institute legal proceedings.

7. *Privileges and Immunities*

ESRO and its personnel shall be accorded the status, privileges, exemptions and immunities indicated in the following subparagraphs:

A. *Customs Duties*
    The United States will, upon request, take the necessary measures to facilitate the admission into the United States of material, equipment, supplies, goods or other items imported by or for the account of ESRO in connection with the station and ESRO programs. Such shipments shall be accorded such exemption from customs duties and internal-revenue taxes imposed upon or by reason of importation, and such procedures in connection

therewith, as are accorded under similar circumstances to foreign governments.

B. *Title to Property*
    Title to all materials, equipment or other items of property used in connection with the station and ESRO programs will remain in ESRO. Material, equipment, supplies, goods or other property of ESRO may be removed from the United States at any time by ESRO free of taxes or duties.

C. *Inviolability and Immunity from Search*
    The archives of ESRO shall be inviolable. The property and assets of ESRO shall, subject to police and health regulations, and applicable United States regulations with regard to radio station inspections, be immune from search, unless ESRO expressly waives such immunity, and from confiscation.

D. *Judicial Immunity*
    ESRO, its property and assets, shall enjoy the same immunity from suit and every form of judicial process as is enjoyed by foreign governments, except to the extent that ESRO may expressly waive its immunity for the purpose of any proceedings or by the terms of any contract.

E. *Other Privileges of ESRO*
    ESRO shall be exempt from the following taxes levied by the United States: federal income tax; federal communications taxes on telephone, telegraph and teletype services in connection with the operation of the station; and federal tax on tickets for air transport of ESRO officers and employees which are purchased by ESRO or ESRO officers and employees in connection with official travel to and from the station.

F. *Privileges of Personnel*
    The United States will facilitate the admission into the United States of such ESRO officers and employees and their families, as may be assigned to or visit the station. ESRO and its officers and employees shall have the same privileges and immunities as those accorded by the United States to officers and employees of foreign governments with respect to laws regulating entry into and departure from the United States, alien registration and fingerprinting, and registration of foreign agents. Officers and employees so assigned shall not exceed in number those necessary for the construction and effective operation of the station.

ESRO will communicate their names to the United States in advance of entry.

Baggage and effects of ESRO officers and employees assigned to the station may be admitted, when imported in connection with the arrival of the owner, into the United States, and may be removed from the United States free of custom duties and internal revenue taxes imposed upon or by reason of importation. Such effects having a significant value shall be sold or otherwise disposed of in the United States only under conditions approved by the United States.

Such ESRO personnel shall be exempt from the payment of United States income tax and federal insurance contributions on wages and expenses paid by ESRO. The privileges and immunities set forth in this subparagraph shall not apply to citizens of the United States or foreign nationals admitted into the United States for permanent residence. However, officers and employees of ESRO, whatever their nationality, shall be immune from suit and legal process relating to acts performed by them in their official capacity and falling within their functions except insofar as such immunity may be waived by ESRO.

8. *Automobile Insurance*

ESRO will ensure that adequate automobile liability insurance is obtained for any of its personnel who operate automobiles in Alaska and will obtain such insurance for any automobiles which ESRO may purchase, lease or borrow. Notwithstanding any other provision of this Agreement, ESRO will waive any immunity which it might otherwise claim with respect to any suit or legal process alleging liability covered by such insurance.

9. *Availability of Data*

ESRO shall, upon request of the United States and at its expense, provide any raw data received by ESRO at the station and any reduced data therefrom. The United States may make use of this data after a period consistent with existing ESRO practice. Any earlier use of this data by the United States shall be subject to prior permission by ESRO. In any use of this data the United States will respect the ESRO rules relating to intellectual property rights.

10. *Station Use*

Apart from utilizing its station for its own satellites, ESRO may utilize its station for the support of satellites of one or more ESRO member states, and, with the prior consent of the United States for the support of other satellites.

11. *Final Clauses*

Supplementary arrangements between the United States and ESRO may be made from time to time as required for the carrying out of the purposes, principles and procedures of this Agreement.

This Agreement may be revised by mutual consent at the request of either party.

The United States and ESRO recognize the desirability, in accordance with international practice, of arbitrating any difference which may arise under this Agreement.

This Agreement shall continue in effect until February 29, 1972, and can be extended for an additional term by prior written agreement.

If the foregoing principles and procedures are acceptable to the European Space Research Organization, I have the honor to propose that this note, together with your note to that effect, shall constitute an Agreement between the United States of America and the European Space Research Organization on this matter which shall enter into force on the date of your note in reply.

I wish to present the renewed assurances of my highest consideration."

I have the honour to confirm that the principles and procedures specified in your note are acceptable to the European Space Research Organization and I concur with your proposal that your note and my present reply shall constitute an Agreement between the United States of America and the European Space Research Organization on this matter, which shall enter into force on today's date.

I have the Honour to be,
with high consideration, your Excellency,
Your obedient Servant,

(signed) Pierre Auger

Executive Order 11227

DESIGNATING THE INTERIM COMMUNICATIONS SATELLITE COMMITTEE AS A PUBLIC INTERNATIONAL ORGANIZATION ENTITLED TO ENJOY CERTAIN PRIVILEGES, EXEMPTIONS, AND IMMUNITIES

By virtue of the authority vested in me by Section 1 of the International Organizations Immunities Act (59 Stat. 669; 22 U.S.C. 288), and having found that the

United States participates in the Interim Communications Satellite Committee pursuant to the authority of the Communications Satellite Act of 1962 (76 Stat. 419; 47 U.S.C. 701–744) and the Agreement Establishing Interim Arrangements for a Global Commercial Communications System, August 20, 1964, TIAS 5646, I hereby designate the Interim Communications Satellite Committee as a public international organization entitled to enjoy the privileges, exemptions, and immunities conferred by the International Organizations Immunities Act, with the following exceptions:

1. The Interim Committee shall not enjoy the privileges, exemptions, and immunities conferred pursuant to Sections 2(b), 2(c), and 6 of that Act.

2. The officers and employees of the Interim Committee shall not enjoy the privileges, exemptions, and immunities conferred pursuant to Section 7(b) of that Act, but representatives to the Interim Committee and their alternates shall enjoy the privileges, exemptions, and immunities conferred pursuant to said Section 7(b).

The designation of the Interim Communications Satellite Committee as a public international organization within the meaning of the International Organizations Immunities Act is not intended to abridge in any respect privileges, exemptions, or immunities which such organization may have acquired or may acquire by treaty or Congressional action.

LYNDON B. JOHNSON

THE WHITE HOUSE,
June 2, 1965.

Agreement between the Government of the Union of Soviet Socialist Republics and the Government of France Concerning Cooperation in the Study and Exploitation of Outer Space for Peaceful Purposes*

[Signed at Moscow, June 30, 1966]

The Government of the Union of Soviet Socialist Republics and the Government of France:

Recognizing the importance of studying and exploiting outer space for peaceful purposes,

Considering that cooperation between the USSR and France in this area will promote the further widening of cooperation between the two countries and respond to the spirit of traditional friendship between the Soviet and French peoples,

Believing that such cooperation in the area of space would be an important step in the work of normalizing European scientific and technical cooperation,

Expressing satisfaction at contacts which have already taken place between interested organizations of the USSR and France in the present area,

Have agreed to the following:

ARTICLE 1.

Both governments have contracted to prepare and carry out programs of scientific and technical cooperation between the USSR and France in the area of the study and peaceful exploitation of outer space. For these purposes they will render support and assistance to interested organizations of both countries.

ARTICLE 2.

This cooperation will be carried out:

—— in the area of the study of outer space, including, in principle, the launching of a French satellite by the Soviet Union;

—— in the area of space meteorology, using the most modern scientific apparatus;

—— in the area of the study of space communications via man-made artificial satellites, as well as joint design and experimental work, and, in particular, in the area of television;

—— by means of the exchange of scientific information, trainees, scientific delegations, and the organization of conferences and symposia.

Scientific data derived in the course of conducting joint experiments shall be accessible to both Contracting Parties and shall be passed on within acceptable periods. The right of first publication will belong to the authors of the experiment.

ARTICLE 3.

Other areas of cooperation may be determined in the future by mutual agreement.

ARTICLE 4.

The program and conditions of cooperation in the areas provided for by Article 2 of the present Agreement will be determined by working protocols.

ARTICLE 5.

The mixed working groups of representatives of scientific and technical organizations of both countries shall ensure the working out and fulfillment of the program of cooperation.

---

* Translated by William E. Butler, member of the District of Columbia Bar. The Russian text of the Agreement was published in *Izvestia,* July 1, 1966, p. 2.

ARTICLE 6.

Each of the Contracting Parties shall notify the other party of the completion of the legislative procedure necessary for the present Agreement to enter into force. The Agreement shall enter into force on the day following notification.

The present Agreement is concluded for a term of ten years. It shall remain in force so long as it is not denounced by one of the parties. In this event it shall terminate two years after the notification of denunciation.

ARTICLE 7.

Clarifications and additions may be made to the present Agreement at the request of one of the Contracting Parties and by their mutual consent.

In witness thereof the representatives of the two Governments have signed the present Agreement and have affixed their seals thereto.

Done in the city of Moscow on June 30, 1966 in two copies, in the Russian and French languages, both texts being authentic.

Upon the authorization of the Government of the Union of Soviet Socialist Republics	Upon the authorization of the Government of France
A. Gromyko	Couve de Murville

Executive Order 11191

PROVIDING FOR THE CARRYING OUT OF CERTAIN PROVISIONS OF THE COMMUNICATIONS SATELLITE ACT OF 1962

By virtue of the authority vested in me by Section 301 of title 3 of the United States Code, and as President of the United States, it is hereby ordered as follows:

SECTION 1. *Definitions.* As used in this order:

(a) The term "the Act" means the Communications Satellite Act of 1962 (76 Stat. 419), and includes, except as may for any reason be inappropriate, that Act as amended from time to time.

(b) The term "the Corporation" means the Communications Satellite Corporation (incorporated on February 1, 1963, under title III of the Act and under the District of Columbia Business Corporation Act).

(c) The term "the Director" means the Director of Telecommunications Management provided for in Executive Order No. 10995 of February 16, 1962.

(d) The term "the Secretary" means the Secretary of State or his designees.

SEC. 2. *Director of Telecommunications Management.* (a) Subject to the provisions of this order, the Director shall generally advise and assist the President in connection with the functions conferred upon the President by the provisions of Section 201(a) of the Act.

(b) The Director shall:

(1) Aid in the planning and development, and aid in fostering the execution, of a national program for the establishment and operation, as expeditiously as possible, of a commercial communications satellite system.

(2) Conduct a continuous review of all phases of the development and operation of such a system, including the activities of the Corporation.

(3) Coordinate the activities of governmental agencies with responsibilities in the field of telecommunication, so as to insure that there is full and effective compliance at all times with the policies set forth in the Act.

(4) Make recommendations to the President and others as appropriate, with respect to all steps necessary to insure the availability and appropriate utilization of the communications satellite system for general Government purposes in consonance with Section 201(a) (6) of the Act.

(5) Help attain coordinated and efficient use of the electromagnetic spectrum and the technical compatibility of the communications satellite system with existing communications facilities both in the United States and abroad.

(6) Prepare, for consideration by the President, such Presidential action documents as may be appropriate under Section 201(a) of the Act, make necessary recommendations to the President in connection therewith, and keep the President currently informed with respect to the carrying out of the Act.

(7) Serve as the chief point of liaison between the President and the Corporation.

SEC. 3. *Secretary of State.* (a) The Secretary shall exercise the supervision provided for in Section 201(a) (4) of the Act and, in consonance with Section 201(a) (5) of the Act, shall further timely arrangements for foreign participation in the establishment and use of a communications satellite system.

(b) The Secretary shall have direction of the foreign relations of the United States with respect to the Act, including all negotiations by the United States with foreign governments or with international bodies in connection with the Act.

SEC. 4. *Annual reports.* The Director shall timely submit to the President each year the report (including evaluations and recommendations) provided for in Section 404(a) of the Act.

SEC. 5. *Assistance and Cooperation.* The Director and the Secretary shall effect such mutual coordination, and all other federal agencies concerned, and the Corporation, shall furnish the Director and the Secretary such assistance and documents, and shall otherwise extend to them such cooperation, as will enable the Director and the Secretary properly to carry out their responsibilities under this order and best promote the implementation of the Act in an orderly and expeditious manner. In connection with his responsibilities under section 3 of this order, the Secretary shall consult with the Director and other federal officers concerned, and, as may be appropriate, with the Corporation.

SEC. 6. *Functions reserved.* The functions, or parts of functions, conferred upon the President by the Act that are not assigned herein are reserved to the President.

LYNDON B. JOHNSON

THE WHITE HOUSE,
January 4, 1965.

Bibliography

A Guide to the Study of the Legal and Political Aspects of Space Exploration including a Selective Topical Bibliography

Kenneth Anderson Finch and H. Peter Kehrberger

This *Guide* is offered primarily to stimulate further research and study by those interested in space law, and consists of (1) a comprehensive list of legal and non-legal research aids available, (2) an enumeration of the major publications of non-governmental institutions, international organizations, and the U. S. government, and (3) an extensive, but still selective, current topical bibliography of American and foreign sources on the law of space.

General Bibliographies on Space Law

"A Guide to the Study of Space Law: Including a Selective Bibliography on the Legal and Political Aspects of Space," compiled by J. C. Hogan, 5 *Saint Louis University Law Journal* 79–133 (Spring 1958).

RAND Report P-1290 (Santa Monica, California, RAND Corporation, 1958), 59 p. Reprinted in full at pp. 291–345, "Space Law: A Symposium," Senate Special Committee on Space and Astronautics, 85th Congress, 2d Session, December 31, 1958, Committee Print (Washington: Government Printing Office, 1959); and in part at

Kenneth Anderson Finch: A.B., St. Louis University, 1952; LL.B., Marquette University, 1956; LL.M., Georgetown University, 1959; member of the International Institute of Space Law; Past Chairman of Federal Bar Association's Space Law Committee.

H. Peter Kehrberger: Junior Barrister in the District of the Hanseatic Supreme Court of Hamburg, Germany; member of the International Institute of Space Law of the International Astronautical Federation.

pp. 330–44, *Legal Problems of Space Exploration: A Symposium,* Senate Committee on Aeronautical and Space Sciences, 87th Congress, 1st Session, March 22, 1961, Senate Document No. 26 (Washington: Government Printing Office, 1961), 1967 GPO Catalog No. 87–1: Senate Document 26. (The latter work is hereinafter referred to as *1961 Senate Symposium.*)

"Bibliography of Space Law," compiled by K. A. Finch, R. C. Hagan *et al.,* at pp. 37–60 in Survey of Space Law, Staff Report of House Select Committee on Astronautics and Space Exploration, 86th Congress, 1st Session, House Document No. 89 (Washington: Government Printing Office, 1959), 1967 GPO Catalog No. 86–1: House Document No. 89. The above-cited sources are acknowledged by L. Lipson and N. deB. Katzenbach in their bibliography at pp. 155–78 in *The Law of Outer Space* (Chicago: American Bar Foundation, 1961), reprinted at pp. 954–82 in *1961 Senate Symposium.*

"Guides to the Study of Communist Views on the Legal Problems of Space Exploration and a Bibliography," compiled by R. D. Crane, at pp. 1011–36 in *1961 Senate Symposium.*

"Selected References on the Legal Problems of Space Exploration," compiled by K. A. Finch, at pp. 1329–92 in *1961 Senate Symposium.* Revised and reprinted as "Space Law Bibliography," Air Force Pamphlet 110–14, July 20, 1961 (Washington, Department of the Air Force, 1961), 79 p.

World Bibliography of Space Law, compiled by M. Smirnoff (Belgrade, Institut za medunarodnu politiku i privredu, 1962), 162 p. (This covers the principal works published from 1910 to the end of 1959, with titles translated into English and Serbo-Croatian).

Worldwide Bibliography for Year 1964 of Space Law and Related Matters, compiled by the International Institute of Space Law of the International Astronautical Federation, edited by E. Pepin, IISL Bibl. No. 1 (Paris, IAF Secretariat, 1965), 33 p.; No. 2, 1966, 64 p.; No. 3, 1967, 43 p.; No. 4, 1968, 48 p.

Legal and Political Implications of Space Research, compiled by H. P. Kehrberger (Hamburg, Verlag Weltarchiv GmbH., 1965), 421 p. (A bibliography of materials published through 1965 on space law and associated political, military, economical and socio-technological aspects of astronautics, contains 6421 citations, and covers literature from 55 nations in 30 languages, with titles translated into English.)

International Space Bibliography, Outer Space Affairs Group of the Secretariat of the United Nations: U.N. Doc. No. A/AC.105/33, December 1966, 166 p. Thirty-five member states have provided a comprehensive list of books published in their individual countries dealing in general with space exploration, international cooperation in space activities, the impact and economic, social, political, and legal implications of space activities. English titles in translation are provided.

Periodical Indexes, Guides, and Other Reference Works

The more important legal and political indexes and reference guides are:

Index to Foreign Legal Periodicals
Index to Legal Periodicals
Index to Periodicals Related to Law
Index to Publications (RAND Corporation)
Index to United Nations Documents
Monthly Catalog of United States Government Publications
American Journal of International Law (Quarterly bibliographies)
Journal of Air Law and Commerce (Quarterly bibliographies)
Useful non-legal indexes are:
Air University Periodical Index
Bulletin of the Public Affairs Information Service
International Index to Periodicals
International Political Science Abstracts
Index to the Times (London)
New York Times Index
Reader's Guide to Periodical Literature
The Current Digest of the Soviet Press
East European Accessions List
Monthly List of Russian Accessions (a monthly record of monographic and periodical publications received by the Library of Congress from these Communist nations.)

Non-legal Periodicals for Lawyers Interested in Policy Background and Global Implications of National Space Research Programs

The following periodicals are among the best published in the English language:

Air Force/Space Digest (monthly)
Air Force Association
1750 Pennsylvania Avenue, N.W.
Washington, D.C. 20006

Air University Periodical Index (Quarterly)
Air University, Maxwell AFB, Alabama

Astronautics and Aeronautics (Monthly)
Journal of Spacecraft and Rockets (Monthly)
AIAA Bulletin (Monthly)
AIAA Journal (Monthly)
American Institute of Aeronautics and Astronautics
1290 Sixth Avenue
New York, New York 10019

Aviation Week and Space Technology (Weekly)
Space Technology International (Quarterly)

McGraw-Hill Publishing Company
330 West 42nd Street
New York, New York 10036

Journal of the British Interplanetary Society (Bi-monthly)
Spaceflight (Monthly)
British Interplanetary Society
12 Bessborough Gardens
London, S.W. 1, England

Broadcasting (Business Weekly of Television and Radio)
1735 DeSales Street, N.W.
Washington, D.C. 20036

Missile/Space Daily (Daily)
Technology Week, including Missiles and Rockets (Weekly)
American Aviation Publications, Inc.
1001 Vermont Avenue, N.W.
Washington, D.C. 20006

Space Business Daily
Space Business Weekly
1426 G Street, N.W.
Washington, D.C. 20005

Space/Aeronautics (Monthly)
Conover-Mast Publications, Inc.
205 East 42nd Street
New York, New York 10017

Space World (Monthly)
Palmer Publications, Inc.
P.O. Box 388
Amherst, Wisconsin 54406

Telecommunications Journal (Monthly)
International Telecommunications Union (ITU)
Place des Nations
1211 Geneva 20, Switzerland

Telecommunications Reports (Weekly)
1208–1216 National Press Building
Washington, D.C. 20004

University Courses Offered Dealing with Space Law

Dr. Eugene Pepin, President of the International Institute of Space Law of the International Astronautical Federation, has conducted a survey of the teaching of Space Law throughout the world. Preliminary reports were issued, and the final report can be obtained upon request. The reports indicate that elements of space law are now incorporated in the teaching of courses in public international law on four continents, in at least the following countries: Argentina, Australia, Belgium, Brazil, Canada, Colombia, Czechoslovakia, France, Germany, Italy, Mexico, Netherlands, Rumania, Spain, Switzerland, United Kingdom, United States, Uruguay, USSR, and Venezuela.

The following university law schools devote or have devoted part of their international law curriculum to space law or have held seminars on specific legal problems of space exploration: California Western, Columbia, Georgetown, George Washington, Harvard, Loyola of Los Angeles, Northwestern, Oklahoma, Rutgers, Saint Louis, Southern California, Southern Methodist, Stanford, Yale, and McGill University in Canada. Professor L. F. E. Goldie describes his syllabus, "Teaching a Course in Space Law," 19 *Journal of Legal Education* 89–101 (1966).

Organizations Active in the Study of Legal and Political Aspects of Space

Information concerning committee membership, publications, and future schedule of meetings may be obtained by writing:
American Astronautical Society
1629 K Street, N.W.
Washington, D.C. 20006

American Bar Association
Section on International and Comparative Law
Committee on Law of Outer Space
1155 East 60th Street
Chicago, Illinois 60637

American Institute of Aeronautics and Astronautics
Technical Committee on Law and Sociology
1290 Sixth Avenue
New York, New York 10019

American Society of International Law
2223 Massachusetts Avenue, N.W.
Washington, D.C. 20008

The David Davies Memorial Institute of International
  Studies
Thorney House, Smith Square
London, S.W. 1, England

Federal Bar Association
Committee on Space Law
1815 H Street, N.W.
Washington, D.C. 20006

Institut de Droit International (Institute of International
  Law)
88 Rue de Grenelle
Paris 7, France

Inter-American Bar Association
1730 K Street, N.W.
Washington, D.C. 20006

International Institute of Space Law
International Astronautical Federation
250 Rue Saint-Jacques
Paris 5, France

International Law Association
3 Paper Building, Temple
London, E.C. 4, England

World Peace Through Law Center
839 17th Street, N.W.
Washington, D.C. 20006

Colloquia, Symposia, and Collections of Articles on Space Law

AMERICAN ASSEMBLY (Columbia University, New York):
Outer Space—Prospects for Man and Society, edited by L.P. Bloomfield. London and Englewood Cliffs, N.J.: Prentice-Hall, 1962. 203 p.

AMERICAN BAR ASSOCIATION, SECTION OF INTERNATIONAL AND COMPARATIVE LAW, COMMITTEE ON LAW OF OUTER SPACE:
Report of the Committee on Law of Outer Space. ABA 81st Annual Meeting, Los Angeles, August 25–29, 1958. Published in *1958 Proceedings,* pp. 143–53. Reprinted in *1959 Senate Symposium,* pp. 472–84.
Report of the Committee on Law of Outer Space. ABA 82d Annual Meeting, Bal Harbour-Miami Beach, August 24–28, 1959. Published in *1959 Proceedings,* pp. 215–33. Reprinted in *1961 Senate Symposium,* pp. 571–94.
Report of the Committee on Law of Outer Space. ABA 84th Annual Meeting, St. Louis, August 7–11, 1961. Published in *1961 Proceedings,* pp. 292–304. *ABA Annual Report 1961,* Vol. 86, pp. 738–50.
Report of the Committee on Law of Outer Space. ABA 85th Annual Meeting, San Francisco, August 6, 8–11, 1962. Published in *1962 Proceedings,* pp. 294–305; *ABA Annual Report 1962,* Vol. 87, pp. 882–93.
Report of the Committee on Law of Outer Space. ABA 86th Annual Meeting, Chicago, August 12, 14–16, 1963. Published in *1963 Proceedings,* pp. 312–29; *ABA Annual Report 1963,* Vol. 88, pp. 738–55.
Report of the Committee on Law of Outer Space. ABA 87th Annual Meeting, New York, August 7–12, 1964. Published in *1964 Proceedings,* pp. 321–23. Also see pp. 61–65.
Report of the Committee on Law of Outer Space. ABA 88th Annual Meeting, Miami Beach, August 9–13, 1965. Published in *1965 Proceedings* at p. 248. See also *Report of Committee on International Communications,* pp. 52–75.

AMERICAN BAR FOUNDATION (Chicago):
Report to the National Aeronautics and Space Administration on the Law of Outer Space. Project Reporters: L. Lipson and N. deB. Katzenbach. Chicago: American Bar Foundation, 1961, 179 p. Reprinted in *1961 Senate Symposium.*

AMERICAN SOCIETY OF INTERNATIONAL LAW (ASIL):
50th Annual Meeting, "Legal Problems of Upper Space" (Washington, D.C., 1956), published in *ASIL Proceedings,* pp. 84–115.
52nd Annual Meeting, "Recent Technological Developments; Political and Legal Implications for the International Community" (Washington, D.C., 1958), published in *ASIL Proceedings,* pp. 26–47, 136–45, 229–80.
55th Annual Meeting, "Current Developments in Air Space and Outer Space: Law Science and Policy" (Washington, D.C., 1961), published in *ASIL Proceedings,* pp. 163–86.
57th Annual Meeting, "The Status of Competing Claims to Use Outer Space" (Washington, D.C., 1963), published in *ASIL Proceedings* pp. 173–207.
61st Annual Meeting, "International Cooperation in Satellite Communication Systems" (Washington, D.C., 1967), published in *ASIL Proceedings* pp. 24–29.

AMERICAN INSTITUTE OF AERONAUTICS AND ASTRONAUTICS (AIAA) (New York):
Communication Satellite System Technology, edited by R. B. Marsten, Vol. 19, "Progress in Astronautics & Aeronautics," chapter 6, pp. 927–1051. New York: Academic Press, 1966.

BRITISH INSTITUTE OF INTERNATIONAL AND COMPARATIVE LAW (London):
"Current Problems in Space Law: A Symposium," *Report of Space Law Conference,* London, May 4, 1965; Special Publication No. 9 (London, British Institute of International and Comparative Law, 1966) 168 p.

CARNEGIE ENDOWMENT FOR INTERNATIONAL PEACE (New York):
Space and Society. Studies for Seminar on Problems of Outer Space, Edited by H. J. Taubenfeld. Dobbs Ferry, N.Y.: Oceana Publications, 1964, 172 p.

DAVID DAVIES MEMORIAL INSTITUTE OF INTERNATIONAL STUDIES, STUDY GROUP ON THE LAW OF OUTER SPACE (London):
"Draft Code of Rules on the Exploration and Use of Outer Space," (London, David Davies Memorial Institute of International Studies, 1962), 17 p. Reprinted in 29 Journal of Air Law and Commerce 141–150 (Spring 1963), and in *Law and Politics in Space* (Montreal, McGill University Press, 1964), pp. 153–67.
"Draft Rules Concerning Changes in the Environment of Earth," (London, David Davies Memorial Institute of International Studies, 1964), 14 p.
"Draft Code of Rules on the Exploration and Use of Outer Space," (London, David Davies Memorial Institute of International Studies, 1966), 20 p.

INSTITUT DE DROIT INTERNATIONAL ("INSTITUTE OF INTERNATIONAL LAW"):
"The International Law of Outer Space," *Preliminary Report to the Second Commission of the Institut de Droit International.* August 4, 1962, C. W. Jenks, Reporter. 260 p. (mimeo). Published and discussed by members of the Second Commission (in French), Annuaire de l'Insti-

tut de Droit International, Vol. 50–I, pp. 128–496 (1963).

Le Droit international des espaces célèstes: Rapport definitif et projects de resolution de M. C. Wilfred Jenks du 1er Mars 1963 ("The International Law of Outer Space: Definitive Report and Draft Resolutions of March 1, 1963 by Mr. C. Wilfred Jenks"). Annuaire de l'Institut de Droit International, Vol. 50–I, pp. 384–433 (1963); Discussion of Report, Vol. 50–II, pp. 60–187 (1963).

Resolution: The Legal Regime of Outer Space (Second Commission), Annuaire de l'Institut de Droit International, Vol. 50–II, pp. 369–72 (1963).

INTERNATIONAL ASTRONAUTICAL FEDERATION, INTERNATIONAL INSTITUTE OF SPACE LAW (IISL):

First Colloquium on the Law of Outer Space, The Hague, Netherlands, August 29, 1958; edited by A. G. Haley and W. Heinrich. Vienna: Springer-Verlag, 1959. 126 p.

Second Colloquium on The Law of Outer Space, London, England, September 4, 1959; edited by A. G. Haley and W. Heinrich. Vienna: Springer-Verlag, 1960. 176 p.

Third Colloquium on The Law of Outer Space, Stockholm, August 15, 1960; edited by A. G. Haley and K. Gronfors. Stockholm: AB Aetatryck, Ahlen & Akerlunds Trycherier, 1961. 160 p.

Fourth Colloquium on The Law of Outer Space, Washington, D.C., October 3–4, 1961; edited by A. G. Haley and M. D. Schwartz. Norman: University of Oklahoma Research Institute, 1963. 413 p.

Fifth Colloquium on The Law of Outer Space, Varna, Bulgaria, September 25–28, 1962; edited by A.G. Haley. Washington, D.C.: 1963, 570 p.

Sixth Colloquium on The Law of Outer Space, Paris, France, September 26–28, 1963; edited by A. G. Haley. Washington, D.C.: 1964. 880 p.

Seventh Colloquium on The Law of Outer Space, Warsaw, Poland, September 9–10, 1964; edited by A. G. Haley and M. D. Schwartz. Norman: University of Oklahoma Research Institute, 1965. 425 p.

Eighth Colloquium on The Law of Outer Space, Athens, Greece, September 14–15, 1965; edited by A. G. Haley and M. D. Schwartz. Norman: University of Oklahoma Research Institute, 1966. 475 p.

Ninth Colloquium on The Law of Outer Space, Madrid, Spain, October 11–14, 1966; edited by M. D. Schwartz. Davis: University of California Law School, 1967. 221 p.

Tenth Colloquium on The Law of Outer Space, Belgrade, Yugoslavia, September 1967, 6 p. (mimeo); edited by M. D. Schwartz. Davis: University of California Law School.

(Information on publications and future colloquia may be obtained by writing International Institute of Space Law of the I.A.F., 250 Rue Saint-Jacques, Paris 5, France.)

INTERNATIONAL LAW ASSOCIATION (ILA) (London):

Report of the Air Law Committee on the Limitations of Air Sovereignty. D. Goedhuis: Rapporteur. Forty-seventh Conference, Dubrovnik, Yugoslavia. 1956, pp. 163–75. 196–215 (includes Report, Discussion, and ILA Resolution).

Report of the Air Law Committee on Air Sovereignty and the Legal Status of Outer Space. D. Goedhuis: Rapporteur. Forty-eighth Conference, New York, 1958, pp. 246–71, 320–30 (includes Report, Discussion, and ILA Resolution).

Report of the Air Law Committee on Air Sovereignty and the Legal Status of Outer Space. D. Goedhuis: Rapporteur. Forty-ninth Conference, Hamburg, 1960, pp. 245–89 (includes Report, Discussion, and ILA Resolution).

Report of the Air Law Committee, Sub-Committee on Air Sovereignty and the Legal Status of Outer Space. D. Goedhuis: Rapporteur. Fiftieth Conference, Brussels, 1962, pp. 31–100 (includes Report, Discussion, and ILA Resolution).

Report of the Space Law Committee. D. Goedhuis: Rapporteur. Fifty-first Conference, Tokyo, 1964. 101 p. with Annexes (includes Report, Discussion, ILA Resolutions, and six Annexes).

Report of the Space Law Committee. D. Goedhuis: Rapporteur. Fifty-second Conference, Helsinki, 1966, 42 p. with four Annexes (includes Report, Discussion, ILA Resolutions, and six Annexes).

INTER-PARLIAMENTARY UNION (IPU, Geneva):

Report and Draft Resolution on Space Law. Presented on behalf of the Parliamentary and Juridical Committee by P. de Montesquieu, 52d Interparliamentary Conference, Belgrade, September 12–20, 1963, 52 Compte Rendu IPU (Geneva) 13–14, 259–60, 433–41, 801–56 (1964).

MC GILL UNIVERSITY, INSTITUTE OF AIR AND SPACE LAW (Montreal):

"Law and Politics in Space: Specific and Urgent Problems in the Law of Outer Space" in *Proceedings of the First McGill Conference on the Law of Outer Space,* Montreal, April 12–13, 1963; edited by M. Cohen (Montreal: McGill University Press, 1964), 221 p.

NORTHWESTERN UNIVERSITY, SCHOOL OF LAW:

Proceedings of the Conference on the Law of Space and of Satellite Communications: A Part of the Third NASA Conference on the Peaceful Uses of Space, Chicago, May 1–2, 1963. 58 Northwestern University Law Review 215–76, 618–43 (1963); NASA SP-44 (Washington, D.C.: Government Printing Office, 1964), 205 p.

UNIVERSITY OF OKLAHOMA:

Proceedings of the Conference on Space Science and Space Law, University of Oklahoma, Norman, June 18–20, 1963, edited by M. D. Schwartz. South Hackensack, N.J.: 1964. 176 p.

WORLD RULE OF LAW CENTER, DUKE UNIVERSITY:

International Organizations and Space Cooperation, edited by L. E. Schwartz, Durham, N.C.: World Rule of Law Center, 1962. 108 p.

RAND CORPORATION

International Political Implications of Activities in Outer Space: Report of a Conference, Santa Monica, California (RAND Corporation), October 22–23, 1959, edited by J. M. Goldsen. RAND Report R-362-RC, May 5, 1960, 209 p. Enlarged and revised as *Outer Space in World Politics.* New York: Praeger, 1963. 180 p. (Other RAND Corporation publications are listed in the attached Selective Topical Bibliography).

UNITED STATES AIR FORCE, OFFICE OF THE JUDGE ADVOCATE GENERAL:

The Legal, Socio-technological Problems of Space Exploration: A National Colloquium. Presented by the United States Air Force Judge Advocate General's Department, Reserve, in Conjunction with the First Annual Meeting of the American Institute of Aeronautics and Astronautics, Washington, D.C., July 2, 1964. Summary published 6 *USAF JAG Bulletin* 11–23 (September–October 1964). Full proceedings to be published.

"Symposium on the Law of Outer Space," Special International Law Issue 7 *USAF JAG Law Review* 1–45 (September–October 1965); 9 *USAF JAG Law Review* 3–56 (September–October 1967).

UNITED STATES CONGRESS, SENATE COMMITTEE ON AERONAUTICAL AND SPACE SCIENCES:

Legal Problems of Space Exploration: A Symposium, edited by E. Galloway. Senate Committee on Aeronautical and Space Sciences, 87th Congress, 1st Session, Senate Document No. 26, March 22, 1961. Washington, D.C.: Government Printing Office, 1961. 1392 p. GPO Catalog No. 87–1: Senate Document 26.

UNION OF SOVIET SOCIALIST REPUBLICS

Na Puti k Kosmicheskomu Pravu ("The Way to Space Law") by I. I. Cheprov and F. N. Kovalev. Moscow: Institut Mezhdunarodnykh Otnoshenij [Institute of International Relations], 1962. 179 p. English translation, 135 p.*

Kosmos i Mezhdunarodnoye Pravo ("Space and International Law") edited by Y. A. Korovin. A Symposium by the Committee on the Legal Problems of Outer Space of the Academy of Sciences, USSR. Moscow: Izdatel'stvo Institut Mezhdunarodnykh Otnoshenij [Publishing Office of the Institute of International Relations], 1962. 182 p. English translation, 145 p.*

Kosmos i Mezhdunarodnoye Sotrudnichestvo ("Space and International Cooperation"), edited by G. P. Zhukov. A Symposium by the Committee on the Legal Problems of Outer Space of the Academy of Sciences, USSR. Moscow: Izdatel'stvo Institut Mezhdunarodnykh otnoshenij (Publishing Office of the Institute of International Relations), 1963. 256 p. English translation, 261 p.*

"Kosmos i Problema Vseobshchego Mira" ("Space and the Problem of a General Peace"); edited by G. P. Zadorozhnyi. A Symposium by the Institute of State and Law of the Academy of Sciences, USSR. Moscow: Izdatel'stvo Nauka (Publishing Office Science), 1966. 196 p. English translation, 224 p.*

Books (English Language)

American Bar Foundation. Project Reporters, Lipson, L. and Katzenbach, N. deB. *The Law of Outer Space: Report to the National Aeronautics and Space Administration on the Law of Outer Space.* Chicago: American Bar Foundation, 1961. 179 p. Reprinted in *1961 Senate Symposium,* pp. 779–983.

Christol, C. Q. *The International Law of Outer Space: International Law Studies,* U.S. Naval War College, 1962. Washington, D.C.: Government Printing Office, 1966, 513 p.

Haley, A. G. *Space Law and Government.* New York: Appleton-Century-Crofts, 1963. 584 p.

Jenks, C. W. *Space Law.* New York: Praeger, 1965. 476 p.

Jessup, P. C., and Taubenfeld, H. J. *Controls for Outer Space and the Antarctic Analogy.* New York: Columbia University Press, 1959. 379 p.

McDougal, M. S., Lasswell, H. D., and Vlasic, I. A. *Law and Public Order in Space.* New Haven, Conn.: Yale University Press, 1963. 1147 p.

Morenoff, J. *World Peace through Space Law.* Charlottesville, Va.: Michie, 1967. 329 p.

Seara Vasquez, Modesto. *Cosmic International Law.* Translated by E. Malley. Detroit, Mich.: Wayne State University Press, 1965. 293 p.

Verplaetse, J. C. *International Law in Vertical Space: Air, Outer Space, Ether.* South Hackensack, N.J.: F. B. Rothman, 1960, 502 p.

United States Government Publications

Congressional documents, hearings, and reports are published by the U.S. Government Printing Office (GPO), Washington, D.C., as are the publications of other government agencies, unless otherwise specified. In January 1967, the Superintendent of Documents, Government Printing Office, published the Frst Edition of Price List 79A, entitled "Space," which indicated that many of the listed congressional and NASA publications were still available for purchase.

---

* Translations of the four above Soviet Symposia were distributed to the Library of Congress, interested Congressional Committees, NASA, and other law libraries by Kenneth A. Finch, past Chairman and Vice-Chairman of the Federal Bar Association's Committee on the Legal Problems of Space Exploration. Information on their possible re-publication may be obtained from the FBA, National Headquarters, 1815 H Street, N.W., Washington, D.C. 20006.

See also *Monthly Catalog of United States Government Publications.* Depository libraries are listed annually in the September issue of the catalog. The catalog contains complete information on how to order publications, price and catalog number, whether the document is for sale from the Superintendent of Documents or being distributed by the Issuing Office, i.e., the Congressional Committee, or the House or Senate Document Room, or government agencies, and finally indicates whether the document has been sent to so-called Depository Libraries. Over 500 university, college and public libraries are currently designated by Congress as depositories for Government publications.

PRESIDENT OF THE UNITED STATES:

Report to the Congress from the President of the United States, United States Aeronautics and Space Activities: 1958, 25 p.; 1959, 141 p.; *1960, 186 p.; 1961, 107 p.; 1962, 139 p.; 1963, 148 p.; 1964, 161 p.; 1965, 172 p.; 1966, 171 p.; 1967, 145 p. (Annual Report* includes space programs, budgets, and achievements of some 15 US departments, agencies, and councils; 1958–61 published by GPO, 1962–67 by National Aeronautics and Space Council, Washington, D.C.).

SENATE SPECIAL COMMITTEE ON SPACE AND ASTRONAUTICS:

National Aeronautics and Space Act: A Bill to Provide for Research into Problems of Flight Within and Outside the Earth's Atmosphere; Hearings on S. 3609, May 6–8, 13–15, 1958, 85th Congress, 2d Session, two parts, 413 p.

National Aeronautics and Space Act of 1958: A Report of Mr. Johnson to Accompany S. 3609; 85th Congress, 2d Session, 1958, Senate Report No. 1701, 26 p.

Space Law: A Symposium. Staff Report edited by Eilene Galloway, 85th Congress, 2d Session, December 31, 1958, Committee Print, 573 p. (revised edition 1961).

SENATE COMMITTEE ON AERONAUTICAL AND SPACE SCIENCES:

Investigation of Governmental Organization for Space Activities; Hearings Before the Subcommittee on Governmental Organization for Space Activities, 86th Congress, 2d Session, 1959, Committee Print, 762 p.

Governmental Organization for Space Activities; Report of the Subcommittee on Governmental Organization for Space Activities, 86th Congress, 1st Session, 1959, Report No. 805, 58 p.

Radio Frequency Control in Space Telecommunications; Staff Report edited by Edward Wenk, Jr., 86th Congress, 2d Session, March 19, 1960, Committee Print, 235 p.

Policy Planning for Space Telecommunications; Staff Report, 86th Congress, 2d Session, December 4, 1960, Committee Print, 207 p.

Legal Problems of Space Exploration: A Symposium; Staff Report edited by Eilene Galloway, 87th Congress, 1st Session, March 22, 1961, Senate Document No. 26, 1392 p.

*Communication Satellites: Technical, Economic, and Inter-**national Developments; Staff Report,* 87th Congress, 2d Session, February 25, 1962, Committee Print, 287 p.

Communications Satellite Legislation; Hearings on S. 2650 and S. 2814, February 27, 28, and March 1, 5, 6, 7, 1962, 85th Congress, 2d Session, 485 p.

Communications Satellite Act of 1962; Report on S. 2814, 87th Congress, 2d Session, (S. Report 1319), April 2, 1962, 9 p.

Soviet Space Programs: Organization, Plans, Goals, and International Implications; Staff Report. 87th Congress, 2d Session, May 31, 1962, Committee Print, 399 p.

Nominations of the Incorporators of the Communications Satellite Corporation; Hearings, 88th Congress, 1st Session, March 19, 1963, 127 p.

Documents on International Aspects of the Exploration and Use of Outer Space, 1954–1962; Staff Report. 88th Congress, 1st Session, May 9, 1963, Senate Document No. 18, 407 p.

United States International Space Programs: Texts of Executive Agreements, Memoranda of Understanding, and Other International Arrangements, 1959–1965; Staff Report edited by Eilene Galloway, 89th Congress, 1st Session, July 30, 1965, Senate Document No. 44, 575 p.

International Cooperation and Organization for Outer Space; Staff Report edited by Eilene Galloway, 89th Congress, 1st Session, August 12, 1965, Senate Document No. 56, 589 p.

National Communications Satellite Programs; Hearings, January 25 and 26, 1966, 89th Congress, 2d Session, Committee Print, 85 p.

Soviet Space Programs, 1962–65, Goals and Purposes, Achievements, Plans and International Implications; Staff Report. 89th Congress, 2d Session, December 30, 1966, Committee Print, 919 p.

Space Treaty Proposals by the United States and USSR; Staff report edited by Eilene Galloway, 89th Congress, 2d Session, July 1966, Committee Print, 52 p.

Treaty on Principles Governing the Activities of States in the Exploration and Use of Outer Space, Including the Moon and Other Celestial Bodies: Analysis and Background Data; Staff Report edited by Eilene Galloway, 90th Congress, 1st Session, March 1967, Committee Print, 84 p.

SENATE COMMITTEE ON COMMERCE:

Space Communications and Allocation of Radio Spectrum; Hearings Before the Communications Subcommittee, August 1, 23, 24, 1961, 87th Congress, 1st Session, 1961, Committee Print, 315 p.

Communications Satellite Act of 1962; Hearings on S. 2814, April 10–26, 1962, 87th Congress, 2d Session, Committee Print, 413 p.

Communications Satellite Act of 1962; Report to Accompany H.R. 11040, 87th Congress, 2d Session, June 11, 1962, Senate Report No. 1584, Committee Print, 61 p.

Satellite Communications; Hearings before the Communications Subcommittee, February 18, 19, and 27, 1963, 88th Congress, 1st Session, Committee Print, 95 p.

Communication Satellite Incorporators; Hearings before the Communications Subcommittee, March 11, 1963, 88th Congress, 1st Session, Committee Print, 91 p.

Air Law and Treaties of the World; Staff Report by the Law Library, Library of Congress, edited by Wm. S. Strauss, Assistant General Counsel, Library of Congress, 89th Congress, 1st Session, July 1, 1965, Committee Print, Three Volumes, 4483 p.

Weather Modification and Control; Report prepared by Legislative Reference Service, Library of Congress, 89th Congress, 2d Session, April 27, 1966, Senate Report No. 1139, 181 p.

Progress Report on Space Communications (and Ford Foundation Proposal for a Broadcasters Non-Profit Domestic Satellite Service); Hearings before the Communications Subcommittee, August 10, 17, 18, and 23, 1966, 89th Congress, 2d Session, Committee Print, 245 p.

SENATE JUDICIARY COMMITTEE:

Antitrust Problems of Space Communications Systems; Hearings Pursuant to Senate Resolution 258, Subcommittee on Antitrust and Monopoly, March 29–April 19, 1962, 87th Congress, 2d Session, two parts, 757 p.

SENATE SELECT COMMITTEE ON SMALL BUSINESS:

Space Satellite Communications; Hearings, August 2–11, and November 8–9, 1961, 87th Congress, 1st Session, two parts, 755 p.

HOUSE COMMITTEE ON SCIENCE AND ASTRONAUTICS:

International Control of Outer Space; Hearings, March 5, 6, 11, 1959, 86th Congress, 1st Session, 108 p.

Satellites for World Communication; Hearings, March 3 and 4, 1959, 86th Congress, 1st Session, Committee Print No. 9, 122 p.

Satellites for World Communication; Report prepared by staff consultant P. B. Schuppener, 86th Congress, 1st Session, 1959, House Report No. 343, 9 p.

U.S. Policy on the Control and Use of Outer Space; House Report No. 353, 86th Congress, 1st Session, April 1959, 11 p.

Current Developments in the Law of the Sea and Outer Space; Report prepared by G. J. Feldman, 86th Congress, 2d Session, June 21, 1960, Committee Print, 13 p.

Outer Space, Road to Peace: Observations on Scientific Meetings and International Cooperation; Compilation of Data; 86th Congress, 2d Session, 1960, 53 p.

Proposed Studies on Implications of Peaceful Space Activities for Human Affairs; prepared for the National Aeronautics and Space Administration by D. McMichael of the Brookings Institution, 87th Congress, 2d Session, April 18, 1961, House Report No. 242, 272 p.

Military Astronautics (Preliminary Report); Report prepared by C. S. Sheldon II, 87th Congress, 1st Session, May 4, 1961, 37 p.

Air Laws and Treaties of the World; annotated compilation by W. S. Strauss, Assistant to General Counsel, Library of Congress, 87th Congress, 1st Session, May 11, 1961, 1476 p. (revised edition, 1965).

Communication Satellites; Hearings, May 8, 9, 10, July 13–17, August 1, 9–10, 1961, 87th Congress, 1st Session, two parts, 908 p.

Practical Values of Space Exploration; Report prepared by P. B. Yeager, 87th Congress, 1st Session, 1961, 74 p.

Commercial Applications of Space Communications Systems; Report prepared by F. R. Hammill, 87th Congress, 1st Session, October 11, 1961, Committee Print, 29 p.

Commercial Communications Satellites; Hearings, September 18–21, 27, and October 4, 1962, 87th Congress, 2d Session, Committee Print, 182 p.

Project Advent—Military Communications Satellite Programs; Hearings, August 15–17, 1962, 87th Congress, 2d Session, Committee Print, 140 p.

Project Advent—Military Communications Satellite Programs; House Report No. 2558, 87th Congress, 2d Session, November 1, 1962, 9 p.

Communication Satellite Experiments; House Report No. 2560, 87th Congress, 2d Session, December 3, 1962, 9 p.

NASA-DOD Relationship; Report, Subcommittee on NASA Oversight, 88th Congress, 2d Session, 1964, Committee Print, 97 p.

Summary Report Future Programs Task Group: A Report by NASA to the President, 89th Congress, 1st Session, 1965, Committee Print, 109 p.

Future National Space Objectives; Staff Study, Subcommittee on NASA Oversight, prepared by J. E. Wilson and J. M. Felton, 89th Congress, 2d Session, July 1966, Committee Print, 439 p.

Review of the Soviet Space Program with Comparative United States Data; prepared by C. S. Sheldon, II, Science Policy Research Division, Legislative Reference Service, Library of Congress, 1967, 90th Congress, 1st Session, November 10, 1967, Committee Print, 138 p.

HOUSE SELECT COMMITTEE ON ASTRONAUTICS AND SPACE EXPLORATION:

Astronautics and Space Exploration; Hearings on H. R. 11881, April 15, 16, 17, 18, 21, 22, 23, 24, 25, 26, 29, 30, May 1, 5, 7, and 12, 1958, 85th Congress, 2d Session, 1542 p. (For discussion of space law see pp. 1262–1464.)

Astronautics and Space Exploration: Summary of Hearings, April 15–May 12, 1958; Staff Report on Hearings, 86th Congress, 1st Session, 1958, House Document No. 87, 46 p.

International Cooperation in the Exploration of Space; House Report No. 2709, 85th Congress, 2d Session, 1959, 16 p.

Space Handbook: Astronautics and Its Applications; Staff Report, 86th Congress, 1st Session, 1959, House Document No. 86, 252 p.

The Next Ten Years in Space 1959–1969; Staff Report, 86th Congress, 1st Session, 1959, House Document No. 115, 221 p.

Survey of Space Law; Staff Report prepared by S. M. Beresford and P. B. Yeager, 85th Congress, 2d Session, 1958, Committee Print; 86th Congress, 1st Session, 1959, House Report No. 89, 60 p. (contains "Bibliography of Space Law" annexed at pp. 37–60: Reprint of "Space Law Bibliography," Air Force Pamphlet No. 110–1–4).

HOUSE COMMITTEE ON GOVERNMENT OPERATIONS (& MILITARY OPERATIONS SUBCOMMITTEE):

Military Communications Satellite Program; Subcommittee Hearings, April 23, 1963, 88th Congress, 1st Session, Committee Print, 51 p.

Satellite Communications—1964; Subcommittee Hearings March 17–26, April 7–16, May 21–28, August 6–11, 1964, 88th Congress, 2d Session, Committee Print, two parts, 793 p.

Satellite Communications (Military-Civil Roles and Relationships); Subcommittee Report, 88th Congress, 2d Session, October 1964, Subcommittee Print, 160 p.

Satellite Communications (Military-Civil Roles and Relationships); Second Report of Committee on Government Operations, 89th Congress, 1st Session, March 17, 1965, House Report No. 178, 161 p.

Government Operations in Space (Analysis of Civil-Military Roles & Relationships); Thirteenth Report of Committee on Government Operations, 89th Congress, 1st Session, June 4, 1965, House Report No. 445, 136 p.

Government Use of Satellite Communications; Hearings August 15–31, September 1–14, 1966, 89th Congress, 2d Session, Committee Print, 850 p.

Government Use of Satellite Communications; Forty-third Report of Committee on Government Operations, 89th Congress, 2d Session, October 19, 1966, House Report No. 2318, 105 p.

Government Use of Satellite Communications—1967; Subcommittee Hearings July 24–25, 1967, 90th Congress, 1st Session, Committee Print, 157 p.

Government Use of Satellite Communications—1967; Seventh Report of Committee on Government Operations, 90th Congress, 1st Session, August 28, 1967, House Document No. 613, 14 p.

HOUSE COMMITTEE ON INTERSTATE AND FOREIGN COMMERCE:

Communications Satellites; Hearings, July 25–28, 1961, 87th Congress, 1st Session, 1961, Committee Print, 343 p.

Communications Satellite Act of 1962; Report to Accompany H.R. 11040, 87th Congress, 2d Session, April 24, 1962, House Report No. 1636, 27 p.

Communications Satellites; Hearings, March 13–22, 1962, 87th Congress, 2d Session, 1962, Committee Print, two parts, 711 p.

Communications Satellite Act of 1962—The First Year, 88th Congress, 1st Session, October 3, 1963, House Report No. 809, 40 p.

FEDERAL COMMUNICATIONS COMMISSION:

In the Matter of an Inquiry into the Administrative and Regulatory Problems Relating to the Authorization of Commercially Operable Space Communications Systems, Docket No. 14024 (3 Volumes); Notice of Inquiry (FCC 61–427, released April 3, 1961); First Report and Order (FCC 61–767, released May 24, 1961); Report of the Ad Hoc Carrier Committee (Released October 13, 1961).

In Matter of Application of Communications Satellite Corporation for Authority to Use and Operate a Communications-satellite Earth Station at Andover, Maine, in conjunction with a Synchronous Communications-satellite in Orbit over the Atlantic Ocean to Provide Commercial Communications Services, and for Approval of the Technical Characteristics thereof, File No. 1-CSS & CSG-L-65; Memorandum Opinion, Order and Authorization (FCC 65–550, June 23, 1965), 38 FCC Reports 1298–1314.

In Matter of Amendment of Part 25 of the Commission's Rules and Regulations with Respect to Ownership and Operation of Initial Earth Stations in the United States for Use in Connection with the Proposed Global Commercial Communications-satellite System, Docket No. 15735, FM-644 (5 volumes); Report and Order (FCC 65–401, released May 13, 1965), 38 FCC Reports 1104–1126; Memorandum Opinion and Order (FCC 66–176, February 26, 1965), 2 FCC2d Reports 658–666; Second Report and Order (FCC 66–1133, released December 8, 1966), 5 FCC2d Reports 812–22.

In Matter of Authorized Entities and Authorized Users under the Communications Satellite Act of 1962, Docket No. 16058 (2 Volumes); Notice of Inquiry (FCC 65–523, released June 16, 1965); Public Notice (FCC 66–563, released June 23, 1966), 4 FCC2d Reports 12–13; Memorandum Opinion and Statement of Policy (FCC 66–677, released July 20, 1966), 4 FCC2d Reports 421–36.

In Matter of Tariff Bearing Designation FCC No. 1 Filed by the Communications Satellite Corporation on May 28, 1965, Docket No. 16070 (2 Volumes); Memorandum Opinion and Order (FCC 65–549, released June 23, 1965), 38 FCC Reports 1286–97.

In Matter of Amendment of Part 25 of the Commission's Rules and Regulations to Provide for the Issuance of Authorizations to Developmental Stations in the Communications-satellite Service, Docket No. 16220 (1 Volume); Notice of Proposed Rule Making (FCC 65–895, released October 8, 1965); Report and Order (FCC 67–13, released January 6, 1967), 6 FCC2d Reports 250–53.

In Matter of the Establishment of Domestic Non-common Carrier Communication-satellite Facilities by Non-government Entities, Docket No. 16495 (4 Volumes); Notice of Inquiry (FCC 66–207, released March 3, 1966), 2 FCC2d Reports 668–671; Supplemental Notice of Inquiry (FCC 66–926, released October 21, 1966), 5 FCC2d Reports 354–56.

NATIONAL AERONAUTICS AND SPACE ADMINISTRATION:

Proceedings of the First National Conference on the Peaceful Uses of Outer Space, Tulsa, Oklahoma, May 26–27, 1961 (NASA-SP-5), 184 p.

Proceedings of the Second National Conference on the Peaceful Uses of Outer Space, Seattle, Washington, May 8–10, 1962 (NASA SP-8), 282 p.

Proceedings of the Conference on the Law of Space and of Satellite Communications: Part of the Third National Conference on the Peaceful Uses of Outer Space, Chicago, May 1–2, 1963 (NASA SP-44), 205 p.

Proceedings of the Fourth National Conference on the Peaceful Uses of Outer Space, Boston, April 29-May 1, 1964 (NASA-SP 51), 225 p.

Proceedings of the Fourth National Conference on the Peaceful Uses of Outer Space, St. Louis, Missouri, May 25–28, 1965 (NASA SP-82), 200 p.

(The Proceedings of the Sixth and Seventh Conferences had not been published as of June 1968; however, the 1967 GPO. Catalog indicates the first five are still available.)

The Legal Status of Outer Space—Freedom or Sovereignty: The Aerospace Boundary Question in International Law

American Bar Association: Section on International and Comparative Law. *Report of the Committee on Law of Outer Space—Recommendations, Proceedings of 82d Annual ABA Meeting,* Miami, 1959, pp. 215–33. Reprinted in the *1961 Senate Symposium,* pp. 571–94. Includes comments by Cooper, Halley, Knauth.

American Bar Foundation. *Report to the National Aeronautics and Space Administration on the Law of Outer Space,* L. Lipson and N. Katzenbach, Project Reporters. Pp. 8–27, 37–58, 65–81, 92–133. Chicago: American Bar Foundation, 1961. 179 p. Reprinted in *1961 Senate Symposium,* pp. 779–983.

Becker, L. E. "Major Aspects of the Problem of Outer Space." Statement made by the Legal Adviser, Department of State, before the Senate Committee on Space and Astronautics, May 14, 1958, *1961 Senate Symposium,* pp. 396–403.

————"United States Foreign Policy and the Development of Law for Outer Space," *Journal of the Judge Advocate General* (US Navy), February 1959, pp. 4–7.

Beresford, S. M. "The Future of National Sovereignty." *Second Colloquium on Law of Outer Space,* London,

1959, pp. 5–10. Reprinted in *1961 Senate Symposium,* pp. 601–12.

Cheng, B. "International Law and High Altitude Flights: Balloons, Rockets and Man-made Satellites," 6 *International and Comparative Law Quarterly* (London) 487–505 (July 1957). Reprinted in *1961 Senate Symposium,* pp. 141–55.

————"From Air Law to Space Law," *Current Legal Problems* (London) 228–54 (1960).

————"United Nations Resolution on Outer Space: Instant International Customary Law," 5 *Indian Journal of International Law* (New Delhi) 23–48 (January 1965).

Christol, C. Q. " 'Innocent Passage' in the International Law of Outer Space," 7 *USAF JAG Law Review* 22–29 (September/October 1965).

Cooper, J. C. "Roman Law and the Maxim, 'Cujus Est Solum' in International Air Law," *McGill Law Journal* 23–65 (1955).

————"High Altitude Flight and National Sovereignty." Address, Escuela Libre de Derecho, Mexico City, January 5, 1951. Reprinted in *1961 Senate Symposium,* pp. 1–7.

————"Legal Problems of Upper Space." Paper, 50th ASIL Annual Meeting, April 26, 1956, Washington, D.C., Reprinted in *1961 Symposium,* pp. 66–73.

————"The Problems of a Definition of 'Air Space.' " *First Colloquium on Law of Outer Space,* The Hague, 1958, pp. 38–44.

————"International Control of Outer Space—Some Preliminary Problems." Memorandum Submitted to the Eleventh International Astronautical Congress, Stockholm, August 13–20, 1960. *Third Colloquium on Law of Outer Space,* IISL, Stockholm, 1960, pp. 21–25.

————"Fundamental Questions of Outer Space Law." Paper, University of Leyden, Netherlands, October 10, 1960. Reprinted in *1961 Senate Symposium,* pp. 764–72.

————"The Passage of Space Craft Through the Air Space." *Sixth Colloquium on Law of Outer Space,* IISL, Paris, 1963, 13 p.

————"The Upper Airspace Boundary Question." Report, IISL Working Group I *Sixth Colloquium on Law of Outer Space,* IISL, Paris, 1963, 8 p.

————"Legal Problems of Spacecraft in Airspace," *Festschrift Riese* 465–74 (1964).

————"Aerospace Law—Subject Matter and Terminology," 29 *Journal of Air Law and Commerce* 89–94 (Spring 1963).

————"Contiguous Zones in Aerospace—Preventive and Protective Jurisdiction," 7 *USAF JAG Law Review* 15–21 (September/October 1965).

————"The Manned Orbiting Laboratory: A Major Legal and Political Decision," 51 *American Bar Association Journal* 1137–40, (1965).

Goedhuis, D. "Air Sovereignty and the Legal Status of Outer Space." *Reports, International Law Association,*

New York, 1958, pp. 320–29. Discussion and remarks by: Cheng, Cooper, Goedhuis, McDougal, A. Meyer, Tomsic, Roy, Machowski, Lissitzyn, Lipson, Monaco, Gorove, pp. 246–70. Resolution: p. 271.

————"Air Sovereignty and the Legal Status of Outer Space." *Reports, International Law Association,* Hamburg, 1960, pp. 272–89. Discussion: pp. 245–67, 269. Resolution: pp. 267–68.

————Report of the Subcommittee of the Air and Space Law Committee on Air Sovereignty and Legal Status of Outer Space. *Reports, International Law Association,* Brussels, 1962, pp. 69–91. Discussion and remarks by: Berezowski, Cheng, Fasan, Focseanu, Georgiades, Goedhuis, E. Glaser, La Pradelle, Latey, Lipson, Mateesco, Matte, Meyer, Rode-Verschoor, Rosevear, Sandiford, Szegö-Bokor, Vignes, pp. 31–68. Resolution adopted on Air and Space Law; p. viii.

————"The Legal Regime of Outer Space: Questionnaire." *Report of the Space Law Committee, International Law Association,* Tokyo, 1964, Annex I, pp. 5–20. Replies and remarks by Bodenschatz, Chauveau, Cooper, Fasan, Guerreri, Huber, Lissitzyn, Meyer, Pepin, Zylicz, and Zhukov, Annex V, pp. 91–93, Draft Resolution on the Question of the Upper Limit of National Space and of Innocent Passage of Foreign Space Vehicles through Such Space.

————"Reflections on the Evolution of Space Law," 13 *Nederlands Tijdschrift voor International Recht* (Leyde) 109–49 (1966).

Gorove, S. "On the Threshold of Space: Toward a Cosmic Law: Problems of the Upward Extent of Sovereignty." *First Colloquium on Law of Outer Space,* The Hague, 1958, pp. 69–76.

Haley, A. G. "Survey of Legal Opinion on Extra-terrestrial Jurisdiction." *Third Colloquium on Law of Outer Space,* IISL, Stockholm 1960, pp. 37–92.

————"Sovereignty in Space," 7 *Review of Contemporary Law* (Brussels) 13–21 (December 1960).

————"National Consent to Overflight," chapter 3, pp. 40–74, and "The Limits of National Sovereignty," chapter 4, pp. 75–117, in *Space Law and Government.* New York: Meredith Publishing Company, 1963. (These two chapters update and summarize Mr. Haley's major contributions on these questions.)

Hannover, W. H. "Air Law and Space," 5 *St. Louis University Law Journal* 11–69 (Spring 1958). Reprinted in *1961 Senate Symposium,* pp. 271–329.

————"Problems in Establishing a Legal Boundary between Airspace and Space." *First Colloquium on Law of Outer Space,* The Hague, 1958, pp. 28–30.

————"Sovereignty in Space." *Fourth Colloquium on Law of Outer Space,* IISL, Washington, 1961, 119–29.

Hingorani, R. C. "La Souveraineté sur l'éspace extra-atmosphérique," 20 *Revue Générale de l'Air* (Paris) 248–52

(1957). Reprinted in English: "Attempt to Determine Sovereignty in Upper Space," 26 *University of Kansas City Law Review* 5–13 (December 1957).

Hogan, J. C. "Legal Terminology for the Upper Regions of the Atmosphere and for the Space Beyond the Atmosphere," 51 *American Journal of International Law* 362–75 (April 1957). Reprinted in *1961 Senate Symposium,* pp. 129–40.

Homburg, R. "Droit astronautique et droit aèrien" ("Astronautical Law and Air Law"), 21 *Revue Générale de l'Air* (Paris) 11–16 (1958).

Ikeda, F. "Toward the Principle of 'Freedom of Outer Space,'" 7 *Japan Annual of Law and Politics* 158–60 (1959).

Jenks, C. W. "International Law and Activities in Space," 5 *International and Comparative Law Quarterly* (London) 99–114 (January 1956). Reprinted in *1961 Senate Symposium,* pp. 33–45.

Johnson, J. A. "Current Developments in Air Space and Outer Space: Law, Science, and Policy." Remarks, *Proceedings of the American Society of International Law, 1961,* pp. 167–69.

————"Remarks in Connection with the Report of Working Group No. 1." *Fourth Colloquium on Law of Outer Space,* IISL, Washington, 1961, pp. 352–60.

————"The Freedom of Outer Space: Some Problems of Sovereignty, Control, and Jurisdiction." *Proceedings of the Conference on the Law of Space and Satellite Communications,* Northwestern University Law School, Chicago, May 1963 (NASA SP-44, 1964), pp. 34–44. Comments by Beresford and Cohen, pp. 45–57.

————"The Developing Law of Space Activities," 3 *Virginia Journal of International Law* 75–100 (1963).

Kislov, A. K. and Krylov, S. B. "State Sovereignty in Airspace," 2 *International Affairs* (Moscow) 35–44 (March 1956). Reprinted in 1961 Senate Symposium, pp. 1037–46.

Kopal, V. "Two Problems of Outer Space Control: The Delimitation of Outer Space and the Legal Ground for Outer Space Flights," *Third Colloquium on Law of Outer Space,* IISL, Stockholm, 1960, pp. 107–12. Reprinted in *1961 Senate Symposium,* "Sovereignty of States and Legal Status of Outer Space." pp. 1118–1126.

Korovin, E. A. "International Status of Cosmic Space," 5 *International Affairs* (Moscow) 53–59 (January 1959). Reprinted in *1961 Senate Symposium,* pp. 1062–71.

————, Osnitskaya, G. A., Zadorozhnyy, G. P., and Zhukov, G. P. "Conquest of Outer Space and Some Problems of International Relations," 5 *International Affairs* (Moscow) 88–96 (November 1959). Reprinted in *1961 Senate Symposium,* pp. 1072–84.

Kovalev, F. N., and Cheprov, I. I. "National Aerospace Sovereignty," chapter 1, pp. 23–73 (Russian text), pp. 17–55 (English translation) in *Na Puti k Kosmoche-*

skomu Pravu ("The Way to Space Law"). Moscow: Institut Mezhdunarodnykh Otnoshenij (Institute of International Relations), 1962.

Larsen, P. B. "Space Activities and Their Effect on International Civil Aviation." *Ninth Colloquium on Law of Outer Space,* IISL, Madrid, 1966, pp. 159–67.

Latchford, S. "Freedom of the Air: Early Theories: Freedom, Zone, Sovereignty," in *Documents and State Papers,* Vol. 1, pp. 303–22 (1948). Reprinted in *1961 Senate Symposium,* pp. 1219–45.

————"The Bearing of International Air Navigation Conventions on the Use of Outer Space," 53 *American Journal of International Law* 405–11, (April 1959). Reprinted in *1961 Senate Symposium,* pp. 493–99.

Leopold, G. V., and Scafuri, A. L. "Orbital and Super-Orbital Space Flight Trajectories—Jurisdictional Touchstones for a United Nations Space Authority," 36 *University of Detroit Law Journal* 514–34 (June 1959). Reprinted in *1961 Senate Symposium,* pp. 520–39.

McDougal, M. S. "The Emerging Customary Law of Space," *Proceedings of the Conference on the Law of Space and Satellite Communications,* Northwestern University Law School, Chicago, May 1963 (NASA SP-44, 1964), pp. 2–28. Comment by Christol, pp. 28–33.

————, Laswell, H. D., and Vlasic, J. A. "Claims Relating to Access and Competence in Outer Space," chapter 3, pp. 193–359; "Claims Relating to Jurisdiction over Space Activities and Spacecraft," chapter 6, pp. 646–748 in *Law and Public Order in Space,* New Haven, Conn.: Yale University Press, 1963.

————and Lipson, L. "Perspectives for a Law of Outer Space," 52 *American Journal of International Law* 407–31 (July 1958). Reprinted in 1961 *Senate Symposium,* pp. 410–31.

McMahon, J. F. "The Legal Aspects of Outer Space: The Problem of Sovereignty," 18 *World Today* 328–34 (August 1962).

————"Legal Aspects of Outer Space," 38 *British Yearbook of International Law* (London) 339–99 (1962).

Machowski, J. "The Legal Status of Unmanned Space Vehicles." *Second Colloquium on Law of Outer Space,* London, 1959, pp. 111–19. Reprinted in *1961 Senate Symposium,* pp. 1204–12.

————"Selected Problems on National Sovereignty with Reference to the Law of Outer Space." *Proceedings of the American Society of International Law,* 1961, pp. 169–74.

————"Certain Aspects of the Question of Innocent Passage of Space Vehicles." *Fourth Colloquium on Law of Outer Space,* IISL, Washington, 1961, pp. 57–69.

Markov, M. G. "Kvoprosu O Granicach Vozdusnoj Territorii V Mezdunarodnom Prave" ("On the Question of the Boundaries of Air Space in International Law"), 31

Sovetskoe Gosudarstvo i Pravo (Soviet State and Law) (Moscow) pp. 95–102 (August 1961).

Menter, M. "Astronautical Law." Thesis, Industrial College of the Armed Forces, Fort McNair, Washington, D.C., May 1959, 94 p. (Thesis No. 86). Reprinted in *1961 Senate Symposium,* pp. 349–97.

Meyer, A. "Legal Problems of Flight into the Outer Space," Address to Third International Astronautical Congress, Stuttgart, September 5, 1952. Reprinted in *1961 Senate Symposium,* pp. 8–19.

————"Legal Problems of Outer Space." *1961 Senate Symposium,* pp. 500–10.

————"Airspace Sovereignty and Outer Space Developments: Comments on the Article of Professor Cooper, The Chicago Convention—After 20 Years" (in German and English), 14 *Zeitschrift für Luftrecht und Weltraumrechtsfragen* (Cologne) 296–311 (October 1965).

Milde, M. "Considerations on Legal Problems of Space Above National Territories," 5 *Review of Contemporary Law* (Brussels) 5-22 (June, 1958). Excerpt reprinted in *1961 Senate Symposium,* pp. 1102–08.

Osnitskaya, A. G. (same as A. Galina). "Some Legal Aspects of Flights in Outer Space: On the Question of Interplanetary Law." *1961 Senate Symposium,* pp. 1051–58.

————"International Law Problems of the Conquest of Space." *1961 Senate Symposium,* pp. 1088–94.

Pepin, E. "The Legal Status of the Airspace in the Light of Progress in Aviation and Astronautics," 3 *McGill Law Journal* 70–77 (Autumn 1956). Reprinted in *1961 Senate Symposium,* pp. 188–94.

————"Legal Problems Created by the Sputnik," 4 *McGill Law Journal* 66–71 (Autumn 1957). Reprinted in *1961 Senate Symposium,* pp. 182–87.

————"Space Penetration (Recent Technological Developments: Political and Legal Implications for the International Community)." *Proceedings of the American Society of International Law,* 1958, pp. 229–36. Reprinted in *1961 Senate Symposium,* pp. 232–38.

Quigg, P. W. "Open Skies and Open Space," 37 *Foreign Affairs* 95–106 (October 1958). Reprinted in *1961 Senate Symposium,* pp. 463–71.

Reintanz, G. "Air Space and Outer Space." *1961 Senate Symposium,* pp. 1134–40.

Roberts, C. A. "Outer Space and National Sovereignty," 12 *Air University Quarterly Review* 53–65 (Spring (1960).

Schrader, G. D. National Sovereignty in Space, 27–100–17 *Military Law Review* 41–81 (July 1962). Reprinted in *Proceedings of Fifth Colloquium on Law of Outer Space,* IISL, Varna, 1962, 40 p.

Seara Vasquez, M. "The Functional Regulation of the Extra-Atmospheric Space." *Second Colloquium on Law of Outer Space,* London, 1959, pp. 139–46.

Smirnoff, M. "The Need for a New System of Norms for Space Law and the Danger of Conflict with the Terms of the Chicago Convention." *First Colloquium on Law of Outer Space,* The Hague, 1958, pp. 105–109.

Strauss, W. S. *Air Law and Treaties of the World,* Senate Committee on Commerce, 89th Congress, 1st Session, July 1, 1965, 3 vols., 4483 p. (Washington, D.C., GPO, 1965).

Szutucki, J. "Security of Nations and Cosmic Space." *1961 Senate Symposium,* pp. 1164–1203.

————"On the So-Called Upper Limit of National Sovereignty." *Fifth Colloquium on Law of Outer Space,* IISL, Varna, 1962, 11 p.

Taubenfeld, H. J. "Regime for Outer Space," 56 *Northwestern University Law Review* 129–67, (March/April 1961).

————"Status of Competing Claims to Use of Outer Space: An American Point of View." *Proceedings of 57th Annual Meeting of American Society of International Law,* 1963, pp. 173–86. Revised at pp. 141–60 in *Space Law and Society.* New York: Oceana Publications, 1964.

————and Jessup, P. C. "International Controls for Outer Space," Part III, chapter 7–9, pp. 194–282 in *Controls for Outer Space and The Antarctic Analogy,* New York: Columbia University Press, 1959.

Woetzel, R. K. "Sovereignty and Sovereign Rights in Outer Space and on Celestial Bodies." *Fifth Colloquium on Law of Outer Space,* IISL, Varna, 1962, 44 p.

Yeager, P. B., and Stark, J. R. "Decatur's Doctrine—A Code for Outer Space?" 83 *U.S. Naval Institute Proceedings* 931–37 (September 1957). Reprinted in *1961 Senate Symposium,* pp. 156–63.

Young, R. W. "The Aerial Inspection Plan and Air Space Sovereignty," 23 *George Washington Law Review* 565–89, (April 1956). Reprinted in *1961 Senate Symposium,* pp. 46–64.

Zadorozhnyi, G. P. "Artificial Satellite and International Law," Translation T-78, No. 12, Santa Monica, California: the RAND Corporation, 1957, 5 p. Reprinted in *1961 Senate Symposium,* pp. 1047–49.

Zhukov, G. P. "Problems of Space Law at the Present Stage," *Fifth Colloquium on Law of Outer Space,* IISL, Varna, 1962, 37 p.

————"Freedom of Space and Its Limits." *Sixth Colloquium on Law of Outer Space,* IISL, Paris, 1963, 7 p.

————"The Problem of the Definition of Outer Space." Paper presented to the Scientific-Legal Liaison Committee of the International Institute of Space Law and the Academy of Astronautics, Congress of the International Astronautical Society, Belgrade, September 26, 1967, 7 p. mimeo.

Zourek, J. "Jaky je Pravni Rezim Vesmiru?" ("What is the Legal Status of the Universe?") 3 *Casopis pro Mezinarodni Pravo* (Journal of International Law), Prague 35–43 (January 1959). Reprinted in *1961 Senate Symposium,* pp. 1109–17.

Assistance, Rescue, and Return of Astronauts and Spacecraft

Berger, H. "Legal Elements of Astronaut and Space Vehicle Assistance and Return and Liability for Damage," 28 *Shingle* 81–84 (April 1965).

————"Space Vehicles and Astronaut Assistance and Liability for Damages." *Eighth Colloquium on Law of Outer Space,* Athens, 1965, pp. 10–14.

Cheprov, I. I. "Legal Regulation of Activity in Outer Space (Rescue and Return of Cosmonauts and Space Vehicles)," pp. 47–73 (English Translation) in *Kosmos i Mezhdunarodnoye Sotrundnichestvo* (Space and International Cooperation). A Symposium: Committee on Legal Problems of Outer Space of the Academy of Sciences, USSR, Moscow: Publishing Office of the Institute of International Relations, 1963. 256 p.

Dembling, P. G., and Arons, D. M. "Space Law and the United Nations: The Work of the Legal Subcommittee of the United Nations Committee on the Peaceful Uses of Outer Space," 32 *Journal of Air Law and Commerce* 329–49 (Summer 1966).

————"The Treaty on Rescue and Return of Astronauts and Space Objects," 9 *William and Mary Law Review* 630–63 (Spring 1968).

Doolittle, J. W. "Man in Space: the Rescue and Return of Downed Astronauts," Remarks in Panel of the Developing Aerospace Law of American Bar Association, Section on International and Comparative Law, Honolulu, Hawaii, August 8, 1967, published in Supplement to Air Force Policy Letter for Commanders, No. 9–1967, pp. 21–24, (September 1967).

Finch, K. A. "Extension of Remarks." *Sixth Colloquium on Law and Outer Space,* IISL, Paris, 1963, pp. 31–37.

Goedhuis, D. "Assistance to and Rescue of Astronauts and Space Vehicles in Distress." *Reports, International Law Association,* Tokyo, 1964, Annex IV, pp. 94–101.

Haley, A. G. "Space Salvage—Artifacts and Personnel in Space and on Terrestial Jurisdiction." *Eighth Colloquium on Law of Outer Space,* IISL, Athens, 1965, pp. 119–30.

Ivanyi, J. "Convention on International Cooperation for Rescue—a Timely Problem of Law Making for Outer Space." *Sixth Colloquium on Law of Outer Space,* IISL, Paris, 1963, 4 p.

————"Sauvetage des Astronauts en Détresse avec la Cooperation des Services de Telecommunication" ("Rescue of Astronauts in Distress by Cooperation of Telecommunications Services"), 31 *Journal des Telecommunications* (Telecommunications Journal, Geneva) 134–36 (May 1964).

Ivanyi, J., Misur, G., and Partli, I. "Draft Rules on International Cooperation for Rescue of Astronauts and Space Vehicles in Distress." *Sixth Colloquium on Law of Outer Space,* IISL, Paris, 1963, 4 p.

Krivickas, D. and Rusis, A. "Preparation of International Agreements on Assistance and Return of Space Vehicles and International Liability," pp. 509–21, 525, in "Soviet Space Programs, 1962–1965: Goals and Purposes, Achievements, Plans, and International Implications," *Staff Report, Senate Committee on Aeronautical and Space Sciences,* 89th Congress, 2d Session, December 30, 1966.

Osnitskaya, G. A. "International Law Problems of the Conquest of Space," *1961 Senate Symposium,* pp. 1088–94.

Rudolf, A. "Müssen in Fremden Staatsgebieten Niegergegangene Unbemannte Raumfahrzeuge Oder Teile Davon Zuruckgegeben Werden?" (Must Unmanned Spacecraft or Parts Thereof Which Fall on Foreign Territory Be Returned?) 9 *Zeitschrift für Luftrecht und Weltraumrechtsfragen* (Cologne) 273-86, (October 1960).

Vasilevskaya, E. G. "Aid to Crews of Space Vehicles in Distress," *Sixth Colloquium on Law of Outer Space,* IISL, Paris, 1963, 7 p.

————"International Law Problems of the Guarantee of Security of Flights in Outer Space," Chapter III, pp. 63–100 in *Kosmos i Problema Vseobschego Mira* (Space and Problems of a General Peace). Moskva: Institut Gosudarstva i Pravo, Akademiya Nauk SSSR, 1966 (Moscow, Institute of State and Law, Soviet Academy of Sciences), 195 p.

Winchester, J. H. "Space Rescue," 9 *NATO's Fifteen Nations* 24–32 (December 1964/January 1965).

Zhukov, G. P. "Problems of Space Law at the Present Stage." Memorandum, *Fifth Colloquium on Law of Outer Space,* IISL, Varna, 1962, 37 p.

————"Mezhdunarodnoye Sotrudnichestvo po Spaseniju Kosmonavtov" (International Cooperation for the Rescue of Cosmonauts), 47 *Avieciju i Kosmonavtika* (Aviation and Astronautics, Moscow) 41–44 (October 1964).

Comments on Soviet and East Bloc Space Law Writings

Chiu, H. "Communist China and the Law of Outer Space," 16 *International and Comparative Law Quarterly* 1135–38 (October 1967).

Christensen, R. A. "Soviet Views on Space Law: A Comparative and Critical Analysis." Paper, American Rocket Society Space Flight Rep. 1961, 33 p.

Cox, D. W. "A Comparison of US and USSR Views on Space Law." Thesis, Air War College, Air University, Maxwell AFB (January 1963), 68 p.

Crane, R. D. "Guides to the Study of Communist Views on the Legal Problems of Space Exploration and a Bibliography." *1961 Senate Symposium,* pp. 1011–36.

————"Soviet Attitude toward International Space Law," 56 *American Journal of International Law* (Washington) 685-723 (July 1962).

————"The Beginnings of Marxist Space Jurisprudence," *American Journal of International Law* (Washington) 616–25 (July, 1963).

————"Basic Principles in Soviet Space Law: Peaceful Cooperation, and Disarmament," 29 *Law and Contemporary Problems* (Durham, N.C.) 943–55 (Autumn 1964).

Kehrberger, H. P. "Rechtsfragen der Eroberung des Weltraums im Osteuropaischen Schrifttum" (Legal Questions of the Conquest of Outer Space in the East-European Literature), 4 *Die Wichtigsten Gesetzgebungsakte in den Landern Ost-Sudost-Europas und in den Ostasiatischen Volksdemokratien* (The Most Important Statutes in the Countries of East and Southeastern Europe and in the East Asia Peoples Democracy), (Hamburg) 162–73 (September 1962). Includes a bibliography.

Kos-Rabcewicz-Zubkowski, L. "Los Puntos de Vista Sovieticos Sobre el Derecho Internacional del Espacio" (The Soviet Standpoints on the International Law of Space), 16 *Boletin del Instituto de Derecho Comparado de Mexico* (Mexico) 597–610 (September/December 1963).

————"La Notion Sovietique du Droit International Spatial" (The Soviet Concept of International Space Law), 19 *Revue Française de Droit Aérien* (Paris) 190–200 (April/June 1965).

Krivickas, D., and Rusis, N. "Soviet Attitude towards Space Law," chapter 6, pp. 493–528 in "Soviet Space Programs, 1962–1965, Goals and Purposes, Achievements, Plans, and International Implications," *Staff Report Senate Committee on Aeronautical and Space Sciences,* 89th Congress, 2d Session, December 30, 1966.

Kucherov, S. "Legal Problems of Outer Space: U.S. and Soviet Viewpoints," *Second Colloquium of Law of Outer Space,* London, 1959, pp. 64–74.

————"The USSR and Sovereignty in Outer Space," 12 *Bulletin of the Institute for the Study of the USSR* (Munich) 25–33 (1965).

Lipson, L. "The USSR and Outer Space," 9 *Problems of Communism* 70–71 (September/October 1960).

Meyer, A. "Die Rechtsprobleme des Weltraums unter Berucksichtigung von Stellungnaman der Vereinigten Staaten von Amerika und der Sowjetunion" (Legal Problems of Outer Space in the Light of U.S. and Soviet Statements), 10 *Aussenpolitik Zietschrift für Internationale Fragen* (Stuttgart) 645–53 (1959).

Neumann, H. G. "The Legal Status of Outer Space and the Soviet Union, Air Intelligence Information Report," IR 1184–57 (February 18, 1957). Reprinted in *1959 Senate Symposium,* pp. 495–503.

Rehm, G. W. "Einige Volkerrechtliche Betrachtungen zum Sowjetischen Souveranitatsanspruch im luftraum" (Some Observations in International Law with Regard to the

Soviet Claim of Sovereignty in Air Space), 8 *Zeitschrift fuer Luftrecht und Weltraumrechtsfragen* 174–82 (1959).

———"Sowjetunion und Weltraum" (The Soviet Union and Outer Space), 5 *Osteuropa-Recht* 99–103 (October 1959).

Sand, P. H. "Die Entwicklung des Luftfahrrechts in der Sowjetunion" (The Development of Air Navigation Law in the Soviet Union), 10 *Osteuropa-Recht* 157–210 (September 1964).

Swatkowski, A. "The Soviet Attitude on Outer Space," 9 *Problems of Communism* 19–24 (May/June 1960).

Woetzel, R. K. "Comments on U.S. and Soviet Viewpoints Regarding the Legal Aspects of Military Use of Outer Space," *Proceedings of the American Society of International Law* (Washington) 195–203 (1963).

———"Legal Aspects of Military Use of Space" in *Soviet and American Essays, Space and Society,* edited by H. J. Taubenfeld (New York: Oceana Publications, 1964) 121–40.

Copyright and Patent Rights in the Space Age

Alnutt, R. F. "Patent Policy for Communications Satellites: A Unique Variation," 46 *Marquette Law Review* 63–78 (Summer 1962).

Alnutt, R. F. and O'Brien, G. D. "Patents and the Public Interest: Developments and Trends in the Space Age," 6 *South Texas Law Journal* 67–76 (Spring 1962).

Behr, O. M. "Relay by Communications Satellites: A Special Situation in Copyright Infringement," 31 *Journal of Air Law and Commerce* 311–26 (Autumn 1965).

Dembling, P. G. "Patent Provisions of the National Aeronautical and Space Act of 1958." Conference on Space Technology: Discovery, Identification, and Protection of New Ideas: A Joint Presentation by University of California, Los Angeles, September 30, 1960, and University of Oklahoma, Norman, October 3, 1960.

Doctors, S. I. "Transfer of Space Technology to the American Consumer: The Effect of NASA Patent Policy," 52 *Minnesota Law Review* 789–818 (March 1968).

Herbert, H. A. "Property Rights in Inventions Useful in Space Under Department of Defense Contracts." Conference on Space Technology: Discovery, Identification, and Protection of New Ideas; A Joint Presentation by University of California, Los Angeles, September 30, 1960, and University of Oklahoma, Norman, October 3, 1960.

Johnson, J. A. "Rights to Inventions under NASA Contracts," 21 *Federal Bar Journal* 37–49 (Winter 1961).

Maltby, W. R. "The National Aeronautics and Space Act of 1958 Patent Provisions," 27 *George Washington Law Review* 49–75 (October 1958).

O'Brien, G. D. "The Patent Provisions of the National Aeronautics and Space Act of 1958," 41 *Journal of the Patent Office Society* 651–55 (September 1959).

O'Brien, G. D. and Parker, G. "Property Rights in Inventions under the National Aeronautics and Space Act of 1958," 19 *Federal Bar Journal* 255–67 (July 1959).

Criminal Law and Space Activities

Delmas Saint-Hilaire, J. P. "Reflexions sur le droit penal aérien et de l'espace" (Reflections on Penal Air and Space Law), 28 *Revue Générale de l'Air* (Paris) 84–91 (January 1965).

Fasan, E., and Gross, F. "Zivil und Strafrecht im Weltraum" (Civil Law and Penal Law in Outer Space), 10 *Zeitschrift für Luftrecht und Weltraumrechtsfragen* 106–109 (April 1961).

Glaser, Stefan, " 'Aggression spatiale' à la lumiere du droit international penal" ("Space Aggression" in the Light of International Penal Law), 77 *Schweizerische Zeitschrift für Strafrecht* (Bern) 129–61 (1961).

Haughney, E. W. "Criminal Responsibility in Outer Space," *Proceedings of the Conference on Space Science and Space Law,* University of Oklahoma, Norman, June 20, 1963, pp. 146–50.

McDougal, M. S., Lasswell, H. D., and Vlasic, I. A. "Claims Relating to Jurisdiction over Space Activities and Spacecraft," chapter 6, esp. pp. 695–704, in *Law and Public Order in Space,* New Haven, Conn.: Yale University Press, 1963.

Legal Status of Astronauts, Space Vehicles, and Space Stations

Bauza-Araujo, Alvaro. "Hacia un Derecho Astronautico: Problemas Juridicas que Originaran los Satelites Artificiales, Astronaves y Bases Especiales" (Towards Astronautical Law: Legal Problems Created by Artificial Satellites, Space Ships and Space Platforms), Montevideo, 1957, 223 p.

Bueckling, A. "Die Rechtsstellung Kunstlicher Erdsatalliten" (The Legal Status of Artificial Earth Satellites), 15 *Osterreichische Juristen-Zeitung* (Vienna) 533–37 (October 21, 1960).

Chandrasekharan, M. "The Gemini Program and the Manned Orbiting Laboratory in Space: An Appraisal," 5 *Indian Journal of International Law* (New Delhi) 334–41 (July 1965).

Christol, C. Q. "Space Stations—A Lawyer's Point of View," 4 *Indian Journal of International Law* (New Delhi), 488–99 (October 1964).

Cocca, A. A. "El Jurista Frente al Astronauta: Diferencia en la Naturaleza Juridica del Cohete y del Proyectil Teleguiado" (The Lawyer vis-à-vis the Astronaut: Difference in Legal Nature of the Rocket and the Guided Missile) 3 *Fuerza Aerea* 67–110 (1956).

———"Legal Status of the Astronaut." *Fourth Collo-*

quium on Law of Outer Space, IISL, Washington, 1961, pp. 138–52.

Cooper, J. C. "Legal Problems of Spacecraft in Airspace," *Festschrift Riese* 465–74 (1964).

————Replies to Questionnaires on "The Legal Regime of Outer Space," "The Legal Status of Space Vehicles," "Rules of Liability for Injury or Loss Caused by Space Vehicles," *ILA Space Law Report,* 1964, pp. 29–33, 67–70, 85–95.

————"The Manned Orbiting Laboratory: A Major Legal and Political Decision," 51 *American Bar Association Journal* 1137–40 (1965).

Haley, A. B. "Legal Problems of Manned Lunar International Laboratory." *Seventh Colloquium on Law of Outer Space,* IISL, Warsaw, 1964, pp. 62–116.

————"Space Vehicle Regulations," chapter 7, pp. 136–59 in *Space Law and Government.* New York: Meredith, 1963.

Hall, R. C. "Comments on Traffic Control of Space Vehicles," 31 *Journal of Air Law and Commerce* (Chicago) 327–42 (Autumn 1965).

————Comments on Salvage and Removal of Man-made Objects from Outer Space." *Ninth Colloquium on Law of Outer Space,* IISL, Madrid, 1966, pp. 117–26.

Horsford, C. E. S. "The Need for a Moon Treaty and Clarification of the Legal Status of Space Vehicles." *Ninth Colloquium on Law of Outer Space,* IISL, Madrid, 1966, pp. 48–49.

Jennings, R. Y. "The Legal Status of Space Vehicles," *Report, International Law Association,* Tokyo, 1964, pp. 61–68. Reply comments by: Cooper, Huber, Pepin, Guerreri, Zylicz, pp. 69–76.

Kopal, V. "Some Problems of the Present Space Legal Terminology." *Ninth Colloquium on Law of Outer Space,* IISL, Madrid, 1966, pp. 145–47.

Lopez-Gutierrez, J. J. "Legal Status of Space Vehicles: Nationality (Unilateral Decisions) v. Internationality (Multilateral Operation)." *Ninth Colloquium on Law of Outer Space,* IISL, Madrid, 1966, pp. 132–42.

Lyon, J. T. "Space Vehicles, Satellites and the Law," 7 *McGill Law Journal* (Montreal) 271–86 (June 1961).

Machowski, J. "The Legal Status of Unmanned Space Vehicles." *Second Colloquium on Law of Outer Space,* London, 1959, pp. 111–19. Reprinted in *1961 Senate Symposium,* pp. 1204–12.

Mankiewicz, R. H. "Legal Regime and Conditions for the Use of Space Vehicles," 7 *Review of Contemporary Law: Law in the Service of Peace* (Brussels) 22–50 (December 1960).

Meyer, A. "The Interpretation of the Term 'Peaceful' with Regard to the Announcement of President Johnson To Establish 'Military Manned Orbiting Laboratories' (MOLS)," 15 *Zeitschrift für Luftrecht und Weltraumrechtsfragen* 36–39 (January 1966).

Reed, W. D. "Nationality of Spacecraft," McGill University, Institute of Air and Space Law, Montreal, LL.M. thesis, 1963, 40 p.

Schweickhardt, A. "Report of the Legal Committee . . . Spacecraft," 32 *International Air Transport Association Bulletin* 88–92 (1964).

Sztucki, J. "Some Preliminary Problems of the Legal Status of Space Objects." *Eighth Colloquium on Law of Outer Space,* IISL, Athens, 1965, pp. 444–55.

————"Legal Status of Space Objects." *Ninth Colloquium on Law of Outer Space,* IISL, Madrid, 1966, pp. 108–116.

Verplaetse, J. G. "On the Definition and Legal Status of Space Craft," 29 *Journal of Air Law and Commerce* (Chicago) 131–40 (Spring 1963).

Zylicz, M. "Sytuacja prawna statku przestrzeni—skrot referatu wygloszonego w pta dn 30, IV, 1957" (The Legal Status of Space Craft; Summary of a Report at the PTA [Polish Astronautical Society] April 30, 1957), 7 *Biuletyn Informacyjny Polskiego Towarzystwa Astronautycznego* (Warsaw) 14–20 (July 1957).

Legal Status of Celestial Bodies

Brooks, E. "National Control of Natural Planetary Bodies, Preliminary Considerations," 32 *Journal of Air Law and Commerce* 315–28 (Summer 1966).

————"Ingredients of an International Planetary Organization." *Ninth Colloquium on Law of Outer Space,* IISL, Madrid, 1966, pp. 17–43.

Cocca, A. A. "Legal Status of Celestial Bodies and Economic Status of the Celestial Products." *Seventh Colloquium on Law of Outer Space,* IISL, Warsaw, 1964, pp. 15–23.

————"Basic Statute of the Moon and Heavenly Bodies." *Fifth Colloquium on Law of Outer Space,* IISL, Varna, 1962, 5 p.

Cooper, J. C. "Who Will Own the Moon: The Need for an Answer," 32 *Journal of Air Law and Commerce* 155–66 (Spring 1966)

Csabafi, I. "Selected Chapters from Space Law in Making: The Status of Celestial Bodies." *Seventh Colloquium on Law of Outer Space,* IISL, Warsaw, 1964, pp. 176–85.

Fasan, E. "The Legal Nature of Celestial Bodies." *Fourth Colloquium on Law of Outer Space,* IISL, Washington, 1961, pp. 267–93.

————"Law and Peace for Celestial Bodies." *Fifth Colloquium on Law of Outer Space,* IISL, Varna, 1962, 14 p.

————"Basic Principles Regarding the Celestial Bodies." *Sixth Colloquium on Law of Outer Space,* IISL, Paris, 1963, 8 p.

Finch, K. A. "Territorial Claims to Celestial Bodies." Paper presented to *Second Colloquium on Law of Outer Space,* London, 1959, 58 p. Printed in *Sixth Colloquium on Law of Outer Space,* IISL, Paris, 1963, 58 p. Revised article reprinted in *1961 Senate Symposium,* pp. 626–36.

Haley, A. G. "Sovereignty Over Celestial Bodies," Chapter 5, pp. 118–35 in *Space Law and Government*. New York: Appleton-Century-Crofts, 1963.

Ikeda, F. "The Legal Status of Planets," 5 *Japanese Annual of International Law* 25–30 (1961).

Kiss, J. "The Law of Outer Space and Celestial Bodies in the Legal Order of International Space." *Sixth Colloquium on Law of Outer Space*, IISL, Paris, 1963, 7 p.

_____"General Principles for International Law of Celestial Bodies." *Seventh Colloquium on Law of Outer Space* IISL, Warsaw, 1964, pp. 287–91.

_____"Moon Charter." *Eighth Colloquium on Law of Outer Space*, IISL, Athens, 1965, pp. 234–38.

Knauth, A. W. "If We Land There Soon Who Owns the Moon?" 45 *American Bar Association Journal* 14–16 (January 1959).

Kopal, V. "Pronikani do vesmiru a mezinarodni pavo. Z jakych zasad bude vychazet pravni rezim mesice a dalsich dosazenych kosmickych teles?" (Space Penetration and International Law. What Will Be the Legal Status of the Moon and Other Celestial Bodies?) 4 *Mezinarodni Politika* (International Politics) (Prague) 242–46 (April 1960).

Markov, M. G. "Moon Landing and International Law." *Sixth Colloquium on Law of Outer Space*, IISL, Paris, 1963. Printed in 3 Diritto Aeroeo 23–46 (1964).

_____"La Lune et le droit international" (The Moon and International Law), 68 *Revue Générale de Droit International Public* (Paris) 413–45 (April/June 1964).

Menter, M. "Jurisdiction Over Landmasses in Space." *Fourth Colloquium on Law of Outer Space*, IISL, 1961, Washington, pp. 294–310. Reprinted in 32 United States Air Force Judge Advocate General Bulletin 34–46 (1962).

Osnitskaya, G. A. "The Doctrine of International Law and Space Conquest," pp. 71–91 (English translation) in *Kosmos i Mezhdunarodnoye Pravo* (Space and International Law). A Symposium by Committee on Legal Problems of Outer Space of the Academy of Science of the USSR. Moscow: Publishing Office of Institute of International Relations, 1962.

Rehm, G. W. "Gebietserwerb im Weltraum" (Acquisition of Territory in Outer Space) 9 *Zeitschrift für Luftrecht und Weltraumrechtsfragen* (Cologne) 1–10 (January 1960).

Smirnoff, M. S. "The Legal Status of Celestial Bodies," 28 *Journal of Air Law and Commerce* 385–404 (Autumn 1961–62).

_____Reports of the Chairman of the IISL's Working Group III on The Legal Status of Celestial Bodies (includes comments by working group members and select bibliography). *Fourth Colloquium on Law of Outer Space*, IISL, Washington, 1961, pp. 361–391; *Fifth Colloquium on Law of Outer Space*, IISL, Varna, 1962, 20 p.; *Sixth Colloquium on Law of Outer Space*, IISL, Paris,

1963, 11 p.; *Seventh Colloquium on Law of Outer Space*, IISL, Warsaw, 1964, pp. 347–360; *Eighth Colloquium on Law of Outer Space*, IISL, Athens, 1965, pp. 464–473; *Ninth Colloquium on Law of Outer Space*, IISL, Madrid, 1966, pp. 8–16, 44–49, 54–65.

Sontag, P. M. "Der Erwerb von Hoheitsrechten im Weltraum und Auf Himmelskorpern" (The Acquisition of Territorial Rights in Outer Space and on Celestial Bodies), 1964 *Jahrbuch für Internationales Recht* (Kiel, Hamburg) 272–300 (1965).

Tunkin, G. "Le droit international des espaces célestes: Observations" (The International Law of Outer Space: Observations), 50 *Annuaire de l'Institut de Droit International* (Brussels) 484–89 (1963).

Verplaetse, J. G. "Can Individual Nations Obtain Sovereignty Over Celestial Bodies?" *Fourth Colloquium on Law of Outer Space*, IISL, Washington, 1961, pp. 311–328.

Woetzel, R. K. "Sovereignty and Sovereign Rights in Outer Space and on Celestial Bodies." *Fifth Colloquium on Law of Outer Space*, IISL, Varna, 1962, 44 p.

Yaeger, P. B. "The Moon—Can Earth Claim It?" *1961 Senate Symposium*, pp. 757–63.

Zadorozhnyi, G. P. "Fundamental Problems of the Science of Space Law," pp. 17–70 (English translation) in *Kosmos i Mezhdunarodnove Pravo* (Space and International Law). A Symposium by Committee on Legal Problems of Outer Space of the Academy of Science of the USSR. Moscow: Publishing Office of Institute of International Relations, 1962.

Liability for Damages Caused by Space Activities

Beresford, S. M. "Liability for Ground Damages Caused by Spacecraft," 19 *Federal Bar Journal* 242–54 (July 1959). Reprinted in *1961 Senate Symposium*, pp. 540–52.

_____"Principles for Spacecraft Liability." *Third Colloquium on Law of Outer Space*, IISL, Stockholm, 1960, pp. 152–57.

_____"Requirements for an International Convention on Spacecraft Liability." *Sixth Colloquium on Law of Outer Space*, IISL, Paris, 1963, 12 p.

Berezowski, C. "Rules of Liability for Injury or Loss Caused by the Operation of Space Vehicles." *Reports, International Law Association*, Brussels, 1962, pp. 96–100.

_____"Rules of Liability for Injury or Loss Caused by the Operation of Space Vehicles." *Reports, International Law Association*, Tokyo, 1964, pp. 77–83. Replies by: Bodenschatz, Cooper, Guerreri, Pepin, pp. 84–90.

_____"Responsabilité Resultant d'Activites Spatiales" (Responsibility Resulting from Activities in Space). *Eighth Colloquium on Law of Outer Space*, IISL, Athens, 1965, pp. 131–37. Comments on report by: Cooper, Pelegri, Verplaetse, pp. 138–42.

Berger, H. "Some Aspects of Civil Liability for Space Craft and Vehicle Accidents," 33 *Pennsylvania Bar Association Quarterly* 301–305 (March 1962).

————"Space Vehicle Accidents and Civil Liability under American Law." *Fifth Colloquium on Law of Outer Space,* Varna, 1962, 12 p.

Bodenschatz, M. "Proposals Relating to an International Convention Concerning the Liability for Damage Caused by Space Vehicles, with a View, in Particular, to the Activities of Private Operators." *Eighth Colloquium on Law of Outer Space,* Athens, 1965, pp. 15–22.

Bourley, M. G. "International Organizations for Cooperation in Space and the Problem of Liability for Space Activity." *Eighth Colloquium on Law of Outer Space,* IISL, Athens, 1965, pp. 1–10.

Bueckling, A. "Staatshaftung fuer Raumfahrtschaden (Government Liability for Space Damages), 17 *Neue Juristische Wochenschrift* (Munich) 527–30 (1964).

Cooper, J. C. "Memorandum of Suggestions for an International Convention on Third Party Damage Caused by Space Vehicles." *Third Colloquium on Law of Outer Space,* IISL, Stockholm, 1960, pp. 141–44. Reprinted in *1961 Senate Symposium,* pp. 680–83.

————"Liability for Space Damage—United Nations— The Rome Convention." *Eighth Colloquium on Law of Outer Space,* IISL, Athens, 1965, pp. 172–77.

Csabafi, I. "The Question of International Responsibility of States Before the U.N. Committee on the Peaceful Uses of Outer Space and Some Suggestions." *Sixth Colloquium on Law of Outer Space,* IISL, Paris, 1963, 22 p.

————"Space Legal Liability." *Eighth Colloquium on Law of Outer Space,* Athens, 1965, pp. 103–15.

Dembling, P. G., and Arons, D. M. "Space Law and the United Nations: The Work of the Legal Subcommittee of the United Nations Committee on the Peaceful Uses of Outer Space," 32 *Journal of Air Law and Commerce* 329–38, 349–86 (Summer 1966).

Fitzgerald, F. G. "Participation of International Organizations in the Proposed International Agreements on Liability for Damage Caused by Objects Launched into Outer Space," 3 *Canadian Yearbook of International Law,* 265–80 (1965).

Goldie, L. F. E. "Some Problems of Liability Arising Out of Space Activities." *Sixth Colloquium on Law of Outer Space,* IISL, Paris, 1963, 27 p.

————"Liability for Damage and the Progressive Development of International Law," 14 *International and Comparative Law Quarterly* 1189–1264 (1965).

Guerreri, G. "Interference Between Aircraft and Space Vehicles and Liability Thereof." Paper, International Law Association, Hamburg, 1960, 11 p.

Gutteridge, J. A. C. "Responsibility for Damage Caused by Objects Launched into Outer Space." Brit. Inst. Internat'l & Comp. Law, Spec. Pub. No. 9, 35 (1966).

Haley, A. G. "Space Vehicle Torts," 36 *University of Detroit Law Journal* 294–314 (February 1959).

————"Liability for Personal and Property Damages in Space Activities," Chapter 8, pp. 233–73 in *Space Law and Government.* New York: Meredith Publishing Company 1963.

Herczeg, I. "Some Legal Problems of Liability in Connection with Outer Space Activities." *Eighth Colloquium on Law of Outer Space,* IISL, Athens, 1965, pp. 229–33.

————"The Exploration of Outer Space and the Safety of States." *Fifth Colloquium on Law of Outer Space,* IISL, Varna, 1962, 4 p.

Horsford, C. E. S. "Legal Liability in Space: An English View," 17 *Journal of the British Interplanetary Society* 440–42 (December 1960).

————"Liability for Damage Caused by Space Operations," 2 *International Relations* 657–69 (October 1964).

Kopal, V. "Problems of Legal Responsibility for Space Activities; Problems of Liability for Damage Caused by Spacecraft," 11 *Studie z mezinarodniho prava* (Studies in International Law) 65–102, Prague (1966).

Lay, S. H., and Taubenfeld, H. G. "Liability and Space Activities: Causes, Objectives and Parties," 6 *Virginia Journal of International Law* 252–88 (April 1966).

Lay, S. H., and Poole, R. E. "Exclusive Government Liability for Space Accidents," 53 *American Bar Association Journal* 831–36 (September 1967).

McDougal, M. S., Lasswell, H. D., and Vlasic, J. A. "The Nationality of Spacecraft and Promotion of Optimum Order in Space," chapter 5, particularly pp. 587–625 in *Law and Public Order in Space.* New Haven, Conn.: Yale University Press, 1963.

Parry, E. F. "Surface Impact Liability of Space Vehicles," 14 *Oklahoma Law Review* 89–98 (February 1961).

Pepin, E. "Damage to Third Parties on the Surface Caused by Space Vehicles." *Third Colloquium on Law of Outer Space,* Stockholm, 1960, pp. 131–33. Comments by: Cooper, Verplaetse, Beresford, von Rauchhaupt, 133–37.

Poulantzas, D. M. "The Rule of Exhaustion of Local Remedies and Liability for Space Vehicle Accidents." *Sixth Colloquium on Law of Outer Space,* IISL, Paris, 1963, 6 p.

————"The Chambers of the International Court of Justice and Their Role in the Settlement of Disputes Arising Out of Space Activities." *Seventh Colloquium on Law of Outer Space,* IISL, Warsaw, 1964, pp. 186–90.

Prusa, V. "Odpovednost za skodu zpusobenou pri vyzkumu a vyuzivani kosmickeho prostoru" (Liability for Damage Caused by Exploration and Use of Outer Space), 10 *Casopis pro mezinarodni pravo* (Czechoslovak Journal of International Law) 14–48 (1966).

Rauchhaupt, F. W., von. "The Problem of Damages in Space Law," in *1961 Senate Symposium,* pp. 755–56.

————"The Damages in Space Law: The Report of Working Group IX of the IISL," *Fifth Colloquium on Law of Outer Space*, IISL, Varna, 1962, 6 p.

Rode-Verschoor, I. H. P., de. "The Responsibility of States for the Damage Caused by Launched Space Bodies," *First Colloquium on Law of Outer Space*, The Hague, 1958, pp. 103–104. Reprinted in *1961 Senate Symposium*, pp. 460–61.

————"Observations on Comparing the Responsibility for Damage Caused by Spacecraft and That Caused by Nuclear Powered Ships." *Fourth Colloquium on Law of Outer Space*, IISL, Washington, 1961, pp. 329–35.

————"General View on the Problems Studied and Still to Be Studied in Connection with the Responsibility for the Damage Caused by Spacecraft," *Fifth Colloquium on Law of Outer Space*, IISL, Varna, 1962, 5 p.

————"Some Suggestions Regarding a Separate Convention on the Liability for Damages Caused by Space Craft," *Sixth Colloquium on Law of Outer Space*, IISL, Paris, 1963, 3 p.

————"Recent Developments Regarding Liability for Damage Caused by Spacecraft." *Seventh Colloquium on Law of Outer Space*, IISL, Warsaw, 1964, pp. 251–55.

Rosenthal, A. J., Korn, H. L., and Lubman, S. B. "Catastrophic Accidents in Government Program: A Report Prepared as an Independent Research Project Under the Auspices of the Legislative Drafting Research Fund of Columbia University for the National Security Industrial Association" (Washington, D. C., NSIA, 1963), 175 p. (see especially pp. 23–30).

Rubin, A. P. "Liability for Damage and the Need for Domestic Legislation," 7 *USAF JAG Law Review* 30–37 (September/October 1965).

Rusis, A., Gsovski, V. "Liability Under Soviet Law for Damage or Personal Injury Caused by Space Vehicles," Library of Congress, European Law Division Study, 38 p. (mimeo).

Schrader, G. D. "Space Activities and Resulting Tort Liability," *Sixth Colloquium on Law of Outer Space*, IISL, Paris, 1963, 33 p. Reprinted in 17 *Oklahoma Law Review* 139–58 (May 1964).

Seara Vasquez, M. "Responsibility in Space Law," chapter 3, pp. 69–90 in *Cosmic International Law*. Detroit, Mich.: Wayne State University Press, 1965.

Tager, T. E. "Liability for Space Activity," McGill University Institute of Air and Space Law, 1963, 45 p. (mimeo).

United Nations General Assembly: Committee on the Peaceful Uses of Outer Space. *Report of the Legal Sub-committee on the Work of Its Sixth Session (June 19–July 14, 1967) to the Committee on the Peaceful Uses of Outer Space.* A/AC.105/37. Annex II, 40 p. Proposals, amendments and other documents relating to liability for damage caused by the launching of objects into outer space, and comparative table (A/AC.105/C.2/L.7/Rev. 3), The United States of America (A/AC.105/C.2/L.19) and Hungary (A/AC.105/C.2/L.10/Rev. 1 and A/AC.104/C.2/L.24 and Add.1).

Vasilevskaya, E. G. "Liability for Damages Caused by Space Activities," chapter 4, pp. 101–128 in *Kosmos i Problema Vseobshchego Mira* (Space and the Problem of a General Peace). Moscow: Institut Gosudarstva i Prava, Akademiya Nauk SSSR (Institute of State and Law of the Soviet Academy of Sciences, USSR), 1966. 195 p.

Wimmer, H. H. "Suggestions for an International Convention on Damages Caused by Space Vehicles." *Fifth Colloquium on Law of Outer Space*, IISL, Varna, 1962, 7 p.

Zhukov, G. P. "Problema Otvetstvennosti za Uscerb v Kosmiceskom Prave" (The Problem of Liability for Damages in Space Law), 35 *Sovetskoe Gosudarstvo i Pravo* (Soviet State and Law) 67–73 (June 1965).

National Security and Military Uses of Outer Space

Baker, A. S. *Military Implications of Space, Current Problems of Space Law: A Symposium* (London: British Institute of International and Comparative Law, 1966), pp. 73–78. Comments by: Cheng and Bond, pp. 83–86.

Bilder, R. B., Kerley, E. L., Ristau, B. A., and Rubin, A. P. "Contemporary Practice of the United States Relating to International Law—Outer Space," 57 *American Journal of International Law* 118–28, (January 1963).

Boodey, C. W. "National Claims to the Use of Outer Space for Military Purposes and the Development of the Public International Law of Space," Doctoral Dissertation, New York University (1964).

Bousky, H. A. "Blueprints for Space," 11 *Air University Quarterly Review* 16–29 (Spring 1959).

Brennan, D. G. "Arms and Arms Control in Outer Space," pp. 123–49 in *Outer Space: Prospects for Man and Society*. Englewood Cliffs, N.J.: Prentice-Hall, 1963.

Cagle, M. W. "The Navy's Future Role in Space," 89 *United States Naval Institute Proceedings* 87–93 (January 1963).

Chandrasekharan, M. "The Gemini Program and the Manned Orbiting Laboratory in Space: An Appraisal," 5 *Indian Journal of International Law* (New Delhi) 334–41 (July 1965).

Cheprov, I. I., and Kovalev, F. N. "The Problem of the Military Use of Space," Chapter 3, pp. 75–107 (English translation) in *Na Puti k Kosmocheskomu Pravu* (The Way to Space Law). Moscow: Institut Mezhdunarodnykh Otnoshenij (Institute of International Relations) 1962. 179 p.

Christol, C. Q. "Space Stations—a Lawyer's Point of View." 4 *Indian Journal of International Law* (New Delhi) 488–99 (October 1964).

Cooper, J. C. "The Manned Orbiting Laboratory: A Major Legal and Political Decision," 51 *American Bar Association Journal* 1137–40 (1965).

————"Self-Defense in Outer Space and the United Nations," 45 *Air Force/Space Digest* 51–56 (February 1962). Reprinted in 4 *Spaceflight* 164–68 (September 1962), and in 11 *Zeitschrift für Luftrecht und Weltraumrechtsfragen* 186–204 (1962).

Crane, R. D. "Law and Strategy in Space," 6 *Orbis* 281–300 (Summer 1962).

————"Basic Principles in U.S. Space Policy," 22 *Federal Bar Journal* 163–78 (Summer 1962).

————"Soviet Attitude Toward International Space Law," 56 *American Journal of International Law* 685–723 (July 1962).

————"The Beginnings of Marxist Space Jurisprudence," 57 *American Journal of International Law* 616–25 (July 1963).

————"Basic Principles in Soviet Space Law: Peaceful Coexistence, Peaceful Cooperation, and Disarmament," 29 *Law and Contemporary Problems* 943–55 (Autumn 1964).

Forman, B. "Why a Military Space Program?" *Proceedings of the Conference on Space Science and Space Law,* University of Oklahoma, Norman, June 18–20, 1963. South Hackensack, N.J.: F. B. Rothman, 1964. Pp. 68–77.

Galloway, E. "World Security and the Peaceful Uses of Outer Space," *Third Colloquium on Law of Outer Space,* IISL, Stockholm, 1960, pp. 93–101. Reprinted in *1961 Senate Symposium,* pp. 684–693.

Gore, A. "United States Policy on Outer Space," 48 *Department of State Bulletin* 21–29 (1963).

————"Contemporary Practice of the United States Relating to International Law, Outer Space and Military Uses," 57 *American Journal of International Law* 428–30 (1963).

Gotlieb, A. E. "Nuclear Weapons in Outer Space," 3 *Canadian Yearbook of International Law,* 3–35 (1965).

Kittrie, N. N. "Aggressive Uses of Space Vehicles—Remedies in International Law," *Fourth Colloquium on Law of Outer Space,* IISL, Washington, 1961, pp. 198–217.

Kopal, V. "The Problem of Neutralization and Demilitarization of Outer Space." *Fourth Colloquium on Law of Outer Space,* IISL, Washington, 1961, pp. 336–45.

————"Pravni Rezim Oblasti Vyhrazenych Mirovym Cilum" (Legal Status of Areas Reserved for Peaceful Purposes), 10 *Casopis pro Mezinarodni Pravo* (Czechoslovak Journal of International Law) 205–25 (1966). Summary in English.

————"Problems of Legal Responsibility for Space Activities," 11 *Studiez Mezinarodniho Prava* (Studies in International Law), Prague 65–87 (1966).

————"Some Problems of the Present Space Legal Terminology," *Ninth Colloquium on Law of Outer Space,* IISL, Madrid, 1966.

Korovin, E. A. "The Neutralization and Demilitarization of Outer Space," 5 *International Affairs* (Moscow) 82–92 (December 1959). Reprinted in *1961 Senate Symposium,* pp. 1085–87.

————"Peaceful Cooperation in Space," 8 *International Affairs* (Moscow) 61–63, (March 1962).

————"International Law through the Pentagon's Prism," 8 *International Affairs* (Moscow) 3–7 (December 1962).

————"Outer Space Must Become a Zone of Real Peace," 9 *International Affairs* (Moscow) 82–92 (September 1963).

————"The Struggle for Space and International Law," pp. 3–16 (English translation) in *Kosmos i Mezhdunarodnoye Provo* (Space and International Law), A Symposium. Committee on Legal Problems of Outer Space of the Academy of Science, USSR, Moscow: Publishing Office of the Institute of International Relations, 1962, 182 p.

Larionov, V. "The Doctrine of Military Domination in Outer Space," 10 *International Affairs* (Moscow) 25–30 (October 1964).

Lazarev, M. I. "O Probleme Zaprescenija Ispol'zovanija Kosmiceskogo Prostranstva v Voennych Celach" (On the Question of the Prohibition of the Use of Outer Space for Military Purposes). Remarks, Second Annual Meeting, S.A.M.P., Moscow, 1959. 2 *Sovetskij Ezegodnik Mezdunarodnogo Pravo* (Soviet Yearbook of International Law) Moscow, 409–10 (1959).

Markov, M. G. Notes Concerning the Remarks of Dr. Alex Meyer Made at the Brussels Conference, August 19–26, 1962 (concerning the interpretation of the term "peaceful uses"). *Fifth Colloquium on Law of Outer Space,* Varna, 1962, 3 p.

McNaughton, J. T. "Space Technology and Arms Control in Law and Politics in Outer Space," *Proceedings of First McGill Conference on Law of Outer Space,* April 1963, pp. 63–74. Comments by: Fisher, Wright, Spingarn, Woetzel at pp. 85–93.

Meyer, A. "Remarks Concerning the Interpretation of the Terms 'Legal Status of Outer Space' and 'Peaceful Uses' ", *Reports,* ILA, Brussels 1962, pp. 40–43.

————"The Interpretation of the Term 'Peaceful' with Regard to the Announcement of President Johnson to Establish 'Military Manned Orbiting Laboratories' (MOLS)," 15 *Zeitschrift für Luftrecht und Weltraumrechtsfragen* 36–39 (January 1966).

Milstejn, M. "The USA Plan Military Use of Outer Space," 5 *International Affairs* (Moscow) 44–49 (May 1959).

Osnitskaja, G. A. "Legal Aspects of the Conquest of Space," 7 *Review of Contemporary Law* (Brussels) 51–59 (December 1960).

Pechorkin, V. "The Pentagon Theoreticians and the Cosmos," 7 *International Affairs* (Moscow) 32–36 (March 1961).

RAND Corporation. "Some Implications for US National

Security of Activities in Outer Space—an Interim Report," RM–2004 (1957), 71 p.

————*International Political Implications of Activities in Outer Space: A Report of a Conference,* October 22–23, 1959, edited by J. M. Goldsen, R–362–RC (May 5, 1960), 209 p.

————"Current Problems of Space Control and Cooperation: An Analytical Summary," L. Lipson, RM–2805, July 1, 1961, 81 p.

Reed, W. D., and de Saussure, H. "Self-defense: A Right in Outer Space," 7 *USAF Judge Advocate General Law Review,* 38–45 ("Symposium on the Law of Outer Space"), September/October 1965.

Robinson, D. "Self-restriction in American Military Use of Space," 9 *Orbis* 116–39 (1965).

Sheldon, C. S. *Report on Military Communications Satellite Program,* House of Representatives, Committee on Science and Astronautics, 87th Congress, 2d Session, 1962.

————"Science, Astronautics and Defense: 1961 Review of Scientific and Astronautical Research and Development in the Department of Defense," House of Representatives, Committee on Science and Astronautics, 87th Congress, 1st Session, 1961, 68 p. (Committee Print).

Sztucki, J. "Security of Nations and Cosmic Space," *1961 Senate Symposium,* pp. 1164–1203.

Tager, T. E. *Legal Control of Military Uses of Spacecraft, Current Problems of Space Law.* A Symposium. (London: British Institute of International and Comparative Law, 1966), pp. 79–82. Comments by: Cheng, pp. 83–86.

Taubenfeld, H. J. "The Status of Competing Claims to Use Outer Space: An American Point of View," *Proceedings of 57th Annual Meeting of American Society of International Law,* pp. 173–86 (1963).

Wehringer, C. K. "Space, Law and War," 4 *Lex et Scientia* 191–206 (Oct.-Dec. 1967).

Woetzel, R. K. "Military Uses of Space," 2 *International Relations* (London) 417–26 (1960–63).

————"Comments on U.S. and Soviet Viewpoints Regarding the Legal Aspects of Military Uses of Outer Space," *Proceedings of the American Society of International Law,* pp. 195–203 (1963).

————"Legal Aspects of Military Use of Space in Soviet and American Essays," in *Space and Society,* edited by H. J. Taubenfeld. New York: Oceana Publications, 1964. Pp. 121–40.

Zacharov, M. "Space for Military Purposes of the West," 3 *Mirovaja Edonomika i Mezhdunarodnij Otnoshenija* (World Economy and International Relations) 106–109 (March 1962).

Zadorzhnyy, G. P. "Fundamental Problems of the Science of Space Law," pp. 17–70 (English translation) in *Kosmos i Mezhdunarodnoye Pravo* (Space and International Law). A Symposium: Committee on Legal Problems of

Outer Space of the Academy of Science, USSR. Moscow: Publishing Office of the Institute of International Relations, 1962. 182 p.

Zhukov, G. P. "International Cooperation in Peaceful Use of Outer Space," pp. 92–121 (English translation) in *Kosmos i Mezhdunarodnoye Pravo* (Space and International Law) A Symposium: Committee on Legal Problems of Outer Space of the Academy of Sciences, USSR. Moscow: Publishing Office of the the Institute of International Relations, 1962. 182 p.

————"Legal Regime of Outer Space at the Contemporary Level," pp. 9–46 (English translation) in *Kosmos i Mezhdunarodnoye Sotrudnichestvo* (Space and International Cooperation). A Symposium: Committee on Legal Problems of Outer Space of the Academy of Sciences, USSR. Moscow: Publishing Office of the Institute of International Relations, 1963. 256 p.

————"Iadrenaia Demilitarizatsua Kosmosa" (Nuclear Demilitarization of Outer Space) 34 Sovetsko Gosudarstvo i Pravo 79–89 (1964).

————"The Soviet Program of Disarmament—the Real Way for the Prohibition of the Use of Outer Space for Military Purposes," chapter 1, pp. 7–46 (English translation) in *Kosmos i Problema Vseobshchego Mira* (Space and Problems of a General World Peace). Moscow: Institute Gosudarstva i Prava, Akademiya Nauk SSSR (Institute of State and Law, Soviet Academy of Sciences) 1966. 195 p.

————"Legal Order in Space—a Vital Necessity," chapter 2, pp. 47–62 (English translation) in *Kosmos i Problema Vseobshchego Mira* (Space and Problems of a General World Peace). Moscow: Institut Gosudarstva i Prava, Akademiya Nauk SSSR, (Institute of State and Law, Soviet Academy of Sciences) 1966. 195 p.

————"Amerikanskie Plany Ispol'sovanija Kosmosa v Agressivnych Celjach i Bezopasnost' Gosudarstv" (American Plans for the Use of Outer Space with Aggressive Purposes and the Security of States), 4 *Sovetskij Ezegodnik Mezhdunarodnogo Prava* (Soviet Yearbook of International Law) 171–207 (1961). English summary, pp. 202–207.

————"Demilitarizacija i Nejtralizacija Kosmiceskogo Prostranstva" (Demilitarization and Neutralization of Cosmic Space), 32 *Sovetskoe Gosudarstvo i Pravo* (Soviet State and Law) 62–72 (May 1962).

————"Problems of Space Law at the Present Stage: Memorandum." *Fifth Colloquium on Law of Outer Space,* IISL, Varna, 1962, 37 p.

————"Problema Mirnogo Ispol'zovanija Kosmosa" (The Problem of the Peaceful Use of Outer Space), *Mezhdunarodnyj Ezegodnik, Politika i Ekonomika* (International Yearbook, Politics and Economy) 92–106 (1962).

————"Practical Problems of Space Law," 9 *International Affairs* (Moscow) 27–30 (May 1963).

Reconnaissance Satellites, Space Surveillance, and International Law

Bentivoglio, L. M. "Spionaggio Aereo e Diritto Internazionale" (Aerial Espionage and International Law), 16 *Diritto Internazionale* 228–41 (1962).

Beresford, S. M. "Surveillance of Aircraft and Satellites: A Problem of International Law," 27 *Journal of Air Law and Commerce* 107–18 (Spring 1960).

———"High Altitude Surveillance in International Law." *Third Colloquium on Law of Outer Space*, IISL, Stockholm, 1960, 26 p. (mimeo).

Bolstridge, L. I. "Legal Aspects of Space Surveillance over Foreign Territory in Times of Peace," Maxwell Air Force Base, Air University, Air War College Thesis No. 2414, Academic Year 1963–64, 108 p.

Cheprov, I. I., and Kovalev, F. N. "The Problem of the Military Use of Space," chapter 3, pp. 75–107 (English translation) in *Na Puti k Kosmocheskomu Pravu* (The Way to Space Law), Moscow: Institutu Mezhdunarodnykh Otnoshenij (Institute of International Relations), 1962. 179 p.

Cooper, J. C. "Self Defense in Outer Space and the United Nations," 45 *Air Force/Space Digest* 51–56 (February 1962).

Crane, R. D. "Law and Strategy in Space," 6 *Orbis* 281–300 (Summer 1962).

———"Basic Principles in U.S. Space Policy," 22 *Federal Bar Journal* 163–78 (Summer 1962).

———"Soviet Attitude toward International Space Law," 56 *American Journal of International Law* 616–25 (July 1963).

———"The Beginnings of Marxist Space Jurisprudence," 57 *American Journal of International Law* 616–25 (July 1963).

Falk, R. A. "Space Espionage and World Order: A Consideration of the Samos-Midas Program," pp. 45–82 in *Essays on Espionage in International Law*, R. I. Stranger, editor. Columbus: Ohio State University Press, 1962.

———"Toward a Responsible Procedure for the National Assertion of Protested Claims to Use Space," pp. 91–120 in *Space and Society*, edited by H. J. Taubenfeld. New York: Oceana Publications, 1964.

Gabrovski, T. "Reflections on the Juridical Problems of the Extra-Aeronautical Space and the Reconnaissance Satellites." *Fifth Colloquium on Law of Outer Space*, IISL, Varna, 1962, 7 p.

Gal, G. "Some Legal Aspects of the Uses of Reconnaissance Satellites." *Fifth Colloquium on Law of Outer Space*, IISL, Varna, 1962, 6 p.

Gatland, K. W. "Surveillance from Orbit," 98 *Aeroplane and Astronautics* (London) 678–79, (June 3, 1960). Reprinted in *1961 Senate Symposium*, pp. 670–74.

Horsford, C. E. S. "Spy Satellites and the Law," 2 *International Relations* (London) 308–10 (April 1962).

Korovin, E. A. "Aerial Espionage and International Law," 6 *International Affairs* (Moscow) 49–50 (June 1960).

———"Bor'ba za Kosmos i Mezdunarodnoe Pravo (The Struggle for the Cosmos and International Law) pp. 5–22 in *Kosmos i Mezdunarodnoe Pravo: Sbornik Statej* (Space and International Law: A Collection of Articles), E. A. Korvin, editor. Moscow: Institut Mezhdunarodnykh Otnoshenij (Institute of International Relations), 1962. 184 p. English translation, pp. 2–16.

———"International Law through the Pentagon's Prism," 8 *International Affairs* (Moscow) 2–7 (December 1962).

Kraus, J. "Legal Aspects of Space Communications and Space Surveillance," 29 *Journal of Air Law and Commerce* 230–40 (Summer 1963).

Leopold, G. V. "Cosmic Surveillance by Space Flight Momentum," 6 *Wayne Law Review* 311–39 (Summer 1960).

Lipson, L. "An Argument on the Legacy of Reconnaissance Satellites," *Proceedings of the American Society of International Law*, pp. 174–76 (1961).

Lissitzyn, O. J. "Treatment of Aerial Intruders in Recent Practice and International Law," 47 *American Journal of International Law* 559–89 (October 1953).

———"Some Legal Implications of the U–2 and RB–47 Incidents," 56 *American Journal of International Law* 135–42 (January 1962).

Meeker, L. C. "Observation in Space," pp. 75–84 in *Law and Politics in Space*. Montreal: McGill University Press, 1964. Discussion and comments by: Fisher, Wright, Spingarn and Woetzel, pp. 85–94.

Milde, M., and Potocny, M. "Letecka Spionaz a Mezinarodni Pravo" (Aerial Espionage and International Law), 4 *Mezinarodni Politika* (International Politics, Prague) 504–506 (1960).

Milstein, M. "The U.S.A. Plan Military Use of Outer Space," 5 *International Affairs* (Moscow) 44–49 (May 1959).

Morenoff, J. "Reconnaissance in Airspace and Outer Space: A Legal Analysis and Prognosis," Doctoral Thesis, George Washington University, 1965.

———*World Peace through Space Law*. See Part III (D), "Sovereignty Considerations of Reconnaissance from Outer Space—Reconnaissance Satellites," pp. 151–215, and Part IV, "Reconnaissance as a Justifiable Activity in the Development of World Peace through Space Law," pp. 219–303. Charlottesville, Va.: Michie Co., 1967.

———"Reconnaissance in Outer Space: A Sentinel for World Peace," pp. 726–32, in *World Peace through Law*. Washington Conference. St. Paul, Minn., West Publishing Co., 1967.

Morrison, F. P. "The Navy and the Space Age Surveillance," 87 *United States Naval Institute Proceedings* 42–45 (February 1961).

Note. "Legal Aspects of Reconnaissance in Airspace and Outer Space," 61 *Columbia Law Review* 1074–1102 (June 1961).

Osnitskaya, G. A. "Legal Aspects of the Conquest of Space," 7 *Review of Contemporary Law* (Brussels) 51–59 (December 1960).

————"Na Putjach k Kosmiceskomu Pravu" (Toward a Law of Space), 5 *Izvestija Vyssych Ucebnych Zavedenij Serija Pravovedenie* (Informations from the High Schools Legal Series) (Moscow) 105–10 (1961).

————*Osvoenie Kosmosa i Mezhdunarodnoe Pravo* (The Conquest of Space and International Law). Moscow: Gosjurizdat, 1962. 72 p.

————"Doktrina Mezhdunarodnogo Prava i Osvoenie Kosmosa" (The Doctrine of International Law and the Conquest of Space) pp. 88–113 in *Kosmos i Mezhdunarodnoe Pravo: Sbornik Statej* (Space and International Law: A Collection of Articles), E. A. Korovin, editor. Moscow: Institut Mezhdunarodnykh Otnoshenij (Institute of International Relations), 1962. 184 p. English translation, pp. 71–91.

Petrov, G. A. (alias Zhukov, G. P.) "Sputniki-shpiony i Mezhdunarodnoe Pravo" (Spy Satellites and International Law), pp. 171–82 in *Kosmos i Mezhdunarodnoe Pravo: Sbornik Statej* (Space and International Law: A Collection of Articles), E. A. Korovin, editor. Moscow: Institut Mezhdunarodnykh Otnoshenij (Institute of International Relations), 1962. 184 p. English translation, pp. 137–45.

Seara Vasquez, M. "Aspectos Juridocos de Reconocimiento por Medio de Satelites" (Legal Aspects of Reconnaissance by Satellites), 15 *Boletin del Instituto de Derecho Comparado de Mexico* (Mexico) 75–89 (January/April 1962).

Soraghan, J. R. "Reconnaissance Satellites: Legal Characterization and Possible Utilization for Peace-keeping," 13 *McGill Law Journal* 458–93 (1967).

Taubenfeld, H. J. "Status of Competing Claims to Use Outer Space: An American Point of View," *Proceedings of the American Society of International Law,* pp. 173–86 (1963).

————"Surveillance from Space: The American Case for Peace-keeping and Self-defense," 47 *Air Force/Space Digest* 54–57 (October 1963).

Young, R. W. "The Aerial Inspection Plan and Air Space Sovereignty," 23 *George Washington Law Review* 565–89 (April 1956). Reprinted in *1961 Senate Symposium,* pp. 46–64.

Zadorozhnyi, G. P. "Osnovnye Problemy Nauki Kosmiceskogo Prava" (Basic Problems of the Science of Space Law), pp. 23–87 in *Kosmos i Mezdunarodnoe Pravo: Sbornik Statej* (Space and International Law: A Collection of Articles), E. A. Korovin, editor, Moscow; Institutu Mezhdunarodnykh Otnoshenij (Institute of International Relations), 1962, 184 p. English translation, pp. 17–70.

Zhukov, G. P. "Space Espionage Plans and International Law" 6 *International Affairs* (Moscow) 53–57 (October 1960). Reprinted in *1961 Senate Symposium,* pp. 1095–1101.

————"Mezhdunarodnoe Sotrudnicestvo v Mirnom Ispol'zovanii Kosmosa" (International Cooperation in the Peaceful Uses of Outer Space), pp. 114–52 in *Kosmos i Mezdunarodnoe Pravo: Sbornik Statej* (Space and International Law: A Collection of Articles), E. A. Korovin, editor, Moscow, Institut Mezhdunarodnykh Otnoshenij (Institute of International Relations), 1962, 184 p. English translation, pp. 92–121.

Space Communications, National Regulatory Policy, and International Law Aspects

Boskev, B. "Monopoly and Anti-Trust Aspects of Communication Satellite Operations." *Proceedings of the Conference on the Law of Space and Satellite Communications,* Northwestern University Law School, Chicago, May 1963 (NASA SP-44, 1964), pp. 80–90. Comments by Fulda, Schlotterbeck, and Cook, pp. 91–110.

Bosak, J. "Radiokomunikace a Kosmicky Prostor" (Radio Communications in Outer Space), 4 *Casopis pro Mezinarodni Pravo* (Prague), pp. 268–72 (July 1960). Reprinted in English in *1961 Senate Symposium* pp. 1127–33.

————"Mezinarodnepravni Aspekty Spojovych Druzic" (International Law Aspects of Communications Satellites), 7 *Casopis pro Mezinarodni Pravo* (Prague), pp. 308–19 (1963).

————"Some Legal Aspects of Satellite Communications," 31 *Telecommunications Journal* (Geneva), pp. 276–80 (October 1964).

————"Mezinardodni Dohoda o Spojovych Drusicich" (International Agreement on Communication Satellites), 9 *Casopis pro Mezinarodni Pravo* (Prague), 256–63 (1965).

Chayes, A. "International Satellite Communications: Questions for 1969." Speech at the Conference on Peaceful Uses of Space, Stanford University, August 1967, 15 p. (mimeo.). Reprinted in *New York Law Journal,* p. 158, November 21–22, 1967.

Cheprov, I. I. "Some Legal Problems of International Space Communications." *Seventh Colloquium on Law of Outer Space,* IISL, Warsaw, 1964, pp. 10–14.

Clark, A. C. "The Social Impacts of Communications Satellites." *Fourth Colloquium on Law of Outer Space,* IISL, Washington, 1961, pp. 70–85.

Cocca, A. A. "Legal Problems of Telecommunications by Satellites." *Eighth Colloquium on Law of Outer Space,* IISL, Athens, 1965, pp. 143–48. Comments by Verplaetse, Fasan, Scifoni, Caplan, and Haley, pp. 149–66.

————"Legal Problems of Telecommunications by Satellites." *Ninth Colloquium on Law of Outer Space,* IISL, Madrid, 1966, pp. 66–71.

————"Legal Problems Arising from the Establishment of One or Several Systems of Telecommunications by Satellites: An Introductory Report." *Tenth Colloquium on Law of Outer Space,* IISL, Belgrade, 1967, (mimeo.).

Colino, R. R. "Global Satellite Communications and International Organization: A Focus on Intelsat." *Tenth Colloquium on Law of Outer Space,* IISL, Belgrade, 1967, (mimeo.).

Dirlam, J. B., and Kahn, A. E. "Merits of Reserving the Cost Savings from Domestic Communications Satellites for Support of Educational Television," 77 *Yale Law Journal* 494–519 (January 1968).

Doyle, S. E. "Legal Problems Arising from the Establishment of One or Several Systems of Telecommunications by Satellite: The Record Up to the Present Time." *Tenth Colloquium on Law of Outer Space,* IISL, Belgrade, 1967, (mimeo.).

————"Communications Satellites: International Organization for Development and Control," 55 *California Law Review* 431–48 (May 1967).

Drury, C. M. *A Domestic Satellite Communication System for Canada,* Ottawa, Queen's Printer, March 28, 1968. 94 p.

Estep, S. D. Some International Aspects of Communication Satellite System. *Proceedings of the Conference on the Law of Outer Space and Satellite Communications,* Northwestern University Law School, Chicago, May 1963 NASA SP–44, 1964), pp. 154–84. Comments by Cohen and McDougal, pp. 184–96.

————"International Lawmakers in a Technological World: Space Communications and Nuclear Energy," 33 *George Washington Law Review* 162–80 (October 1964).

Estep, S. D., and Kearse, A. L. "Space Communications and the Law: Adequate International Control After 1963?" 60 *Michigan Law Review* 873–904 (May 1962).

Faller, E. W. "European Perspectives on Satellite Communications." 19 *Progress in Astronautics and Aeronautics* 1033–51 (An AIAA Series), New York: Academic Press, 1966.

Federal Communications Commission, In the Matter of an Inquiry into the Administrative and Regulatory Problems Relating to the Authorization of Commercially Operable Space Communications Systems, Docket No. 14024 (3 Volumes); Notice of Inquiry (FCC 61–427, released April 3, 1961); First Report and Order (FCC 61–767, released May 24, 1961); Report of the Ad Hoc Carrier Committee (released October 13, 1961).

————In Matter of Application of Communications Satellite Corporation for Authority to Use and Operate a Communications-Satellite Earth Station at Andover, Maine, in conjunction with a Synchronous Communications-Satellite in Orbit over the Atlantic Ocean to Provide Commercial Communications Services and for Approval of the Technical Characteristics thereof, File No. 1–CSS & CSG-L–65; Memorandum Opinion Order and Authorization (FCC 65–550, June 23, 1965), 38 FCC Reports 1298–1314.

————In Matter of Amendment of Part 25 of the Commission's Rules and Regulations with Respect to Ownership and Operation of Initial Earth Stations in the United States for Use in Connection with the Proposed Global Commercial Communication-Satellite System, Docket No. 15735, RM–644 (5 Volumes); Report and Order (FCC 65–401, released May 13, 1965), 38 FCC Reports 1104–26; Memorandum Opinion and Order (FCC 66–176, February 26, 1965), 2 FCC2d Reports 658–66; Second Report and Order (FCC 66–1133, released December 8, 1966), 5 FCC2d Reports 812–22.

————In Matter of Authorized Entities and Authorized Users under the Communications Satellite Act of 1962, Docket No. 16058 (2 Volumes); Notice of Inquiry (FCC65–523, released June 16, 1965); Public Notice (FCC 65–563, released June 23, 1966), 4 FCC2d Reports 12–13; Memorandum Opinion and Statement of Policy (FCC 66–677, released July 20, 1966), 4 FCC2d Reports 421–36.

————In Matter of Tariff Bearing Designation FCC N. 1 Filed by the Communications Satellite Corporation on May 28, 1965, Docket No. 16070 (2 Volumes); Memorandum Opinion and Order (FCC 65–549, released June 23, 1965), 38 FCC Reports 1286–97.

————In Matter of Amendment of Part 25 of the Commission's Rules and Regulations to provide for the Issuance of Authorizations to Developmental Stations in the Communications-Satellite Service, Docket No. 16220 (1 Volume); Notice of Proposed Rule Making (FCC 65–895, released October 8, 1965); Report and Order (FCC 67–13, released January 6, 1967), 6 FCC2d Reports 250–53.

————In Matter of the Establishment of Domestic Non-common Carrier Communication-Satellite Facilities by Non-government Entities, Docket No. 16495 (4 Volumes); Notice of Inquiry (FCC 66–207, released March 3, 1966), 2 FCC2d Reports 668–671; Supplemental Notice of Inquiry (FCC 66–926, released October 21, 1966), 5 FCC2d Reports 354–56.

Feldman, G. "International Arrangements for Satellite Communications," pp. 23–28, in *Law and Politics in Space.* Montreal: McGill University Press, 1964. Comments and discussion by Schlei and Taubenfeld, pp. 29–34.

Finch, K. A. "Space Communications: Catalyst for International Understanding." *Sixth Colloquium on Law of Outer Space* IISL, Paris, 1963, 40 p. Attachments I–VII (100 Pages) include, relevant ITU Resolutions, Recommendations, Allocation of Frequencies for Space Research and Communications, and U.S. Proposals for 1959 Ordinary and 1963 Extraordinary; ITU Administrative Radio Conference for Space Radio Communications and Radio Astronomy.

Glazer, J. H. "The Law Making Treaties of the International Telecommunications Union Through Time and Space," 60 *Michigan Law Review* 269–316 January 1962.

————"Infelix ITU—The Need for Space-Age Revisions to the International Telecommunication Conventions," 23 *Federal Bar Journal* 1–36 (Winter 1963).

————"Some Interpretive Grapeshot Concerning the Application of the International Telecommunications Conventions to Military Radio Installations" 25 Federal Bar Journal 307–14 (Summer 1965).

Haley A. G. "A Basic Program for the 1963 Extraordinary Administrative Radio Conference on Space Communications." *Proceedings of the 11th IAF Congress,* Stockholm, 1960, pp. 175–98. Reprinted in *1961 Senate Symposium,* pp. 694–718.

————"Space Communications—Some Legal and Sociological Challenges." *Fifth Colloquium on Law of Outer Space,* IISL, Varna, 1962, 31 p.

————"Space Communications," chapter 7, pp. 159–232 in *Space Law and Government,* New York: Appleton-Century-Crofts, 1963.

————"Communications in Space: Existing Structures and Foreseeable Problems." *Eighth Colloquium on Law of Outer Space,* IISL, Athens, 1965, pp. 34–99.

————"Space Age Frequency Allocations," 4 *Astronautics and Aeronautics* 66–75 (May 1966).

————"Reports of the Chairman of IISL's Working Group VII—Space Communications" (includes comments by working group members and select bibliography). *Fourth Colloquium on Law of Outer Space,* IISL, Washington, 1962, pp. 396–405, and *Seventh Colloquium on Law of Outer Space,* IISL, Warsaw, 1964, pp. 361–425.

Hult, J. L. "Satellite and Future Communications, including Broadcast, Commercial Utilization of Space," Thirteenth Annual Meeting of American Astronautical Society, Dallas, May 1, 1967, 20 p. (RAND Corporation Print).

Istvan, E. J. "Organization and Program of Intelsat," chapter 6, in 19, *Progress in Astronautics and Aeronautics* 929–40 (An AIAA Series). New York: Academic Press, 1966.

Ivanyi, J. "Thoughts on Legal Provisions to Improve and Safeguard Space Communications." *Fifth Colloquium on Law of Outer Space,* IISL, Varna, 1962, 7 p. Revision printed in 30 *Telecommunications Journal* (ITU, Geneva) 73–76 (March 1963).

————"Rescue of Astronauts in Distress by Cooperation of Telecommunication Services," 31 *Telecommunications Journal* (ITU, Geneva) 134–36 (May 1964).

————"The Topical Legal Problems of Space Communications," *Eighth Colloquium on Law of Outer Space,* IISL, Athens, 1965, pp. 298–319.

Ivanyi, J., Szadefzky-Kordoss, L. and Mora, I. "Legal Aspects of Telecommunication and Meteorological Activities Connected with Space Research." *Ninth Colloquium on Law of Outer Space,* IISL, Madrid, 1966, pp. 78–85.

Johnson, J. A. "Satellite Communications: The Challenge and Opportunity for International Cooperation," 19 *Federal Communications Bar Journal* 88–96 (1965).

————"International Cooperation in Satellite Communication Systems." *Proceedings of the American Society of International Law,* 61st Annual Meeting, April 1967, pp. 24–28. Discussion by Dumbald, More, Rubin, Doyle, Belknup, Aten, Schwartz, Nimer, Deener, and Rao, pp. 42–49.

————"International Cooperation in Satellite Communications," 13th Annual Meeting of American Astronautical Society, Dallas, May 2, 1967, 18 p. (mimeo.).

Kraus, J. "Legal Aspects of Space Communications and Space Surveillance," 29 *Journal of Air Law and Commerce* 230–40 (Summer 1963).

Lessing, L. "Cinderella in the Sky," 76 *Fortune* 131–33, 196–208 (October 1967). Reprinted in 21 *Federal Communications Bar Journal* 92–110 (1967).

Levin, H. J. "Organization and Control of Communications Satellites," 113 *University of Pennsylvania Law Review* 315–57 (January 1967).

Lukin P. I. "Use of Artificial Earth Satellites for Creation of World Wide System of Communications," chapter 5, pp. 129–51; "Satellite Communications and International Relations," chapter 6, pp. 152–73; "The International Legal Regime of Communications Satellites," chapter 7, pp. 174–84, in *Kosmos i Problema Vseobshchego Mira* (Space and the Problem of a General Peace), Institut Gosudarstva i Prava, Akademiya Nauk SSSR (Institute of State and Law of the Soviet Academy of Sciences), 1966. 195 p.

Marks, L. R. "Domestic Communication Satellites and International Cooperation." *Proceedings of the American Society of International Law* 61st Annual Meeting, April 1967, pp. 36–42, discussion at pp. 42–49.

Markov, M. G. "Satellite de communications: Elements de dissidence ou de rapprochement." *Eighth Colloquium on Law of Outer Space,* IISL, Athens, 1965, pp. 456–63. Reprinted in 5 *Dirretto Aero* (Rome) 47–57 (1966).

Morenoff, J. "Communications in Orbit: A Prognosis for World Peace." *Ninth Colloquium on Law of Outer Space,* IISL, Madrid, 1966, pp. 86–90. Revised edition, chapter 6, 19, *Progress in Astronautics and Aeronautics* 1011–31 (An AIAA Series). New York: Academic Press, 1966.

Moulton, H. P. "Commercial Space Communications," pp. 73–90 in *Space Law and Society.* New York: Oceana Publications, 1964.

Paglin, M. D. "Some Regulatory and International Problems

Facing the Establishment of Communication Satellite Systems," 6 *Journal of Broadcasting* 285–94 (Fall 1962).

_____ "The Establishment of Satellite Communication Systems," 70 *Public Utilities Fortnightly* 606–13 (October 25, 1962).

RAND Corporation. "Communication Satellites and Public Policy: An Introductory Report," by J. M. Goldsen, L. S. Lipson, B. H. Klein, W. H. Meckling, and S. H. Reiger; RM–2925 (December 1961), 138 p.

_____ "Foreign Participation in Communications Satellite Systems: Implications of the Communications Satellite Act of 1962," by M. D. Schwartz and J. M. Goldsen; RM–384–RC (February 1963), 91 p.

_____ "Communications Satellites: Technology, Economics, and System Choices," by S. H. Reiger, L. B. Dews, and R. T. Nichols; RM–3487–RC (February 1963), 101 p.

Rosenblum, V. G. "Regulations in Orbit: Administrative Aspects of the Communications Satellite Act of 1962." *Proceedings of the Conference on the Law of Space and Satellite Communications,* Northwestern University Law School, Chicago, May 1963, (NASA SP–44, 1964), pp. 111–31. Comments by Paglin, Johnson, Plesent, Nathanson, Strassburg, Beresford, and Cook, pp. 131–153.

Sawitz, P. H. "Communications Satellites and Free Enterprise." *Fifth Colloquium on Law of Outer Space,* IISL, Varna, 1962, 16 p.

Schick, F. B. "Space Law and Communications Satellites," 16 *Western Political Quarterly* 14–33 (March 1963).

Schrader, G. D. "Communications Satellite Corporation: A New Experiment in Government and Business," 53 *Kentucky Law Journal* 532–742 (Summer 1965).

_____ "ComSat, the Carriers, and the Earth Stations: Some Problems with Melding Variegated Interests," 76 *Yale Law Journal* 441–84 (January 1967).

Segal, B. G. "Communications Satellites: Progress and the Road Ahead," 17 *Vanderbilt Law Review* 677–704 (June 1964).

Silverman, C. E. "The Little Bird That Casts a Big Shadow," 75 *Fortune* 108–11, 223–28 (February 1967).

Simsarian, J. "Interim Arrangements for a Global Communications Satellite System," 59 *Journal of International Law* 344–51 (April 1965).

Smythe, D. E. "Communication Satellites in Communications Explosion," Programs for Policy Studies in Science and Technology, No. 9, pp. 1–25 (Washington, D.C.: George Washington University, 1965).

Stashevski, G. S. "Role of Specialized U.N. Institutions in the Development of International Cooperation in Mastering Outer Space for Peaceful Purposes," pp. 108–33 (English Translation) in *Kosmos i Mezhdunarodnoye Sotrudnichestvo* (Space and International Cooperation). A Symposium: Committee on Legal Problems of Outer

Space of the Academy of Sciences, USSR. Moscow: Publishing Office of International Relations, 1963. 256 p.

_____ "Sputniki Svjazi i Mezhdunarodnoe Pravo" (Communication Satellites and International Law), 34 *Sovetskoe Gosudarstvo i Pravo* (Moscow) 57–66 (1964).

Throop, A. E. "Some Legal Facets of Satellite Communications," 17 *American University Law Review* 12–40 (December 1967).

Trooboff, P. D. "INTELSAT: Approaches to the Renegotiation," 9 *Harvard International Law Journal* 1–84 (Winter 1968).

Woetzel, R. K. "International Cooperation in Telecommunications for Educational and Cultural Purposes," *Proceedings of the American Society of International Law,* 61st Annual Meeting, April 1967, pp. 29–36, discussion at 42–49.

Yerigan, D. D. "The Question of Assignment and International Regulation of Radio Frequencies for Space Service," pp. 134–157 (English translation) in *Kosmos i Mezhdunarodnoye Sotrudnichestvo* (Space and International Cooperation). A Symposium: Committee on Legal Problems of Outer Space of the Academy of Science, USSR. Moscow: Publishing Office of the Institute of International Relations 1963. 256 p.

Zhukov, G. "World-wide Telecommunication System by Satellite (Legal Aspects)," *Ninth Colloquium on Law of Outer Space,* IISL, Madrid, 1966, pp. 91–95.

_____ "Legal Problems of Space Radio Communications" chapter 7, pp. 178–222, in *Kosmicheskoye Pravo* (Space Law) Moscow: Institut Mezhdunarodnoye Otnoshenij (Publishing Office of the Institute of International Relations), 1966.

Space Meteorology and the Law

Gardner, R. N. "Space Meteorology and Communications: A Challenge to Science and Diplomacy," 48 *Department of State Bulletin* 740–46 (1963).

Herczeg, I. "Problems of International Law in Formulating the Legal Principles Governing Activities in Outer Space," 2 *Questions of International Law* (Budapest, Hungarian Branch of International Law Association) 42–64 (1964).

Staskevskiy, G. S. "Role of Specialized U.N. Institutions in the Development of International Cooperation in Mastering Outer Space for Peaceful Purposes," pp. 108–133 (English translation) in *Kosmos i Mezhunarodnoye Sotrudnichestvo* (Space and International Cooperation). A Symposium: Committee on Legal Problems of Outer Space of the Academy of Sciences, USSR. Moscow: Publishing Office of the Institute of International Relations, 1963. 256 p.

Szadecky-Kardoss, L. "Legal Aspects of Meteorological Problems in Space Exploration." *Sixth Colloquium on Law of Outer Space,* IISL, Paris, 1963.

Taubenfeld, H. "Weather Modification and Control: Some International Legal Implications," 55 *California Law Review* 493–506 (May 1967).

Vasilevskaya, E. G. "Meteorological Satellites and International Law Questions," Chapter VIII, pp. 185–95 (English translation) in *Kosmos i Problema Vseobshego Mira* (Space and Problems of General World Peace). Moscow: Institut Gosudarstvo i Pravo, Akademiya Nauk SSSR (Institute of State and Law, Academy of Sciences of the USSR). Moscow: Science, 1966. 195 p.

————"Perspecktivy Pravovogo Regululirovaniya Kosmicheskoy Meteorologii" (Outlook for the Legal Regulation of Space Meteorology) 36 *Sovetskoe Gosudarstvo i Pravo* (Soviet State and Law) (Moscow) 64–72 (1966), English translation, 18 p. (mimeo.).

Whelan, J. C. "Soviet Attitude towards International Cooperation in Space," (World Meteorological Organization and Space Meteorology) pp. 476–80, 481–92 in "Soviet Space Programs, 1962–1965; Goals and Purposes, Achievements, Plans and International Implications," *Staff Report, Senate Committee on Aeronautical and Space Sciences,* 89th Congress, 2d Session, December 30, 1966.

The United Nations and Space Law

Bueckling, A. "Entschliessungen der Vereinten Nationen für das Weltraumrecht: Rechtsnatur und Bedeutung" (Resolutions of the U.N. on Space Law: Legal Nature and Significance), 13 *Zeitschrift fuer Luftrecht und Weltraumrechtsfragen* (Cologne) 193–202 (1964).

Cheng, B. The United Nations and Outer Space, 14 *Current Legal Problems* (London) 247–79 (1961).

Cooper, J. C. "Aerospace Law: Progress in the United Nations," 2 *Astronautics & Aeronautics,* 42–46 (March 1964).

Cox, D. W. and Stoiko, M. "The Need for a United Nations Space Law," chapter 13, pp. 196–210 in *Spacepower—What it Means to You* (Philadelphia: Winston, 1958) 262 p. Reprinted in *1961 Senate Symposium,* pp. 239–51.

Csabafi, I. "The Question of International Responsibility of States Before the U.N. Committee on the Peaceful Uses Of Outer Space and Some Suggestions," *Sixth Colloquium on Law of Outer Space,* IISL, Paris, 1963.

————"The U.N. General Assembly Resolutions on Outer Space as Sources of Space Law," *Eighth Colloquium on Law of Outer Space,* IISL, Athens, 1965, pp. 337–61.

Dembling, P. G., and Arons, D. M. "Space Law and the United Nations: The Work of the Legal Subcommittee of the United Nations Committee on the Peaceful Uses of Outer Space," 32 *Journal of Air Law and Commerce* 329–86 (Summer 1966).

————"The Evolution of the Outer Space Treaty," 33 *Journal of Air Law and Commerce* 419–56 (Summer 1967).

————"The Treaty on Rescue and Return of Astronauts and Space Objects," 9 *William and Mary Law Review* 630–63 (Spring 1968).

————"The United Nations Celestial Bodies Convention," 32 *Journal of Air Law and Commerce* 535–50 (Autumn 1966).

Feldman, G. J. "The Report of the United Nations Legal Committee on the Peaceful Uses of Outer Space: A Provisional Appraisal." *Second Colloquium on Law of Outer Space,* London, 1959, 19–23.

Fitzgerald, F. G. "Participation of International Organizations in the Proposed International Agreements on Liability for Damage Caused by Objects Launched into Outer Space," 3 *Canadian Yearbook of International Law* (Vancouver) 265–80 (1965).

Gal, G. "Az E.N.S. es a Vilagus" (The U.N. and Outer Space), pp. 179–207 in *Az Urrepules es a Tudomany* (Spaceflight and Science: An Essay on Legal Problems of Space Research). Budapest: Kossuth Konyvkiado, 1962. 240 p.

Galloway, E. "The United Nations Ad Hoc Committee on the Peaceful Uses of Outer Space: Accomplishments and Implications for Legal Problems." *Second Colloquium on Law of Outer Space,* London, 1959, pp. 30–41. Reprinted in *1961 Senate Symposium,* pp. 613–25.

————"United Nations Committee on the Peaceful Uses of Outer Space." *Fifth Colloquium on Law of Outer Space,* IISL, Varna, 1962, 16 p.

————"International Regulations of Outer Space Activities," *Seventh Colloquium on Law of Outer Space,* IISL, Warsaw, 1964, pp. 55–61.

————"United States International Space Programs: Texts of Executive Agreements, Memoranda of Understanding, and Other International Arrangements, 1959–1965," *Staff Report, Senate Committee on Aeronautical and Space Sciences,* 89th Congress, 1st Session, July 30, 1965, Senate Document No. 44, 575 p.

————"International Cooperation and Organization for Outer Space," *Staff Report, Senate Committee on Aeronautical and Space Sciences,* 89th Congress, 1st Session, August 12, 1965, Senate Document No. 56, 580 p.

Gardner, R. N. "Status of the Law of Outer Space in the United Nations: Outer Space Problems of Law and Power." Paper, Sixth Space Law Symposium, American Bar Association, August 10, 1963. Reprinted in 49 *Department of State Bulletin* 367–71 (September 2, 1963).

Gorove, S. "Toward a Cosmic Law: Hope and Reality in the United Nations," 5 *New York Law Forum* 333–47 (October 1959).

Herczeg, I. "The Legal Character of UN Resolutions."
Seventh Colloquium on Law of Outer Space, IISL, Warsaw, 1964, pp. 273–383.

Holcombe, A. N. "Relationship of the United Nations to
Outer Space," *1961 Senate Symposium*, pp. 195–197.

Jaffe, M. S. "Recent Developments in the International Law
of Space: Observation at Another Station." *Seventh Colloquium on Law of Outer Space*, IISL, Warsaw, 1964. pp.
193–213. Reprinted in 38 Temple Law Quarterly 263–78
(Spring 1964).

Jessup, P. C., and Taubenfeld, H. J. "Outer Space, Antarctica and the United Nations," 13 *International Organization* 363–79 (Summer 1959).

_____ "The United Nations Ad Hoc Committee on the
Peaceful Uses of Outer Space," 53 *American Journal of
International Law* 877–81 (October 1959).

_____ "Controls for Outer Space and the Antarctic
Analogy." New York: Columbia University Press, 1959.
279 p. Excerpts reprinted in *1961 Senate Symposium*, pp.
553–70.

Kemp, J. "Evolution towards a Space Treaty: An Historical
Analysis," NASA Publication HHN–64 (Washington,
NASA, 1966), 221 p.

Kopal, V. "O.S.N. a Mirove Vyuziti Kosmickeho Prostory"
(The U.N. and the Peaceful Uses of Outer Space) 6
Casopis pro Mezinarodni Pravo (Journal of the Interna-
tional Law, Prague) 335–50 (1962).

_____ "Questions Raised at the Sessions of the United
Nations Committee on the Peaceful Uses of Outer Space
and Its Legal Subcommittee 1962." *Fifth Colloquium on
Law of Outer Space*, IISL, Varna, 1962, 9 p.

Kovalev, F. N. "Problema Kosmosa i O.O.N. v 1961 g"
(The Problem of the Cosmos at the U.N. in 1961) 5
Sovetskij Ezigodnik Mezhdunarodnogo Pravo (Soviet
Yearbook of International Law) 260–62 (1962).

_____ "Komitet O.O.N. po Ispol'zovaniju Kosmiceskogo
Prostranstva" (The U.N. Committee on the Peaceful
Uses of Outer Space), pp. 77–109 in *Kosmos i Mezh-
dunarodnoye Sotrudnichestvo* (Space and International
Cooperation), Moscow: Institut Mezhdunarodnykh
Otnoshenij (Institute of International Relations), 1963.
256 p. English translation, pp. 74–107.

Lipson, L. "Space Technology and the Law of International
Organizations." *Reports, International Law Association*,
Tokyo, 1964, Annex II, pp. 53–56. Replies by: Lowen-
feld and Pepin, pp. 56–60. Draft Resolution on the Legal
Value of U.N. Resolution 1963 (XVIII) by ILA Space
Law Committee, Annex V, pp. 91–93.

Litvine, M. "Première Session du Sous-comite Juridique du
Comite des Utilisations Pacifiques de l'Espace Extra-
atmospherique" ("First Session of the Legal Subcommittee of the Committee on the Peaceful Uses of Outer
Space"), 18 *Revue Française de Droit Aérien* (Paris)
305–18 (October/December 1962).

Lopez-Gutierrez, J., and Tapia Salinas, L. *International
Texts on Space*, Madrid, 1966. 600 p.

Rybakov, J. "Rassmotrenie v Organach O.O.N. v 1962–
1963 gg. Provovych Voprosov Osvoenija Kosmosa"
(Examination by U.N. Agencies of Questions of Space
Law in 1962 and 1963), *Sovetskij Ezegodnik Mezhduna-
rodnogo Pravo 1963* (Soviet Yearbook of International
Law), 1965, pp. 519–23.

Schick, F. B. "Problems of a Space Law in the United Nations," 13 *International and Comparative Law Quarterly*
(London) 969–86 (July 1964).

Simsarian, James. "Outer Space Cooperation in the United
Nations," 57 *American Journal of International Law*
854–67 (October 1963).

Stashevskiy, G. S. "Rol' Specialisirovannych Ucrezdnij
O.O.N. v Razvitii Mezdunarodnogo Sotrudnicestva po
Osvoeniju Kosmiceskogo Prostranstva v Mirnych Celjach" (The Role of the Specialized Organizations of the
U.N. in the Development of International Cooperation in
the Conquest of Space for Peaceful Purposes), pp. 110–34
in *Kosmos i Mezhdunarodnoye Sotrudnichestvo* (Space
and International Cooperation), Moscow: Institut Mezhdunarodnykh Otnoshenij (Institute of International Relations), 1963. 256 p. English translation, pp. 108–33.

Taubenfeld, H. J. "Consideration at the United Nations on
the Legal Status of Outer Space," 53 *American Journal of
International Law* 400–405 (April 1959).

Toth, J. "Les Activités de l'Organisation des Nations Unies
Concernant le Droit de l'Espace" (The Activities of the
U.N. in the Field of Space Law), 91 *Journal du Droit
International* (Paris, Clunet) 58–64 (January/March
1964).

United Nations, General Assembly: Committee on the
Peaceful Uses of Outer Space Review of the Activities
and Resources of the United Nations, of Its Specialized
Agencies and of Other Competent International Bodies
Relating to the Peaceful Uses of Outer Space, U.N. Docu-
ment No. A/AC.104/L.29, August 17, 1966, 81 p.

_____ Review of National and Co-operative International
Space Activities, A/AC.105/L.36, June 5, 1967, 181 p.
Addendum 1, Poland, July 13, 1967, 5 p. Addendum 2,
Argentina, August 22, 1967, 33 p.

_____ Report of the Ad Hoc Committee on the Peaceful
Uses of Outer Space. U.N. Document No. A/4141, July
14, 1959, 26 p. Report of Legal Subcommittee contained
in Part III; reprinted in *1961 Senate Space Symposium*,
pp. 1246–72.

_____ Report of the Legal Subcommittee on the Work of
Its First Session (May 28–June 20, 1962) to the Committee on the Peaceful Uses of Outer Space. U.N. Document No. A/AC.105/6, July 9, 1962, 16 p. with Annexes.

_____ Report of the Legal subcommittee on the Work of
Its Second Session, (April 16–May 3, 1963) to the Committee on the Peaceful Uses of Outer Space. U.N. Docu-

ment No. A/AC.105/C.2/12, May 6, 1963, 25 p. with Annexes.

_____Report of the Legal Subcommittee on the Work of Its Third Session (March 9–26, 1964) to the Committee on the Peaceful Uses of Outer Space. U.N. Document No. A/AC.105/19, March 26, 1964, 66 p. with Annexes.

_____Report of the Legal Subcommittee on the Work of Its Third Session, 2d Part (October 5–23, 1964) to the Committee on the Peaceful Uses of Outer Space. U.N. Document No. A/AC.105/21, October 23, 1964, 172 p. with Annexes.

_____Report of the Legal Subcommittee on the Work of Its Fourth Session (September 20–October 1, 1965) to the Committee on the Peaceful Uses of Outer Space. U.N. Document No. A/AC.105/29, October 1, 1965, 44 p. with Annexes.

_____Report of the Legal Subcommittee on the Work of Its Fifth Session (July 12–August 4, September 12–16, 1966) to the Committee on the Peaceful Uses of Outer Space. U.N. Document No. A/AC.105/35, September 16, 1966, 50 p. with Annexes.

_____Report of the Legal Subcommittee on the Work of Its Sixth Session (June 19–July 14, 1967) to the Committee on the Peaceful Uses of Outer Space. U.N. Document No. A/AC.105/37, July 14, 1967, 81 p. with Annexes.

_____Report of the Legal Subcommittee on the Work of Its Special Session (December 14–15, 1967) to the Committee on the Peaceful Uses of Outer Space. U.N. Document No. A/AC.105/43, December 15, 1967, 5 p. with Annexes.

(Mimeographed or processed U.N. documents, such as these listed above, may be consulted at depository libraries in the United States. Printed U.N. publications may be purchased from: United Nations, Sales Section, United Nations Plaza, New York, New York. For further information on the reports and proceedings of the U.N. Committee on the Peaceful Uses of Outer Space consult the monthly Index to United Nations Documents.)

Vereshchetin, V. S. "Legal Forms of International Cooperation of the USSR in Peaceful Exploration of Outer Space." *Ninth Colloquium on Law of Outer Space* IISL, Madrid, 1966, pp. 213–18.

Zhukov, G. "O.O.N. i Problema Mirnogo Ispol'zovanija Kosmiceskogo Prostranstva," 3 *Sovetskij Ezegodnik Mezhdunarodnoyo Pravo* (Soviet Yearbook of International Law, Moscow) 177–85 (1960). English summary, "The U.N. and the Problems of the Peaceful Use of Outer Space," pp. 186–88.

_____"Mezdunarodnoe Sotrudnicestvo v Mirnom Ispol'zovanii Kosmosa" (International Cooperation in the Peaceful Uses of Outer Space), pp. 114–52 in *Kosmos i Mezdunarodnoe Pravo: Sbornik Statej* (Space and International Law: A Collection of Articles), E. A. Korovin,

editor. Moscow: Institut Mezhdunarodnykh Otnoshenij (Institute of International Relations), 1962. 184 p. English translation, pp. 92–121.

_____"Pravovoj Rezim Kosmiceskogo Prostranstva na Sovremennom Etape" (The Legal Regime of Outer Space at the Present Stage) pp. 10–48 in *Kosmos i Mezhdunarodnoye Sotrudnichestvo* (Space and International Cooperation) Moscow, Institut Mezhdunarodnykh Otnoshenij (Institute of International Relations), 1963. 256 p. English translation, pp. 9–46.

————"The Moon, Politics, and Law," 12 *International Affairs* 32–37 (September 1966).

————"Basic Stages and Immediate Prospects of the Development of Outer Space Law," *Seventh Colloquium on Law of Outer Space,* IISL, Warsaw, 1964, pp. 315–25.

Treaty on Outer Space: Problems of Interpretation and Definition

Adams, T. R. "Outer Space Treaty: An Interpretation in Light of the No-Sovereignty Provision," 9 *Harvard International Law Journal* 140–57 (Winter 1968).

Berger, H. "Background Aspects of Treaty Governing the Exploration and Use of Outer Space," 38 *Pennsylvania Bar Association Quarterly* 320–27 (March 1967).

Cooper, J. C. "Some Critical Questions Concerning the Space Treaty: A Commentary," 50 *Air Force/Space Digest* 104–11 (March 1967).

Dembling, P. G. and Arons, D. M. "Evolution of the Outer Space Treaty," 32 *Journal of Air Law and Commerce* 419–56 (Autumn 1966).

_____"Space Law and the United Nations: The Work of the Legal Subcommittee of the United Nations Committee on the Peaceful Uses of Outer Space," 32 *Journal of Air Law and Commerce* 329–86 (Summer 1966).

_____"The United Nations Celestial Bodies Convention," 32 *Journal of Air Law and Commerce* 535–50 (Autumn 1966).

_____"Treaty on Rescue and Return of Astronauts and Space Objects," 9 *William and Mary Law Review* 630–63 (Spring 1968).

Finch, E. R., Jr. "Outer Space for 'Peaceful Purposes,'" 54 *American Bar Association Journal* 365–67 (April 1968).

Galloway, E. "Space Treaty Proposals by the United States and USSR," *Staff Report, Senate Committee on Aeronautical and Space Sciences,* 89th Congress, 2d Session, July 1966, Committee Print, 52 p.

_____"Treaty on Principles Governing the Activities of States in the Exploration and Use of Outer Space, Including the Moon and Other Celestial Bodies: Analysis and Background Data," *Staff Report, Senate Committee on Aeronautical and Space Sciences,* 90th Congress, 1st Session, March 1967, Committee Print, 84 p.

_____"Interpreting the Treaty on Outer Space," *Tenth*

Colloquium on Law of Outer Space, IISL, Belgrade, 1967, 11 p. (mimeo.).

————— "The Definition of Outer Space," Paper for presentation at the meeting of the Scientific-Legal Liaison Committee of the IISL and the International Academy of Astronautics, Eighteenth Congress of the International Astronautical Federation, Belgrade, September 26, 1967, 7 p. (mimeo.).

Herczeg, I. "Problems of Interpretation of Space Treaty of 27 January 1967; Introductory Report," *Tenth Colloquium on Law of Outer Space,* IISL, Belgrade, 1967, 9 p. (mimeo.). Also contains comments on rapporteur's report by working group members, E. Galloway and M. G. Bourely.

Kopal, V. "The Space Treaty of January 27, 1967 and Related Problems," McGill University, Institute of Air and Space Law, 1967, 60 p. (mimeo.).

Leavitt, W. "The Proposed Space Treaty: Is There Less There Than Meets the Eye?" 50 *Air Force/Space Digest* 43–46 (January 1967).

Menter, M. "Developing Law for Outer Space," 53 *American Bar Association Journal* 703–707 (August 1967).

————— "National Security and the Space Law Treaty," Remarks at Space Law Seminar of Federal Bar Association's Space Law Committee, San Francisco, California, July 27, 1967, published in Supplement to Air Force Policy Letter for Commanders, No. 9–1967, pp. 25–27 (September 1967).

Reed, W. D. "Outer Space Treaty: Freedoms, Prohibitions, Duties," 9 *USAF JAG Law Review* 26–37 (Sept./Oct. 1967).

Senate Committee on Foreign Relations, *Treaty on Outer Space; Executive Report No. 8,* 90th Congress, 1st Session, April 18, 1967, Committee Print (Washington, GPO, 1967), 6 p.

————— *Treaty on Outer Space: Hearings on Executive D, May 7, 13, and April 12, 1967,* 90th Congress, 1st Session, Committee Print, (Washington, GPO, 1967), 162 p.

Vereshchetin, V. S. "Scientific and Technical Agreements on Space: Do They Constitute a Source of Space Law?" *Tenth Colloquium on Law of Outer Space,* IISL, Belgrade 1967, (mimeo.).

Vlasic, I. A. "The Space Treaty: A Preliminary Evaluation," 55 *California Law Review* 507–19, (May 1967).

Zhukov, G. P. "The Problem of Legal Status of Scientific Research Stations on the Moon," *Tenth Colloquium on Law of Outer Space,* IISL, Belgrade, 1967, mimeo.

————— "The Problem of the Definition of Outer Space, paper for presentation at a meeting of the Scientific-Legal Liaison Committee of the IISL and the International Academy of Astronautics," *Eighteenth Congress of the International Astronautical Federation,* Belgrade, September 26, 1967, 7 p. (mimeo.).

Index